Studying Native America

Sponsored by the American Indian Studies Advisory Panel
of the Social Science Research Council

Studying Native America

Problems and Prospects

Edited by
Russell Thornton

THE UNIVERSITY OF WISCONSIN PRESS

The University of Wisconsin Press
2537 Daniels Street
Madison, Wisconsin 53718

3 Henrietta Street
London WC2E 8LU, England

Library of Congress Cataloging-in-Publication Data
Studying native America: problems and prospects /
    edited by Russell Thornton.
      464 pp.   cm.
    Based on a conference sponsored by the Social Science Research
Council and held in May of 1997 at Stanford University.
    Includes index.
    ISBN 0-299-16060-2 (cloth: alk. paper)
    ISBN 0-299-16064-5 (pbk.: alk. paper)
1. Indians of North America—Study and teaching.   2. Indians—
Study and teaching.   3. Indigenous peoples—America—Study and
teaching.   I. Thornton, Russell, 1942–   .   II. Social Science
Research Council (U.S.)
E76.6.S78   1998
970.004′97—dc21   98-20733

In memory of
Vee Salabiye
(1948–1996)

The Great Spirit is good to all His children, but it seems He loves His white children most. He has never shown my people how to do the many wonderful things His white children are doing.

Plenty Coups (Aleekchea'ahoosh), 1928

Contents

Preface   xi

Contributors   xv

Introduction and Overview   3
Russell Thornton

Part 1. Native Americans Today

1. The Demography of Colonialism and "Old" and "New"
   Native Americans   17
   Russell Thornton

2. Perspectives on Native American Identity   40
   Raymond D. Fogelson

3. Native Americans and the Trauma of History   60
   Bonnie Duran, Eduardo Duran, and Maria Yellow Horse Brave Heart

Part 2. The Development of Native American Studies

4. Institutional and Intellectual Histories
   of Native American Studies   79
   Russell Thornton

**Part 3. Native American Studies and the Disciplines:
Literature, Linguistics, Anthropology, and History**

5. Literature and Students in the Emergence
   of Native American Studies   111
   Robert Allen Warrior

6. "Writing Indian": American Indian Literature and the Future
   of Native American Studies   130
   Kathryn W. Shanley

7. Linguistics and Languages in Native American Studies   152
   J. Randolph Valentine

8. Native American Studies and the End of Ethnohistory 182
Melissa L. Meyer and Kerwin Lee Klein

9. Using the Past: History and Native American Studies 217
Richard White

Part 4. Five Topics for Native American Studies

10. The Eagle's Empire: Sovereignty, Survival, and Self-
Governance in Native American Law and Constitutionalism 247
Rennard Strickland

11. Truth and Tolerance in Native American Epistemology 271
John H. Moore

12. Kinship: The Foundation for Native American Society 306
Raymond J. DeMallie

13. Directions in Native American Science and Technology 357
Clara Sue Kidwell and Peter Nabokov

14. Who Owns Our Past? The Repatriation of Native American
Human Remains and Cultural Objects 385
Russell Thornton

A Final Note 416
Russell Thornton and C. Matthew Snipp

Index 425

Preface

When does the beginning begin? The beginning of this volume for me was in 1991 when Al Reiss, Jr., a sociologist at Yale, asked me about work on American Indians in conjunction with work he was doing with a national panel. I sent him a copy of my and Mary Grasmick's *Sociology of American Indians: A Critical Bibliography,* in which we detail the disciplinary imbalances in the study of Native Americans and discuss sociological research and writings on Native Americans. Responding to the need for appropriate research on Native Americans, Reiss wrote to the sociologist David Featherman, then president of the Social Science Research Council (SSRC), and urged a SSRC project. Featherman decided to undertake an initiative on Native Americans and Native American studies.

Featherman convened a small interdisciplinary group of scholars of Native Americans in Santa Fe, New Mexico, in February 1992. It was co-chaired by Gary Sandefur of the University of Wisconsin–Madison, and Matt Snipp, then at the same campus; Alfonso Ortiz of the University of New Mexico was the local host. Participants were David Edmunds, then of Indiana University, Charlotte Heth, then of UCLA, Fred Hoxie of the Newberry Library, Ted Jojola of the University of New Mexico, Ron Trosper of Northern Arizona University, Blair Stonechild of Saskatchewan Indian Federated College, and myself, then at the University of California, Berkeley. Local guests were Kathryn Tijerina and Roger Buffalohead of the Institute of American Indian Arts. The SSRC was represented by David Featherman and Annette Dieli. We discussed the need for new directions in the study of Native Americans and presented various scholarly and professional needs. Particularly important research needs were reconstructing pre-Columbian societies and populations, exploring the "ethnohistory" of early America, examining Native American resettlement patterns, and understanding the dynamics of contemporary Native Americans and their communities.

Following the meeting, in the summer of 1993, the SSRC submitted a proposal to the Ford Foundation to develop a guide for resources in Native American studies research. The project was eventually funded.

Under the new project's auspices, a SSRC American Indian Studies Advisory Panel was formed, headed by Matt Snipp and composed of Fred Hoxie, Charlotte Heth, Joseph Jorgensen of the University of California, Irvine, Clara Sue Kidwell, then at the National Museum of the American Indian, Spero Manson of the University of Colorado, James Merrell of Vassar College, James Nason of the University of Washington, Blair Stonechild, and myself. The panel met in Dallas in the spring of 1994. The SSRC was represented by Felix V. Matos Rodriguez and Jamie A. Castaneda. We discussed in much detail the initiative funded by the Ford Foundation and agreed to broaden the mandate considerably to focus on the intellectual side of Native American studies while also compiling a guide to scholarly resources. Having decided to undertake an edited volume, the panel developed an outline and identified potential authors. I agreed to edit the work.

In February 1996, Matt Snipp, I, and the contributors to the planned volume met in the Department of Anthropology at UCLA to discuss their chapters. Ramon Torrecilha represented the SSRC at the meeting. We briefly presented our respective projects, discussed them with other authors, and also considered adding some chapters, which was done.

Besides the reviewers who read the manuscript for the University of Wisconsin Press, many others read and commented on specific chapters: Thomas Biolsi, Robert Brightman, Robert Edgerton, Morris Foster, Eva Garroutte, Lynne Goldstein, Richard Grounds, Alexandra Harmon, Douglas Hollan, Dell Hymes, Elaine Jahner, Jennie Joe, Clara Sue Kidwell, Teresa LaFromboise, James Merrell, Melissa Meyer, John Moore, LaVonne Brown Ruoff, Gary Sandefur, Greg Sarris, Kate Shanley, Bruce Smith, Matt Snipp, Blair Stonechild, Robert Williams, and Craig Womack. The assistance of all is much appreciated.

In May 1997 the SSRC sponsored a conference at Stanford University to consider, among other issues, some of the ideas raised in the volume. Participants provided helpful comments. Those attending were Thomas Biolsi, Ray DeMallie, Ray Fogelson, Eva Garroutte, Angela Gonzales, Gabriela Gomez-Carcamo, M. Annette Jaimes-Guerrero, Clara Sue Kidwell, Kerwin Klein,

Teresa LaFromboise, Colleen Larrimore, Jim Larrimore, Richard Little Bear, Tsanina Lomawaima, Cheryl Metoyer, John Moore, Betty Parent, Kate Shanley, Matt Snipp, Jay Stauss, Ramon Torrecilha, Robert Warrior, David Wilkins, William Willard, Rosita Worl, and myself.

The result of this journey for me is the present volume. I hope it is worthy of the effort committed to it. I would like to thank Al Reiss and David Featherman for their concern about Native Americans and Native American scholarship and Matt Snipp for chairing all the panels guiding the eventual project. Ramon Torrecilha was a pleasure to work with during the latter phases of the volume; Jamie Castaneda, his former assistant, was helpful and cheerful in handling various arrangements and problems, as was Gabriela Gomez-Carcamo, his next assistant. I thank all of them. Scott Waugh, dean of social sciences at UCLA, provided some small but greatly appreciated course relief for me while I undertook my commitments to the project. I thank him. Finally, I would like to acknowledge funds provided by the Committee on Research at UCLA that provided for research assistance during 1995. My research assistants from time to time on the project, Robert Collins in anthropology and Michael Fickes in history, eased many tasks greatly. Thank you both. The Ford Foundation provided the major support for the project, and I am most grateful to them for their interest in Native American studies. Rosalie Robertson of the University of Wisconsin Press was both very helpful and a pleasure to work with in turning the manuscript into this volume.

UCLA, 1997   RUSSELL THORNTON

Contributors

MARIA YELLOW HORSE BRAVE HEART (Hunkpapa and Oglala Lakota) is associate professor at the University of Denver Graduate School of Social Work. She is also the Director and Co-founder of the Takini Network for Lakota Holocaust Survivors. She has lived and worked on the Standing Rock Lakota and Dakota Reservation providing clinical mental health services, has been as Associate Director at Denver Indian Health and Family Services, and is a national consultant on historical trauma among Native people. Her publications include six journal articles and several book chapters.

RAYMOND J. DEMALLIE is professor of anthropology at Indiana University and director of its American Indian Studies Research Institute. He has published widely on North American Indians and is editor of the forthcoming volume 13, *Plains,* of the *Handbook of North American Indians.*

BONNIE DURAN (Opelousas/Coushatta) has had extensive experience working with the Native American community as a public health direct service provider and researcher. She is currently an assistant professor at the University of New Mexico School of Medicine, Department of Family and Community Medicine. She co-authored, with her husband, Ed, *Native American Postcolonial Psychology.*

EDUARDO DURAN (Tewa/Apache) has worked as a clinician, administrator, researcher, and theoretician in Indian Country for fifteen years. Presently, he is a psychologist in the Behavioral Health Department at Rehobeth/McKinley Hospital in Gallup, New Mexico. He is author of the books *Transforming the Soul Wound* and *Native American Postcolonial Psychology,* the latter co-authored with his wife, Bonnie.

RAYMOND D. FOGELSON is professor of anthropology at the University of Chicago, where he has trained many scholars of North American Indians. He is an authority on Cherokee and other North American Indians.

CLARA SUE KIDWELL (Choctaw/Chippewa) is director of the Native American Studies Program at the University of Oklahoma. She is former associate director of cultural resources at the National Museum of the American Indian. She is the author of *Choctaws and Missionaries in Mississippi, 1818–1918* and, with Charles Roberts, *The Choctaws: A Critical Bibliography.*

KERWIN LEE KLEIN earned his Ph.D. in history from UCLA. He is now assistant professor of history at the University of California, Berkeley, and the author of *Frontiers of Historical Imagination: Narrating the European Conquest of Native America, 1890–1990.*

MELISSA L. MEYER is associate professor of history at UCLA, having received her Ph.D. in history from the University of Minnesota. A social historian of Native Americans, she is author of *The White Earth Tragedy: Ethnicity and Dispossession at a Minnesota Anishinaabe Reservation, 1889–1920.*

JOHN H. MOORE is chair and professor of anthropology at the University of Florida in Gainesville. He has done fieldwork or served as consultant to a large number of Native North American tribes and nations, including the Cheyennes, Mvskokes, Kiowas, Arapahoes, Cherokees, Chickasaws, Crees, Blackfeet, and Sarsis. He is the author or editor of seven books and monographs, including *The Cheyenne Nation: A Social and Demographic History.*

PETER NABOKOV is associate professor in the Department of World Arts and Cultures and the American Indian Studies Program at UCLA. He is the author of *Native American Architecture, The Architecture of Acoma Pueblo, Indian Running,* and *Two Leggings: The Making of a Crow Warrior,* among other books.

KATHRYN W. SHANLEY (Assiniboine) is associate professor in the Department of English and the American Indian Program at Cornell University. She has published widely on American Indian writers and literature, and has written a forthcoming book on James Welch.

C. MATTHEW SNIPP (Cherokee/Choctaw) is professor of sociology at Stanford University. His many publications include *American Indians: The First of This Land.*

RENNARD STRICKLAND (Osage/Cherokee) is currently dean and Philip H. Knight Professor of Law at the University of Oregon School of Law. Strickland served as editor-in-chief of the revised edition of Felix Cohen's *Handbook of Federal Indian Law.* He is the author of many books, including *The Indians in Oklahoma* and *Fire and the Spirits: Cherokee Law from Clan to Court.*

RUSSELL THORNTON (Cherokee) was born and raised in Oklahoma. Currently, he is professor of anthropology at UCLA. His books include *We Shall Live Again, American Indian Holocaust and Survival,* and *The Cherokees: A Population History.*

J. RANDOLPH VALENTINE received his Ph.D. in linguistics from the University of Texas, Austin, in 1994. He presently is assistant professor of linguistics and American Indian studies at the University of Wisconsin–Madison.

ROBERT ALLEN WARRIOR (Osage) teaches American Indian literature and intellectual history in the Department of English, Stanford University. He is the author of the books *Tribal Secrets: Recovering American Indian Intellectual Traditions,* and, with Paul Chaat Smith, *Like a Hurricane: The Indian Movement from Alcatraz to Wounded Knee.*

RICHARD WHITE is professor of history at Stanford University. He is currently a MacArthur fellow. His books include *The Middle Ground: Indians, Empires, and Republics in the Great Lakes Region, 1650–1815* and *The Roots of Dependency: Subsistence, Environment, and Social Change Among the Choctaws, Pawnees, and Navajos.*

Studying Native America

Russell Thornton

Introduction and Overview

Three sentences written by the Lakota writer Luther Standing Bear have intrigued me since I read them first two decades ago: "The White man does not understand the Indian for the reason that he does not understand America. He is too far removed from its formative process. The roots of the tree of his life have not yet grasped the rock and soil." [1] These are sweeping assertions—that America before the Europeans is part of America today, and that to understand America one must understand both America as a land and its first people. Were peoples and cultures transferred here from Europe and elsewhere transformed by the Native Americans they encountered? Are America's roots as firmly in native America as in transferred cultures? It is an interesting argument for the importance of Native American studies. At the least, America was created as a series of frontiers where Europeans, later Euro-Americans, interacted with diverse Native American peoples. Understanding these frontiers is important in understanding Europeans here, the Euro-Americans they became, and Native Americans after European arrival, and how each became transformed to form America.

In the final chapter of his *Land of the Spotted Eagle,* Luther Standing Bear discusses the education needed by native youth, one that includes understanding both traditional and modern life. The Native American "should become his own historian," he argues, "giving his account of the race—fairer and fewer accounts of the wars and more of statecraft, legends, languages, oratory,

3

and philosophical conceptions." [2] He then asks: "Why not a school of Indian thought, built on the Indian pattern and conducted by Indian instructors? . . . Why should not America be cognizant of itself; aware of its identity? In short, why should not America be preserved?" [3] What Standing Bear advocated in 1933 was Native American studies to educate both Native American and non–Native American youth about their respective Americas.[4]

What Is Native American Studies?

Decades after Standing Bear's book, scholars began to define Native American studies as it was being established in colleges and universities. In 1978, I expressed it thus: "American Indian studies is the endogenous consideration of traditional and contemporary Indian societies located in the Western Hemisphere." [5] This endogenous consideration would provide new perspectives on the study of Native Americans, additional topics to be studied, and new issues to be discussed. If this occurred, I asserted, Native American studies could become a distinct academic discipline. Later, in 1986, Vine Deloria, Jr., defined Native American studies as "encompassing all the relevant knowledge and information concerning the relationship between American Indians and the rest of the world, be it the federal government, other religions, the world of art and music, or international and domestic economies." [6]

Other scholars have occasionally addressed the problem of definition. In his chapter in this volume, Robert Allen Warrior discusses Elizabeth Cook-Lynn's suggestion that Native American studies should be "doing the intellectual work of the tribes," with "indigenousness" and its implications central to Native American studies as a unique area.[7] Yet, Cook-Lynn argues, Native American studies has drifted away from that mandate. Virtually everyone has agreed that the impact of colonialism on Native Americans and their societies must be considered and that Native American studies needs to bring new, postcolonial perspectives on the Native American past, present, and future.[8]

The latter point is important, since examining colonialism is critical in understanding Native Americans, as examining racism is critical in understanding African Americans. The racism of being denied full access to American society is the best description of the situation of African Americans in the United States. Indeed, the civil rights movement of the 1960s and 1970s and on to today is about lessening the discrimination that prevents African Americans from participating in American society to the same extent as white Americans. Colonialism, in contrast, typically involves imposing a society—a "way of life"—upon a land and its people while exploiting one or the other or both. "Colonialism" is a more appropriate term than "racism" for describing the situation of Native Americans within historical and contemporary American society. African Americans had another culture imposed upon them, and the civil rights movement has lessened this colonialism while lessening racism toward them. Although Native Americans have experienced racism in many forms, a different emphasis is crucial to understanding each group. Native Americans were colonized on their land, the one land to which they trace their social, cultural, and religious origins. They are the indigenous people of this hemisphere. To understand Native Americans is to understand both this fact and also the fact that Native Americans seek to remain as both sovereign tribes and people distinct from American society while participating in it.

Native Americans often must choose between life in Native American post-colonial societies and cultures and life in more mainstream American society. The choice is not always easy. The classic English novel *Brave New World* alludes to the contemporary dilemma for Native Americans. Like Aldous Huxley's "Savage," Native Americans are "offered only two alternatives, an insane life in Utopia, or the life of a primitive in an Indian village, a life more human in some respects, but in others hardly less queer and abnormal." [9] Many Native Americans consider life in the mainstream of America to be "insane"; yet the poverty, violence, and hopelessness of some postcolonial reservations are not attractive alternatives.

The objective of Native American studies can be best stated as follows: to understand Native Americans, America, and the world from the Native American indigenous perspective and by that understanding to broaden the knowledge and education of both Native Americans and non–Native Americans. Not just Native Americans are to be understood in Native American studies, though to understand them and their histories, societies, and cultures is critical. In Native American studies, as Marlys Duchene has written, "generations of dreams, crises, adjustments, and ancient roots should surface." [10] Native American studies must also contain an understanding of America and the wider world as Native Americans and Native American tribes understand both. Therefore, Native American studies — the study of *Native* America — differs from the traditional study of Native Americans in the various academic disciplines.

Interdisciplinary, multidisciplinary, and comparative approaches are particularly important. At one conference of Native American studies directors, all agreed "that Native American cultures have a holistic conception of the world and the place of humans in it, which is reflected in the idea of Native American Studies as a liberal arts field." [11] They concluded, moreover, that "the connectedness of Indian cultures on all levels is the underlying philosophical motivation of the field, and sufficient to warrant calling it a discipline." [12] Interdisciplinary and multidisciplinary approaches incorporate the "holistic" perspective characteristic of Native American cultures. Many scholars also advocate a comparative perspective, arguing that the experience of Native Americans can be fully understood only when compared with the experiences of other indigenous people. This "indigenism," according to M. Annette Jaimes, "exerts precisely the sort of impetus required to move AIS [American Indian Studies] toward being a valid and *autonomous* discipline, rather than a rubber stamp of others." [13]

Native American studies should not be limited in either regard, however. While the traditional disciplines are useful and helpful, Native American studies can be more than their sum, and must be more to accomplish the mandate of "indigenousness" and study America and the world from the native perspective. Comparative approaches are important but should not mask the crucial task of articulating Native American America, discovering the impact of colonialism on Native Americans and their societies, and articulating Native American efforts to deal with issues of the postcolonial period, particularly sovereignty.

What Has Gone Wrong?

Perhaps many agree that Native American studies has rich intellectual potential, and that knowledge from and about Native American societies and cultures can be very important to the scholarly function of higher education in our society. Perhaps many agree also that Native American studies is crucial to the education of all about Native Americans, Native America, America, and even the world. Some may even agree that Native American studies has made important intellectual contributions to academe. Some scholarship discussed here would prove that is the case. However, the potential importance of Native American studies in higher education is far from realized.

Why is this so? In part, the potential of Native American studies is hindered by many of the same things that hinder Native Americans in American society. These factors encompass romantic, fantasy-driven, and stereotyped notions about, lack of appreciation and respect for, and even a rejection of Native Americans. In colleges and universities, this tendency can be translated into a failure to understand and appreciate Native Americans, their societies, cultures, and uniqueness, to respect Native American studies, and to demand that Native American studies be a first-rate intellectual endeavor. It is telling that major national universities have not committed to developing Native American studies as an academic endeavor equal to others, including the incorporation of many leading Native American scholars and the creation of doctoral programs emphasizing Native Americans. (The University of Arizona has recently moved in this direction.) Universities have made such efforts for African-American studies, women's studies, and many, many area studies, but not Native American studies. What Native Americans have gotten are some commitments to educate Native Americans at the undergraduate level (e.g., Dartmouth College), the graduate level (e.g., Harvard University), or both levels (e.g., Stanford University), and Native American studies programs often not equal to other academic units on campus, in terms of both intellectual quality and necessary resources.

It must be noted, however, that part of the fault lies with Native American studies. Sometimes faculty members in Native American studies departments or programs do not appreciate or understand the system of higher education. Sometimes they, too, fail to understand Native American peoples, especially traditional or tribal ones. They may be influenced by romanticized, stereo-typed notions of Native Americans, or they may be non-Indians who want to "help the poor Indian," generally in ways they think Native Americans should be helped, or who are "Indian sniffers," wanting merely to associate themselves with Native Americans. They may not be committed to Native American studies, but may view it as a career vehicle if unable to compete in the traditional academic disciplines. To appreciate and understand both academe and Native American peoples and their diversity is critical for Native American studies. It makes no sense to be involved in higher education if one is unwilling to embrace the values and objectives of higher education, including high standards for research and scholarship along with teaching and service. It makes no sense to be involved in Native American studies without a real understanding, appreciation, and acceptance of Native Americans.

Native American studies, we hear often, has little in the way of an intellectual agenda. Jaimes has even characterized it as "a structurally and conceptually rudderless discipline." [14] Native American studies still seems to survive on the politics and polemics of the sixties. Some agenda is needed if we are to incorporate the full intellectual richness of Native Americans, and their societies and cultures, into colleges and universities. As described above, that agenda must include a full understanding of colonialism in America, the contemporary "postcolonial" period, and comparative colonialism. And, as most contributors to this volume discuss, topics within Native American studies generally need to be examined from multi- and interdisciplinary perspectives using diverse methodologies. However, Native American studies must not be limited to these approaches in its quest to address the Native Americans as indigenous, sovereign peoples of America. Native American issues, definitions, perspectives, and concepts should be at the forefront.

Native American Studies or American Indian Studies?

In most colleges and universities in the United States, the discipline is named either "American Indian studies" or "Native American studies." The terms "Native American studies" and "Native American" are generally used throughout the present work. This choice is not based on contemporary fashion or political correctness—I prefer "American Indian"—but on inclusiveness.

"Native American" encompasses all the indigenous peoples of the Western Hemisphere: American Indians, Inuit (Eskimo), Aleutian Islanders (Aleuts), and Native Hawaiians. Although this volume focuses on American Indians, contributors on occasion refer to other Native Americans or to Hawaiian or Native Alaskan studies. Using the term "Native American" recognizes the distinctiveness of the several native peoples of the hemisphere.

Overview

This volume offers perspectives on Native American studies—what it is has been, what it is, and what it may be. Writers assess its past, analyze its present, and suggest future directions. They discuss scholarly successes and failures, examine old areas of inquiry, and propose new ones. Native American studies does, or can, embrace all the topics discussed in this volume.

Contributors have attempted to consider the uniqueness of Native American studies and the importance of incorporating native views into it while remaining cognizant of the nature of higher education. Some have been involved in Native American studies programs of one type or another; others have not, but are scholars of Native Americans. Most authors have considered the impact of European and Euro-American colonialism on Native Americans and how it may be incorporated into Native American studies, along with the relevance of Native American studies to the postcolonial period. In keeping with the goal of a fully interdisciplinary approach, authors represent, besides Native American studies, the traditional disciplines and professions of anthropology, demography, English and literature, history, law, social work, linguistics, public health, psychology, and sociology. Most authors draw freely from ideas and scholarship in various disciplines and, of course, from their knowledge of Native America.

The volume is organized in four parts. Part 1 asks who Native Americans are today. In the initial chapter, one of several I wrote for this volume, I provide an overview of the demographic impact of colonialism on the Native American population and consider how various forms of colonialism combined with disease reduced their numbers. (What happened to the native peoples of this hemisphere is only one facet of the larger picture of the demographic effects of European colonialism.) I then examine implications of that impact for how the Native American population is defined today and may be defined in the future, and suggest how this may affect Native American identity. Important in this examination is a discussion of contemporary tribal membership requirements—particularly variations in "blood quantum."

In Chapter 2, Raymond Fogelson considers Native American identity from three perspectives—blood, land, and community. He emphasizes the historical continuity of identity for Native Americans and considers identity as the presentation of self-images. Fogelson also discusses historic "tribal" forms of Native American organization as they relate to identity. Native American studies itself, of course, presents an image of Native Americans to others.

Bonnie Duran, Ed Duran, and Maria Yellow Horse Brave Heart write about the psychological impact of European and Euro-American colonialism in Chapter 3. They draw upon research among Native Americans in California and survivors of the Nazi holocaust to argue that Native Americans will never be "psychologically sound" until they and American society deal with how the past affected Native Americans and continues to affect Native American identity today. Native American studies can play an important educational role for both Native American and other students in this regard.

Part 2 consists of one chapter, a detailed consideration of the emergence of Native American studies. In Chapter 4 I examine the institutional and intellectual histories of Native American studies and its incorporation into the system of higher education. The history of Native American education in the United States includes the first colonial attempts to Christianize and "civilize" the peoples Europeans encountered, the establishment of the system of higher education in America, the boarding school period, and contemporary educational self-determination. Encompassed within this story are the development of Native American studies per se and the study of Native Americans by Europeans and Americans as their intellectual life and science developed over the past several centuries. In offering perspectives on the incorporation of Native American studies in higher education and the incomplete intellectual development of Native American studies, I am critical of both the colleges and universities that have embraced Native American studies and some individuals who have been a part of the field over the past three decades. There is much to praise and much to criticize, and I pull few punches (but I do pull some).

Part 3 considers Native American studies in terms of four disciplines important to its development: literature, linguistics, anthropology, and history. Native American literature is one of the real success stories of both Native Americans in academe and Native American studies, and is, along with "ethnohistory," a critical area in Native American studies. Robert Warrior looks at the important role of Native American literature in the emergence of Native American studies in higher education (Chapter 5), with particular emphasis on N. Scott Momaday, Vine Deloria, Jr., and other Native American writers. He also illustrates the role Native American students played in the incorporation of Native American literature in colleges and universities, and contrasts literature with the disciplines of anthropology and history. Native American literature, he suggests, presents Native Americans as they are envisioned by the writer. The same might be said for Native American studies, which presents Native Americans, their societies, cultures, and histories, as envisioned by the faculty and students of Native American studies.

Certainly, one important task of Native American studies is to present issues, concerns, problems, definitions, and the like from Native American tribal perspectives. In Chapter 6, Kathryn Shanley focuses on "writing Indian": that is, how may Native American literature and thus Native American studies become really "Native American"? It is not an identity issue, she asserts, though it has frequently been defined in this way, to our confusion. "It might be a matter of 'seeing' things a certain way," she writes, but probably "the experience is a full sensory one." The answers she seeks for Native American studies are, as she says, not simple ones. In seeking those answers, Shanley relates literature ("writing Indian") and Native American studies to the important topics of identity, place, kinship, and tribalism. One answer for her is to develop regionally based programs combining place and tribe with Native American studies.

J. Randolph Valentine considers languages, linguistics, and Native American studies in Chapter 7. Native American languages are at the very heart of Native American peoples. (Consider, by way of example, the concerted attempt to suppress Native American languages during the boarding school period.) Yet many Native American studies programs do not consider languages, much less actively teach a Native American language. As Valentine illustrates, this is an extremely important area, one requiring unique methods and goals. He notes that linguistics for Native American studies is different from "mainstream" linguistics, unique in its focus on documentation and need to be relevant to the communities where the languages are spoken. These are two worthy goals. A discussion of some exemplary language programs draws upon Valentine's experiences in Ojibwe and Cree language programs over the years. Many tribal peoples today are concerned with reviving or preserving their languages, often developing tribal language programs. The involvement of Native American studies in such endeavors seems natural.

Melissa Meyer and Kerwin Klein examine the relationship of Native American studies to anthropology and history, drawing upon the history of the study of Native Americans in both disciplines. They also examine the "old and ambivalent relationship" of the two. Meyer and Klein discuss and critique in some detail the product of this relationship—"ethnohistory." Why, they ask, should the study of Native Americans be removed from mainstream scholarship in history? Why should a special type of history—ethnohistory—be reserved for Native Americans, while "history" is for other types of people? They then suggest areas in the study of Native Americans that should naturally incorporate history and anthropology (including archaeology).

Richard White's chapter is complementary to Meyer and Klein's. In Chapter 9 he discusses the creation and writing of Native American history by contemporary scholars, and its relationship to the wider discipline of history. He notes how Native Americans are generally considered either "outside of history" or, for academe, "against history," and how they have appeared in debates critiquing the discipline of history. However, polemicized history still plagues Native American studies from time to time, and this is more problematic when the "history" written by people in Native American studies does not conform to the tenets of solid historical scholarship.

The current debate about the influence of the Iroquois Confederacy upon the U.S. Constitution is a case in point for White. I do not know whether the Constitution was influenced by the Iroquois form of governance, but from my own reading of some of the literature, I would say that influence has not been proven.[15] Like White, I wonder why this connection is so important to many Native Americans. As a young Iroquois woman at Dartmouth College pointed out: if the U.S. Constitution were really patterned after the Iroquois, then the clan mothers would be electing the President![16]

Part 4 considers topics important or potentially important to Native American studies as an intellectual enterprise. Rennard Strickland writes in Chapter 10 on the history of Native American tribal sovereignty and the related issues of self-governance and constitutionalism. He suggests that the survival of the concept of sovereignty is crucial for the survival of Native Americans, but rarely addressed by Native American studies at the microlevel of tribal operations. "We need scholars," he asserts, "who are prepared to step beyond the theory of sovereignty and explore it in practice. . . . It is a truly rich field that provides an opportunity for scholarship in the grand tradition." Such scholarship within the confines of Native American studies programs is, of course, exactly what the field needs. Also needed is the other facet of Strickland's suggestion — studies of the actual operation of Native American tribes. Studying the many and complex facets of contemporary tribal operations and politics is an obvious, and much needed, undertaking. Of related importance are studies of historical periods of tribal governance, or lack thereof: for example, the history of the western Cherokee between land allotment in the first decades of this century and tribal resurgence in the 1960s and 1970s.

John Moore examines the place of Native American epistemology in Native American studies (Chapter 11). He notes the great differences both between Native American and western epistemologies and among Native American ones themselves. He also contrasts Cheyenne and Creek cosmology. Moore describes a surprisingly small number of basic principles of Native American cosmology and religion, focusing on the natural world and its spirits and creatures. He also offers insightful suggestions for teaching Native American epistemology in the classroom, here again drawing in part upon differences between the Cheyenne and the Creek. Strategies for instruction, he argues, must ensure that the Native American people in question are comfortable with both what is taught and how it is taught.

Raymond DeMallie considers Native American families and kinship, in many ways the essence of Native American peoples, and he says, "the necessary starting point" for understanding them. (Kinship might even be, as Shanley asserts, the essence of individual identity for Native Americans.) One important reason this is so, DeMallie notes in Chapter 12, is that kinship in most Native American societies is a cognitive structure describing the "relationship of human beings to all other forms of existence in a vast web of cosmic interrelationship in which humans stand at the bottom or on the periphery." Kinship and family, however, have not received due attention from Native American studies. DeMallie begins by describing types of Native American kinship systems, then discusses how they work, what they mean, and how they are used. As DeMallie illustrates, Native American studies could embrace many important topics and issues in the examination and study of kinship and family.

Clara Sue Kidwell and Peter Nabokov write in Chapter 13 about Native American science and technology, examining how the two terms might apply to Native American cultures before European contact. They draw their examples from present-day Mexico and Central and South America and the present-day United States and Canada. Science and technology seem a natural way for the academic system to relate to Native American peoples, and a means by which their knowledge may be shared with and potentially benefit the wider society. In Native American culture, science and religion, art and technology, are intermingled. This is perhaps important for all of us to remember in our increasing fragmented societies. Simply studying Native American science and technology can greatly expand our knowledge base, as, for example, Bruce Smith has done recently in his *Rivers of Change*,[17] a study of the transition to agriculture in eastern North America. Kidwell and Nabokov also examine the current state of scholarship, then suggest some new avenues for investigation within the context of Native American studies.

In the final chapter of this section, I examine the recent movement for the repatriation of Native American human remains and cultural objects, drawing on my experiences since 1990 as chair of the Smithsonian Institution's Native American Repatriation Review Committee. Based primarily on federal laws but also upon state laws, such repatriations are ending longstanding grievances. The repatriation movement is also revitalizing native communities, forming new working relationships between Native Americans and scholars and new intellectual relationships between oral history, written history, and archaeology, and forcing nonnatives to consider Native American conceptions of property and ownership.

As Meyer and Klein also suggest, I assert that archaeology, including physical anthropology, precontact or otherwise, has much to offer to Native American studies and Native Americans. Important roles for Native American studies in this regard would include the synthesis of archaeological studies and site reports and the consideration of archaeological findings as they relate to Native American oral traditions and written histories. Similarly, physical anthropology can provide insights into affinities among Native American peoples and between them and other peoples of the world, and, thus, help in the writing of Native American history, before and after European contact. Repatriation has forced archaeologists and physical anthropologists to relate in new ways to Native Americans, as anthropologists and Native Americans forged new relations after the sixties and the establishment of Native American studies. Native American studies could help direct and foster these new relationships.

In a closing note about the future of Native American studies, Matt Snipp and I return to the past, echoing calls made at the First Convocation of American Indian Scholars in 1970 and a Round Table of Native American Studies Directors held in 1980, and then suggest some new paths to follow. As Native American scholars, we have much to do and formidable obstacles to overcome, but many will benefit from our actions.

Notes

1.   Luther Standing Bear, *Land of the Spotted Eagle* (Lincoln: University of Nebraska Press, 1978 [1933]), 248.

2.   Ibid., 254.

3.   Ibid., 254–55.

4.   Standing Bear surely knew what he was talking about. Probably a Brule Lakota from South Dakota (though he referred to himself as Ogalala), he was born in the mid-1860s and was in the initial class of the Carlisle Indian School in 1879. (His young name was Plenty Kill; renamed at the school, he was given his father's name, Standing Bear, as a surname.) He learned tinsmithing at Carlisle, but returned to South Dakota, working variously at the Rosebud and Pine Ridge reservations, and eventually receiving an allotment at Pine Ridge. In the early 1900s, he toured with Buffalo Bill's Wild West show, then moved to California, before returning to Pine Ridge in 1931 after an absence of sixteen years. *Land of the Spotted Eagle* was undoubtedly a response to the conditions he witnessed on his reservation (see Richard N. Ellis, "Foreword," ibid., vii–xiv). Standing Bear was also perhaps influenced by both the Meriam Report of 1928 and national Native American leaders of the early twentieth century—for example, Charles Eastman (Ohiyesa), Carlos Montezuma, Laura Cornelius Standing, and Arthur C. Parker—as well as such non–Native Americans as Fayette Avery McKenzie of Ohio State University (who was on the staff that prepared the Meriam Report of 1928). Standing Bear apparently did not participate in their activities, although his brother, Henry Standing Bear, did. Yet Standing Bear's ideas were actually reflected in the careers of some of these individuals, since he advocated professional training for Native Americans who would work on reservations. A discussion of these and other intellectuals and their efforts may be found in Hazel W. Hertzberg, *The Search for an American Indian Identity: Modern Pan-Indian Movements* (Syracuse: Syracuse University Press, 1971), 1–209.

5.   Russell Thornton, "American Indian studies as an academic discipline," *American Indian Culture and Research Journal*, 2 (1978), 10.

6.   Vine Deloria, Jr., "Indian studies — The orphan of academia," *Wicazo Sa Review*, 2 (1986), 6.

7.   Elizabeth Cook-Lynn, "Who stole Native American studies?" *Wicazo Sa Review*, 12 (1997), 9–22.

8.   See, for example, Ward Churchill, "White studies: The intellectual imperialism of contemporary U.S. education," *Integrateducation*, 19 (1982), 51–57; M. Annette Jaimes, "American Indian studies: Toward an indigenous model," *American Indian Culture and Research Journal*, 11 (1987), 1–16.

9.   Aldous Huxley, *Brave New World* (New York: HarperCollins, 1992 [1932]), viii.

10.   Marlys Duchene, "The relevancy of Indian studies in higher education," in *American Indian Issues in Higher Education* (Los Angeles: American Indian Studies Center, UCLA, 1981), 17.

11.   Roxanne Dunbar Ortiz, ed., *Final Report from the Round Table of Native American Studies Directors in Forming the Native American Studies Association* (Albuquerque: Native American Studies Association with the Institute for Native American Development, University of New Mexico, 1980), 20.

12.   Ibid., 21.

13.   Jaimes, "American Indian studies," 14.

14.   Ibid., 4.

15.   See Elisabeth Tooker, "The United States Constitution and the Iroquois League," *Ethnohistory*, 35 (1988), 305–36; Bruce E. Johansen, "Native American societies and the evolution of democracy in America, 1600–1800," *Ethnohistory*, 37 (1990), 279–90; Elisabeth Tooker, "Rejoinder to Johansen," *Ethnohistory*, 37 (1990), 291–97.

16.   Similarly, I happen to think the demographic history of Native Americans after colonialism should speak for itself, without deflating or inflating aboriginal Native American population size, though I have been accused of both crimes. For some, the more Indians who suffered and died at the hands of the colonial Europeans and Euro-Americans, the better. It seems the best history is the history of the greatest atrocity, real or otherwise. We do not know the "real" story of the population decline of Native Americans following European contact, but we know enough to know that whatever it "really" was, it is horrific enough, without supplying critics of Native American studies with examples of inferior scholarship. I have empathy for those Native Americans who suffered and had short or unlived lives, and hope their number was small, though I do not think it was.

17.   Bruce D. Smith, *Rivers of Change: Essays on Early Agriculture in Eastern North America* (Washington, D.C.: Smithsonian Institution Press, 1992).

PART 1

NATIVE AMERICANS TODAY

1 *Russell Thornton*

The Demography of Colonialism and "Old" and "New" Native Americans

The demographic impact of European populations on indigenous populations has taken many forms. Following European expansion and colonization, the indigenous population might grow, often quickly, though sometimes after an initial decline. This occurred, according to A. M. Carr-Saunders, in India, Java and Madura in the Netherlands Indies, Egypt, Formosa, Algeria, and the Philippines.[1] In other cases indigenous populations were destroyed, or greatly reduced, more or less permanently. Examples here include the aboriginal population of Tasmania, the Maori of New Zealand, the Australian Aborigines, and Native Hawaiians.[2] Of course, ascertaining indigenous population growth or decline depends on knowing what the pre-European populations actually were. Estimates are generally tenuous and may vary widely. There is not much information, for example, on the population of the Netherlands Indies prior to the nineteenth century; the same may be said for Algeria.[3] Moreover, problems of definition and enumeration arise because of intermarriage between indigenous and immigrant populations as well as social and cultural changes obscuring the nature of native populations, such as loss of tribalism or language, and the formation of new ethnic or even racially defined groups.

The Native American population of the Western Hemisphere underwent drastic decline following European contact and its associated colonialism. Some recovery occurred, but how much is debated, since aboriginal population estimates for the hemisphere vary widely—from a mere 8.4 million (suggested by Alfred L. Kroeber) to 53.9 million (William Denevan) to more than 100 million (Henry Dobyns). Some 75 million seems a reasonable estimate, as I have argued.[4] Population recovery is also a function of how historic and contemporary indigenous populations are defined. Such definitions vary considerably from country to country in the hemisphere; for example, the censuses of different countries enumerate Native Americans differently, and the way in which a country enumerates Native Americans may vary from census to census.[5] As a result, we have no good figures for the current Native American population of the Western Hemisphere as a whole, and it is often unclear how current definitions of the populations relate to aboriginal populations. Certainly, the total population is smaller than the estimated 75 million circa 1492. It can be said with certainty only that specific populations were destroyed, were more or less "permanently" reduced, or declined sharply but experienced some subsequent population growth. (And some populations, under some definitions, are far larger today than in 1492.) It may be pointed out, however, that the overwhelming majority of the more than 5.5 billion people alive in the world today are descendants of those five hundred million or so people living in the Eastern Hemisphere in 1492. The past five hundred years have witnessed nonparalleled population growth for those of the Eastern Hemisphere, while the Native Americans of the Western Hemisphere have struggled to survive as distinct populations.

Native North America

The size of the aboriginal population of America north of present-day Mexico is debated by scholars; hence, the magnitude of population decline is debated as well.

The classic estimate of the aboriginal population for this area is by James Mooney. Early in this century, he estimated individual Native American tribal populations, summed them by regions, and then totaled the regions to arrive at an estimate of 1,153,000 for North America north of the Rio Grande at first (extensive) European contact.[6] Generations of subsequent scholars generally accepted Mooney's estimate, although Kroeber considered it excessive for the California area and lowered it to barely more than 1 million.[7] "Mooney's total of about 1,150,000, reduced to 1,025,000 by the California substitution, will ultimately shrink to around 900,000, possibly somewhat farther," Kroeber suggested.[8]

In 1966, Dobyns worked backwards using depopulation ratios derived from assorted aboriginal population sizes and nadir populations to arrive at an aboriginal population size for America north of Mexico of 9.80 to 12.25 million.[9] In 1983, Dobyns used depopulation ratios from epidemics and also considered possible carrying-capacities of Native American environments and technologies to propose a population of 18 million aboriginal Native Americans north of Mesoamerica (an area including northern Mexico as well as the present-day United States, Canada, and Greenland).[10]

The vast majority of scholars now agree that Mooney significantly underestimated the aboriginal population for the area north of the Rio Grande and thus also the baseline from which aboriginal population decline may be fully assessed. The problem is that he did not consider the possibility of significant population decline prior to his dates of first extensive European contact, which ranged from A.D. 1600 to 1845 depending on the region in question.[11]

Most scholars also consider Dobyns's estimates to be far excessive.[12] Alternative estimates have varied from around 2 million by Douglas Ubelaker to almost 4 million (reduced from an earlier estimate of almost 4.5 million) by Denevan to the slightly more than 7 million I arrived at and continue to use.[13] My estimate includes about 5 million people for the coterminous United States and about 2 million for present-day Canada, Alaska, and Greenland combined.

Such dissension notwithstanding, substantial depopulation did occur after European arrival and colonization; there is no argument about this point. The Native American population of the United States, Canada, and Greenland combined reached a nadir of perhaps 375,000 around 1900.[14]

During the past decade, "holocaust" has emerged as the metaphor describing the population collapse of Native Americans that accompanied European expansion into this hemisphere. Likewise, this "holocaust" has emerged as crucial to understanding the full impact of colonialism upon Native Americans and the social, cultural, biological, and perhaps psychological changes they subsequently underwent. Native American societies and cultures and Native Americans as biological and psychological entities were all affected by demographic collapse following 1492. The social and cultural collapse accompanying demographic change is well known. Not so well known are the biological changes that occur through selective mortality in epidemics and "population bottlenecks" whereby populations contract then expand. Native American postcolonial psychology, an emerging field, is even attempting to relate contemporary psychological problems to the long history of colonialism, including its demographic history.

Few topics within Native American studies today can afford to overlook this demographic history. There is much room for solid scholarship on Native American demography and epidemiology, both contemporary and historical, in Native American studies. Native scholars and demographers such as Gary Sandefur, Matthew Snipp, and myself, all of whom have been organizationally involved in Native American studies at points in our careers, have long realized this. Yet most Native American studies programs do not contain demographic or epidemiological components, although issues within the two topics are important to academe, Native American peoples, and the larger American society.[15] (Training and research in demography and epidemiology must be rigorous, however; here, as in other areas, no scholarship is preferable to poor scholarship.)[16] Comparing demographic histories between North American groups and comparing these histories with Native American groups elsewhere in the hemisphere and with indigenous groups around the world is also important to Native American studies. The resulting demography of colonialism could be expanded to include the experiences of other populations around the world in the wake of colonialism in its various forms.

Population Decline and the Epidemic Disease "Myth"

The effects of "Old World" diseases on Native American populations of this hemisphere have been important in the debate on aboriginal population size and decline, and their role has been extensively discussed. There were considerably fewer infectious diseases here than in the other hemisphere. New diseases that affected native populations here include smallpox, measles, the bubonic plague, cholera, typhoid, diphtheria, scarlet fever, whooping cough, malaria, and yellow fever, as well as some venereal diseases. America was not a "disease-free" paradise before the Europeans arrived, however; serious diseases, particularly tuberculosis and treponemal infections, were present. Nevertheless, one scholar concludes "that the two worlds of disease were different enough so that the post-Columbian effects of Old World diseases on the Native Americans was [sic] devastating." [17]

Scholars have also shown that the life expectancies of Native Americans did not differ much from those of their European counterparts. Life expectancies for Native Americans — who generally died in their twenties or early thirties — were kept relatively low by famine, nutritional deficiency diseases (e.g., pellagra), warfare, parasites, dysentery, influenza, fevers, and other ailments, in addition to tuberculosis and treponemal infections.[18]

The relative dearth of infectious diseases in this hemisphere is not fully understood. Reasons surely include the existence of fewer domesticated animals, from which many human diseases arise, and perhaps the absence of many large centers of population concentration, which foster diseases; a low overall population density probably hindered the survival of many diseases.

It is generally thought that humans came first to America from Asia, and the Native American descendants of the first humans here have common ancestors with contemporary Asian peoples. Most argue that the *Homo sapiens sapiens* who would become Native Americans migrated across cold and barren Beringa (the land bridge connecting the hemispheres at certain times) and moved into the interior of North America across present-day Alaska and Canada, probably along the eastern edge of the Canadian Rocky Mountains. (Some argue, however, that humans came here first by boat, along the northwest coast of North America.) There were perhaps three migrations: the Paleo-Indians arrived as long as 40,000 years ago; the Na-Dine, as recently as 12,000 years ago; and the Eskimo [Inuit] and Aleutian Islanders, about 9,000 to 10,000 years ago. These migrations across Beringa (or over water) may have served as a filter restricting pathogens from entering the Western Hemisphere, as such organisms cannot survive in extremely cold temperatures.[19]

In any event, Native Americans lacked prior exposure to diseases from Europe and Africa such as smallpox and measles, which typically confer lifelong immunity on anyone who recovers from them. In the Western Hemisphere these diseases produced "virgin soil epidemics" whereby a new disease spreads to virtually all members of a population (and may be particularly virulent).[20] Native Americans here in 1492 also seem to have been genetically homogeneous to a remarkable degree, causing viral infections to be preadapted to successive hosts rather than encountering a wide variety of new immune responses.[21] Technically, they had "a lack of genetic polymorphism in the MHC (major histocompatibility complex) alleles," as a young Passamaquoddy immunologist expressed it to me. (This characteristic reflects a lack of historic contact with many diseases whereby Native American immune systems would "adapt" to them and made Native Americans more susceptible to the diseases from the other hemisphere.) Certainly, such diseases and this relative homogeneity caused widespread population reduction. There is no question about this.

The timing and magnitude of "Old World" disease episodes and subsequent depopulation in North America, however, are still being debated. Soon after Europeans arrived in the Western Hemisphere, diseases devastated American Indian populations in areas of present-day Mexico, the Caribbean, and Central and South America. Yet it also has been argued that diseases moved northward early in the sixteenth century from European settlements in the Caribbean and Mesoamerica and spread to North America through early European explorations, colonies, slave raids, shipwrecks, and other native contacts. The diseases, according to this argument, infected native populations in both the Southeast and the Southwest of the present-day United States during the initial decades of the sixteenth century, and frequently culminated in epidemics and pandemics that devastated Native American populations of these regions and others as well. This theory suggests that the aboriginal population of North America was exceedingly large, but was reduced greatly by epidemic disease prior to significant historical documentation.[22]

Scholarly research has generally refuted arguments regarding continent-wide pandemics of smallpox and other diseases during the sixteenth century.[23] As Clark Spencer Larsen summarizes the information regarding smallpox,

"Archaeological, historical, and bioarchaeological studies provide compelling evidence that the arrival of Europeans did not occasion a sudden pandemic of smallpox in the early sixteenth century." [24]

Significant population decline in the Southeast, and perhaps in the Southwest, did begin *sometime* during the sixteenth century.[25] Some research supports the notion that epidemic disease in the Southeast (and Mississippi Valley region) was responsible;[26] similarly, it is possible that smallpox was present early in the Southwest.[27] Still debated is whether sixteenth-century diseases in the Southeast—and by implication, the Southwest—occurred as region-wide pandemics or more isolated epidemics or even mere episodes.[28] More likely, the pattern of disease "was a patchwork affair, striking some populations and not others at various times." [29] Neither the epidemic disease pattern in North America nor the depopulation of Native American peoples by epidemic disease is fully understood by scholars, however.

Human populations constantly change in composition as members are born, die, or move into or out of the population. As discussed elsewhere,[30] the underlying population patterns may be termed a "demographic regime"—determinants of fertility, mortality, and migration that, interacting together, produce population growth, decline, or stability over a particular time. Such patterns tend to be relatively stable and influence the population's ability to respond to disturbances such as those caused by disease episodes.[31]

It was likely not the *direct* effects of any single epidemic or even any single disease that produced the long-term population reduction of most Native American groups. Disturbances such as epidemics may result in short-term population decline, but populations may return to predisease levels of population growth, decline, or stability. For example, I have simulated this process for smallpox epidemics; D. Ann Herring has illustrated recovery of a Native American population following the influenza epidemic of 1918–19; and Robert Boyd has shown the temporary effects of a smallpox epidemic as well as the longer effects of a measles epidemic.[32] Similarly, the historian William McNeill concluded that "the period required for medieval European populations to absorb the shock of renewed exposure to plague seems to have been between 100 and 133 years, that is, about five to six human generations." [33] Population recovery may even occur following repeated cycles of different diseases. The "Black Death" in Europe (1347–52) caused huge population losses through cyclic recurrence of the plague and the occurrence of other diseases such as typhus, influenza, and measles. European populations did not recover until late in the fifteenth century; however, they did recover.[34]

The indirect effects of disease episodes appear more important in population decline—the social disruption accompanying epidemics (as described by James Neel and others among the Yanomamo Indians of South America and discussed by Janet McGrath), and decreased fertility due to the disease itself or to marital disruption (e.g., loss of a spouse).[35] The nature of Native American societies, including preexisting patterns of social organization, also influenced population reduction and/or recovery, as I have shown regarding the Tolowa of northern California.[36]

Native American population decline resulted not only from European and African diseases, but also from the many effects of colonialism, subtle or otherwise. As Larsen comments, the emphasis on disease "has overshadowed a host of other important consequences of contact such as population relocation, forced labor, dietary change, and other areas." [37] Colonialism also interacted with disease to produce population decline; hence, Cary Meister notes that "later population decline resulting from disease was made possible because Indians had been driven from their land and robbed of their other resources." [38]

Native American societies were removed and relocated, warred upon and massacred, and undermined ecologically and economically. All of these products of colonialism caused population decline due to fertility decreases as well as mortality increases, as I have pointed out and as David Stannard has analyzed in the case of the Native Hawaiians.[39] For example, the Cherokee "Trail of Tears" from the Southeast to Indian Territory produced substantial population losses, partly through diseases such as cholera, but also through malnutrition, starvation, and decreased fertility.[40] Southern California Indians were missionized, confining them in new disease environments that took a demographic toll via both fertility and mortality,[41] and eventually displaced, resulting in selective outmigration and lower fertility as well as assimilation;[42] northern California Indians were subjected to pseudo-war and outright genocide as well as the destruction of their traditional patterns of subsistence.[43] While it is hard to address direct effects on mortality and fertility, plains Indians lost much of their social and cultural life and most of their economic basis when the great herds of buffalo were destroyed.[44]

It is important to note as well that small population declines over extended periods of time may ultimately produce large population reductions, as I have illustrated.[45] For example, a population decline from Mooney's estimated 1.153 million circa 1492 to 375,000 at the beginning of this century would require only a 0.28 percent annual decrease; even a decline starting from Dobyns's 18 million would require only a 0.97 percent annual decrease, which could have been produced by very small increases in mortality and decreases in fertility. Thus large population declines could have been produced by relatively small but long-term alterations in Native American societies whereby mortality and fertility levels changed modestly, not dramatically. Spectacular long-term mortality from epidemic disease, therefore, is unnecessary to account for either large aboriginal Native American populations or their decimation.

One task of Native American studies is to fully understand this differential impact of colonization upon Native Americans rather than subscribing to simple, inadequate explanations of disease history since 1492. Another important task—one having far-reaching implications for Native Americans and Native American studies—involves the full significance of the eventual population recovery and resulting demographic changes in the Native American population. One important consequence, examined below, relates to definitions of the Native American population and Native American identity.

Population Recovery

After some 400 years of population decline beginning soon after the arrival of Columbus in the Western Hemisphere, the Native American population north of Mexico began to increase around the turn of the twentieth century. The U.S. Census decennial enumerations indicate nearly continuous growth for the Native American population since 1900 (although the 1918–19 influenza epidemic caused serious losses, and some changes were made in enumeration procedures) to more than 1.4 million by 1980 and to more than 1.9 million by 1990.[46] To this may be added some 740,000 Native Americans in Canada in 1986 (575,000 American Indians, 35,000 Inuit [Eskimos], and 130,000 *Métis*), and perhaps 30,000 Native Americans in Greenland. Allowing for some increase to the present day, the total then becomes some 2.75 million in North America north of Mexico. This is obviously a significant increase from perhaps fewer than 400,000 around the turn of the century, about 250,000 of whom were in the United States, but far less than the more than 7 million I believe were here circa 1492. It is also but a fraction of the total current populations of the United States (250 million in 1990) and Canada (more than 25 million in 1990).[47]

U.S. Census enumerations also provide self-reported tribal affiliations and ancestries. The 1990 census reported the ten largest tribal affiliations in the United States as Cherokee, 308,000; Navajo, 219,000; Chippewa (Ojibwe), 104,000; Sioux, 103,000; Choctaw, 82,000; Pueblo, 53,000; Apache, 50,000; Iroquois, 49,000; Lumbee, 48,000; and Creek, 44,000.[48]

This population recovery was in part a result of lower mortality rates and increases in life expectancy as the effects of "Old World" disease and associated colonialism lessened.[49] For example, some data indicate that Native Americans' life expectancy at birth increased from 51.6 years in 1940 to 71.1 years in 1980, compared with a change from 64.2 to 74.4 years in the life expectancy of whites during the same four decades.[50]

In addition, changing fertility patterns and adaptation through intermarriage with nonnative peoples during this century meant that American Indian birth rates have remained higher than those of the average North American.[51] Early in the twentieth century, at around the point of the Native American population nadir in the United States, the fecundity and fertility of Native Americans—

particularly "full bloods"—was of considerable concern to government officials.[52] Soon, however, fertility increased.[53] (Mortality decreases have also
occurred.) In 1980, for example, married American Indian women 35 to 44
years of age had 3.61 children (mean number ever born), compared with 2.77
for the total U.S. population and only 2.67 for the white segment of the population.[54] Intermarried American Indian women generally had lower fertility
rates in 1980 than American Indian women married to American Indian men;
however, even intermarried American Indian women had higher fertility than
the total U.S. population.[55]

The very nature of this population history and recovery has had and continues to have profound effects upon Native Americans, and particularly on
who Native Americans are and how they define themselves on both the group
and the individual level.

For example, many remnant American Indian groups in the eastern United
States joined with the Iroquois and were adopted by them, as were the Tuscarora who fled northward from the Carolinas to escape the slave trade. Similarly, the migration of various tribes into the Mississippi River Valley and their
amalgamation there has been illustrated: Jeffrey Brain noted that the Natchez
changed marriage rules to adopt other Indians as relatives.[56] My earlier study of
the Tolowa and Yuki Indians of northern California indicates that depopulation
in and of itself was not the only factor determining tribal survival. Also significant was a difference in reservation experiences: the Yuki were placed on
a reservation with other tribes and intermarried with them, thereby becoming
merged with other tribes of the Covelo Indian Community of Confederated
Tribes of the Round Valley Indian Reservation. Preexisting patterns of social
organization were also important: Tolowa kinship patterns allowed the easy
incorporation of outsiders into the tribe through marriage but with offspring
defined as Tolowa, since Tolowa society is both patrilocal and patrilineal.[57]

New "Native American" groups were created in response to the demographic events of Euro-American contact. The *Métis* of Canada and the
United States–Canadian border are the best-known: this Indian–white "racially
mixed" group was created, they say, "nine months after the first white man set
foot in Canada." New peoples also include the Lumbee, historically prominent
tribes such as the Catawba, and many and varied triracial groups throughout the Atlantic, southeastern, and southern states. Mooney surveyed many
of these peoples for the Smithsonian in the early 1900s and found a strong
sense of Indian identity along with a fear of being absorbed into the African-
American population.[58] William Harlen Gilbert, Jr., of the Library of Congress
surveyed such communities in the mid-1940s and found "little evidence for
the supposition that they are being absorbed to any great extent into either
the white or the Negro groups." [59] In fact, he found that they were increasing
in size.[60]

"Old" and "New" Native Americans

The twentieth-century increase in the Native American population reflected in successive censuses of the United States was due in part to changes in the identification of individuals as "Native American." The U.S. Census enumerates individuals as belonging to one race, and since 1960 it has relied on self-identification to ascertain race. Although the *American Indian* population (excluding Eskimos [Inuit] and Aleuts) increased from 523,591 in 1960 to 792,730 in 1970 to 1.37 million in 1980 to more than 1.8 million in 1990, much of the apparent growth occurred because people who had not identified themselves as American Indian in an earlier census did so in a later one.[61] About 25 percent of the population "growth" of American Indians from 1960 to 1970, about 60 percent of the 1970–80 "growth," and about 35 percent of the 1980–90 "growth" may be accounted for by these changing identifications.[62] (Put in other words, the "error of closure" — the difference between a natural increase and the enumerated population from one time to another, assuming no migration — was 8.5 percent in the 1970 census count, 25.2 in the 1980 count, and 9.2 in the 1990 count.)[63]

Why did this occur? The political mobilization of Native Americans in the sixties and seventies along with other ethnic pride movements may have lifted part of the stigma attached to a Native American racial identity. This would be especially true for persons of mixed ancestry who formerly might have declined to disclose their Native American background because of that stigma. Conversely, individuals with minimal Native American background may have identified as Native American out of a desire to affirm a marginal or romanticized ethnic identity.[64]

Tribal Membership Requirements

Many different criteria may be used to delimit a population. Language, residence, cultural affiliation, recognition by a community, degree of "blood," genealogical lines of descent, and self-identification have all been used at some point in the past to define both the total Native American population and specific tribal populations. Each measure produces a different population, and which variables are ultimately employed is an arbitrary decision. The implications for Native Americans can be enormous, however.

Native Americans are unique among ethnic and racial groups in their formal tribal affiliations and in their relationship with the U.S. government. Today, 317 American Indian tribes in the United States are legally recognized by the federal government and receive services from the U.S. Bureau of Indian Affairs.[65] (Some tribes are recognized by states but not by the federal government. In addition, some 217 Alaska Native Village Areas identified in the 1990 census contain a total of 9,807 American Indians, 32,502 Inuit [Eskimo], and 4,935 Aleuts.)[66] Between 125 and 150 tribes are now seeking federal recognition, and dozens of others may do so in the future.[67] Contemporary American Indians typically must be enrolled members of one of the 317 federally recognized tribes to receive benefits from either the tribe or the federal government. To enroll, they must meet various criteria for tribal membership, which vary from tribe to tribe and are typically set forth in tribal constitutions approved by the Bureau of Indian Affairs. Upon membership, individuals are normally issued tribal enrollment (or registration) numbers and cards that identify their special status as members of a particular American Indian tribe.

The process of enrollment in a tribe has historical roots that extend back to the early nineteenth century. As the U.S. government dispossessed native peoples, treaties established specific rights, privileges, goods, and money to which those party to a treaty — both tribes as entities and individual tribal members — were entitled. The practices of creating formal censuses and keeping lists of names of tribal members evolved to ensure an accurate and equitable distribution of benefits. Over time, Native Americans themselves established more formal tribal governments, including constitutions, and began to regulate their membership more carefully, especially in regard to land allotments, royalties from the sale of resources, distributions of tribal funds, and voting. In the twentieth century, the U.S. government established further criteria to determine eligibility for benefits such as educational aid and health care.

The Wheeler–Howard Act of June 18, 1934 (Indian Reorganization Act), under which most current tribes are organized, was "the culmination of the reform movement of the 1920s led by John Collier." It "reversed the policy of allotment and encouraged tribal organization" [68] and written constitutions containing a membership provision.[69] Generally, these constitutions were either established or modified after the act of 1934. (A few groups, however, have no written constitution; the Pueblo of Taos, for example, say they have "a traditional form of Government.")[70]

Court cases have tested tribal membership requirements. From the disputes, American Indian tribal governments won the right to determine their own membership: "The courts have consistently recognized that in the absence of express legislation by Congress to the contrary, an Indian tribe has complete authority to determine all questions of its own membership." [71]

Individuals enrolled in federally recognized tribes also receive a Certificate of Degree of Indian Blood (referred to as a CDIB) from the Bureau of Indian Affairs. The bureau uses a specific degree of Indian blood — generally one-fourth degree of Native American ancestry — or tribal membership or both to recognize an individual as Native American. However, each tribe has a particular set of requirements — generally including a blood quantum — for membership (enrollment) in the tribe. Typically, a blood quantum is established by

Table 1.1. Blood quantum requirement of American Indian tribes by reservation basis and size

	Blood quantum requirement		
	More than ¼	¼ or less	No minimum
Number of tribes	21	183	98
Reservation-based	85.7%	83.1%	63.9%
Median size	1,022	1,096	1,185

Note: Information not available on 15 tribes.

Source: U.S. Bureau of Indian Affairs, unpublished tribal constitutions and tribal enrollment data obtained by the author.

tracing ancestry back through time to a relative or relatives on earlier tribal rolls or censuses where the relative's proportion of Native American blood was recorded. In such historical instances, more often than not it was simply self-indicated.

When enrollment criteria have changed over time, often the change has been made to establish minimum blood quantum requirements. For instance, in 1931 the Eastern Band of Cherokee Indians established a one-sixteenth blood quantum requirement for those born thereafter.[72] Tribes may establish higher or lower requirements. The Confederated Salish and Kootenai Tribes have tightened their membership requirements since 1935 and in 1960 established that only those born with a one-quarter or more blood quantum could be tribal members.[73] Conversely, tribes may reduce or even eliminate their blood quantum requirements. "The general trend of the tribal enactments on membership is away from the older notion that rights of tribal membership run with Indian blood, no matter how dilute the stream," Felix Cohen writes. "Instead it is recognized that membership in a tribe is a political relation rather than a racial attribute." [74] Blood quantum requirements vary widely. The Walker River Paiute require at least a one-half Indian (or tribal) blood quantum; the Navajo require a one-fourth blood quantum; some tribes in California and Oklahoma require a one-eighth or one-sixteenth or one-thirty-second blood quantum; and many tribes have no minimum blood quantum requirement but only require a documented tribal lineage.[75] A summary of the blood quantum requirements for federally recognized tribes is presented in Table 1.1.

In 1990 about one-fourth of the Native American population, some 437,079 American Indians (and 182 Inuit [Eskimo] and 97 Aleuts), lived on 314 reservations and trust lands; about half of them, some 218,290 American Indians (and 25 Inuit [Eskimo] and 5 Aleuts), lived on the 10 largest reservations and trust lands: Navajo Reservation and trust lands, 143,405; Pine Ridge Reservation and trust lands, 11,182; Fort Apache Reservation, 9,825; Gila River Reservation, 9,116; Papago Reservation, 8,480; Rosebud Reservation and trust lands, 8,043; San Carlos Reservation, 7,110; Zuni Pueblo, 7,073; Hopi Pueblo and trust lands, 7,061; and Blackfeet Reservation, 7,025.[76] (Alaskan Eskimos [Inuit] and Aleuts present a somewhat different picture than American Indians. Most are tied to small, local communities representing ancestral grounds rather than government reservations.)[77]

American Indian tribes located on reservations tend to have higher blood quantum requirements than those not located on reservations. As indicated in Table 1.1, more than 85 percent of tribes requiring more than one-quarter blood quantum for membership are reservation-based, whereas less than 64 percent of the tribes having no minimum requirement are reservation-based. Those tribes on reservations seem to have been able to maintain *exclusive* membership by setting higher blood quanta, since their location has generally served to isolate the tribe from non-Indians and intermarriage with them. Tribes without a reservation basis have maintained an *inclusive* membership by setting lower blood quanta for membership, since their populations interacted more with non-Indian populations and intermarried with them. As indicated in Table 1.1, tribes with more restrictive blood quantum requirements tend to be somewhat smaller than those with less restrictive ones, although the differences are not particularly striking.

In the early 1980s the total membership of federally recognized tribes was about 900,000. Therefore, many of the 1.37 million individuals identifying themselves as American Indian in the 1980 census were not actually enrolled members of federally recognized tribes. In fact, only about two-thirds were. In the late 1980s the total membership of these tribes was somewhat more than 1 million;[78] hence, only about 60 percent of the more than 1.8 million people identifying themselves as American Indian in the 1990 census were actually enrolled in a federally recognized American Indian tribe.

Differences between self-identification and tribal enrollment varied considerably from tribe to tribe. Most of the 158,633 Navajos enumerated in the 1980 census and the 219,198 Navajos in the 1990 census were enrolled in the Navajo Nation; however, only about one-third of the 232,344 Cherokees enumerated in the 1980 census and the 308,132 Cherokees in the 1990 census were actually enrolled in one of the three Cherokee tribes (the Cherokee Nation of Oklahoma, the Eastern Band of Cherokee Indians [of North Carolina], or the United Keetoowah Band of Cherokee Indians of Oklahoma).[79] Thus the Navajo Nation is the American Indian tribe with the largest number of enrolled members, but more individuals identifying as Native American called themselves "Cherokee" in the 1980 and 1990 censuses than any other tribe.[80]

The nature of the Native American population recovery has produced Native American populations that are different and distinctive along both "racial" and tribal lines. A "racial" heterogeneity has been produced whereby many individuals with few "Native American genes" are included within the Native American population, defined either tribally or by the U.S. Census (or by most other methods). It has also produced tribal variations, not only in terms of membership requirements but, more importantly, in terms of whether or not an individual is an enrolled tribal member. A dichotomy has emerged between Native Americans and tribal Native Americans.

Implications of Urbanization and Intermarriage

By the beginning of the twentieth century, surviving Native American groups in the United States had been redistributed. Much of this redistribution occurred during the nineteenth century through Native American removals, the establishment of the reservation system, and the subsequent elimination and allotment of some reservations. According to the 1990 census, the ten states with the largest Native American populations were: Oklahoma, 252,000; California, 242,000; Arizona, 204,000; New Mexico, 134,000; Alaska, 86,000; Washington, 81,000; North Carolina, 80,000; Texas, 66,000; New York, 63,000; and Michigan, 56,000.[81]

Another redistribution has occurred through urbanization. Only 0.4 percent of the American Indians in the United States lived in urban areas in 1900. By 1950, this had increased to only 13.4 percent; in 1990, however, 56.2 percent of American Indians lived in urban areas.[82] Some migration to urban areas occurred under the Bureau of Indian Affairs relocation program, which began in 1950 to assist American Indians in moving from reservation (and rural) areas to selected urban areas.[83] U.S. cities with the largest Native American populations are New York City, Oklahoma City, Phoenix, Tulsa, Los Angeles, Minneapolis–St. Paul, Anchorage, and Albuquerque.[84]

Urbanization and its partner, intermarriage, will bring about heightened "racial" and tribal threats to Native Americans in the twenty-first century.

The above-described pattern of requiring low percentages of Indian blood for tribal membership and dealing with the federal government to certify it may be seen in part as a result of the demographic legacy of 1492. As the numbers of Native Americans declined and Native Americans came into increased contact with whites, blacks, and others, Native American peoples increasingly married non-Indians. As a result, they have had to rely more and more on formal certification as proof of their "Indianness." This pattern has accelerated as urbanization has expanded the numbers of nonnatives that Native Americans have encountered and thus increased intermarriage rates. Today, almost 60 percent of all American Indians are married to non-Indians. I would argue that the "new Native Americans" who changed their census definitions of themselves are more likely to be intermarried.

Urbanization also seems to have brought about a decreased emphasis on Native American tribal identity. Overall, about 20 percent of American Indians enumerated in the 1970 census reported no tribe, but only about 10 percent of those on reservations reported no tribe, while about 30 percent of those in urban areas reported no tribe. (Comparable data from the 1980 and 1990 censuses are not available: the 1980 census indicated that about 25 percent reported no tribal affiliation;[85] the figure for 1990 was between 10 and 15 percent.) As indicated in the 1990 census, only about one-fourth of all American Indians speak an Indian language at home; however, census enumerations also indicate that urban residents are far less likely than reservation residents to speak an Indian language, or even participate in tribal cultural activities.

If these trends continue, both the genetic and the tribal distinctiveness of the total Native American population will be greatly lessened. A Native American population consisting primarily of "old" Native Americans strongly attached to their tribes will change to a one dominated by "new" Native American individuals who may or may not have tribal attachments or even tribal identities. It may even make sense at some point in the future to speak mainly of Native Americans as people of Native American ancestry or ethnicity.

Such pan-Native Americanism is replacing the pan-Indianism of the past, whereby tribal groups formed alliances along lines of common interest. Among contemporary Native Americans we may observe various forms of pan-Indianism. The first is the original form—tribal groups joined together for common interest. More recently there has emerged a pan-Indianism of tribal members sharing common issues and identities as "Native Americans" in American society. Third is a "posttribal" phenomenon whereby Native Americanism has replaced all vestiges of tribal life. A continuity with the past has been diminished; to be Native American is to be ancestrally tribal, as others are American with English or German or Irish or African or Japanese or Chinese ancestry.

Taking into account the high rates of intermarriage, it has been projected that within the next century the percentage of American Indians of one-half or more blood quantum will decline to only 8 percent of the American Indian population, while the percentage with less than one-fourth blood quantum will increase to around 60 percent. Moreover, these individuals will be increasingly unlikely to be enrolled as tribal members. Even if they are, traditional cultural distinctiveness may be replaced by mere social membership if language and other important cultural features of American Indian tribes are lost. Certainly the total Native American population as a distinctive segment of American society will be in danger. If individuals who identify as Native American cannot meet established blood quantum enrollment criteria, they will have no rights to benefits. Stricter requirements will operate to restrict the eligible Native American population as well as, ultimately, the number of federally recognized Native American entities. As long as reservations exist, there will undoubtedly be a segment of the Native American population that is quite distinct—genetically and culturally—from the total U.S. population. However, for the U.S. government, decreasing blood quanta may be perceived as meaning that the Native Americans to whom it is responsible have declined in number.

Eduardo Duran and Bonnie Duran have asserted that developing a new Native American identity is important in the postcolonial period because " 'Indian,' in its popular cultural meaning, is not an ethnicity but a stage in a social evolutionary ladder. This meaning precludes people of indigenous descent from ever living up to the image of Indianness and in the process inscribes a lost relations to nature or spiritual connectedness." [86] I agree with this and with the Durans' insistence that Native Americans must take it upon themselves to develop their own "postcolonial identity." But what will that identity be? If Native Americans become only people with native ancestry, then five centuries of colonialism will have succeeded.

The upcoming U.S. census in A.D. 2000 will eliminate the forced-choice race question in favor of allowing individuals to specify more than one race. This is simply reflective of the fast-growing number of racially mixed people in American society. If this occurs, some people labeled "Native Americans" in earlier censuses will become "racially mixed," although their numbers may not be large. With greater awareness of race mixture, might some Native Americans simply become racially mixed people of Native American and other ancestry? They will not even occupy the category "Los Indios," as they were defined by Europeans from the beginning, but will be descendants of "Los Indios." "Posttribalism" may mean "post-Indianism" for some.

Conclusion

Native Americans in the United States (and Canada) experienced a population recovery during the twentieth century but may face new demographic and tribal dangers during the twenty-first. Intermarriage with non–Native Americans may continue to undermine their basis as a distinctive racial and cultural population. The key in the next century to who is distinctively Native American may very well be tribal membership, irrespective of how that is determined. Tribes with high blood quantum requirements may find themselves with a shrinking population base unless they manage to control marriages between tribal members and non–Native Americans (or even Native American nontribal members). Or, of course, unless they lower their blood quantum requirements. Continued urbanization probably will produce more intermarriage while also further diminishing Native Americans' identity as distinctive tribal peoples tied to specific geographic areas.

Native Americans need to find new ways to adapt to these challenges. Certainly tribal membership as the defining characteristic of Native Americans is a way of retaining a distinctiveness from other Americans while total blood quanta are diminishing. New ways of maintaining tribalism are perhaps needed for urban Native Americans. There is no reason why "new" Native American tribes or branches of existing tribes cannot develop in urban areas: the history of Native American population collapse and removal and relocation is filled with the formation of new tribes. Already pan-Indian urban centers and associated activities such as powwows are firmly established in many cities. In the next century, with the consent if not the help of U.S. government policymakers, perhaps the next step might occur whereby urban Native Americans coalesce into new, distinctive Native American tribes with their own membership requirements as well as distinctive social and cultural characteristics linked to tribal pasts. If so, then Native Americans will have made yet another significant adaptation to European colonialism and its legacy.

Notes

This chapter is a modification of my "Tribal membership requirements and the demography of 'old' and 'new' Native Americans," *Population Research and Policy Review,* 7 (1997), 1–10; it also appeared in *Changing Numbers, Changing Needs: American Indian Demography and Public Health,* Gary D. Sandefur, Ronald R. Rindfuss, and Barney Cohen, eds. (Washington, D.C.: National Academy Press, 1996). The introduction and other parts of the present chapter are drawn freely from my "Population history of native North Americans," in *A Population History of North America,* Michael R. Haines and Richard H. Steckel, eds. (New York: Cambridge University Press, in press).

1. A. M. Carr-Saunders, *World Population* (Oxford: Clarendon Press, 1936), 260–94.

2. Edward Nelson Palmer, "Cultural contacts and population growth," *American Journal of Sociology,* 53 (1948), 262.

3. Tasmania: Carr-Saunders, *World Population,* 295; New Zealand: D. Ian Pool, *The Maori Population of New Zealand, 1769–71* (Auckland: Auckland University Press, 1977); Australia: Noel Butlin, *Our Original Aggression* (Sydney: George Allen & Unwin, 1983); Hawaii: Eleanor C. Nordyke, *The Peopling of Hawai'i* (Honolulu: University of Hawaii Press, 1989; Robert C. Schmitt, *Demographic Statistics of Hawaii: 1778–1965* (Honolulu: University of Hawaii Press, 1968); and David E. Stannard, *Before the Horror* (Honolulu: University of Hawaii Press, 1989).

4. See A. L. Kroeber, *Cultural and Natural Areas of Native North America,* University of California Publications in American Archaeology and Ethnology, Vol. 38 (Berkeley: University of California Press, 1939), 164–66; Henry F. Dobyns, "Estimating aboriginal American population: An appraisal of techniques with a new hemispheric estimate," *Current Anthropology,* 7 (1966), 395–416; William Denevan, "Native American populations in 1492: Recent research and a revised hemispheric estimate," in *The Native Population of the Americas in 1492,* 2d ed., William Denevan, ed. (Madison: University of Wisconsin Press, 1992 [1976]), xvii–xxix; Woodrow Borah, "The historical demography of aboriginal and colonial America: An attempt at perspective," in Denevan, *Native Population,* 13–34; Russell Thornton, *American Indian Holocaust and Survival: A Population History Since 1492* (Norman: University of Oklahoma Press, 1987), 22–25.

5. See, for example, Doreen S. Goyer and Elaine Domschke, *The Handbook of National Population Censuses: Latin America and the Caribbean, North America and Oceania* (Westport: Greenwood Press, 1983).

6. James Mooney, "The aboriginal population of America north of Mexico," in *Smithsonian Miscellaneous Collections,* Vol. 80, John R. Swanton, ed. (Washington, D.C.: U.S. Government Printing Office, 1928); see also James Mooney, "Population," in *Handbook of American Indians North of Mexico,* Frederick W. Hodge, ed. (Washington, D.C.: U.S. Government Printing Office, 1910). Douglas Ubelaker has examined Mooney's methodology in Douglas H. Ubelaker, "The sources and methodology for Mooney's estimates of North American Indian populations," in Denevan, *Native Population,* 243–88.

7. Kroeber, *Native North America,* 131–66, especially 131–34.

8. Ibid., 134.

9. Dobyns, "Estimating aboriginal American population."

10. Henry F. Dobyns, *Their Number Become Thinned: Native American Population Dynamics in Eastern North America* (Knoxville: University of Tennessee Press, 1983), 34–45.

11. See Ubelaker, "Mooney's estimates," 287–88; Thornton, *American Indian Holocaust,* 25–28.

12. There have been many criticisms of Dobyns's methodologies, particularly those in the 1983 book but also those in his 1966 paper. Criticisms of his paper may be found in Harold E. Driver, "On the population nadir of Indians in the United States," *Current Anthropology,* 9 (1968), 330; and Russell Thornton and Joan Marsh-Thornton, "Estimating prehistoric American Indian population size: Implications of the nineteenth-century population decline and nadir," *American Journal of Physical Anthropology,* 55 (1981), 47–53. Criticisms of his book may be found in William B. Fawcett, Jr., and Alan C. Swedlund, "Thinning populations and population thinners: The historical demography of Native Americans," *Reviews in Anthropology,* 11 (1984), 264–69; David Henige, "Primary source by primary source? On the role of epidemics in New World depopulation," *Ethnohistory,* 33 (1986), 293–312; David Henige, "Their number become thick: Native American historical demography as expiation," in *The Invented Indian: Cultural Fictions and Government Policies,* James A. Clifton, ed. (New Brunswick: Transaction, 1990), 169–91; Dean R. Snow and Kim Lanphear, "European contact and Indian depopulation in the Northeast: The timing of the first epidemics," *Ethnohistory,* 35 (1988), 15–33; Russell Thornton, "But how thick were they?" *Contemporary Sociology,* 13 (1984), 149–50.

13. Douglas H. Ubelaker, "North American Indian population size, A.D. 1500 to 1985," *American Journal of Physical Anthropology,* 77 (1988), 289–94; Douglas H. Ubelaker, "North American Indian population size: Changing perspectives," in *Disease and Demography in the Americas,* John W. Verano and Douglas H. Ubelaker, eds. (Washington, D.C.: Smithsonian Institution Press, 1992), 169–76; Denevan, "Native American populations in 1492"; Thornton and Marsh-Thornton, "Estimating prehistoric American Indian population size"; see also Thornton, *American Indian Holocaust,* 25–32. For a recent, thorough consideration of North American estimates, see John D. Daniels, "The Indian population of North America in 1492," *William and Mary Quarterly,* 49 (1992), 298–320.

14. Thornton, *American Indian Holocaust,* 42–43; see Ubelaker, "North American Indian population size," for a higher nadir figure.

15. See, for example, Gary D. Sandefur, Ronald R. Rindfuss and Barney Cohen, eds., *Changing Numbers, Changing Needs: American Indian Demography and Public Health* (Washington, D.C.: National Academy Press, 1996), recently published by the National Research Council.

16. The demographic chapter in M. Annette Jaimes's *The State of Native America* is embarrassing for its polemical approach and lack of scholarship, though I find some of the other chapters in the volume good. See Lenore A. Stiffarm and Phil Lane, Jr., "The demography of native North America: A question of American Indian survival," in *The State of Native America: Genocide, Colonization, and Resistance,* M. Annette Jaimes, ed. (Boston: South End Press, 1992).

17. Charles F. Merbs, "A new world of infectious disease," *Yearbook of Physical Anthropology,* 35 (1992), 36.

18. Thornton, *American Indian Holocaust,* 37–41; Marshall T. Newman, "Aboriginal New World epidemiology and medical care, and the impact of Old World disease imports," *American Journal of Physical Anthropology,* 45 (1976), 667–72; Karl J. Reinhard, "Archaeoparasitology in North America," *American Journal of Physical Anthropology,* 82 (1990), 145–63.

19. Thornton, *American Indian Holocaust,* 40–41.

20. Alfred W. Crosby, "Virgin soil epidemics as a factor in the aboriginal depopulation in America," *William and Mary Quarterly,* 33 (1976), 289–99.

21. Francis L. Black, "Why did they die?" *Science,* 258 (December 11, 1992), 1739–40.

22. See Dobyns, "Estimating aboriginal American population"; Dobyns, *Their Number Become Thinned,* 15–23; Henry F. Dobyns, "Disease transfer at contact," *Annual Review of Anthropology,* 22 (1993), 273–91; Steadman Upham, "Smallpox and climate in the American Southwest," *American Anthropologist,* 88 (1986), 115–28; David E. Stannard, *American Holocaust: Columbus and the Conquest of the New World* (New York: Oxford University Press, 1992).

23. See, for example, Ann F. Ramenofsky, *Vectors of Death: The Archaeology of European Contact* (Albuquerque: University of New Mexico Press, 1987); Snow and Lanphear, "European contact and Indian depopulation"; Dean Snow and William Starna, "Sixteenth-century depopulation: A view from the Mohawk Valley," *American Anthropologist,* 91 (1989), 142–49; Russell Thornton, Jonathan Warren, and Tim Miller, "Depopulation in the Southeast after 1492," in Verano and Ubelaker, *Disease and Demography,* 187–95; D. Ann Herring, "Toward a reconsideration of disease and contact," *Prairie Forum,* 17 (1992), 154–65; Clark Spencer Larsen, "In the wake of Columbus: Native population biology in the postcontact Americas," *Yearbook of Physical Anthropology,* 37 (1994), 109–54.

24. Larsen, "In the wake of Columbus," 109.

25. See Ramenofsky, *Vectors of Death;* Thornton, Warren, and Miller, "Depopulation in the Southeast"; Marvin T. Smith, *Archaeology of Aboriginal Culture Change in the Interior Southeast* (Gainesville: University Press of Florida/Florida Museum of Natural History, 1987).

26. See Ramenofsky, *Vectors of Death;* Smith, *Aboriginal Culture Change.*

27.   See Upham, "Smallpox and climate"; Daniel T. Reff, "The introduction of smallpox in the greater Southwest," *American Anthropologist,* 89 (1987), 704–8; Steadman Upham, "A reply to Reff," *American Anthropologist,* 89 (1987), 708–10.

28.   See Smith, *Aboriginal Culture Change;* Robert L. Blakely and Betinna Detweiler-Blakely, "The impact of European diseases in the sixteenth-century Southeast: A case study," *Midcontinental Journal of Archaeology,* 14 (1989), 62–89; Thornton, Warren, and Miller, "Depopulation in the Southeast"; Ezra Zubrow, "The depopulation of native America," *Antiquity,* 64 (1990), 754–65.

29.   Larsen, "In the wake of Columbus," 109.

30.   Russell Thornton, Tim Miller, and Jonathan Warren, "American Indian population recovery following smallpox epidemics," *American Anthropologist,* 93 (1991), 20–38.

31.   For a fuller discussion, see E. A. Wrigley, *Population and History* (London: Weidenfeld and Nicolson, World University Library, 1969); Alan Bideau, "Autoregulating mechanisms in traditional populations," in *Population and Biology,* Nathan Keyfitz, ed. (Liege: Ordina Editions, 1984), 117–31.

32.   Thornton, Miller, and Warren, "Population recovery"; D. Ann Herring, " 'There were young people and old people and babies dying every week': The 1918–1919 influenza pandemic at Norway House," *Ethnohistory,* 41 (1994), 73–105; Robert T. Boyd, "Population decline from two epidemics on the northwest coast," in Verano and Ubelaker, *Disease and Demography,* 249–55.

33.   William H. McNeill, *Plagues and Peoples* (Garden City, N.Y.: Anchor Doubleday, 1976), 150.

34.   See Robert S. Gottfried, *The Black Death* (New York: Free Press, 1983), xv–xvi, 129–35, 156–59.

35.   See James V. Neel, W. R. Centerwell, Napoleon A. Chagnon, and H. L. Casey, "Notes on the effect of measles and measles vaccine in a virgin-soil population of South American Indians," *American Journal of Epidemiology,* 91 (1970), 418–29; James V. Neel and Kenneth M. Weiss, "The genetic structure of a tribal population, the Yanomama Indians, XII: Biodemographic studies," *American Journal of Physical Anthropology,* 42 (1975), 25–51, 418–29; James V. Neel, "Population structure of an Amerindian tribe, the Yanomama," *Annual Review of Genetics,* 12 (1978), 365–413; Janet W. McGrath, "Biological impact of social disruption resulting from epidemic disease," *American Journal of Physical Anthropology,* 84 (1991), 407–19.

36.   Russell Thornton, "Social organization and the demographic survival of the Tolowa," *Ethnohistory,* 31 (1984), 187–96; Russell Thornton, "History, structure and survival: A comparison of the Yuki (*Unkomno'n*) and Tolowa (*Hush*) Indians of northern California," *Ethnology,* 25 (1986), 119–30; see also Zubrow, "Depopulation of native America", Jody F. Decker, "Depopulation of the northern plains natives," *Social Science and Medicine,* 33 (1991), 381–93; Boyd, "Population decline from two epidemics", Larsen, "In the wake of Columbus."

37.   Larsen, "In the wake of Columbus," 110.

38.   Cary W. Meister, "Demographic consequences of Euro-American contact on selected American Indian populations and their relationship to the demographic transition," *Ethnohistory,* 23 (1976), 161–72.

39.   Russell Thornton, Discussion of the session entitled "A return to old killing

grounds: Recent epidemiological studies of North American Indians," Annual Meeting of the American Society for Ethnohistory, 1988, Williamsburg, Va.; David E. Stannard, "Disease and infertility: A new look at the demographic collapse of native populations in the wake of western contact," *Journal of American Studies,* 24 (1990), 325–50.

40.   Russell Thornton, "Cherokee population losses during the Trail of Tears: A new perspective and a new estimate," *Ethnohistory,* 31 (1984), 289–300.

41.   Philip L. Walker and John R. Johnson, "The decline of the Chumash Indian population," in *In the Wake of Contact: Biological Responses to Conquest,* C. S. Larsen and G. R. Milner, eds. (New York: Wiley-Liss, 1994), 109–20.

42.   M. R. Harvey, "Population of the Cahuilla Indians: Decline and its causes," *Eugenics Quarterly,* 14 (1967), 185–98.

43.   Thornton, "Social organization and demographic survival"; Thornton, "History, structure and survival"; Philip L. Walker and Russell Thornton, "Health, nutrition, and demographic change in native California," paper presented at the Second Conference on a History of Health and Nutrition in the Western Hemisphere, 1996, Columbus, Ohio.

44.   Thornton, *American Indian Holocaust,* 51–53.

45.   Russell Thornton, "Aboriginal North American population and rates of decline, ca. A.D. 1500 to 1900," *Current Anthropology,* 38 (1997), 310–15.

46.   Changing definitions and procedures for enumerating Native Americans used by the U.S. Bureau of the Census also had an effect on the enumerated population size from census to census during this century.

47.   Russell Thornton, "Population," in *Native Americans in the Twentieth Century: An Encyclopedia,* Mary B. Davis, ed. (New York: Garland, 1994), 461–64.

48.   U.S. Bureau of the Census, *We the . . . First Americans* (Washington, D.C.: U.S. Government Printing Office, 1993), fig. 2. It should be noted that over 10 percent of those individuals identifying as Native American in the 1990 census did not report a tribal affiliation.

49.   See Thornton, *American Indian Holocaust,* 159–85; C. Matthew Snipp, *American Indians: The First of This Land* (New York: Russell Sage, 1989), 66–69.

50.   Snipp, *American Indians,* 67–69.

51.   Russell Thornton, Gary D. Sandefur, and C. Matthew Snipp, "American Indian fertility history," *American Indian Quarterly,* 15 (1991), 359–67.

52.   U.S. Bureau of the Census, *Indian Population of the United States and Alaska, 1910* (Washington, D.C.: U.S. Government Printing Office, 1915).

53.   Thornton, Sandefur, and Snipp, "American Indian fertility."

54.   Ibid., 390, table 1.

55.   Ibid., 362, 364–65.

56.   Jeffrey P. Brain, "The Natchez 'paradox,' " *Ethnology,* 10 (1971), 215–22.

57.   Thornton, "History, structure and survival."

58.   James Mooney, "The Powhatan Confederacy, past and present," *American Anthropologist,* 9 (1907), 129–52.

59.   William H. Gilbert, Jr., "Memorandum concerning the characteristics of the larger mixed-blood racial islands of the eastern United States," *Social Forces,* 24 (1946), 438.

60.   The total population of these groups in 1960 was estimated at 100,000 by Brew-

ton Berry in *Almost White: A Study of Certain Racial Hybrids in the Eastern United States* (New York: Macmillan, 1963), 57.

61.   The 1980 U.S. Census obtained information that some 7 million Americans had some degree of Native American ancestry. Native American ancestry ranked tenth among the total U.S. population in 1980. In descending order, the ten leading ancestries were: English, German, Irish, Afro-American, French, Italian, Scottish, Polish, Mexican, and Native American.

62.   See Jeffrey S. Passel, "Provisional evaluation of the 1970 census count of American Indians," *Demography,* 13 (1976), 397–409; Jeffrey S. Passel and Patricia A. Berman, "Quality of 1980 census data for American Indians," *Social Biology,* 33 (1986), 986, table 1; Thornton, *American Indian Holocaust,* 220–21; David Harris, "The 1990 census count of American Indians: What do the numbers really mean?" *Social Science Quarterly,* 15 (1994), 583, tables 1–2; Karl Eschbach, "The enduring and vanishing American Indian: American Indian population growth and intermarriage in 1990," *Ethnic and Racial Studies,* 18 (1995), 89.

63.   See Passel, "Provisional evaluation"; Passel and Berman, "Quality of 1980 census," 164; Harris, "The 1990 census count," 583, table 2.

64.   See, for example, Russell Thornton, *The Cherokees: A Population History* (Lincoln: University of Nebraska Press, 1977), 178–203.

65.   U.S. Bureau of Indian Affairs, "Indian entities recognized and eligible to receive services from the United States Bureau of Indian Affairs," *Federal Register,* 58 (1993), 54364–69. Criteria used to establish whether a Native American group may become federally recognized are discussed in Thornton, *American Indian Holocaust,* 195–96.

66.   U.S. Bureau of the Census, *1990 Census of Population: General Population Characteristics: American Indian and Alaskan Native Areas* (Washington, D.C.: U.S. Government Printing Office, 1992), table 2.

67.   U.S. Bureau of Indian Affairs, personal communication.

68.   Francis Paul Prucha, ed., *Documents of United States Indian Policy* (Lincoln: University of Nebraska Press, 1975), 222.

69.   Felix S. Cohen, *Handbook of Federal Indian Law* (Albuquerque: University of New Mexico Press, n.d. [1942]), 136.

70.   Pueblo of Taos, personal communication.

71.   Cohen, *Handbook,* 136.

72.   Ibid., 5.

73.   Ronald L. Trosper, "Native American boundary maintenance: The Flathead Indian Reservation, Montana," *Ethnohistory,* 3 (1976), 256.

74.   Cohen, *Handbook,* 136.

75.   See Thornton, *American Indian Holocaust,* 190.

76.   U.S. Bureau of the Census, *We the . . . ,* 1, fig. 12.

77.   Around 60 percent of the Native American population of Alaska live in "Alaskan Native villages." The Bureau of Indian Affairs recognizes 222 Native American villages, communities, and other entities in Alaska (Bureau of Indian Affairs, "Indian entities").

78.   U.S. Bureau of Indian Affairs, unpublished data.

79.   Thornton, *The Cherokees,* 170–72; Thornton, "Population."

80.   The situation in Canada is somewhat different. In Canada one must be registered under the Indian Act of Canada to be an "official" Indian. Canadian Indians fall
into two categories: status (or registered) Indians, those recognized under the act, and
nonstatus (or nonregistered) Indians, those who had never registered under the act or
who gave up their registration (and became "enfranchised"). Depending on whether the
group has ever entered into a treaty relationship with the Canadian government, status
Indians are subdivided into treaty and nontreaty Indians. (There are also the *Métis,* individuals of Indian and white ancestry not legally recognized as Indians.) Some 500,000
of the 575,000 Canadian Indians in the mid-1980s were registered. About 70 percent
of Canadian Indians live on one of 2,272 reserves. There were 578 bands of Canadian
Indians in the early 1980s, most containing fewer than 500 members. Only three bands
had more than 5,000 members: Six Nations of the Grand River, 11,172; Blood, 6,083;
and Kahnawake, 5,226. See Thornton, "Population." The largest Canadian "group" in
terms of language and culture is the Chippewa-Ojibwe.

81.   U.S. Bureau of the Census, *We the . . . ,* fig. 3. Canadian provinces with the
largest number of Native Americans are Ontario, British Columbia, Saskatchewan, and
Manitoba. See Russell Thornton, "Urbanization," in Davis, *Encyclopedia,* 670–71.

82.   U.S. Bureau of the Census, *American Indian and Alaskan Native Areas;* Thornton, "Tribal membership requirements," 12.

83.   Thornton, "Urbanization," 670–71.

84.   Ibid. Around 40 percent of Canadian Native Americans lived in cities in the
mid-1980s, particularly Vancouver, Edmonton, Regina, Winnipeg, Toronto, and Montreal. This was an increase from the 30 percent who lived in cities in the early 1970s,
and the mere 13 percent who lived in cities in 1961. Today, however, only about 20 percent of Canadian Inuit (Eskimos) live in cities, and only about 30 percent of the status
Indians do so.

85.   Thornton, *American Indian Holocaust,* 238.

86.   Eduardo Duran and Bonnie Duran, *Native American Postcolonial Psychology*
(Albany: SUNY Press, 1995), 136.

2 *Raymond D. Fogelson*

Perspectives on
Native American Identity

Native American identity is central to the concerns of Native American studies programs. This chapter offers some perspectives on this complex topic. Perspectives are ways of viewing or lines of vision. To gain perspective, one usually steps back in space and time. The perspectives on identity offered here are conceptual and historical. By "conceptual" I mean that the idea of identity is neither singular nor monolithic but has many dimensions that may be usefully separated for purposes of analysis. The presentation followed here is loosely historical in that I am interested in the development of external images, as well as self-reflection, of Indianness through time. However, I am not a (or an) historian, so that specific dating, contextual circumstances, and complete citations may often be lacking. One commentator on an earlier draft of this chapter noted that it needs more Indian "voices." I agree. Hopefully what I have to say will provoke the critical acumen of historical colleagues as well as raise Native American voices from both the living and the dead.

I begin with some general considerations of the meaning of identity. Next I survey names that have been collectively applied to the native inhabitants of the New World. A discussion of three primary attributes of Native American identity follows: blood and descent, relations to land, and sense of community. Many other attributes of identity are recognized by Indians and non-Indians, including language usage, cultural participation and performances, dress, physical features, consumption of Indian foods, and particular styles of life. However, blood, land, and community remain the *sine qua non* for legal recognition as tribal Indians, whereas other identity markers tend to be employed more flexibly: they can be lost and regained or, if I may be excused, invented or reinvented.[1]

General Considerations on Identity

We hear and read much about identity politics, identity struggles, and ethnic identity, but rarely is identity itself clearly or consistently defined. One set of meanings refers to an image or set of images of oneself or one's group. The basic notions of identity in these usages involve communication of a sense of oneself or one's group intrapsychically to oneself or projected outwardly to others. Identity in this regard may contain several components. For instance, Anthony F. C. Wallace and R. D. Fogelson recognize that an individual, and by extension a group, may comprise an ideal identity, an image of oneself that one wishes to realize; a feared identity, which one values negatively and wishes to avoid; a "real" identity, which an individual thinks closely approximates an accurate representation of the self or reference group;[2] and a claimed identity that is presented to others for confirmation, challenge, or negotiation in an effort to move the "real" identity closer to the ideal and further from the feared identity.[3]

These identity components can be arranged in a lineal or ordinal fashion. Thus, in a particular situation a Native American's ideal identity might be that of full blood, a feared identity might be a Wannabee, a "real" identity is a person having three-eighth's blood quantum, and a claimed identity is a person with a nine-sixteenths degree of Indian blood. However, identity components are rarely so ordinal or quantifiable. A group of protesting Native Americans might see their ideal identity as that of traditional warriors, have a feared identity as self-serving "radishes," a "real" identity as a disenfranchised minority fighting for their rights, and a claimed identity, claimed by black T-shirts with a distinctive logo, as active members of the American Indian Movement (AIM). The total image may be instantaneous, although micro-shifts in the relations and content of these identity components might occur in the process of interaction. Identity in this sense is primarily synchronic, concerning the here and now.

I want to emphasize that identity struggles are more social than individual psychological phenomena. Identities are negotiated through interaction with another person or group. Let me produce an imagined scenario to make my point. There is a large discourse about the legal aspects of the Native American Graves Protection and Repatriation Act (NAGPRA), but we have few ethnographic accounts of the implementation of its provisions. One can imagine a confrontation between a Native American tribal representative and a museum anthropologist that takes the form of an identity struggle. The Native American may have an ideal image of himself as an altruistic champion of his tribe, a feared identity as a publicity-seeking fraud representing only himself, a "real" identity as someone trying to reclaim tribal patrimony from the museum, and a claimed identity, marked by braids and shades, a headband, and a finger-woven sash, as a traditional leader. In contrast, the museum anthropologist has an ideal identity as a professional curator responsible for the collections in his or her care and responsive to the politico-legal situation surrounding them. The anthropologist may have a feared identity as a despised "anthro" with an anachronistic colonial mentality who assumes unwarranted expertise. The "real" identity centers on being someone who is negotiating in good faith to return artifacts and physical remains to their rightful heirs. The claimed identity, signaled by a long white coat, an identification badge, and calipers or other tools of the trade, is that of Dr. Science, the dispassionate arbiter of objectivity. It is these two claimed identities that meet in the museum storeroom. The potential for misunderstanding and bitter conflict is great, but mutual understanding may be achieved by compromise and through the very process of interaction. Hopefully claims and counterclaims can be settled amicably before a painful and prolonged court case ensues in which nobody really "wins." In short, identities can change through social interaction.

The term "identity" was given a different emphasis by Erik Erikson, who introduced the concept into the social science literature.[4] For Erikson, identity was a processual or historical concept representing the cumulative effects of a series of life cyclical nuclear conflicts. Although the individual changed throughout the life course, identity was held together by threads of continuity. Indeed, in its etymological sense "identity" means "sameness." (Thus, Erikson's conception of identity resembled William Wordsworth's dictum "the child is father to the man" or Dylan Thomas's image of a "green fuse" that predetermined the pattern of a plant's exfoliation.)

Erikson explained the ethos and ego structure of members of two Native American tribes in terms of unresolved childhood conflicts. Sioux ego identity was epitomized by the skewering of the pectoral muscles in the Sun Dance, reflecting, Erikson thought, an externalized feminine superego. Alas, the poor Yuroks found themselves up the alimentary canal without a paddle, as they worked out their anal fixations in adult litigiousness and other forms of mean-spiritedness.[5]

This extreme psychological reductionism seems ludicrous, if not libelous, today. Nevertheless, the basic thrust of Erikson's scheme, shed of its shoddy and stereotypic psychodynamics, is relevant to contemporary legal considerations of Native American identity that stress historical continuity. To be recognized as an American Indian tribe by the U.S. government, unbroken descent from a historically known tribe must be demonstrated, as well as a continuous form of political organization or community.[6] It is assumed that there exists a linkage forged by a chain of blood and continuous social inter-action between historical tribes and their modern descendants, even though there may be such radical discontinuity that present-day Yuroks or Sioux would have a difficult time recognizing, let alone identifying with, the cultures of their ancestors. The "ancient ones" would seem like aliens.

The two conceptions of identity—the communication of self-images and the epigenetic or historical unfolding of identity—are not mutually exclusive. The identity dynamics of presenting self-concepts to others, be they Euro-Americans or other Native Americans, produced counterimages that might be accepted, rejected, or partially assimilated by the individual or group in ques-tion. This dialectic, working itself out over long periods of time, could give rise to a sense of historical identity in Erikson's sense of contingent continuity.

Collective Names for Native North American Peoples

The story of how the European-styled "New World" was named in honor of a self-promoting Florentine adventurer, Amerigo Vespucci, requires neither additional retelling nor retailing.[7] Columbus's geographic miscalculation, which resulted in labeling the newly found lands the Indies and its people the Indians ("Los Indios"), is equally well known. "American Indians," used to distinguish those so referred to from Asian or East Indians, became the most general term for the native inhabitants of the United States. Sometimes the term "American Indian" was contracted, à la Euro-American, into "Amerind," but this never received much acceptance from either American Indians or whites (perhaps because it sounds like the peel of an exotic fruit). In the late 1950s there was a brief effort to invert the word order by using the expression "Indian Americans." This shift apparently was an effort to deemphasize the racial, legal, and historical distinctiveness of Native Americans and allow them to achieve parity with, if not become a parody of, other assimilated ethnic groups, such as Italian Americans or Japanese Americans. It is not surprising that contemporary efforts at establishing a binomial taxonomy utilizing conti-nent of origins as genus and continent of current residence as species, such as Asian American or African American, or the agglutinatively congealed Euro-American, has avoided the redundancy of American Americans.[8]

Today, the politically correct, and in many cases official, designation is "Native Americans." However, there may be a gradual shift back toward the simpler term "Indians." Indeed, the preference for "American Indians" by many tribal leaders and others may reflect the legal language of treaties and other documents securing Indian rights, which references "Indians" and not "Native Americans."[9] One rarely hears Native Americans refer to themselves as Native Americans. "Indians" (sometimes with unvoiced *d*) seems the term of choice in local discourse. Such differences between official and vernacular terms raise the question of appropriate usage. Native Americans can call Native Americans "Indians" as well as a whole host of other terms generally regarded as derogatory (e.g., "bloods," "skins," "long hairs"), but others use such terms, especially the derogatory ones, at their own peril.

"Anthros," a term popularized by Vine Deloria and Floyd Westerman, is taken as a token of derision and calculated disrespect for anthropologists, since it calls into question the moral dimensions of the profession. Anthropologists find it particularly appalling when historians get on the bandwagon and tauntingly refer to them as "anthros"; they sometimes counterattack in kind by referring to historians as "histos," with a long drawn-out sibilant *s*. If anthropologists refer to each other as "anthros," however, it marks a kind of privileged joking relationship. The situation is not unlike the current mascot controversy, which really at base is a problem of totemism. Activists protest against the appropriation of Native American names for sports teams, such as "Indians," "Braves," "Chiefs," "Redskins," "Siwash." One can sympathize with such resentment and recognize the bitter irony in the fact that the people who coined the term "totem" (a Central Algonquian root, usually having reference to a spiritual animal) have become totemized themselves. However, activists conveniently ignore the kind of autototemism (not Pontiacs, Jeep Cherokees, or Sun Dances) manifested in the frequent use of terms like "Indians," "warriors," "braves," "chiefs," and more by sports teams at Native American schools and colleges. Without disparaging or belittling the mascot protest, one can observe that when it comes to using stereotypical labels for people's identity, it makes a big difference who calls whom what.

The Attributes of Native American Identity

Native American identity is minimally premised, both endogenously and exogenously, on three prerequisites: blood and descent, land, and community.

Blood and Descent

While many Native Americans possessed elaborate theories about the symbolic significance of blood, including theories of procreation, taboos regarding menstrual blood, the function of blood in health and illness, its association with warfare, and its connections with death, the idea of blood quantum as a marker of identity was foreign. For Native Americans identity was primarily associated with kinship. Kinship not only included those with whom one could trace familiar common descent, but could be extended to include more ramifying groups like clans, moieties, and even nations. Moreover, besides biological reproduction, individuals and groups could be recruited into kinship networks through naturalization, adoption, marriage, and alliance. Identity encompassed inner qualities that were made manifest through social action and cultural belief.

In contrast, Euro-American assessments of Native American identity tended to proceed from outside to inside. Skin color and head and body hair figured prominently in early European efforts to classify American Indians and locate their place in nature and the human family. (It will not be reviewed here how Native Americans became red, nor how long head hair and sparse body hair were interpreted as indices of inferiority.)[10] External traits were soon conjoined to more determinate inner physical and psychical entities and processes. The nature of the American Indian "soul" and its relationship to character and salvation were the subject of much debate, as were considerations of mental dispositions, passions, and reason.

For Euro-Americans, blood was thought both to symbolize ideally and to embody materially genetic or racial differences. Blood was understood as more than a metaphor for descent; it was believed to be intrinsically important in human generation and regeneration. Female blood was thought to be directly deposited in the fetus, while the male blood was distilled in the testes into semen or seed.[11] These beliefs, which are rooted in western folk biology, bestowed on blood an abiding inherency and transgenerational permanence. Modern science perpetuates these attitudes by employing blood typing as a stable measure of descent, population differences, and individual identity, but, as we learned in the O. J. Simpson trial, such measures are hardly foolproof.

The "myth of blood," as Juan Comas terms it, gave rise to ideas of racial purity as a quality to be preserved and to a view of miscegenation as "unnatural," abominable, and polluting.[12] For example, fifteenth-century Spanish ecclesiastical policy considered Spanish intermixture with Moors or with Jews to be defiling to *limpieza de sangre* or "clean blood."[13] The "myth of blood" diffused to the New World along with European flora, fauna, pathogens, and the institution of slavery. Throughout Latin America there developed elaborate classification codes to distinguish degrees of racial admixture between whites and blacks. A person possessing three-quarters black blood was referred to as a "griffe" or "sambo," while seven-eighths blacks were called "sacatris" or "mangos." "Mulatto" designated persons who were one-half black and one-half white; a "quadroon" was one-quarter black; and an "octoroon" was one-eighth black. In some areas the classification went further to include terms for individuals with one-sixteenth, one-thirty-second, or one-sixty-fourth degree of black blood.[14] This complex terminology had only minor utility for Anglo-America. North of Mexico, the proverbial "one drop of black blood" was sufficient to classify a person as black. However, colonial records in Virginia report that one-eighth black blood made one legally a Negro, while in North Carolina the rule was one-sixteenth[15] (and thus the "stigma" of being black might be erased in four or five generations, respectively, and one could legally pass as white provided no additional black blood was acquired).

It is tempting to see the Spanish/Portuguese conception of race mixture as directly ancestral to the development of notions of blood quantum in identifying degrees of Native American ancestry. A similar mindset may be at work, but as Frederick Lomayesva argues, blood quantum arose as a means to define Indian identity for purposes of legal jurisdiction over criminal defendants and went back to the Trade and Intercourse Act of 1834.[16] Also, as Paul Spruhan points out, blood quantification is clearly present in English common law regulating property inheritance by upper-class heirs of different degrees of blood relationship. Finally, quantitative degrees of relationship were also well established by breeders of livestock.[17]

Intermarriage between whites and Native Americans was generally considered by Euro-Americans to be less degrading and unnatural than miscegenation with blacks. However, at different times and places such unions were looked upon with scorn. Thus, whites with American Indian wives were sometimes called "squaw men"; whites with American Indian husbands were referred to as "buck women"; and the offspring of such unions were sometimes derisively referred to as "mixed breeds" or "white Indians." The term "mustee," derived from *mestizo,* is sporadically reported from colonial Virginia, the Carolinas, and New York to indicate tribally unrecognized people of mixed American Indian–white or American Indian–black descent.[18] Such people, also referred to as "remnant groups," *mestizos,* or "triracial isolates," have become more visible in recent years as they seek state or federal recognition as American Indian tribes.[19]

In some sections of the colonial and antebellum South (and elsewhere), marriage with American Indians was positively valued. Starting with Pocahontas and John Rolfe, such marriages were often considered, at least temporarily, as politically advantageous for Indians and whites alike. Traders found it both convenient and economically expedient to have Native American wives and mixed-blood children. Later some southern intellectuals, such as William Gilmore Simms, argued that an infusion of American Indian blood might invigorate the local white population.[20] Intermarriage with American Indians was also regarded by some as a solution to the so-called Indian problem, which was at base a white problem. Intermarriage was viewed as an irreversible step along the path to civilization and the inevitable physical incorporation and cultural assimilation of native peoples. Symbolically, intermarriage with American Indians retroactively legitimized the occupation of Indian territory and assimilated Euro-Americans to the landscape, while distancing them from their European origins.

By the nineteenth century the European "myth of blood" became transmogrified into the calculation of a blood quantum to ascertain degree of

"Indianness." [21] Less a deliberate "divide and conquer" strategy, blood quantum functioned more as an administrative mechanism for effecting policies of inclusion and exclusion, entitlement and disqualification in such issues as child custody, receipt of health benefits and scholarships, artistic license to authenticate one's work as Indian art, political and criminal jurisdiction, eligibility for health care, settlements of land claims, mining and other resource royalties, and local and federal taxation.[22] However, the long-term consequences of policies employing blood quantum created, and continue to generate, social structural strain and psychological stress, as mixed-bloods often became liminal figures, neither fully American Indian nor fully white. Some mixed-bloods were able to bridge the two culture systems, and they often rose to prominence as political leaders and cultural brokers. Nevertheless, just as frequently mixed-blooded individuals and classes became ready scapegoats for the ills of American Indian communities from the perspectives of both whites and Native Americans. They were taken as degenerate examples of the evils of miscegenation. Later schisms in Indian societies were, of course, marked by opposition between mixed-bloods and/or progressives on one hand and full bloods and/or traditionalists on the other. Yet one must always be cautious in equating blood quantum with cultural and political orientations.

The U.S. government, according to Thomas Jefferson Morgan, the Commissioner of Indian Affairs in the late nineteenth century, was advised to maintain "a liberal and not technical or restrictive construction" with regard to the recognition and rights of mixed-blooded Indians.[23] Thus, many mixed-bloods of varying degrees who were recognized as tribal members by the tribes themselves were declared eligible for property settlements and other benefits due to tribal members from the federal government. This seeming anticipation of Native American self-determination was not as liberal as it appears, for if blood quantum had been construed narrowly in property rights and other benefits, then most, if not all, treaties that American Indian tribes had entered into with the federal government would have to be declared void and invalid, since mixed-bloods were often instrumental in negotiating treaties and were significant signatories.

The federal government and the courts seemed to favor, at least through the 1930s, a norm of one-half Indian blood for recognition as an American Indian; this was subject, of course, to qualification by already recognized tribes, who might choose to set blood quantum much lower.[24] In fact, the government tried mightily to transform the "myth of blood" into scientific reality by employing physical anthropologists to conduct anthropometric studies and to utilize newly developed serological tests to ascertain blood quantum with scientific precision. Fortunately or unfortunately, such government scientists as Ales Hrdlicka and Frank Setzler were not up to these challenges. After the Indian New Deal under Commissioner of Indian Affairs John Collier in the 1930s and early 1940s, responsibility for setting blood quantum requirements for tribal membership was increasingly vested in individual tribal governments.

Relations to Land

A second defining attribute of Native American identity is land or, better, relations to land. For Europeans, land has always possessed a close and at times metaphysical connection to kinship and descent, as can be inferred from such notions as *fatherland* and *motherland*. Eastern European immigrants from a common town or region often felt themselves bound together by special ties as *landsmen*. Land and descent merge as identity indicators in such expressions as "our boys fight for the land of their fathers and often pay for that land in blood." Europeans had definite ideas of land ownership, whether that ownership was vested in the individual living upon or working the land or whether ultimate ownership rested with a lord, or literally a landlord, a sovereign, or the Lord God of Hosts.[25]

Most of these ideas about land were alien to Native Americans when Europeans first set foot on their shores. Even more strange, surely, were the curious landing rituals the invaders reenacted when they claimed the territory in the name of their country, king, and God and left an effigy or some other marker to memorialize the event.[26] Native Americans certainly had notions of land tenure, land and group boundaries, and right of usage. Moreover, many Native Americans maintained an attachment to land in which their ancestors were buried. NAGPRA is not a recent reflex of political correctioness but a delayed response to longstanding Indian grievances. As early as Thomas Jefferson's *Notes on the State of Virginia,* there is reference to Indians making regular pilgrimages to burial mounds; Plains Indians frequently complained about white desecration of scaffold burial sites; and the Iroquois had a taboo against eating the meat of animals that burrowed into graveyards (by the same logic they would probably have avoided eating archaeologists).[27]

The idea that land was property that could be exclusively possessed, expropriated, or alienated was foreign to native North America. The notion of real estate was as unreal as the demarcation of the seas or the sale of rights to the air. Nevertheless, Native American identity was connected to the land as a site of origination in narratives of ethnogenesis, as a home area where life was lived, and as the final resting place of mortal remains. Later, Native Americans came to accept Euro-American conceptions of land as a commodity that could be alienated through sale during treaty negotiations and be a source of recompensation through decisions of the Indian Claims Commission. Land lost through conquest or purchase continued to have sentimental value for those who once inhabited the area and their descendants.

Regarding indigenous ideas of private property, much controversy has been aroused over whether ownership of hunting territories was a pre-Columbian institution among northern Algonquian hunters or whether the practice only emerged in connection with the fur trade.[28] Obviously the issue hinges on what is understood by "ownership." The Naskapis, studied by Julius Lips in the 1930s, believed that the local animal "bosses" or masters of the game "owned" the territory;[29] specific human individuals were empowered to treat with the local animal spirits through special ceremonies, knowledge of which was usually transmitted transgenerationally through family lines and may represent in terms of both descent and locality the source of totemism. Other groups seem to have respected the boundaries of the hunting territory, less out of deference to its human caretakers and more out of fear of giving offense to the spiritual landlords, the masters of the game. Similar ideas seem to have been present in the Northwest with regard to fishing stations, berry patches, and other resource sites.

Just as the "myth of blood" helped promote the idea that American Indians were a separate race of people, so the "myth of nomadism" played a major role in justifying Euro-American claims to lands that had previously been controlled by Indians. This "myth" appears early. Certainly it was strongly represented in the divinely ordained rhetoric of the buckle-headed Puritans, and it has proven remarkably persistent. Essentially the myth avows that Indians are habitually migratory, cannot settle down, have a restless urge to move on; they do not cultivate the soil nor make their mark on the landscape, and thus they are *on* the land but not *of* the land. The "myth of nomadism" conveniently ignores the facts that many, if not most, Indians traditionally lived a settled existence in semipermanent villages and became unsettled mainly in response to direct and indirect Euro-American pressures or in order to take advantage of new lifestyles made possible by horses, firearms, or steel traps. Only now are we beginning to appreciate the extent to which precontact Native Americans transformed their environments and cultivated the soil to produce plants that would help revolutionize the world economy.

Around Thanksgiving Day, schoolchildren are often taught to recite a long grocery list of plants that the American Indians bestowed upon their white friends as "gifts." [30] Doubtless the most valuable "gift" of all was the land, since this was a gift that kept on giving. It is difficult to imagine how the government of the American Republic was financed before the establishment of corporate income taxes in 1909 and personal income taxes in 1913. The sale of Indian lands was a significant source of government funding, and ironically Native Americans indirectly contributed to the endowment of an American Republic that scorned them, patronized them, impoverished them, and fully expected to bury them in the alienable ground.

The Euro-American claim to Indian land and "the myth of nomadism" are clearly articulated in Indian Commissioner Morgan's 1890 report:

On account of their ignorance, their savage condition, and their customs and habits, the Indians were never deemed to have the right of property in the soil of the portion of the country over which the tribe or band had established by force of strength the right to roam in search of game, etc. or which had been set apart for its use by treaties with the United States, act of Congress, or Executive order, but only to have the right to occupy said portion of country. The fee in the land of the country occupied and roamed over by the Indians was deemed to be first in the European sovereigns or countries, but now held to be in the Government of the United States.[31]

Morgan goes on to note that, despite the ultimate claim to the land by the United States, the Native American right of occupancy was recognized and had to be purchased. (It is impossible here to explicate all the assumptions, contradictions, and secondary rationalizations contained in this statement of government policy regarding land.)

The displacement of American Indians took place historically in two fashions. First, Native American populations were removed ever westward and resettled behind natural boundaries, like the Appalachian Mountains or the Mississippi River, or behind artificial lines where they were promised perpetual freedom to roam and pursue accustomed lifeways without interference. Secondly, Native American groups were encircled and placed on reservations where they could be confined, controlled, civilized, and Christianized.[32] However, even reservation lands proved not to be inalienable, as title was extinguished through usurpation, allotment, and termination.

Nevertheless, collective possession of land became an important attribute of tribal identity, in terms of both external recognition and sense of self. Reservation land, especially if located in the same general vicinity where first contact with whites occurred, assumed a primordial quality replete with sacred and historic sites. With over two-thirds of the present Native American population residing off-reservation, reservations have come to resemble holy lands, pilgrimage destinations, and retirement homes. To counteract the diaspora, many tribes have instituted annual fairs or powwows that function as homecomings to renew ties to the base community.

Continuity of land occupancy is one of the criteria considered in petitions for U.S. federal recognition as an American Indian tribe. For example, the decisive factor leading to the recognition of the Mashantucket Pequots was the fact that the last few acres of their original colonial reserve continued to be occupied by the elderly George sisters after all other relatives and tribespeople had left, mostly to seek gainful employment. The Mashantuckets, with their sudden casino wealth, are actively purchasing land to restore the original boundaries of their reservation, as well as buying other choice properties in the area for investment purposes. This does not please white neighbors, since lands added to the reservation are removed from local tax rolls. The reacquisition of land by wealthy Indian tribes reverses long-term historical trends and looms large in future identity politics.

Sense of Community

In addition to blood and land, a sense of community constitutes a third de-fining attribute of Native American identity. To a large extent one is identified as a Native American because one lives in or has close connections to an Indian community. The idea of communities is preferable to the idea of tribes, since tribes are politico-legal entities rather than direct face-to-face interactive social groups. Furthermore, in aboriginal and neo-aboriginal times there were very few true tribes, in the sense of institutions with clear lines of political authority, chiefs, councils, and strict membership criteria. Rather, as Mor-ton Fried argues,[33] tribes as discernible units mostly arose out of the contact with Europeans. Tribes were not primordial polities but institutions created to facilitate interaction with states. However, the "myth of the tribe" as an eternal and enduring entity is subscribed to by Euro-Americans and Native Americans alike. For the former, belief in the existence of tribes is of opera-tional value in that it postulates a political entity with which to treat and to enter into binding agreements on a government-to-government basis.

In earlier eras, when American Indians were still regarded as possessing considerable autonomy, military power, and political might, the term "nation" was frequently applied to Native American polities. (The term was sometimes, however, reserved for larger, more complex societies and suggested greater equivalence with European nation-states or their colonies than smaller tribes or bands.) When the balance of power shifted and Native Americans were considered as dependent nations or wards of the U.S. government, the term "tribe" became more widespread. In addition, for Euro-Americans "tribes" connoted an earlier evolutionary stage of social development and cultural progress. Even when an American Indian society became highly acculturated and assimilated white values and institutions, it remained a tribe, albeit a "civi-lized tribe," which if not oxymoronic seems to suggest an unstable liminality in which forces for further progress contended with pressures to return to a more tribal existence. Tribalism reflected not only a state of society but an appropriate mentality. Civilization was seen as a thin patina covering a less refined tribal mentality that would burst forth under the right conditions. For example, during the U.S. Civil War observers wondered whether Cherokee soldiers, fighting for the Union or for the Confederacy, would revert to scalp-ing in the heat of battle.

Notions of tribe and tribalism convey an inferior, primitive, or negative identity in certain areas of white discourse, but these very same terms are valued positively by Native Americans. Tribal sovereignty is vigorously defended, and the federal government is held strictly accountable for the fulfillment of treaty and other legal obligations. The tribe becomes the site of one's identity and distinctiveness not only vis-à-vis whites but also with respect to other Native American tribes. Members are felt to be united not only by blood, a common land base, and law, but also by a sense of belonging to a moral community with a shared history and destiny. Participation in this moral community entails practical and emotional costs, but, as with American Express, membership has its privileges, be they health care, tax-free status for certain items, Bureau of Indian Affairs services, or license to operate gambling facilities, and these privileges are jealously guarded and strongly defended. The upshot is that if tribes did not exist aboriginally, they most surely do exist today.

One may very well ask what forms of social organization prevailed in aboriginal America in lieu of the tribe. Certainly there were distinctive peoples speaking different languages and participating in different cultures. They belonged to what could be called a peoplehood, as a pluralized form of personhood.[34] Peoplehoods comprised widely spread networks of differentially connected individuals having reciprocal rights and duties toward one another and sharing a collective sense of community.

The social structure of peoplehoods, of course, varied from area to area in aboriginal North America. The native inhabitants of the eastern seaboard whom the English settlers first encountered appear to represent loose federations of related, interdigitated local groups extending from the Carolina coast to Massachusetts, all speaking Algonquian dialects. Elite intermarriage seems to have been an important mechanism for linking these groups together. Most resided in settled villages but were often seasonally mobile. The Lenapes knew about the summer attractions of the seashore long before Philadelphians became bilocal. Small-scale chiefdoms rose and fell with a fair degree of regularity, yet Powhatan was no emperor and Philip no king. The Iroquois Confederacy probably existed before the coming of whites, but it was a loose and fragile alliance at best, and not the formidable political and military machine it became during the colonial period.

In the interior of the Southeast, individual towns or linked sets of towns, not tribes, were the autonomous political units. Complex chiefdoms emphasizing hierarchy and central control characterized societies in the Caddoan and Mississippi drainage areas, while village organization prevailed in much of the Midwest. To the north, family and composite bands were the norm, as was the case in the pedestrian Plains and the Great Basin. In the Southwest, then as now, individual Pueblos were the loci of political authority. The groups of the lower Colorado River and the Mohave may have approximated "true" tribes, but in densely populated California, the units of political organization were what Alfred L. Kroeber aptly called "tribelets." [35] On the Northwest Coast and into the Plateau, villages or regional districts were the main units of individual and group identity, while, within the villages, households provided the specific locus of identity.

The major mechanism holding all of these diverse peoplehoods together was kinship. Kinship truly was a model of and a model for political integration. In some instances, where there was a ruling elite, we may be dealing directly with kinship and consanguineal systems of descent. Elsewhere, kinship served as a metaphor for social and political relations that could be inwardly intensive, such that everyone was related to everyone else through direct descent, clan affiliation, or adoption, and could be outwardly extensive, such that the idiom of kinship could be used as a means to establish and structure relations with strangers and alien societies.

In expanding the world of personhood, rituals of adoption and diplomatic protocol with outside groups nearly always involved the manipulation of symbols of identity. It is doubtful whether the proverbial blood brotherhood, in which actual blood was exchanged through mutual incision, was widely practiced, but intermarriage surely reflected symbolic exchanges of blood. Very often adoption rituals involved the trading of clothing. Clothing was sympathetically related to its wearer through principles of contagion and represented an exchange of skin. Animal skins, of course, became measurable wealth during the fur trade. On some more profound level, personified animal spirits bestowed their skins on human persons to reveal and reassert primordial kinship and identity relations with human beings. Diplomatic embassies were frequently concerned with adjudicated territorial boundaries and might even involve transactions of land, the second major attribute of identity discussed in this chapter. Increasingly in historical time, Indian–white diplomatic relations focused on land issues, either because whites were seeking to acquire more land through cessions or American Indians were complaining about white boundary jumpers and seeking redress.

Finally, with respect to adoption and diplomacy, cultural exchange was manifested in gift giving, feasting, and other acts of hospitality. Whites took this treatment as their due or as an instance of inherent native generosity. Native Americans, however, viewed these events as efforts to expand the community, to extend personhood by establishing or renewing relationships. They expected reciprocity on the part of whites to sustain the relationship. When they were disappointed in this expectation and reciprocity was not forthcoming, communalism was destroyed, identity was threatened, and the speeches of whites were perceived as the deliberate deceptions of a "forked tongue." Whites reacted by referring to their formerly generous hosts and hostesses as "Indian givers," and the identity struggle began anew.

Conclusion

In this chapter, Native American identity is considered in terms of three defining attributes: blood and descent, land, and community. Some of the subjective aspects of these attributes are suggested, but more emphasis is placed on political and legal dimensions, since these have been used to offer supposedly objective criteria for determining who and what is a Native American. This is a problem that is, or should be, of central concern to Native American studies programs.

Today, the assumptions underlying the effort to employ stable and objective measures of Native American identity are under fire. Blood quantum is being questioned not only because it reduces identity to biology and race, but also because the original information on which it was based may be flawed or erroneous. Scientific measures of blood type, DNA, anthropometry, and earwax texture are often unreliable and invalid identity markers. Land holdings can be ascertained, but the subjective associations with land are harder to evaluate. Finally, measures of community integration, which may include the structure and functioning of political organizations, voting behavior, church attendance, powwow participation, visiting patterns, telephone records, and other sociological indicators of community and communication, cannot provide conclusive evidence of a "sense of community."

The Branch of Acknowledgment and Recognition of the Bureau of Indian Affairs holds implicitly that once Indian tribal identity is lost or surrendered, it can never be regained. This notion is also problematic from a worldwide perspective. Cultural revivals, ethnic renewals, and nationalistic movements are rampant today. One has only to look at the breakup of the Soviet Union, the dismemberment of the former Yugoslavia, and the less brutal division of Czechoslovakia, at efforts by the Sami, the Maori, and other Fourth World peoples to gain sovereignty, at separatist movements in Wales, Scotland, and Ireland, as well as in Hawaii, Papua New Guinea, and Guatemala. Similar phenomena recur in the Middle East, South America, South and Central Africa, and many parts of Asia. A few generations ago most colonial powers viewed detribalization as an inevitable evolutionary trend on a one-way street leading to assimilation into the modern nation-state. Now the demands for independence and the movement toward retribalization and ethnic revival have forced social scientists and philosophers of history to reconfigure their theories of social change.

The determination of Native American identity has increasingly become the responsibility of federally recognized tribes. Some have chosen to tighten blood quantum requirements, while others apply different criteria to determine tribal membership. However, given the current diaspora of Native Americans in which perhaps as much as 70 percent of the population now resides off-reservation and far from tribal territories, specific tribal identity comes to take on more of a symbolic than a pragmatic reality. Nevertheless, many Native Americans do regroup in the cities to form multitribal communities and build new institutions as connections with former "home" communities become attenuated.

The growth of the Native American population in the United States has been phenomenal in recent decades. Substantial natural increase has been greatly supplemented with ever larger numbers of individuals claiming Native American identity in the decennial censuses. Many of these people are "Wannabees"; others claim partial Native American descent; still others are members of federally nonrecognized tribes. Such claims are a cause of concern for federally recognized tribes, who feel that their own special status vis-à-vis the federal government may be threatened. Indeed, the State of Georgia, which pressed for the removal of American Indians from its borders in the 1820s and 1830s, leading to the tragic Trail of Tears, recently reversed its policy by giving state recognition to scores of groups dubiously claiming to be Cherokees, much to the consternation of recognized Cherokee tribal officials in North Carolina and Oklahoma.

The times they are a-changing. However, it would be premature to predict the demise of tribes in the next century, as did Commissioner of Indian Affairs Thomas Jefferson Morgan in 1893 at the World's Columbian Exposition.[36] Issues of Native American identity will continue to be actively debated during the next millennium. Native American studies programs are strategically situated to monitor and interpret the ongoing identity struggle over who and what is an Indian. These will be interesting times.

Notes

I would like to thank Russell Thornton for his patience and encouragement in helping me complete this chapter. When he originally suggested that I write something on Native American identity, I realized that the course was uncharted and would be difficult to navigate, but I never thought I would be at sea, out of sight of land, for so long. Anne Straus and Raymond DeMallie offered useful dialogue, and I also appreciate the commentary of acerbic and fitful readers who helped me keep my bearings. Paul Spruhan was an important interlocutor and bibliographic source.

1. The notion of "reinvented culture" is irksome, since it not only sounds like a mechanical "clink," but suggests a lack of authenticity, a fraud perpetrated by "phony folk." Culture is always being reinvented. Who invents the reinventors? See Erik Hobsbawm and Terence Ranger, eds., *The Invention of Tradition* (Cambridge: Cambridge University Press, 1983), for discussion and examples of this approach.

2. "Real" is placed in quotation marks because all identities are real in some sense.

3. See Anthony F. C. Wallace and Raymond D. Fogelson, "The identity struggle," in *Intensive Family Therapy: Theoretical and Practical Aspects,* Ivan Boszomenyi-Nagy and James L. Framo, eds. (New York: Harper and Row, 1965), 365–406.

4. See, for example, Erik H. Erikson, *Childhood and Society,* 2d ed. (New York: Norton, 1963 [1950]); Erik H. Erikson, *Identity and the Life Cycle: Selected Papers,* Psychological Issues, vol. I, no. 1 (New York: International Universities Press, 1967 [1959]; Erik H. Erikson, "Identity, Psychosocial," in *International Encyclopedia of the Social Sciences,* vol. 7, David L. Sills, ed. (New York: Macmillan, 1968), 61–63.

5. Erikson, *Childhood and Society,* 114–86.

6. See Frank W. Porter III, "Nonrecognized American Indian tribes: An historical and legal perspective," *Newberry Library Center for the History of the American Indian Occasional Paper Series,* no. 7 (Chicago: Newberry Library, 1983).

7. Soon after European colonization, the "New World" also became a new world for surviving Native Americans. See James Merrell, *The Indians' New World: The Catawbas and Their Neighbors from European Contact Through the Era of Removal* (Chapel Hill: University of North Carolina Press, 1989); Richard White, *The Middle Ground: Indians, Empires, and Republics in the Great Lakes Region, 1650–1813* (Cambridge: Cambridge University Press, 1991).

8. Other terms prevail in other parts of the Americas. "First People" is the preferred term in Canada, although to a badly attuned ear this sounds too grammatical, as in first person plural, or "we"; "Indigenista" is widely used in Latin America; and occasionally one hears "American Aborigines" or, much more rarely (thank goodness), "American Autochthons."

9. I am indebted to one of the anonymous reviewers of an earlier draft of this chapter for this observation.

10. For a discussion of some of these matters see Raymond D. Fogelson, "Interpretation of the American Indian psyche: Some historical notes," in *Social Contexts of American Ethnology, 1840–1984,* 1984 Proceeding of the American Ethnological Society, June Helm, ed. (Washington, D.C.: American Anthropological Association, 1985), 4–27.

11. Winthrop D. Jordan, *White Over Black: American Attitudes Toward the Negro* (Chapel Hill: University of North Carolina Press, 1968), 166.

12. Juan Comas, *Racial Myths* (Westport: Greenwood, 1976 [1951]).

13. J. H. Elliot, *Imperial Spain, 1469–1716* (Baltimore: Penguin, 1990), 107.

14. See Jordan, *White Over Black;* Russell Thornton, *American Indian Holocaust and Survival: A Population History Since 1492* (Norman: University of Oklahoma Press, 1987), 187; and Jack D. Forbes, *Africans and Native Americans: The Language of Race and the Evolution of Red-Black Peoples,* 2d ed. (Champaign: University of Illinois Press, 1993 [1988]), for excellent discussions of these systems of fractionated descent.

15. Jordan, *White Over Black,* 168.

16. Frederick K. Lomayesva, "Indian identity and degree of Indian blood," *Red Ink,* 3 (1995), 33–37.

17. Paul Spruhan, "Quantum of power: Historical origins of blood identification in United States Indian policy" (M.A. thesis, Master of Arts Program in the Social Sciences, University of Chicago, 1996).

18. Jordan, *White Over Black,* 168–69; Forbes, *Africans and Native Americans,* 215–18, 221–33.

19. For discussions of some of these groups, see James Mooney, "Indian tribes of the District of Columbia," *American Anthropologist,* 2 (1889), 259–66; Roland M.

Harper, "A statistical study of the Croatans," *Rural Sociology,* 2 (1937), 444–56; Brewton Berry, "The Mestizos of South Carolina," *American Journal of Sociology,* 51 (1945), 34–41; William H. Gilbert, Jr., "Memorandum concerning the characteristics of the larger mixed-blood racial islands of the eastern United States," *Social Forces,* 24 (1946), 438–47; William H. Gilbert, Jr., "Surviving Indian groups of the eastern United States," *Annual Report of the Smithsonian Institution* (Washington, D.C.: U.S. Government Printing Office, 1948); Edward T. Price, "A geographic analysis of White-Indian-Negro racial mixtures in the eastern United States," *Annals of the Association of American Geographers,* 43 (1953), 138–55; Brewton Berry, *Almost White: A Study of Certain Racial Hybrids in the Eastern United States* (New York: Macmillan, 1963); Forbes, *Africans and Native Americans;* Joel Williamson, *New People: Miscegenation and Mulattoes in the United States* (New York: New American Library, 1975), 178.

20.   Simms's remarks appear in an 1845 review of two works by the early American ethnologist Henry Rowe Schoolcraft, which is reprinted in Abraham Chapman, ed., *Literature of the American Indians: Views and Interpretation* (New York: New American Library, 1975), 178.

21.   Perhaps the best critical review of the issue of blood quantum is Terry P. Wilson, "Blood quantum: Native American bloods," in *Racially Mixed People in America,* Maria P. P. Root, ed. (Newbury Park, Calif.: Sage, 1992), 108–25. See also Spruhan, "Quantum of power," which is a fine recent overview of the historical origins of blood quantum and its uses and abuses in U.S. Indian policy. Blood quantum first appears in a legal context to determine jurisdiction over criminal defendants. The key case is *United States v. Rogers* (1846). William Rogers, white, moved to Indian Territory, married a Cherokee woman, and was adopted into the Cherokee Nation. He was accused of killing another white man who had been similarly adopted. The court ruled that although his adoption made him a legitimate member of the Cherokee Nation, he was still a white man and subject to federal prosecution. See Lomayesva, "Indian identity," for further details.

As is well known, blood quantum later was employed to establish tribal rolls, particularly in connection with implementing the Allotment Act in the 1890s and the later Indian Reorganization Act of the 1930s. See David Beaulieu, "Curly hair and big feet: Physical anthropology and the implementation of land allotment on the White Earth Chippewa reservation," *American Indian Quarterly,* 7 (1984), 281–313; Melissa L. Meyer, *The White Earth Tragedy: Ethnicity and Dispossession at a Minnesota Anishinaabe Reservation, 1889–1920* (Lincoln: University of Nebraska Press, 1994), for detailed accounts of the implementation and consequences of allotment based upon blood quantum in a northern Chippewa community.

22.   The most spirited defender of the position that employment of blood quantum was a deliberate effort by the federal government to divide American Indians and ultimately bring about genocide is M. Annette Jaimes. See her "Federal Indian identification policy: A usurpation of indigenous sovereignty in North America," in *The State of Native America: Genocide, Colonization and Resistance,* M. Annette Jaimes, ed. (Boston: South End Press, 1992), and her article "American Indians, American racism: On race, eugenics, and 'mixed bloods,' " in *Occasional Papers in Curriculum Series,* 17 (Chicago: Newberry Library, 1995).

C. Matthew Snipp usefully contrasts administrative definitions of race with mystical and biological definitions in his *American Indians: The First of This Land* (New York: Russell Sage, 1989), 28–35. Snipp favors tribal determination of who is and who is not an Indian and is rightfully suspicious of biological tests of identity. Compared with Jaimes, however, his view of governmental intentions in employing blood quantum is less conspiratorial.

The final chapter, "The problematic of American Indian ethnicity," in Joanne Nagel's *American Indian Ethnic Renewal: Red Power and the Resurgence of Identity and Culture* (New York: Oxford University Press, 1996), offers a useful summary of many of the issues debated here.

23. U.S. Commissioner of Indian Affairs, *Annual Report of the Commissioner of Indian Affairs to the Secretary of the Interior for the Year 1890* (Washington, D.C.: U.S. Government Printing Office, 1890), 37.

24. For one attempt by a Native American to consider some of these issues, see Frell M. Owl, "Who and what is an American Indian?" *Ethnohistory,* 9 (1962), 265–84. William T. Hagen, "Full blood, mixed blood, generic, and ersatz: The persisting problem of Indian identity," *Arizona and the West,* 27 (1985), 309–26, offers useful historical understandings. Chapters 1 and 2 in Snipp, *American Indians,* provide lucid discussions of identity issues. For a recent attempt to consider the resurgence of American Indian identity, see Joanne Nagel, "Politics and the resurgence of American Indian ethnic identity," *American Sociological Review,* 60 (1995), 947–65. For related issues, see Steven Pratt, "Being an Indian among Indians," (Ph.D. diss., University of Oklahoma, 1985); D. Lawrence Wieder and Steven Pratt, "On being a recognizable Indian among Indians," in *Cultural Communication and Intercultural Contact,* Donal Carbaugh, ed. (Hillsdale, N.J.: Lawrence Erlbaum Associates, 1990), 45–64; D. Lawrence Wieder and Steven Pratt, "On the occasioned and situated character of member's questions and answers: Reflections on the question, "Is he or she a real Indian," ibid., 65–75.

25. See, for instance, M. J. Field, *Angels and Ministers of Grace: An Ethnopsychiatrist's Contribution to Biblical Criticism* (London: Longman, 1971), especially 6–19, for a provocative interpretation of early western views of land ownership.

26. See especially Patricia Seed, *Ceremonies of Possession in Europe's Conquest of the New World, 1492–1640* (Cambridge: Cambridge University Press, 1995), and also L. C. Green and Olive P. Dickason, *The Law of Nations and the New World* (Edmonton: University of Alberta Press, 1989), 7–17.

27. Thomas Jefferson, *Notes on the State of Virginia* (New York: Harper and Row, 1964 [1787]), 95–96; F. W. Waugh, *Iroquois Foods and Food Preparation,* Memoir 86, no. 12, Anthropological Series (Ottawa: Government Printing Bureau, 1916), 131.

28. Some of the more important contributions to this controversy include Frank G. Speck, "The family hunting band as the basis of Algonkian social organization," *American Anthropologist,* 17 (1915), 289–305; Frank G. Speck and Loren C. Eiseley, "The significance of hunting territory systems of the Algonkian in social theory," *American Anthropologist,* 41 (1939), 269–80; John M. Cooper, "Is the Algonquian family hunting ground system pre-Columbian?" *American Anthropologist,* 41 (1939), 66–90; Eleanor B. Leacock, *The Montagnais "Hunting Territory" and the Fur Trade,* American Anthropological Association, Memoir no. 78 (Washington, D.C.: American Anthropological Association, 1954); Charles A. Bishop and Toby Morantz, eds., "Who owns the beaver? Northern Algonquian land tenure reconsidered," Special Issue of *Anthropolo-*

gica, 28 (1986), 1–219; Adrian Tanner, *Bringing Home Animals: Religious Ideology and Mode of Production of Mistassini Cree Hunters* (New York: St. Martin's Press, 1979); Harvey A. Feit, "The construction of Algonquian hunting territories: Private property as moral lesson, policy advocacy, and ethnographic error," in *Colonial Situations: Essays on the Contextualization of Ethnographic Knowledge,* G. W. Stocking, ed. (Madison: University of Wisconsin Press, 1991), 109–34; Richard B. Lee and Richard H. Daley, "Eleanor Leacock, Labrador, and the Politics of Gatherer-Hunters," in *From Labrador to Samoa: The Theory and Practice of Eleanor Burke Leacock,* C. R. Sutton, ed. (Washington, D.C.: American Anthropological Association, 1993), 33–46.

29. Lips is cited in Tanner, *Bringing Home Animals,* 107.

30. My late friend Alfonso Ortiz would feign befuddlement at references to these "gifts." "What gifts?" he would ask. "They stole those things." Indeed, the expression "Indian giver" goes back to mid-eighteenth-century New England and is less indicative of Native American mendacity than of the Puritan failure to comprehend the reciprocity involved in gift giving.

31. Commissioner of Indian Affairs, *Annual Report for 1890,* 33.

32. The first reservations date back to the first half of the seventeenth century in colonial New England, but the reservation system did not become fully institutionalized as a federal governmental responsibility until the nineteenth century.

33. Morton H. Fried, "On the concepts of 'tribe' and 'tribal society,' " in *Essays on the Problem of Tribe,* June Helm, ed. (Seattle: University of Washington Press, 1968), 3–20; Morton H. Fried, *The Notion of Tribe* (Menlo Park, N.J.: Cummings, 1975). See also Raymond D. Fogelson, "The context of American Indian political history: An overview and critique," *Occasional Papers in Curriculum Series,* no. 11 (Chicago: Newberry Library, 1989), 8–21.

34. The notion of personhood employed here derives from Marcel Mauss's pioneering conceptualization (1938), which has been retranslated and discussed from several angles in Michael Carrithers, Steven Collins, and Steven Lukes, eds., *The Category of the Person: Anthropology, Philosophy, History* (Cambridge: Cambridge University Press, 1985). For the author's understanding of personhood and related concepts, see Raymond D. Fogelson, "Self, person, and identity: Some anthropological retrospects, circumspects and prospects," in *Psychosocial Theories of the Self,* Benjamin Lee, ed. (New York: Plenum Press, 1982), 67–109.

35. A. L. Kroeber, "Nature of the land-holding group," *Ethnohistory* 2 (1955), 303–14.

36. Thomas J. Morgan, "The Indian tribes will disappear," in *Today Then: America's Best Minds Look 100 Years Into the Future on the Occasion of the 1893 World's Columbian Exposition,* Dave Walter, compiler (Helena: American and World Geographic Publishing, 1992), 43–44. Morgan did, however, predict a Native American population of a million or so by 1993, and: "There will be here and there wandering bands of blanket beggars. These aboriginal tramps will perpetuate the absurdities and enormities of Indian life either as a profession or as a providential object lesson for students of history." (I am not certain whether Morgan here is envisioning the gypsy life of some Ph.D.s in anthropology or history or professors in Native American Studies programs!)

3 Bonnie Duran, Eduardo Duran, and Maria Yellow Horse Brave Heart

Native Americans and the Trauma of History

We can affirm that for people so remote and lacking contact with polished Spanish lands there has been no people on earth, who lived in their paganism with such harmony, good organization, and social orders as this nation. . . . It is my opinion that, no matter how beastly, they practiced their religion and its precepts well.

Fray Diego Duran, *The History of the Indies of New Spain*

An extensive body of literature deals with the Native American life world—the everyday background knowledge that informs and guides our interpretations of reality and interactions in sociocultural and interpersonal spheres.[1] Much less, however, has been written about the effects of colonialism on that life world and the implications of postcolonialism for it. How have Native Americans reacted to the system of colonization? Here we offer a broad answer to that question and illustrate how understanding this history and the intergenerational trauma it produced is a vital part of the healing and regenerative process for Native American peoples today.

Although the construct of intergenerational trauma has long been known to healers and elders in Native American communities, and is known from clinical studies of Jewish Holocaust survivors, it is new to many disciplines. Similarly, postcolonial thinking is relatively new within the social sciences, but it is old and well known in many Native American communities. That Native Americans have often resisted an "academic colonial process" and the identities prescribed by academic institutions bears witness to an ongoing legacy of counterhegemonic ideology in Native American communities themselves.

We realize that some scholars have and will continue to have problems with particular themes discussed here, in part because of the scarcity of research supporting them. In response to a need for quantitative data, recently we completed a nine-year study of cases from an urban Indian clinic that repeatedly validated our ideas. These data provide empirical evidence that intergenerational trauma exists and that its effects manifest themselves through present-day symptomatology. In addition, the study shows that some of the solutions we propose here have had positive results.[2] Particularly important is the fact that the hybrid form of treatment discussed below is remarkably more effective than any other treatment approach discussed in the literature.

Students of Native American studies should engage in critical thinking, and to do so they must have various literatures available to them. It is not acceptable to exclude consideration of some of the counterhegemonic thinking present in "Indian Country." Many conferences being held in the United States and Canada on Native American "healing" incorporate many of the general ideas presented here. Specifically, gatherings addressing alcoholism, suicide, and men's and women's issues have incorporated intergenerational trauma and its resolution.

Although Native American life worlds are not monolithic, many Native American peoples face similar challenges to their physical, spiritual and psychological health. Alcohol and other drug-related problems are particularly prevalent, contributing to more than 60 percent of the morbidity and mortality among Native American people.[3] Many Native American families are plagued by the symptomatology of alcoholism, poverty, learned helplessness and dependence, violence, and the breakdown of values that correlate with healthy living.

Historical trauma or intergenerational trauma, then, is offered as a paradigm to explain, in part, problems that have plagued Native Americans for many generations. In addition to analyzing some present problems within a sociohistorical context, we also propose strategies to ameliorate the effects of trauma. Our strategies are derived from empirical research such as the study mentioned above, psychological and public health practice, and a close analysis of contemporary Native American discourses.

The terms "colonialism" and "colonized" have been used by scholars to signify similar processes and effects occurring in different historical times at different analytical levels: physical, social, cultural, and psychological. Edward Said, a leading postcolonial scholar, defines colonialism as an effect of imperialism that results in settlements in distant territories. Imperialism means the "practice, the theory, and the attitudes of a dominating metropolitan center." [4] Most Native American populations in the United States have been subjected to all or a combination of these processes during the past five hundred years.

We are not advocating romanticized remembering of the past. Even without the devastation of colonialism, there would have been changes within Native American structures and systems over time. However, those changes would have taken place within the context of cultural change and development. We discuss here some of the subjugated knowledge of the events that led to the present life world of Native Americans and their families. In the process we hope to provide space for reimagining the present—also an important component of Native American studies.

We realize that not all tribes or all Native American people were subjected to the same amount of trauma. Our purpose here is to illustrate the effects of trauma on the tribes and people who suffered as colonization occurred. The problems that our communities face today are a result, at least in part, of not being given the time and resources to resolve the trauma. When people attribute present symptomatology to deficiencies within the Native American community, this belief is itself a form of epistemic violence that only exacerbates the problem.

If a person is traumatized, the trauma must be resolved for the person to be psychologically healthy. Not resolving the trauma will typically result in psychological symptoms, particularly depression, anxiety, and psychosomatic disorders. Memories of the trauma do not have to be kept alive through conscious awareness. Some practitioners argue that it is best to "let things be" and not disturb memories of things that happened long ago. As many clinical studies of Jewish survivors of the Holocaust have shown, however, trauma is often passed on to subsequent generations whether it is a conscious memory or not.

The Historical Legacy

European contact decimated the indigenous populations of this hemisphere.[5] The impact upon the Native American psyche may be understood as a "colonization of the life world." [6] Colonization of the life world occurs when the colonizers interfere with the mechanisms needed to reproduce the life world domains—culture, social integration, and socialization—of the colonized. Here, the creation and expansion of America produced an inevitable disintegration of the rationality of everyday Native American life. This disintegration is at the root of many present-day social and health problems.

The Trauma of Colonialism

The trauma of colonialism took various forms. The physical space of many tribes was systematically colonized, diseases were introduced, and military actions were frequent. Native American elders and the very young—depositories of cultural, spiritual, and medicinal knowledge and the hope for the future, respectively—were often disproportionate casualties of warfare and disease. The rapid succession of traumatic events sometimes prevented an adequate period of grieving and bereavement.[7] Native American peoples and families suffered the loss of their subsistence economy. Loss of territory and game not only created physical hardship but also bankrupted many meaning structures that informed identity and mechanisms of sociocultural reproduction and control. Life worlds were colonized by European rationality, engrossed as the colonizers were in economic and bureaucratic control over this hemisphere. The U.S. government sometimes carried out policies through military means; surviving Native American peoples and families were frequently removed from traditional homelands by force, suffering symptoms of refugee syndrome as they were displaced.

Traditional homelands provided familiar sources of sustenance for both physical and spiritual needs; relocation sites were often barren and harsh, and geographically based cultural and spiritual systems were difficult to maintain. Loss of relationship to a traditional environment was a severe spiritual and psychological injury. Many Native American familial and kinship systems were produced and reproduced in seasonal congregation, and language and ritual were closely tied to geography and the ability to move freely. The imposition of boundaries under the reservation system kept people from moving from one place to another and exacerbated what we call the "soul wound" (see below).

To further its "civilizing mission," the U.S. government enacted policies systematically attacking the core of identity—language and the family system. Removal of Native American children from their parents and placing them in distant boarding schools became a widespread practice.[8] This disruption of family life further eroded the production and reproduction of family systems and cultural mechanisms of social control. Socialized into neither the mainstream cultural system that devalued them and their potential nor the Native American systems from which they were physically distanced, Native American youths were often lost in no-man's-land.

Just as Native American people were starting to catch their breath in the twentieth century, an additional encroachment into the family and tribe occurred. During the 1950s, many Native American people were recruited into urban relocation programs. They went to the cities with an already large accumulation of historical trauma, and the urban situation created additional stress—economic, social, and spiritual—on Native American families. The intent was to assimilate native people, particularly to wage labor, and many Native Americans expected to become fully functioning middle-class, "white" Americans. Facing a concerted lack of economic and health resources, many soon returned to their reservations; others remained based in the cities, often developing a lifestyle of going back and forth between the city and the home reservation.

Cultural Genocide

Genocide of Native Americans has taken different forms, and there is growing attention to cultural genocide. "Cultural genocide" refers to actions that threaten the integrity and viability of social groups. Prohibition of religious freedom, for example, is a form of cultural genocide that continues to this day for Native Americans. Family and extended kinship rituals and ceremonies are a large part of religious life and ensure family cohesion and clan unity. It was only with Joint Senate Resolution 102 in 1978, the American Indian Religious Freedom Act (AIRFA), that Native American peoples were guaranteed the right to practice their religion without fear of reprisal by state and federal governments.[9] However, colonization of the life world continues as Native American religious beliefs and practices are obstructed by concerns that take precedence over Native American religious issues.

The Soul Wound

For two decades, the idea of the "soul wound" has circulated within the mental health discourse of Native American and other colonized peoples. Current synonymous terms include "historical trauma," "historical legacy," "Native American holocaust," and "intergenerational posttraumatic stress disorder." [10] Although these terms are new to the mental health literature, the concept has been an integral part of indigenous lay knowledge for generations. Many Native American people understand their problems in contemporary life by reference to traumatic events of the past.

The notion of the soul wound emerged when Native American people were asked about the problems plaguing them in central California in the late 1970s. Following a needs assessment study occurring over more than three years, a content analysis was done on the reported dreams of Native American community members. Though more than 800 themes were listed, the overwhelming message of the dreams was the hostility of the environment or the world. Many Native American people understood the effects of colonization as a spiritual injury, since spirituality remains a cornerstone of Native American cultures:

It is apparent that the psyche of the community recognized the wounding of the environment, and that this awareness in turn was perceived as a wounding of the psyche. Harmony had become discord and the community's unconscious perception was that the world was unfriendly and hostile. The problems that were manifested and verbalized were merely symptoms of a deeper wound—the soul wound.[11]

Historical trauma and its effects are complex, multigenerational, and cumulative. A constellation of features that occur in reaction to multigenerational, collective, historical, and cumulative psychic wounding over time—over the lifespan and across generations—historical trauma is characterized as incomplete mourning and the resulting depression absorbed by children from birth onward.[12] Unresolved trauma is intergenerationally cumulative, thus compounding the mental health problems of succeeding generations.

These phenomena are not exclusive to Native American or even other indigenous populations. Evidence suggests that the depressive and emotional breakdowns of the descendants of survivors of the Holocaust of Nazi Germany are always linked to Holocaust experiences.[13] The "survivor's child complex" is a constellation of features resulting from the intergenerational transmission of parental traumatic experiences and responses. Martin Bergman and Milton Jucovy conclude that, despite the possibility of adaptation and sublimation, the mental health of most children of survivors is at risk and that they are scarred by the psychic reality of the Jewish Holocaust.[14] Cardinal themes of parental survival, persecution, and deaths of relatives, at times unconscious, were manifested in their analyses.[15] Judith and Milton Kestenberg describe a "survivor's child complex" that includes the Holocaust's impact upon psychic structure, fantasies, and identification.[16] The Kestenbergs regard post-Holocaust experiences of oppression as further affecting parental survivorship and quality of transmission to offspring. Features associated with the complex are depression, suicidal ideation and behavior, guilt and concern about betraying the ancestors by being excluded from their suffering, as well as internalized obligation to share in the ancestral pain. Other features include feeling obliged to take care of and be responsible for survivor parents, identification with parental suffering, and a compulsion to compensate for the genocidal legacy, persecutory and intrusive Holocaust memories and also grandiose fantasies, dreams, and images, and a perception of the world as dangerous. Many of these themes were also found in the dreams of the Native Americans recorded in the needs assessment referred to earlier.

The description of the survivor's child complex was congruent with features identified by Gordon Macgregor and Erik Erikson among the Lakota:[17] persecutory fantasies and a perception of the world as dangerous, the fantasy of the return of the old way of life, analogous to compensatory fantasies, paranoia, apprehension, shame, withdrawal, grandiosity in daydreams, and anxiety about aggressive impulses.[18]

Historical trauma is a continuing process, maintained via the pressures of acculturative stress. "Acculturative stress" refers to anxiety produced through the process of acculturation, often resulting in depression, feelings of marginality and alienation, heightened psychosomatic symptoms, and identity confusion. Acculturative stress may undermine individuals' physical, psychological, and social health.[19] While historical trauma includes acculturation stress, it goes much deeper and encompasses the aftereffects of racism, oppression, and genocide.

Although experts urge caution in the assertion of a "survivor syndrome," the mental health literature acknowledges the existence of special features among the clinical population of trauma survivors. Addressing criticisms of the survivors' syndrome, Eva Fogelman asserts that, although more empirical studies are needed, the pain and psychological impairment of survivors are not captured by standardized personality tests.[20]

Fogelman and Maria Brave Heart outline aspects of the experiences of Jewish survivors that are relevant for Native Americans. These include difficulty in mourning over a mass grave, the dynamics of collective grief, and the importance of community memorialization,[21] all experienced by the Lakota descendants of the Wounded Knee Massacre in 1890. As Jews in European countries live "among the perpetrators and murderers of their families," [22] Native Americans live in a colonized country where similar patterns of grief have emerged. Fogelman asserts that

Jews in Europe have not found . . . effective means of coping, integration, and adaption. Most are in a stage of complete denial and stunted mourning of their losses. . . . They feel a great need to control their emotions, because they feared that if their intense emotions were given free rein, they might go insane. . . . Survivors feared the uncontrollable rage locked within them, they feared they would be devoured by thoughts of avenging the deaths of their loved ones. These repressions result in psychic numbing.[23]

Fogelman's research distinguishes the healthier communal grief process of American Jews from the delayed and impaired grief of European Jews. For Native Americans, the U.S. government is the perpetrator of their holocaust. Whereas other oppressed groups can emigrate to escape further psychic genocide, Native Americans have not had this option. "Where was America for American Indians?" Alice Beck Kehoe asks. "No other country welcomed them as immigrants, no other country promised them what their native land had denied them." [24]

Problems brought on by the devastation of the Native American holocaust are further complicated by this lack of validation from the world community and its failure to offer an escape route. These dynamics require a repressed psychology that can only be expressed through symptoms. Native American people are aware of the conspiracy of silence that invalidates the pain they endured. It is yet another level of ongoing trauma that must be confronted.

Consider the example of a fifteen-year-old Pueblo girl referred for a suicide attempt from an aspirin overdose. She said that she did not want to kill herself but that she felt an overwhelming sadness that she could not share with her parents: "I just can't talk to my parents. I don't want to burden them with my problems and feelings. They have so much pain of their own. I just can't bring myself to do that, but I felt like I had no one to talk to." [25] In another case, a young man reported walking in his homeland and finding himself in the middle of a massacre, engulfed by horses and cavalry. He saw old Indian women and children huddled against the river bank and trying to shield themselves from the sabers and the bullets. When he shared this vision with some of the elders of his community, they informed him that a massacre had occurred over a hundred years ago on that very spot.[26]

Such cases are common in clinical settings where Native American people are seen for treatment. Often clients completely deny or shut down their emotions, since their surfacing would elicit extreme anger. When that anger is manifested, externally or internally, the resulting need for anesthetic self-intervention behaviors such as alcohol abuse, drug abuse, domestic violence, or suicide makes psychological sense.

A Note on Pre-Columbian Family Systems

A tremendous diversity existed and exists in family and kinship systems in Indian Country. In this chapter we must generalize, without wanting to reduce the cultural richness of Native kinship systems. As Spero Manson states, "First, members aid and protect one another; their collective liability for the other's actions regulates individual behavior." [27] This collective liability speaks to tribal or collective behavioral sanctions that were in place to regulate the society.[28]

In addition to strict behavior codes, Native American family and kinship were heavily influenced by a deep sense of relationship. Instead of breaking the family into role units, it would be more accurate to differentiate the family according to relationships. Robert Thomas makes this point: "Well, an Indian family is not a structure in a system of roles. It is a system of relationships, first, from which the activities emerge. It is not a role system. To see it as a role system is a distortion. Now there are activities there, but they emerge from the relationship. Indian families are first a system of personal, definitive relationships. By tradition there are activities connected with those relationships. That is what gives them a role-like appearance. That's not central. What is central is the relationship." [29]

Native American peoples and families have always had human problems. The full spectrum of health and pathology existed in the pre-Columbian Native American family. The difference between then and now is that typically there were systems in place to deal with and resolve problems in a way that ensured the healthy functioning of the family and culture. Because of the holocaust suffered by Native Americans, these systems were broken down and replaced with foreign, dysfunctional ones, or not replaced at all. An early account reflects this breakdown:

Because neither do you understand us, nor do we understand you. And we do not know what it is that you want. You have deprived us of our good order and way of government, and the one with which you have replaced it we do not understand. Now all is confusion and without order and harmony. The Indians of Mexico have given themselves to fighting because you have brought it upon them. Those who are not in contact with you do not fight; they live in peace. And if during the time of our "paganism" there were fights and disputes, they were very few. And they were dealt with justly and settled quickly because there used to be no difficulties in finding out which of the parties was right, nor were there any delays and cheating as there are now.[30]

These words were recorded very soon after contact with colonialism. Even at this early stage, there is a clear understanding that many societal problems were direct effects of the colonial process. The speaker acknowledges that problems existed before colonial contact, as well as systemic solutions to the problems.

Particularly damaging has been the systematic destruction of the initiation ceremonies of many (though not all) tribes. Among the Apache, there were ceremonies for every step of child development, used to invoke the assistance of supernatural powers to protect the child.[31] A lack of such ceremonies contributes to problems faced by contemporary Native American youth. Traditional initiation ceremonies have given way to other undifferentiated methods of initiation, conducted away from family and tribe and sometimes involving unhealthy activities. One of the major initiations for Native American youth has involved the use of alcohol, with devastating effects.

Healing Native Americans and Their Families

Western psychology and other forms of social service intervention are useful but not sufficient to provide a future for and to heal Native Americans. An intellectual colonization persists in the representations of Native Americans in some social science research and mental health literature. New approaches are needed.

Standard Psychotherapeutic Approaches

The sociocultural, behavioral, and disease theories that public and Indian Health Service officials apply to interpret and intervene in some problems affecting Native Americans,

however useful, are not neutral insights and assessments of Native [problems] but rather venture to explain and predict behavior based on a very historically and culturally specific mode of representation—realism—which erroneously assumes unity between the sensible and intelligible. Embedded within this Eurocentric mode of representation is a biased assessment of non-Western cultures. Behavioral theories decontextualize and individualize social problems and many socio-cultural theories continue European representations of native peoples that have origins in the politics of the colonial and early American era. Insofar as these approaches are cultural products—a form of literature—we can say that they are hegemonic. By this we mean that they partake in ideological/cultural domination by the assertion of universality and neutrality and by the disavowal of all other cultural forms or interpretations.[32]

Researchers and practitioners using western methodologies fail to realize how incompletely their methods capture the truth of Native American tribal lives and pathology. Western methods infiltrate Native American life worlds as epistemic violence,[33] replacing Native American with foreign idioms, definitions, and understandings. Social scientists have been rewriting tribal rituals via anthropology and other disciplines for centuries and thereby have produced meanings that have changed and distorted tribal understandings or forced them underground. Western empirical research and theory are based on the illusion of objectivity with a transhistorical, transcultural orientation. It operates within an *a priori,* essentialist Cartesian model of a unified, rational, autonomous subject. Here, the objectification of Native American families deprives the Native American life world of its material history and context and so of a crucial aspect of its truth and potential.

Typically, clinical interventions attempting to relieve problems caused by historical trauma have been inadequate; low utilization rates are consistently found in studies of the mental health service delivery system. Most Native American people drop out of treatment before three sessions. In one study, the authors discuss how exposure to western therapy alone may be harmful to Native American people.[34] Although historical distrust, language,[35] and class barriers are important issues in the development of cultural competency, in many clinical settings they are nonexistent issues.[36]

A recent attack on the Native American family has taken the form of extracultural adoption. Until the passage of the Indian Child Welfare Act in 1978, many religious organizations actively recruited Native American parents to give up their children for adoption.[37] This incursion had its roots in the assimilation/termination policies of the U.S. government from 1900 to 1960.[38] Adoption has had a devastating impact on individual children, families, and tribes.

Irving Berlin observes that Native American children adopted into white families are at higher risk for suicide or the emergence of other pathology during adolescence and young adulthood. These children feel rootless and often believe that as Native American people they are not valued by the dominant culture. When they become adolescents, he notes, they feel that they have no ties to either their own or the majority culture. He estimates that their suicide rate is twice that of the American Indian youth living on reservations.[39]

So compelling was the evidence of the destructiveness of extracultural placement that in 1975 the American Academy of Child Psychiatry urged against placing American Indian children in white homes. Berlin warns that "what may be advantageous developmentally for the small child may rob him of his cultural heritage and be devastating to him in his later development. Judges must learn to recognize that loss of ties with their tribal customs and culture leaves these children without an identity and can result in an adult life of estrangement from both worlds." [40] Even with this strong warning, social workers and judges continue to place Indian children away from their families and tribes. Currently, the Indian Child Welfare Act itself is threatened in Congress, marking a shift away from the ideals of cultural diversity.[41]

Although some progress has been made, there are still overtones of paternalism in the delivery of health services. While the Indian Health Service is responsible for providing health services to tribal and urban communities, Congress has inconsistently provided funds for appropriate levels of functioning.[42]

Restoration of the Life World: Postcolonial Practice

And as I looked and wept, I saw that there stood on the north side of the starving camp a Sacred man who was painted red all over his body, and he held a spear as he walked into the center of his people, and there he laid down and rolled. And when he got up it was a fat bison standing there, and where the bison stood a Sacred herb sprang up right where the tree had been in the center of the nations' hoop. The herb grew and bore four blossoms on a single stem while I was looking—a blue, a white, a scarlet and a yellow—and the bright rays of these flashed to the heavens.—Black Elk

When the young Black Elk saw this vision, he understood it as the restoration of the nations' hoop—the healing of the Indian nations.[43] Black Elk also understood that the healing would take place seven generations after Wounded Knee—our generation today.

Many successful programs currently operating among Native American groups use Native American epistemology as the root metaphor for theoretical and clinical interventions. Postcolonial practice integrates indigenous knowledge and therapies with Euro-American models of therapy. Native American therapies need wider acceptance from mainstream sources, not only to expand availability and gain adequate funding, but also to adapt and grow in this postmodern cultural context.

Many present-day indigenous interventions have been recommended by our Native American ancestors for centuries and are still in use in individual treatment by medicine people. In addition, new therapies based on postcolonial thought have emerged. By "postcolonial thought" we mean a critical orientation to scholarship and practice that, first, recognizes a social criticism of the unequal process of representation by which the historical experience of the once colonized became framed by the colonizers and, second, incorporates the subjected knowledge of marginalized groups in developing posttraditional methods. These therapies based on postcolonial thought do not operate on the logic of equivalence (A:non-A) but rather on a logic of difference (A:B), thus celebrating diversity rather than comparing people to what they are not.

Two approaches to individual and community mental health practice may be highlighted.

Hybrid Therapy: The Community Clinic Model

The first approach, a hybrid or a community clinic model, uses staff who are trained in both western and Native American treatment and epistemological systems. Western-trained Native American and other psychotherapists work alongside traditional Native American healers. This bicultural approach accomplishes multiple goals: it allows a historically inclusive psychological approach that acknowledges the roots of betrayal and anger; it moves the patient toward a more acceptable cultural system of sanctions and rewards that prescribes appropriate behavior; and it focuses on issues of internalized oppression and adoption of negative stereotypes, thereby creating space for reimaging the self.

Healers from each side (western and Native American) must be sincerely respectful and appreciative of what the other has to offer. If the practitioners do not live a lifestyle that follows some traditional forms or genuinely believe in the healing powers of both traditional and western approaches, the interventions will be seen as offensive caricatures by the staff and clients and their families and communities.

A typical protocol for a family may be as follows:

1. The family is referred to or contacts either a traditional provider (an indigenous therapist) or a psychologist for intervention. Referrals are made by a full range of community agencies.
2. The traditional counselor or psychologist makes an assessment of the client and immediately has a conference with the other providers. Assessment includes mental health functioning, level of acculturation, spiritual functioning or problems, and general health.
3. The family then receives psychotherapy and participates in traditional ceremonies as appropriate. A client who needs help from a medicine person is referred to one from his or her traditional belief system if possible. In urban areas it is difficult to provide tribal-specific medicine people. It becomes imperative, then, that the medicine people available be able to generalize their interventions so that the client can participate in and make sense of the intervention. Education by the medicine people is an integral part of the intervention. The therapy is designed to help the client understand the process itself. Many Native American clients have been so acculturated that often one important focus of the therapy is to reconnect them to a traditional system of belief and make sense of their life world from a traditional perspective.
4. The family is evaluated and recommendations are made for ongoing therapy or participation in traditional ceremonies, or both.

Insight-oriented treatment has been a very effective modality in treating Native American people within urban and rural settings. Native American people utilize dream-oriented therapy, and frequently this insight-oriented intervention allows other modalities to be effective. Insight-oriented treatment, especially a hybrid model in which Jungian approaches are integrated with Native American therapeutic modalities, is successful in large part because this model validates many Native American psychological experiences.

Once the client has engaged in hybrid therapy, it becomes easier to implement other modalities. Common strategies that have been successful in this model include cognitive behavioral, behavioral, client-centered, psychoanalytic, and addictions treatment. The critical point is that these western therapies were made effective because the hybrid model is inclusive of both western and Native American strategies.

Healing Rituals

The second model incorporates healing rituals for the entire community. For example, the Lakota have brought back a traditional approach to individual, family, and community-wide healing of historical trauma and other mental suffering. They undertook a communal memorialization through the Tatanka Iyotake (Sitting Bull) and Wokiksuye (Bigfoot) Ride, which traced the path of the Hunkpapa and Miniconju massacred at Wounded Knee.[44] The Lakota intervention model includes catharsis, abreaction, group sharing, testimony, opportunities for expression of traditional culture and language, ritual, and communal mourning. Wounded Knee and the generational boarding school trauma cannot be forgotten.

Brave Heart found that education about the historical trauma leads to an increase in awareness of that trauma, its impact, and the grief-related effects. The process of sharing these effects with others of similar background and within a traditional Lakota context leads to a cathartic sense of relief. A healing and mourning process results in a reduction of grief effects, an experience of more positive group identity, and an increased commitment to continuing healing work on both an individual and a community level.[45]

Brave Heart found that the Lakota intervention helped with everyone's grief resolution, and almost 75 percent found it very helpful in other aspects of their mental health. Ninety-seven percent felt that they could now make a constructive commitment to the memory of their ancestors. All respondents felt better about themselves after the intervention, with some 75 percent expressing high agreement that the intervention helped them overcome feelings of cultural shame.

Brave Heart's intervention model, culturally syntonic grief resolution and healing, identifies and incorporates features congruent with treatment for Nazi

Holocaust survivors and their descendants: (1) facilitating mourning as the primary task; (2) helping the patient tolerate effects that accompany the traumatic memories and the process of working through; (3) codification in self- and object representations as well as world representations; and (4) validation and normalization of the trauma response and techniques such as visualization and pseudohypnotic suggestibility. Other techniques involve exploration of pre-Holocaust family history.

Brave Heart describes her treatment as a group treatment model. The restorative factors incorporate sharing experiences, providing hope, collective mourning, and social support. Advantages of group treatment include bonding through sharing common traumatic experiences and mutual identification. Developing awareness of intergenerational transfer processes inhibits the transmission of psychopathology.[46]

Conclusion

Both Native American self-determination and cultural revitalization are furthered by the study of and intervention in Native Americans and their family systems. Family- and community-based intervention programs based on participatory, postcolonial research capture prescriptions for healthy family roles and include them alongside mainstream socialization. In contrast to assimilation or segregationist alternatives, posttraditional visions are inherently hybrid and self-reflective. Through an awareness of both negative and positive representations that colonize and, in part, determine subjectivity, self-determination is enacted through Native Americans' choice of identity—those meanings, values, and social and cultural systems that constitute Native American ethnicity.

Western approaches that focus on illness and pathology do not consider community assets. Unless the strengths of Native American family structures are included in therapy and other forms of intervention, there will always be resistance to adopting a pathologized self. One important source of intervention is simply the education of Native Americans and others about this process, in Native American studies programs and elsewhere.

Notes

1. Jurgen Habermas, *The Theory of Communicative Action,* Vol. 1: *Reason and the Rationalization of Society,* Thomas McCarthy, trans. (Boston: Beacon Press, 1984).

2. The study data are available in an Indian Health Service (IHS) report of December 1996. The study was conducted by Eduardo Duran and Susan Yellowhorse-Davis. Also see other quantitative and qualitative data in Maria Yellow Horse Brave Heart, "The return to the sacred path: Healing the historical trauma and historical unresolved grief response among the Lakota," *Smith College Studies in Social Work,* 68(1998), 287–305; Maria Yellow Horse Brave Heart, "Oyate Ptayela: Rebuilding the Lakota

Nation through addressing historical trauma among Lakota parents," in *Voices of First Nations People: Considerations for Human Services* (New York: Hawthorn Press, 1998); "Wakiksuyapi: Carrying the historical trauma of the Lakota," *Tulane Studies in Social Welfare* 11–12 (1998). See Brave Heart, 1998 and Maria Yellow Horse Brave Heart and Lemyra DeBruyn, "The American Indian Holocaust: Healing historical unresolved grief," *American Indian and Alaska Native Mental Health Research*, 8(1998), 56–78.

3. Everett Rhoades et al., "The Indian burden of illness and future health interventions," *Public Health Reports*, 102 (1987), 461–68.

4. Edward Said, *Culture and Imperialism* (New York: Knopf, 1993).

5. See Dee Brown, *Bury My Heart at Wounded Knee: An Indian History of the American West* (New York: Holt, Rinehart & Winston, 1971), for a popular account; for scholarly accounts, see Wilbur Jacobs, *Dispossessing the American Indian: Indians and Whites on the Colonial Frontier* (Norman: University of Oklahoma Press, 1972); Richard White, *The Roots of Dependency: Subsistence, Environment and Social Change Among the Choctaws, Pawnees, and Navajos* (Lincoln: University of Nebraska Press, 1983); Russell Thornton, *American Indian Holocaust and Survival: A Population History Since 1492* (Norman: University of Oklahoma Press, 1987); Patricia Limerick, *The Legacy of Conquest: The Unbroken Past of the American West* (New York: Norton, 1987); Roy Harvey Pearce, *Savagism and Civilization: A Study of the Indian and American Mind* (Berkeley: University of California Press, 1988); Lyman Legters, "The American genocide," *Policy Studies Journal*, 16 (1988), 768–77; David Stannard, *American Holocaust: Columbus and the Conquest of the New World* (New York: Oxford University Press, 1992); see also Maria BraveHeart-Jordan and LeMyra DeBruyn, "So she may walk in balance: Integrating the impact of historical trauma in the treatment of Native American women," in *Racism in the Lives of Women: Testimony, Theory, and Guides to Anti-Racist Practice*, Jeanne Adleman and Gloria Enguidanos, eds. (New York: Haworth Press, 1995).

6. Habermas, *Theory of Communicative Action*, 1: 25–50.

7. Clinical research has found that if trauma is not resolved, there will always be a movement from the person/family toward resolution. If ritualized healing or therapy is not available, individuals will resort to other ways of dealing with the injury. Often the approaches taken to resolve trauma exacerbate the problem at both the individual and the collective level, as when the impulse to anesthetize pain involves the use of alcohol. See Brave Heart and DeBruyn, 1998.

8. Brave Heart-Jordan's examination of traumatic boarding school experiences among the Lakota are generalizable to many other tribes. She finds that many boarding schools were operated like prison camps, with American Indian children being starved, chained, and beaten. Children were forbidden to speak Native American languages, practice Native American religions, or to convey or enact anything that might remotely resemble Native American lifestyles, beliefs, or customs. Children were taught that Native American cultures and religions were inferior, even evil, and were influenced to be ashamed of their parents, their family and kinship systems, their language, their way of worship, and other remaining facets of Native American identity. See Brave Heart and DeBruyn, 1998; Legters, Lyman, "The American genocide," *Policy Studies Journal*, 16(1988).

9. See Francis Paul Prucha, *The Great Father: The United States Government*

and the American Indians, abridged ed. (Lincoln: University of Nebraska Press, 1986 [1984]), 368–69. Prucha notes that "Indian religious rights were further recognized in the Archaeological Resources Protection Act of 1979." See Brave Heart and DeBruyn, 1998.

10.   See Brave Heart-Jordan and DeBruyn, "So she may walk in balance"; Maria Brave Heart-Jordan, "The return to the sacred path: Healing from historical trauma and historical unresolved grief among the Lakota" (Ph.D. diss., Smith College, 1995); Eduardo Duran and Bonnie Duran, *Native American Postcolonial Psychology* (Albany: SUNY Press, 1995); Brave Heart, 1998. Reprints available through the Takini Network c/o Maria Yellow Horse Brave Heart, University of Denver Graduate School of Social Work, 2148 S. High St., Denver, CO 80208.

11.   Duran and Duran, *Postcolonial Psychology,* 26.

12.   Brave Heart-Jordan, "Return to the sacred path"; Tamar Shoshan, "Mourning and longing from generation to generation," *American Journal of Psychotherapy,* 43 (1989), 193–207; Brave Heart, 1998.

13.   Zahuva Solomon, Moshe Kotler, and Mario Mikulincer, "Combat related post-traumatic stress disorder among second-generation Holocaust survivors: Preliminary findings," *American Journal of Psychiatry,* 145 (1988), 865–68.

14.   See Martin Bergman and Milton Jucovy, eds., *Generations of the Holocaust* (New York: Columbia University Press, 1990).

15.   Judith Kestenberg and Milton Kestenberg, "The experience of survivor-patients," ibid. See also Danieli Yael, "Mourning in survivors and children of survivors of the Nazi Holocaust: The role of group and community modalities," in *The Problems of Loss and Mourning: Psychoanalytic Perspectives,* D. R. Dietrich and P. C. Shabad, eds. (Madison: International University Press, 1989).

16.   Kestenberg and Kestenberg, "The experiences of survivor-patients."

17.   Gordon Macgregor, *Warriors Without Weapons* (Chicago: University of Chicago Press, 1975); Erik H. Erikson, *Childhood and Society,* 2d ed., revised and enlarged (New York: Norton, 1963 [1950]), 114–65.

18.   Carolyn Williams and John Berry, "Primary prevention of acculturative stress among refugees: Application of psychological theory and practice," *American Psychologist,* 46 (1991), 634; Brave Heart, 1998; Brave Heart-Jordan, 1995.

19.   Ibid.

20.   Eva Fogelman, "Mourning without graves," in *Storms and Rainbows: The Many Faces of Death,* A. Medvene, ed. (Washington, D.C.: Lewis Press, 1991).

21.   Ibid.; Brave Heart-Jordan, "Return to the sacred path."

22.   Fogelman, "Mourning without graves," 94; Brave Heart and DeBruyn, 1998.

23.   Ibid.

24.   Alice Beck Kehoe, *The Ghost Dance: Ethnohistory and Revitalization* (New York: Holt, Rinehart and Winston, 1989), 133.

25.   Brave Heart and DeBruyn, 1998, 62.

26.   Duran and Duran, *Postcolonial Psychology.*

27.   Spero Manson, "Indian family and kinship systems: With special reference to the Northwest Coast," manuscript, White Cloud Center, 1979, 4.

28.   Ibid.

29.   Robert Thomas, "Alternative paradigms for research," in *The American Indian*

Family: Strengths and Stresses, Proceedings of the Conference on Research Issues, John Red Horse, August Shattuck, and Fred Hoffman, eds. (Isleta, N.Mex.: American Indian Social Research and Development Associates, n.d.), 96–97.

30.   Alonso de Zurita, *Breve y sumaria relacion de documentos para la historia de Mexico,* vol. 3, Salvador Chavez Icazbalceta, ed. (Hayhoe, Mexico: 1941), 110.

31.   See Bryce Boyer, *Childhood and Folklore: A Psychoanalytic Study of Apache Personality* (New York: Library of Psychological Anthropology, 1979).

32.   Duran and Duran, *Postcolonial Psychology,* 110.

33.   Guyatri Spivak, "Can the subaltern speak," in *Marxism and the Interpretation of Culture,* Cary Nelson and Lawrence Grossberg, eds. (Urbana: University of Illinois Press, 1988), 271–313.

34.   T. D. LaFromboise and W. Rowe, "Skills training for bicultural competence: Rationale and application," *Journal of Counseling Psychology,* 30 (1983), 589–95.

35.   Miguel Barrera, "Mexican American mental health service utilization: A critical examination of some proposed variables," *Community Mental Health Journal,* 4 (1978), 35–45.

36.   Barbetta Lockart, "Historic distrust and the counseling of American Indian and Alaskan Natives," *White Cloud Journal,* 2 (1981), 31–34.

37.   See David Fanshell, *Far from the Reservation: The Transracial Adoption of American Indian Children* (Metuchen, N.J.: Scarecrow Press, 1972); Beaver Pierce, "Protestant churches and the Indians," in *Handbook of North American Indians,* Vol. 4: *History of Indian–White Relations,* Wilcomb Washburn, ed. (Washington, D.C.: Smithsonian Institution, 1988), 430; John Price, "Mormon missions to the Indians," ibid., 469.

38.   William Cingolani, "Acculturating the Indian: Federal policies," *Social Work,* 18 (1973), 24–28.

39.   Irving Berlin, "Effects of changing Native American cultures on child development," *Journal of Community Psychology,* 15 (1978), 218.

40.   Ibid., 214.

41.   The authors thank Dr. Michael Villanueva for his help with this section on adoption.

42.   Policy-makers appropriate funds based on their need to maintain bureaucratic systems without considering needs assessment data. These decisions have a direct impact on the delivery of mental health services that would address some of the trauma discussed in this chapter; in 1990, for example, a meager 2 percent of the Indian Health Service budget was devoted to mental health.

43.   John G. Neihardt, ed., *Black Elk Speaks* (New York: Simon and Schuster, 1959), 81.

44.   Brave Heart-Jordan, "Return to the sacred path"; Brave Heart, 1998; Brave Heart and DeBruyn, 1998.

45.   Ibid.

46.   Yael Danieli, "The treatment and prevention of long term effects and intergenerational transmission of victimization: A lesson from Holocaust survivors and their children," in *Trauma and Its Wake,* Charles R. Figley, ed. (New York: Brunner/Mazel, 1985); Brave Heart, 1998; Brave Heart and DeBruyn, 1998.

PART 2

THE DEVELOPMENT OF NATIVE AMERICAN STUDIES

Institutional and Intellectual Histories of Native American Studies

Americans were brought face to face with the glaring problems in America during the 1960s and 1970s. The movement for racial civil rights emerged and changed racial relations in our society; the student movement emerged and changed the nature of student relationships to the academic system in our society; the women's movement emerged and changed gender relationships in our society; and the protest against the war in Vietnam emerged and changed the fundamental nature of our society. Native American studies was a creation of this time, and it is important to understand this.

Native American studies was also a new chapter in the long history of the education of Native Americans and a new chapter in the long history of the study of Native Americans. The two histories were important to the eventual implementation of Native American studies within higher education. Here, I present brief overviews of both, culminating in the incorporation of Native American studies into higher education.

The Education of Native Americans

Traditional Native American societies had their own form of education—that is, practices whereby new generations become full members of society—as described a half-century ago by George Pettitt.[1] Formal education of Native Americans began when Europeans sought to convert to Christianity and educate ("civilize," as they defined it) the native peoples of this hemisphere. This began virtually at first arrival: the date and place generally given for the initial attempt to educate Native Americans of what is now the United States are 1568 and Havana, Cuba. The Jesuits then and there established a school to educate the Indians of *La Florida* (which extended far above present-day Florida).[2] Other sixteenth-century efforts included the Spanish Jesuit mission in Virginia, founded around 1570, and missions in the Southwest. Spanish, French, and English efforts to Christianize and educate the native people expanded as European colonization of North America expanded.

In the seventeenth century, there were French schools on the St. Lawrence River and educational communities of "praying Indians" in New England. Plans were made for the East India School ("East Indy Schoole") for Indians at Charles City, Virginia, and schools were actually established in *La Florida,* Virginia, and elsewhere by both Catholics and Protestants. The efforts were very much a part of European (later Euro-American) colonization: "Indians could not be Christians until they first abandoned native habits and accepted 'civilized' customs. . . . 'Civilization and salvation' was the credo of nearly every North American missionary, which often proved to be a euphemism for cultural invasion and tribal decline." [3] Later, in 1769, the first California mission was established at San Diego. What became the California mission system was an extension of an earlier system established in Baja California, it eventually reached north of San Francisco before its demise in the mid-1800s. Missions had such a profound effect upon Native Americans that even today many native groups in southern California are known as "Mission Indians."

Early Colleges

Early seventeenth-century European plans for the education of Native Americans included not only mission schools but colleges. The objectives were basically the same; the colleges sought to train an elite group of natives who would then teach their own people "civilization and salvation."

In 1617, only a few days after the death of Pocahontas in England, King James I, some say at the suggestion of Pocahontas herself, called for building schools and churches to educate "the children of those Barbarians in Virginia." Funds were collected and a university proposed near Henrico, Virginia; a few years later some 10,000 acres were appropriated for the university, including 1,000 acres for an "Indian College." George Thorp was sent to establish the above-mentioned East India School at Charles City and Henrico College, to which the school would channel its students. In 1622, in a battle with the Virginia Indians, led by the Powhatan chief Opechancanough, many colonists, including Thorp, were killed. Two years later, the Virginia charter was revoked and control of the colony transferred to the crown; as a result, the educational efforts failed.[4] Several decades later, in 1660–61, the Virginia Assembly passed legislation to establish a new college but never did so.[5] The early seventeenth-century effort in Virginia was not the only failed attempt at a Native American college. Sometime before the mid-1630s, Dr. John Stoughton proposed a college in New England "for learninge the language and instructing heathen and our owne and breeding up as many of the Indians children as providence shall bring into our hands."[6]

The system of higher education that developed in the United States and Canada was created, in part, to educate Native Americans. In 1637, after ten years of planning, a structure was started at the fort in Quebec to house the Jesuit College of Quebec, consisting of a college for the French and a seminary for the Huron. It existed until 1768.[7] Similarly, the University of Saskatchewan grew out of Emmanuel College, established for Native Americans.

Early colleges of the future United States expressed the goal of educating Native American youth in their charters. Harvard's Charter of 1650 commits the college to "the education of the English and Indian youth of this country in knowledge: and godliness."[8] Whatever the objective, few natives enrolled and considerably fewer graduated. A separate "Indian College" was built in the 1650s in Harvard Yard (then College Yard); by 1675, however, it housed other students and a printing press, because of "the death and failing of Indian scholars."[9] Virginians waited until the founding of the College of William and Mary so that their "Youth may be piously educated in good Letters and Manners, and that the Christian Faith may be propagated amongst the Western Indians, to the Glory of Almighty God," as its 1693 charter states.[10] (The Brafferton Building, built in 1723 to house Native American students at William and Mary, still stands!)

Native Americans did not necessarily see the benefits of such an education. According to Benjamin Franklin, the Iroquois declined a 1744 invitation from the Virginia government to send six young men to William and Mary: "Several of our young people were formerly brought up at the Colleges . . . ; but, when they came back to us, they were bad Runners, ignorant of every means of living in the Woods, unable to bear either Cold or Hunger, knew neither how to build a Cabin, take a Deer, or kill an Enemy, spoke our Language imperfectly, . . . were totally good for nothing. . . . However, . . . if the Gentlemen of Virginia will send us a Dozen of their Sons, we will take great Care of their Education, instruct them in all we know, and make *Men* of them."[11] Nor did Native Americans given a Christian education in early colleges necessarily stay Christian (though they may have stayed "educated"). William Byrd wrote of Native American students educated at William and Mary: "They have been taught to read and write, and have been carefully Instructed in the Principles of the Christian Religion, till they came to be men. Yet after they return'd home, instead of civilizeing and converting the rest, they have immediately Relapt into Infidelity and Barbarism themselves." [12] Byrd also noted that some of the educated natives used their education "by employing it against their Benefactors. Besides, as they unhappily forget all the good they learn, and remember the Ill, they are apt to be more vicious and disorderly than the rest of their Countrymen." [13]

After some 250 years of higher education, Dartmouth is the early college best known for its commitment to the education of Indian youth. Its 1769 charter states that it is "for the education & instruction of Youth of the Indian Tribes in this land in reading, writing, & all parts of Learning which shall appear necessary and expedient for civilizing & christianizing Children of Pagans as well as in all liberal Arts and Sciences; and also of English Youth and any others." [14] Its motto is *Vox clamantis in deserto,* translated as "a voice calling in the wilderness." ("Wilderness" is a European conception of land not being used in their fashion; America was not wilderness before the Europeans arrived.) Its seal depicts a light shining on two Native Americans, one holding a book, as they walk from the woods toward a college building.

The history of Dartmouth College's relations with Native Americans is particularly interesting. In 1755 Eleazar Wheelock founded More's Indian Charity School in Lebanon, Connecticut, naming it after its benefactor, Joshua More of Mansfield, Connecticut.[15] (The name was later changed to Moor.) It enrolled both male and female Native American students. In 1765 Wheelock sent his protégé, the Mohegan minister Samson Occom, accompanied by Nathaniel Whitaker, to England and Scotland to plead for funds for the school and the education of Native Americans.[16] The trip proved highly successful: The pair raised 9,497 pounds in England and 2,529 pounds in Scotland.[17] Much to Occom's dismay, Wheelock took the funds and used them to establish Dartmouth College in 1769. ("As early as 1775 the Continental Congress appropriated $500 for the education of Indians at Dartmouth, and this was increased to $5,000 five years later.")[18] Dartmouth College enrolled only male Native Americans (and other students) for two centuries. Occom's name is much used at Dartmouth and around Hanover, New Hampshire, although he never set foot on the campus or in the town, as far as anyone knows. In the ensuing centuries, few Native Americans attended Dartmouth and considerably fewer graduated. Some notable ones did, including Charles Eastman. (Two hundred years after its founding, Dartmouth reaffirmed its commitment to the education of Native Americans, began to enroll more native students, and created a Native American studies program.)

Government Schools

As Euro-Americans struggled with the idea of the new country they were creating in America, they sought to place Native Americans within it. It became important for enlightened thinkers, like the revolutionary founding fathers, to believe that Native Americans could attain equality with Euro-Americans through proper training. Their success would demonstrate to the world that America was carrying out its announced mission as a "New World" for all. Henry Knox, an early architect of U.S. federal Indian policy, wrote (probably in 1792) to Anthony Wayne, "If our modes of population and War destroy the tribes the disinterested part of mankind and posterity will be apt to class the effects of our Conduct and that of the Spaniards in Mexico and Peru together." [19]

The enlightened thinker Thomas Jefferson advocated intermarriage as well as promoting the adoption of Euro-American lifestyles through training. After telling a gathering of Indians to adopt farming and private property, he predicted, "You will become one people with us; your blood will mix with ours: and will spread with ours over this great island." [20] The price of Jefferson's generous offer would be forfeiture of native societies, cultures, and ways of life. Intermarriage was allowable, as Native Americans were viewed differently from Africans. In Euro-American minds, Native American blood, which is, of course, a metaphor for genetics, did not operate the same way as African and African-American blood. For them, even a drop of African-American blood "contaminated" other blood, making any descendant African or African-American. Native American blood was conceived of as less potent, able to be counteracted by Caucasian blood. Thus, intermarriage with Euro-Americans would "uplift" the entire Native American race. The problem was the Native American insistence on being "Indians" and living un-Euro-American lifestyles. The solution became training and education for all Native Americans.

Often this goal was incorporated into treaties. The first mention of education in a treaty between Native Americans and the U.S. government appears in the 1794 treaty with the Oneida, Tuscarora, and Stockbridge; other references followed in treaties with the Creek Confederacy in 1801, with the Kaskaskia (an Illinois group) in 1803, and with the Delaware in 1804.[21] Soon other groups began to establish their own schools. The Choctaw Academy was established in the vicinity of Georgetown, Kentucky—a considerable distance from Choctaw lands—and "flourished from 1825 to 1842." [22] The Cherokees established a school system after most were forced to migrate to what is now Oklahoma in 1838–39. They did so by an Act of the National Council on December 16, 1841, establishing eleven schools,[23] having two years earlier made all schools in the nation "subject to such supervision and control of the National Council as may be provided." [24] Two years later, in 1843, seven additional schools were called for, making a total of eighteen.[25] In 1848, "manual labor schools" for orphans were established;[26] later the Cherokees would establish schools for "freedmen" (former African-American slaves). The apex of the Cherokee educational system was represented by the Cherokee Male Seminary and the Cherokee Female Seminary, established in 1846.[27] Education in the seminaries mirrored high school educations elsewhere in the United States at that time. Others of the so-called Five Tribes—the Choctaws, the Chickasaws, the Creeks, the Seminoles—established their own schools. (By about this time, the total number of Indian schools run by the U.S. government had increased to thirty-seven.)[28]

At some schools manual arts were taught as well as regular academics and, of course, Christianity; typically, students were required to work in the fields to produce food. Such schools included the Presbyterian Union among the Osage in Indian Territory, the Methodist Episcopal Society school for the Shawnee at Levenworth, Kansas, the Methodist New Hope Academy (women) and Fort Coffee (men) in Indian Territory for Choctaw, and the Presbyterian school for Winnebagos in Minnesota. (By 1881, there were 106 schools run by the U.S. government.)[29]

The first all–Native American college in North America was Bacone College in Muskogee, Oklahoma, founded in 1880 by the Baptist Home Mission Board in Tahlequah and named after its head, Almon C. Bacone, a former teacher at the Cherokee Male Seminary. The following year Bacone appealed to the Muscogee-Creek Nation to locate the school near Muskogee. The motion to do so narrowly passed the House of Warriors, which was the lower house of the Muscogee-Creek Nation's legislative body. The House of Kings, the upper house, then passed the bill and provided 160 acres of land, stipulating that it be open to all Native American students.[30] Bacone "thereby became the one land-grant institution of higher learning established by any Indian nation," as John Williams and Howard Meredith observe.[31] Not until 1885, however, did the move from Tahlequah to Muskogee occur, after the construction of Rockefeller Hall at Bacone; the enrollment was 109 students. Several academies were then established to provide students for Bacone: the Cherokee Academy, the Choctaw Academy, the Seminole Female Academy, the Waco Baptist Academy for the Wichita (at Anadarko), and The Lone Wolf Mission among the Kiowa.[32]

Pembroke State University was established in 1887 at Lumberton, North Carolina, solely for the education of Native Americans. Originally an elementary and secondary school, Pembroke became a two-year, then four-year college, and was the only four-year, state-supported college in the United States exclusively for Native Americans. (It became a university in 1969.) Both Bacone and Pembroke State eventually expanded their mandate to include non–Native Americans. Haskell Indian Nations University (formerly Haskell Institute) in Lawrence, Kansas, was first established as the United States Indian Industrial Training School in 1884; it was a boarding school focused on agricultural education. A decade later it changed its name to Haskell Institute as it expanded its training. In 1970 it became Haskell Indian Junior College; its current name was taken in 1993 after it received accreditation to offer a bachelor's degree in education. It is still only for Native Americans and "provides higher education to federally recognized tribal members." In 1995 it had (the "full-time equivalent" of) 890 students, representing some 147 tribes.

More recently, additional tribal colleges have been established either solely or primarily for Native Americans; typically, they are two-year community colleges. Included in this category are the first tribally controlled Native American college, Navajo Community College in Tsaile, Arizona (1969), Salish Kootenai College in Pablo, Montana (1977), Sisseton Wahpeton Community College at Old Agency Village, South Dakota (1979), Fort Belknap College in Harlem, Montana (1984, but affiliated with Salish Kootenai College until 1987), Fond du Lac Tribal and Community College in Cloquet, Minnesota (1987), and College of the Menominee Nation at Keshena, Wisconsin (1991). Deganiwidah-Quetzalcoatl University was established in Davis, California, in 1971, for the education of indigenous peoples. (Its name should not be spoken; it is known as DQU.)[33] The schools offer associate degrees in academic disciplines and vocational and technical areas; they also have programs in Native American studies, frequently focused on a specific tribe; for example, Lakota or Dakota studies, Anishinaabe studies. (Other, two-year community colleges, not wholly tribally run but located in areas with high Native American populations, offer instruction in Native American studies: Murray State College in Tishomingo, Oklahoma, Yavapai College in Prescott, Arizona, the College of Ganado in Ganado, Arizona, and Northwest Community College in Nome, Alaska, among others.)

When one thinks of the history of the education of Native Americans, one perhaps thinks first of the Native American boarding and day schools provided by the U.S. government primarily for elementary and secondary education and vocational and technical training. The schools began after the U.S. Civil War; a number were on reservations. In 1878, a group of Native American students were sent to the Hampton Normal and Agricultural Institute (now Hampton University) in Virginia, established in 1868 for former slaves. They were Kiowa, Comanche, and Cheyenne former prisoners from the so-called Outbreak of 1874—members of southern plains tribes who had been imprisoned at Fort Marion, Florida, during the winter of 1874–75. (This event is represented in the Dohasan Kiowa Winter Count by a picture of "Big Meat," who was killed by soldiers. Above his head is a drawing of Fort Sill, I.T. [now Oklahoma], where some Kiowa were also imprisoned.)[34] Other Native American students soon followed, and Native Americans continued to attend Hampton until 1923.

Carlisle Indian School, of football and Jim Thorpe fame, was established at Carlisle, Pennsylvania, in 1879 under Richard H. Pratt. This was the first Native American off-reservation boarding school. It restricted students' access to their families, and gave them half a day of education and half a day of work; its outing system placed students with a white family to work for three years. Other boarding schools included the Chilocco Industrial School in Oklahoma (founded in 1884), Albuquerque Indian School (1886), Santa Fe School (1890), Phoenix School (1892), Pipestone Indian Training School in Minnesota (1893), Chamberlain School in South Dakota (1898), and Riverside School in California (1902).

A 1903 report describes 221 government schools on reservations (93 boarding schools and 128 day schools), in addition to schools provided by states and schools in Indian Territory under the auspices of the Five Tribes: Cherokee Nation, 140 day schools, an orphan academy, a "colored" high school, and two seminaries; Creek Nation, 52 day schools, six boarding schools, two "colored" boarding schools, one orphan home, and one "colored" orphan home; Choctaw Nation, 190 day schools and five academies; Chickasaw Nation, 16 day schools, three boarding schools, and one orphan home; and unknown numbers of schools in the Seminole Nation. Also listed are 26 off-reservation boarding schools and five off-reservation day schools.[35]

A quarter-century later it was realized that such schools were not providing the appropriate type of education. The well-known Meriam Report of 1928 noted "that the whole Indian problem is essentially an educational one," [36] and called for the redirection of the education of Native Americans. The 1930s were a turning point in the education of Native Americans, as educational objectives became more sympathetic to Native American cultures. Slowly, schools established for Native Americans began to incorporate aspects of Native American history and culture into their curricula.

Boarding schools declined as students were increasingly channeled to day schools and especially public schools. Many boarding and day schools were closed immediately before, during, and after World War II. For example, "on the Navajo Reservation almost twenty day schools had ceased operation by 1944. At least one of the older boarding schools had been shut down by the end of the war; others were partially or completely abandoned shortly thereafter." [37] (Today almost 100 Native American day and boarding schools remain.)

By mid-century, public school education for Native Americans had become more prevalent, following the developing policy of termination—that is the ending of a federal relationship with a tribe, and the relocation of Native Americans to urban areas, "thus dumping many thousands of additional Indian students into the *public* school system." [38] (There were still, however, well over 200 schools run by the U.S. government.) In 1967, the U.S. Office of Education began the National Study of Indian Education, under the direction of Robert J. Havighurst. The four-year endeavor involved the study of thirty-nine schools in twenty-six different Native American communities between

1968 and 1970.[39] At this time, the education of Native Americans in the United States was, in the words of the U.S. Senate Special Subcommittee on Indian Education, "a national tragedy." [40] The solution was a greater involvement of Native Americans in their own schools. The Indian Education Act of 1972 and the Indian Self-Determination and Educational Assistance Act of 1975 were passed. In the same decade, the American Indian Movement (AIM) established "survival schools," primarily in urban areas (e.g., Heart of the Earth in Minneapolis and The Red Schoolhouse in St. Paul), but also on reservations.

Native American Studies

The civil rights movement emerged fully in the 1960s, accompanied by heightened ethnic consciousness. Not only black became beautiful—any shade became beautiful and any ethnic origin became meaningful. These forces changed the American academic system. Students became important decision-makers in their own education and educational institutions. Formerly all-male colleges became coed; and colleges and universities became more racially and ethnically integrated. As increasing numbers of "minority students" entered higher education, ethnic studies developed organizationally if not intellectually: ethnic studies courses found their way into curricula, and ethnic studies programs, departments, and degrees were created. Once new numbers of African-American students called for African-American studies programs, other groups followed their lead.

The impetus for the development of Native American studies came from new numbers of Native American students on campus. They formed organizations, associations, and the like and lobbied university faculties and administrators for academic programs to accompany the student support programs that were developing, and to gain their place in the ethnic studies spectrum. In 1968, the year Martin Luther King, Jr., was assassinated, N. Scott Momaday published *House Made of Dawn,* for which he won the Pulitzer Prize in 1969.[41] This recognition perhaps provided some support for the idea of Native American studies.[42]

By the mid-1970s seventy-six out of 100 colleges and universities surveyed had courses dealing with Native American concerns.[43] Native American studies was a result of the period; yet it had roots in the history of Native American education, which by this time was focused on Native American input into, if not control over, the process.

The academy adopted numerous ways of incorporating Native American studies, as institutions coped with the new mandate. However, Native American studies' involvement in student support services presented a problem. Indeed, Native American studies was, and frequently still is, plagued with being all things to all (native) people. Academics had to exist side by side with student support programs. Few, if any, efforts envisioned Native American studies standing side by side with a college or university's other intellectual endeavors.

The University of Minnesota, after much discussion, decided to offer a bachelor of arts degree in American Indian studies and accordingly established a Department of American Indian Studies within the College of Liberal Arts in 1969, the first in the country and still one of the few separate departments. (Other organizational arrangements, particularly a program structure, were rejected in favor of a department with a full-time faculty.) [44] The University of California, Berkeley, adopted a different arrangement. Following protests, particularly from African-American students but also from other groups, including a strike and the barricading of campus, the university established its Ethnic Studies Department in 1969, comprising programs in Afro-American studies, Chicano studies, Asian-American studies, and Native American studies. As was the case at Minnesota, faculty appointments were within the department; in fact, the entire department was "outside" the College of Letters and Sciences at Berkeley. [45] (Later, Afro-American Studies "split off," moved to the College of Letters and Sciences, and became a separate department; Ethnic Studies later followed suit.) Other programs in Native American studies within "ethnic studies" were established at Washington State University (as "Comparative American Cultures"), Humboldt State University, University of California, Irvine (as "Comparative Cultures"), and University of California, Riverside.

Another model developed at UCLA. The American Indian Studies Center was established in 1969 "to develop Native American leadership, train Native professionals, seek Native solutions to problems, and to disseminate accurate information about Native Americans," according to a former director. [46] It was one of several ethnic studies centers established, with faculty appointments in traditional academic departments at UCLA. At Dartmouth, a Native American studies program was established in 1972, after a well-publicized statement about returning partially to its original mandate to educate Native Americans. The Dartmouth program was organized around joint appointments with several departments, including history, anthropology, and English. The same year, the Native American Studies Program was established in the Law School at the University of Wisconsin–Madison; it moved to the School of Education in 1976. In 1988, after changing its name to the American Indian Studies Program, it moved to the College of Letters and Sciences. It developed into a premier Native American studies program, reflecting both a high percentage of native faculty members and a cadre of serious, well-respected scholars and teachers: "It seeks to provide and maintain the highest levels of education, scholarship, leadership, and support to all students, staff, faculties at the University." (Some faculty members have appointments in traditional disciplinary departments; some have joint appointments in American Indian studies.)

Native American Studies was established at the San Francisco State University and the University of California, Davis, in 1969. At Davis, it eventually developed into a department with a unique focus on indigenous people of the Western Hemisphere, not just Native Americans north of present-day Mexico. Other Native American studies endeavors occurred at the University of New Mexico, University of Montana, Montana State University, University of South Dakota, University of North Dakota, University of Tulsa (Oklahoma), Oklahoma State University, Dakota Wesleyan University (South Dakota), Bemidji State University (Minnesota), Harvard University, University of Wisconsin, Milwaukee, and Cornell University, where the Native American studies program is located in the College of Agriculture and Life Sciences. Native American studies was also established at Pembroke State University (as a department), Northeastern State University (in Tahlequah, Oklahoma, on the site of the former Cherokee Female Seminary), University of Alaska, Fairbanks (as an Alaskan Native Studies Program, including Inuit [Eskimos] and Aleuts, and now also an Alaskan Native and Rural Development Department), Palomar College (California), University of Washington (as a "center" within the Department of Anthropology), and San Diego State University (where it was apparently not a product of political turmoil, but, according to a former director, "emerged 'like a dusty moth from a cocoon' ").[47] In the 1980s, an American Indian Studies Research Institute was established at Indiana University, an institution with few native students or scholars. The University of Colorado's Center for Studies of Ethnicity and Race in America has established an American Indian Studies Program, with several faculty members. The University of Oklahoma hired Clara Sue Kidwell in 1995 to develop an expanded American Indian studies program which offers a bachelor's degree. In addition, the University of North Carolina has recently hired Michael Green to develop a program of Native American studies.

Hawaiian studies, a program considering indigenous Hawaiians, has developed at the University of Hawai'i. There is a School of Hawaiian, Asian and Pacific Studies as well as an ethnic studies program in the College of Social Sciences at the university's Manoa campus, and a Hawaiian Studies Department at its Hilo campus.

In Canada similar efforts frequently fall under the rubric of native studies. Departments or programs were established at, for instance, the University of Saskatchewan, University of Manitoba, University of Northern British Columbia (as First Nations studies), University of Calgary, and University of Lethbridge. In 1976, the Saskatchewan Indian Federated College (SIFC) was established with the University of Regina, under the jurisdiction of the Indian governments of Saskatchewan. The college, "dedicated to offering quality university education on a foundation of First Nations traditions," has Departments of Indian Studies, Indian Education, Indian Fine Arts, and Indian Languages, Literatures, and Linguistics.

Various undergraduate "degrees" reflecting Native American studies have developed at various colleges and universities, reflecting to some extent varying institutional arrangements. One may obtain a bachelor's degree in American Indian studies at the University of Minnesota, and even concentrate on a Native American language, typically Dakota or Ojibwe. It is also possible to do a "double major" in American Indian studies and another discipline. At the University of Washington, Native American studies students may major in anthropology with an emphasis in American Indian studies. Some Native American studies programs give students "certificates" (e.g., the University of Tulsa), a "minor" (e.g., Iowa State University), or a "topical concentration" (e.g., Colgate University) in Native American studies while requiring them to major in one or another traditional discipline.

Some graduate degrees are also available. There is a master's degree program in American Indian studies at UCLA as well as one in First Nations studies at the University of Northern British Columbia. The University of Arizona has just established a Ph.D. program in American Indian studies. Students must study across at least three of four areas — American Indian Law and Policy, American Indian Languages and Literatures, American Indian Societies and Cultures, and American Indian Education — and ultimately concentrate in one of them. The University of California, Davis, offers a designated emphasis in Native American studies associated with Ph.D. programs in anthropology, comparative literature, education, geography, history, psychology, Spanish, and sociology. The University of California, Berkeley offers a Ph.D. degree in ethnic studies with a concentration on American Indian studies. At the University of Minnesota, a Ph.D. degree in American Studies includes the possibility of focusing on Native American studies, as well as African-American, Chicana/o and Hispanic, and Asian-American studies. (The same is true in Canadian Studies at the University of Calgary, but at the undergraduate level.) Some applied or professional degrees have special Native American components: for example, the Indian Law Institute at the University of New Mexico's School of Law, the Indigenous Law Program of the Faculty of Law at the University of Alberta, and the Native American Forestry Program at Northern Arizona University.

The Study of Native Americans

Europeans quickly developed intellectual interests in the native peoples of this hemisphere. They had to explain where the natives came from; they were also awed by native customs and cultures. European interest in the peoples of North America dates from at least 1502, when Gaspar Corte-Real sent fifty-seven Native Americans back to Portugal. Books and observations about the people of this hemisphere were offered to the peoples of Europe, including the accounts of such early explorers of North America as Álvar Núñez Cabeza de Vaca (1527–37), Hernando De Soto (1539–43), and Francisco Coronado (1540–41).

Observations about the physical appearance of Native Americans often stressed the homogeneity (to European eyes) of their appearance. For example, the Spaniard Antonio de Ullola wrote in 1772, "Visto un Indio de qualquier region, se puede decir que se han visto todos en quanto al color y contextura," meaning, "If you have seen one Indian, you have seen them all." (It was not until 150 years later that the physical homogeneity of Native Americans was extensively questioned by the disciplines.[48] Now we know that the Native American population is physically diverse.)

As intellectual writings developed in Europe and as European colonization expanded into North America, Europeans sought to integrate Native Americans into their study of human history, society, and culture. Thomas Malthus in his 1798 *Essay on the Principle of Population,* discussed Native Americans and demographic events in the former colonies in terms of his theory;[49] he expanded the discussion in later editions.[50] His observations did little to elicit respect for Native Americans. He noted, for example, that "the wretched inhabitants of Tierra del Fuego have been placed by the general consent of voyagers at the bottom of the scale of human beings." [51] Malthus concluded about North America that "the greatest part . . . was found to be inhabited by small independent tribes of savages, subsisting . . . on the products of unassisted nature." [52] Perhaps he had not heard of corn or potatoes. In any event, it was only a couple of decades later that G. W. F. Hegel asserted that Native Americans lacked history and would disappear.[53]

Later in the nineteenth century, Lewis Henry Morgan wrote several works on Native Americans, including *League of the Ho-de-no-sau-nee, or Iroquois* (1851) and *Ancient Society* (1877), taking the idea of social evolution from Herbert Spencer and applying it to social development.[54] European intellectuals like Emile Durkheim, Sigmund Freud, Karl Marx, and Frederick Engels drew upon such Native American institutions as totemism and the family in their formulations and attempts to understand the essence of human social life.[55] Responding to Morgan, both Europeans and Americans saw Native Americans and other indigenous people as representing lower stages of social history; hence, they could study the roots of their own past through studying contemporary native peoples. Morgan even argued that America was "the richest of all continents in ethnological, philological and archaeological materials, illustrative of the great period of barbarism." [56] Morgan thought humans had a single origin and that the course of development of all groups has been similar; therefore, "the history and experience of the American Indian tribes represent, more or less nearly, the history and experience of our remote ancestors when in corresponding conditions." [57]

Europeans and Americans had a longstanding interest in the visible signs of ancient Native Americans, particularly the mounds in the eastern United States and the cliff dwellings and pueblo ruins in the Southwest. Morgan noted their importance but had a more urgent task on his hands: "While fossil remains buried in the earth will keep for the future student, the remains of Indian arts, languages and institutions . . . are perishing daily, and have been perishing for upwards of three centuries. . . . After a few more years, facts that may now be gathered with ease will become impossible of discovery." He urged "Americans to enter this great field and gather its abundant harvest." [58]

Intellectuals turned away from social evolution early in the twentieth century. Nevertheless, Morgan's call to document "diminishing" Native American societies and cultures continued to be heeded. Without Morgan's historical perspective, it was not too long before the focus in anthropology—and sociology—shifted to the way in which elements of societies and cultures were integrated to form a coherent whole.[59]

Anthropology was now separating itself from sociology in the United States, with implications for the study of Native Americans. Few distinctions may be made between anthropologists and sociologists up to the early twentieth century; the two had intellectual traditions in common, and Weber, Durkheim, Marx, and others are important to each. They also shared common methodologies and theoretical perspectives, at least in the "functional period," which lasted through the mid-twentieth century. Both studied Native Americans, although this interest was quickly lost by sociology. Early in this century, Fayette Avery McKenzie, who was involved with the leading Native American intellectuals of his time and a member of the staff of the Meriam Report, called for sociology to give more attention to Native Americans. In a paper published in the *American Journal of Sociology,* McKenzie pleaded, "We have eminent professors who as anthropologists, ethnologists, and historians study the Indian of the past. Should we not have men who can devote themselves to the problem of the Indian as he now is, and to the problems of the means by which he may realize his highest possibilities as a citizen and fellow worker? . . . The nation and the continent call for this great new chair in sociology. Do we not owe this to people we have so largely dispossessed?" [60] (In fact, despite McKenzie's view, some anthropologists had shown an interest in and concern for contemporary Native Americans.)

Anthropology and history eventually rejoined forces, primarily to study Native Americans. The U.S. Indian Claims Commission helped promote the union. Under the Commission, created in 1946, native groups established aboriginal rights to geographic areas within the present-day United States using anthropology—including archaeology and physical anthropology—and history. In the 1950s, there was an attempt to consummate the union of anthropology and history and produce Native American studies. On March 29, 1952, The Newberry Library in Chicago held a Conference on Indian Studies. Ten historians and eight anthropologists were convened to consider a letter written in 1806 by John Norton Teyoninhokarawen, a man described by the Newberry as a "Cherokee half-breed and a chief in the Mohawk tribe since 1800." [61] The letter was to a Mr. Owen, the principal secretary of the British and Foreign Bible Society; in part, the letter considered how temperance was gaining ground at the Grand River Reservation. The question presented to the conference was: "What at first sight seems to be the importance of this document? What in this document can be trusted? What distrusted?" [62] The letter was thus used to stimulate discussion of methodology, specifically differences between the methodologies of anthropology and history: "It had always been the method of anthropologists to rely on nothing so much as on personal observations. . . . Historians, on the other hand, were wont to gather their evidence about the past from documents in preference to most other sources." [63] The two groups did indeed perceive the letter differently: the anthropologists distrusted it because it was not objective; the historians embraced it because of the personal involvement of the writer but also evaluated it without taking the content at face value. The anthropologist Anthony F. C. Wallace summarized the reciprocal benefits of the two disciplines in the study of Native Americans: "While the anthropologist could widen his horizon with the help of techniques of the historian, the historian would find in the results of anthropology material whose immediacy gave it a scientific solidity not always attainable in the historian's own conclusions." [64] The result might be "the three-dimensional history of the American Indians which was badly needed but did not yet exist." [65]

Combining ethnology with history, the idea of an "ethnohistory" focused on Native Americans soon formally developed. The American Indian Ethnohistoric Conference was founded in 1954 at Indiana University and began to publish the journal *Ethnohistory;* Indiana University held a symposium in 1960 to achieve a consensus on the term "ethnohistory"; and the Conference changed its name to American Society for Ethnohistory in 1966, reflecting its broader mandate.[66] Ethnohistory might be simply considered as "the history of the peoples normally studied by anthropologists." [67] Native Americans have been studied by historians as well as anthropologists for a long time; hence, the term seems more favored in anthropology than in history; many historians would say "ethnohistory" is either "just good history" or part of the newly emerged "social history." Historians did, however, respond with an increased use of oral history in formulating their histories of native peoples, as anthropology became more interested in written documents.

During this period Native Americans became more involved in setting national agendas for education and other social issues. The American Indian Chicago Conference, for example, was held in 1961 at the University of Chicago. It drew over 450 delegates from some ninety tribes to consider events since the 1928 Meriam Report. Topics included education, termination, the Bureau of Indian Affairs, health, economic development, and law.[68] A decade later, in 1970, the First Convocation of American Indian Scholars was held at Princeton University; almost all of the 200 participants were Native Americans.[69] The convocation addressed many intellectual issues, setting agendas for colleges and universities. A year later the Second Convocation of American Indian Scholars, held at the Aspen Institute for Humanistic Studies in Colorado, was almost exclusively Native American.[70]

When Native American studies entered the academic system in the late 1960s and early 1970s, however, it was primarily a reaction to the intellectual traditions of studying Native Americans, rather than a positive force in its own right. It particularly opposed the type of research conducted by anthropologists and the virtual "all-inclusiveness" of anthropology as a discipline where Native Americans were studied. One important problem was anthropology's focus on Native Americans at the point of the "ethnographic present," as if frozen in time with little prior history and certainly no significant subsequent history as "real" Native Americans. Native American studies also strongly objected to the anthropological technique of establishing friendships with Native Americans for anthropology's purposes (i.e., research), and to historians' failure to include Native Americans as part of mainstream American history. The backwater subarea of Native American history all too often focused on wars, battles, and Native American warriors but relied little on Native American views or the oral record. Equally important, Native American history was virtually limited to writing about Native American–Euro-American relationships, as if Native Americans had no other histories. And, finally, Native American studies reacted against the neglect of Native American societies and cultures by other disciplines in the social sciences and humanities—sociology, political science, psychology, art, music, literature, religion, or philosophy.

The main emphasis of the new area became Native American history, a topic that seems to be present in every Native American studies program. The importance to Native Americans of defining their own history is well summed up by the English writer George Orwell in *1984*. During the "reeducation" of Winston Smith by his antagonist, Inner Party Member O'Brien, Smith is strapped to a bed; O'Brien is looking down at him.

> "There is a Party slogan dealing with the control of the past," he said. "Repeat it, if you please."
> " 'Who controls the past controls the future; who controls the present controls the past,' " repeated Winston obediently.

" 'Who controls the present controls the past,' " said O'Brien, nodding his head with slow approval. "Is it your opinion, Winston, that the past has real exis tence? . . . Does the past exist concretely, in space? Is there somewhere or other a place, a world of solid objects, where the past is still happening?"

"No."

"Then where does the past exist, if at all?"

"In records. It is written down."

"In records. And———?"

"In the mind. In human memories."

"In memory. Very well, then. We, the Party, control all records, and we control all memories. Then we control the past, do we not?" [71]

Focusing on history was also a means of going beyond the traditional anthropological approach, recognizing that Native Americans were real people with significant pasts and futures. The newly emerged ethnohistory was waiting in the wings, a natural cure for the ills of both anthropology and history when it came to studying Native Americans. In 1975, the historian Wilcomb Washburn would write, citing some important recent works, "The increasingly sophisticated melding of anthropology and history in these books can be deemed the distinguishing characteristic of Indian studies as it is now emerging." [72]

Other areas were important, but had little foundation: they merely sought to present the Native American view, whatever that might be. A new Native American literature was emerging; there was interest in presenting and describing native cultures, religions, art, music, customs, and practices; and contemporary issues were considered. Other subjects included federal Indian law (typically not "Native American law," as traditionally practiced), the education of Native Americans, and Native American languages and linguistics.

The same mix of topics is present thirty years later, although some—for example, Native American economic development—have been added. "Native American" literature is at the forefront of the humanities component of Native American studies; Native American history, in the form of "ethnohistory," remains at the forefront of the social science component. There is even today a new impetus for ethnohistory and Native American studies. The repatriation of Native American human remains, grave goods, sacred objects, and objects of cultural patrimony from museums, colleges and universities, and elsewhere, as mandated by the Native American Graves Protection and Repatriation Act (NAGPRA) of 1990, as well as the National Museum of the American Indian (NMAI) Act of 1989 (which limited its provisions to the Smithsonian Institution), has greatly expanded the importance of ethnohistory, particularly to native peoples but also to museums and educational institutions. Critical to the repatriation process under both NAGPRA and the NMAI Act is establishing cultural affiliation between contemporary groups and historical groups represented by the remains or objects. "Cultural affiliation" is defined by law as "a relationship of shared group identity that can be reasonably traced historically or prehistorically between a present day Indian tribe or Native Hawaiian organization, and an identifiable earlier group." Thus Native American groups may, and often must, present different types of evidence to establish cultural affiliation: archaeological evidence, including physical anthropology, written history, oral traditions, or ethnography. Thus archaeology also tells about the past, a source of history not considered by either Winston Smith or O'Brien. For repatriation, archaeology and physical anthropology are important components of ethnohistory, accompanying anthropology and history. The archaeological record and the written record may eventually be reconciled with Native American memories, in oral traditions or otherwise.[73]

Native American Studies in Colleges and Universities

Thorstein Veblen, the astute early twentieth-century observer and critic of the American higher education system, noted in *The Higher Learning in America* that all societies have esoteric knowledge, which is always more important than the material culture.[74] Such knowledge "makes up the substantial core of the civilization in which it is found, and it is felt to give character and distinction to that civilization" and "to embody a systematization of fundamental and eternal truth." [75] Veblen observes that the care of this knowledge is entrusted to a select group of people, ranging from scientists to shamans. For Veblen, the problem with the academic system in the early twentieth century was that the wrong people—the businessmen—were shaping it.

Has Native American studies been shaped by the wrong people during its thirty-year history? It is undeveloped in many ways, and not enough knowledge from Native America has found its way into higher education as a result of Native American studies.

An Assessment

During that thirty-year period, I have been both a direct participant in and an outside observer of Native American studies. From time to time I have also assessed and evaluated it. In 1978, a decade after its initial incorporation into a university, I thought that it had much to offer but had not developed intellectually, so I suggested some intellectual topics to be explored under the rubric of Native American studies: oral traditions, treaties and treaty rights, tribal governments, and epistemology, among others.[76] A few years later, attending a conference on Native American studies, I found participants pessimistic about its development into a scholarly discipline, as Vine Deloria, Jr., observed.[77] The following year I was asked to give the keynote address at UCLA's Fourth Annual Conference on Contemporary American Indian Issues, and to update views from 1978. The update was easy; little had happened.[78] Ensuing years have seen the survival of Native American studies but not a focus or uniqueness, although most would agree that both are needed and possible. In the late 1980s, Annette Jaimes of the University of Colorado called it "a structurally and conceptually rudderless discipline, generally isolated both within the academic environment and from its own cultural roots, and functioning all too often as a career ladder for those who wish to 'work with Indians,' rather than as an intellectual enterprise for Indians themselves."[79] A decade later, Elizabeth Cook-Lynn, professor emerita of Eastern Washington University, asserted, "Native American Studies in American universities has not been nurtured in appropriate ways nor has it been actualized since its inception in the way that other epistemologies have been, Feminism, for example, or Black Studies which has produced major African-American intellectuals speaking out on all manner of national issues."[80]

There has been important scholarship on Native Americans during the last three decades, however. Much has been by scholars inside and outside the academic system without an affiliation or with only a loose affiliation with Native American studies departments, programs, or centers. Most of the contributors to this volume are in this category; I myself am a professor of anthropology at UCLA, not involved in Native American studies as it is *organized* there. Native American studies appears intellectually more dependent upon this group of scholars than upon those formally involved in its institutional arrangements, although many of the latter have produced solid, innovative scholarship on Native Americans.

An important exception is Native American literature. Much of it is hybrid literature, developed in and around Native American studies. Literary invention has occurred within it; the subfield is alive and well and productive. However, fiction is a form unknown in traditional Native American societies, so in some views it suffers from not being "truly Native American" in this very limited sense. Many traditional, tribal Native Americans find some of these writings insulting. Accompanying this fiction has been a rapid increase in biographies and autobiographies of native people, which is an important development. This literature presents Native Americans as real people and real actors in Native American history.

Aside from literature, Native American studies as a separate intellectual entity in higher education is underdeveloped, it would seem. Perhaps it has been in the wrong hands. This does not mean that acceptable courses are not offered (though little innovation may be shown in the courses), that important community service and applied activities are not performed, that students are not adequately advised, and even that important research and writings have not been accomplished. All these good things have, to one degree or another, been done. Native American studies even has some journals devoted to it: *Ameri-*

can Indian Quarterly, Northeast Indian Studies, American Indian Culture and Research Journal, and *Wicazo Sa Review.* However, the full potential of Native American studies is unrealized in most Native American studies programs, in whatever fashion they are organized.

Some Observations

Why hasn't Native American studies emerged as an important intellectual area? The answer is simple—a single statement about the nature of academe. At the same time, the answer is complex—a thousand individual stories about involvement in Native American studies at a hundred colleges and universities.

Native American studies arose out of politics and pressure and polemics, and it has yet to escape this heritage. It was a football punted back and forth between academic administrators and Native American studies' faculty, staff, and students. Native Americans, especially Native American students, were concerned that Native American studies "be" and "be in the right hands," because it was important symbolically. This too often meant political and polemical correctness. Too many times Native American studies was overly influenced by students and others unfamiliar with the academic system, and this actually kept some Native American scholars away from it. Academic responses, in turn, were political or at best applied as institutions sought easy, simple, and inexpensive paths to create Native American studies. This frequently meant combining teaching and student services, admitting sometimes unqualified Native American students, hiring as faculty one or two Native Americans, occasionally with minimal academic credentials, and adding a few nonnative faculty members—sometimes to be "watchdogs"; the result was then served up as Native American studies. It became the "Indian showboat" on campus. Some institutions created separate Native American studies programs with their own faculty, thereby "protecting" the regular academic departments from having to consider Native American issues or hire Native American teachers. I interviewed a group of Native American students at Berkeley in 1990 as part of a study of diversity on the campus. The students thought that it was good that Berkeley had a Native American studies program, but one asked, "Why isn't American Indian history taught in the History Department?" Few faculty or administrators saw the promise of coming to grips in fundamental ways with Native American peoples, societies, cultures, histories, and problems. Fewer still saw the promise of incorporating this effort into higher education in a way that would make sense to native peoples while being fully understood by academics. No major college or university decided that Native American studies had rich intellectual promise and that it would build a first-rate scholarly endeavor, comparable to others at the institution.

Sometimes special student services for Native Americans were established without creating Native American studies programs or hiring native faculty. Harvard University and Stanford University are examples here. Harvard has had significant numbers of Native Americans at the graduate level recently; Stanford is known for having relatively large numbers of Native Americans at both the graduate and undergraduate levels. Neither institution has many Native American faculty members or Native American courses. Education for Native Americans mostly mirrors the education of nonnatives, and neither group learns very much about Native Americans and America from the Native American perspective. I was involved in the discussions a few years ago when Stanford and Dartmouth were developing an exchange program for native undergraduates. When I met with some of the Dartmouth students, I asked them, "Why do you want to go to Stanford? It doesn't even care enough about you to teach your own history!"

A Department of American Indian Studies was created at the University of Minnesota in response to pressure from Native American students and the Native American "community." The department's mandate included developing courses and training students, serving as a resource base for the Native Americans in the area, and assisting students.[81] Nowhere was scholarship mentioned. In 1979, the dean of the College of Liberal Arts actually told the faculty that he hoped the department would concentrate on community service. The following year, the novelist and critic Gerald Vizenor, by then a member of the department, observed: "There have been four scholarly 'official' evaluations of the department, all of which have recommended more administrative support with an emphasis on research. But the administration has not accepted these recommendations. . . . Instead, various deans have emphasized the importance of community service rather than research." [82]

Unfortunately, Minnesota illustrates another problem of incorporation. Some administrators are determined to "help the poor Indian." An administrator told me, "Don't take this the wrong way, but Native Americans here in Minnesota are a little different from other minority groups, they're considered 'our Indians.' " Such administrators may support Native American studies but want to control it. I am reminded of writings about and by nineteenth-century Indian agents: "These are our Indians. We know what's good for them. And they are going to get it whether they want it or not."

Today, the department struggles with its identity and existence. It seems committed to the language component, the heart and soul of the department. Whether it will develop beyond this remains to be seen; perhaps it will just be important regionally, similar to the program at Cornell. That university has modified its American Studies program to include Native American studies and other ethnic studies at the graduate level; hence, variations as well as modalities in American society are considered. Intellectually, this makes some sense, but Native Americans are the indigenous people of America, distinct from all others in American society—is it appropriate to include them in American studies? Other universities continue to consider this model.

Native American studies must frequently face negative, perverted, and fantasy-dominated views about Native Americans. A person would phone the department at Minnesota regularly and say, "The only good Indian is a dead Indian," then hang up. Dartmouth, however, displays more perversions and fantasies about Native Americans than any other institution of which I am aware. The examples are many; here I offer some particularly note-worthy items.

The so-called Hovey Murals at Dartmouth depict Eleazer Wheelock and a group of drunken Native Americans, including young, bare-breasted, bare-buttocked native women, one of whom is holding a book upside down. The works represent what might be called "bar art." Dartmouth's Native American students eventually succeeded in having the murals covered up, but not permanently removed. They cannot be exposed for teaching purposes; when alumni cocktail parties are held in the room, however, they have been uncovered at some expense so that graduates of the college can surround themselves with these images of Native Americans and sing this song (to the tune of "The Battle Hymn of the Republic"):

> Oh, Eleazar Wheelock was a very pious man,
> He went into the wilderness to teach the Indian.
> With a Gradus ad Parnassum, a Bible and a drum,
> And five hundred gallons of New England rum.

> Fill the bowl up! Fill the bowl up!
> Drink to Eleazar and his primitive Alcazar
> Where he mixed drinks for the heathen,
> In the goodness of his soul.

> The big chief that met him was the sachem of the Wah-hoo-wahs.
> If he was not a big chief there was never one you saw who was.
> He had tobacco by the cord, ten squaws, and more to come,
> But he never yet had tasted of New England rum.

> Chorus: Fill the bowl up!

> Eleazar and the big chief harangued and gesticulated.
> They founded Dartmouth College and the big chief matriculated.
> Eleazar was the faculty and the whole curriculum
> Was five hundred gallons of New England rum.

> Chorus: Fill the bowl up!

Some discussion has occurred about uncovering the murals permanently and including "appropriate explanations" about their history. As of this writing, they remain covered. The murals do not, of course, say anything about

Native Americans, but only about Dartmouth, as the pornographic perversions some men have about women's bodies do not say anything about women, only about the men.

Fantasies about Native Americans abound in Hanover, New Hampshire, as well. One is particularly telling. At the beginning of a two-year stay at Dartmouth, I was invited over to an administrator's house for dinner. While dinner was being prepared, I was escorted into his basement office to see pictures of Native Americans he had taken during a trip to the West. He was particularly proud of a picture of one old Indian man. None of this was, I am sure, intended to offend me. But would one consider this to be appropriate behavior with anyone but Native Americans? Using typical stereotypes, would one invite African Americans to the house for dinner and show them a picture of a black man taken during a trip to Mississippi? Who would show a Chicano a Chicano man's picture from a trip to Texas? Or an Asian American a similar picture from a trip to California? What about showing a Jew a Jewish man's picture from a trip to New York? Or a Catholic a Catholic's from a trip to Boston? What about asking a gay person to look at a picture of a gay man from a trip to San Francisco? What about a white man? Who would invite a white person over to dinner and say to them, "Come down to my basement. I want to show you some pictures of whites I took on a trip to Des Moines!"

Why do people, and institutions such as Dartmouth, fantasize so much about Native Americans? And is it appropriate to convey their fantasies to Native American individuals? How can institutions incorporate Native American studies if they do not accept Native Americans as real, multidimensional people, but regard them only as objects of fantasy and perversion? How can Native Americans incorporate themselves into institutions that do not respect them?

Native American studies can be in the hands of the wrong faculty, to be sure. Some Native American faculty members fail to appreciate or understand the academic system; some may be unqualified for it. Colleges and universities have sometimes scrambled to hire people of native background, but because of the paucity of qualified native faculty, they sometimes hire Native Americans of less-than-stellar quality. Genes have sometimes been more important than scholarship. Conversely, even native faculty members without roots in tribal or Native American communities can fail to appreciate or understand other Native Americans. They may see involvement in Native American studies as legitimizing, if not actually creating, a native identity. Other Native American academics have turned their backs on their people, selling out in return for minor recognition from a nonnative academy rather than attempting to develop Native American studies.

Another, particularly serious problem is the low number of Native American faculty in some programs. For example, I spoke to an advisory board at Dartmouth a few years ago. A member asked what I thought was unique about Native American studies at Dartmouth. I didn't take long to reply: "the low proportion of native faculty!" Recent faculty lists from three large Native American studies programs show the following percentages of Native Americans: University of Arizona, 70 percent; University of Wisconsin–Madison, 46 percent; and UCLA, 24 percent. (American Indian studies at UCLA recently had two faculty positions to fill; both were offered to non-Indian males.) Sometimes involvement in Native American studies is merely a career vehicle for nonnative scholars who would be unable to succeed otherwise at particular levels of the higher education system.

"I say again that Indians should teach Indians," wrote Standing Bear.[83] I agree, but I do not agree that Native American studies should have only Native American faculty. And because of demographics, Native American studies will probably always have a high proportion of non–Native American faculty, higher than the proportions of nonmembers of the group in African-American and other ethnic study programs. Yet an acceptable Native American studies unit where less than half of the faculty is Native American is hard to imagine. Too many positions in Native American studies have gone to non–Native Americans, who typically see themselves as "friends of Native Americans." Some are, in the truest sense of the word; others have the patronizing attitude of "wanting to help the Indians"; still others are simply using Native American studies for their own limited agendas. Unfortunately, there are numerous Native American studies programs with too many friends and not enough Indians.

No matter who is on the faculty, scholarship should be appreciated. "Men instinctively seek knowledge, and value it," wrote Veblen.[84] This is as true of Native Americans as of other people; Native Americans, "traditional" or otherwise, are not anti-intellectual. However, Native American studies programs cannot allow polemics to replace research, chronology to replace history, and application to replace scholarship. How can the academic system respect Native American studies if Native American studies does not embody the highest intellectual standards of the system? It cannot. Conversely, Native American studies programs cannot allow studying sociology or anthropology to replace studying Native American societies or cultures, writing novels with Native American characters to replace writing novels that examine and interpret Native America, and creating histories about Native Americans to replace creating histories of Native Americans. How can Native Americans respect Native American studies if it does not attempt to understand them on their own terms? They will not. They should not.

Notes

1.   George A. Pettitt, *Primitive Education in North America,* University of California Publications in American Archaeology and Ethnology, vol. 43 (Berkeley and Los Angeles: University of California Press, 1946).

2.   Brewton Berry, *The Education of American Indians: A Survey of the Literature* (Washington, D.C.: U.S. Government Printing Office, 1969), 5; see also Hildegard Thompson, "Education among American Indians: Institutional aspects," *Annals of the American Academy of Political and Social Science,* 311 (1957), 95.

3.   James P. Ronda and James Axtell, *Indian Missions: A Critical Bibliography* (Bloomington: Indiana University Press, 1978), 30.

4.   See Samuel Eliot Morison, *The Founding of Harvard College* (Cambridge: Harvard University Press, 1935), 411–14; Frederick Rudolph, *The American College and University* (New York: Knopf, 1962), 7–8; Margaret Connell Szasz, *Indian Education in the American Colonies, 1607–1783* (Albuquerque: University of New Mexico Press, 1988), 59–62.

5.   Rudolph, *College and University,* 8.

6.   Morison, *Founding of Harvard,* 415.

7.   Ibid., 416–17.

8.   Edward C. Elliott and M. M. Chambers, eds., *Charters and Basic Laws of Selected American Universities and Colleges* (New York: Carnegie Foundation for the Advancement of Teaching, 1934), 210.

9.   Samuel Eliot Morison, *Harvard in the Seventeenth Century, Part 1* (Cambridge: Harvard University Press, 1936), 340–45.

10.   Edgar W. Knight, ed., *A Documentary History of Education in the South Before 1860,* vol. 1 (Chapel Hill, N.C.: University of North Carolina Press, 1949), 5.

11.   Albert Henry Smyth, ed., *The Writings of Benjamin Franklin,* vol. 10: *1789–1790* (New York: Macmillan, 1907 [1784]), 98–99.

12.   *William Byrd's Histories of the Dividing Line Betwixt Virginia and North Carolina,* with introduction and notes by William K. Boyd (Raleigh, N.C.: North Carolina Historical Commission, 1929), 118.

13.   Ibid.

14.   Elliott and Chambers, *Charters and Basic Laws,* 179.

15.   Kenneth C. Cramer, "The American Indian and Eleazar Wheelock," *Dartmouth College Library Bulletin,* November 1976, 27.

16.   Ibid., 28.

17.   Burr Richardson, *An Indian Preacher in England* (Hanover, N.H.: University Press of New England, 1939), 20.

18.   Berry, *Education,* 10.

19.   Richard C. Knopf, ed., *Anthony Wayne: A Name in Arms* (Pittsburgh: University of Pittsburgh Press, 1960), 165.

20.   Thomas Jefferson, Address to Captain Hendrick, the Delawares, Mohicans, and Muncies, December 1808, Records of the Office of the Secretary of War, Letters Sent, Indian Affairs, B, pp. 394–97, File Microcopies of Records in the National Archives, no. 15, roll 2.

21. Berry, *Education,* 10.

22. Ibid.

23. "An act relative to public schools," in *The Constitution and Laws of the Cherokee Nation: Passed at Tahlequah, Cherokee Nation, 1839–41* (Oklahoma City: Oklahoma Publishing Co., 1969 [1852]), 59–61.

24. Ibid., 30.

25. "An act further to amend an act relative to public schools," in *Cherokee Nation,* 101–2.

26. "An act establishing manual labor schools for the benefit of the destitute orphans," in *Cherokee Nation,* 182–83.

27. "An act for the establishment of two seminaries or high schools: One for the education of males, and the other of females, and for the erection of buildings for their accommodation," in *Cherokee Nation,* 146–47.

28. Francis Paul Prucha, ed., *Documents of United States Indian Policy* (Lincoln: University of Nebraska Press, 1975), 254.

29. Ibid.

30. John Williams and Howard L. Meredith, *Bacone Indian University: A History* (Oklahoma City: Western Heritage, 1980), 11–12.

31. Ibid., 12.

32. Ibid., 17.

33. Other tribal colleges are Bay Mills Community College (Brimley, Mich.), Blackfeet Community College (Browning, Mont.), Cheyenne River Community College (Eagle Butte, S.D.), College of the Menominee Nation (Keshena, Wisc.), Crownpoint Institute of Technology (Crownpoint, N.M.), Dull Knife Community College (Lame Deer, Mont.), Fort Berthold Community College (New Town, N.D.), Fort Peck Community College (Popular, Mont.), Lac Courtes Oreilles Ojibwa Community College (Hayward, Wisc.), Leech Lake Tribal College (Cass Lake, Minn.), Little Big Horn College (Crow Agency, Mont.), Little Hoope Community College (Fort Totten, N.D.), Nebraska Indian Community College (Winnebago, Nebr.), Northwest Indian College (Bellingham, Wash.), Oglala Lakota College (Kyle, S.D.), Sinte Gleska (Rosebud, S.D.), Southwest Indian Polytechnic Institute (Albuquerque, N.M.), Standing Rock College (Fort Yates, N.D.), Stone Child College (Box Elder, Mont.), Turtle Mountain Community College (Belcourt, N.D.), and United Tribes Technical College (Bismark, N.D.). These colleges, including D-Q U, the federally sponsored Haskell University (Lawrence, Kans.) and Institute of American Indian Arts (Santa Fe, N.M.), Navajo Community College and others listed in the text, and the Canadian Red Crow Community College (Cardston, Alberta) form the American Indian Higher Education Consortium (AIHEC), founded in 1972. The American Indian College Fund, established in 1989 by AIHEC, helps raise funds for the colleges in the United States. In 1996 President Clinton signed an executive order to facilitate federal funding for the U.S. colleges; "29 Tribal Colleges in West Will Get Expanded Access to Federal Assistance," *New York Times* (October 17, 1996).

34. *A Chronicle of the Kiowa Indians (1832–1892)* (Berkeley: R. H. Lowie Museum of Anthropology, University of California, n.d.), 10, 18, footnote O.

35. U.S. Bureau of Indian Affairs, *Statistics of Indian Tribes, Agencies, and Schools, 1903* (Washington, D.C.: U.S. Government Printing Office, 1903).

36.   Lewis Meriam, *The Problem of Indian Administration* (Baltimore: Johns Hopkins Press, 1928), 348.

37.   Margaret Connell Szasz, *Education and the American Indian: The Road to Self-Determination Since 1928* (Albuquerque: University of New Mexico Press, 1979 [1974]), 109.

38.   Jorge Noriega, "American Indian education in the United States: Indoctrination for subordination to colonialism," in *The State of Native America: Genocide, Colonization, and Resistance,* M. Annette Jaimes, ed. (Boston: South End Press, 1992), 386.

39.   See Robert J. Havighurst, "Indian education since 1960," *Annals of the American Academy of Political and Social Science,* 436 (1978), 13–26; see also Estelle Fuchs and Robert J. Havighurst, *To Live on This Earth: American Indian Education* (Garden City, N.Y.: Anchor Press/Doubleday, 1973).

40.   See Prucha, *Documents,* 253–56, for the introduction to the report *Indian Education: A National Tragedy—A National Challenge,* Senate Report no. 501, 91st Congress, 1st session, serial 12836–1).

41.   N. Scott Momaday, *House Made of Dawn* (New York: Harper and Row, 1968).

42.   Undoubtedly important, too, were other, earlier events shaping the place of Native Americans in contemporary American society: for example, the formation of the National Congress of American Indians in 1944, the establishment of the Indian Claims Commission by Congress in 1946, the American Indian Chicago Conference, held at the University of Chicago in 1961, and the above-mentioned Senate Report on Indian education of 1968.

43.   Patricia Locke, *A Survey of College and University Programs for American Indians* (Boulder: Western Interstate Commission for Higher Education, 1974), 169–75.

44.   Frank C. Miller, "Involvement in an urban university," in *The American Indian in Urban Society,* Jack O. Waddell and O. Michael Watson, eds. (Boston: Little, Brown, 1971), 313–40.

45.   Clara Sue Kidwell, "Native American studies: Academic concerns and community service," *American Indian Cultural and Research Journal,* 2 (1978), 4–9.

46.   Roxanne Dunbar Ortiz, ed., *Final Report from the Round Table of Native American Studies Directors in Forming the Native American Studies Association* (Albuquerque, N.M.: Native American Studies Association with the Institute for Native American Development, University of New Mexico, 1980), 8.

47.   Ibid., 12.

48.   Douglas H. Ubelaker and Richard L. Jantz, "Biological history of the aboriginal population of North America," *Rassengeschichte der Menschheit,* Lieferung 11: *Amerika I: Nordamerika, Mexico* (Munchen: R. Oldenbourg, 1986), 12.

49.   Thomas Malthus, *An Essay on the Principle of Population* (New York: Penguin, 1985 [1798]), 81, 104–8.

50.   See, for example, Thomas Malthus, *An Essay on the Principle of Population,* 2 vols., Patricia James, ed. (Cambridge: Cambridge University Press, 1989 [1803, 1806, 1807, 1817, and 1826]).

51.   Ibid., 1:25.

52.   Ibid., 1:30.

53.   G. W. F. Hegel, *The Philosophy of History* (New York: Dover, 1956 [1822]).

54.   Lewis Henry Morgan, *League of the Ho-de-no-sau-nee or Iroquois* (New York:

Burt Franklin, 1966 [1851]); *Ancient Society* (Tucson: University of Arizona Press, 1985 [1877]).

55. See, for example, Emile Durkheim, *The Elementary Forms of Religious Life* (New York: Free Press, 1965 [1922]); Sigmund Freud, *Totem and Taboo* (New York: Norton, 1952 [1913]); Friedrich Engels, *The Origin of the Family, Private Property and the State* (New York: International Publishers, 1970 [1884?]).

56. Morgan, Preface, *Ancient Society,* xxxi.

57. Ibid.

58. Ibid., xxxii.

59. Elisabeth Tooker, Foreword, in Morgan, *Ancient Society,* xxv–xxvii.

60. Fayette Avery McKenzie, "The assimilation of the American Indian," *American Journal of Sociology,* 19 (1914), 775.

61. "The Newberry Library Conference on Indian Studies," *Newberry Library Bulletin,* 3 (1952), 30. The historians were Stanley Pargellis and Ruth L. Butler (both of the Newberry Library), Vernon Carstensen (University of Wisconsin), Randolph C. Downes (University of Toledo), Charles Gibson (State University of Iowa), Ernest S. Osgood (University of Minnesota), Howard H. Peckham (Illinois Historical Bureau), Roy M. Robbins (Butler University), Albert T. Volwiler (Ohio University), and Morris Wardell (University of Oklahoma); the anthropologists were John C. Ewers (Smithsonian Institution), William N. Fenton (National Research Council), Floyd G. Lounsbury (Yale University), Alexander Spoehr (Chicago Natural History Museum), David B. Stout (State University of Iowa), Mr. and Mrs. Charles F. Voegelin (Indiana University), and Anthony F. C. Wallace (University of Pennsylvania).

62. Ibid.

63. Ibid., 31.

64. Ibid., 35.

65. Ibid.

66. James Axtell, "The ethnohistory of early America: A review essay," *William and Mary Quarterly,* 35 (1978), 112–13, 115.

67. William C. Sturtevant, "Anthropology, history, and ethnohistory," *Ethnohistory,* 13 (1966), 6–7.

68. See *The Voice of the American Indian: Declaration of Indian Purpose—American Indian Chicago Conference* (Chicago: University of Chicago, 1961).

69. For a report of the convocation, see *Indian Voices: The First Convocation of American Indian Scholars* (San Francisco: Indian Historian Press, 1970).

70. See *Indian Voices: The Native American Today—The Second Convocation of American Indian Scholars* (San Francisco: Indian Historian Press, 1974).

71. George Orwell, *1984* (New York: Penguin, 1992 [1949]), 204–5.

72. Wilcomb E. Washburn, "American Indian studies: A status report," *American Quarterly,* 27 (1975), 270. Washburn cites Warren Cook, *Flood Tide of Empire: Spain and the Pacific Northwest, 1543–1819* (New Haven: Yale University Press, 1973); Joseph G. Jorgensen, *The Sun Dance Religion: Power for the Powerless* (Chicago: University of Chicago Press, 1972); Richard Slotkin, *Regeneration Through Violence: The Mythology of the American Frontier, 1600–1860* (Middletown: Wesleyan University Press, 1973); Gary Nash, *Red, White, and Black: The Peoples of Early America* (Englewood Cliffs, N.J.: Prentice-Hall, 1974).

73. An excellent example of this is Roger C. Echo-Hawk, "*Kara Katit Pakutu:* Exploring the Origins of Native America in Anthropology and Oral Traditions" (M.A. thesis, University of Colorado, 1994).

74. Thorstein Veblen, *The Higher Learning in America* (New York: Hill and Wang, 1957 [1918]).

75. Ibid., 1. Veblen elaborates that "it is evident to any outsider that it will take its character and its scope and method from the habits of the group, from the institutions with which it is bound in a web of give and take."

76. Russell Thornton, "American Indian studies as an academic discipline," *Journal of Ethnic Studies,* 5 (1977), 1–15.

77. Ortiz, *Final Report,* 5.

78. Russell Thornton, "American Indian studies as an academic discipline: A revisit," in *American Indian Issues in Higher Education* (Los Angeles: American Indian Studies Center, 1981), 3–10.

79. M. Annette Jaimes, "American Indian studies: Toward an indigenous model," *American Indian Culture and Research Journal,* 11 (1987), 4.

80. Elizabeth Cook-Lynn, "Who stole Native American studies?" *Wicazo Sa Review,* 12 (1997), 9–22.

81. See, for example, Miller, "Involvement," 332.

82. Ortiz, ed., *Final Report,* 15.

83. Luther Standing Bear, *Land of the Spotted Eagle* (Lincoln: University of Nebraska Press, 1933), 252.

84. Veblen, *Higher Learning,* 4.

PART 3

NATIVE AMERICAN STUDIES AND THE DISCIPLINES: LITERATURE, LINGUISTICS, ANTHROPOLOGY, AND HISTORY

5 *Robert Allen Warrior*

Literature and Students in the Emergence of Native American Studies

The defining moment for Native American literature occurred in 1969 when Kiowa author N. Scott Momaday won the Pulitzer Prive for his novel *House Made of Dawn*.[1] A stunning cascade of events followed Momaday's breakthrough. Editors in New York publishing houses immediately saw Native American writing in an entirely new light; teachers of English were confronted by a new world of experience most had not previously considered, even if that world was being presented by one of their own. (Momaday earned a Ph.D. in English at Stanford and was teaching in California when *House Made of Dawn* appeared.)

For an emergent group of Native American artists, Momaday's achievement revealed the possibility of recognition and success. Laguna Pueblo writer and critic Paula Gunn Allen in fact credits Momaday's work with literally saving her life; her frustration at her inability to direct her creative impulses and anguish had led her to the brink of suicide. Reading *House Made of Dawn,* she claims, showed her a path away from despair and into her own literary and academic career.

Though the reverberations of his work were soon well beyond his control, Momaday's achievement in 1969 continued to have impact into the next decade and the present. Momaday himself has gone on to fill a role as an important literary figure in American life, and is arguably the most distinguished Native American humanist of the twentieth century.

Here, I discuss how Native American literary studies since Momaday have affected Native American studies. First, I look at the emergence of Native American literature as part of an answer to the larger issue of the emergence of Native American voices in contemporary society. Second, I discuss the complex ways Native American students, Native American writers, and literary critics helped to institutionalize Native American literature in English departments. Third, I turn to the literary texts themselves and discuss written Native American literature as a crucial development in establishing the historical and contemporary condition of Native American people struggling to find terms and possibilities for the future. Finally, I discuss some professional issues that face Native American and non–Native American critics working in this area.

Native American Literature and the Importance of Native Voices

A subject often lost amid discussions of the stunning breadth of the post-Momaday scene is what was happening in Native America educationally, socially, politically, and artistically in 1969. That was, after all, the year in which Vine Deloria, Jr.'s *Custer Died for Your Sins* came out and was a best-seller.[2] On campuses around the country, a discernible youth movement had emerged in American Indian affairs and was nearing a critical mass. In California, for example, the University of California saw a tremendous increase in the number of Native American students on its various campuses in the fall of 1969.[3]

In 1969 a radical Native American presence was clearly a part of any large gathering in American Indian affairs. The erstwhile calm corridors and meeting rooms of the annual convention of the National Congress of American Indians had by then become thoroughly noisy venues, with activists like Lehman Brightman from Berkeley, Russell Means from Cleveland, and Dennis Banks and Clyde Bellecourt from the Twin Cities demanding attention to the needs of Native Americans in cities and to the demands of radicals everywhere.[4]

Near the end of 1969, the percolating rage of Native American youth boiled over into public consciousness. Around eighty Native Americans, mostly students recently recruited by colleges and universities, took over and occupied Alcatraz Island, in the first of dozens of widely noticed, spectacular actions.[5]

A way of pulling this together is to say that in 1969 and afterward Native Americans emerged as contemporary people with contemporary issues, who could do for themselves what some believed they must be dependent on others for, and who demanded that historical wrongs and contemporary injustices be addressed. Sometimes focusing on the events, the demands, the personalities, and the twists and turns of that extraordinary time causes us to lose sight of perhaps the most important development: the emergence of a new voice for

Native Americans and a new recognition of how critical that voice was, is, and will be to the future of Native American peoples, cultures, and communities.

The importance of the idea of Native voices at that juncture is evident in the titles of a number of books from the era. Deloria's second book, for instance, was *We Talk, You Listen,* Gerald Vizenor's anthology of Ojibwe writing was called *The Everlasting Sky: New Voices from the People Named the Chippewa,* and Jack Forbes published a book in 1967 called *Nevada Indians Speak.*[6] Other examples are bountiful in the journalism of the period and in the popular culture. This preoccupation with Native Americans speaking (and, in Deloria's case, others listening) presupposes a previous absence of that voice.

One telling artifact from the period also is framed this way. Produced on the cusp of Momaday's Pulitzer, a 1969 issue of the *South Dakota Review* was devoted to what is now called Native American expressive culture. When it was published later that year as a book, editor John R. Milton called it *The American Indian Speaks.*[7] Milton, in introducing the volume, testifies to the hopefulness of the time: "It seems only fair (and even intelligent) to let the minority groups speak for themselves once in a while. And so I have omitted all the white experts . . . and what we have in this issue . . . is the Indian speaking to us. . . . Since—thank heavens—there are no outside interpreters, the reader may listen directly." [8] Actually finding and listening to that Native American voice have, of course, been more complicated than Milton suggests, but the way he poses the issue shows how crucial it was during that time.

This foregrounding of Native voices speaking is one way of understanding the importance of literature in the development of Native American studies. While Native American representation has been important in other areas of Native studies, Native literature has been, from its origins in the academy, presumed to be a realm in which the Native voice would be the central object of inquiry.[9]

The cover of our first example here—*The American Indian Speaks*—is reminiscent of the first edition of *House Made of Dawn,* a novel Milton no doubt had read, since he acknowledges Momaday's help in his introduction.[10] The original jacket of the novel that launched Native American literature runs counter to subsequent editions, which foreground the novel's Native American subject through stereotyped border patterns and images.[11] The first edition features sans serif black type on a white background with a single figure of someone running as if being pursued (a theme in the novel and much of Momaday's work). The photo on the back features Professor Momaday seated at a desk wearing a dress shirt, a cardigan sweater, and black plastic-frame glasses. A ceramic mug of coffee is nearby; the professor is reading a book. Hanging on the wall, only partially in the frame, is a weaving evoking the Southwest, the only indication on front or back that Indians are the novel's subject.

Milton was working with a smaller budget than Momaday's publisher, and he announces the Native American subject with his book's title, but his cover embodies the same minimalism. The typefaces of *The American Indian Speaks* are plain, the background is neutral, and the figures are contemporary, not replications of traditional tribal symbols. Neither a mythic past nor an exotic present is foregrounded.

The cover is a reflection of the contents of the anthology, which demonstrate that Native American artists were using the same modernist forms to express the contemporary experiences of Native American people as was Momaday. In an essay and interview entitled "A New Ballet," for example, Quapaw/Cherokee composer Louis Ballard writes about bringing together traditional Native American instruments with orchestras in composing symphonic music that expresses Native American realities.[12] He describes his work in much the same way critics have talked about Momaday's bringing together of traditional Native American material and the formal elements of novels.[13]

The core of the book, Milton says, is a set of submissions from the Institute of American Indian Arts (IAIA), then a residential high school in Santa Fe, New Mexico, for Native American students pursuing visual and literary arts.[14] (It has since become an institution of higher education.) He impressively fills out that core with pieces by young Blackfoot poet and novelist James Welch, Ballard (then teaching at IAIA), Acoma poet Simon Ortiz, Dakota scholar Bea Medicine (then in graduate school), future novelist Janet Campbell (later Hale), and well-known Native American visual artists R. C. Gorman, Fred Beaver, Richard W. West, Sr., and Oscar Howe. Already, in this moment before Momaday's Pulitzer changed everything, the literary future was poised to step into its own.

The IAIA played a crucial role, not just in Milton's volume, but in subsequent developments in Native American literature. Creek poet and musician Joy Harjo, now among the handful of major American Indian poets, was a student there in this period, as was Spokane poet and critic Gloria Bird. In contrast to Momaday's experience of developing as a writer in the midst of a non–Native American literary community, Harjo (like others at the IAIA) experienced what she has described as a profound sense of belonging to a Native aesthetic community.[15]

Many other contributors were coming from schools or cities with communities of young Native American people actively working for social change. Contemporary Native American writers, then, did not emerge from a vacuum and did not come forward only after Momaday showed the way. Clearly, Native American literature would have developed without Momaday's signal breakthrough, although much of the fanfare would have been missing.

An event on the other side of the 1969 threshold offers another example of the eagerness in that time to hear Native American voices expressing Native American points of view. The Convocation of American Indian Scholars had its first meeting in March 1970. The proceedings, published by the Native American-run Indian Historian Press (in San Francisco), were entitled *Indian Voices: The First Convocation of American Indian Scholars.* Cahuilla historian Rupert Costo and his wife, Jeannette Henry, operated the Indian Historian Press, published a journal named *The Indian Historian,* and ran the American Indian Historical Society. Costo and Henry, along with Bea Medicine, Alfonso Ortiz, Edward Dozier, Joseph Senungetuk, Fritz Scholder, and Robert Kaniatobe, made up the event's steering committee.

Costo wrote of the event in *Indian Voices:* "The Convocation was conceived, organized, and directed entirely by Native Americans. No Federal or other governmental agency was involved in any part of the preparations, organization, or conduct of the Convocation. No political organization, social agency, or church was involved in any way." [16] After discussing the various panels, keynote addresses, and other sessions that occurred over four days, Costo calls the event "a milestone in the history of the Native Americans, and indeed it was a milestone in the history of this nation. The event proved beyond doubt that leadership exists among the Native American people, for all the purposes of education, administration, economic development, and the general betterment of the American Indian." [17]

Even allowing for some self-aggrandizement in Costo's glowing review of an event for which he was the major organizer, this exceptional gathering deserves a place in the annals of Native American intellectual history. It was held at Princeton University because of Professor Alfonso Ortiz's academic appointment there. Keynote speakers were Ortiz himself, Deloria, still riding the wave of popularity for *Custer Died for Your Sins,* and Momaday, who had so recently broken through onto the national literary scene. Momaday, in fact, delivered one of his most important (and most often misunderstood) essays, "The Man Made of Words," to the convocation. (Most people read it in anthologies, out of context, and do not see that Momaday's audience consisted of 200 Native American scholars and almost no non-Native Americans.) [18]

In reading the proceedings, even in their edited format, we are treated to extraordinary moments. Richard West, Jr., now director of the Smithsonian Institution's National Museum of the American Indian but then a Stanford law student, asks Alfonso Ortiz about differences between Native American and Christian conceptions of nature and human domination. Vine Deloria, D'Arcy McNickle, William Demmert, Herb Blatchford, and Robert Bennett exchange thoughts about the direction of federal Indian policy. The proceedings are filled with a sense of the importance of the occasion: people participating in a new kind of intellectual engagement with each other and for their constituents in Native American communities. Momaday, who eschewed the kind of politics with which the more radical Native American studies programs seemed to be suffused, appears to be completely engaged in this different endeavor.[19]

Deloria, still years away from heavy involvement in the vagaries of academic programs, is similarly engaged. And Costo, a difficult and sometimes dogmatic figure, seems happy that this event had somehow become even larger and more vibrant than his already expansive conception.

Crow Creek Dakota scholar and novelist Elizabeth Cook-Lynn sees a significant confluence of ideas, personalities, and program in the Princeton meeting. She finds there a strong commitment to the idea that Native American studies is, at its base, defined by its function of "doing the intellectual work of the tribes." [20] In some ways this goal is as nebulous as the commitment of the American Indian Movement (AIM), the activist group that was beginning to make itself known nationally at the time of the convocation, to go anywhere, anytime, to defend Native Americans. Yet Cook-Lynn finds in that impulse the only justifiable version of Native American studies available to us.

Cook-Lynn's position is bolstered by history. The next convocation, which Costo had said should happen only when events called for it, was occasioned by a crisis over water rights in Indian Country. Although an interesting meeting, the second gathering did not carry the same weight as the first. It did, however, occur because of a great need that affected the health and welfare of Native Americans living in real time.[21]

The title of Cook-Lynn's essay on the first meeting asks the pointed question, "Who stole Native American studies?" It suggests that somehow the early 1970s agenda of doing the intellectual work of the tribes has been hijacked. She points to multiculturalism, a fascination with questions of identity, and other culprits, then argues that only a return to the kinds of questions scholars were confronting at the time of the first convocation will give Native American studies an appropriate agenda.

I argue that the change in Native American studies has been part of a larger concern over the emergence of Native American voices into contemporary public and academic life. It is important that many of the voices demonstrate that they are not the boisterous, angry ones that have regularly stood as a barrier to the progress of Native American studies. Momaday, Ortiz, Deloria, and others took seriously their role as the first wave of Native Americans to cross the threshold into spaces that had previously been closed to most Native Americans.

I concur, nevertheless, with Cook-Lynn that we in Native American studies must continue to pay attention to the effects of our work in the lives of Native Americans and their communities. I believe also that we must continue to pay attention to the need for more Native American voices in all areas of academic life. In the remainder of this chapter, I look at how literary studies has addressed and is addressing these issues.

Literary Critics and Native Students in the Genealogy
of Native American Studies

In the early 1970s, University of Oklahoma English professor Alan Velie met with a group of Native American students. Like their peers at other schools, these students were frustrated with the paucity and low quality of courses on Native American subjects. They asked Velie if he would offer a course on Native American literature. He replied he would be happy to, but they would have to provide a reading list, since he knew next to nothing about the subject. Velie taught the course and has gone on to make significant contributions to the study of Native American literature, despite his unconventional entry into the field. Without those students, he likely would have not done so.[22]

Scholars like Velie have had to do the hard work of making Native American literature a legitimate field of academic inquiry, a glacial process that could not be conducted by students: attending scholarly meetings, giving papers, organizing panels at workshops, lobbying governing committees, writing proposals for summer seminars, working through the various bureaucracies involved in developing a curriculum, and the myriad other tasks. Often, then as now, Native American students did what they could to press the process forward and discuss how to shape and mold what scholars did.

I doubt that those students who approached Velie (and those involved in similar events at other colleges and universities) were concerned about or even aware of the absence of Native American literary studies from Native American studies as it then existed. They merely wanted to read in their classes material that was not available to them in their history and anthropology courses about Native Americans — works about Native Americans written by Native Americans.

As a teacher of Native American literature fortunate enough to teach many Native American students, I can attest to the fact that most Native American students are not primarily drawn to Native American literature because it is literature. Like most American college students, Native American students are typically not fond of the novels and poems that make up the reading lists of literature courses. Instead, they want both to understand their tribal histories and to develop ways to understand their place in their tribal cultures. History and anthropology, therefore, have had and will continue to have a central role to play in Native American studies.

Simultaneously, a critical component of what American Indian students demand is that universities offer courses not only *about* American Indians but with books *by* American Indians on the syllabuses. Those same Native American students (and I was once one of them) have shown themselves to be willing and able to learn from books by people who are not Native American and to acknowledge the fine work done by many non–Native American scholars. Nevertheless, a legitimate wish to read books by other Native Americans has been a part of the enterprise of Native American studies since the first programs started in the late 1960s (and earlier by some accounts).

Starting perhaps as early as the beginning of the 1970s, teachers of literature—but not of history or anthropology or other disciplines—had the potential to offer courses that featured almost exclusively books by Native American writers. Students just like Velie's but seeking an anthropology course taught through works by Native American anthropologists would have been limited in the 1970s to a few works: Alfonso Ortiz's *Tewa World*,[23] some monographs by Edward Dozier, some articles by Robert Thomas, some books by D'Arcy McNickle (who was not a credentialed scholar), and other works by Native American anthropologists and informants (including Francis LaFlesche, Ella Deloria, J. N. B. Hewitt, and George Bushotter) that remain relatively unknown within anthropology departments even today.[24]

The situation in history was even more dire then (and in many ways remains so). Though he was perhaps the most important American Indian historian of his generation, Rupert Costo (Cahuilla) never held a position of prominence in academe and is far from required reading in history departments now.[25] One of the most interesting examples of history from a tribal perspective (I am showing my own ethnocentric biases here), John Joseph Mathews's *Osages: Children of the Middle Waters,* has been all but ignored by academic historians because it lacks source notes.[26] Jack Forbes's early work, which spanned history and anthropology, is one of the few examples of Native American scholarly work that emerged essentially into the mainstream of academe.[27]

These states of affairs in anthropology and history are addressed elsewhere in this volume; I will not comment more upon what the future might hold. Suffice it to say that what can be done should be done to advance the careers of Native American people working toward credentials, appointments, and promotions in these fields and others along the spectrum. The health of Native America depends in no small part on the ability of Native American people to participate in all professions and occupations.

The desire of a broad range of people, from frosh people to provosts, to hear a Native American voice in person, on the site, rather than through the prism of a government or foundation-sponsored report, has validity. To put things simply, the desire of Native American students to read and learn from writings by Native American writers is legitimate. Further, non–Native American students often express a desire to hear in a more direct way what Native American people actually think about their own experience. Knowing that the vast majority of texts about Native Americans have been written by outsiders, they share in the frustration.

Literary studies has been one area where Native American voices have been heard. Consequently, scholars within literary studies have had to live with the consequences. Today, many major college and university departments of English or ethnic studies programs include scholars who research and teach Native American literature: for example, Dartmouth, Stanford, Cornell, the University of Wisconsin at Madison, Milwaukee, and Green Bay, the University of Michigan, University of Arizona, and the University of California at Los Angeles (three positions), Berkeley (two positions), and Davis. My informal count may be off by a few, but of these positions, the vast majority are held by Native American scholars. That presence of Native scholars has changed the field in literary studies, making it perhaps the first field in Native studies to have such strong Native representation.

Native American students have played an integral role in the development of this new area of academic concern with Native American subjects. Native American students have been a pool of talent from which successful artists (and a few critics) have emerged. Native American students have been on the front lines of those demanding that universities offer courses that feature works by Native American authors. And Native American students have been a consistent, if sometimes frustrating, barometer of whether or not academic representations of Native American life reveal or even approach the realities of the lives they have known. For these reasons, especially the last, critics of all stripes should be grateful.

Literary Criticism and Native Literature

Academic fields have to be legitimized by scholars among other scholars. Students may be representatives on committees and help energize debates over the importance of various topics, but at certain steps along the way, only the votes and signatures of the faculty are important. Native American literature has established itself as an academic field through the hard work done by its champions among literary scholars. In the Modern Language Association, that most tony and publicity-hungry of academic associations, Native American literature enjoys a status more permanent than that of either Asian-American or Chicana/o literatures. Like African-American literature, Native American literature is no longer struggling to convince the association of its merits; it has established its presence among other permanent fields. This did not just happen; rather, it reflects the long, hard work of many dedicated scholars, especially LaVonne Brown Ruoff.[28]

The story of how those scholars established a foothold in academe is impressive. In the early 1970s, the study of Native American literature involved a few novels and poems by contemporary writers and the always looming question of the relationship of those writings to the oral traditions of Native American communities. Not only has the number of contemporary writers grown quickly, but now scholars study writings by Native Americans from three centuries, many languages, and a large set of genres, including autobiography, nonfictional prose, and translations. We can now look at a field in which specialists in nineteenth-century Native American writing, oral traditions, the contemporary novel, Native American autobiography, and early twentieth-century writers could work side by side on quite different sorts of scholarship. Scholars in Native American literature face the exciting prospect of defining how future generations of scholars will think about the central questions of the area.

An obvious but important factor in the relative success of Native American literature is the willingness of English departments to allow that turn of events. Major native authors have held major appointments in major universities. Beyond that, many Native American writers have made careers as members of writing faculties in English departments. This reflects another reality in Native American literature: the ability of English departments with creative writing programs to give regular faculty appointments to people whose credentials are their artistic works rather than the usual doctorate and scholarly publications. Thus, in spite of facing the same difficulty as other departments in finding scholars with the credentials and record of scholarly work to make it through their university's appointment process, English departments have had an alternative route to take.

This does not mean that all is well. Literary studies as a discipline does not automatically embrace every new trend that emerges into its purview. At the curricular level, English departments teach a set of courses that are split, usually, into British and American literatures. Within British literature, departments offer courses in medieval, renaissance, early modern, eighteenth-century, Victorian, and twentieth-century writing; on the American side, pre-colonial, early Republic, nineteenth-century, and twentieth-century make up the menu.

During the past twenty years we have seen an unprecedented pressure to add to these lists. Women's literature and gay and lesbian literature have become important areas in all these subfields, while becoming areas of literary and theoretical concern in and of themselves. On the British side, postcolonial studies and literature from the British Commonwealth compete for attention with the traditional areas. On the American side, the pressure is perhaps even more intense. In America, African-American literature now commands an impressive share of the American literary audience and has had an impressive literary history. Richard Wright, Ralph Ellison, Zora Neale Hurston, James Baldwin, Alice Walker, and Toni Morrison represent the highest level of literary achievement. Add to this list narratives written by former slaves, the poetry of Phyllis Wheatley, and the works of figures such as Frederick Douglass and Booker T. Washington, and there is an amazingly rich and recognizable literary tradition.[29] Chicana/o or Latina/o studies and Asian-American studies are also now included in that mix, though these groups have a shorter history within the United States and thus a shorter history of written, published work.[30]

The study of Native American literatures has had to fit into these structural constraints. Since the 1970s the growing body of work has lived in symbiosis with literary scholars' readiness to write about the emerging literature and, most importantly, assign it to students. Without that embrace, many Native American authors would not have secured their place on the literary scene.

Many if not most scholars who think about Native American literature at all assume that criticism of Native American literature will follow the pattern of African-American literature. In fact, what is emerging is something of a hybrid between American ethnic-style criticism and postcolonial criticism, the latter being concerned with issues of nonintegrative nationalism, for which native nations continue to strive. In other words, what is often labeled "separatist" for other non-European groups in the Americas is, in fact, government policy for native groups. That reality has made its way into at least some criticism of Native American literatures.[31]

Further, contemporary literary theory and cultural studies make deeper and deeper inroads into Native American literary studies with each successive cohort of graduate students. While many early critics of the literature assumed (to ill effect) that the keys to unlock the levels of meaning of contemporary Native American writing would come from folklorists and anthropologists, scholars within the unsettled parameters of the field today make fewer assumptions and are usually willing to consider a larger number of options.[32] Whether those parameters will become more stable anytime soon remains to be seen. What does seem clear, though, is that Native American literary studies will remain a working field for at least the next several generations of scholarship.

Native American Literature and Self-Representation

However we understand the development of Native American literary studies, the unarguable linchpin of its success over the past three decades has been Native American writers and artists and their steady flow of work. Native American traditions have been of interest to both American writers (as material for their writing) and critics (as a minor subject of literary inquiry), but only with the recent success of Native American novelists and poets has the secondary function of criticism of their works become a possibility.

Plenty of that literary output has been deeply flawed, found to have been produced by authors of fraudulent or at least suspicious identity, and disdained by those who hold the keys to the kingdom of literary taste. Still, a significant amount of that output, most notably the writings of N. Scott Momaday, Leslie Marmon Silko, Louise Erdrich, and Joy Harjo, has been recognized as belonging to the upper echelon of contemporary world literature. Indeed, other than the film actors Russell Means, Graham Green, and Wes Studi, Native American writers are perhaps the most famous Indians in our celebrity-centric contemporary world. All of the writers mentioned above except Erdrich have held or currently hold distinguished positions in English departments in American universities, and Erdrich's base of operations for many years was Dartmouth College, where her late collaborator and spouse Michael Dorris held an appointment. Momaday and the others were among the first Native Americans to hold such eminent positions in American universities.

Native American writers have clearly been for at least a century and a half important representatives of Native American realities to nonnative society. Books like Helen Hunt Jackson's *A Century of Dishonor*[33] and hybrid works like John Neihardt's *Black Elk Speaks*[34] will continue to play important roles in helping us understand the complex ways in which the experiences of Native Americans came before a national public. However, the published output of writers like Samson Occom in the eighteenth century, the Cherokee intellectuals of the first part of the nineteenth century, various Native American missionary writers of the nineteenth century, Native American women who wrote in the nineteenth and twentieth centuries, and many others provide increasing proof of the presence and importance of Native American writing in Native American history. What that tradition offers Native American studies is a set of representations from Native American points of view of the crucible of modern Native American existence. Those realities are not anthropological ones, except perhaps for ethnographic novels such as Ella Deloria's *Waterlily*.[35] Those realities are not historical ones, except for the specific genre of historical fiction as practiced in James Welch's *Fools Crow*[36] or John Joseph Mathews's *Wah'Kon-Tah: The Osage and the White Man's Road*.[37]

Most Native American novels involve both cultural and historical material, but what few scholars inside or outside the field emphasize is that novelists are mostly concerned with their own kind of truth, not the truth anthropologists, historians, or even literary critics tell. Perhaps the view is a romantic one. Nevertheless, I assert that what the novelist or poet offers is not a fulfillment of its readers' expectations but a truth that the particular novelist or poet sees and represents.

As far as this is true, identifying a work's audience is, at best, of secondary importance. If some Native American people have bookshelves on which books on Native American history by nonnative authors predominate, this means to me that they are not interested in novels, but in history. Native American authors appropriately feel as much commitment to their vision of writing the truth as they do to their sense of what a Native American audience wants to read. The Native American novelist, poet, or critic engages the contemporary situation of Native American people as Native American lawyers, doctors, and other professionals do—in the role of a Native American who has learned to occupy a position within a remade Native America, one in which Native Americans in Native American communities will, perhaps, have a future. Like their counterparts in the law or in medicine, they do not necessarily believe in the superiority of their new role. Nor do they believe that their role will necessarily supplant similar roles within the tribal cultures to which they are connected. In other words, they are neither the harbingers of the end of oral Native American literature nor the supplanters of the traditional storytellers in traditional communities.

Because representing the lives of members of Native American communities in words so closely impinges on some features of traditional, oral literatures, and because so many Native American writers have turned to those traditions for source material, many readers and critics have assumed that they seek a spot within their communities similar to the position of those who have traditionally passed such stories along to the next generation. Whatever the authors' intentions are, I have yet to meet a Native American novelist or poet who has successfully combined the two functions. Some, perhaps, have managed to work at both levels as novelists and storytellers, but that is different from combining them. And those who achieve spectacular financial success from writing novels do what most such people in America do: they move to the most comfortable and most expensive place they can afford (in the mountains or the desert, usually).

Thus Native Americans have filled the roles they have been asked to fill. New commitments to Native American novelists and poets have resulted in roundly praised work by genuinely talented people. Few are suggesting that Native American literature has supplanted Shakespeare. Nevertheless, anyone who suggests that Native American people have not mastered the challenge, have not occupied the same positions as other contemporary novelists and poets, is simply wrong.

Another assumption that plagues contemporary criticism of Native American literature is the notion that somehow these various writers share a view of their vocation as writers. Instead, they seem to have no single view of anything as a group, although nearly every novelist or poet, regardless of origin, starts out as a devoted if not fanatical reader of novels or poems. Native American novelists and poets run the gamut from frighteningly assimilationist to staunchly traditional and tribal. Their diversity, in fact, is one of the things that makes their works such rich material for critics.

Novels and poems are particular kinds of responses to our times. They are responses that have emerged from the anxieties of the modern condition—loneliness, the overwhelming pace of change, and the seemingly endless descent into meaninglessness. Is it any surprise that Native American people have found a voice in these genres that respond, and often respond profoundly, to those anxieties and realities, given the dizzying impact of modernity? The continually growing body of creative writing, contemporary visual arts, and (to a much lesser extent) criticism by Native Americans is adequate evidence of the rich and profound response these conditions have provoked.

People who do not read contemporary Native American literature commonly wonder how any novel or poem can be Native American, given that the writing of novels and modern poems is not a traditional practice in any Native American cultural group. This quandary, still puzzling to some, especially newcomers, once preoccupied scholars and students in the field. Those looking for highly detailed descriptions of the traditions and life ways of tribal cultures can easily come away from reading contemporary Native American literature greatly disappointed.

The problem, though, lies with the readers—critic Elaine Jahner has called it a "tyranny of expectations." [38] I sometimes ask undergraduates to imagine taking a trip to the American South and using as your travel guide a novel by William Faulkner. You would enter Oxford, Mississippi, expecting to find a set of eccentric, dysfunctional citizens speaking in incredibly long, nearly incomprehensible, sentences. However, you would not find them. Unfortunately, too many readers expect just that kind of travelogue experience from Native American literature.

As a genre of literature, novels are a feature of modernity. Native Americans are people struggling, along with most people, to come up with ways of dealing with the realities of modernity. Those who express surprise at or disdain for contemporary Native American literature and other arts are, frankly, denying to Native American people one thing they need desperately—visible inclusion in the contemporary world. In many ways, such a stance is the equivalent of denying Native American people opportunities to become accountants, engineers, or other kinds of professionals.

Ironically, Native American literature has been one significant way of making those experiences available to the contemporary world. Because the literature is a response to the conditions of modernity, much is represented in it that fails to make it into other kinds of written work. Perhaps the best example is the urban existence now lived by more than half of Native American people. The story of why and how so many Native Americans relocated to cities is as poignant as the story of how people who only (fill in the blank) years ago existed in tribal consciousness now must confront new realities or cease to exist.

No Native American person I have ever met needs to be told that his or her contemporary existence is radically different from that of many generations ago, or that his or her tribal group was rocked by the demands and destructiveness of modern realities. In spite of this, Native Americans are virtually bombarded with reminders, and the contemporary culture sends an overwhelming message that all Indians are dead Indians; or, if their descendants are still around, they can at best only simulate ways of life that are not viable in the world of today. What most people — including many Native Americans — want to hear is how things used to be, not how things are now, or how they might be in an imagined future.

To live in a world in which the *now* has next to no status is quite thorny. Native American literary artists often give voice to that thorniness and remind their readers of just how bewildering the world is. And that is as true for William Apess in the 1830s and E. Pauline Johnson at the turn of the past century as it is for Leslie Marmon Silko in our own time. The ethnographer has most often sought to understand the way things were before the disastrous interaction of Native Americans and Europeans; the historian has usually tried to piece together some believable account of events in difficult times. Both offer increasingly valuable knowledge to which Native Americans have access.

Testimony about the responses of contemporary Native American people to the conditions that they face now will be at least as important to those who will come after. If nothing else, people of the future will need to know that people of today were at least thinking of these things, even if they could not solve them. Contemporary Native American literature, perhaps only in some small way, is helping to ensure just that.

Conclusion: Challenge and Responsibility

Native American literary studies have grown synergistically with Native American studies in American universities over the thirty years since N. Scott Momaday won his Pulitzer. They both have a generative moment in the complex mix of societal shifts, movement activism, campus politics, and organic growth that is the lasting legacy of the 1960s and 1970s. As a new century approaches and that heady period becomes more and more distant, native literary studies is really only now coming into its own as a field of academic endeavor.

As critics charting the continued emergence of a literature, those of us who do native literary studies have taken on a challenge and a responsibility. The challenge is to continue to develop ways of understanding how native voices have found expression in literature even as the scope of that literature expands. Far from the small set of novels and poems available in the early 1970s, we now have available to us the early and late works of native authors whose careers span decades. We have access to the dozens of writers who engaged in literary production before Momaday. And we have the always growing list of new native authors who make their way into the public eye through their literary work.

Our responsibility is to reflect in our work the same fullness of life that native literary artists have represented in their art. That fullness includes aspects of contemporary life that have all too often been ignored in Native

American studies. Issues of gender and sexuality, which continue to exist on the margins of other fields, have become more and more a part of native literary studies. Native literary artists have portrayed the roughest edges and the most transcendent beauties of Native American life. Indeed, perhaps it is that aspect of literature which allows rough edges and beauty to be coeval that makes native literary expression such a compelling phenomenon.

As with other fields in contemporary literary studies, Native American literature faces an uncertain future. The challenge of what has come to be called cultural studies has been felt no more acutely than in literature departments. And alongside the questions confronting the broader discipline of literary studies, native literature continues to face its own set of thorny issues. What is the relationship between oral and written literatures? How do other aspects of expressive culture, such as the visual and ceremonial arts, challenge us to alter the critical categories of literary studies? To what extent can we make distinctions between various sorts of literature, such as the most serious works (Momaday and Harjo, for instance) and those more obviously of a popular or amateur sensibility?

These questions and many others confront those who work in Native American literature. As with so much of the scholarly enterprise, the challenge is as much in the asking as it is in the answering. The creativity and determination of Native American artists have given scholars that most rare opportunity of being present at a critical stage in the establishment of a field. What remains to be seen is how literary scholars will continue to respond to that wonderful opportunity.

Notes

1. See N. Scott Momaday, *House Made of Dawn* (New York: Harper and Row, 1968).

2. Vine Deloria, Jr., *Custer Died for Your Sins: An Indian Manifesto* (New York: Macmillan, 1969).

3. Smith and Warrior, *Like a Hurricane,* 3.

4. Ibid., 132.

5. Ibid., passim.

6. Vine Deloria, Jr., *We Talk, You Listen: New Tribes, New Turf* (New York: Macmillan, 1970); Gerald Vizenor, *The Everlasting Sky: New Voices from the People Named the Chippewa* (New York: Crowell-Collier Press, 1972); Jack Forbes, *Nevada Indians Speak* (Reno: University of Nevada Press, 1967).

7. John R. Milton, ed., *The American Indian Speaks* (Vermilion, S.D.: Dakota Press, 1969). The contents of the book are identical to issue number 2 of the *South Dakota Review,* 7 (1969).

8. John R. Milton, "Indians speak for themselves," in Milton, *The American Indian Speaks,* 3.

9. See A. LaVonne Brown Ruoff, *American Indian Literatures: An Introduction,*

Bibliographic Review, and Selected Bibliography (New York: Modern Language Association, 1990), 148–49. Ruoff's text remains the best introduction to the literature, and her thoroughness means that I need not rehash every twist and turn of the development of Native American literature. Although her work is showing signs of age, it remains a better basic source than, for instance, Andrew Wiget's recent *Handbook of Native American Literature* (New York: Garland, 1996), and more attuned to what is happening in the field.

10. Milton, interestingly, did a second volume of Native American writing two years later. In contrast, the second iteration features a much less contemporary image on the cover—a realistic line drawing of a Native American woman in traditional dress with her head slightly bowed. See John R. Milton, ed., *American Indian II* (Vermilion, S.D.: Dakota Press, 1971), which is identical to issue number 2 of *South Dakota Review,* 9 (1971).

11. The cover of an early, post-Pulitzer paperback edition of *House Made of Dawn* has drawn figures and scenes from the novel in a sort of Hollywood montage centering on Abel, the protagonist, who wears a broad windband around his head and an expression of deep alienation on his face. One of the figures is presumably Angela St. John, the non-Indian woman with whom Abel has sex; she stands seductively with pursed lips while taking off her dress. A quote from the *New York Times* above the montage reads, "The magnificent, heartbreaking novel of a proud stranger in his native land— the American Indian." 'Superb.' " See *House Made of Dawn* (seventh printing, New York: Signet, 1969). A German edition features four figures on horseback wrapped in wool blankets against bitterly cold wind and snow. In the background is the Empire State Building and the skyline of New York City, with orange hues of dawn in a hazy sky. Neither shivering Indians on horseback nor New York City appears in the text of the novel. See N. Scott Momaday, *Haus aus Morgen Dammerung,* trans. Jochen Eggert (Munich: Eugen Diederichs, 1988 [1969]).

12. Louis Ballard, "A new ballet," in Milton, *The American Indian Speaks,* 22–26.

13. See, for instance, Matthias Schubnell, *N. Scott Momaday: The Cultural and Literary Background* (Norman: University of Oklahoma Press, 1985).

14. Milton, "Indians speak," 4.

15. Joy Harjo and Robert Allen Warrior, "Tribal Aesthetics in Native Literature: A Conversation," presented at the Stanford Humanities Center, Stanford University, Stanford, California, January 18, 1996.

16. *Indian Voices: The First Convocation of American Indian Scholars* (San Francisco: Indian Historian Press, 1970), vii.

17. Ibid.

18. Other presenters included Bea Medicine on "Red Power," Fritz Scholder on Native American arts, Roger Buffalohead on Native American studies programs, and former Bureau of Indian Affairs Commissioner Robert Bennett on economic development. Other participants included Samuel Billison, Herb Blatchford, George Crossland, Philip Sam Deloria, William Demmert, Jr., Adolph Dial, John E. Echohawk, Gloria Emerson, Charles Loloma, Chris McNeil, D'Arcy McNickle, Simon Ortiz, Ann Rainer, Jack Ridley, Buffy Sainte-Marie, Joe Sando, James West, and Richard West, Jr. Thirty-one artists, including Blackbear Bosin, Allan Houser, Yeffe Kimball, and Al Momaday, appeared in an exhibition concurrent with the convocation.

19.   See Peter Nabokov, "The Indian Oral Tradition" (interview with N. Scott Momaday), Pacifica Radio Archives, North Hollywood, California, 1969; N. Scott Momaday, "The man made of words," in *Indian Voices,* 49–84.

20.   Elizabeth Cook-Lynn, "Who stole Native American studies?" *Wicazo Sa Review,* 12 (1997), 9–22.

21.   See *Indian Voices: The Native American Today: The Second Convocation of Indian Scholars* (San Francisco: Indian Historian Press, 1974).

22.   Velie relates this story in the introduction to his *Four American Indian Literary Masters: N. Scott Momaday, James Welch, Leslie Marmon Silko and Gerald Vizenor* (Norman: University of Oklahoma Press, 1982).

23.   Alfonso Ortiz, *The Tewa World: Space, Time, Being, and Becoming in a Pueblo Society* (Chicago: University of Chicago Press, 1969).

24.   For discussions of these figures, see Warrior, *Tribal Secrets.*

25.   Costo and Jeannette Henry created the American Indian Historical Society in the 1960s. The society put out the *Indian Historian* and later a national newspaper, named *Wassaja* after an earlier newspaper put out by the Apache physician and activist Carlos Montezuma. Under the imprint of the Indian Historian Press, the society published a number of books in the 1960s and 1970s. Costo's library and papers are available at a center named for him at the University of California, Riverside. UC Riverside and the Indian Historian Press published Costo's *Natives of the Golden State* posthumously, in 1995.

26.   John Joseph Mathews, *The Osages: Children of the Middle Waters* (Norman: University of Oklahoma Press, 1961).

27.   Examples of Forbes's early work are: *Apache, Navaho, and Spaniard* (Norman: University of Oklahoma Press, 1960); *The Indian in America's Past* (Englewood Cliffs, N.J.: Prentice Hall, 1964); and *Warriors of the Colorado: The Yumas of the Quechan Nation and Their Neighbors* (Norman: University of Oklahoma Press, 1965). Forbes has been perhaps the most prolific Native American scholar of the century. His wide-ranging works have included journalistic columns, poems, short stories, monographs, and historical studies.

28.   As far as I know, no account of the twists and turns of this process exists. Hopefully, Professor Ruoff or someone with intimate knowledge of what happened and when will produce such an account.

29.   For an account of the rise and contemporary status of literary studies in African-American studies, see, among many others, Henry Louis Gates, Jr., *The Signifying Monkey: An Afro-American Theory of Literary Criticism* (New York: Oxford University Press, 1988).

30.   Perhaps the most significant breakthrough critical text in Chicana/o literary studies has been Gloria Anzaldúa, *Borderlands (La Frontera): The New Mestiza* (San Francisco: Spinsters/Aunt Lute, 1987). Jose David Saldivar, *The Dialectics of Our America: Genealogy, Cultural Critique, and Literary History* (Durham: Duke University Press, 1991), and Ramon Saldivar, *Chicano Narrative: The Dialectics of Difference* (Madison: University of Wisconsin Press, 1990), have also been influential works in the field.

31.   Gerald Vizenor, ed., *Narrative Chance: Postmodern Discourse on Native American Literatures* (Albuquerque: University of New Mexico Press, 1989), is one collection

that demonstrates the different contours of Native American literature. My book *Tribal Secrets: Recovering American Indian Intellectual Traditions* is an extended engagement with these issues of culture, separatism, and sovereignty.

32.   See, for instance, Charles Larson, *American Indian Fiction* (Albuquerque: University of New Mexico Press, 1978).

33.   Helen Hunt Jackson, *A Century of Dishonor: A Sketch of the United States Government's Dealings with Some of the Indian Tribes* (Norman: University of Oklahoma Press, 1995 [1881]).

34.   John G. Neihardt, *Black Elk Speaks: Being the Life Story of a Holy Man of the Ogalala Sioux* (Lincoln: University of Nebraska Press, 1979 [1932]).

35.   Ella Deloria, *Waterlily* (Lincoln: University of Nebraska Press, 1988).

36.   James Welch, *Fools Crow* (New York: Penguin, 1987 [1986]).

37.   John Joseph Mathews, *Wah'Kon-Tah: The Osage and the White Man's Road* (Norman: University of Oklahoma Press, 1932).

38.   See Elaine Jahner, "American Indian writers and the tyranny of expectations," *Booklist,* 5 (1981), 343–48.

"Writing Indian"
American Indian Literature and the
Future of Native American Studies

Imperialist nostalgia occurs alongside a peculiar sense of mission, "the white man's burden," where civilized nations stand duty-bound to uplift so-called savage ones. In this ideologically constructed world of ongoing progressive change, putatively static savage societies become a stable reference point for defining (the felicitous progress of) civilized identity.

Renato Rosaldo, *Culture and Truth*

When the white men come onto Indian land
and try to lead by forlorn example,
I want to laugh and cry at the same time.
If only they understood:
the savages don't want to be tamed!
    Adrian Louis, *Among the Dog Eaters*

Anyone who knows anything about what it means to be Indian in the United States in the late twentieth century knows what an Indian car looks like.[1] Rez Indians and urban Indians alike know. Anglos who live on reservations eventually come to know. Anglo academics who make forays into Indian Country in search of data and encounters with Indians-in-the-know know, if they stick around long enough. But people are not as quick to recognize an Indian dog. There's something about how you can really talk to an Indian dog, talk Indian —even if you only speak English. One of the most famous of such conversations ever recorded in Native American literature occurs in James Welch's *Death of Jim Loney,* when Jim Loney says to his deaf dog, Swipesy, "You don't even hear me, but I think you understand everything about life. . . . You live clean and you never abuse yourself. You're an example to me, Swipesy. I just wish I was as smart as you." [2] The late Ron LaFrance, Mohawk educator and former director of the American Indian Program at Cornell, claimed he sometimes felt like a junkyard dog, but we knew what he really meant was "Indian dog." [3] He was merely trying to translate Indian talk into something non-Indians would understand, a roughly equivalent term. In fact, what non-Indians might regard as a yardful of junk, Indians might think of as storage space and reusable parts. Where I'm from (Poplar, Montana), the dogs howl in chorus every night at 10 P.M. when the old siren blows, the siren that used to mean "no Indians allowed on the street after ten." Those Poplar dogs can't help singing—they must remember their Coyote roots. Whatever . . . the sound translates.

But cross-cultural translation is such a tricky business. The many nuances of Indian philosophy regarding Indian dogs—perhaps we could call it Indian dogology—can be easily missed. Among the people of my own and my cousin tribes (Nakota, Dakota, and Lakota), for example, anthropologists have identified in us something they term an "ambivalence" toward The Dog. As Adrian Louis, the displaced Paiute poet who teaches at Oglala Lakota College, can tell you, being among the Dog Eaters is an experience unlike any other,[4] but ambivalence of any sort is *not* something we'd quickly own up to. So what makes a dog an *Indian* dog? Is it important to figure it out? Or, perhaps, a prior question: is it true that such a creature as an Indian dog exists? Ontologically concerned minds want to know.

By now, you have no doubt figured out that I'm joking (sort of). To sustain a philosophical discussion in this vein and tone would tax me beyond my capacity for satire, irony, and the like. I do believe, nonetheless, that Indian dogs exist and that only certain people (some being Indian themselves and others not) are able to recognize an Indian dog when they see one, and that whatever it is that separates Indian-dog-recognizers from nonrecognizers is important to our understanding of Native American studies and the place of literature within it. But the something that sets the two apart gets lost or confused in debates and discussions on American Indian identity per se. It might be a matter of "seeing" things a certain way, though I suspect the experience is a full sensory one. It probably has to do with the difficulty of putting some things into words, particularly academic words. One thing is sure: recognizing Indian dogness is a skill best cultivated by first learning "to hold the question in your mind"—that is, not to leap to quick, easy answers, then run with them like hot coins in your pocket to the nearest bank.[5]

Talking Indian, Writing Indian

A definition of "writing Indian," like "talking Indian," is elusive.[6] Yet "writing about Indians" is not the same as "writing Indian"—most of us know that. Since the 1960s, the American studies disciplines within the academy have been trying to grasp what that difference means, how form should in some sense match content.[7] The American cultural revolution of the Vietnam/civil rights era issued a new call to "get real, get down," a populist spur to move

American institutions, including academia, in the direction of intellectual honesty and social justice. Discussions of ethnopoetics, on the one hand, and discourse analysis, on the other, were (and still are) academic movements that have attempted to elucidate the issues involved in rendering cross-cultural thought and experience into writing, while being careful to maintain an ethical responsibility to the people and individuals being represented. (At least that is the ideal.) Ethnopoetics, helped along by anthropologists/poets such as Dell Hymes, Dennis Tedlock, Jerome Rothenberg, and others, moved the study of American Indian poetic forms out of the category of the "primitive" and granted those linguistic expressions a fuller respect for their complexity. Discourse analysis, helped along by European thinkers like Michel Foucault and Mikhail Bakhtin, enabled a recognition of the power relations inherent in all discourse as well as a questioning of the position, even "existence," of the "author" in creating meaning. Positionality has since then gradually become a part of the struggle by scholars to own the perspectives from which their work has been generated, their world views, personal and cultural. Some Native Americans were part of the academic movements mentioned above (e.g., Simon Ortiz, Jr., participated in ethnopoetics projects associated with the journal *Alcheringa*),[8] and others had their own movements (e.g., the building of Native American studies programs within universities and the founding of tribal colleges, at least three of which also published books on Native American subjects). I do not have the space to review the highlights of those movements (temporal and thematic), nor do I want to duplicate what others in this volume say;[9] nonetheless, I evoke the memory of that historical stream of thought here in order to broach the subject of recognition of Indianness as a poetic and a politic within Native American studies and mainstream academia.

Simply to utter the words "Indianness as a poetic and a politic" is sure to rankle those who diligently (and I think, rightly) argue against racial essentialist thinking, and at the same time those words sound a call to arms for the would-be identity police force. I must emphasize that my position is one of a *strategic* essentialism, a positing of an "essential" difference for the sake of shifting the center of power. Non-Indians have always been predominant in the study of Native American cultures, as part of the privilege that goes along with colonialism. (A treatise on the education of Native Americans through forced-assimilationist policies [and beyond] might partially illuminate that history and help to explain why relatively few Native Americans have pursued college degrees and academic appointments at major research institutions until recently.)[10] While the quality of the work and thinking produced in Native American studies has probably ranged as widely as the work of any pool of people on any subject, the perspectives derived from indigenous people had, for the most part, been absent, marginalized, or mediated until the advent of Native Americans themselves writing and teaching in significant numbers.

(The significance of the numbers can, of course, be disputed, and the relative newness of the field of study also must be taken into account in any assessment of the achievements of Native American studies.

For at least the past decade, Native Americans have begun to enter more fully into academic roles in which they can participate in the shaping of Native American studies programs as well as of the field of study itself. I must add, though, that many (but certainly not all) of the non-Indian Native American studies scholars I know within the field have supported the inclusion of Native Americans with credentials of every type from the "hard knocks" school to Harvard; however, the biggest obstacle to instilling Indianness as a poetic and a politic in institutions of higher learning rests with the system itself. A new round of thinking and talking in which Indian voices are central is needed (and is happening) to produce a different paradigm, one that avoids both essentialist and monological perspectives, yet does not shun an advocacy role. Elizabeth Cook-Lynn puts it well:

Indian America has always had its own quiet word(s) and language(s) which it has used and composed and clung to in an attempt to assert its own distinction in the age of empire. This quiet voice, tribal by nature, is at the core of all that is wrong yet all that is right about America's literature and art; its absence has been a failure [on the part of Euro-Americans] to accept the whole phenomenon of humanity.[11]

When we look around the proverbial table, indigenous people, who ought to be there to lend their most quiet of voices, are conspicuously absent. The painful irony of the situation is that if present at "the table" at all, indigenous peoples are most often there to offer the opening prayer (best delivered in a language the hosts' ancestors fought so hard to destroy); rarely are indigenous people there to deliver the keynote address.

A central concern in building institutional longevity for and intellectual excellence within Native American studies programs or departments[12] therefore ought to be the building of a recognition of and respect for indigenous difference in a range of arenas from philosophy to law; such building should function to promote cultural survival. By "range of arenas" I refer not merely to academic disciplines, but also to ontological spheres. When my son's kindergarten teacher, for example, asked me to do a presentation to her class, to show the four- to six-year-olds Indian-made jewelry and other art objects I own, she was quick to add, "I want the children to know that Indians are alive today and not necessarily like the Indians they read about in storybooks or see on T.V." To have her recognize the living, changing vitality of American Indian life was refreshing to me, since most often I feel that I am going against a very deep grain in American culture that disallows recognition of and respect for contemporary Indians. However obliquely, what we do in institutions of higher education eventually filters down to kindergarten teachers, writers for local newspapers, businesspeople in and around Indian communities—in short, people in all walks of life. As an educator, I have to believe that.

In this chapter, I am discussing the role literature and literary theory play in assuring that Indianness is recognized and thereby preserved, rather than merely mimed or staged and thereby destroyed. What Alfonso Ortiz says of revisionary Indian history holds as well for American Indian literary study: "The kind of history of which I speak is one that recognizes that Indian people have always been multidimensional and fully sentient human beings. It is also a history that would take up the Indian people's side of the historical encounter and tell their story fully." [13] Literature is primarily about storytelling, and the story gets told fully only in a dialogical way—that is, by studying the many stories of a community. As Louis Owens writes, "American Indian novelists are revising fundamentally the long-cherished, static view of Indian lives and cultures (or noncultures) held by people around the world." [14]

Although it should be obvious that Native American people are "multidimensional and fully sentient" human beings, remarks made by students often indicate otherwise. The responses of two non-Indian students stand out in my mind: a student expressing surprise that some Indians identify as gay or lesbian, and another student imagining that the course was going to teach him how to become a shaman who could then go into an Indian community and "heal the people." Apparently, the thinking goes: what is best in indigenousness is open for the taking, and what is complex behaviorally *must* be a corruption of that pristine, simple, lost past life. Both ideas imply a sort of crude social Darwinism that is prevalent in the popular culture available to youth. The challenge of contravening such thinking requires a significant quantity and quality of varied educational materials, but also a number of guideposts or points from which to proceed. The first important guidepost is to "revisit" place, or, more specifically, place-centeredness, to help all students gain a more complex understanding of connectedness to local geographies.

The Mind of the Earth, the Earth of the Mind

Each Native American studies program/department is destined to be unique depending on its location within its institution, region, and nation. I would argue for building programs (departments or centers when and where possible) around and through regional diversity, rather than emulating standard Euro-American universalizing models. Whether or not it is consciously built into a program's design, location helps shape a program's community, and therefore its focus and concerns. That happens through many factors: the number of Native American students; students' ages, sexes, gender orientations, and marital statuses; their educational preparation as well as goals; the tribal affiliations of students, staff, and faculty; settler and colonial histories of the non-Indians (whites) in the region; the settler and colonial histories of other nonwhite ethnic minorities in the region, and the languages spoken, to name the most obvious factors. Since other chapters in this volume take up more fully the topic of how Native American studies programs should be shaped and what their mission and scope ought to be, I will limit myself to issues most relevant to literary study, except to make the point that since no single model fits all places, interinstitutional cooperation and collaboration assist the creative use of personnel and other educational resources.

To recap my point, the strongest relation a Native American studies program can have toward American Indian social realities is to be clear in its mission to serve the regional Native American communities as best it can. That is, of course, a matter of resources as well as good intentions, but the point I want to stress is that Native American studies must be an entity that does not shy away from advocacy. Inasmuch as one goal of American Indian higher education ought to be the production of future leaders, their empowerment must not "constitute a contradiction to the people." [15] A dialogue must be set in place through which Native American students, staff, and faculty communicate with community leaders. It is in that spirit that I advocate for regionally centered American Indian studies/Native American studies programs.

By that I do not mean to suggest that studies cannot or should not be global in perspective or that students, faculty, and staff should only be from a particular region—such a thing would be absurd. The study of American Indian literatures in relation to theories of postcoloniality, for example, can prove quite fruitful. A term such as "anti-imperial translation," from Arnold Krupat's essay "Postcoloniality and Native American Literature," [16] gives us a way of talking about contemporary American Indian writing in English that assumes "complex acts of translation" of Indian identity and difference. What I am suggesting relative to a literal space within the academy has to do with reclaiming our territories in equally concrete yet also metaphorical ways. Building a community, like restoring an ecosystem, involves working with those peoples (in the broad sense of connectedness) who have the greatest investment in making a place habitable and with whom reciprocity of purposes and actions holds the greatest hope. Literature fits handily into such efforts.

Karl Kroeber, in his book on the relationship between ecology and literature, expresses well the connections I am drawing between community-building and local knowledge, as well as literature's place within an academic program/department and the world beyond the academy. Ecological literary criticism, according to Kroeber, denies the view that art is practically trivial and of no significance to physical, social, or ethical problems,

and is sympathetic to the romantic premise that the imaginativeness essential to poetry is the primary human capability enabling us to interact in a responsible manner with our environment. Acts of imagination such as are realized in poems, therefore, may contribute to the resolution of practical social and ethical difficulties, and commentators should endeavor to speak not to an elite or a coterie but to as wide an audience as possible. The [English] romantics never forgot what today we too frequently overlook, that the most important elements of our environment are our fellow human beings— most of whom, thank goodness, are not academic critics.[17]

In the context of Kroeber's remarks, poetry means something other than the rarefied artifact of a "high" culture. Poems created by indigenous people have always functioned both *practically* to fulfill "the people's" responsibility toward Nature and each other and *aesthetically* to please the senses. In fact, most poetry occasions in traditional Indian settings are multimedia events. Poetic imagination, as Kroeber envisions it, fits into the seamless whole of connectedness to the environment. The "ecosystem" of any particular piece of literature consists of all the verbal expressions that mother it into existence— jokes, chants, anecdotes, autobiographical tales, naming stories, myths, gossip, tales of quest, historical memoirs, songs, even rallying cries. Understanding a piece of written literature ideally requires that fullness of perspective, much as assuring the survival of a species of bird requires certain trees, flowers, and climatic conditions.

Beginning with the curriculum, the subjects taught should reflect the unique cultural knowledge of that place and should involve significant participation of the Native American individuals and communities in the region. While it is not always possible in the current academic climate to find Native Americans from a particular region with the kind of academic credentials that satisfy research universities, positions can be created for regional writers, language specialists, and storytellers, not to mention the variety of adjunct or visiting appointments possible for faculty. For indigenous knowledge and its practitioners ultimately to be recognized within the academy, positions would have to be filled on a basis other than the one currently in use.[18] As K. Anthony Appiah argues, liberal democracies operate under a moral imperative to recognize their citizens as equally possessed of human dignity, and, therefore, equally deserving of representation (i.e., expression, voice); according to that line of reasoning, liberal democracies should not create second-class citizens by virtue of institutional structure or policy.[19] Neither Native American studies departments and programs nor native faculty should remain "adjunct" to what is considered core to the vision and mission of universities to educate and to produce knowledge.

American Indians have been, in effect, second-class citizens in universities, even—or especially—in programs set up to study their cultures. "Real" Indians can and do earn Ph.D.'s, can and do enter broad-ranging intellectual discussions beyond the "song and dance" of their own cultures, and can and do maintain connections to their own and other Indian communities. But they often find themselves misunderstood by people on both sides of an unnecessarily imposed line between universities and communities. Krupat describes it well: "For Native critics, the impossible situation concerns the fact that when they speak as insiders, they may be seen as lacking in academic 'objectivity,' yet when they speak 'objectively,' from the outside, they may be seen as having abandoned their people or their experientially privileged position." [20] As double binds go, the call for "objectivity" from the usually supposed object is clearly a failure to recognize difference and, at the same time, a refusal to see commonality.

For centuries the ideological construction of "savagery" (as opposed to "civilization") has served as the justification for excluding indigenous cultures (philosophies, politics, etc.) from the mainstream of what is thought to be "the best that has been known and said in the world," according to Matthew Arnold's definition of culture. The political lobbying to institutionalize indigenous knowledge (and I use the term "institutionalize" guardedly) would logically result from a collaboration among university-wide advocates, Native American studies faculty, and regional Indian leaders, as an insider/outsider partnership for the benefit of all. While that may sound somewhat utopian, it is occurring all of the time on the level of pedagogy. For instance, teachers of American Indian literature since the so-called Native American renaissance of the 1960s and 1970s, many of them non-Indian, have worked to transform standard literary curricula to correspond to the needs of the Indian communities surrounding their institutions and the Indian students seeking an education therein.[21] Many National Endowment for the Humanities (NEH) Summer Seminars for college teachers, taught by such people as Larry Evers (University of Arizona), A. LaVonne Brown Ruoff (University of Illinois, Chicago Circle), and Kenneth Roemer (University of Texas, Arlington), have been geared to enable teachers to accommodate growing bodies of both American Indian literatures and students. Lawanna Trout's NEH-sponsored summer seminars for high school and tribal college teachers, held at the Newberry Library for twenty-some years, focused on presenting American Indian literatures and their authors to teachers.[22] As the body of pan-Indian texts available to teachers has grown, so has the body of culturally specific, place-centered texts. (I will take up the former category of literature later.)

To speak of Native Americans in relation to place, earth, land, or any other geographic location courts cliché, yet the definition of "indigenous" entails place: "having originated in and being produced, growing, living, or occurring naturally in a particular region or environment." [23] When Paula Gunn Allen talks about indigenous people's connectedness to the land, her comment at first sounds as if it is going in the direction of cliché: "We are the land. To the best of my understanding, that is the fundamental idea embedded in Native American life and culture in the Southwest. More than remembered, the earth is the

mind of the people as we are the mind of the earth." As Allen elaborates the
symbiotic relation she envisions between humans and the rest of creation, she
gradually makes clear that the tie entails a dynamism:

> It is not the ever-present "Other" which supplies us with a sense of "I." It is rather
> a part of our being, dynamic, significant, real. It is ourself, in as real a sense as such
> notions as "ego," "libido," or social network, in a sense more real than any conceptual-
> ization or abstraction about the nature of human being can ever be. . . . Nor is this rela-
> tionship one of mere affinity for the Earth. It is not a matter of being "close to nature."
> The relationship is more one of identity, in the mathematical sense, than of affinity.[24]

Much as Freud conceives of an artificially static division of the individual
psyche into "id," "ego," and "super-ego," in order to see the pattern of the
constitutive parts of a whole human being, Allen sees "the Earth" as part of
who native people are. The model developed further includes individual, extended family, and community, which would also be considered parts of the
whole individual, as Raymond DeMallie indicates in Chapter 12. In poststructuralist thought what Allen posits would not seem so far out, since theorists
following Jacques Derrida assert a "decentered self," an interactive, dynamic
subjectivity, rather than an isolated thinking, choosing self.[25] Elsewhere, as in
The Sacred Hoop, Allen expands the idea that indigenous peoples base their
existence on earth-centered living and interconnectedness (and reciprocity)
with two- and four-legged kin, the elements, and the like.

Many of the writings by American Indians make place, particularly home-
land, a primary theme, something more than setting: N. Scott Momaday's *The
Way to Rainy Mountain*, D'Arcy McNickle's *The Surrounded*, James Welch's
Fools Crow (actually his first three novels), Leslie Marmon Silko's *Ceremony,*
Ray Young Bear's *Black Eagle Child*, Louise Erdrich's *Tracks*, Thomas King's
Medicine River, Beth Brant's *Mohawk Trail*, Louis Owens's *Sharpest Sight,*
Elizabeth Cook-Lynn's *From the River's Edge*, N. Scott Momaday's *House
Made of Dawn*, Simon Ortiz's *Woven Stone* and *After and Before the Light-
ning,* John Joseph Mathews' *Talking to the Moon,* and Elizabeth Woody's
Seven Hands, Seven Hearts. William Bevis captures the essence of such literary choices and cultural imperatives well when he writes, "Both 'plot' and
'nature' lead to culturally conditioned concepts and to pervasive differences
in white and Native American points of view. As we shall see in their 'homing' plots and their surprisingly 'humanized' nature, these works are drenched
in a tribalism most whites neither understand nor expect in the works of contemporary Indians, much less when they are professors (all four novelists have
taught at universities)." [26] Alienation, also identified frequently as a theme in
American Indian writing (even in the works of the authors mentioned above),
past and present, always involves a component of dis-ease in relation to geography, regional flora and fauna, and cultural rituals based on maintenance of

a proper balance between humans and the rest of creation. In a sense these place-centered novels are in the tradition of Lakota "At Home Songs," songs sung at the beginning and end of a day when a person is away from home.[27]

Place-centeredness, I would argue, figures broadly into American Indian identity even in the case of urban Indians, who live away from their ancestral homeland, by virtue of kinship ties, ancestral burial sites, political and social centers, and other connections. (It is remarkable how human beings can overcome loss, and what they can keep alive in themselves.) I would also argue that once individuals or families lose their conscious cultural connection to the natural world and their valuing of kinship or extended family—as can happen with generations of urban or suburban living—they cease to be indigenous. It is impossible to decide when a person ceases to be of a particular cultural perspective, and to try to decide such a thing for someone else seems both absurd and disrespectful. Nonetheless, if we find a need to define collective identities and their constituents, those definitions are best kept loose.[28]

Leave it to Gerald Vizenor to illustrate how to keep definitions loose. In his recent novel *Dead Voices,* he develops the theme of an individual's earth-connectedness within an urban environment in intriguing ways, ways that refuse the binary thinking of urban/rural, civilization/wilderness. As is typical of Vizenor's work, *Dead Voices* first turns the notion of "wild" upside down, then turns it inside out, leaving his readers without easy judgments about where and how Indians can or should live. Vizenor's humorous, carnivalesque vision provides alternative ways of keeping imaginations fluid and judgments at bay, while offering counterimages to prevalent stereotypes. *Dead Voices* also contains its own theory on whether or not it takes spoken as opposed to written language to effect healing. Returning for a moment to an issue I raised early on in this chapter about whether form should somehow match content, it strikes me that that may be the central question for all art, and that Vizenor's yes *and* no is also always the answer. We must, like Vizenor's character Bagese, adopt a "plural first-person pronoun in writing," something "used to be sure nature is not separated from humans." [29]

To Write/Sight/Sound It Out

In our contemporary world, an ever-increasing hypervisualism sets images in the American cultural psyche without mediation by fact. Not surprisingly, Indians seem to be affected by hypervisualism as readily as non-Indians are. Being so accustomed to seeing bastardized, even comical versions of American Indians' relation to the natural world,[30] we can easily lose sight of what connectedness and reciprocity mean in concrete, pragmatic terms. The ideological power of contemporary American media can be illustrated by examining attitudes toward artifacts such as headdresses. (This example perhaps speaks more to me at the moment than any other because I attended a powwow this weekend, and generally find the pride the people present take in every aspect of the event encouraging.) Most Americans need new eyes to see the beauty in an authentic headdress, how it stands for honor and courage and is made to be distinctive to a particular individual's life and culture, as well as visually stunning and evocative. All Native American cultures do not produce headdresses like the ones depicted in the recent U.S. postage stamp series, perhaps because different birds are indigenous to different areas. Feathered headdresses other than the Plains versions also exist. The fact that many people are indifferent to Indians' arguments against the use of headdresses and tomahawks by fans of the Atlanta Braves and other baseball teams, and fail to recognize that such appropriation of Indian artifacts is degrading, is an indication of the extent to which American ideology blinds many American people to American Indian life, past and present.[31] What is true for artifacts is doubly true for Indian people themselves. As Vine Deloria, Jr., remarked back in the 1960s in *Custer Died for Your Sins,* Indians too easily become either invisible or transparent, relics of a romanticized past Americans want to be a part of or contemporary undesirables Americans want to do away with. The ironies layer deeply, as when contemporary groups such as the Lumbees cannot gain the support of other groups, "because" as one Lumbee woman claims, "we ain't got feathers and beads." [32]

It has become much easier to tackle the problems of colonialist representations of Indians in the past decade or so thanks to the cultural studies movement (which chiefly began in England with the work of Roland Barthes). Cultural studies is centered in English departments (or interdisciplinary programs such as American studies) and enables a broader interpretation of a wider range of cultural artifacts using more appropriate, interdisciplinary critical tools than the conventional tools of literary criticism. Cultural studies enables us to discuss headdresses in the context of dime novels and Mark Twain as well as American baseball, in other words. In a recent discussion in the *PMLA* of the whys and wherefores of cultural studies, William Thornton of National Cheng King University remarks on the importance of seeing literature as it has been situated in elitist cultural terms: "The colonial erasure of the local, whether modern or postmodern, could go unchallenged for so long because it was assumed that reality exists in great books." To some extent, the belief that "great" books contain the distillation of the greatest wisdom in the world continues in the efforts of conservative educators such as William Bennett to press for greater "cultural literacy." Global stereotypes of native people serve to erase the local peoples and their literatures by not assigning to those peoples the capacity to produce "great books" in the first place. As Thornton continues:

From the colonial vantage, the mission of a literary education is to take locals elsewhere, a will to exile that reaches far beyond any geographic positioning of the colonial–postcolonial contest. It is as much a First World as a Fourth World issue. Broadly construed, colonialism operates where local voices are systematically muted. It prevails wherever local subjects are de-realized in the name of a literature that displaces common culture.[33]

Cultural studies enables an "ecosystemic" approach to Native American studies. Moving away from the narrow set of literary questions previously thought appropriate for texts, we can ask about a text's features of localness and its aliveness within a human context.

A more holistic philosophy of scholarly endeavor and/or expression, not unlike indigenous thinking or performative art, is emerging through cultural studies. Krupat cites Stephen Tyler's vision of a radically new form through which to present nonwestern cultures to westerners:

> One would here abandon the Western aim of *representing* (and so of *knowing* or *understanding*) culture and instead seek to *evoke* cultural world views, a kind of anthropological poetics rather than an anthropological science — but, to be sure, a particular *kind* of poetics, one that sees the poem as a quasi-mystical embodiment or incarnation of — whatever. . . . Something of this sort might also be said for the hope of writing history, at least the history of Native Americans, from an Indian point of view.[34]

Ultimately, as Krupat also notes, anthropological poetics may be more easily thought of than realized. In an article forthcoming in a special issue of the *American Indian Quarterly* on cultural property rights, Kimberly Blaeser contrastingly asserts that, at least as far as contemporary Indian literature is concerned, a suitable way of analyzing texts is always already contained within them in their circularity of form — the distinctively indigenous view of time as cyclical. Whatever the case may be, Tyler's and Blaeser's (and others') calls for radically rethinking representation will give more collaborative texts a chance to come to life.

In that way, not only can the living literatures of regional American Indian groups potentially enhance any Native American studies curricular offerings, but Native American peoples' critical language or metalanguage can open worlds for comparative study. This metalanguage, which can be key to the literature, is most often evident in a people's names for things, in their stories of how the world came to be and how the human community should be ordered. *Yaqui Deer Songs,* by Larry Evers and Felipe S. Molina is an exemplary literary work, one that reflects native and nonnative collaboration on the individual and institutional levels, and also one that presents an American Indian metalanguage in practice.[35] The importance of this particular text can be more fully appreciated by first recognizing the images it counters. In speaking of the predominance in public spheres of the Yaqui deer singer image, Evers writes, "These are public images, and they are fixed, immobile, and silent. What speaks are the political and economic motives that cluster around them. They

serve as an aboriginal connection for the politicians, a romantic lure for the
admen, the borderlands equivalent, in many ways, to the warbonneted Plains
Indian horsemen of the Wild West." [36] The goals Molina and Evers set for
themselves in writing the text were to enable "the continuation of deer songs
as a vital part of life in Yaqui communities and . . . their appreciation in all
communities beyond." [37] In addition, the authors express their hope that their
work together will be a model for others who wish to embark on fully collaborative projects.

A text such as Molina and Evers's not only presents an example of a fruitful
collaboration but also potentially serves as a center around which to build a
literary "ecosystem." In a survey course in American Indian literature, *Yaqui
Deer Songs* could be taught alongside Refugio Savala's *Autobiography of a
Yaqui Poet* and *A South Corner of Time: Hopi, Navajo, Papago, and Yaqui Tribal
Literature* (the latter edited by Larry Evers). *Yaqui Women: Contemporary Life
Histories,* edited by Jane Holden Kelly, could function as a transition to a text
such as *Papago Woman,* which in turn could be linked to Ofelia Zepeda's
contemporary poetry, *Ocean Power: Poems from the Desert.* In my Southwest
native literatures section, I frequently assign a wonderful piece by Gary Paul
Nabhan, "Plants Which Coyote Steals, Spoils, and Shits On," to show how
interwoven the philosophy of Coyoteness is within O'odham (Papago) culture.
Nabhan writes, "*Bankaj* refers to any coyote-like quality, such as 'yelling like
a coyote.' *Banma* describes one who is being greedy. *Banmad* is a verb meaning 'to cheat somebody.' *Banmakam* is a glutton. *S-banow* is the superlative
for the bad breath of someone who 'sure stinks like a coyote.' " [38] Many plants
take the name of Coyote one way or the other and for better or for worse,
and the fact that the root word for Coyote, *ban,* is sprinkled throughout the
O'odham language indicates just how that Coyote gets around. Remembering
Coyote at every turn must bring a smile to the native speaker's face when he
or she least expects to be touched by something so common, yet profoundly at
home in that world.

A contemporary collection of southwestern American Indian writing edited
by Evers and Zepeda, *Home Places,* would nicely round out a section of regional study that could provide a model for students to emulate in studying
other regions. I frequently assign students to compile an annotated bibliography of at least four types of Native American literature from a region or tribal
group we did not have time to cover in class. The work of Edward Spicer,
a historian who has written extensively on the history of Yaqui and other
southwestern Indian peoples, would be an important resource for supplemen-
tal historical background material. Teaching such a course at a place like the
University of Arizona could involve class visits by Yaqui or Tohono O'odam
elders, writers, and educators, visits to sites, and other experiences designed
to bring together the region's history, literature, and religion (categories that
might themselves seem somewhat alien in their indigenous cultural context).

Teaching *Yaqui Deer Songs* in an American Indian literature class outside the Southwest calls for reliance on visual aids and other supportive materials to enable the reader to "picture" the flora, fauna, and climate better, since the very sounds of the rasps that accompany the music reflect the environment from which they originate. A tape of the songs contained in the book is also available. Each region could have any number of similar units, based on its cultural and historical particulars, but I prefer in general to teach American Indian regional literatures with a chronological mix of materials in many genres, so that at the close of a unit we do not feel we have left all the "real" Indians behind as we end in the contemporary period. Giving up the idea that Indians are exotic can be a painful but necessary process, but it should never occasion the complete abandonment of the idea that indigenous or tribal people are nonetheless different from what Elizabeth Cook-Lynn (in response to Krupat's use of the term) calls "cosmopolitans." [39] Most importantly, when non-Indian students are made aware of the Indian people who continue to inhabit certain geographic regions, particularly the students' own, they begin to recognize that they are part of an ongoing, living history of how Indians are treated by the dominant culture.

It is important to emphasize that the regionalism of which I speak is not to be confused with what in literary study commonly passes under the heading of "regional literature" — that is, a literature that reflects the language customs (vernacular, dialect, predominant genres, etc.) of a particular place along with other aspects of "local color." Although the knowledge base of which I speak may include those features of locale, features (by the way) that have often drawn derision from scholars for their parochial (i.e., not universal) quality, what I mean is more accurately termed "bioregionalism." As M. Annette Jaimes notes, "Bioregionalism, with its emphasis on natural systems as eco-systems, can be identified as a significant attribute of Indian identity and survival." Native American studies programs (and departments) predicated on advocacy would, understandably, explore the ways identity is "linked to the land and the environment as an indigenous homeland, . . . [and is] also essential to the Native concept of nationhood predicated on kinship and land-based religions." [40] The marginalization of indigenous knowledge within predominantly white academic institutions mirrors the political marginalization (not to mention destruction!) of indigenous groups struggling to maintain an ecologically sound separatism.

On Not Being Dogged about Recognizing Dogness

When we conceive of a "politics of equal dignity" as based merely on the "recognition of our universal capacities," we risk bringing upon ourselves something as equally homogenizing as the colonial stereotypes have been. [41] As Charles Taylor states, "There must be something between the inauthentic and homogenizing demand for recognition of equal worth, on the one hand, and the self-immurement within ethnocentric standards on the other." [42] The literary solution to the dilemma of over-versus underinscribed and "-read" Indianness that I would propose involves what Clifford Geertz terms thick description. The more you know, the less you know for sure, but the richer what you know becomes. Many American Indian literary critics and cultural studies scholars have been asserting their ideas of what constitutes an Indian (sometimes tribally specific) criticism or critical theory; a brief survey of their ideas will illustrate what I mean by thick description. Greg Sarris writes, in *Keeping Slug Woman Alive*, "I will etch out a way to read the text [in this case, *Autobiographies of Three Pomo Women*] so that I can see the text as well as myself as reader, so that I might inform the text and allow the text to inform me." [43] Although Sarris comes from Pomo Indian heritage (as well as Miwok, Jewish, and Filipino heritages), these texts seem to him to be at so much of a cultural remove as to require a cross-cultural reading. In other words, he does not want to presume cultural knowledge.

For Beth Brant, "theory" gets embedded in storytelling, and storytelling should be abundant and full as long as there are tellers to carry on the tradition. Brant sees great healing potential in shaping our centuries-old experiences in words. She writes, "Much of the self-hatred we carry around inside us is centuries old. This self-hatred is so coiled within itself, we often cannot distinguish the racism from the homophobia from the sexism." [44] Even or especially the "ugly and terrorizing" stories must be told, according to Brant, alongside the "beautiful testaments to endurance and dignity. We must learn to emulate this kind of testimony." Brant is a Mohawk woman whose father migrated to Detroit to work in the auto industry; she grew up working-class in a multi-ethnic neighborhood and married and divorced young—after giving birth to three girls. Brant raised her daughters as a single, working-class parent, and despite not having finished high school began writing at the age of forty. She insists that none of her complexity as a human being be overlooked: she is "mother, grandmother, Mohawk, lesbian, feminist, working-class, mammal and on and on." [45] The last words in *Writing as Witness* say a lot about what she thinks writing ought to be: "I've done my job." [46] No other Indian writer, save Simon Ortiz, makes working-class concerns the focus of her or his work as Brant does. When she was asked to edit a volume of North American Indian women's writings, she pulled from her own background and experience and canvassed the places she knew she could find Native North American women's voices—reservations, prisons, urban Indian centers, and the like. The result is *A Gathering of Spirit* (1984), perhaps the most diverse and thereby powerful anthology of native women's writings published to date.

Like Beth Brant, Anna Lee Walters combines personal reflection and autobiography with political statement, fiction, and literary criticism in her book

Talking Indian: Reflections on Survival and Writing (1992). Author of several other books of fiction and nonfiction, including *Ghost Singer* (1994) and *The Sun Is Not Merciful* (1989), Walters is among the most prolific of contemporary native women writers. *Talking Indian* explains much of her philosophy toward writing and how such achievement is not anathema to her as a Pawnee and Oto woman. An earlier work, *The Sacred: Ways of Knowledge, Sources of Life* (1977), co-authored with Peggy V. Beck, provides much useful information on American Indian or tribal beliefs, particularly for teachers who often do not know how to approach the teaching of Native American literary texts.

Robert Warrior sets for himself a much different task: to elucidate forerunners in American Indian intellectualism, most notably John Joseph Mathews and Vine Deloria, Jr. Warrior concerns himself first and foremost with "the ways American Indian intellectuals write about and speak to each other about the role of intellectual work." [47] For Warrior, discourse is more a matter of content than form, and he bemoans the fact that the discourse of native and nonnative alike has been "preoccupied with parochial questions of identity and authenticity, while the major achievements of American Indian writers such as Russell Bates, Martin Cruz Smith, and Will Rogers go unnoticed, unsung." [48] He tries for an engagement with Mathews's and Deloria's work that will inspire native writers to read each other and write *to* each other in a way that builds a more functional Indian critical vocabulary than has previously existed. It is not altogether possible to move beyond identity questions, however, as Warrior hopes, if we intend to posit a political need for authentic representation and recognition.

Whom Indians recognize as their own—if in any sense the generalized term "Indian" can apply here—is fraught with controversy. There are destined always to be contradictions in our complaints, hopes, and expectations around identity issues, since "authenticity" tends to be its most recognizable when it is its most static. Nevertheless, all determinations of Indianness need to be seen as somewhere on a continuum of traditional indigenous knowledge, whether or not the full range possible is known to us. Several other Indian critics and writers have written "notes toward a definition" pieces related to American Indian identity in Indian written literature: Michael Dorris, Ward Churchill, Gerald Vizenor, Kim Blaeser, Jack Forbes, William Willard, Elizabeth Cook-Lynn, Simon J. Ortiz, Jr., Vine Deloria, Jr., Craig Womack, Michael Wilson, Jeane Breinig, and others. But in many ways Native Americans have just begun to write a range of criticism from local, tribal, national, hemispheric, and global perspectives; mixed-blood identities, such as are reflected in the work of Ines Hernandez-Avila and Janice Gould (both poets and critics), also figure in the larger picture of American Indian literary study. Blaeser and I have written single-author studies on Gerald Vizenor and James Welch respectively, and Paula Gunn Allen's work on American Indian women's place within tribal societies continues to be studied for its reassertion of the "feminine principle" in indigenous life. Louis Owens's *Other Destinies,* an excellent study of American Indian novels, follows Mikhail Bakhtin's theories regarding the nature of the novel as a many-storied dialogue. The ever-increasing production of Native American literary texts and the growing body of literary criticism generated by Native American critics, writers, and educators bode well for the future of American Indian literary study within American Indian studies. We have come a long way since the days when our literary predecessors could be listed in a few lines: Samson Occum, William Apess, Zitkala Ša, Mourning Dove, Ella Deloria, Charles Eastman, John Joseph Mathews, and D'Arcy McNickle.

Studying American Indians, as I commented earlier, has obviously and primarily been the purview of non-Indians, as has been the institution building that has supported such study—that is an important and central fact in discussing Native American studies and literature. Having said that, I must immediately insist that academic culture is not any other "real thing" but its own quasi-cultural space, and we must not lose sight of that fact. Even a space created for (and by) Indians within the academy tends to feel alien, *not* culturally Indian. But what is "Indian," after all, can only at best, be vaguely gestured, like a blunt pointing of the lips in one direction rather than another.[49] I do not mean to imply that "there are no real Indians left," nor that Indian intellectualism does not exist. Indians and Indian intellectualism continue as they have for millennia. Exactly whose "culture" the academy is may be subject to debate; yet, for Indians, developing a sense of belonging within mainstream institutions will be the prerequisite to redefining that space—actual and intellectual—as Native American. However that is done, it will be a long time before the numbers of Indians will constitute a critical mass.

For the time being, the received wisdom is that in some ways it is easier to say what a thing is *not* than to say what it is. The necessary recognition I hinted at in the beginning of this chapter will come together that way. For there are taboos against naming certain realities or personages, as if to do so would disempower the personage or bring a curse upon the namer. At the present historical moment, questions of American Indian identity seem to be flooding our carburetors such that it is difficult to move forward, but we will tire of those discussions and press for broader visions, whether from the vantage point of the microscope or the satellite. As Renato Rosaldo says in the opening of his book *Culture and Truth,* "These days questions of culture seem to touch a nerve because they quite quickly become anguished questions of identity. Academic debates about multicultural education similarly slip effortlessly into the animating ideological conflicts of this multicultural nation." [50] Just as the abundantly obvious fact that multiculturalism exists has begun to make an impression on dominant power forces, the radical nature of indigenous thought will also become a legitimate way of seeing, knowing, being.

An important first step in the recognition of American Indian cultural concerns involves an avoidance of what Rosaldo terms "imperialist nostalgia" — quite simply, "yearning for what one has destroyed." [51] Certain cultural values, when viewed through "imperialist nostalgia," miss how a people can both revere dogs and eat them; how a people can regard The Dog of dogs, Coyote, as both a creator of sorts without whom the world as we know it simply would not exist and, at the same time, a rascal whom we should avoid, if we know what is good for us. The same people who regard Coyote as a culture hero would also not hesitate to shoot the four-legged coyote when the sheep in their pastures are threatened by his appetite.[52]

Literature, one of Coyote's frequent haunts, can be a place of "free play" in the postmodern sense as well as a means of bringing history to life. Literature can thwart the comfort of an imperialist nostalgic perspective by disrupting expectations in several ways: by presenting the voices and perspectives of Indians to contradict or counter stereotypes; by adding validity and emphasis to the points made by historical facts; and, most of all, by rendering Indians as "multidimensional and fully sentient human beings." [53] Those features alone make the study of American Indian literature central to Native American studies curricula and philosophy. The growing popularity of American Indian flute music reminds me how most Indian music has remained unassimilable to mainstream American cultures, how translating it into European melodic structures does not work—as Frances Densmore's enthusiastic students soon discovered. Literature, like much of Indian music, can be that unassimilable thing. But that is not all literature can and should do or be. As Louis Menand remarks in his article on visual representations:

The true pleasure of representation does not come from its indistinguishability from the real thing. It comes from its distinguishability. An Elvis impersonator gives pleasure precisely because he's not Elvis, and it is crucial to the effect that we never forget he's not. The moment we mistake him for Elvis, the frisson is lost.[54]

Representation in art and representation in politics can have seemingly opposite connotations, but recognition of cultural difference requires an astute sense of the pleasure and play in not being so easy to pin down. As Menand says, "For truth and authenticity, we have the subway." [55] Somewhere between the unreal and the real, beyond but not yet become the hyperreal, resides Coyote, in a place where you have to talk Indian, write Indian, and think Indian dog if you hope to get home safe.

Notes

1. Elizabeth Woody captures the charisma of Indian cars well in her short story "Buckskin," in *Seven Hands, Seven Hearts* (Portland: Eighth Mountain Press, 1994), 21–24. Woody writes, "The name Buckskin was chosen, not to honor our Native

American heritage, but because she was a bona fide, temperamental, restless warhorse, an Indian car. In that legacy, she had to earn her name" (21).

2.   James Welch, *The Death of Jim Loney* (New York: Harper and Row, 1979), 18.

3.   Ron LaFrance passed on to the spirit world in July of 1996. For him, education was a fighting creed, a determination to keep his own Mohawk traditions, and all American Indian traditions, alive. This chapter is dedicated to his memory.

4.   Adrian Louis, *Among the Dog Eaters* (Albuquerque: West End Press, 1992).

5.   The phrase comes from something I have been drafting on what I term an American Indian pedagogical model.

6.   Anna Lee Walters entitles her book on writing as an Indian (Walters is Pawnee/ Otoe), *Talking Indian: Reflections on Survival and Writing* (Ithaca: Firebrand Books, 1992).

7.   An important revisitation of the topic is Hayden White, *The Content of the Form: Narrative Discourse and Historical Representation* (Baltimore: Johns Hopkins University Press, 1987). Earlier, in the field of literary studies, M. H. Abrams explored a similar topic in *The Mirror and the Lamp: Romantic Theory and the Critical Tradition* (New York: Oxford University Press, 1953). The title page of the first edition tellingly presents the idea of objectivity as a western intellectual religious construct in an epigraph from W. B. Yeats: "It must go further still: that soul must become / its own betrayer, its own deliverer, the one / activity, the mirror turned lamp." That is actually an old question, dating back at least to Plato in western thought. Among other issues related to Romanticism and literary criticism, Abrams traces through eighteenth- and nineteenth-century European thought the idea that the "primitive" urge (raw emotion) gave birth to poetry—indeed, to language itself.

8.   See Arnold Krupat, *The Turn to the Native: Studies in Criticism and Culture* (Lincoln: University of Nebraska Press, 1996), 1–29.

9.   See James Clifford and George E. Marcus, eds., *Writing Culture: The Poetics and Politics of Ethnography* (Berkeley: University of California Press, 1986).

10.   Jorge Noriega, "American Indian education in the United States: Indoctrination for subordination to colonialism," in *The State of Native America: Genocide, Colonization and Resistance,* M. Annette Jaimes, ed. (Boston: South End Press, 1992), 371–402.

11.   Elizabeth Cook-Lynn, "The relationship of a writer to the past," in *Why I Can't Read Wallace Stegner and Other Essays* (Madison: University of Wisconsin Press, 1996), 64.

12.   Organizers of the American Indian Program at Cornell University had to decide whether to have the word "studies" in their name and thereby risk being seen as primarily a studies program; they reasoned that serving Indian students in noncurricular ways and working with Indian communities would be as important as their academic curriculum, and so they opted to bypass all the implications of appropriation of Indian experience by being seen as a studies program. To my knowledge there are only two Native American Studies departments per se in the country—at the University of Minnesota and at the University of California, Davis.

13.   Alfonso Ortiz, "Indian/white relations: A view from the other side of the frontier," in *Indians in American History,* Frederick E. Hoxie, ed. (Wheeling, Ill.: Harlan Davidson, 1988), 1.

14.   Louis Owens, *Other Destinies: Understanding the American Indian Novel* (Nor-

man: University of Oklahoma Press, 1992), 28. Also see James Ruppert, *Mediation in Contemporary Native American Fiction* (Norman: University of Oklahoma Press, 1995).

15. Paulo Freire, *Pedagogy of the Oppressed* (New York: Herder and Herder, 1972), 165.

16. *Yale Journal of Criticism,* 7 (1994), 164.

17. Karl Kroeber, *Ecological Literary Criticism: Romantic Imagining and the Biology of Mind* (New York: Columbia University Press, 1994), 21.

18. For a discussion of Indians' place with the larger debate around recognition of cultural collectivities within liberal democracies, see my article, "The thinking heart: American Indian discourse and the politics of recognition," in *Race, Ethnicity, and Nationality in the United States: Toward the Twenty-first Century,* Paul Wong, ed. (forthcoming from Westview Press, 1998). As the argument goes, liberal democracies operate under a moral imperative to recognize their citizens as equally possessed of human dignity, and therefore as equally deserving of representation (i.e., expression, voice). According to that line of reasoning, liberal democracies should not create second-class citizens by virtue of institutional structure or policy.

19. Charles Taylor, *Multiculturalism* (Princeton: Princeton University Press, 1994), xx. The central issue of the text, as Jurgen Habermas conceives it, is: "While modern law establishes a basis for state-sanctioned relations of intersubjective recognition, the rights derived from them protect the vulnerable integrity of legal subjects who are in every case individuals. . . . Can a theory of rights that is so individualistically constructed deal adequately with struggles for recognition in which it is the articulation and assertion of collective identities that seems to be at stake?" (107).

20. Krupat, *The Turn to the Native,* 13.

21. Kenneth Lincoln, *Native American Renaissance* (Berkeley: University of California Press, 1983), first coined the term in an effort to describe the emergence of many new American Indian writers around the time of the publication of N. Scott Momaday's *House Made of Dawn.* In my opinion, it is a misnomer, since there had never been a pan-Indian writing movement like the one spawned by the events of the 1960s and 1970s.

22. Many important reference texts have resulted from those years, including Paula Gunn Allen, ed., *Studies in American Indian Literature* (New York: Modern Language Association of America, 1983); A. LaVonne Brown Ruoff, *American Indian Literatures: An Introduction, Bibliographic Review, and Selected Bibliography* (New York: Modern Language Association, 1990); Gretchen Bataille and Kathleen Sands, *American Indian Women, Telling Their Lives* (Lincoln: University of Nebraska Press, 1984); and Kenneth Roemer, ed., *Teaching Approaches to The Way to Rainy Mountain* (New York: Modern Language Association of America, 1988). Three of the four works mentioned above were published by the Modern Language Association, and their publication corresponded with the institutionalization of the study of American Indian literatures within that organization of over 30,000 members, the primary professional organization for literary study in the United States and Canada.

23. *Webster's Ninth New Collegiate Dictionary* (Springfield, Mass.: Merriam-Webster, 1989), 614.

24. As quoted by Robert M. Nelson, *Place and Vision: The Function of Landscape in Native American Fiction* (New York and San Francisco: Peter Lang, 1993), 1.

25. See Eduardo Duran and Bonnie Duran, *Native American Postcolonial Psychol-*

ogy (Albany: SUNY Press, 1995), 26. In an odd twist of logic, however, the decentered self envisioned lacks religious foundation. Duran and Duran write, "Some postmodern theorists have gone so far as to say once we give up metaphysical attempts to find a true self for man [*sic*], we can only appear as the contingent historical selves we find ourselves to be" (26). In other words, the move *away* from western individualism does not imply a move *toward* tribal views of the self.

26. William Bevis, "Native American novels: Homing in," in *Recovering the Word: Essays on Native American Literature,* Brian Swann and Arnold Krupat, eds. (Berkeley: University of California Press, 1987), 580–81. Also see Louis Owens, "Earthboy's Return: James Welch's Acts of Recovery," in *Other Destinies: Understanding the American Indian Novel* (Norman: University of Oklahoma Press, 1992), 128–66.

27. Peggy V. Beck and Anna L. Walters use one such song as an epigraph to the seventh chapter of their book *The Sacred: Ways of Knowledge, Sources of Life,* entitled "The world out of balance" (Tsaile, Ariz.: Navajo Community College Press, 1977). The text is a good example of the indigenous-knowledge books published by that tribal college press.

28. For a full discussion of identity issues, see Kathryn Shanley, "The Indian American loves to love and read," forthcoming in the *American Indian Quarterly,* special issue on cultural property rights, edited by David L. Moore. In that article I argue that "representational politics" requires a definition of Native American identity that is a combination of recognition by a group and self-identification. In an epistemological sense, native or indigenous identity is defined by a sense of connectedness to the natural world, and from that connectedness derives a different value or view of materiality and spirit as well as a profound belief in the importance of kinship.

29. Krupat, *Turn to the Native,* 86.

30. An expression that itself seems alienating, as if humans are not themselves natural.

31. According to the article "Mascot replaced with mockingbird," in *Native Wind,* 2 (1997), 9, a Chattanooga, Tennessee, team gave up its mascot, Chief Moccanooga, who is described as wearing a long feather headdress, suede-fringed pants, a Mocs jersey, and moccasins. His face was painted brownish-red with white, yellow, and blue "war paint." Some things do change!

32. Quoted in Fergus M. Bordewich, *Killing the White Man's Indian: Reinventing Native Americans at the End of the Twentieth Century* (New York: Doubleday, 1996), 62.

33. William Thornton, letter in "Remarks," *PMLA,* 112 (1997), 262.

34. Arnold Krupat, "Introduction," in *The Voice in the Margin: Native American Literature and the Canon* (Berkeley: University of California Press, 1989), 11.

35. I regard Felipe Molina's traditional religious and educational institutions as equivalent in cultural sanction and authority to Larry Evers's university.

36. Larry Evers and Felipe S. Molina, *Yaqui Deer Songs, Maso Bwikam: A Native American Poetry* (Tucson: University of Arizona Press, 1987), 7.

37. Ibid., 8.

38. Gary Paul Nabhan, *The Desert Smells Like Rain: A Naturalist in Papago Indian Country* (San Francisco: North Point Press, 1987), 79.

39. See Elizabeth Cook-Lynn, "The American Indian fiction writers: Cosmopolitanism, nationalism, the third world, and first nation sovereignty," in *Why I Can't Read*

Wallace Stegner, 78–96. Since this chapter has to do with Indian-centered writing, "writing Indian," I am not listing the many many indispensable studies in the field done by non-Indians; a longer work would allow for such a comprehensive survey.

40. M. Annette Jaimes, "Native American identity and survival: Indigenism and environmental ethics," in *Issues in Native American Cultural Identity,* Michael K. Green, ed. (New York: Peter Lang, 1995), 277.

41. I am paraphrasing Charles Taylor's thought in *Multiculturalism,* 51.

42. Ibid., 72.

43. Greg Sarris, *Keeping Slug Woman Alive: A Holistic Approach to American Indian Texts* (Berkeley: University of California Press, 1993), 83.

44. Beth Brant, *Writing as Witness: Essay and Talk* (Toronto: Women's Press, 1994), 63.

45. Ibid., 79.

46. Ibid., 124.

47. Robert Allen Warrior, *Tribal Secrets: Recovering American Indian Intellectual Traditions* (Minneapolis: University of Minnesota Press, 1995), xvi.

48. Ibid., xix–xx.

49. Two essays that discuss the difficulties of a term such as "Indian" and a rubric such as "American Indian literature" are Michael Dorris, "Native American literature in an ethnohistorical context," *College English,* 41 (1979), 147–62; and Jack Forbes, "Colonialism and Native American literature: Analysis," *Wacazo Sa Review,* 3 (1987), 17–23. In this essay, I have chosen to use the terms "American Indian," "Indian," "Native American," "indigenous," etc., fairly interchangeably, although I do recognize that "Native American" generally includes Alaskan Natives and Native Hawaiians; my field of specialization is American Indian literature, the indigenous peoples from the lower forty-eight states, and that term seems most apt.

50. Renato Rosaldo, *Culture and Truth: The Remaking of Social Analysis* (Boston: Beacon Press, 1993 [1989]), xxi.

51. Ibid., 71. In his critique of the positionalities of social analysts, Rosaldo also makes it clear that he does not expect perfection, that is, political correctness: "Under imperialism, metropolitan observers are no more likely to avoid a certain complicity with domination than they are to avoid having strong feelings toward the people they study. Such recognitions need not lead either to confessional breast-beating or to galloping bias. If social analysts realize that they cannot be perfectly 'clean,' they no more should become as 'dirty' as possible than airline pilots, invoking limitations of human fallibility, should blind their eyes" (69).

52. Some critics dispute the validity of the "culture hero" designation when used to refer to "trickster figures," another disputed term. For a discussion of the relationship between contemporary writing about trickster figures and the place of the trope within traditional cultures, see Franchot Ballinger, "Living sideways: Social themes and social relationships in Native American trickster tales," *American Indian Quarterly,* 13 (1989), 15–30.

53. Ortiz, "Other side of the frontier," 1.

54. "Get unreal," *New Yorker* (March 17, 1997), 12.

55. Ibid.

7 *J. Randolph Valentine*

Linguistics and Languages in Native American Studies

In this essay I will discuss the role of linguistics within a program of Native American studies. Motivated by the alarming rates of attrition among Native American languages, I argue that such programs need comprehensive, clearly articulated research and teaching strategies, with a goal of thoroughly documenting all aspects of language pattern and usage, using integrated linguistic, anthropological, literary, and folkloristic methods. I will also sketch the history of the study of Native American languages to show the place that it has had in the development of North American linguistics and anthropology, and the reasons that its goals and methods differ from, but complement, those of current theoretical linguistics. Mainstream contemporary theory by its nature fails to address what it means to describe a language in all its fullness, because the emphasis on what is universal in human language necessarily plays down comprehensive attention to what is specific to individual languages, at least in our present state of knowledge. Although theoretical models are important in guiding research, comprehensive documentation must be rooted in well-articulated, inductive methodologies that seek to account for the full gamut of a language's resources. That is, Native American linguistic research must be informed by a theory of grammatical documentation involving a proper understanding of the relationship of language to culture and society, as well as by a theory of universal grammar. Such an undertaking requires knowledge that is spread over many academic disciplines and must be integrationist in orientation. I also stress the collaborative relationship that must exist between the academy and the communities whose languages are at issue, with regard to program design and administration, the nature and extent of documentary research, the character and content of university language programs, and the training of students in skills of value to ongoing community language programs. At the end of this chapter I describe some institutional programs exemplifying these broadly defined goals of rich documentation and collaborative community.

The State of American Indian Languages

Michael Krauss, director of the Alaska Native Language Center at the University of Alaska, Fairbanks, has been a prominent voice in recent expressions of concern over the precipitous, unprecedented decline of not just Native American languages, but minority languages around the world. Against all odds, approximately 200 of the 300 or more languages spoken in North America at the time of contact with Europeans are still used in some form today, though only a fraction of these are likely to survive for very long. Approximately 175 indigenous languages are spoken within the boundaries of the United States. Krauss makes the following observations on their relative vitality, though: only about 20 languages are still being learned by children, and so have a reasonable chance of surviving for several generations; about 30 languages are spoken today only by adults, but are not being learned by children; another 70 languages are spoken only by the elderly; and another 50 or so are spoken by only a very few of the oldest members of communities.[1] This means that within the next generation approximately 25 percent of the surviving languages will be gone; within two generations well over half will disappear.[2]

Concern to preserve and promote what remains has long influenced linguists and anthropologists working with Native American languages. Americanist luminaries such as Edward Sapir and Leonard Bloomfield are respected as much for their descriptive work as for their theoretical contributions. Part of the motivation for Americanists has always been the scientific and historical value of the languages they work with, but many linguistic scholars of the past and present consider their work to be an ethical matter, as well, since the decline of these languages has been accelerated and exacerbated by social programs designed to assimilate Native Americans into American society. The longstanding system of off-reservation schools worked to distance children physically and psychologically from their communities and traditions, in part by the promotion of English at the expense of Native American languages.[3] A snapshot of one child's boarding school experience is provided by Andrew Medler, an Ojibwe from Walpole Island, Ontario, who attended the infamous Carlisle Indian School. In 1938 Medler provided materials for Bloomfield's sketch of Eastern Ojibwe, some including personal anecdotes of childhood experiences. In the following account Medler reflects on the time long ago when, as a student at Carlisle, he heard from a schoolmate that there was a young Menomini woman in residence who spoke Ojibwe. Medler wanted to know if this was true, and when his student job as handyman took him to the girl's quarters one day, he devised a strategy to find out. He describes the meeting as follows:

Ngii-maajaa dash gii-zhaayaan widi Girls' Quarters. Mii dash gii-waabmag maaba Menomini girl dzhi-gziibiignang waasechganan.

So I started off and went to the Girls' Quarters. There I saw this Menomini girl washing windows.

Mii dash besho eni-yaayaan maa endnakmigzid. Gaa waya ekwaabid nwaabmaasii.

Then I go near to where she was working. I did not see anyone keeping watch.

Mii dash gii-gnoonag. "Megwaa sa ggiziibiigsagnige!"

So I spoke to her. "I see you're washing woodwork!"

Mii dash gii-nkwetwid. "Enh, megwaa," kido.

Then she answered me. "Yes, so I am," she said.[4]

This is the extent of the exchange that Medler records in this account, though in another he mentions eventually having a second opportunity to speak with his Menomini schoolmate, which allowed him to draw the conclusion, "Mii dash nhendamaan geget sa gii-gkenmag sa Wjibwemod" — "And then I knew for certain that she spoke Ojibwe." Medler seems to show no bitterness in these accounts, but relates straightforwardly a memorable childhood experience in which he had a chance to speak Ojibwe with another student, which at Carlisle Indian School entailed risks that could be circumvented only by careful planning.

The History of the Study of American Indian Languages

While residential schools were striving to distance Native American children from their ancestral languages and cultures, American scholars were working to preserve a record of what remained. In the earliest periods of European contact, the study of these languages served the purposes of missionaries seeking to convert Native American populations to Christianity. Grammars and dictionaries written in European languages were compiled as aids to missionaries, and scriptures, missals, and hymnals were translated into indigenous languages. In the late eighteenth century, nationalist movements began to sweep Europe, giving rise to the intensive study of national languages and their folk traditions as embodiments of cultural ethos and identity. Scientific methods for the study of historical and comparative relationships between languages were developed in Europe, and the oral folk traditions of various nations were gathered, most famously perhaps the collection compiled by the eminent German philologists Jakob and Wilhelm Grimm. In North America, interest developed in reconstructing the histories of the languages and cultures of the continent's aboriginal peoples. Native Americans presented an enigma for Europeans seeking to reconcile their existence with the Biblical record, and a common hypothesis was that they represented the lost tribes of Israel. The vast differences between indigenous languages and cultures and their European counterparts made the task of reconstruction difficult, though, and no directly interpretable written records existed.[5]

The study of indigenous language and culture became a popular pastime of early American intellectuals, partly out of curiosity, and partly because of the role indigenous traditions could play in the emergent ideology of the American state.[6] Benjamin Franklin arguably drew from the Iroquoian tradition in conceptualizing the relationship between state and federal authority codified in the U.S. Constitution. While president, Thomas Jefferson designed the linguistic and ethnological research questionnaire that Lewis and Clark used on their expedition to explore the recently acquired territory of the Louisiana Purchase. Jefferson's questionnaire included vocabulary items to be gathered for comparative historical purposes.[7] Many such vocabularies were eventually assembled, and the material and linguistic artifacts of the continent's indigenous peoples were deemed important enough to justify the founding of an institutional base for their archive and systematization, realized in the creation of the Smithsonian Institution in 1846. The early nineteenth century also saw a blossoming European interest in Native American oral traditions, in part for their literary and cultural-historical value, and in part for the insight they allegedly provided into the Native American psyche, which might prove helpful in programs of assimilation.[8]

When the Bureau of American Ethnology (BAE) was founded in 1879, its first director, John Wesley Powell, continued to emphasize linguistic research in the documentation of Native American cultures. In 1891, Powell and his colleagues produced the first complete classification of North American languages, divided initially into 55 independent stocks and later revised to 58.[9] Powell's assessment was limited to the comparison of vocabulary lists because of erroneous but widely held beliefs about the uniformity of grammar in American Indian languages. In 1819 Peter Duponceau had coined the term "polysynthetic" in reference to the elaborate structures of the words in many Native American languages, and in 1838, in an influential essay, he asserted the uniformity of grammar in American Indian languages. Since language structure was held to correlate directly with cultural evolution, and Native American cultures were assumed to be less advanced than their European counterparts, polysynthetic structure was considered somehow representative and indicative of the "primitive" cultures of Native Americans. According to Regna Darnell, this view was so pervasive that structural features of language were largely neglected by students of culture history on the grounds that such structures were determined by psychological rather than historical principles.[10]

In the late nineteenth century, American linguistic and ethnological studies became increasingly professionalized under the guidance of Franz Boas, a German immigrant working at Columbia University. In 1889 Boas published a seminal paper that argued that the variability researchers were recording in the phonetics of Native American languages did not support claims to the languages' evolutionary primitiveness and indeterminateness, but rather reflected the interference of the recorder's own native phonological system.[11] Boas's argument epitomized his belief in cultural relativism, the notion that individual languages and cultures must be studied on their own terms, and that differences should not be projected onto a one-dimensional cline of relative quantitative or qualitative evolution or value. Boas championed the view, in John Fought's terms, that "cultural and linguistic categorization is imposed on experience in ways that differ from language to language and that these different categorizations have claims on the attention of science." [12] The Boasian program entailed careful, detailed linguistic transcription of ethnologically relevant texts. Boas sought too to compile standardized grammatical sketches of the languages that could serve as a basis for their comparison. His interest in cultural diffusion resulted in extensive study of the geographical distribution of features of material and intellectual culture, including myths and other linguistic artifacts.[13]

The philosophy of cultural and linguistic relativism and the need for explicit methodologies to address the vast diversity of linguistic structures in North American languages led to the development of the descriptive methods that underlie twentieth-century linguistics. Boas trained a generation of scholars whose documentary research serves as a historical record of many languages, sometimes the only record there will ever be. Boas standardized the documentation of a language to include a grammar, a dictionary, and a text collection, which is still considered normative. He was responsible for the *Handbook of American Languages,* which contained twenty lengthy grammatical studies of languages representing different families in Powell's genetic classification. Boas trained many outstanding students, including Edward Sapir, Robert Lowie, Paul Radin, Melville Jacobs, Gladys Reichard, Leo Frachtenberg, and A. L. Kroeber, who were prominent in the development of the disciplines of linguistics and anthropology in North America, largely based on their work with Native Americans. In linguistics, Sapir was preeminent. He carried out extensive field research on Wishram, Takelma, Yana, Southern Paiute, Nootka, Sarsi, Hupa, Sutchin, and Navajo. In 1929, he proposed a grouping of North American languages into six super-stocks, which he labeled Eskimo-Aleut, Nadene, Algonkin-Wakashan, Penutian, Hokan-Siouan, and Aztec-Tanoan.[14] Although tentative and sometimes tenuous, Sapir's classification has provided a useful framework for the investigation of genetic relationships. Sapir is also well known for his interest in the relationship between language, culture, and cognition, an issue that continues to be controversial to this day.

Another prominent figure in American linguistics in the first half of this century was Leonard Bloomfield, who worked extensively with Algonquian languages, producing grammars, dictionaries, and text collections. His posthumous grammar of Menomini is still one of the most comprehensive grammars of any Algonquian language.[15] From a comparison of Fox, Menomini, Cree, and Ojibwe, Bloomfield was also able to reconstruct the parent language of the Algonquian language family, Proto-Algonquian, showing the power of the comparative linguistic method to determine to a fine degree of detail the histories of languages even in cases where no written records existed.[16] Bloomfield was also prominent in the founding of the Linguistic Society of America (LSA), which reflected a growing distance between linguistics and anthropology. The success of the structural linguistic methods developed by Bloomfield and his peers became the envy of the social sciences, though the very success of these methods fostered a rift between the study of the internal structures of language and the study of language's relationship to culture and society.

World War II brought another shift in emphasis, away from Native American languages and toward those languages that could aid the war effort. An intensive program to provide language training for military purposes was carried out on fifty-five campuses in the United States, resulting in a substantial increase in the number of linguistics departments nationwide, while at the same time accelerating the separation of linguistics and anthropology, a process that Harry Hoijer described in 1973 as "almost complete." The paradigm shift in linguistics that has taken place since the publication in 1957 of Noam Chomsky's *Syntactic Structures* has deepened the rift between the two disciplines, with unfortunate consequences for the study of Native American languages. I take up this issue below.

The Scope of Contemporary Linguistics: Theory and Description

Contemporary linguistics is a complex and convoluted field, largely because of the explosion of theoretical perspectives that has occurred in the last forty years, and the explicitness and sophistication of methodologies that scholars such as Sapir, Bloomfield, and Chomsky have brought to the discipline as a whole. The core areas of linguistic research have traditionally included phonetics, phonology, morphology, syntax, and semantics. Briefly, phonetics addresses the ways in which human speech sounds are produced and perceived, and the classification of sounds according to their modes of production and perception; phonology deals with the ways in which sounds pattern distinctively within a given language and across languages, and the structure and behavior of larger phonological entities such as syllables, words, and intonational groups; morphology deals with the structure of words and word components, called morphemes; syntax is concerned with principles that govern the structures and function of phrases, clauses, and sentences; semantics addresses the meanings of words, phrases, and sentences, both in terms of their fundamental constituency and representation and in terms of the derivation of the meanings of larger structures from their component constituents. The relative structural and functional autonomy of each of these subcomponents of language has also become a focus of much research and theorizing in recent years.

The study of all aspects of language can be undertaken comparatively as well, whether examining a given language or group of languages at different points in time (the domain of historical and comparative linguistics) or related dialects and languages across geographical or social space (the focuses of dialectology and sociolinguistics, respectively). There is also a diverse assortment of linguistic research and application gathered under the rubric of applied linguistics, including computational approaches to language, language teaching methodologies, and the planning of language and literacy programs at local and national levels.

Many theoretical perspectives exist for each of the subcomponents of linguistics outlined above, most prominently the generative structural paradigm of Noam Chomsky and its many offshoots (e.g., generative semantics, lexical-functional grammar, relational grammar, auto-lexical syntax), but also an assortment of functional, cognitive, and typological approaches.[17] As with any contemporary discipline, theories emerge and undergo significant changes over the brief span of a few years, so that scholars working within a given theoretical tradition may differ in their views on the basis of when they undertook their formative training and research. Generative grammar has been particularly subject to mutation, largely because of the vast amount of productive research and theorization it has inspired.

Generative linguistic theory argues that human linguistic competence must be innate, involving a distinctly *linguistic* cognitive capacity, given the ease with which children acquire language. The goal of generative linguistics, then, is to articulate the nature of this faculty by means of "universal grammar," a set of principles shared by all languages. Where individual languages appear to differ radically from one another, the divergence is held to reflect variable settings of simple, systemic parameters. For example, Ojibwe and English appear quite different in that the grammatical relations of subject and object are determinable in English on the basis of syntactic structure, whereas in Ojibwe they are not. Thus, in English, the subject commonly precedes the verb and the object follows it, and there is a demonstrable syntactic constituent traditionally called the "predicate," consisting of the verb and its object. In Ojibwe, however, the subject, verb, and object can occur in any order with respect to each other, and the syntactic evidence for a predicate constituent is much weaker. This difference between the two languages is addressed in generative grammar with the binary parameter of *configurationality,* which groups languages into two types: one in which subject and object are structurally (configurationally) determined, as in English, and one in which they are not, as in Ojibwe. Many other aspects of the syntactic behavior of a language fall out in predictable ways on the basis of its setting for the configurationality parameter. A related parameter, dubbed the polysynthesis parameter by its proponent, Mark Baker, provides a unitary explanation of such disparate phenomena in Ojibwe as reflexives, reciprocals, mechanisms for distinguishing third persons, and restrictions on person combinations in the rich inflectional structure of Ojibwe transitive verbs.[18] These generalizations would probably go unnoticed without the particular "gaze" of generative theory.

The empirical methodology of generative grammar hinges on a speaker's ability to make qualitative judgments of the grammaticality of test sentences. For example, "It seems to be raining" would be accepted by a speaker of English as grammatical, while "It seems John to be ill" would not. The theory then attempts to provide a motivated account of such judgments by means of its independently motivated principles and parameters, which, when properly characterized, will license all and only those sentences that are grammatical, while ruling out those that are not. Because gramaticality judgments often involve finely graded nuances, they can be made confidently only by native speakers, and most typically, by the native-speaking linguists posing the questions. Consider, for example, the sentences "I wonder who John expected to hurt himself" and "As successful as Mary, I don't think that John will ever be" from Chomsky.[19] Only a native speaker could say with certainty that these sentences are grammatical, and even then not without a little head-scratching. This is not, however, to deny the efficacy of such sentences as data for the explication of English grammar. But because of the need for native speaker intuition and the difficulty of getting reliable grammaticality judgments of such complex constructions from others, most linguists working on Native American languages do not have access to such information, since they are rarely native speakers of the languages they study. When such research is attempted, it commonly involves the methodologically perilous practice of translating batteries of focal English sentences into the language being studied, which can produce unnatural and misleading results.

By contrast, traditional structural grammars of Native American languages were "descriptive," proceeding inductively from the relatively concrete particularities of specific languages, recognizing categories, their constituent members, and broader syntagmatic patterns within each language on the basis of a sifting of a representative corpus of words, sentences, and discourses, supplemented with direct translation of the sort cautioned against above. For example, a descriptive study of English might soon discover the need to distinguish between two classes of verbs on the basis of how past tenses are formed: one class in which a change of vowel occurs, as in "sing/sang" and "write/wrote," and a much larger, more productive class that adds a suffix, as in "cook/cooked" and "help/helped."

Concern with the grammatical particularities of specific languages puts the descriptive approach in distinct contrast to contemporary theoretical approaches, which, as we have seen, seek to discern and account for broad grammatical principles applicable to *all* languages. The two approaches are in theory capable of producing almost complementary results, as suggested by Chomsky in the following passage:

Take a good traditional grammar: it presents those phenomena which have a "human" interest; for example, irregular verbs. Irregular verbs, that's amusing. But traditional grammar does not take interest in what some generative grammarians term the *specified subject condition,* because the phenomena which are excluded by this condition have no "human interest."

For example, the sentence . . . "*John seems to the men to like each other,*" is excluded by the specified subject condition. But I doubt any traditional grammar, even the most comprehensive one, would trouble to note that such sentences must be excluded. And that is quite legitimate, as far as traditional grammars of English are concerned; these grammars appeal to the intelligence of the reader instead of seeking explicitly to characterize this "intelligence." One can suppose that the specified subject condition — or any other principle which excludes this phrase — is simply an aspect of the intelligence of the speaker, an aspect of universal grammar; consequently, it does not require explicit instruction to the person who reads a traditional grammar.

For the linguist, the opposite is true. The linguist is interested in what the traditional grammars don't say; he is interested in the principles — or at least that is what should interest him, in my opinion.[20]

An agenda of the sort that Chomsky argues for presents problems for the study of Native American languages, however, precisely because it is "human interest" that motivates much of the attention given to these languages, whether the goal is to document a dying language, assist in revival efforts, or contribute to maintenance programs. This is not to say that Americanists do not share Chomsky's interest in general linguistic theory, as the work of Kenneth Hale, Jerrold Sadock, Anthony Woodbury, Marianne Mithun, Wallace Chafe, Mark Baker, and many, many others testifies. But comprehensive description is necessarily much more prominent in Americanist linguistic studies than it is in general linguistics, since the Americanist goal so often is to capture as much as possible of a language before it is gone.

Many modern grammars of Native American languages do double duty, serving both as comprehensive descriptions and as applications and examinations of theory. A good example is Keren Rice's monumental grammar of the Athapaskan language Slave, which runs to nearly 1,400 pages and, though couched in particular theoretical assumptions, includes a 500-page "chapter" on the verb that, as one might suppose, is rather rich in descriptive content.[21] The landscape is strewn, however, with descriptively impoverished grammars written in a particular theoretical vein that has become passé, constituting little more than doctoral rites of passage. This is not an issue for a robust language such as English, but in "endangered" languages in need of substantive, concrete documentation, it is indeed regrettable.

The ascendancy of generative grammar in the politics and practice of the academy has resulted in a shift away from the areas of field methods and comprehensive documentary research, chiefly due to the theory's introspective methods and its promotion of the general over the specific. The theory of the *documentation* of a language today is still largely at the same level of sophistication that Boas established nearly a century ago: a grammar, a dictionary, and a collection of texts, with no comprehensive strategies to guide in the research and compilation of these materials. The content of many grammars is now based on whatever theory is in vogue, and dictionaries still typically consist of alphabetically ordered lists with telegraphic English glosses, reminiscent of the word lists that dominated nineteenth-century documentation. Text collections rarely include stylistic and contextual information on the performances, and are still typically cast in the block paragraph form of expository prose, with little attention to their aesthetic structural properties. The evaluative system of the scholarly community encourages short theoretical monographs, rather than comprehensive treatments of languages, which promotes superficiality of treatment and lack of integration.

Sound theories of language must be grounded in a solid knowledge of many languages, which requires accurate, thorough, well-designed descriptive work. At the same time, categories of analysis in documentation invariably rely on the understandings supplied by particular theoretical approaches. There is no atheoretical description of language. Theory provides descriptive bearings and makes hypotheses about the structure and integration of individual components of language. The absence of such bearings can leave important components of a language undocumented. This is evident in the lack of sophistication of the dictionaries and text collections of many Native American languages, mentioned above, mostly because few modern linguists receive *any,* much less *adequate,* training in lexicographic, anthropological, and folkloristic principles, and because such knowledge is often not considered properly "linguistic" from a disciplinary point of view.

The main reason for these problems is that the study of language has become something of a Solomonic child within the disciplines of linguistics and linguistic anthropology, which now have almost complementary perspectives, and students of language typically receive training in one or the other tradition but not both. Yet both perspectives are immensely important to an understanding of what human language is about and, hence, what its documentation entails. For example, linguistic anthropologist Dell Hymes,[22] reacting to Chomsky's aggressively autonomous casting of language as something residing in the head of an idealized individual speaker, proposed that languages must also be studied in terms of their *communicative* functioning, and defined a well-articulated program of research to investigate communicative competence, the ethnography of communication, which has as its goal the delineation of a set of "cross-culturally valid concepts and theories for interpreting and explaining the interaction of language and social life." [23] Theories of language that focus on its computational properties, such as those of Bloomfield and Chomsky, have almost nothing to say about the interaction of language and social life.

In the matter of texts, Hymes has also been instrumental in new approaches to the representation of Native American oral traditional materials, particularly myths and ritual discourse. While such materials have long been recorded, the presentational form has usually consisted of block paragraphs in the manner of European prose, and the motivations for recording them have been their ethnological value, the tokens of vocabulary and syntax they might contain, and their utility in the study of patterns of cultural diffusion. In recent years, though, under the inspiration of Hymes and fellow linguistic anthropologist Dennis Tedlock, traditional oral literature has increasingly been appreciated for its formal aesthetic aspects, especially its prosodic and parallelistic structures, and much ingenuity has been shown in representing these patterns in visually revealing ways. The primary means of doing this exploits the line-based format of European poetry, along with various typographic conventions that highlight the prosodic dynamics.[24] Tedlock especially has focused on prosodics, attending to such features as the interplay of speaking and silence, cadence, and variation in pitch and loudness. Hymes, working only with written transcriptions of languages no longer spoken, discovered recurrent, culturally significant, numerically constrained patterns of repetition at work in the mythic structures of languages such as Tonkawa and Chinook. "Hidden within the margin-to-margin printed lines," he observes, "are poems, waiting to be seen for the first time." [25] "Seeing" is the key here, because the *written* form now takes on a long overdue validity through the power of its intersemiotic, visual representation of the aural, grammatical, and rhetorical patterning of spoken words.

Joel Sherzer and Anthony Woodbury make a key observation regarding the role of linguistics in the study of verbal aesthetic traditions: "Native American verbal art can only be truly appreciated by means of attention to linguistic detail, and at the same time linguistic structures can only be adequately and completely described by paying attention to their function and pattern within verbal art and other natural discourse." [26] Here again we see the power of linguistic methodology as a tool of critical attentiveness.

A Distinctively Americanist Linguistics

Native American studies provides a forum in which the issues of comprehensive documentation discussed above could be productively addressed. Where assistance in language documentation is desired by Native American communities, long-term, comprehensive projects can be undertaken, involving the cooperation of communities and academics of all disciplinary backgrounds, including linguists, anthropologists, folklorists, and historians. The quantity of data accumulated should be massive by contemporary standards for Native American languages, and serious attention should be given to the development of general research instruments to facilitate descriptive thoroughness. There is a profound need for articulated guidelines in documentary method and content. At present linguistic research is guided by precedent within a particular language family's tradition, or by the exigencies of theory, or by a very modest number of taxonomic descriptive models, such as Comrie and Smith's questionnaire.[27] Much more attention should be given to what is involved in the comprehensive documentation of a language's grammar, vocabulary, and discourse.

Central to a documentary project of the sort I am suggesting is an electronic corpus of textual materials drawn from all identifiable spoken and written discourse genres. Such an instrument would provide a framework for documentation, as well as the citation database necessary for a comprehensive, detailed account of a language's grammar. For example, there are very few collections of conversational materials for Native American languages, and yet this is by far the most common form of discourse in any living language. Knowledge of both the primary linguistic structures used in conversation (such as how questions are formed and the linguistic cues for taking turns) and the social structure of conversation (such as the factors governing politeness strategies) is fundamental to knowing a language, yet these areas are neglected in most grammatical descriptions because of a historical tradition that views language too narrowly, in both social and linguistic terms, as canonically expository and declarative.

Existing corpora of European language texts can guide initial conceptualizations, though they too are undoubtedly impoverished by the standards that I am advocating, since they are usually based on written forms of language. One such example is the set of materials constituting the Birmingham corpora, which consists of more than twenty million words and was used for the *Collins Cobuild English Grammar*.[28] Analytical schemata can draw from the categories inductively determined by a rigorous structural parsing of the language, as well as from the categories and insights provided by contemporary theoretical approaches, not limited to any one but seeking to take advantage of all in the interest of thoroughness. In cooperation with local communities, not only linguistic, but social, ethnological, and folklorist categories as well could be considered in gathering and organizing data. This, too, will encourage a comprehensiveness that is now lacking. For example, how is a conversation between a grandparent and grandchild different from that of two teenagers? A parent and a child? What sorts of traditional tales are told, who tells them, when, where, and under what social and ambient circumstances? What linguistic resources are used in aesthetic discourse? Answers would attend to phonological, morphological, lexical, syntactic, and discourse features, and, of course, the interplay of each of these linguistic subsystems. What part of a particular performance of a traditional tale represents the teller's contribution and what part reflects tradition? What stylistic features reflect this particular teller's verbal art? How is a performance contextualized for a particular audience? How does women's speech differ from men's, structurally and socially? What linguistic resources exist for talking about one's emotions, and what is appropriately shared in differing contexts of intimacy? What about the proxemics and kinesics of these various kinds of linguistic interaction?

Finally, serious thought should also be given to the development of annotational instruments that will allow for detailed and comprehensive query of the database, including social, geographic, linguistic, anthropological, and folkloristic indexing.

Theory, Description, and Pedagogy

To this point I have mentioned two fundamental types of grammars, the theoretical and the descriptive. A third type of grammar is the *pedagogical*. Such a grammar ideally organizes the materials of a descriptively rich grammar in ways that facilitate the teaching and learning of a language, including communicative as well as structural linguistic aspects. The design of pedagogical grammars and dictionaries must take explicit account of their intended audiences as well, since materials produced for adults necessarily differ from those intended for children of varying age groups, and materials designed for use in a community where the language is still spoken daily will differ from those designed for people with limited access to natural speaking contexts. To be most effective, pedagogical grammars require input from education specialists, linguists, and the teachers who will be using them.

Linguistic theory and pedagogy are related too in that theoretical linguistic approaches inform theories of language pedagogy. This can be seen quite saliently in the theories of S. D. Krashen, who argued on the basis of certain premises of generative theory that drawing the language learner's conscious attention to linguistic patterns imposed a disruptive and dysfunctional analytic "monitor" between the speaker and speaking. On this basis many programs of language learning shunned conscious attention to linguistic structures, with a direct impact on the structure and content of pedagogical grammars.[29]

The three types of grammar outlined here exist on a rather obvious cline of usefulness to Native American communities seeking resources for the teaching and preservation of their languages. Pedagogical grammars are the most immediately useful, since they directly address the desire to teach the language to children. Ideally, pedagogical grammars could be developed by community language workers using theoretical and even descriptive grammars as bases. This is usually not practical, though, because scholarly grammars rely critically on discipline-specific linguistic terminology that creates a barrier for the uninitiated, whether speakers or scholars. Such works are far more comprehensible to linguists working in other language traditions than to speakers of the target languages who lack linguistic training, or even academics specializing in other disciplines. How to resolve this problem is not at all clear, since linguists must demonstrate academic rigor if their work is to be recognized by the scholarly community. What often seems to happen in the Algonquian languages I work with is that two parallel strands of documentation develop, one professional and the other community or individually rooted, with very little communication between the two. What sharing there is generally comes through short-term university courses in which attempts are made to teach students linguistic terminology to clarify for them the salient structures of their languages, usually with only modest success.

The main problem seems to be that pedagogy is best addressed in terms of concrete functional and communicative categories, but that most popular contemporary linguistic approaches are extremely abstract and structural in their orientation. Unable to make the leap from the structures presented in the classroom to the functions needed in the community, language teachers sometimes resort to adapting primary-level English materials, which are often structurally and culturally at odds with the languages and cultures being taught. But it is important to recognize that professional linguists need to know much more about language function and usage than they presently do if they really wish to be of help to language programs. An unhealthy asymmetry in professional and community interactions often undermines the productivity of the relationship.

Linguists working with Native American languages experience a considerable amount of ambivalence, since the politics of the academy exerts very strong pressure to take a theoretical or theory/descriptive approach, while the community of speakers is most immediately interested in the practical needs of functional pedagogy, and stands to benefit most from just such material. Faced with such conflicts of interest, Americanist linguists try to assist in the development of a variety of materials covering the gamut of community, institutional, and professional needs. As a result, linguistic work in Native American communities is usually based on extensive field contact and long-term relationships between the researchers and the community. Long work with particular languages tends to make Americanists into generalists with regard to their knowledge of linguistics and specialists with regard to the particular language or group of closely related languages they work with. Americanist linguists most commonly make theoretical contributions by subjecting data from their languages of interest to a theory and offering evaluation and revision on that basis. Because the languages they work with are not widely known, their arguments have limited accessibility and their work does not usually enjoy a wide audience. Only those familiar with the particular language and theory at issue can properly appreciate and assess the validity of an analysis. Languages are complex, and theoretical arguments commonly hinge on levels of detail that require extensive systemic knowledge of the object language for their proper evaluation. Yet the need to have "theoretical" credentials exerts vast pressure on professional linguists and their departments and detracts from the time they can commit to more enduring aspects of language work.

Because of their long acquaintance with the languages they study, Americanists can aspire to become fluent speakers. Learning to speak the language that you are ostensibly helping others learn to speak is a great way to gain perspective.

Bloomfield had a useful plan for researching and documenting Native American languages, which Charles Hockett mentions in his introduction to Bloomfield's posthumous Menomini grammar. Bloomfield half-jokingly maintained that linguists should neither marry nor teach, but dedicate their summers to gathering data and the rest of the year to organizing and analyzing it. With such devotion, he speculated, each linguist could adequately cover perhaps three languages in his or her lifetime. Specialists committed to the thorough documentation of even one language over their professional lifetimes could accomplish much, particularly if their program of scholarship included the ongoing training of additional field workers. Michael Krauss eloquently states the vastness of the task before us with the observation that "a hundred linguists working for a hundred years could not get to the bottom of a single language." [30] It would be nice to try, though.

Indigenous Language Programs

While linguists can assist in local and regional language projects, I myself have found too much may be expected of the academic linguist, the assumption being that we are somehow specialists in language teaching methods by virtue of our knowledge of linguistics. Knowledge of a language's structure hardly bestows a mantle of insight into the best ways to teach it, whether the goal is to instruct children or adults. For such purposes, educational programs are needed that provide culturally sensitive foundations, materials, and teaching methods, the kinds of knowledge that, within the academy, can only come through the cooperative work of education sciences with local communities or, through programs of study specifically addressing language teaching.[31] Linguists can advise such enterprises but on the whole lack the knowledge to design and implement them; they may actually impede progress by holding out a false promise of constructively addressing the issue, when, in fact, they cannot.[32]

While recognizing its limitations, linguistic input is nonetheless important to such programs in order to ensure that the curricula are sensitive to the genius of the object languages and cultures, and not based on the structure and vocabulary of some dominant European language, which sometimes happens when linguistic input is lacking. Educators seem to fare no better than linguists when left to their own devices, and native language teachers in communities, lacking training and materials, are often forced to resort to English-based instructional materials and methods that may be neither culturally nor linguistically appropriate. Linguists can provide structured language materials such as topical word lists, dictionaries, grammars, and text collections. They can also assist in the development of practical orthographies and help with local literacy programs and other aspects of language planning. University programs can provide personnel and venues for regional workshops pertaining to language and cultural retention, drawing on the varied expertise provided by broad faculty bases.

On another level, several recent studies by linguists have addressed aspects of acquisition in Native American languages structurally very differently from European languages.[33] Such studies also have a role in the design of language maintenance programs.

The goals and implementation of a retention program will be determined by the local language situation and by the available resources. In the urgent cases of California languages facing imminent extinction, one approach links highly motivated young adults in indigenous communities with fluent elders, and through small grants provides subsistence stipends that allow the apprentice and master to immerse themselves for months at a time without interruption in the targeted languages and cultures.[34] This strategy shows some initial promise, but it is, of course, a desperate measure, since it does not perpetuate speech communities, the lifeblood of any language, but only isolated individual bearers of language traditions.

The situation in much of California can be contrasted with that of British Columbia, where the University of Northern British Columbia is assisting in a very substantial program of language and culture promotion, presently involving the languages Nisga'a, Haisla, Coast Tsimshian, and Carrier. Working with tribal educational institutions, a variety of courses are offered at regional campuses and in local communities with the goal of developing community expertise. The curriculum is designed to offer up to four levels of courses in both language and culture, and at present classes are co-taught either by an academic linguist and a native speaker of the language or by native speakers alone.

The Nature of University Language Courses

Courses in regional Native American language presentation and instruction should be core components of any Native American studies program because of the central relationship between language and culture, the importance of recognition and representation of the languages in multicultural curricula, and the immense inherent interest of the languages themselves. The form these courses take will be determined on the basis of available resources, particularly the availability of university-certified native speakers to serve as instructors, the relative proximity of the university to communities of speakers, and the relative robustness of the languages. Language courses seem logically to fall into two distinguishable types: those that emphasize cultural content and those that focus on linguistic structures. The former tend to be conversational and social-functional in orientation, and contemporary in their scope; the latter, the explicitly linguistic courses, should focus on documentation and methodology, and initially perhaps be historical and philological in orientation, especially in their efforts to "repatriate" [35] the linguistic materials existing for most languages that were gathered in the past. A text-based presentational approach will also clarify the need for ethnological and folkloristic knowledge as components of adequate documentation and exposition, and encourage their development. A common and persistent problem in the study of Native American oral tradition is the myopic view that there is one way to tell a story, one way to interpret it, and one set of conditions under which it is told. This is rarely true.

The need for comprehensive treatments of literature was made particularly clear to me when I had the occasion to teach a course on oral traditional literature to a group of Ojibwe-speaking language specialists from communities throughout Ontario. We used several stories from a collection of texts gathered at the turn of the century by William Jones, a Fox Indian and student of Boas.[36] The texts represented dialects of Ojibwe spoken along the western shores of Lake Superior and points inland. The students presented the full gamut of fluency in their heritage languages, and one spoke no English. They were from widely divergent geographic and cultural contexts, and traditional stories had played very different roles in their lives. One woman recalled listening as a child to similar stories late at night, through cracks in the floor as elders gathered below to preserve their traditions beyond the disapproving gaze of the church. Another insisted on the impossibility of introducing such stories into the curriculum in her community because of endemic factionalism between Christians and traditionalists. Others spoke of having learned these stories from their parents on long boat trips and, more recently, of relating them to their own children under the same circumstances, to edify and to entertain. It is commonly alleged that the Ojibwes tell such stories only in winter, and some adhered to this practice; others stated that telling stories particularly about *frogs* out of season would invite misfortune; another stated that in her communities such stories could only be told after having been heard at least four times over four seasons from the same source; others stated that seasonal restrictions did not exist for them or were no longer in effect. It became clear as we examined these stories that Ojibwe people varied extensively in their interpretations and understandings, and in the confidence with which they expressed these. The need for the cultural and personal contextualization of the stories was acute, even for, and perhaps *especially* for, Ojibwe people.

A multitiered program that includes advanced courses in the study of the oral and written literature of the language in its native forms would seem to be of particular value. Such a program of study would have broad appeal, attracting students from linguistics, literature, composition, Native American studies, anthropology, and folklore. Most importantly, it offers the possibility of training Native American students, who can then apply the skills learned in their studies to the needs of the communities they come from, ultimately carrying research far beyond its present humble state. Storytellers should be invited to the classroom, and their performances recorded whenever acceptable, as a means of archiving language materials, and as resources for both university and community language programs. In all cases, though, every effort must be made to honor the sensibilities and desires of the communities whose languages are being studied. Such programs can only be effectively undertaken in close cooperation with such communities.

Access to Language Materials

There is also a great need for concise, pedagogically sensitive introductions to the languages, with the student of oral literature in mind. As mentioned above, most of the grammars of Native American languages are too technical to be of use to any but a few specialists. Concise, coherent sketches could be developed for some of the regionally prominent Native American languages at least, and perhaps even standardized in their organization to facilitate comparative studies. There should be some way for students to gain an understanding of the grammatical basics of a language without having to commit years of study to the enterprise. Students cannot do this, so they end up encountering Native American texts only in translation. Lucid, well-organized, well-presented guides to the languages would be invaluable. Many institutions teach comparative Native American culture courses, but the lack of accessible handbooks precludes comparable approaches to the languages.

Inaccessibility is not merely due to pedantry. Constraints imposed by publishers often limit the quantity and quality of textual annotation to such a degree that published versions of texts become interpretable only by linguists working on the same or a closely related language. Ideally, texts should be presented in a variety of formats, including at the very least a narrowly annotated interlinear and a rhetorically sensitive display, and serious attention must be given to situating grammatical terminology within a language's systemic contrasts. Anything less severely restricts the usefulness of the text. To understand how this is so, consider the following fragment of an Algonquin (a dialect of Ojibwe) story told by Albert Mowatt of Pikogan, Quebec:

> Amik anicinaabewigoban.
> Gegapiich babaamosegoban.
>
> Beaver was once a human, according to tradition.
> And he was walking around, according to tradition.

Such a presentation is of very limited utility, since anyone lacking knowledge of the language will not be able to read the Algonquin, and anyone able to read the Algonquin will probably not need the translation. While it may be useful for the reader to know that the orthographic representation of the Algonquin meaning "Beaver was once a human, according to tradition" is *Amik anicinaabewigoban,* the reader unfamiliar with the language will not know how to pronounce these words, nor what each word contributes to the meaning. Yet this is the way that an overwhelmingly large percentage of Native American texts are presented in published form. In the most accessible renderings, the source language materials and the English are presented on facing pages. As a result, the reader hews to the English, and only occasionally refers to the source language. The Algonquin text ultimately seems to serve only as proof that the translation is based on a source text, and not a fabrication of the analyst.

Problems such as these are typically addressed by providing an interlinear annotation, such as the following:

Amik	anicinaabewigoban
beaver.NA.PROX	be.human.VAI.IND.PDUB.3.PROX
Gegapiich	babaamosegoban
then	walk.around.VAI.IND.PDUB.3.PROX

Elsewhere, one can usually find a key to the abbreviations used in the interlinear, such as the following:

3	third person animate
IND	independent order
NA	noun, animate independent
PDUB	preterit dubitative mode
PROX	proximate
VAI	verb, animate intransitive

This interlinear too will be of little use to any but a few Algonquianists because the linguistic categories referred to have meaning only within the system of oppositions that they participate in within a given language, and terminology is often idiosyncratic and specific to the scholarly traditions of particular language families. Thus, the gloss for NA, "noun, animate independent" makes sense only when one knows that Algonquin groups nouns into two classes or genders, conventionally called animate and inanimate, the former consisting of those referring to humans, spirits, animals, trees, many plants, and a variety of other objects. Nouns can also be subclassified according to whether or not they obligatorily take a possessor; those that do are designated dependent, and those that do not, independent. The gloss "according to tradition" is based on the presence of inflectional marking for the preterit dubitative mode of the two verbs, but without knowledge of the system of modal contrasts, or even what a mode *is,* the translation remains mysterious. Even linguists have difficulty with such categories because of the variation in usage that exists. The appreciation of Native American literatures in the source languages will never blossom until such fundamental issues of presentation are addressed. With careful, well-thought-out presentation, the grammars of diverse Native American languages could come alive, and become accessible to nonspecialists.

Computer presentation of materials shows promise for overcoming some of these problems, and goes even further in making oral performances accessible in aural and visual forms, by virtue of the computer's capacity to play back digitized sound and video. The teaching of Native American languages and cultures could benefit immensely from treatments such as that of the Perseus Project, an interactive multimedia digital library of classical Greek now under the direction of the Tufts University Classics Department. Perseus integrates Greek literature, linguistics, ethnology, art, history, geography, and archaeology in pedagogically exciting ways. It contains a vast number of texts annotated at the morphological level. How wonderful it would be to have a collection of Ojibwe texts in digital form, with various kinds of linguistic, ethnological, and literary information available at the click of a button on a computer screen. For that matter, Oneida, Lakota, Dogrib, Tsimshian, Yupik—how rich our language programs could be if we had collections of such materials from a variety of languages, in user-friendly formats that allowed students ready access to their grammars and verbal art.

Some Exemplary Programs

Work in Canada shows the power of Native American studies programs with well-provisioned linguistic components involving a team of dedicated specialists, including linguists who are native speakers of the languages being studied. The University of Manitoba's program of research in Cree and Ojibwe represents a striking example of what can be done. H. Christoph Wolfart, a linguist, has worked extensively to document Cree with his former student, Freda Ahenakew, a native speaker of Plains Cree and now on the Manitoba faculty. Facilitated by her fluency in Cree, Ahenakew has interviewed monolingual elders about various aspects of Cree life. These interviews are often conducted in the context of university guest-lectureship programs or extension programs where academic knowledge is taken to regional centers or communities as a means of fostering local language and literacy projects. A fine example of such work is Wolfart and Ahenakew's 1993 book,[37] which contains transcriptions and translations of a series of lectures delivered by the late Sarah Whitecalf, a monolingual Cree elder, at La Ronge, Saskatchewan. As Wolfart and Ahenakew point out in their introduction, these lectures differ from most collections of indigenous texts in that their purpose is not to "tell stories but to explicate Cree practices and beliefs." [38] The lectures are published in both syllabic and Roman Cree transcriptions, the latter provided with facing-page English translations. The syllabic transcription makes the text accessible to Cree readers. Extensive glossaries of both Cree to English and English to Cree correspondences for each word used in the texts are provided as aids to language learners. Such a work provides cultural and linguistic documentation, and honors and includes, in a formal academic setting, the voice of a community-recognized authority on Cree cultural tradition. At the same time, the philological apparatus of multiple transcriptions and glossaries makes the words of the elder accessible to speakers and language learners alike. Such documents can also provide a much-needed textual foundation for research in Cree philosophy and world view.

The Ojibwe program at the University of Manitoba illustrates other aspects of an excellent program. Courses are taught in conversational Ojibwe by native-speaking linguist Patricia Ningewance, who has authored a pedagogical grammar of her native dialect of Lac Seul, Ontario. She works closely as well with linguist John Nichols and others to produce substantive descriptive and pedagogical grammars for use in Manitoba and Ontario Ojibwe communities. Nichols, working with native-speaking linguist Earl Nyholm, has produced a dictionary of Minnesota Ojibwe used widely in language programs throughout Minnesota and Wisconsin.[39] He has edited several collections of texts told by the late Maude Kegg,[40] who was from Mille Lacs, Minnesota, an esteemed elder and a recipient of a National Heritage Fellowship from the National Endowment for the Arts. Kegg's reminiscences as recorded by Nichols cover most of the twentieth century, depicting in quiet terms the struggle of Mille Lacs Ojibwe to maintain their social and cultural autonomy. As with his colleagues' work, Nichols provides Ojibwe transcriptions with facing-page English translations and an extensive glossary to aid language learners and speakers of other dialects. Nichols has also worked to repatriate old texts, including narratives by Angeline Williams, an Ottawa speaker who was from northern Michigan, collected as part of a field methods course taught by Leonard Bloomfield and Charles Voegelin in 1941.[41] Here again, transcription, translation, and an extensive glossary are provided.

Nichols also works in forensic linguistics — that is, the use of linguistic evidence in legal proceedings. In a prominent case in Canada, the government argued that the Temagami Ojibwe Indians of eastern Ontario had no rights to land that the government desired for commercial development, on the grounds that the Temagami had only in relatively recent times moved to their present location from an area farther west, where, the government argued, the Ojibwes had ceded their claims to land in 1830. Nichols conducted a dialectological survey of dozens of communities in the relevant areas and provided unequivocal linguistic evidence that Temagami vocabulary and grammar were entirely congruous with those of other Ojibwe groups in the region of their present location, suggesting long residence in the area.[42] The disaggregating nature of traditional Ojibwe life created vast amounts of dialect variation, resulting in a richly textured fabric of interconnected dialects stretching from Quebec to Alberta. Any given community's language patterns fit quite specifically into the general mosaic, much as a single piece of a puzzle fits into the puzzle as a whole. The Temagami lost the case, though, when the court brazenly declared the expert evidence to be nebulous, and stated that it was inconceivable that King George III would have granted ownership of large tracts of land to the Indians. In another prominent case, however, when the Mille Lacs Band of Ojibwe sued the state of Minnesota to defend their right to hunt and fish off the reservation, Nichols's linguistic testimony was instrumental to their success. Linguistic data can be crucial in land claims disputes, but can only be used if the languages are well documented, the data are recognized as a legal resource by litigants, and the proper institutional bases exist to legitimate the evidence such data provide.

Many other kinds of research and advocacy in Algonquian languages are part of the ongoing language program of the University of Manitoba. Another Algonquianist, David Pentland, edits the annual proceedings of the Algonquian conference; Nichols publishes a quarterly newsletter containing an extensive bibliography of Algonquian and Iroquoian linguistic and language education resources. The university publishes an Algonquian text series, under the direction of its linguistic and Native Studies faculties. This is the kind of institutional base and program approach that is needed for other Native American languages.

Another Algonquian program carrying out noteworthy research is that of Lakehead University in Thunder Bay, Ontario. Lakehead is the home of the Native Language Instructors' Program, which provides training and certification to Native American language teachers throughout Ontario. A staff of native-speaking and nonnative linguists works in the development of a variety of materials documenting regional languages. The most exciting research presently being undertaken is the development of a large electronic corpus of language materials drawn from a broad sample of sources, to be used for practical and research purposes and, perhaps most significantly, as the foundation for a monolingual Oji-Cree (a dialect of Ojibwe) dictionary, the first of its kind in North America. Somewhat surprisingly, few if any linguistic materials have been written in Native American languages. Grammars are written in European languages such as English, so the study of the language can be carried out only within the context of European (usually English) terminology and conceptualizations. English linguistic terminology exerts a de facto hegemony, and linguistic scholarship for Native Americans thus becomes a matter of mastering an esoteric variety of English.

Whether we want it to be or not, the voice of linguistics is a monologic voice of academic English dominance, in the Bakhtinian sense, constraining the possibilities of Native American linguistic discourse by means of active domination.[43] This is a vexing problem. Most dictionaries of Indian languages are not really dictionaries in important senses, either, but bilingual glossaries, and provide neither definitions nor relationships between meanings, but only rough English correspondences to indigenous vocabulary. These documents, too, for all their value, impose external conceptualizations on the object languages, since the indigenous semantics are usually organized around the English translations, at least in Algonquian languages, and probably in most polysynthetic languages.[44] A properly constituted monolingual dictionary will provide definitions of culturally salient terms from within the language and culture, and if based on naturally occurring usage, will exemplify concepts in culturally appropriate ways. Native language metalanguage developed to provide the dictionary infrastructure can be applied to other areas of grammar, thus initiating a program of true indigenous-language linguistics.

Programs such as those of the University of Manitoba and Lakehead University are blessed with situations in which the languages being studied still have large numbers of fluent speakers of all ages, many of whom hold university degrees in relevant specialties. Many places lack such resources, and the approaches exemplified by these programs cannot be implemented on such a scale. Still, with ingenuity, many of the methods they use can be applied in most situations: careful linguistic documentation and publication of language materials; the cooperation of university and Native American communities; and the development of electronic text corpora as a basis for linguistic and cultural research.

Conclusion

Dell Hymes has assailed the current state of linguistic documentation of Native American languages:

> The bibliographies of the languages grow, but there is hardly to be found anywhere a comprehensive, cogent presentation of what is known about a language, so that what is known can be used by anthropologists, folklorists, even just other linguists. There are no handbooks that interpret, reconcile, codify the various orthographies, vocabularies, grammatical discussions that make what is collectively known a means to further knowledge.[45]

Despite our best efforts, there are no such presentations, to my knowledge, of *any* aspect of research on Algonquian languages, whether linguistic, anthropological, or folkloristic. There are also no comprehensive accessible reference grammars of any Algonquian languages, though these languages have been the objects of critical attention since the earliest periods of the European colonization of North America. The most complete coverage of any dialect of Ojibwe is arguably still Bishop Frederick Baraga's grammar published in 1850 and now long out of print, and fraught with a characteristic nineteenth-century chauvinism that is disturbing to Ojibwe readers seeking guideposts to the study of their language. Yet these ancient missionary works are being replaced by useful contemporary treatments at too slow a pace, evidently because the comprehensiveness required in such endeavors does not fit well with academic schedules of productivity. How else do we explain their absence, given our deep desire that they exist?

As suggested already, linguistics within a Native American studies program, properly conceived, offers a way to address some of these problems. Productive programs will be carried out in cooperation with local communities. Ideally, the university can train local students, perhaps from the communities where indigenous languages are still spoken, in linguistic methodologies that they can then use in their communities to document the languages. One of the challenges in documenting Native American languages has been the vast amount of local variation. Local training could alleviate the burden, ideally providing researchers whose interests and sensibilities would be in complete harmony with those of the local community. Linguists associated with such programs can function as guides to theory and method, collocate data, and propose research topics. Such an undertaking will require a well-designed language program, stressing the diverse knowledge and methods necessary for comprehensive documentation, including field and theoretical linguistics, ethnography, and folklore.[46] Training must emphasize the accurate transcription of naturally occurring language, sound analytic and collection methods, rich ethnological annotation, and a careful accounting of all aspects of language use. Such an approach to textual documentation is illustrated by a recent compilation of Lushootseed texts by Crisca Bierwert, a linguistic anthropologist, which was produced in collaboration with several linguists, an Upper Skagit elder, and an ethnomusicologist.[47] I am reminded too of Julie Cruikshank's collaborative work with three Yukon elders, in which personal narratives alternate with traditional stories and together constitute the "life histories," or autobiographies, of the three women.[48] Here a collaboration of a different order—between the interviewer and interviewees—shaped the research itself and its final product.

Many of the narratives in Cruikshank's collaborative work were told in English, which provides an opportunity to make another point about the nature of Native American languages—namely, that the varieties of English that have arisen in Native American communities through processes of language shift are worthy of serious attention and appreciation in their own right, and should not be construed merely as sources of disadvantage, as spoken varieties of English so often are in American popular opinion. Dell Hymes points out in an essay entitled "Report from an Underdeveloped Country" that two kinds of freedom are at stake in American attitudes toward linguistic variety, one positive and the other negative.[49] Negatively, no speaker of any variety of English should be denied opportunity on the basis of language; positively, speakers must have the freedom to find satisfaction and means of imaginative expression in their own forms of language. William Leap's study of American Indian English suggests that there exist distinct varieties of English for each of the tribal languages that formed a substratum as speakers of these languages began to speak English, each in its way a creative adaptation.[50] Furthermore, many writers and poets of Native American descent, such as Ray Young Bear, Roberta Hill, N. Scott Momaday, Gerald Vizenor, and Louise Erdrich, have chosen to express themselves in the medium of English.

The development of electronic textual corpora will allow for better archiving, better research, better analysis, and better presentation of linguistic and cultural materials. We cannot know what is missing until we have a decent idea of what there is. A solid program of regional research could produce materials of value to community language programs, if not directly, then in organized databases of linguistic information, made available to communities in electronic form allowing query and retrieval for pedagogical applications.

Linguistics and anthropology grew up in the United States by means of rigorous search for inductive methodologies that could account for the structures and histories of the "exotic" languages and cultures of the continent. Documentation has always been primary, and field methods have been a central concern. One way that Americanist linguistics can make a significant contribution to the understanding of human language is to seriously address the nature of documentation and description, asking what is involved in a comprehensive account of a human being's knowledge of a *particular* language, and developing tools to begin to investigate such questions.

The tools that linguistics offers can benefit anthropologists, folklorists, literary analysts, historians, legal scholars, and others, and these disciplines, in turn, can benefit linguistic scholarship. Properly constituted, Native American studies programs present a structure and an agenda in which such interdisciplinary work has some hope of actually being realized, because, ideally, such programs address particular languages from a comprehensive viewpoint, culturally and linguistically, theoretically and pedagogically. Every program should insist on such collaboration and carefully consider ways in which it can be fostered within broader program goals and structure.

Notes

The perspective I bring to this volume is that of an Algonquian linguist with many years of work in Ojibwe and Cree language programs. I would like to thank Victor Golla for valuable discussion on many aspects of this chapter, though I have no doubt that he will recognize hardly anything in the form it has taken here. Thanks, too, to Dell Hymes for copious, very useful notes on an earlier draft. All flaws of fact and presentation, of course, remain the responsibility of the author. Mea culpa, mea maxima culpa.

1. Michael Krauss, "Studies of Native American language endangerment," in *Stabilizing Indian Languages,* Gina Cantoni, ed. (Flagstaff: Northern Arizona Press, 1996), 16–21.

2. Cantoni, *Stabilizing Indian Languages,* is a fine collection of articles on endangered languages, representing a wide variety of perspectives. See also Heather Blair, "Do not go gentle into that good night: Rage, rage against the dying of the light," *Anthropology and Education Quarterly,* 26 (1995), 1–23; James Crawford, "Endangered Native American languages: What is to be done, and why?" *Bilingual Research Journal,* 19 (1995), 17–38; Kate Freeman, "Ojibwe, Mohawk, and Inuktitut alive and well? Issues of identity, ownership and change," *Bilingual Research Journal,* 19 (1995), 39–70; Kenneth Hale, "Language endangerment and the human value of linguistic diversity," *Language,* 68 (1992), 35–42.

3. Francis Paul Prucha, *The Great Father: The United States Government and the American Indians* (Lincoln: University of Nebraska Press, 1984), provides a useful account of the philosophies and practices of off-reservation schools.

4. Leonard Bloomfield, *Eastern Ojibwa: Grammatical Sketch, Texts, and Word List* (Ann Arbor: University of Michigan Press, 1958), 186. I have transliterated Bloomfield's transcription into contemporary Ojibwe orthography.

5. Conventionalized ideographic systems exist in many cultural traditions, but these are not directly useful to linguistic reconstruction.

6. These notes owe a great debt to Harry Hoijer, "History of American Indian linguistics," in *Linguistics in North America,* Current Trends in Linguistics, vol. 10, Thomas A. Sebeok, ed. (The Hague: Mouton, 1973), 657–76, and Regna Darnell, "American linguistics: Anthropological origins," in *Encyclopedia of Language and Linguistics,* R. E. Asher, ed. (New York: Pergamon, 1994), 93–97; see also Regna Darnell,

19. Noam Chomsky, *The Minimalist Program* (Cambridge: MIT Press, 1995), 36, 47.

20. Noam Chomsky, *Language and Responsibility,* translated from the French by John Viertel (New York: Pantheon, 1979), 60–61.

21. Keren Rice, *A Grammar of Slave* (New York: Mouton de Gruyter, 1989).

22. My discussion of linguistics and linguistic anthropology might seem to suggest that those who study language can be neatly classified into complementary sets, one consisting of "linguists" and the other, "anthropologists." This would be extremely misleading, since many socially oriented scholars consider themselves to be "linguists," and would object that the generative approach is reductionist, narrow, and fundamentally flawed in its failure to take into account the social nature of language. They might also strenuously object to my appearing to represent the interests of "autonomous" linguistics as "core" linguistics. My apologies to any who feel slighted by my usage, which is strictly for expository convenience. I hope it is clear from my exposition that I deeply value all perspectives that provide insight into human language, and feel that current "linguistic" training fails to give remotely enough prominence to the social.

23. G. Philipsen, "Ethnology of speaking," in Asher, *Encyclopedia,* 1156.

24. See Dell Hymes, *"In vain I tried to tell you"*: *Essays in Native American Ethnopoetics,* Studies in Native American Literature, vol. 1 (Philadelphia: University of Pennsylvania Press, 1981); Dennis Tedlock, *The Spoken Word and the Work of Interpretation* (Philadelphia: University of Pennsylvania Press, 1983); Joel Sherzer and Anthony C. Woodbury, eds., *Native American Discourse: Poetics and Rhetoric* (New York and Cambridge: Cambridge University Press, 1987).

25. Dell Hymes, "Tonkawa poetics: John Rush Buffalo's 'coyote and eagle's daughter,' " in Sherzer and Woodbury, *Native American Discourse,* 19.

26. Sherzer and Woodbury, *Native American Discourse,* 2.

27. Bernard Comrie and Norval Smith, "Lingua descriptive studies questionnaire," *Lingua,* 42 (1976), 7–72.

28. *Collins Cobuild English Grammar* (London: Collins, 1990). This grammar is a fascinating piece of inductive scholarship, illustrating well many of the issues I discuss in this chapter, such as the relationship of theory to description and the nature of comprehensive grammatical description. I am thankful to John Nichols for alerting me to its value as a model for practical reference grammars.

29. See, for example, S. D. Krashen, "The monitor model of second-language acquisition," in *Second Language Acquisition and Foreign Language Teaching,* R. Gringras, ed. (Washington, D.C.: Center for Applied Linguistics, 1978).

30. Krauss, "Studies," 16.

31. A useful source for general discussion of the relationship of education, linguistics, and anthropology is Dell Hymes, *Ethnography, Linguistics, Narrative Inequality: Toward an Understanding of Voice* (Bristol, Pa.: Taylore and Francis, 1996), which gathers together Hymes's various publications on the subject.

32. On a broader level, of course, the efficacy of language acquisition in classroom settings needs to be addressed as well.

33. See, for example, Marianne Mithun, "The acquisition of polysynthesis," *Journal of Child Language,* 16 (1989), 285–312; Clifton Pye, "The acquisition of ergative

languages," *Linguistics,* 28 (1990), 1291–330; Lourdes de Leon, "Exploration in the acquisition of geocentric location by Tzotzil children," *Linguistics,* 32 (1994), 857–84.

34.   See Leanne Hinton, *Flutes of Fire: Essays on California Indian Languages* (Berkeley: Heyday Books, 1994), 234–47, for documentation of this program.

35.   See Dell Hymes, "Custer and linguistic anthropology," *Journal of Linguistic Anthropology,* 1 (1991), 5–11.

36.   See *Ojibwe Texts,* 2 vols., William Jones, comp., Truman Michelson, ed. (New York: G. E. Stechert, 1917–19).

37.   H. C. Wolfart and Freda Ahenakew, eds., *kinehiyawiwininaw nehiyawewin: The Cree Language Is Our Identity—The La Ronge Lectures of Sarah Whitecalf,* trans. and with a glossary by H. C. Wolfart and Freda Ahenakew (Winnipeg: University of Manitoba Press, 1993).

38.   Ibid., ix.

39.   John D. Nichols and Earl Nyholm, *A Concise Dictionary of Minnesota Ojibwe* (Minneapolis: University of Minnesota Press, 1995).

40.   Maude Kegg, *Portage Lake: Memories of an Ojibwe Childhood* (Edmonton: University of Alberta Press, 1991).

41.   Leonard Bloomfield, ed., *The Dog's Children: Anishinaabe Texts Told by Angeline Williams,* newly edited, with a glossary by John Nichols (Winnipeg: University of Manitoba Press, 1991).

42.   The case is summarized in J. K. Chambers, "Forensic dialectology and the Bear Island land claim," *Annals of the New York Academy of Sciences,* 606 (1990), 19–31.

43.   See Mikhail M. Bakhtin, *The Dialogic Imagination* (Austin: University of Texas Press, 1980 [1935]), cited in Jane Hill, "The grammar of consciousness and the consciousness of grammar," in *The Matrix of Language: Contemporary Linguistic Anthropology,* Donald Brenneis and Ronald Macaulay, eds. (Boulder: Westview Press, 1996), 307–23, which is an excellent account of linguistic, political, and economic relationships between Mexicano (Aztec) and Spanish in central Mexico.

44.   In Algonquian languages, this is an unfortunate consequence of their polysynthetic nature, and the analytic nature of English. So, for example, if one wants to determine whether lexical means exist in Ojibwe to express the concept equivalent to English "hand," there is no way to determine this within a "flat" Ojibwe–English listing in the dictionary, since the morphemes realizing this concept will occur at different locations within the word, and thus not fall into any sequential alignment on the basis of the alphabetization of dictionary entries. Looking at the English–Ojibwe listing, however, draws one much nearer to the desired information, since the Ojibwe words containing the concept in their definitions will be listed adjacently on the basis of their sharing of the English lexeme "hand" in their definitions. This is not a minor matter, because bilingual children using the dictionary are much more likely to look words up using the English side of the dictionary, which not only hampers the learning of the indigenous language, but suggests that English is primary and the indigenous language secondary. Topical organization of the Algonquian listing can go a long way to alleviate this problem. Thanks to John Nichols and John O'Meara for much discussion of these aspects of Algonquian lexicography.

45.   Hymes, "Tonkawa poetics," 17–18.

46.   While I do not discuss folklore at any length in this chapter, I have benefited

particularly from Stith Thompson, "The Star-Husband tale," *Studia Septentrionalia,* 4 (1953), 93–163, reprinted in Alan Dundes, *The Study of Folklore* (Englewood Cliffs, N.J.: Prentice-Hall, 1965), 414–74, in *Tales of the North American Indians,* selected and annotated by Stith Thompson (Bloomington: Indiana University Press, 1966 [1929]), and in *The Folktale* (Berkeley: University of California Press, 1977 [1946]); Alan Dundes, *The Morphology of North American Indian Folktales* (Helsinki: Suomalainen Tiedeakatemia [distributed by Akateeminen Kirjakauppa], 1964); Dundes, *Study of Folklore;* Alan Dundes, "North American Indian folklore studies," *Societe des Americanistes,* 56 (1967), 53–79; Richard Bauman, *Verbal Art as Performance* (Prospect Heights, Ill.: Waveland Press, 1977); Richard Bauman, *Story, Performance, and Event: Contextual Studies of Oral Narrative* (Cambridge: Cambridge University Press, 1986); and Richard Bauman, ed., *Folklore, Cultural Performances, and Popular Entertainments: A Communications Centered Handbook* (New York: Oxford University Press, 1992); see also Richard Bauman and Charles Briggs, "Poetics and performance as critical perspectives on language and social life," *Annual Review of Anthropology,* 19 (1990), 59–88.

47. Crisca Bierwert, ed., *Lushootseed Texts: An Introduction to Puget Salish Narrative Aesthetics* (Lincoln: University of Nebraska Press, 1996).

48. Julie Cruikshank, in collaboration with Angela Sidney, Kitty Smith, and Annie Ned, *Life Lived Like a Story* (Lincoln: University of Nebraska Press, 1990).

49. In Hymes, *Ethnography.*

50. See William Leap, "American Indian English and its implications for bilingual education," in *Georgetown University Round Table on Language and Linguistics 1978: International Dimensions of Bilingual Education,* James E. Alatis, ed. (Washington, D.C.: Georgetown University Press, 1978), 657–69.

Melissa L. Meyer and Kerwin Lee Klein

Native American Studies and the End of Ethnohistory

The study of Native Americans has long been a meeting place for historians and anthropologists. Scholars here affiliate across departmental fences more than in any other subfield of either discipline. They often have a Ph.D. in one profession but substantive training in the other. Two primary organizational networks help to maintain this intellectual commons: the American Society for Ethnohistory with its annual conference and journal, and the D'Arcy McNickle Center for the History of the American Indian at the Newberry Library in Chicago, which has held workshops and conferences and granted fellowships to academic and public scholars alike. Increasingly, the Western History Association annual conference offers common ground. In Native American studies, historians and anthropologists still argue about what "ethnohistory" is, but in general they share a common professional territory even as they attend the "mainstream" conferences in their respective disciplines. That sort of institutionalized collaboration, though, is a recent phenomenon.

Indeed, the convergence of history and anthropology has more than its share of ironies. More than a century and a half ago, when Georg W. F. Hegel delivered his *Lectures on the Philosophy of World History,* he told his students that the indigenous peoples of Africa and America (who lacked nation-states and writing) were people without history, and thus doomed to disappear beneath the rising historical tide of the west.[1] Few of us today share that belief, but the antinomy of people with and without history, an idea much older than Hegel, has left its institutional imprint. In fact, history and anthropology have served as its departmental manifestation, and so their postcolonial convergence deserves some critical attention. In this chapter we sketch a map of the historical relations of history and anthropology, note some current dominant trends in the literature, and suggest some directions for future research. Ultimately, we argue that if history and anthropology have reconciled, then we have surely reached the end of ethnohistory.

The *Rapprochement* of History and Anthropology

History and anthropology have an old and ambivalent relationship. Painting in the broadest of narrative strokes, we might render it as follows. In the mid-nineteenth century, history and anthropology were interwoven. In the early twentieth century, they separated as topics, methods, and disciplines. By mid-century, the two words were virtual antonyms. Today, conflicted narratives of reconciliation dominate our debates.

In the mid-nineteenth century, history and anthropology were fused in the great works of writers like Marx and Engels, Lewis Henry Morgan, and Edward Tylor. Anthropology employed evolutionary rhetoric, and history debated humanity's social origins. Native cultures were viewed as primitive and as representative of the early stages through which all human groups necessarily passed on a unilinear path to the pinnacle of civilization epitomized by western Europe.[2] Before the professionalization of the disciplines, an author like Francis Parkman, although known primarily as a historian, could engage in what would become "participant-observation." Today we remember Parkman for his classist and racialized noble savagism, but his great histories, like *The Conspiracy of Pontiac,* show a certain sensitivity for source criticism and a sense of Native Americans as important historical agents, although tragically doomed or villainous ones.[3] In later decades, few historians showed any interest at all in Native America. Disciplinization effectively separated history and anthropology by method: historians studied people who had left written records, and anthropologists studied people who had not. Since those divisions were imagined primarily along racial lines, they reinscribed the old antinomy of people with and without history.[4]

In the early twentieth century, following the different methodological paths represented by Boasians and functionalists, anthropology turned away from history. This was inspired by at least two impulses. One was scientistic, and the other was political.

Modernist anthropology suspected that social evolutionism and its comparative genetic methods were so much priestcraft. The "stages of man" emplotments of Victorian convention looked brutally old-fashioned in a modernist social science. And since many anthropologists believed that social science should produce generalizations that would apply to all cultures in all times and places, or at least to as many as possible, the end of social evolutionism seemed to be the end of history. Take away social evolution's generalizing, and history collapsed into mindless fact-gathering. As functionalists saw it, Boasians made exactly that mistake in their studies of the diffusion of culture traits. In 1933 Bronislaw Malinowski pejoratively described Boasians as "historicist," by which he meant antiquarian.[5] Even today, we sometimes speak of Boasians as "historicists," but that is a remarkably loose usage. Like the functionalists, Boasians generally wrote in a timeless "ethnographic present" that effectively placed American Indians in an eternal pre-Columbian stasis. And functionalist and Boasian revolts against social evolution turned anthropology away from history and toward "science."[6]

The revolt against Victorian historicisms had another, more nearly political component. Many anthropologists carried into the field a sense that studying other cultures was a means for criticizing one's own. Deeper dissatisfactions with the course of modernity—the class conflict of capitalism, the scale of global war, the social costs of rationalization—led many thinkers to imagine "their" tribes as victims of history. If history really was the sweep of the west across the rest of the globe, so much the more reason for suspicion. If anthropology's turn away from Victorian historicism and toward ethnographic presentism represented a quest for scientific rigor, it could also represent a political critique of the course of history. Indeed, many ethnographers acted as if anti-imperialist politics demanded antihistorical discourse.[7]

At mid-century, when two of the more historically minded American anthropologists, Leslie White and Alfred Kroeber, clashed over the legacy and practice of historicism, they could agree that most of their colleagues displayed little intelligent interest in historical issues. In departments of anthropology, history stood for outmoded metaphysics, or the unhappy course of European imperialism, or for the most plodding chronologies of data. Science and history served most ethnographers as antonyms. "The callower our graduate students," lamented Kroeber, "the more interested they are in getting their ethnography 'scientific.'"[8] He was thinking primarily of the various dominant forms of functionalism, but American anthropology was ready to import even more aggressive mixtures of political and scientistic antihistory. In his classic 1962 work, *The Savage Mind,* Claude Lévi-Strauss declared that "history may lead to anything, provided you get out of it," and high structuralism had found its manifesto.[9] For both methodological and political reasons, it was *good* to be without history.

In one of those ironic narrative twists that would have delighted a Francis Parkman, technical problems of political economy actually helped to reintroduce history to anthropology. In the 1930s, the Social Science Research Council had encouraged the study of "acculturation" to facilitate the social engineering of the New Deal. If white America was going to incorporate American Indians into the welfare state, then it had better understand the mechanisms of cultural mixing.[10] Acculturation studies proliferated after the late 1930s, and the formation of the Indian Claims Commission (ICC) in 1946 focused scholarly interest. The ICC evaluated treaty claims made by various tribes against local, state, and federal governments. Adjudicating those claims required the sort of legal documentation that had traditionally been the province of historians. The American Society for the Study of Ethnohistory emerged in large part as a response to the perceived need to train anthropologists in the use of archival data for research related to claims cases.[11]

"Ethnohistory" joined the traditional participant-observation methods of ethnographic fieldwork with the conventional archival research of the historian. In theory, ethnohistory took in historians like Robert Berkhofer and Wilbur Jacobs[12] as well as anthropologists, but, in practice, most ethnohistorians were trained as ethnographers and got their paychecks from departments of anthropology. "Ethnohistorical method" effectively referred to anthropologists writing narrative analyses based on written primary documents. But in the late sixties and early seventies, many history graduate students invested in dissertations on American Indian topics, and scholars heralded the rise of the "New Indian History."[13] The political activism of students, scholars, and local communities led to the establishment of Native American studies programs in many major universities. By 1980, the study of Native Americans was a growth field in many departments of history. Today, historians frequently imagine that growth as an outcome of sixties activism, but it also owes much to two earlier and very different inspirations: the often paternalistic social engineering of the New Deal order, and the actions of Native Americans, who, in pressing their legal claims, forced federal and academic bureaucracies to recognize Native American history.

We can imagine the *rapprochement* of history and anthropology as a series of overlapping phases. The first, social evolutionism, peaked in the nineteenth century, but it never entirely disappeared, and in the early 1960s cultural materialism drew inspiration from evolutionist traditions. The second, acculturation studies, peaked in the late 1940s as anthropologists attempted to adapt functionalism's ahistorical vocabularies for historical accounts of culture change. The third phase, ethnohistory, grew out of acculturation studies, but it quickly created its own institutional niche, occupied primarily by ethnographers willing to brave the archival wilderness. We might imagine the fourth phase, the "New Indian History," as beginning when departments of history adopted ethnohistory as a recognized subfield.

The various syntheses of disciplinary allegiances and languages have had mixed results. On the one hand, they have created bodies of often classic literature that render historical analyses of Native American pasts. And before the recent explosion of multicultural enthusiasm, ethnohistory was one of the few scholarly enterprises that engaged in sympathetic explorations of interethnic relations. These interdiscplinary scholars refined their cross-cultural relativism well before the celebrated discovery of "postmodernism." On the other hand, acculturation studies, ethnohistory, and New Indian History have all shown their limitations as well. The tradition of imagining Native Americans as people without history, combined with the typically antihistorical language of the twentieth-century ethnographies upon which modern ethnohistories must rely, has often produced monographs broken into racialized narrative halves: a precontact "ethnographic" half that fixes aborigines in timeless social stasis and a postcontact "historical" half in which Europeans wreak imperial mayhem.

The ongoing conversations between history and anthropology have opened some promising scholarly avenues, however, and we might speak of a fifth phase of convergence, which, following James Clifford, we might call "ethnographic history." [14] The label scarcely denotes a coherent school, and it is distinguished from the ethnohistorical syntheses of previous decades more by quantitative than by qualitative differences. The main event has been the widespread adoption of historical discourse by anthropologists and the appropriation of ethnographic language and methods by historians who have no institutional loyalties to ethnohistory. Even more remarkable is that the shift sweeps far past the topics of Native American studies to encompass a virtually limitless range of regions and periods. Although we cannot even begin to list topics and titles in the new ethnographic history, we will quickly sketch four of the more suggestive trends.

One is the history of *encounters,* a word that has been much used in recent years, partly because of the immense investments in the Columbian quincentenary. Such histories have given us a widening circle of literature that foregrounds interethnic events and settings. The works of Marshall Sahlins, in particular, have attracted no end of interest. Ethnohistory has been a subfield for years in departments of anthropology, but when one of the most famous ethnographers of the Pacific turned historical, it attracted much attention. *Historical Metaphors and Mythical Realities* and *Islands of History* deployed primary documents, ethnographic upstreaming, and Hawaiian oral literature in a series of provocative essays on European, Hawaiian, and Maori interactions. Sahlins argued that Captain Cook's visit to the islands had created a situation in which native theology, Cook's itinerary, and European behavior fell catastrophically in and out of alignment. Cook unwittingly reenacted the ritualized Hawaiian account of Lono, the dying God. The comic overlap of narrative horizons—the resemblance of Cook's actions to native narrative expectations for Lono, together with the Europeans' expectations that savages might see them as deities—turned tragic (or farcical) when Cook deviated from the ritual calendar, landed in the "wrong" time and place, and was killed in keeping with the native history in which Lono died and elites consumed his flesh in anticipation of his cyclical resurrection and return.[15]

Sahlins's account of the "Apotheosis of Cook" provoked a loud dissent from Gananath Obeyesekere, who took exception to what he termed in his subtitle *European Mythmaking in the Pacific.* Obeyesekere undertook his own readings of the documents, waded through the ethnographies, consulted with members of the local community, and reached a different conclusion. Sahlins had unselfconsciously reproduced the old European expectation of lost kingdoms awaiting the upwardly mobile white professional. The Hawaiians had immediately divined the clay feet of the English, and the death of Cook had little to do with mistaken identity. Clifford Geertz has recently reviewed the Sahlins–Obeyesekere debate, neatly summarized its politics, and concluded that Sahlins was more persuasive. But Geertz suggested that judgments of the dispute would ultimately turn more on aesthetics than evidence.[16]

We might draw somewhat different morals and say that the exchange has been productive for reasons beyond its sheer dialectical quality. Both Sahlins and Obeyesekere interweave oral and written literature, cultural history and biography, political events and social structure in fascinating ways that would have been unimaginable fifty years ago. History does not appear as the rickety staircase of social evolution, as brute chronology, or as the province of a specific racial group. Both scholars imagine Hawaiian historicities, compare and contrast them with European historicity, and differentiate each by politics and class. If their debate has a weakness, it is that neither scholar is as attentive to gender issues as we might wish. Here, Jocelyn Linnekin's *Sacred Queens and Women of Consequence* may help us with its suggestion that the actions of native Hawaiian women, many of whom aligned themselves with Cook's sailors, had special significance for the patriarchal politics of Hawaiian kingship.[17] Whomever we privilege in this dispute, it is pleasing to note that it represents only a fraction of a widening circle of literature exploring interethnic encounters that revise our understandings of historicity.

Having cheered the blurring of the frontiers between history and anthropology, we should point out a second development—namely, a concerted effort to redraw the boundary in more self-conscious ways and create deliberately *mythographic* scholarship. The Lévi-Straussian celebration of people without history still has academic advocates. Among them is Calvin Martin, who had argued, in *The American Indian and the Problem of History* and *In the Spirit of the Earth,* that American Indians (excepting literate, statist peoples like the Nahua and Maya) were and are people of "nature" rather than "history." Invoking modernist antihistoricists from W. B. Yeats to Hayden White, Martin urges us to forsake the colonialist habit of thinking historically about Native Americans and cultivate mythopoesis.[18] Although the Kiowa literary scholar

N. Scott Momaday has expressed some enthusiasm for Martin's thesis, most readers have been more skeptical. Critics have argued that Martin is reproducing pseudo-functionalist conceptions of culture and that such works reify unhappy forms of noble savagism.[19] Whatever one's evaluation of Martin's theses, the exchange encourages a more critical discussion of the return of history. What does it mean to think historically? What does it mean to be in history? We ought not simply to suspend such questions in a flurry of footnotes.

Where anthropologists once used "culture" to destabilize the verities of history and denounce historicism as the prototypical colonial venture, recent literature has employed "history" to undermine the pseudo-positivist sciences of culture and describe anthropology as the imperial discipline *par excellence*. Thinkers as different as Vine Deloria, Jr., and Edward Said have called for the end of anthropology, and people talk about *ethnographic criticism* as if it were a well-defined subfield.[20] Among the many influential works here, the books of James Clifford, particularly *The Predicament of Culture* and his edited anthology *Writing Culture* have won both criticism and acclaim. *The Predicament of Culture* places the history of ethnography and theories of cultural production in global contexts. For Native American studies, the crux of the book lies in its account of the unsuccessful bid of the Mashpee Indians for legal recognition as a tribe. Clifford expertly interweaves trial testimony with analyses of the languages of "culture." The essay shows how theoretical investments structure legal practice, and Clifford argues that the Mashpee suffered from the law's reliance on modern western notions of historical identity that preclude the sort of social improvisation that has characterized Mashpee lives. Ultimately, the state's historicity (linear chronologies anchored by written documents) defeated the Mashpees' historicity (complex genealogies encoded in oral tradition and local practices).[21]

The debates over ethnographic criticism have frequently turned on the politics of "postmodernism," although the exchanges are so conflicted that it would be hazardous to abstract from them a shared definition of that term. Critics sometimes worry that ethnographic criticism undermines the ability of social scientists to sort out "true" stories from "false," or that it promotes a sophomoric skepticism at the very historical moment in which feminist and Third World voices begin to challenge the epistemic authority of the white male academy.[22] For our purposes, we can bracket those arguments and observe that ethnographic criticism in general, and *The Predicament of Culture* in particular, offer several important developments for Native American studies. First, *The Predicament of Culture* shows the value of situating Native American studies within global contexts. And, second, the essay on the Mashpee trial, regardless of one's theoretical reservations, is a virtuoso performance that pulls the voices of native "informants," its author, and contending scholars into a shared conversation. Even the harshest critics of Clifford's theoretical interventions could benefit from careful attention to his mastery of the mechanics of such prosaic aspects of scholarship.

Thus far we have singled out well-publicized texts and topics, but we will end with a development that has not received the attention it deserves from historians and even some cultural anthropologists. In the last thirty years, scholarship in Native American oral literature has effected a quiet revolution in *source criticism*. The development of source criticism—the location, evaluation, and interpretation of historical sources—had been the defining moment in the making of historical method in the early nineteenth century. Victorian source criticism had taken in monuments and archeological artifacts and also written documents. But source criticism was routinized and narrowed as twentieth-century historians focused increasingly upon written documentary sources. Now, innovations in the collection, encoding, and interpretation of oral texts should force us to renovate the foundations of historical scholarship and imagine new forms of postcolonial source criticism. Here, the *rapprochement* of history and anthropology both returns us to our earliest scholarly origins and opens out onto new directions of travel.

Native oral texts typically appear in print after a hidden history of translation, abstraction, and reproduction, but recent studies of the politics and mechanics of those processes encourage us to rethink historicity. Ethnolinguists like Dell Hymes, Dennis Tedlock, and Keith Basso have written high-profile works that urge readers to think of oral texts as social performances the meanings of which lay in their historical situations rather than in some hidden mythic essence.[23] Larry Evers and Felipe Molina's translation and annotation of Don Alfonso Florez Leyva's Yaqui "Testamento" (1992) is a model of postcolonial source criticism that combines ethnographic collection, historical research, and literary criticism. In it, Evers and Molina publish a Yaqui history of the "dividing line" in both English and Spanish with occasional Yaqui interpolations. Evers and Molina take turns accounting for the provenience of the text, telling readers why and how they published it, and explaining how we might read the story. The various oral texts that went into this version of the "Testamento" were probably first typewritten by Yaqui authors between 1920 and the late 1940s to document, explain, and legitimate their political struggle with Mexico over land and identity. But the "Testamento" belongs to an old tradition of Yaqui history that has blended oral and written modes of discourse since at least the seventeenth century. With such texts, we cannot draw straight lines between historical and nonhistorical discourse and experience.[24]

Such works as the Yaqui "Testamento" exemplify the intercultural collaboration that ethnographic criticism calls for, but seldom delivers. Greg Sarris, in *Keeping Slug Woman Alive* and *Mabel McKay*, similarly places oral texts in historical horizons and does a good job of situating its author without lapsing into self-indulgent heroics. Mentioning Sarris (of Pomo, Miwok, Filipino,

positive critiques, consensus historians portrayed Native Americans as the quintessential "Other," whose role consisted of resistance and marginalization. Here lay a thinly veiled resurrection of the savagery-versus-civilization construct. In negative critiques, conflict historians, increasingly in vogue since the 1960s, cast Native Americans as the ultimate victims whose treatment laid bare the paradox and hypocrisy of capitalism and American democracy. In the most crude manifestations, natives became spiritual, environmental saints and Euro-Americans were greedy, vicious, and immoral. Narratives amounted to self-flagellation for conquest.[26]

The social criticism born in the 1960s took other directions as well. Throughout the historical discipline, interest in social history ballooned. Doing history "from the bottom up" became the rage as scholars explored the histories of people previously neglected: African Americans, women, workers, immigrants, and native people. This has probably been the most significant watershed in historical discourse in the twentieth century and has altered the representation of history. Early, conflict historians held sway, and romanticized stories of native saints who were exploited and resisted were reflected in titles like *Bury My Heart at Wounded Knee, The Long Death, The Last Days of the Sioux Nation,* and *Requiem for a People.*[27] When contemporary descendants of miscast victims cried foul, historians and anthropologists alike struggled to create more balanced interpretations that allowed for a greater agency without losing sight of the exploitation inherent in conquest. The focus shifted to emphasize cultural adaptation and persistence. Understanding native perceptions of their experiences gained center stage, as reflected in titles like *Red, White, and Black, The European and the Indian, The Children of Aataentsic, Manitou and Providence, Crown and Calumet, Dawnland Encounters, Calumet and Fleur-de-Lys, Kiva, Cross, and Crown,* and *Cultures in Contact.*[28] Interpretations that shed light on the complexities of religious adaptations abounded: *The Death and Rebirth of the Seneca, Salvation and the Savage, The Primal Mind, The Shawnee Prophet, The Ghost Dance, A Spirited Resistance, Sacred Revolt, Prophetic Worlds,* and *Dreamer-Prophets of the Columbia Plateau.*[29]

At its inception, Native American studies immediately adopted the lingo of acculturation studies. For anthropologists and historians who chose their research topics to allow them to make tangential criticisms of American and western civilization, it seemed to offer the perfect convention for explaining how various types of exotic "Others," from immigrants to southern blacks to American Indians, came to take on some trappings of western society. It was in vogue to eschew the word "assimilation" and its suggestion of total cultural obliteration. But despite the muddled efforts of the Social Science Research Council under the guidance of Ralph Linton to provide clarification, "acculturation" came perilously close to paralleling the notions of "progress" and modernization that lay at its conceptual core.[30] Scholars engaged in fieldwork knew that people did not simply discard one cultural element after another along a continuum that ended just shy of the "A" word, but it took Malcolm McFee in his influential and oft-cited article "The 150% Man . . ." to articulate the problem.[31] One could simultaneously drive a Chevrolet, use Tupperware, carry jish, and conduct healing ceremonies. Just where on an acculturative continuum should we place such a person? Students of revitalization movements could also attest that religions as creative as the Ghost Dance or the Native American Church could not be explained by reference to acculturation.[32]

The Native American studies literature is also riddled with dichotomous labels that bracket descriptively the acculturative endpoints. The pairings are familiar to others who have drawn on the insights of Ferdinand Tönnies:[33] traditional and modern, Christian and pagan, and the ubiquitous "mixed blood" and "full blood," to name a few. Perhaps because the cultural gulf has seemed so much greater, no other field has been characterized by such heavy recourse to oppositional codes to explain cultural change without really explaining anything. Scholars used them uncritically and without comment until the past ten years or so.

In the past decade, scholars have chosen more neutral language as they have embarked on studies that are more sensitive to the complexities of cultural adaptation and persistence. The dichotomous labels have given way to less value-laden terms like "persistence," "change," "adaptation," and "syncretism" (the creative blending of new and old cultural elements) and to symbolic analyses of terms like "mixed blood" and "full blood" instead of assuming a direct correlation between genetic heritage and cultural behavior.[34]

Studies of the fur trade first incorporated native cultural conventions in analyses of behavior. Since natives figuratively and literally incorporated intertribal trading partners as kin, Europeans were forced to present at least a semblance of following suit. Gift-giving became an entrenched part of trade ritual, showing that Europeans learned to function within native conventions even as natives learned to equate items of European manufacture with wampum or "made beaver" and otherwise to understand many aspects of market behavior. We came to understand that native people often had a "ceiling of wants" that failed to correspond to the model of western market rationality assuming unlimited wants. New trade goods, alcohol prominent among them, had to be designed to persuade native hunters to procure ever more pelts.[35]

As we learned that native people shaped their environment in previously unappreciated ways by husbanding and harvesting resources, we also learned that regarding them as inexhaustible market trade items led them to deplete those resources and depend on European products, and so spelled the end of economic autonomy. The process might be slow and halting or swift and complete, but ultimately all native groups were drawn into economic and political relationships with some European power or another forevermore.

Fur trade scholarship was the first genre to introduce the expansion of market capitalism as a powerful engine of change. This led to incorporating the insights of world systems theory to explain the patterns of "dependency" that evolved. This macro-level theory uses a global scale to explain local events in terms of the demand generated for resources from "colonies" by "the metropolis." For world systems theorists, the experiences of those who procured resources firsthand scarcely mattered; they were merely super-exploited victims. It is here that scholars of native experiences are making original contributions to this theoretical discourse by asking more sophisticated questions and showing greater sensitivity toward native experiences. They ask how natives have adapted culturally in the wake of the expansion of market capitalism and seek to discern patterns in the responses.[36]

Efforts to refine the application of world systems theory have led directly to the current major paradigm, termed alternately the "Indians' New World" by James Merrell or the "Middle Ground" by Richard White. Both historians refer to an intermediate world between precontact native cultures and the hegemonic domination of the United States where native actors were primary players and the relationships and conventions formed were as much Native American as Euro-American and as "new" for Indians as for Europeans. In contradistinction to mainstream colonial historians who have largely written indigenous people out of the equation, despite some of the best scholarship the field has to offer, Merrell's and White's depictions allow for societies characterized by nuance and diversity.[37]

Scholars' newfound appreciation of the extent and spiritual foundation of native resource husbandry led them to question Indians' motivations for overhunting. Many felt that this seeming paradox required more explanation than the economic man model allowed. Calvin Martin offered the provocative but poorly researched hypothesis that Indians enacted revenge upon their animal brethren for bringing (European) diseases to humans, thereby breaching their spiritual compact.[38] However, the breakdown of that spiritual relationship was never as swift or complete as Martin suggests. Family hunting territories have been appreciated as an innovation designed to preserve collective access to subsistence game while regulating access to game for commercial purposes. It is more likely that as needs were redefined, animal relatives were expected to respond accordingly by allowing themselves to be taken in greater numbers.[39]

Fur trade scholars also pioneered analyses of women's roles, intermarriage, and people of mixed descent. Pathbreaking studies by Jennifer Brown, Sylvia Van Kirk, and Jacqueline Peterson revealed the powerful mediating roles performed by native women and people of mixed descent (*métis* in Canada), elite marital patterns shifting from native women to *métis* women to Euro-American women, and ultimately "ethnogenesis"—the birth of new ethnic groups composed typically of people of mixed biological and cultural descent. Fur trade scholarship as a whole displays the greatest sophistication in the field and is remarkably free of the dualistic jargon so endemic in the general literature.[40]

Not surprisingly, the denouement of the fur trade, which occurred at different times in different regions, coincided with the onset of hegemonic domination by a European power or the United States. The "middle ground" began to unravel; the world was still "new," but more familiar even as Native Americans found their options constricted. The nineteenth century witnessed increasingly coercive policies toward native people, accompanied by rapid territorial acquisition and tribal dispossession. From the removal policies of mid-century to the genocide accompanying the California gold rush to the bloody Plains wars to the forced assimilation and allotment policies of the late nineteenth and twentieth centuries, the overall balance of power had definitely shifted.

As have scholars of African-American slavery, scholars have sought to uncover and acknowledge native agency even within such coercive and often violent circumstances. We know of creative efforts by Cherokee leaders to use the U.S. Constitution, laws, and courts to overcome removal pressures. We now understand that native warfare was not born of inherent savagery, but reflected their own rational motivations. The Pawnee and Crow were not simply turncoats for allying with the United States; they sought aid against those whom they perceived as a greater threat—the Sioux. Yet despite these and other important understandings, the tenor of histories of this period is one of nearly unrelieved tragedy. Regardless of all creative, often heroic, efforts, native people invariably lost the ability to control their own lives. Death loomed large from coast to coast. Most at the time believed that Native Americans would not survive at all.[41]

Scholars turned their attention to discerning how Native Americans had survived and adapted. As their sights shifted to the late nineteenth and twentieth centuries, so too did the resources available from which to construct their interpretations. Three major types of material are allowing historians of the more recent past to delve more deeply into native history than had ever been possible. First, imagine the Office of Indian Affairs (not the Bureau of Indian Affairs until the late 1930s) as a vast colonial bureaucracy churning out reams of paperwork relating to many facets of Native American lives that it was charged with micromanaging and remaking for much of the time. Serial documentation abounds: far more census material for native people than for the general U.S. population; birth and death registers of varying quality; economic statistics; records of Indian council meetings; inspection reports; and correspondence galore. The bulk of this documentation has never been touched by researchers and requires quantitative skills to manage. Second, classic ethnographies proliferated as anthropologists scrambled to recover what they thought was "traditional" culture before it disappeared, as they thought it would. The field notes and publications are often biased, as are all sources, but they contain a wealth of descriptive, often individually focused materials of which a trained eye can make extensive use. Third, scholars can talk to people who participated in or witnessed past events. Oral history collections exist, and scholars can undertake their own interviewing. Taken together, these resources have enormously broadened the possibilities for research and understanding. They are also daunting. The sheer amount of the research involved in something as basic as a reservation community study becomes a serious consideration as scholars assess their career agendas.[42]

Some fine studies have taught us a great deal, but we must acknowledge that the surface of the recent past has barely been scratched. The further forward we move in time, the fewer the studies with significant temporal perspective. In this arena, anthropologists and historians have become virtually indistinguishable in print. The community study model so popular among social historians has been transplanted to reservations, but no new paradigm, other than placing native historical actors and motivations at center stage, has emerged to replace the arcane tribal history format.[43] Instead, we have many stories crying out for synthesis.

It is perhaps easiest to learn about reservation politics for the same reasons historians focused for so long on great men: They are most visible, generated the greatest volume of documentation, and, as public personas, are more accustomed to being interviewed. Nonetheless, it is a significant contribution to learn that reservation governance has persisted despite concerted efforts by U.S. policy-makers to eradicate tribal governments. In-depth studies reveal leaders' and constituents' creative adaptations to ever-changing conditions. We now have examples of how symbols of authority, social gatherings, rituals, ways of determining leaders, and governing structures have all bent to altered circumstances with astonishing resilience.[44] But we also have examples of how such changes can strain or fracture political governance, rendering normal functions difficult at best, impossible at worst.[45] What explains the differential "success"? Some have suggested that only those governing structures that closely parallel earlier governmental forms can succeed, dooming Indian Reorganization Act tribal councils from the outset. This is reminiscent of the thinking of the old savagery (and not-so-subtly racialist) school, whereby native people are so shackled by a traditional ball and chain that they cannot innovate or adapt. Would anyone argue that American democracy was doomed to failure because it deviated from monarchical and parliamentary procedures? Structuralist arguments have long been abandoned; specific historical circumstances must be considered before offering an explanation for apparent patterns.

Directing our lens at economic conditions reveals a far bleaker portrait. With the major exception of the arid Southwest, most reservations lost most of their land base through allotment policies, the premature removal of protective restrictions, and tax forfeiture proceedings. What remained was managed by the Office of Indian Affairs more for the benefit of the adjacent non-Indian population than with an eye toward native welfare. Few opportunities to engage in new tribally controlled business enterprises existed; even fewer of those attempted succeeded. The mass resort to gaming illustrates most effectively the desperation of reservation economies. Given such conditions, it should come as no surprise that the native population consistently places at the bottom in every index of education, health, wealth, and welfare.[46]

We know strikingly less about Native American social history than about reservation economies and politics. Probably because of the daunting nature of available documentation and the necessity of employing quantitative methods, we can count on two hands the number of studies that can be thus defined.[47] The only well-developed topic that falls under the rubric of social history also straddles the boundary of the history of religion. Revitalization movements, a particular type of cultural change, have received ample attention, from the classic treatments of Anthony Wallace's study of the Seneca Handsome Lake religion and Joseph Jorgensen's study of the Sun Dance to works focusing on the Shawnee Prophet, the Ghost Dance, and the Native American Church. We are now well aware of how frequently native people turned to syncretic religious solutions during times of duress. Some were more successful than others, but all sought some accommodation of native and Euro-American ways, and most condemned the use of alcohol.[48]

Placing contemporary issues in historical perspective is currently a booming area of research and publication, more so than for any other subgroup of the American population. The unique status of Native Americans vis-à-vis federal Indian law and the federal government makes diving into the past a prerequisite for understanding nearly every contentious issue: land and water rights, gaming, the Hopi–Navajo land dispute, recovery of sacred lands, repatriation of skeletal remains and sacred objects from federally funded museums, the institution of modern health care, women's rights versus tribal sovereignty among the Pueblo, blood quantum requirements, and sovereignty disputes among the Haudenosaunee.[49] The topic naturally supports a lively seminar class with individual students' papers focusing on the issue of their choice.

The End of Ethnohistory

Postcolonial source criticism raises questions about the traditional disciplinary boundaries that separate anthropology and history. In some ways, a work like Evers and Molina's treatment of the Yaqui "Testamento" more nearly resembles an exercise in Victorian source criticism than a high modernist ethnography or a classic ethnohistory. The new works simply do not evince any of the differences of method, theory, or language that usually differentiate history from anthropology. In them, the two forms so thoroughly interweave that we should imagine the *rapprochement* of history and anthropology as a point of departure for rethinking older syntheses.

Indeed, we need to rethink the most popular word of all: "ethnohistory." Why call the history of American Indians "ethno-history" at all? Why not just "history"? Or "anthropology"?

Originally, Native Americans fell under the tender care of anthropologists because, as people without history, they needed the special "ethno" methods of participant observation to translate oral interviews, observed behavior, and material culture into a printed past. By the end of the twenties, ethnographers could also point to the culture concept as a boundary marker differentiating their discipline from history. As anthropologists turned away from history, ethnohistory created a space where ethnographers and historians could exchange methods and monographs. By the 1980s, many anthropologists not associated with ethnohistory had turned to historical interpretation. Many historians not associated with ethnohistory interviewed informants and used oral texts as historical evidence. Today, the "library dissertation" and historical narrative are becoming fixtures in anthropology. Oral interviews and the culture concept are commonplaces in history. The transitions have gradually emptied "ethnohistory" of its methodological content. The word no longer points to a method distinct from what other ethnographers and historians do.

In Americanist practice (although things are different in Africanist practice), ethnohistory effectively means Native American history, and it artificially separates Native American studies from other forms of ethnic studies, postcolonial studies, and various other fields. To give one example, Anthony F. C. Wallace is one of the great pioneers of ethnohistorical method, and his *Death and Rebirth of the Seneca* surfaces routinely in bibliographies of ethnohistory. But his study of (predominantly) white laborers, *Rockdale,* which is methodologically akin to his book on the Seneca, is routinely described by historians as "social history." The difference turns on tacit but powerful racial codes: "ethno-" history is red, "social" history is black or white.[50] Ethnohistory has in some situations provided a space for the integration of anthropology and history, but in others it has widened the boundaries that hold them apart.[51] Perhaps the new convergence of ethnographic and historical scholarship may allow us to imagine a post-ethnohistorical future. It may be that "ethnohistory" will follow "acculturation studies" as a label that has served its historical purpose. If we have reconciled history and anthropology, then ethnohistory has reached its end.

Future Directions

The *rapprochement* of history and anthropology has been one of the more creative social science events of recent years, but it is not an unmixed blessing. We should be critical of terms, tropes, and teaching that unselfconsciously re-

inforce the old antinomy of people with and without history, either by natural-
izing terms like "prehistory" or by artificially whitening "history." And while
reconciliation promises to enrich Native American studies, we should concentrate upon the ways in which it can connect us with larger conversations.
Instead of treating the convergence of history and anthropology as an occasion
for creating yet another specialized jargon, discipline, and institutional affiliation, we should embrace it as an opportunity for a more cosmopolitan practice.

A few general but concrete suggestions are in order.

Transnational Contexts

Historians and anthropologists working in Native American studies would
benefit from careful attention to *transnational contexts.* Too often, historians
see the nation-state, and anthropologists see the tribe, chiefdom, or *ethnos,* as
the natural subjects of their studies. In the case of American history, the consequence has been a marginalization of American Indian history. A title like
"Colonial America," whether one is writing a book or teaching a course, effectively naturalizes the arrival of Europeans and leaves Native America before
1492 quite literally out of (the) history. American history surveys commonly
imagine native history as a tragic but peripheral subplot. Native Americans
typically figure in such stories as the marginal subjects of a ritualized token
discussion in the early, colonial portion of the story, and perhaps resurface in
the late nineteenth century as exotic victims of industrial capitalism on the
Great Plains.

Imagining Native American history in terms of world or global history
makes it harder to subordinate cultural conflict and empire building to questions of national policy and character. Few scholars have the training and resources to write monographs whose research bridges places like West Africa
and Arizona, but we might employ the work of specialists from outside our
own localities to provide a greater breadth of context for American tales. We
should consider placing articles in journals like *Comparative Studies in Society
and History* or the *Journal of World History,* where they may help to build
ties across the boundaries of national specialties. We might also benefit from
careful consideration of the debates in subaltern studies, postcolonial studies,
and Third World studies. Anthropologists have traditionally been more dili-
gent than historians when it comes to discussing literature outside one's own
regional focus, but even in ethnographies such discussions are frequently isolated in a brief introduction or buried in notes and bibliography. Making
broader debates and contexts part of the story, rather than an addendum to it,
would help us to cultivate a salutary cosmopolitanism.

Precontact Archaeology

In this vein, specialists in the field need to reach out to incorporate insights emerging from precontact archaeology. The broad outlines have long been sketched in, but proliferating site reports need to be analyzed and conveyed in a synthetic yet humanistic format that does not privilege categorization of ceramic shards over population and group dynamics. *Native Americans Before 1492* and *Ancient Art of the American Woodland Indians* are admirable efforts in this direction that emphasize the continuity of indigenous symbols during the various stages of eastern woodlands and Mississippian cultures, rather than attributing them solely to diffusion from Mesoamerican core areas. It is ironic (and reinforces our first recommendation for further research) that a historian of modern China (Lynda Shaffer) would undertake such a synthetic treatment.[52] Similarly, Bruce Smith in *Rivers of Change* establishes southeastern North America as one of four independent global centers for the domestication of plants by using new dating techniques and synthesizing hundreds of site and scientific reports.[53] The Hohokam, Mogollon, Anasazi sequence in the Southwest awaits such refinement. As scholars increasingly describe even seventeenth-century America as a pluralistic society, understanding what came before assumes greater import. Headway has been made, but constructing balanced lecture courses demands encompassing archaeological research in humanistic fashion.

Historical Demography

Native American historical demography is at a crossroads of sorts. Exaggerated debates about how many people were here in 1492 and what happened to them have been eclipsed by refined studies of specific pathogens and their impacts on local areas. Microbes behave differently and do not affect all types of societies and concentrations of population in the same fashion. Extremely virulent viruses, like Ebola, take a high toll and then burn out very quickly; killing the host is not well suited to long-term survival. Scholars across disciplinary lines are finding considerable variation in the impact of diseases on the indigenous American population. Archaeologists, historical demographers, and epidemiologists report that all viruses in the Americas did not behave in Dobynesque fashion,[54] though they credit Henry Dobyns with stimulating the decades-long debate.[55] Even more startlingly, they suggest that colonization—not European-borne diseases—bears primary responsibility for the failure of the native population of the Americas to recover, as most populations do following demographic crises.

Native American historical demography is wide open for research. Measures like fertility and mortality rates, the age structure of a population, age at first marriage, household size and composition, child-spacing, all central concerns for mainstream historical demography, have attracted very little attention. Aside from rising fertility rates and falling mortality rates, we cannot account for population increase in the twentieth century. More case studies are necessary. Causal factors cannot be pinpointed by examining the aggregate population, because historical circumstances differed so greatly from tribe to tribe.

Changing Social Structure

There is a glaring need for studies of changing social structure. Scholars glibly note that extended families and matrilineal kinship systems gave way to nuclear families and bilateral descent, but invariably chalk this up to Euro-American missionary influence. A closer look at footnotes rarely turns up the substantive evidence upon which such assertions should rest. When Nancy Shoemaker analyzed the 1900 U.S. federal census, she found that the Seneca (as well as the Yakima and Red Lake Ojibwe) had over twice as many extended families as the U.S. population and had not adopted nuclear families, thus raising questions about Anthony Wallace's classic treatment.[56] Clearly, such transitions must have been much more complex than the literature has allowed, and perhaps never so complete as it suggests. Groups like the Cherokee with a rich documentary record, including pre-Removal censuses and property lists, may afford closer inquiry.

Intermarriage, people of mixed descent, ethnogenesis, and issues of identity also beg for further studies; the limited literature in existence more than piques interest. These topics have received attention in relation to the fur trade, but insights should be extended to the Southeast and Southwest. In general, it appears that intermarriage was more extensive in areas where trade lasted the longest, leading at times to ethnogenesis. It is well known that intermarriage as a product of the fur trade resulted in the emergence of the *Métis* in the Red River district of Canada. Did the formation of incipient classes based in part on ethnicity among the Cherokee, Choctaw, Chickasaw, and others in the Southeast eclipse ethnogenesis there? Recent studies that delve more deeply into relationships between natives and African Americans suggest that colonial history was much more pluralistic than the current mainstream paradigm offering a black and white portrait allows. The historical experiences of groups like the Lumbee and Mashpee (formerly labeled "triracial isolates"), who maintained their identity and cohesion to the present time despite legal and academic efforts to define their distinctiveness away, should have relevance for all scholars interested in ethnicity.[57]

Research on native women has been slow to take hold. Just as romantic images of Indians have symbolized the pitfalls of western civilization, the relatively greater status enjoyed by native women has been used by feminist scholars to challenge assumptions of the universality of female subordination and of the steady decline in status accompanying colonization. Only recently have scholars begun to analyze native women's history apart from these meta-agendas.[58]

However, rather than issuing a call for further research on native women, we want to underscore the need for gender studies. Given the undeveloped nature of Native American social history in general, it makes little sense to follow the mainstream course of engaging in compensatory women's history before working toward integration. Men's history cannot truly be understood without women's history, and the converse is also true. Women and men ineluctably made history together. Ironically, this lacuna in Native American history offers the opportunity at the outset to integrate the histories of women and men, with all the variation that cultural and social constructions of gender entail.[59]

No aspect of the forced assimilation campaign of the U.S. government has seemed more inhumane than the incarceration of native children in boarding schools far removed from their families and cultures. The objective—to be attained through harsh military discipline that had the children marching to bells throughout the day—was nothing less than cultural genocide. The daily details of indoctrination in the English language, rudimentary math skills, and American history and culture, together with a gendered division of labor that maintained the schools, are well known. The assault on Indian identity expressed through haphazardly assigning English names and surnames, shearing boys' hair, punishing children for speaking their own languages, and requiring cadet uniforms draws censure today. Surely the presence on the school grounds of graveyards for those who could not survive rampant epidemic diseases or the emotional and psychological trauma of the experience symbolically represents the worst boarding schools had to offer.[60]

Until recently, studies of boarding schools had not explored student culture. K. Tsianina Lomawaima's *They Called It Prairie Light: The Story of Chilocco Indian School* offers a refreshing corrective by combining archival research with oral interviews with Chilocco alumni. The study reveals how students simultaneously found solace in peer group associations that substituted for family relationships and devised ways to outwit the system. Some even retained fond memories of their years at Chilocco.[61]

The problem with this perspective lies not with the story rendered, but with those experiences that cannot be recaptured. Those who rest in the graveyards cannot tell their stories. Some who survived find it too painful to recount those years to third-generation descendants eager to learn of their aging relatives' early twentieth-century experiences. That cohort might be labeled "the lost generation." Future efforts should build on Lomawaima's insights and take extra pains to seek out those who might be reluctant to revisit the boarding school chapters of their lives. This is one place where being of native descent, like Lomawaima, might give a scholar a decided advantage in gathering information.

Over half of all Native Americans now live in cities. Most scholars attribute their presence to the 1950s relocation policy, which went hand-in-hand with federal efforts to "terminate" the special trust relationship between the U.S. government and tribes and ultimately reduce financial obligations. However, the appearance of native people in cities stems more from processes of dispossession than simple policy maneuvers. We are now learning that native people have lived in cities since the early colonial era. Often, the labels used by record-keepers have obscured natives' presence.[62] As their means of subsistence was undermined, native people turned to wage labor and urban opportunities, as did thousands and increasingly millions of other Americans. Native people have been part of the migration of the American population from rural to urban areas that escalated in the late nineteenth and twentieth centuries. The research completed thus far is sketchy, but highly suggestive. What seems clear is that the relocation policy of the 1950s codified and escalated a solution that native people had already worked out for themselves.[63]

Scholars have established that urban Indian communities have employed strategies for self-help very similar to those of immigrants and African Americans. Relatives and friends followed one another in chain migrations so that familiarity eased the transition for later arrivals. They settled in ethnic enclaves and formed voluntary associations to address needs ranging from employment assistance to social welfare to cultural celebration. Nonetheless, studies of urban Indian communities have been scant. Most earlier studies were sociological and overemphasized social disfunction and malaise. No one has illuminated the relationships between urban communities and reservations in a directed fashion. The connection between urban communities and evolving pan-Indian identity also deserves further exploration.[64]

Two initiatives undertaken by the D'Arcy McNickle Center for the History of the American Indian, both featuring unprecedented interdisciplinary collaboration, held promise. The American Indian Family History Project brought together five specialists with training in historical demography and family history; the American Indian Historical Demography Project, funded by the National Science Foundation, drew on experts in archaeology, epidemiology, biostatistics, demography, history, and anthropology, among others, and aspired to develop four co-edited volumes spanning millennia. However, both projects were abandoned by then-director Fred Hoxie, probably because of the very exigencies of coordinating such extensive interdisciplinary collaboration.

Dialogical Narratives

Most of us could improve our work by attending more carefully to Native American texts and voices, thus making our monographs more *dialogical.* Some critics worry about the theoretical justifications for dialogical quests for "voice," and some extravagant claims have been made both for the emancipatory possibilities of dialogism and the impossibility of its achievement, but those debates can only be enriched by growing numbers of monographs that make "native" texts part of their practice as well as their theoretical reflection. Here, linguistic anthropology leads both cultural anthropology and history. There is a growing consensus in ethnolinguistics that scholars should kick the habit of employing anonymous informants and unselfconsciously substituting translated prose glosses for original oral performances. A simple commitment to reproducing the discourse of "informants" (perhaps even crediting those authors) within one's own monograph could do much to improve the dialogical quality of writing in Native American studies. This holds as well for scholars who are themselves Native Americans. Even native scholars are related by differentials of class, gender, age, sexuality, or authority to the worlds and stories of others.

The result might be more block-indented quotation than we have been accustomed to, and more sentences talking about the provenience of sources, but it could have some concrete benefits. First, it would provide other scholars a better look at evidence that would otherwise be hidden in footnotes, and so offer better opportunities to evaluate and revise scholarly interpretation. And, second, it would benefit scholars outside the specialty. More dialogical texts would provide interested outsiders better access to voices that have been largely inaudible in mainstream fields. Further, a deliberate integration of the texts of principals, informants, and interlocutors would offer some interpretive direction to other academics who would like to diversify their own scholarship, but for whom the typical "readings" anthology—with its *Reader's Digest* glosses of Native American oral literature—offers little in the way of guidance.

The clarion call of the past twenty years has been "survival!" Since only a century ago most people predicted the opposite, perhaps this is understandable. But academic scholars of all stripes bear an obligation to present more balanced, honest appraisals. Celebration of survival must be accompanied by sobering demographic analyses of the millions who died or were never born and of the wrenching adaptations undertaken by survivors. Mainstream scholars must display greater receptivity to the outpouring of scholarship that could enrich courses and synthetic treatments. Books like Bernard Bailyn's *The Peopling of British North America* should not omit native people and win awards.[65] There is no quick fix for glossing the diversity of native experiences over the millennia. Specialists in the field must be less parochial and more responsive to appeals from generalists for accessible narratives and synoptic articles. And Native American studies programs and departments should refrain from pressures to foster what amount to polemics in historical disguise. Considering that the Constitution fails to protect native rights, why is the myth of Iroquois precedents a matter of pride? But change is incremental, and every victory should be savored.

Notes

1.   G. W. F. Hegel, *Lectures on the Philosophy of World History: Introduction, Reason in History,* translated from the German ed. of Johannes Hoffmeister by H. B. Nisbet (Cambridge: Cambridge University Press, 1975).

2.   Karl Marx, *Capital: A Critical Analysis of Capitalist Production/Karl Marx,* Frederick Engels, ed. (Moscow: Foreign Languages Publishing House, 1959); Karl Marx, *Capital, the Communist Manifesto and Other Writings of Karl Marx,* Max Eastman, ed. (New York: Carlton House, 1932); Friedrich Engels, *Dialectics of Nature,* Clemens Dutt, trans. and ed. (New York: International Publishers, 1960 [1940]); Friedrich Engels, *The Origin of the Family, Private Property, and the State, in the Light of the Researches of Lewis H. Morgan* (New York: International Publishers, 1942); Friedrich Engels, *Socialism: Utopian and Scientific: With the Essay on "The Mark"* (New York: International Publishers, 1975); Lewis Henry Morgan, *Ancient Society, or, Researches in the Lines of Human Progress from Savagery Through Barbarism to Civilization,* Eleanor Leacock, ed. (Gloucester, Mass.: P. Smith, 1974); Lewis Henry Morgan, *League of the Ho-de-no-sau-nee or Iroquois* (New York: B. Franklin, 1966); Lewis Henry Morgan, *Systems of Consanguinity and Affinity of the Human Family* (Washington, D.C.: Smithsonian Institution Press, 1870); Edward Burnett Tylor, *Anthropology: An Introduction to the Study of Man and Civilization* (New York: D. Appleton, 1898); Edward Burnett Tylor, *The Origins of Culture* (New York: Harper and Row, 1958); Edward Burnett Tylor, *Primitive Culture: Researches Into the Development of Mythology, Philosophy, Religion, Language, Art, and Custom* (New York: Holt, 1889); Edward Burnett Tylor, *Researches into the Early History of Mankind and the Development of Civilization* (London: J. Murray, 1878).

3.   Francis Parkman, *The Conspiracy of Pontiac and the Indian War After the Conquest of Canada* (Boston: Little, Brown, 1898).

4.   For a good review of the literature, see James D. Faubion, "History in anthropology," *Annual Review of Anthropology,* 22 (1993), 35–54. On temporality, see Thomas R. Trautmann, "The revolution in ethnological time," *Man,* 27 (1992), 379–98; Jean-Loup Amselle, "Anthropology and historicity," *History and Theory,* 32 (1993), 12–32. For overviews of the relations of history and anthropology, compare Aron I. Gourevitch, "History and historical anthropology," *Diogenes,* 151 (1990), 75–90; Johannes Fabian, *Time and the Other: How Anthropology Makes Its Object* (New York: Columbia University Press, 1983); Johannes Fabian, *Time and the Work of Anthropology: Critical Essays, 1971–1991* (Philadelphia: Harwood, 1991); Nicholas Thomas, *Out of Time: History and Evolution in Anthropological Discourse* (Cambridge: Cambridge University Press, 1989); Jay O'Brian and William Roseberry, eds., *Golden Ages, Dark Ages: Imagining the Past in Anthropology and History* (Berkeley: University of California Press,

1991); Jean Comaroff and John L. Comaroff, *Ethnography and the Historical Imagination* (Boulder: Westview, 1992); Bernard Knapp, ed., *Archaeology, Annales, and Ethnohistory* (Cambridge: Cambridge University Press, 1992); David William Cohen, *The Combing of History* (Chicago: University of Chicago Press, 1994); Joan Vincent, *Anthropology and Politics: Visions, Traditions, Trends* (Tucson: University of Arizona Press, 1990); Ernest Gellner, *Anthropology and Politics: Revolutions in the Sacred Grove* (Oxford: Basil Blackwell, 1995).

5. Bronislaw Malinowski, "Culture," in *Encyclopedia of the Social Sciences,* Edwin R. A. Seligman, ed. (New York: Macmillan, 1950 [1933]), 621–46; Bronislaw Malinowski, *Argonauts of the Western Pacific: An Account of Native Enterprise and Adventure in the Archipelagoes of Melanesian New Guinea* (London: Routledge & Sons, 1932); Bronislaw Malinowski, *The Sexual Life of Savages in North-western Melanesia: An Ethnographic Account of Courtship, Marriage, and Family Life Among the Natives of the Trobriand Islands, British New Guinea* (London: Routledge & Sons, 1932). For discussions of the relations between anthropology and canonical modernism, see Marc Manganaro, ed., *Modernist Anthropology: From Fieldwork to Text* (Princeton: Princeton University Press, 1990).

6. On the revolts against historicism, see Fabian, *Time and the Other;* Kerwin Lee Klein, *Frontiers of Historical Imagination: Narrating the European Conquest of Native America, 1890–1990* (Berkeley: University of California Press, 1997). On Boasian anthropology, see especially George W. Stocking, Jr., *The Ethnographer's Magic and Other Essays in the History of Anthropology* (Madison: University of Wisconsin Press, 1992); George W. Stocking, Jr., *Race, Culture, and Evolution: Essays in the History of Anthropology* (New York: Free Press, 1968).

7. Klein, *Frontiers of Historical Imagination.* For an introduction to discussions of anthropology and imperialism, see Dell Hymes, ed., *Reinventing Anthropology* (New York: Random House, 1969); Talal Asad, *Anthropology and the Colonial Encounter* (London: Ithaca Press, 1973); Richard G. Fox, ed., *Recapturing Anthropology: Working in the Present* (Santa Fe, N.M.: School of American Research Press, 1991); Micaela Di Leonardo, ed., *Gender at the Crossroads of Knowledge: Feminist Anthropology in the Postmodern Era* (Berkeley: University of California Press, 1991); and Diane Bell et al., eds., *Gendered Fields: Women, Men and Ethnography* (London: Routledge, 1993).

8. Alfred L. Kroeber, "History and evolution," *Southwestern Journal of Anthropology,* 2 (1946), 1–13; Leslie A. White, "History, evolutionism, and functionalism: Three types of interpretation of culture," *Southwestern Journal of Anthropology,* 1 (1945), 215–39; Leslie A. White, " 'Diffusion vs. evolution': An anti-evolutionist fallacy," *American Anthropologist,* 47 (1945), 339–56; Leslie A. White, "Kroeber's 'Configurations of Cultural Growth,' " *American Anthropologist,* 48 (1946), 78–93. See also Alfred L. Kroeber, *Anthropology: Race, Language, Culture, Psychology, Prehistory* (New York: Harcourt, Brace, 1948); Alfred L. Kroeber, *Anthropology* (New York: Harcourt, Brace, 1923); Alfred L. Kroeber, *Area and Climax* (Berkeley: University of California Press, 1936); Alfred L. Kroeber, *Configurations of Culture Growth* (Berkeley: University of California Press, 1944); Alfred L. Kroeber, *The Nature of Culture* (Chicago: University of Chicago Press, 1965 [1952]); Alfred L. Kroeber, *Culture: A Critical Review of Concepts and Definitions* (Cambridge, Mass.: The Museum, 1952); Alfred L. Kroeber, *Ethnographic Interpretations* (Berkeley: University of California

Press, 1957); Alfred L. Kroeber, *An Anthropologist Looks at History* (Berkeley: University of California Press, 1963); Leslie A. White, *The Science of Culture: A Study of Man and Civilization* (New York: Farrar, Straus, 1949); Leslie A. White, *The Concept of Cultural Systems: A Key to Understanding Tribes and Nations* (New York: Columbia University Press, 1975).

9.   Claude Lévi-Strauss, *The Savage Mind* (Chicago: University of Chicago Press, 1966). Compare his earlier statement in *Structural Anthropology,* trans. Claire Jacobson and Brooke Grundfest Schoepf (Garden City, N.Y.: Anchor, 1967 [1958]), especially 1–28, 229–38. See also Kerwin Lee Klein, "In search of narrative mastery: Postmodernism and the people without history," *History and Theory,* 34 (1995), 275–98.

10.   Robert Redfield, Ralph Linton, and Melville Herskovits, "Memorandum on the study of acculturation," *American Anthropologist* 38 (1936), 149–52; Ralph Linton, ed., *Acculturation in Seven American Indian Tribes* (New York: Appleton-Century, 1940); Social Science Research Council Summer Seminar on Acculturation, "Acculturation: An exploratory formulation," *American Anthropologist,* 56 (1954), 974–80; Stocking, *The Ethnographer's Magic,* 142–44, 228–29. On "acculturation," see Philip Gleason, *Speaking of Diversity: Language and Ethnicity in Twentieth-Century America* (Baltimore: Johns Hopkins University Press, 1992); Jon S. Gilkeson, Jr., "The domestication of culture in interwar America, 1919–1941," in *The Estate of Social Knowledge,* JoAnne Brown and David K. van Keuren, eds. (Baltimore: Johns Hopkins University Press, 1991), 153–74.

11.   For a sense of the changes in ethnohistorical consciousness, see the various essays published in the organization's flagship journal: Erminie Wheeler-Voegelin, "An ethnohistorian's viewpoint," *Ethnohistory,* 1 (1954), 155–70; Stanley Pargellis, "The problem of American Indian history," *Ethnohistory,* 4 (1957), 113–24; "Symposium on the concept of ethnohistory," *Ethnohistory,* 8 (1961), 5–30; William N. Fenton, "Ethnohistory and its problems," *Ethnohistory,* 9 (1962), 1–23; William C. Sturtevant, "Anthropology, history, and ethnohistory," *Ethnohistory,* 13 (1966), 1–51. For more recent retrospections, see Bruce G. Trigger, "Ethnohistory: Problems and prospects," *Ethnohistory,* 29 (1982), 1–19; Francis Jennings, "A growing partnership: Historians, anthropologists, and American Indian history," *Ethnohistory,* 29 (1982), 21–34; Raymond D. Fogelson, "The ethnohistory of events and nonevents," *Ethnohistory,* 36 (1989), 133–47; Raymond J. DeMallie, " 'These have no ears': Narrative and the ethnohistorical method," *Ethnohistory,* 40 (1993), 515–39; Shepard Krech III, "The state of ethnohistory," *Annual Review of Anthropology* (1991), 345–75; Helen Tanner, "Erminie Wheeler-Voegelin (1903–1988), Founder of the American Society for Ethnohistory," *Ethnohistory,* 38 (1991), 58–72.

12.   Robert F. Berkhofer, *Salvation and the Savage: An Analysis of Protestant Missions and American Indian Response, 1787–1862* (New York: Atheneum, 1972 [1965]); Robert F. Berkhofer, *The White Man's Indian: Images of the American Indian, from Columbus to the Present* (New York: Vintage, 1978); Wilbur R. Jacobs, *Diplomacy and Indian Gifts: Anglo-French Rivalry Along the Ohio and Northwest Frontiers, 1748–1763* (Stanford: Stanford University Press, 1950); Wilbur R. Jacobs, *Dispossessing the American Indian: Indians and Whites on the Colonial Frontier* (New York: Scribner, 1972); Wilbur R. Jacobs, *Wilderness Politics and Indian Gifts: The Northern Colonial Frontier, 1748–1763* (Lincoln: University of Nebraska Press, 1950).

13.   Robert F. Berkhofer, "The political context of a new Indian history," *Pacific*

Historical Review, 40 (1971), 357–82; R. David Edmunds, "Native Americans, new voices: American Indian history, 1895–1995," *American Historical Review,* 100 (1995), 717–40. See also Sherry Ortner, "Theory in anthropology since the sixties," *Comparative Studies in Society and History,* 26 (1984), 126–66.

14. James Clifford, *The Predicament of Culture: Twentieth-Century Ethnography, Literature, and Art* (Cambridge: Harvard University Press, 1988).

15. Marshall Sahlins, *Historical Metaphors and Mythical Realities: Structure in the Early History of the Sandwich Islands Kingdom* (Ann Arbor: University of Michigan Press, 1981); Marshall Sahlins, *Islands of History* (Chicago: University of Chicago Press, 1985); Marshall Sahlins, *How "Natives" Think: About Captain Cook, for Example* (Chicago: University of Chicago Press, 1995). For an introduction to the vast literature on encounters, see Stuart B. Schwartz, ed., *Implicit Understandings: Observing, Reporting, and Reflecting on the Encounters Between Europeans and Other Peoples in the Early Modern Era* (Cambridge: Cambridge University Press, 1994).

16. Gananath Obeyesekere, *The Apotheosis of James Cook: European Mythmaking in the Pacific* (Princeton: Princeton University Press, 1992); Clifford Geertz, review essay in *New York Review of Books,* 42 (November 30, 1995), 4–7; Clifford Geertz, *After the Fact: Two Countries, Four Decades, One Anthropologist* (Cambridge: Harvard University Press, 1995). Compare also the accounts in Greg Dening, *Performances* (Chicago: University of Chicago Press, 1996).

17. Jocelyn Linnekin, *Sacred Queens and Women of Consequence: Rank, Gender, and Colonialism in the Hawaiian Islands* (Ann Arbor: University of Michigan Press, 1990).

18. Calvin Martin, *The American Indian and the Problem of History* (New York: Oxford University Press, 1987); Calvin Luther Martin, *In the Spirit of the Earth: Rethinking History and Time* (Baltimore: Johns Hopkins University Press, 1992). For a sampling of literature on this topic from outside North America, see Jonathan D. Hill, ed., *Rethinking History and Myth: Indigenous South American Perspectives on the Past* (Urbana: University of Illinois Press, 1988).

19. See especially Susan Hegeman, "History, ethnography, myth: Some notes on the 'Indian-centered' narrative," *Social Text: Theory, Culture, Ideology,* 23 (1989), 144–60; Robert F. Berkhofer, "Cultural pluralism and the new Indian history," in Martin, *The American Indian and the Problem of History,* 34–44; Thomas Biolsi, "Review Article: The American Indian and the Problem of History," *American Indian Quarterly,* 13 (1989), 259–65.

20. Vine Deloria, Jr., *Custer Died for Your Sins: An Indian Manifesto* (New York: Macmillan, 1969); Edward W. Said, *Culture and Imperialism* (New York: Knopf, 1993).

21. James Clifford, *The Predicament of Culture: Twentieth-Century Ethnography, Literature, and Art* (Cambridge: Harvard University Press, 1988); James Clifford and George E. Marcus, eds., *Writing Culture: The Poetics and Politics of Ethnography* (Berkeley: University of California Press, 1986). On the Mashpee, compare Paul Brodeur, *Restitution: The Land Claims of the Mashpee, Passamaquoddy, and Penobscot Indians of New England* (Boston: Northeastern University Press, 1985); Francis G. Hutchins, *Mashpee: The Story of Cape Cod's Indian Town* (West Franklin, N.J.: Amarta Press, 1979); and Jack Campisi, *The Mashpee Indians: Tribe on Trial* (Syracuse: Syracuse University Press, 1991).

22. Among the many critiques of James Clifford, see Micaela Di Leonardo, "Mali-

nowski's nephews," *The Nation,* 248 (March 13, 1989), 350–53; Frances E. Mascia-Lees and Patricia Sharpe, "Culture, power, and text: Anthropology and literature confront each 'other,' " *American Literary History,* 4 (1992), 678–96; P. Steven Sangren, "Rhetoric and the authority of ethnography," *Current Anthropology,* 29 (1988), 405–24; Paul Rabinow, "Representations are social facts: 'Postmodernism' and the social reproduction of texts," in Clifford and Marcus, *Writing Culture,* 234–60; Arnold Krupat, *Ethnocriticism: Ethnography, History, Literature* (Berkeley: University of California Press, 1992), 101–26. See also Klein, "In search of narrative mastery," 275–86; Vincent Pecora, "The sorceror's apprentices: Romance, anthropology, and literary theory," *Modern Language Quarterly,* 55 (1994), 345–82.

    23. For an overview of this immense literature, see David Murray, *Forked Tongues: Speech, Writing, and Representation in North American Indian Texts* (Bloomington: Indiana University Press, 1991). For classic examples of such work, see Dell H. Hymes, *"In vain I tried to tell you": Essays in Native American Ethnopoetics* (Philadelphia: University of Pennsylvania Press, 1981); Dennis Tedlock, *The Spoken Word and the Work of Interpretation* (Philadelphia: University of Pennsylvania Press, 1983); and Keith H. Basso, *Western Apache Language and Culture: Essays in Linguistic Anthropology* (Tucson: University of Arizona Press, 1990).

    24. See "Don Alfonso Florez Leyva's 'Testamento': Holograph, transcription, and translation," and Larry Evers and Felipe S. Molina, "The holy dividing line: Inscription and resistance in Yaqui culture," in *"Hiakim:* The Yaqui homeland," Special Issue of *Journal of the Southwest,* 34 (1992), Larry Evers and Felipe S. Molina, eds., 3–106. See also Larry Evers and Felipe S. Molina, recorded, translated, annotated, *Wo'i bwikam = Coyote Songs: From the Yaqui Bow Leaders' Society* (Tucson: Chax Press, 1989); Larry Evers and Felipe S. Molina, *Yaqui Deer Songs, Maso Bwikam: A Native American Poetry* (Tucson: University of Arizona Press, 1987).

    25. Greg Sarris, *Keeping Slug Woman Alive: A Holistic Approach to American Indian Texts* (Berkeley: University of California Press, 1993); Greg Sarris, *Mabel McKay: Weaving the Dream* (Berkeley: University of California Press, 1994).

    26. The most obvious example is Francis Jennings, *The Invasion of America: Indians, Colonialism, and the Cant of Conquest* (Chapel Hill: University of North Carolina Press, 1975).

    27. Ibid.; Dee Brown, *Bury My Heart at Wounded Knee: An Indian History of the American West* (Fort Worth: Holt, Rinehart and Winston, 1971); Ralph K. Andrist, *The Long Death: The Last Days of the Plains Indians* (New York: Macmillan, 1964); Robert M. Utley, *The Last Days of the Sioux Nation* (New Haven: Yale University Press, 1963); Stephen Dow Beckham, *Requiem for a People: The Rogue Indians and the Frontiersmen* (Norman: University of Oklahoma Press, 1971).

    28. Gary B. Nash, *Red, White, and Black: The Peoples of Early America* (Englewood Cliffs, N.J.: Prentice-Hall, 1974); James Axtell, *The European and the Indian: Essays in the Ethnohistory of Colonial North America* (New York: Oxford University Press, 1981); Bruce G. Trigger, *The Children of Aataentsic: A History of the Huron People to 1660* (Montreal: McGill–Queen's University Press, 1976); Neal Salisbury, *Manitou and Providence: Indians, Europeans, and the Making of New England, 1500–1643* (New York: Oxford University Press, 1982); Colin G. Calloway, *Crown and Calumet: British–Indian Relations, 1783–1815* (Norman: University of Oklahoma Press, 1987); Colin G.

Calloway, *Dawnland Encounters: Indians and Europeans in Northern New England* (Hanover: University Press of New England, 1991); John A. Walthall and Thomas E. Emerson, *Calumet and Fleur-de-Lys: Archaeology of Indian and French Contact in the Midcontinent* (Washington, D.C.: Smithsonian Institution Press, 1992); John L. Kessell, *Kiva, Cross, and Crown: The Pecos Indians and New Mexico, 1540–1840* (Albuquerque: University of New Mexico Press, 1987); William W. Fitzhugh, ed., *Cultures in Contact: The European Impact on Native Cultural Institutions in Eastern North America, A.D. 1000–1800* (Washington, D.C.: Smithsonian Institution Press, 1985).

29. Anthony F. C. Wallace, *The Death and Rebirth of the Seneca* (New York: Vintage, 1972); Berkhofer, *Salvation and the Savage;* Jamake Highwater, *The Primal Mind: Vision and Reality in Indian America* (New York: New American Library, 1981); R. David Edmunds, *The Shawnee Prophet* (Lincoln: University of Nebraska Press, 1983); Weston LaBarre, *The Ghost Dance: The Origins of Religion* (London: George Allen and Unwin, 1972); Gregory Evans Dowd, *A Spirited Resistance: The North American Indian Struggle for Unity, 1745–1815* (Baltimore: Johns Hopkins University Press, 1992); Joel W. Martin, *Sacred Revolt: The Muskogees' Struggle for a New World* (Boston: Beacon Press, 1991); Christopher L. Miller, *Prophetic Worlds: Indians and Whites on the Columbia Plateau* (New Brunswick: Rutgers University Press, 1985); Robert H. Ruby and John A. Brown, *Dreamer-Prophets of the Columbia Plateau: Smohalla and Skolaskin* (Norman: University of Oklahoma Press, 1989).

30. Linton, *Acculturation in Seven American Indian Tribes.*

31. Malcolm McFee, "The 150% man, a product of Blackfeet acculturation," *American Anthropologist,* 70 (1968): 1096–107.

32. LaBarre, *Ghost Dance;* Russell Thornton, *We Shall Live Again: The 1870 and 1890 Ghost Dance Movements as Demographic Revitalization* (New York: Cambridge University Press, 1986); Alice Beck Kehoe, *The Ghost Dance: Ethnohistory and Revitalization* (Fort Worth: Holt, Rinehart and Winston, 1989); Omer C. Stewart, *Peyote Religion: A History* (Norman: University of Oklahoma Press, 1987); Joseph G. Jorgensen, *The Sun Dance Religion: Power for the Powerless* (Chicago: University of Chicago Press, 1972); David F. Aberle, *The Peyote Religion Among the Navaho* (Chicago: Aldine, 1966).

33. Ferdinand Toennies, *Community and Association (Gemeinschaft und Gesellschaft),* translated and supplemented by Charles Loomis (London: Routledge and Paul, 1955).

34. Loretta Fowler, *Shared Symbols, Contested Meanings: Gros Ventre Culture and History, 1778–1984* (Ithaca: Cornell University Press, 1987); Melissa L. Meyer, *The White Earth Tragedy: Ethnicity and Dispossession at a Minnesota Anishinaabe Reservation, 1889–1920* (Lincoln: University of Nebraska Press, 1994); David Rich Lewis, "Reservation leadership and the progressive–traditional dichotomy: William Wash and the Northern Utes, 1865-1928," *Ethnohistory,* 38 (1991), 124–48; William T. Hagan, "Full blood, mixed blood, generic, and ersatz, the problem of Indian identity," *Arizona and the West,* 27 (1985), 309–26; Melissa L. Meyer, "American Indian tribal enrollment: Blood is thicker than family," in *Over the Edge: Mapping the Contours of Western Experience,* Valerie Matsumoto and Blake Allmendinger, eds. (Berkeley: University of California Press, 1998); Melissa L. Meyer and Russell Thornton, "American Indian tribal enrollment: The blood quantum quandary," paper presented at the Annual Meeting of the American Society for Ethnohistory, November 1990, Toronto, Canada, and

at the Annual Meeting of the Pacific Coast Branch of the American Historical Association, August 1991, Kona, Hawaii.

35.   Harold A. Innis, *The Fur Trade in Canada: An Introduction to Canadian Economic History* (New Haven: Yale University Press; rev. eds. Toronto: University of Toronto Press, 1956, 1970); Jacobs, *Wilderness Politics and Indian Gifts;* John C. Ewers, "The influence of the fur trade upon the Indians of the northern plains," in *People and Pelts: Selected Papers of the Second North American Fur Trade Conference,* Malvina Bolus, ed. (Winnipeg: Peguis, 1972); Charles A. Bishop, *The Northern Ojibwa and the Fur Trade: An Historical and Ecological Study* (Toronto and Montreal: Holt, Rinehart and Winston, 1974); Arthur J. Ray, *Indians in the Fur Trade: Their Role as Hunters, Trappers and Middlemen in the Lands Southwest of Hudson Bay, 1660–1870* (Toronto and Buffalo: University of Toronto Press, 1974); Arthur J. Ray and Donald B. Freeman, *"Give Us Good Measure": An Economic Analysis of Relations Between the Indians and the Hudson's Bay Company Before 1763* (Toronto: University of Toronto Press, 1978); David J. Wishart, *The Fur Trade of the American West, 1807–1840: A Geographical Synthesis* (Lincoln: University of Nebraska Press, 1979); Bruce M. White, " 'Give us a little milk': The social and cultural significance of gift giving in the Lake Superior fur trade," in *Rendezvous: Selected Papers of the Fourth North American Fur Trade Conference, 1981,* Thomas C. Buckley, ed. (St. Paul: North American Fur Trade Conference, 1983); Peter C. Mancall, *Deadly Medicine: Indians and Alcohol in Early America* (Ithaca: Cornell University Press, 1995).

36.   J. Leitch Wright, Jr., *The Only Land They Knew: The Tragic Story of the American Indians in the Old South* (New York: Free Press, 1981); Richard White, *The Roots of Dependency: Subsistence, Environment, and Social Change Among the Choctaws, Pawnees, and Navajos* (Lincoln: University of Nebraska Press, 1983); William Cronon, *Changes in the Land: Indians, Colonists, and the Ecology of New England* (New York: Hill and Wang, 1983); Thomas D. Hall, *Social Change in the Southwest, 1350–1880* (Lawrence: University Press of Kansas, 1989); James H. Merrell, *The Indians' New World: Catawbas and Their Neighbors from European Contact Through the Era of Removal* (Chapel Hill: University of North Carolina Press, 1989); Richard White, *The Middle Ground: Indians, Empires, and Republics in the Great Lakes Region, 1650–1815* (Cambridge: Cambridge University Press, 1991); Daniel H. Usner, Jr., *Indians, Settlers, and Slaves in a Frontier Exchange Economy: The Lower Mississippi Valley Before 1783* (Chapel Hill: University of North Carolina Press, 1992).

37.   Merrell, *Indians' New World;* White, *Middle Ground;* James H. Merrell, "Some thoughts on colonial historians and American Indians," *William and Mary Quarterly,* 3rd ser., 46 (1989), 94–119.

38.   E. E. Rich, "Trade habits and economic motivation among the Indians of North America," *Canadian Journal of Economics and Political Science,* 26 (1960), 35–53; Abraham Rotstein, "Trade and politics: An institutional approach," *Western Canadian Journal of Anthropology,* 3 (1972), 1–28; Calvin Martin, *Keepers of the Game: Indian–Animal Relationships and the Fur Trade* (Berkeley: University of California Press, 1978); Shepard Krech, ed., *Indians, Animals, and the Fur Trade: A Critique of Keepers of the Game* (Athens: University of Georgia Press, 1981).

39.   Eleanor Leacock, *The Montagnais "Hunting Territory" and the Fur Trade,* American Anthropological Association, Memoir no. 78 (Washington, D.C.: American

Anthropological Association, 1954); Bruce Cox, ed., *Cultural Ecology: Readings on the Canadian Indians and Eskimos* (Toronto: McClelland and Stewart, 1973); Adrian Tanner, "The significance of hunting territories today," ibid., 101–14; James Van Stone, "The Yukon River Ingalik: Subsistence, the fur trade, and a changing resource base," *Ethnohistory*, 23 (1976), 199–212; Adrian Tanner, *Bringing Home Animals: Religious Ideology and Mode of Production of the Mistassini Cree Hunters* (New York: St. Martin's Press, 1979).

40. Jennifer S. H. Brown, *Strangers in Blood: Fur Trade Company Families in Indian Country* (Vancouver: University of British Columbia Press, 1980); Jennifer S. H. Brown, "Woman as centre and symbol in the emergence of metis communities," *Canadian Journal of Native Studies*, 3 (1983), 39–46; Sylvia Van Kirk, *"Many Tender Ties": Women in Fur-Trade Society in Western Canada, 1670–1870* (Winnipeg: Watson & Dwyer, 1980; Norman: University of Oklahoma Press, 1980); Jacqueline Peterson, "Prelude to Red River: A social portrait of the Great Lakes Metis," *Ethnohistory*, 25 (1978), 41–67; Jacqueline Peterson, "The People in Between: Indian-White Marriage and the Genesis of a Metis Society and Culture in the Great Lakes Region, 1680–1830" (Ph.D. diss., University of Illinois, Chicago Circle, 1980; Ann Arbor: University Microfilms International, 1981); Jacqueline Peterson, "Ethnogenesis: The settlement and growth of a 'new people' in the Great Lakes Region, 1702–1815," *American Indian Culture and Research Journal*, 6 (1982), 23–64.

41. Annie Heloise Abel, *The American Indian as Slaveholder and Secessionist: An Omitted Chapter in the Diplomatic History of the Southern Confederacy* (Cleveland: Arthur H. Clark, 1915); Annie Heloise Abel, *The American Indian as Participant in the Civil War* (Cleveland: Arthur H. Clark, 1919); Annie Heloise Abel, *The American Indian Under Reconstruction* (Cleveland: Arthur H. Clark, 1925); Angie Debo, *And Still the Waters Run: The Betrayal of the Five Civilized Tribes* (Princeton: Princeton University Press, 1940); Angie Debo, *The Road to Disappearance: A History of the Creek Indians* (Norman: University of Oklahoma Press, 1941); Theda Perdue, *Slavery and the Evolution of Cherokee Society, 1540–1866* (Knoxville: University of Tennessee Press, 1979); Michael D. Green, *The Politics of Indian Removal: Creek Government and Society in Crisis* (Lincoln: University of Nebraska Press, 1982); William G. McLoughlin, *Cherokee Renascence in the New Republic* (Princeton: Princeton University Press, 1986); William G. McLoughlin, *After the Trail of Tears: The Cherokees' Struggle for Sovereignty, 1839–1880* (Chapel Hill: University of North Carolina Press, 1993); Tom Hatley, *The Dividing Paths: Cherokees and South Carolinians Through the Revolutionary Era* (Oxford: Oxford University Press, 1995); James J. Rawls, *Indians of California: The Changing Image* (Norman: University of Oklahoma Press, 1984); Albert L. Hurtado, *Indian Survival on the California Frontier* (New Haven: Yale University Press, 1988); George Harwood Phillips, *Indians and Intruders in Central California, 1769–1849* (Norman: University of Oklahoma Press, 1993); Preston Holder, *The Hoe and the Horse on the Plains: A Study of Cultural Development Among North American Indians* (Lincoln: University of Nebraska Press, 1970); Alvin M. Josephy, Jr., *The Nez Perce Indians and the Opening of the Northwest* (New Haven: Yale University Press, 1965); Richard White, "The winning of the West: The expansion of the Western Sioux in the eighteenth and nineteenth centuries," *Journal of American History*, 65 (1978), 319–43; Martha Royce Blaine, *Pawnee Passage, 1870–1875* (Norman: University of

Oklahoma Press, 1990); Anthony McGinnis, *Counting Coup and Cutting Horses: Inter-tribal Warfare on the Northern Plains, 1738–1889* (Evergreen: Cordillera Press, 1990); Katherine A. Spielman, ed., *Farmers, Hunters, and Colonists: Interaction between the Southwest and the Southern Plains* (Tucson: University of Arizona Press, 1991); Angie Debo, *Geronimo: The Man, His Time, His Place* (Norman: University of Oklahoma Press, 1976); Edward H. Spicer, *Cycles of Conquest: The Impact of Spain, Mexico, and the United States on the Indians of the Southwest, 1533–1960* (Tucson: University of Arizona Press, 1962); Frank McNitt, *Navajo Wars: Military Campaigns, Slave Raids, and Reprisals* (Albuquerque: University of New Mexico Press, 1972); Elizabeth A. H. John, *Storms Brewed in Other Men's Worlds: The Confrontation of Indians, Spanish, and French in the Southwest, 1540–1795* (Lincoln: University of Nebraska Press, 1975); Eve Ball, *Indeh: An Apache Odyssey* (Provo: Brigham Young University Press, 1980); William Haas Moore, *Chiefs, Agents and Soldiers: Conflict on the Navajo Frontier, 1868–1882* (Albuquerque: University of New Mexico Press, 1994).

42. Edward E. Hill, comp., *Guide to Records in the National Archives of the United States Relating to American Indians* (Washington, D.C.: National Archives and Records Service, General Services Administration, 1981); Loretto Dennis Szucs and Sandra Hargreaves Luebking, *The Archives: A Guide to the National Archives Field Branches* (Salt Lake City: Ancestry Publishing, 1988); *American Indians: A Select Catalog of National Archives Microfilm Publications* (Washington, D.C.: National Archives Trust Fund Board, National Archives and Records Administration, 1995); George P. Murdock, *Ethnographic Bibliography of North America* (New Haven: Yale University Press, 1941); George P. Murdock, *Ethnographic Bibliography of North America* (New Haven: Human Relations Area Files Press, 1953); George P. Murdock, *Ethnographic Bibliography of North America* (New Haven: Human Relations Area Files, 1960); George P. Murdock and Timothy O'Leary, *Ethnographic Bibliography of North America* (New Haven: Human Relations Area Files Press, 1975); William Hodge, *A Bibliography of Contemporary North American Indians: Selected and Partially Annotated with Study Guide* (New York: Interland, 1976); Frederick E. Hoxie, "The view from Eagle Butte: National Archives field branches and the writing of American Indian history," *Journal of American History,* 76 (1989), 172–80; Meyer, *White Earth Tragedy,* "Bibliographic essay," 297–313; Melissa L. Meyer and Russell Thornton, "Indians and the numbers game: Quantitative methods in Native American history," in *New Directions in American Indian History,* Colin G. Calloway, ed. (Norman: University of Oklahoma Press, 1988), 5–29; Cary Meister, "Methods for evaluating the accuracy of ethnohistorical demographic data on North American Indians: A brief assessment," *Ethnohistory,* 27 (1980), 153–68.

43. Peter Iverson, "Indian tribal histories," in *Scholars and the Indian Experience: Critical Review of Recent Writing in the Social Sciences,* W. R. Swagerty, ed. (Bloomington: Indiana University Press, 1984), 205–22; James Clifton, "The tribal history: An obsolete paradigm," *American Indian Culture and Research Journal,* 3 (1979), 81–100.

44. Loretta Fowler, *Arapaho Politics, 1851–1978: Symbols in Crises of Authority* (Lincoln: University of Nebraska Press, 1982); Fowler, *Shared Symbols, Contested Meanings;* Morris Foster, *Being Comanche: A Social History of an American Indian Community* (Tucson: University of Arizona Press, 1991); M. Estellie Smith, *Governing at Taos Pueblo,* Eastern New Mexico University Contributions in Anthropology, vol. 2, no. 1, C. Irwin-Williams, ed. (Portales: Eastern New Mexico University Press, 1969);

and Jewish descent) also highlights the unhappiness of routinely imagining academic cultures as white and informant cultures as Native American. If the works of Molina (who is Yaqui) and Evers (who is not) create intercultural texts by bringing together editor-authors from different ethnic communities, the writings of scholars like Sarris suggest that we need to complicate our sometimes facile accounts of anthropology/history as colonialist discourse. While few scholars have the expertise for this sort of redaction and criticism, all of us benefit from having such texts available as sources, and they should help us to reconsider the ways we use older ethnographies and collections. At the very least, the new work suggests that we might benefit from raising to the textual surface at least some critical processes we usually consign to footnotes or bibliographies.[25]

What Have We Learned? Genres and Insights

Native American studies emerged only recently as an outgrowth of several trends. Most importantly, the convergence of the civil rights movement and the ongoing American Indian renaissance of the past twenty-five years gave new urgency to the goal of placing native historical actors at center stage. Benchmark events are the founding of Native American studies programs at the University of Minnesota and UCLA in 1969, and at Berkeley in 1972. New Deal social engineering and cases brought before the Indian Claims Commission since the late 1940s provided long-term impetus, but the demands of Native American university students and their supporters gave birth to Native American studies programs and departments. Anthropology and history together could offer no more than a handful of Native American Ph.D.'s as professors and role models; American Indians are still the most underrepresented group among university faculty members and students.

Earlier scholarship lay outside the domain of these political struggles. Much of it provides at best a foundation for later studies to build upon and at worst glaring examples of the sins of omission. Today's university students can easily grasp the inadequacies of earlier research.

Most older scholarship embraced the savagery-versus-civilization dichotomy in an unabashed celebration of colonial conquest. Even in more enlightened times, most studies fell into four groupings: (1) warfare between Indians and Euro-Americans; (2) the history of U.S. policy toward Indians; (3) attitudes toward and stereotypes about Indians; and (4) formulaic tribal histories that began in the timeless ethnographic present, ended around 1900, skimmed over watershed policy changes along the way, and were without native individuals or endogenous perspectives. As scholarship about attitudes toward Native Americans amply shows, Native Americans have long been used as foils for scholars' critiques of the United States and western civilization. In

Mischa Titiev, *The Hopi Indians of Old Oraibi: Change and Continuity* (Ann Arbor: University of Michigan Press, 1972); Peter M. Whiteley, *Deliberate Acts: Changing Hopi Culture Through the Oraibi Split* (Tucson: University of Arizona Press, 1988); John D. Loftin, *Religion and Hopi Life in the Twentieth Century* (Bloomington: Indiana University Press, 1991); Barbara Tedlock, *The Beautiful and the Dangerous: Encounters with the Zuni Indians* (New York: Viking Penguin, 1992); Alfonso Ortiz, "The dynamics of Pueblo cultural survival," in *North American Indian Anthropology: Essays on Society and Culture,* Raymond J. DeMallie and Alfonso Ortiz, eds. (Norman: University of Oklahoma Press, 1994) 296–306; Triloki Nath Pandey, "Patterns of leadership in Western Pueblo society," ibid., 328–39; Frederick E. Hoxie, *Parading Through History: The Making of the Crow Nation in America, 1805–1935* (Cambridge: Cambridge University Press, 1995).

45. Ernest L. Schusky, *The Forgotten Sioux: An Ethnohistory of the Lower Brule Reservation* (Chicago: Nelson-Hall, 1975); James A. Clifton, *The Prairie People: Continuity and Change in Potawatomi Indian Culture, 1665–1965* (Lawrence: Regents Press of Kansas, 1977); Terry P. Wilson, *The Underground Reservation: Osage Oil* (Lincoln: University of Nebraska Press, 1985); John H. Moore, *The Cheyenne Nation: A Social and Demographic History* (Lincoln: University of Nebraska Press, 1987); Thomas Biolsi, *Organizing the Lakota: The Political Economy of the New Deal on the Pine Ridge and Rosebud Reservations* (Tucson: University of Arizona Press, 1992); Meyer, *White Earth Tragedy;* Jeffrey Burton, *Indian Territory and the United States, 1866–1906* (Norman: University of Oklahoma Press, 1995).

46. The literature emphasizing this is too vast to be cited. Instead, it might be refreshing to consider strategies that have proven effective as correctives to these bleak conditions. See, for example, Robert H. White, *Tribal Assets: The Rebirth of Native America* (New York: Holt, 1990); Stephen Cornell and Joseph P. Kalt, eds., *What Can Tribes Do? Strategies and Institutions in American Indian Economic Development* (Los Angeles: American Indian Studies Center, UCLA, 1992).

47. Hurtado, *Indian Survival on the California Frontier;* Moore, *Cheyenne Nation;* Fowler, *Shared Symbols, Contested Meanings;* Merrell, *Indians' New World;* White, *Middle Ground;* Meyer, *White Earth Tragedy;* Foster, *Being Comanche;* Hoxie, *Parading Through History;* Peterson, "The People in Between"; Van Kirk, *"Many Tender Ties";* Brown, *Strangers in Blood.*

48. See nn. 29 and 32 above.

49. American Friends Service Committee, *Uncommon Controversy: Fishing Rights of the Muckleshoot, Puyallup, and Nisqually Indians* (Seattle: University of Washington Press, 1970); Jerry Kammer, *The Second Long Walk: The Navajo–Hopi Land Dispute* (Albuquerque: University of New Mexico Press, 1980); Charles T. DuMars, Marilyn O'Leary, and Albert E. Utton, *Pueblo Indian Water Rights: Struggle for a Precious Resource* (Tucson: University of Arizona Press, 1984); Daniel Raunet, *Without Surrender, Without Consent: A History of the Nishga Land Claims* (Vancouver: Douglas & McIntyre, 1984); Brodeur, *Restitution;* Imre Sutton, ed., *Irredeemable America: The Indians' Estate and Land Claims* (Albuquerque: University of New Mexico Press, 1985); Fay G. Cohen, *Treaties on Trial: The Continuing Controversy over Northwest Indian Fishing Rights* (Seattle: University of Washington Press, 1986); Ken Harper, *Give Me My Father's Body: The Life of Minik, the New York Eskimo* (Iqaluit, Northwest Terri-

tory: Blacklead Books, 1986); Charles F. Wilkinson, *American Indians, Time, and the Law: Native Societies in a Modern Constitutional Democracy* (New Haven: Yale University Press, 1987); Catherine Feher-Elston, *Children of Sacred Ground: America's Last Indian War* (Flagstaff: Northland, 1988); Gail H. Landsman, *Sovereignty and Symbol: Indian–White Conflict at Ganienkeh* (Albuquerque: University of New Mexico Press, 1988); Robert Doherty, *Disputed Waters: Native Americans and the Great Lakes Fishery* (Lexington: University of Kentucky Press, 1990); Paul Tennant, *Aboriginal Peoples and Politics: The Indian Land Question in British Columbia, 1849–1989* (Vancouver: University of British Columbia Press, 1990); Larry Krotz, *Indian Country: Inside Another Canada* (Toronto: McClelland and Stewart, 1990); Lloyd Burton, *American Indian Water Rights and the Limits of Law* (Lawrence: University Press of Kansas, 1991); Campisi, *Mashpee Indians;* R. C. Gordon-McCutchan, *The Taos Indians and the Battle for Blue Lake* (Santa Fe: Red Crane, 1991); Rick Hornung, *One Nation Under the Gun: Inside the Mohawk Civil War* (New York: Pantheon, 1991); Edward Lazarus, *Black Hills, White Justice: The Sioux Nation Versus the United States, 1775 to the Present* (New York: HarperCollins, 1991); H. Marcus Price III, *Disputing the Dead: U.S. Law on Aboriginal Remains and Grave Goods* (Columbia: University of Missouri Press, 1991); George C. Shattuck, *The Oneida Land Claims: A Legal History* (Syracuse: Syracuse University Press, 1991); Christopher Vecsey, ed., *Handbook of American Indian Religious Freedom* (New York: Crossroad, 1991); George Wenzel, *Animal Rights, Human Rights: Ecology, Economy and Ideology in the Canadian Arctic* (Toronto: University of Toronto Press, 1991); Thomas R. McGuire, William B. Lord, and Mary G. Wallace, ed., *Indian Water in the New West* (Tucson: University of Arizona Press, 1993); Emily Benedek, *The Wind Won't Know Me: A History of the Navajo–Hopi Land Dispute* (New York: Knopf, 1992); Bruce E. Johansen, *Life and Death in Mohawk Country* (Golden, Colo.: North American Press, 1993); Tamara L. Bray and Thomas W. Killion, eds., *Reckoning with the Dead: The Larsen Bay Repatriation and the Smithsonian Institution* (Washington, D.C.: Smithsonian Institution Press, 1994); Malcolm Ebright, *Land Grants and Lawsuits in Northern New Mexico* (Albuquerque: University of New Mexico Press, 1994); Peter H. Eichstaedt, *If You Poison Us: Uranium and Native Americans* (Santa Fe: Red Crane, 1994); Rick Whaley with Walter Bresette, *Walleye Warriors: An Effective Alliance Against Racism and for the Earth* (Philadelphia: New Society Publishers, 1994).

50. Wallace, *Death and Rebirth of the Seneca;* Anthony F. C. Wallace, *Rockdale: The Growth of an American Village in the Early Industrial Revolution* (New York: Norton, 1978).

51. Merrell, "Some thoughts."

52. Lynda Shaffer, *Native Americans Before 1492: The Moundbuilding Centers of the Eastern Woodlands* (Armonk, N.Y.: M. E. Sharpe, 1992); David S. Brose, James A. Brown, and David W. Penney, *Ancient Art of the American Woodland Indians* (New York: H. N. Abrams, in association with the Detroit Institute of Arts, 1985).

53. Bruce D. Smith, *Rivers of Change: Essays on Early Agriculture in Eastern North America* (Washington, D.C.: Smithsonian Institution Press, 1992).

54. Russell Thornton, Jonathan Warren, and Tim Miller, "Depopulation in the Southeast after 1492," in *Disease and Demography in the Americas,* John W. Verano and Douglas H. Ubelaker, eds. (Washington, D.C.: Smithsonian Institution Press, 1991), 187–95; Russell Thornton, Tim Miller, and Jonathan Warren, "American Indian popu-

lation recovery following smallpox epidemics," *American Anthropologist,* 93 (1991), 20–38; Dean R. Snow and Kim Lanphear, "European contact and Indian depopulation in the Northeast: The timing of the first epidemics," *Ethnohistory,* 35 (1988), 15–33; Russell Thornton, *American Indian Holocaust and Survival: A Population History Since 1492* (Norman: University of Oklahoma Press, 1987); Ann F. Ramenofsky, *Vectors of Death: The Archaeology of European Contact* (Albuquerque: University of New Mexico Press, 1987).

55.   Henry F. Dobyns, "Estimating aboriginal American population: An appraisal of techniques with a new hemispheric estimate," *Current Anthropology,* 7 (1966), 395–416; Henry F. Dobyns, *Their Number Become Thinned: Native American Population Dynamics in Eastern North America* (Knoxville: University of Tennessee Press, 1983); Wilbur R. Jacobs, "The tip of an iceberg: Pre-Columbian Indian demography and some implications for revisionism," *William and Mary Quarterly,* 31 (1974), 123–32; William M. Denevan, ed., *The Native Population of the Americas in 1492,* 2d ed. (Madison: University of Wisconsin Press, 1992 [1976]).

56.   Nancy Shoemaker, "From longhouse to log house: Household structure among the Senecas in 1900," *American Indian Quarterly,* 15 (1991), 329–39; Wallace, *Death and Rebirth of the Seneca.*

57.   Karen I. Blu, *The Lumbee Problem: The Making of an American Indian People* (Cambridge: Cambridge University Press, 1980); J. Leitch Wright, Jr., *Creeks and Seminoles: The Destruction and Regeneration of the Muscogulge People* (Lincoln: University of Nebraska Press, 1986); Jack D. Forbes, *Africans and Native Americans: The Language of Race and the Evolution of Red-Black Peoples* (Urbana: University of Illinois Press, 1993); Gerald M. Sider, *Lumbee Indian Histories: Race, Ethnicity, and Indian Identity in the Southern United States* (Cambridge: Cambridge University Press, 1993); Daniel F. Littlefield, *Rice and Slaves: Ethnicity and the Slave Trade in Colonial South Carolina* (Baton Rouge: Louisiana State University Press, 1981); Daniel F. Littlefield, *Africans and Creeks: From the Colonial Period to the Civil War* (Westport: Greenwood Press, 1979); Daniel F. Littlefield, *Africans and Seminoles: From Removal to Emancipation* (Westport: Greenwood Press, 1977); Daniel F. Littlefield, *The Cherokee Freedmen: From Emancipation to American Citizenship* (Westport: Greenwood Press, 1978); Daniel F. Littlefield, *The Chickasaw Freedmen: A People Without a Country* (Westport: Greenwood Press, 1980); William Loren Katz, *Black Indians: A Hidden Heritage* (New York: Atheneum, 1986).

58.   The best overview of the status of the field is Nancy Shoemaker, "Introduction," in *Negotiators of Change: Historical Perspectives on Native American Women,* Nancy Shoemaker, ed. (New York: Routledge, 1995). See also Patricia Albers and Beatrice Medicine, eds., *The Hidden Half: Studies of Plains Indian Women* (Washington, D.C.: University Press of America, 1983); Laura F. Klein and Lillian A. Ackerman, eds., *Women and Power in Native North America* (Norman: University of Oklahoma Press, 1995).

59.   For discussions of gender and sexuality, see Walter L. Williams, *The Spirit and the Flesh: Sexual Diversity in American Indian Culture* (Boston: Beacon Press, 1986); Will Roscoe, *The Zuni Man-Woman* (Albuquerque: University of New Mexico Press, 1991).

60.   Michael Coleman, *American Indian Children at School, 1850–1930* (Jackson:

University Press of Mississippi, 1993); Sally McBeth, *Ethnic Identity and the Boarding School Experience of West-Central Oklahoma American Indians* (Washington, D.C.: University Press of America, 1983); Francis P. Prucha, *The Churches and the Indian Schools* (Lincoln: University of Nebraska Press, 1979); Margaret Szasz, *Education and the American Indian: The Road to Self-Determination, 1928–1973* (Albuquerque: University of New Mexico Press, 1974); Robert Trennert, *The Phoenix Indian School: Forced Assimilation in Arizona* (Norman: University of Oklahoma Press, 1988); John Williams and Howard L. Meredith, *Bacone Indian University: A History* (Oklahoma City: Western Heritage Books, 1980).

61.   K. Tsianina Lomawaima, *They Called It Prairie Light: The Story of Chilocco Indian School* (Lincoln: University of Nebraska Press, 1994). See also Donal Lindsey, *Indians at Hampton Institute, 1877–1923* (Urbana: University of Illinois Press, 1995); Devon A. Mihesuah, *Cultivating the Rosebuds: The Education of Women at the Cherokee Female Seminary* (Urbana: University of Illinois Press, 1993).

62.   Forbes, *Africans and Native Americans.*

63.   Jean M. O'Brien, *Dispossession by Degrees: Indian Land and Identity in Natick, Massachusetts, 1650–1790* (Cambridge: Cambridge University Press, 1997); Michael L. Fickes, " 'They could not endure that yoke': The colonial captivity of Pequot women and children after the War of 1637" (M.A. thesis, University of California, Los Angeles, Department of History, 1996); James Drake, "Severing the ties that bind them: A reconceptualization of King Philip's War" (Ph.D. diss., University of California, Los Angeles, 1996); Usner, *Indians, Settlers, and Slaves;* George Phillips, "Indians in Los Angeles, 1781–1875: Economic integration, social disintegration," *Pacific Historical Review,* 49 (1980), 427–51; Henry Dobyns, Richard Stoffle, and Kristine Jones, "Native American urbanization and socio-economic integration in the southwestern U.S.," *Ethnohistory,* 22 (1975), 155–79; Rolf Knight, *Indians at Work: An Informal History of Native Indian Labour in British Columbia, 1858–1930* (Vancouver: New Star, 1978); Meyer, *White Earth Tragedy;* Nancy Shoemaker, "Urban Indians and ethnic choices: American Indian organizations in Minneapolis, 1920–1950," *Western Historical Quarterly,* 19 (1988), 431–47; Alice Littlefield and Martha Knack, ed., *Native Americans and Wage Labor: Ethnohistorical Perspectives* (Norman: University of Oklahoma Press, 1996).

64.   Elaine M. Neils, *Reservation to City: Indian Migration and Federal Relocation,* Research Paper, no. 131 (Chicago: University of Chicago, Department of Geography, 1971); Arthur Margon, "Indians and immigrants: A comparison of groups new to the city," *Journal of Ethnic Studies,* 4 (1977), 17–28; Shoemaker, "Urban Indians and ethnic choices"; Joan Weibel-Orlando, *Indian Country, L.A.: Maintaining Ethnic Community in Complex Society* (Urbana: University of Illinois Press, 1991).

65.   Bernard Bailyn, *The Peopling of British North America: An Introduction* (New York: Knopf, 1986).

9 *Richard White*

Using the Past
History and Native American Studies

History is not the only way of using the past. The current fascination among historians with myth, public memory, and tradition acknowledges that there are alternative and rival creations of the past. But the response of historians to rivals is imperial. Historians recognize alternative ways of using the past in order to historicize them, domesticate them, and make them part of history itself. Within the academy, other uses of the past have not succeeded in invading the turf history claims, challenging its authority and procedures, and trying to set themselves up as rivals. Or rather, they have not done so except in Native American studies.[1]

I neither wish to exaggerate this challenge nor denigrate other ways of using the past. My intent is much more modest: I want to look at explicit challenges to both history itself and conventional historical understandings that too often fail to get the respectful scrutiny they deserve. (Even as I recognize academic history's limits and shortcomings, I remain very much an academic historian. My own sympathies are with academic history.) There are two reasons why the challenges Native American studies has presented to historians have failed to get much critical examination. The first lies in attitudes many historians share with non-Indians overall. The second lies within the practices of historians themselves.

Most American historians, like most modern Americans, are pious about Native American peoples, but they do not take Native Americans very seriously. Most nonnatives relegate Native Americans to the past. Living Native Americans become invisible; dead Native Americans become visible without becoming historical. In both popular culture and the academy, Native Americans are people who either have no significant history or exist outside history.

Popular understandings make Native Americans ahistorical by reflexively granting Native Americans a certain "spiritual" or "traditional" knowledge. This knowledge is timeless; it seemingly appeared whole at some point far in the past and now can only erode. It cannot be added to. In this formulation Native Americans do not learn; they only forget and disappear.

This inherited spiritual knowledge serves to make Native Americans nearly identical with nature itself. When Native Americans speak, nature speaks. So, in yet another version of the old western story of savagery—noble and ig-noble—Native Americans merge with nature. They become "primal peoples" at one with the world around them. Only whites and assorted other non-Indians are peoples of history: this is why our flattery of "primal peoples" and their traditional knowledge—for we do intend to flatter—is an act of such immense condescension. For in a continent and a country defined by change, we regard non–Native Americans as the only people who make a difference. At best, Native Americans matter only as a litmus test to determine if our actions are good or bad. But, as they become one with nature, they also cease to matter as either historical or modern peoples. They stand outside history.

Even historians who do not share such attitudes reflect in their practice another kind of exclusion of Native Americans from history. Native Americans are outside history because their history does not matter much to our under-standings of the modern world. Most historians make the case by omission. If Native American history mattered, Native Americans would be an indispens-able part of our narration of the past and not a tragic sidebar.

With both popular assumptions and historical practice pushing Native Americans to the margins of history, it is not surprising that challenges to aca-demic history find fertile ground in Native American studies and that such challenges can proceed without attracting much response from American his-torians overall. If such arguments had challenged groups judged more central to the American experience, or if they had developed in the heart of the disci-pline of history itself, there would have been controversy. But not only have Native Americans seemed inconsequential to larger historical understandings; many antihistorical arguments have developed outside history in anthropology and cultural studies.

The challenge to conventional academic history is still very much in flux, but it takes two broad forms. One is a challenge to historical understand-ing itself. This challenge either draws on European intellectual traditions that claim traditional American Indian understandings as critical evidence, or it claims to represent those traditional understandings themselves.

The second challenge does not necessarily repudiate historical understandings per se; rather, it attacks particular narrative forms and conclusions embraced by most academic historians. This alternative history defines itself as anticolonialist. Here, again, Native American studies borrows from the outside. This alternative history has perhaps been most thoroughly developed in subaltern studies, a branch of historical writings still not commonly read by American historians. It has moved into Native American studies under the broader rubric of postcolonial studies.

Distinguishing these two broad approaches is useful as a heuristic device, but in actual practice there is considerable mixing and matching of arguments. This eclecticism, with all the contradictions it sometimes entails, is a mark of the current state of Native American studies. It makes developments in the field distinctive; few elements of the arguments within the field are original, but they often form a unique mix.

Anthropology and Cultural Studies

The academic construction of Native Americans as a people standing against, rather than just being outside, history has a distinguished intellectual pedigree. Native Americans have provided ammunition for two of the most influential and sophisticated late twentieth-century critiques of history: structuralism and postmodernism. Neglected by historians, Native Americans have appeared in scholarly debates as peoples who offer alternatives to history itself. Claude Lévi-Strauss used Native Americans as a model of peoples who constructed mythic pasts that had not yet descended into history. Jean-François Lyotard used Native Americans to attack metanarratives of the kind that characterizes most western history.[2]

Structuralism explicitly and most famously placed traditional societies outside history. When Lévi-Strauss divided the world between cold and hot societies—that is, traditional and modern societies—he marked off sharp differences between societies of myth and timelessness on the one hand and those of history and chronology on the other. He not only classified American Indians on the side of tradition; they were among his primary examples.[3]

Within Native American history and Native American studies, Calvin Martin has been the leading advocate of defining "real" American Indians as a people outside history. He has combined Lévi-Straussian structuralism with New Age seeking into an idiosyncratic mix. Two of Martin's controversial books, *The American Indian and the Problem of History* and *In the Spirit of the Earth,* represent forays against history itself.[4]

Martin, himself a prize-winning academic historian, gives a pessimistic assessment of academic histories of Native American peoples. It is an assessment shared by some academic historians discouraged by the slight impact of

Native American history on the discipline as a whole.[5] Most American historians, Martin wrote, have dismissed American Indian history as a quaint sideshow, a depressing and "endless tale of woe and atrocity." [6] According to Martin, historians of Native American peoples deserve such disdain because they themselves have neglected the true nature of Native Americans. Historians, by turning American Indians into a "people of history," have distorted their essence: "Native Americans traditionally subscribed to a philosophy of history, and of time, profoundly different from ours and our forebears." [7] Indians, Martin has claimed, were primal and biological. Europeans are historical and anthropological.[8] To write of Native Americans as if they were historical peoples is an act of ideological colonization.[9] Real American Indians were and are a product of a mythic world in which all of life's "effective and responsible acts" were revealed at creation and still exist.[10] The only significant history is the "sacred history" of creation. Secular history can neither add to nor subtract from this sacred history.[11]

Martin wants an acknowledgment of the old structuralist division between hot and cold societies. Native Americans are not people of history, and so historians "need to get out of history, as we know it, if we wish to write authentic histories of American Indians." [12] Historians have to escape time and grasp an unchanging eternal reality, an "eternally flowing present." [13]

The issue for Martin is moral, not just intellectual. History is an attempt of humans to assert their autonomy from nature. The effort is, according to Martin, arrogant, mad, and doomed.[14] Historical consciousness has become "the greatest enemy of true progress." [15] American Indians and other traditional people point the way back to nature.

Martin is fully aware of the echoes of noble savagery in all this, and he insists that this is not yet another version of that old iconic version of Native Americans, even as he replicates nearly all of its key tenets. Martin merges Native Americans and nature. Knowledge is primal knowledge.[16] Martin differs only in going the old account of corruption by modernity one better. Calvin Luther Martin writes of the Fall. Eden was the Paleolithic. The Fall was the Neolithic. In disavowing history, he writes a supposed history of the descent into history, a lament for the Paleolithic that was largely lost in the triumph of Neolithic farmers.[17] Martin widens the realm of primal peoples beyond Native Americans. In *Spirit of the Earth* he divorces primal knowledge from most living Native Americans and seeks to make it available to New Age seekers, but insofar as some true Native Americans remain possessed of primal knowledge, Martin retains the very conception of Native Americans against which many academic historians write.

In Martin's writing there is, as Susan Hegeman notes "a pure, authentic, trans-historical essence to Native American culture and thought which existed before the European encounters and which continues today, in an obscured form." [18] Hegeman sees a search for the "authentic, original, authoritative" at the root of both Martin's rendering of Native Americans as radically Other and attempts by other historians to write "Indian-centered" narratives.[19] Native Americans exist to rescue the rest of us from ourselves. Standing against this in much recent historical writing and anthropology are Native Americans as the impure, historical, and negotiated. This does not, of course, make them any less Native American.

Martin appealed not to anthropology, but to a specific structuralist anthropology that even as he wrote had come under devastating attack. Both historians and poststructuralist anthropologists mounted attacks on non-European societies as "Other," as pure and authentic, and painted them as just as impure and contingent as Europe itself. Poststructuralists mounted a vigorous attack on distinctions between hot and cold societies. An anthropological critique challenged the structuralist formulation by using Lévi-Strauss's own examples—South American Indians—against him. Native narratives of the past, these scholars argued, certainly contained ahistoric and mythic narratives, but they also included historical narratives, and complicated mythohistorical narratives.[20]

At the same time that scholars asserted that traditional societies did indeed possess historical consciousness as well as historical agency, other scholars quite independently argued that modern societies embodied understandings of the past other than history. Concern with popular memory, particularly studies of sites of memory (*les lieux de mémoire*), to use Pierre Nora's term, emphasized memory not as a personal synonym for history, but as a rival to historical constructions of the past.[21] Scholars looking at American narratives of the past, many of them featuring Native American peoples, argued that American myths disseminated by mass media existed alongside history in an advanced industrial society where history supposedly should have held full sway.[22]

There was thus an ironic twist involved in breaking down the structuralist distinction between hot and cold societies: it was not an unmitigated triumph for history. Both history and myth extended their reach. History, particularly academic history, was but one way of understanding the past; others were also constantly at work in the world.

This twist allowed a second critique of history to emerge from what seemed to be the ruins of structuralism. As structuralism yielded to poststructuralism, the distinction between societies without history and societies with history was resurrected in a new form on the level of narrative. Lyotard features Native American peoples as exemplars of local narratives that stand against the universalizing metanarratives of most history. This has not always been Lyotard's position. Kerwin Klein has in effect historicized Lyotard's own account of the production of master or metanarratives and local narratives, arguing that Lyotard's own position has changed over time.[23]

Lyotard's critique of the master or metanarratives of historians has theoretically allowed an opening in which local narratives can function to throw not only particular historical constructions of the past but history itself into doubt. In practice the result has been more complicated.

This sense of multiple constructions of the past colliding and intersecting has become a central part of James Clifford's work. Clifford, who is in fact a historian, is also one of the most representative practitioners of what is often labeled poststructuralist anthropology. His article on the Mashpee Indians' suit to gain recognition as an Indian tribe is heavily cited by scholars involved in Native American studies.

On one level Clifford's account of the Mashpees is a poststructuralist narrative in which local knowledge confronts metanarratives, but the end result is something less than a challenge to academic history. Clifford portrays Mashpee identity as contingent and contextual, a combination of loss and invention. His account is about ways of looking.[24] Mashpee witnesses, however, do not regard their identity that way. As Clifford admits, for them "culture and tradition are continuities, not inventions." [25] Mashpees do speak in Clifford's article. The article is purposefully narrated to reflect multiple positions. It rejects a God's eye view. "Mistrustful of transparent accounts," Clifford wants his writing "to manifest some of its frames and angles, its wavelengths." [26]

On one level the article is indeterminate, but it is a contrived indeterminacy. Clifford ultimately engages in a radical historicization, not only of the objects of study—Indian peoples—but of the historians and their own systems of knowledge. It seems as much a self-conscious extension of the historicizing enterprise as a challenge to history itself.[27] And, in the end, Clifford reaches historical conclusions. He is convinced that "organized Indian life had been going on in Mashpee for the past 350 years." [28]

Clifford's narratives do not remain indeterminate. He controls his account. He structures it. But he does not control the outcome of the actual clash of competing narratives in any real world sense: the jury in the Mashpee case that Clifford covered reached conclusions opposite his own. What Clifford is doing, and he does it in a very interesting and intelligent manner, is organizing and orchestrating a variety of ways of constructing the past to put them to the ultimate service of a history. It is Clifford who is in control, and it is Clifford's construction of identity, not those of the Mashpees or their opponents, that dominates his text.

Ethnohistory and Tradition

Clifford's technique of historicizing history itself is, of course, hardly unique. Historians seek to subsume all other narrations of the past by historicizing them, but if *all* things are historicized, then the knowledge of historians is as contingent and situated as that of their subjects—in this case Indian peoples. There is no view from nowhere, as Donna Haraway says. All knowledge is situated knowledge. This is not a statement of relativism, as it is sometimes taken to be. It does not say all accounts are equal, but it is a recognition that all accounts are contingent, imperfect, and judged by changing and variable human standards.

Native American studies has raised the problem of how far historicizing—seeing the past as a constant set of makings and remakings, appearances and disappearances that can be taken in from a vantage point outside the particular cultures under examination—should extend. Within Native American studies, tradition is often pitted against history and historicizing. Perhaps no word appears more often as a description of Native Americans than "traditional." The meaning of tradition is perhaps the greatest site of controversy between scholars bent on historicizing Native Americans, the self-understanding of many Native Americans, and scholars interested in challenging not only the historicizing of Indians but history itself.

Historians recognize other ways of ordering the past in order to historicize and dominate them. Critics see in this historicizing not only a disciplinary domination, but a colonial domination that is both a reflection of and a constituent part of Europe's colonization and domination of the world. History, critics say, dominates even when it claims to liberate.

The discussion of this dominance within Native American history has been more implicit than explicit, but the issue has appeared in a theoretically explicit manner in the "other" Indian history—the history of the Indian subcontinent and subaltern studies.[29] Through them, it is filtering back into Native American studies.[30] Ashis Nandy, for example, provides an argument easily transferable to Native American studies. Nandy argues that historical consciousness with its relentless historicizing abets colonialism, removes the opportunity for self-definition, and is complicit in the violence that has characterized modernity. By a very different reasoning and for different ends, he reaches a conclusion similar to Calvin Martin's: traditional societies are outside history and historical consciousness and should remain there.[31]

Historians certainly are bent on historicizing tradition. Benedict Anderson's influential *Imagined Communities* and his paper in the collection *The Invention of Tradition,* edited by Eric Hobsbawm and Terence Ranger question both its origins and its construction.[32] Tradition is not what a supposedly ancient group carried down unchanging from a timeless past; instead, it is often a relatively recent invention of a quite recently constituted group of people. Tradition, in any case, is always subject to change as it is passed down and readjusted to current circumstances. When Sam Gill historicized the concept of Mother Earth and argued that it was the product of "the complex history of the encounter between Native Americans and Americans of European ancestry," and not a construction of the pre-Columbian past, he hit a cultural trip wire. He struck at a tradition supposedly buried deep in the mists of time and at the heart of much Native American religion.[33]

"Tradition" is a malleable word. As used by and about Native American peoples, it can be the great essentialist category: it can signify the unchanging essence of a group.[34] This is often at the heart of popular uses of the word in regard to Native Americans. It can also refer to cultural practices that make a group distinctive. Such practices date from a previous generation, but they are not necessarily either unchanging or original to the group.[35] Most traditions are oral, and belong to a specific cultural entity, but "traditions" can also refer to a rather abstract set of assumptions supposedly once shared by many Native American groups. Ronald Trosper thus talks about "Traditional American Indian Economic Policy." "Community, Connectedness, the Seventh Generation (consideration of descendants), and Humility" were supposedly the marks of a traditional knowledge that he admits he had to synthesize out of the scholarly literature.[36]

It is around the issue of traditions that some of the most fruitful ferment in Native American studies has occurred. The questions of whether and how Native American understandings of the past can, or should, be assimilated into academic narratives remains a very live issue in Native American studies.[37]

Precisely because most historians recognize the constructedness of any version of the past, they are skeptical of received knowledge and willing to see their own constructions as tentative. Practicing historians have long recognized that they write as if they are describing the world as it was, but they are actually describing the world that they have created from the debris of the past. They interpret the traces that the past leaves in the present by using the intellectual tools they possess and following rules of their collective devising. The weight they give to certain kinds of evidence, the questions they ask, and the issues they explore are inextricably tied up with the concerns of their own society. Historians make maps of vanished countries. There are only the maps; the past is gone and cannot be recreated.

In seeking to understand the past as a past and not just a reflection of the present, historians give agency to people who lived there and try to understand their motivations as particular and contextual rather than as universal. People's motivations in the past depended in part on their understanding of the world, including their own understanding of their pasts. These understandings not only often differ from our current understandings but involve assertions about actions and events that we now regard as impossible. Incorporating past, and current, understandings that violate our own sense of the world into our historical narratives is a problem common to most histories, but it is particularly acute in Native American history because very often aspects of Native American understanding differ so dramatically from that of the historian.

Raymond DeMallie's thoughtful consideration of William Cronon's equally thoughtful analysis of historical narrative can illustrate the way in which Native American history confronts common scholarly problems in quite dramatic forms.[38] DeMallie has argued that in writing Lakota ethnohistory, scholars confront documents that preserve "complementary perspectives based on different cultural premises; in a fundamental sense they represent conflicting realities, rooted in radically different epistemologies. The challenge of ethnohistory is to bring these two types of historical data together to construct a fuller picture of the past." [39] The ethnohistorical account thus is a hybrid; it replicates neither perspective but ideally contains both. It is itself a new narrative that constructs yet a third perspective on past events: that of the ethnohistorian.

This is a reasonable, if general, description of the process and its goal, but it runs into some illuminating difficulties in practice. DeMallie cites three of Cronon's propositions about the evaluation of historical narratives: they "cannot contravene known facts about the past," stories "must make ecological sense," and they are to be judged not just as narratives but as nonfiction. But, DeMallie asks, how then do we evaluate the work of Father Peter Powell?[40]

Father Powell is a widely admired ethnohistorian who has worked closely with the Northern Cheyenne and has been adopted by them. He intends his histories to reflect a Northern Cheyenne understanding of the world and their own past. But to understand his project only as an attempt to convey a Cheyenne understanding is to oversimplify. Father Powell wants to show how the Cheyenne version of their past and their sacred history is reconcilable with a Catholic view of universal history and salvation.[41]

DeMallie is clear in his own evaluation of Powell. He calls his work "the most thoroughly consistent, culturally grounded interpretation of the history of an American Indian group ever written." It "points the way to alternative narrative modes." [42] According to DeMallie, Powell takes the first steps toward new and more inclusive possibilities of historical narration.

He reaches this conclusion despite Powell's violation of all three of Cronon's propositions. In Powell's account, for example, human beings are transformed into buffalo, contravening "the historian's sense of past reality, of ecology, and of nonfiction." DeMallie thinks Cronon's propositions are misplaced because to criticize Powell according to such criteria is to suggest "that the perspectives of the actors in histories are not legitimately part of the story." [43]

Such a critique would be telling except that (1) it is not really Cronon's position and (2) the criticism undercuts DeMallie's own earlier and quite cogent description of the ethnohistorical narrative as a hybrid that creates a third narrative of the past. Cronon certainly does not deny that a narrative should contain the actor's perspectives. He just distinguishes that perspective from that of the historian, as did DeMallie in his original formulation. The problem here is that Father Powell, in choosing a Cheyenne narrative voice, sometimes conflates his perspective with that of the Cheyenne participants, and sometimes, particularly in his footnotes, he stands apart from it.[44] For Cheyenne actors in the past to believe that humans turn into buffalo is one thing; for Father Powell the historian to believe it is another. It costs him credibility with some readers and reviewers.

Framing the issue this way seems to solve the problem, but does it? It only brings us deeper into issues of narration and the multiple ways humans understand the past. The key issue is not the stance of people in the past, as difficult as recovering their perspective might be; the issue is the difficulty involved in the position of the narrator. Father Powell speaks as an adopted Cheyenne. He also speaks as an "Anglo-Catholic priest." Anglo-Catholic priests, and most Anglo-Catholics, speak from a world view that makes claims about the past that violate Cronon's propositions as thoroughly as do those of the Cheyenne. Virgin births, bodies rising from the dead, and many other Christian beliefs contravene our normal sense of past reality, ecology, and nonfiction. Yet they are claimed as history by many believers. Indeed, any serious Christian perspective cannot regard history as indeterminate: its ultimate point is known. It is a story of redemption and salvation.

If Powell were writing a history of Christianity or of missionary activities among the Cheyenne, would we expect him to distance himself from the perspective of the believers and to interrupt the narrative to assure readers that events Christians believe in could not actually have taken place? Under a strict application of Cronon's criteria, Powell, it would seem, can no more narrate as a Catholic then as a Cheyenne if he wishes to claim status as a historian. But in practice Catholics and other Christians are granted narrative credibility all the time. If Powell can narrate as a Catholic, then logically he can narrate as a Cheyenne. He no more has to disavow people turning into buffalo than he would have to disavow Christ's resurrection or the virgin birth.

But we can complicate this still more by introducing a third element. What if Powell, instead of narrating the history of the Cheyennes, were narrating a history of the Aryan Nation? Would we grant him the same narrative authority that we might now grant to Cheyennes or Catholics if his narration presented American history as a racial struggle between superior Aryans and inferior mud peoples? Or would we then demand a narrative voice and position that, as in DeMallie's original proposition, replicates the world view of the participants without embracing it? Instead, would not we expect him to disavow and critique it and deny him credibility if he failed to? If we treat a Cheyenne, a Catholic, and an Aryan Nation narration differently when each violates an agreed-upon set of rules, are we not then simply applying standards according to our own obvious preferences? And if there is a common set of standards that accepts the Catholic and Cheyenne narration and not the Aryan Nation narration on the basis of, for example, the consequences of each narration in the present, then are we not explicitly tying the truth of the narrative to the present worthiness of the groups embracing the narration?

Such questions are quite immediate in much Native American history. They can be particularly pressing for historians of Native American peoples who happen to be Indian and members of Indian communities. Joe Sando's history of Jemez Pueblo—*Nee Hemish*—can serve as an example. As both a trained academic historian and a member of Jemez Pueblo, Sando sought to accommodate both academic accounts of Hemish origins and accounts of the Hemish themselves. The Hemish, like other Pueblo peoples, claim to have risen from the underground. In their case, they emerged at *Hoa-sjela,* now Stone or Boulder Lake on the Jicarilla Apache Reservation.[45]

A non-Hemish historian would probably simply say that the Hemish believe they emerged from *Hoa-sjela,* but Sando also believes this. He wants to claim Hemish emergence as a potentially valid explanation of Hemish origins. His technique is interesting. He mixes Hemish origin stories with what would seem equally problematic to many historians: a western rise-to-civilization narrative. He gives an account of the multiple theories of Indian origins. He describes origin stories as "vague, mythical, remote, and clouded by the romantic mists of antiquity," but he also writes that "tribal oral history is valuable and sacred for those raised within its confines." He is willing, similarly, to grant some credibility to migration from Asia for some Native American peoples, but he points out the evidentiary problems of such theories and grants them no greater credibility than other academic theories not taken seriously by most historians, anthropologists, and archaeologists. By making all accounts unsubstantiated and indeterminate, he seeks to leave room for Hemish origin stories.[46] It is in some ways a more sophisticated version of tactics used by those who question Darwinian theories of human evolution.

DeMallie's original attraction to Powell's narrative, despite the problems it raises, springs in part from a belief that too many historians sin on the other extreme: they leave out of their narratives the accounts and explanations that violate their own sense of how the world works. To combat the rendering of Native Americans as the exotic, primitive Other, they can introduce omissions and elisions in their narratives that habitually mask certain kinds of evidence— such as claims of Indians turning into buffalo.

In my own book, *The Middle Ground,* I took a narrative approach very different from Powell's, but also full of potential pitfalls. In the book, for example, I cited a document from Paul Radin's field notes that provides an account of some Winnebagos joining Tenskwatawa, the Shawnee prophet. I used it only to show Tenskwatawa's promise of a new medicine. Although the issue of supernatural medicines is clearly part of a distinctive Winnebago world view, I skirted issues that Powell faced more squarely. In the Winnebago account the party walked "as thunders and walk[ed] above the earth." This may be metaphorical. But in the same account the prophet also turned his belt into a snake, which was not, I think, intended to mean a metaphorical snake. I did not mention any of this. I do not believe that the Winnebagos walked above the earth, nor that the prophet turned his belt into a snake, although I do believe that that is what the Winnebagos thought. In making this narrative decision, I failed to convey a full Winnebago understanding of significant events in the way that Powell conveyed a Cheyenne understanding. It is precisely this kind of narrative conundrum that writing Native American history forces historians to face.

Such problems of narration are linked to problems of historical evidence. Much of the evidence in Native American history consists of outsiders from one culture describing the conditions and motivations of people from another. Much of the rest comes from oral accounts. Because oral traditions, like the memory they rely on, are living, their concern is with shaping not just the narration but the evidence itself to suit present purposes. Like written history, they exist to make the world understandable, but unlike written history they are their own source. They do not have to confront intractable material relics from the past in the same way that historical accounts do. They are a very different kind of evidence than written documents or material artifacts and need to be understood according to their own rules and context. They cannot be conflated with written evidence, but the two can perhaps be used in a complementary manner that allows us to see how different societies organize a common past.[47]

These problems of narration, evidence, and multiple ways of organizing the past are hardly unique to Native American history. It is precisely because they occur in many histories that the struggles of historians of Native American peoples to deal with them in often exaggerated forms should be of interest to scholars.[48]

It is easy to agree in principle that the perspective of historical actors is critical and nonetheless slight that perspective in the writing of an actual history when it is quite foreign to our own understandings. It is easy to claim that we will historicize everything, including our own work. It is much harder to do so in practice. It is also surprisingly easy to assume that there is a fundamental epistemological agreement among historians until an issue such as humans turning into buffalo reveals cracks in our set of rules for evaluating past events.

Conflicting Histories

Intellectually, the most interesting challenges to history arise from those who place Native Americans outside history or uphold traditional knowledge against historical knowledge, but arguments that simply challenge conventional interpretations of the past are probably more noticed. Charges of calculated and sustained genocide by the United States, claims that the Iroquois contributed to the federal Constitution, and other demands for a reinterpretation of American history attract more public attention. In these arguments both sides usually claim to follow agreed-on historical methods and rules of evidence, but again the lines are not firm. There are also often claims to tradition.

To understand the present conflicts, a little history is necessary. Over the last thirty years a group of historians, largely within history departments but also within Native American studies departments, criticized other historians for leaving Native Americans out of the national narratives of American history. They achieved some success, but they, in turn, found themselves criticized by other scholars, largely within Native American studies departments, for in effect refusing to incorporate what their critics contended were native viewpoints and ascertainable facts.

The original ambition of incorporating Native Americans into colonial and North American history turned out to be a far more difficult task than historians of Native American peoples imagined. Starting out with the limited aim of taking Native Americans seriously, of restoring their agency, and of incorporating them and their concerns into some larger national narratives, historians have found that their own original aims were in some ways as problematic as the targets they attacked.[49]

Historians of Native American peoples originally saw their targets as the popular and scholarly conceptions of Native Americans as being outside history and the conviction of most academic historians that Native Americans just did not matter very much in national narratives. As a result, Native American historians developed detailed rationales for and defenses of the historicizing of nonwestern peoples. To describe a people as being outside history, historicizers argue, is to naturalize them, to render them powerless. They are not only victims of the modern world—a world that defines itself as historical and always in the act of becoming—but they are reduced to victims who are both incapable of understanding the narratives of their own subjugation (which are historical) and who are liable to be erased from those narratives themselves. They do not matter.

Eric Wolf gave his study of the incorporation of Native Americans and other non-Europeans into a European colonial and market system the ironic title of *Europe and the People Without History.* Wolf sought to attack and deflate three linked positions. First, he took aim by implication at the Hegelian construct of Europe and the rest, with Europe as the darling of the Spirit that worked through history and other societies doomed to disappear or assimilate. Second, he wanted to demolish an anthropological conceit of pristine, isolate cultures that somehow existed apart from history and the upheavals of the modern world. Finally, he wanted to demonstrate the vacuity of the position of some European and American historians that stateless peoples had little recoverable history and certainly none that mattered in the shaping of the modern world.[50] He wanted to restore non-Europeans to central places in a historical narrative of modernity. He wanted, in the most general sense of the word, to historicize them.

Native American peoples were important to Wolf's project, but he was not primarily a scholar of Native American peoples. To make his case in North America, he resorted to a literature sympathetic to his general aims. It was already relatively large and would soon grow rapidly. This literature aspired both to be Native American–centered—Indian peoples were central actors in their own history and not merely the objects of colonialism or U.S., Canadian, and other national policies—and to integrate Native Americans into larger narratives.[51] This literature has become particularly influential in colonial and early national history. The various editions of Gary Nash's *Red, White, and Black* serve to summarize its progress and use. James Axtell, David Edmunds, Donald Fixico, Jack Forbes, Michael Green, Theda Perdue, Colin Calloway, James Merrell, Daniel Richter, Peter Mancall, Daniel Usner, Matthew Dennis, myself, and many others all wrote books in the service of this larger project.[52] Although written about peoples on the periphery of current historical concern, the profession as a whole, if reviews and awards are any measure, seemed to embrace the books and accept a good measure of the critique.

It is this large group of colonial and early national historians, as well an even larger group of historians who have looked at the relations between Native American peoples and more recent American society, that I will, for convenience but rather awkwardly, refer to as the historicizers. Titles such as Peter Iverson's *When Indians Became Cowboys* and Stephen Cornell's *The Return of the Native* convey the concern of scholars working in later periods to counter persistent cultural stereotypes and render Native Americans visible and active historical participants within American society, politics, and culture.[53] These later historicizers portray complicated Native American societies in which, as Melissa Meyer argues for the White Earth Anishinaabeg, distinct Native American ethnic groups have evolved inside reservation communities, and, as Alexandra Harmon details for Puget Sound, Indian and white identities have evolved in complicated historical relation to each other.[54]

Because the historicizers have had their greatest impact on colonial and early national history, I will draw most of my examples from these eras. With Native American peoples as their subjects, the historicizers managed to ride, and indeed help instigate, several significant developments in colonial history. Many of their projects from necessity stepped out of the old national frames in which colonial history serves as a national prelude. Their subjects and histories operated within intersections of empires and native polities. They in many ways find more niches within concepts such as the "Atlantic World" and "borderlands" than in older frameworks that segregate colonies according to their relation to the nation-states that succeeded them.[55]

The works of historians of Native American peoples also tend to thrive when existing formulations of identity are rendered contingent and problematic. Their histories have contributed to making identity itself more problematic, accentuating how Native American identities were also under construction, and how much they were entangled with identity construction in the colonies. They have put Native Americans and nonnatives in contiguous and simultaneous worlds: Native Americans were no longer tradition and the past while whites represented history and progress. Both groups existed simultaneously, side by side, and were responding to similar changes. Their responses were linked and mutually influential.[56]

The newer literature has had considerable impact on the most recent syntheses such as Edward Countryman's *Americans: A Collision of Histories* and Colin Calloway's *New Worlds for All*, but the overall success of this historicizing project remains open to question.[57] The historicizers did not fully appreciate how many different groups might make common cause against them. Daniel Richter recently expressed skepticism about the ability of this "new Indian history" to withstand the indifference of many historians to Native American peoples, attacks by those who continue to insist that Native Americans are outside history, and assertions from within Native American communities that Native American history is a cultural property unavailable to outsiders without permission and restraints.[58]

Richter and other scholars interested in the historicization of Native Americans and their incorporation into the larger national narrative expected resistance from historians who simply did not regard Native Americans as a very significant part of American history. What they did not expect was resistance from scholars who did take Native Americans very seriously and who often identified as Native American themselves. This debate reflected not so much the ideal of incorporation as the terms of incorporation. In part, it reflected tensions between historians teaching in history departments and historians and other scholars teaching in American Indian studies or Native American studies departments. But this is a very rough measure, considering that historians like Donald Fixico and Clara Sue Kidwell and historian-anthropologists like Tsianina Lomawaima and many others taught in Native American studies programs and produced scholarship that seemed very much part of the newer, historicizing literature.[59]

The first and most predictable problem the historicizers faced was the diversion of the issue of the significance of Native American peoples in American history into a newer version of the contributionist school of history. The story of how successive racial and ethnic groups in American society made contributions to the society as a whole is an old staple of melting pot history. In regard to Native American peoples, this might be called the succotash school of history. I remember as a child listening as a teacher listed the contributions of each constituent American group. And Native Americans, she said, gave us succotash. That was it. All those millennia, millions of lives, and what we should know about them was a mixture of vegetables.

The newer contributionist school has set its sights much higher. Native Americans, this new school says, gave us democracy and republican government and inspired our Constitution. Jack Weatherford, in his popular formulation, makes Native Americans instrumental in everything from snack foods to the rise of world capitalism.[60]

Some of this literature has proved very popular with the tribes. The Six Nations, who were the central figures in the theory of American Indian democracy put forward by Bruce Johansen and Donald Grinde, were quick to embrace their role in founding the Republic against whose birth many of their ancestors had, for good reason, fought bitterly.[61] To oppose the American Indian origins of the Constitution was to oppose not just academics but sometimes quite vocal and articulate Native American people. Still, very few historians accepted the Grinde and Johansen thesis. Both historians of Native American peoples and American historians in general have regarded it as a fabric of insinuation, invention, and misreading. Its factual basis was weak and its own portrait of Indian governance simplistic.[62]

In Native American studies, however, the thesis found supporters. Rebecca Robbins fully embraced the constitutional argument, claiming in an essay on Native American governance that "certain of the structures and principles of indigenous governance, notably those drawn from the Haudenousaunee (Iroquois) Confederacy . . . were so advanced that they were consciously utilized as a primary model upon which the United States constitution was formulated and the federal government created." [63] M. Annette Jaimes Guerrero attributed refusal to accept the interpretation to Eurocentric bias.[64]

But it was not just the factual and evidentiary issues around Native American contributions that presented difficulty; arguments about such exchanges raised questions about the nature of contact between different groups. The contributionist school rarely examined the nature of cultural exchange itself. Implicitly, they saw cultural exchange as relatively simple. Human beings saw practices of other human beings and unproblematically adopted those they liked. On some level, this supposed a common way of seeing and understanding the world. It oddly mirrored an old colonialist view of the world in which inferior natives would grasp the superiority of Europeans and seek to imitate them.

Where contributionists saw straightforward exchange, many of the historicizers tried to see complicated reinventions, misunderstandings, and appropriations for new purposes, all within a shifting set of power relations.[65] Exchanges were as likely to be based on misunderstandings as understanding. As in the fur trade, where Native Americans initially took worn metal goods and inferior manufactures while Europeans craved what amounted to the old and worn-out fur clothing of Indians, each side could want what the other valued relatively little.[66]

The historicizers insisted on Indian agency. Peter Mancall saw it even in the liquor trade and in Indian drinking.[67] And it is around issues of historical agency that deeper challenges to the historicizers than those of the contributionists began to appear. Some, such as Shepard Krech, wondered reasonably enough if sometimes the push for agency went too far, slighting historical factors such as virgin soil epidemics that clearly were then beyond the ability of Native American peoples, or any people, to control.[68] Krech's point was well taken, but it could be met without changing the thrust of the newer studies.

A far angrier and more complicated attack came from scholars with a different set of concerns. Scholars who demanded that Native American history become an anticolonialist discourse turned the table on the historicizers and often grouped them into one large, Eurocentric lump with historians who showed little or no interest in Native American peoples.

The anticolonialist position in Native American studies reflects, both indirectly and directly, postcolonialism as it has developed in subaltern studies. It draws far less on the subaltern attacks on history itself cited earlier than on more moderate positions that hope to turn history against colonialism. Dipesh Chakrabarty, for example, criticizes history "as a discourse" because it forces all other histories into variations on "a master narrative that could be called 'the history of Europe.' " [69] But he does not claim that such a master narrative is the inevitable result of historical consciousness or historical thinking; it is merely the result of the present construction of historical studies. Chakrabarty gives a theoretically blunter statement than anything found in Native American studies, but scholars in Native American studies have begun to confront similar issues, and some younger scholars have begun to borrow directly from subaltern studies itself.[70]

The postcolonial position within Native American studies, at least as developed so far, is somewhat contradictory. As it appears in collections such as *The State of Native America: Genocide, Colonization, and Resistance,* or some of the articles published in a special issue of *Historical Reflections/ Reflexions Historiques* in 1995, its program is paradoxical.[71] It is multiculturalist, but the multiculturalism seems quite old-fashioned. By demanding that historians accept, for example, Iroquois contributions to the Constitution, they at least implicitly seem to measure the importance of Native American governance by the extent to which whites copied it. This postcolonialism is an anticolonial denouncement of Eurocentrism, but in Native American studies the literature remains resolutely centered on Europe for the driving force of its own narrative. It simply wants to change the valence of colonialism. It attacks a narrative of "progress and civilization" that does not seem all that typical of most recent historical accounts.[72] It denounces a "Eurocentric scholarship" that "discounts and trivializes" indigenous accomplishments, but its own emphasis seems overwhelmingly on the victimization of Indians and their helplessness before the European onslaught.[73]

Postcolonial and anticolonialist scholarship praises Native American resistance, but its own concern is with atrocity and victimization. It retains the Native Americans' status as pure victim and with it the inevitable corollary: the historical status of whites as simple and malevolent aggressors.

Scholars within Native American studies have, however, exploited a danger at the heart of the scholarship emphasizing American Indian agency: by detailing the complexity of white motivations and the ways in which Native Americans and whites shared a common world, the accounts of historicizers could be read as exculpatory. The newer works could seem to diminish the abuses that Native American peoples have suffered. The historicizers did not attempt to deny, and indeed fully elaborated, the dispossession and subjugation of Native American peoples and the atrocities committed against them, but their own accounts were more interested in Native American actions and how Native American peoples gradually entered into a common world with Europeans. Their narratives were more complicated and ambiguous than both popular pro-Indian narratives such as Dee Brown's *Bury My Heart at Wounded Knee* and the work of many scholars working within Native American studies.

Given the real horrors inflicted on Native American peoples by Europeans, Americans, and Canadians, and the political usefulness of the status of victim in late twentieth-century America, it would be surprising if a history of Native Americans as victims had failed to continue to thrive within Native American studies and Native American history. Particularly in the years surrounding the five-hundredth anniversary of Columbus's voyage to America, accounts of Native American victimization became straightforward assertions of genocide on national and hemispheric scales.[74] M. Annette Jaimes, for example, claimed that American Indian policy was the equivalent of Hitler's policy toward the Jews, that Americans were "Nazis," and that only a lack of suitable technology limited the scope of the slaughter.[75]

Such blanket denunciation of a homogeneous and continuing genocide renders a large historical literature irrelevant. By claiming five hundred years of genocide, proponents equated instances that do appear to be genocide— early American actions in California and southern Oregon, for example—with deaths in battle and deaths in epidemics. If the massacre at Sand Creek stood for all of American policy, then even newer studies of policy were suspect.

Contentions that American policy was genocidal either ignored or brushed aside studies that stressed the complexities of this policy in operation and sought to make Native Americans a central part in the story: peoples who acted and also were acted upon. David Lewis's recent book, *Neither Wolf nor Dog: American Indians, Environment and Agrarian Change,* for example, makes no sense within a framework of genocide. Native Americans appear as agents, actors, and resistors. They are a people who are victimized, but they are hardly simple victims. They partially shape their fate under conditions not of their own choosing.[76]

Newer studies of policy, such as Lewis's, accepted the basic premises of an older policy literature that had largely triumphed among historians by the 1970s and 1980s, but they also offered a critique. They insisted that Native Americans had to be a central part in the story, and that Native American actions were largely missing from earlier accounts. Still, despite such disagreements, nearly all historians of American Indian policy saw marked shifts and conflicts in Indian policy rather than some homogeneous, genocidal impulse.

In a crude way, the genocide argument might seem to echo an older debate about who controlled American Indian policy—Indian-haters or "friends of the Indian"—and whether their intentions were relatively "benign," the peaceful incorporation of Native Americans into American society, or malign, their violent elimination.[77] But even in this debate, Reginald Horsman, who doubted the good intentions of American Indian policy, thought "the formulators of policy in these first years of the new nation . . . wanted land, but they also wanted a good conscience." In the end, the debate had yielded a rough consensus that the so-called friends of the Indian had controlled policy. Although certainly culturally biased and chauvinistic, many were not necessarily racist, and few were genocidal. They largely believed Native Americans were culturally inferior but not racially inferior. They often relentlessly attacked Native American culture, but their goal was to assimilate actual Native Americans in one way or another into American society. As Bernard Sheehan, Clyde Milner, and others argued, the disquieting question of American Indian policy was how philanthropists convinced that they had the best interest of Native Americans at heart could cause such harm to Native Americans.[78] History would have been simpler if Indian-haters dominated American Indian policy.

In this view racism was a powerful force in American society, but overtly racist assumptions did not dominate American Indian policy until the early twentieth century. Only with the rise of scientific racism did officials in control of policy explicitly mark Native American peoples as racially inferior and act accordingly. This was a historical episode, not a constant factor, and the Collier administration of the 1930s and 1940s, whatever its faults, rejected racist policy tenets.[79]

Writing Native American history as the history of victims—at least until the rise of the American Indian Movement (AIM)—negates this more complex account. In the bulk of the new historicizing literature, colonialism emerges as a tangled set of cultural contacts and power relations in which Native American peoples found opportunity mixed with grave danger. They were more than victims. In the anticolonialist position within Native American studies, colonialism is simply subjugation, exploitation, and genocide. It places agency in the hands of the persecutors. And by doing so it conveys the message that only the actions of the persecutors ultimately mattered in shaping the past.

The future, however, is another story; victimization has a double agenda. In denying an effective agency to dead Indians, scholars who emphasize victimization usually seek to secure agency for living Native Americans. Writing Native American history as a history of victims often serves as a preface to a demand that Native American peoples take back control over their own lives. This is at least one of the themes in *The State of Native America,* a volume that seeks to couple a depiction of a past of largely unrelieved genocide with hopes of a resurgent Native American future.[80]

The scholars who contributed to *The State of Native America* seek to make history do work in the world, and this insistence that knowledge has work to do has been one of the real strengths of many Native American studies programs. But the need for knowledge to work in the world is precisely why history cannot simply be a means to be bent to greater ends.

For history to do effective work in the world over the long term, it has to be true to the complexity of the past. Without some commitment to the past on its own terms and a desire to portray its fullness, excursions into the past become an intellectual shopping trip to find what is useful to the present. If historical knowledge is made *simply* tactical, then the past becomes valued *only* as a tool in present struggles. The past loses its integrity. The past as past, as a different country with different concerns and rules, a place where we might actually learn something different from what we already know, vanishes. Such tactical uses of the past discredit those who use them within the academy. Those who do not share the historical shoppers' tastes, and who know the historical shopping district as well as they do, dismiss what they bring back as selective and revealing only of the historian's own prejudices.

Nor does some purely tactical approach serve "Indian" interests even in the short run. "Indian" interests are often diverse and conflicted. Scholars who claim a Native American identity and detail past victimization of Native Americans to influence the present-day situation of Native American peoples often stand in complicated relations to the very communities they seek to empower. To take a simple example, contributors to *The State of Native America* often sympathize with AIM, and in their accounts it often emerges as both a turning point and a model for Indian action.[81] Few tribal governments, however, have ever had much use for AIM, and outside Pine Ridge AIM has only rarely been a significant power in reservation communities. Articles in the *State of Native America* praising AIM and detailing victimization are thus doing more than empowering Indians. They are attacking some Indians and praising others. They are often very critical of tribal governments, which they regard as tools of whites, and sometimes of the very tribal communities their scholarship seeks to empower. They often look nostalgically back on "traditional" governments that by their own accounts of victimization proved incapable of effectively resisting genocidal policies.[82]

The anticolonialist nostalgia for tradition leads to another contradiction. Despite their deep differences, postcolonialists, anticolonialist scholars, and those devoted to other versions of national history are historicizers. All are interested in changing the place of Native Americans within a recognized body of historical scholarship and believe understanding Native American societies is a historical endeavor. But when anticolonialists look at Native American societies before their domination by whites, history and conflict often seem to vanish.

History and Native American Studies

Both within history departments and within Native American studies, writing the history of Native American peoples has become a vastly more complicated, sophisticated—and chastened—endeavor than it was only a generation ago. The early goals of moving beyond histories of Indian policy, of writing history from the Indian point of view, of making the experience of Native American peoples central to narratives of American history, have proved more difficult and tangled than the proponents originally thought. More recent goals of rethinking the relations of history, oral history, and tradition and of creating, if not a postcolonialist, then an anticolonialist discourse are running into tangles of their own.

But, as in any scholarly endeavor, the difficulties scholarship confronts can become yet another source for scholarly investigation. In the case of Native American studies, present problems and controversies throw light on the challenge of doing history. They underline the status of history as one among many ways in which humans organize the past, the variety of the evidence that reveals that past, and the difficulty of interpretation.

There are real opportunities in Native American studies. There is a chance to transcend both the old binary dualisms that created the Indian as the quintessential American "Other"—the Noble Savage victimized by corrupt "civilization"—and the equally simplistic attempts to transcend this otherness by assimilating Indians and their contributions as just another group in an American mosaic. There is, however, also the real possibility that newer studies will just echo, with some new twists, old and tired positions: Indians as anointed spiritual guides uncontaminated by the West, Indians as victims, Indians as the forgers of American democracy, Indians as the voice of nature.

There remains, however, an integrity in the past itself. The histories of Native American peoples are too interesting and too complicated to rest comfortably with such confining constructions. My sympathies obviously lie with the tendency of some of the current literature to depict Native Americans as mixed, impure, inventive, and historical peoples. At least in American history, there have been few peoples as culturally, politically, and socially complicated as Indians. They demand histories worthy of their dense and tangled lives.

Current developments in Native American history and Native American studies, with their questioning of ways of knowing the past and the standing of historians, threaten some scholars who continue to see the past as transparent and the gathering of evidence as, in some sense, scientific. They denounce borrowings from theories that seem arcane and needlessly difficult; they are impatient with the questioning of principles that seem to them mere common sense. They reflexively denounce anything they see as influenced by postmodernism. They see much of the current enterprise as elitist because the problems, language, and arguments are difficult and sometimes hard to follow. They very rarely, however, attempt to confront such problems or meet the arguments. They more often simply denounce those who do and hope the issues will go away.

The current ferment and controversy will, however, not go away soon; and even when it does, it will probably provide the basis for whatever follows. These controversies matter in Native American history, and they matter even for those with little interest in Native American history *per se*. No branch of American history is confronting such explicit challenges to historical understanding itself. Identity history and claims to knowledge based on descent have come relatively late to Native American history; but, having arrived, they give no promise of departing soon. Such claims ironically often conflict with the tribes' success in creating an eminently usable past by successfully mobilizing conventional history and non-Indian scholars to prosecute land claims and treaty rights cases. Practically, ideologically, and theoretically, history matters in Native American studies. How these controversies develop is well worth the attention of historians.

Notes

1. This chapter, like others in this volume, is not intended as a bibliographic article. I make no claim for a systematic survey of the literature. Instead, the idea is to look at salient issues with Native American studies broadly conceived that are, or should be, of interest to scholars within the disciplines. In this case my concern is primarily with historians.

2. Kerwin Lee Klein, "In search of narrative mastery: Postmodernism and the people without history," *History and Theory,* 34 (1995), 275–86.

3. Ibid., 277–80; Claude Lévi-Strauss, *The Savage Mind* (Chicago: University of Chicago, Press, 1966), 16–22, 66–74, 234–44, 258–64.

4. Calvin Martin, "Introduction," in *The American Indian and the Problem of History,* Calvin Martin, ed. (New York: Oxford University Press, 1987), 15; Calvin Martin, *In the Spirit of the Earth: Rethinking History and Time* (Baltimore: Johns Hopkins University Press, 1992).

5. Daniel K. Richter, "Whose Indian history?" *William and Mary Quarterly,* 50 (1993), 379–93.

6. Martin, "Introduction," 9.

7. Ibid., 6.

8. Ibid., 8.

9. Ibid., 9.

10. Calvin Martin, "The metaphysics of writing Indian-white history," in Martin, *The American Indian and the Problem of History,* 33.

11. Martin, "Epilogue," ibid., 195–97.

12. Martin, "Introduction," 15.

13. Martin, "Introduction," 16–17.

14. Martin, "Epilogue," 200.

15. Martin, *Spirit of the Earth,* 120.

16. Martin, "Epilogue," 200–211.

17. Martin, *Spirit of the Earth,* 37–38, 51–52.

18. Susan Hegeman, "History, ethnography, and myth: Some notes on the 'Indian-centered' narrative," *Social Text: Theory, Culture, Ideology,* 23 (1989), 148.

19. Ibid., 144–46.

20. Jonathan D. Hill, "Introduction: Myth and history," in *Rethinking History and Myth: Indigenous South American Perspectives on the Past,* Jonathan D. Hill, ed. (Urbana: University of Illinois Press, 1988), 1–18.

21. Pierre Nora, *Les lieux de mémoire* . . . (Paris: Gallimand, 1984); Pierre Nora, "Between Memory and History: Les Lieux de Mémoire," *Representations,* 26 (1989), 7–25.

22. Richard Slotkin: *Gunfighter Nation: The Myth of the Frontier in Twentieth Century America* (New York: Atheneum 1992), *Regeneration Through Violence: The Mythology of the American Frontier, 1600–1860* (Middletown: Wesleyan University Press, 1974), and *The Fatal Environment: The Myth of the Frontier in the Age of Industrialization, 1800–1890* (Middletown: Wesleyan University Press, 1986).

23. Klein, "In search of narrative mastery," 280–85.

24. James Clifford, "Identity in Mashpee," in *The Predicament of Culture: Twentieth-Century Ethnography, Literature and Art* (Cambridge: Harvard University Press, 1988), 289.

25. Ibid., 290.

26. Ibid., 291.

27. For just two examples of reactions to Clifford's work, see Klein, "In search of narrative mastery," 284–94; Hegeman, "History, ethnography, and myth," 153–58.

28. Clifford, "Identity in Mashpee," 350.

29. Ashis Nandy, "History's forgotten doubles," in "World historians and their critics," Theme Issue of *History and Theory,* 34 (1995), 44–66; a more compelling article is Dipesh Chakrabarty, "Postcoloniality and the artifice of history: Who speaks for 'Indian' pasts?" *Representations,* 37 (1992), 2–26.

30. See, for example, Rachel Buff, "Tecumseh and Tenskwatawa: Myth, historiography and popular memory," *Historical Reflections/Reflexions Historiques,* 21 (1995), 280, for such influence.

31. Nandy, "History's forgotten doubles," 61–66.

32. Benedict Anderson, *Imagined Communities: Reflections on the Origin and Spread of Nationalism* (London: Verso, 1983); Eric Hobsbawm and Terence Ranger, eds., *The Invention of Tradition* (New York: Cambridge University Press, 1984).

33. Sam D. Gill, *Mother Earth* (Chicago: University of Chicago Press, 1987), 6.

34. Theresa Schenck, "William W. Warrens's history of the Ojibway people: Tra-

dition, history and context," in *Reading Beyond Words: Contexts for Native History,* Jennifer S. H. Brown and Elizabeth Vibert, eds. (Peterborough, Ontario: Broadview Press, 1996), 254–55.

35.   Steven J. Crum, *Po'i Pentun Tammen Kimmappeh, The Road on Which We Came: A History of the Western Shoshone* (Salt Lake City: University of Utah Press, 1994), 40.

36.   Ronald Trosper, "Traditional American Indian economic policy," *American Indian Culture and Research Journal,* 19 (1995), 65–95, particularly 66–67.

37.   An argument connected with various subaltern and anticolonialist positions suggests that when various "native" products are collected and codified, they are simply appropriated to the service of the very colonialism that oppressed their makers. For a discussion of such issues, see Matthew Sparke, "Between demythologizing and deconstructing the map: Shawnadithit's New-found-land and the alienation of Canada," *Cartographica,* 32 (1995), 1–21.

38.   Raymond J. DeMallie, " 'These have no ears': Narrative and the ethnohistorical method," *Ethnohistory,* 40 (1993), 515–538; William Cronon, "A place for stories: Nature, history and narrative," *Journal of American History,* 78 (1992), 1347–76.

39.   DeMallie, " 'These have no ears,' " 516.

40.   Ibid., 524–26.

41.   Peter J. Powell, *Sweet Medicine: The Continuing Role of the Sacred Arrows, the Sun Dance, and the Sacred Buffalo Hat in Northern Cheyenne History* (Norman: University of Oklahoma Press, 1969), xx–xxxi.

42.   DeMallie, " 'These have no ears,' " 526.

43.   Ibid.

44.   See, for example, Powell's explanation of an instance of the practice of putting a woman "on the prairie"—that is, exposing an unfaithful wife to gang rape at the husband's invitation. In his interpretation he does far more than simply give a Cheyenne account. Powell, *Sweet Medicine,* 75, n. 8.

45.   Joe S. Sando, *Nee Hemish: A History of Jemez Pueblo* (Albuquerque: University of New Mexico Press, 1982), 4.

46.   Ibid.

47.   Julie Cruikshank, "Discovery of gold on the Klondike: Perspectives from oral tradition," in Brown and Vibert, *Reading Beyond Words,* 433–36, 443, 452–53.

48.   Discussions of such issues show up in Brown and Vibert, *Reading Beyond Words;* see, for example, Daniel Clayton, "Captain Cook and the Spaces of Contact at 'Nootka Sound,' " 95–123; and Maurreen Matthews and Roger Roulette, "Fair Wind's Dream: *Naamiwan Obawaajigewin,* " 330–60.

49.   Robert F. Berkhofer, "The political context of a new Indian history," *Pacific Historical Review,* 40 (1971), 357–82. Two of the first attempts to synthesize Indians into the larger colonial history were Gary Nash, *Red, White, and Black: The Peoples of Early America* (Englewood Cliffs, N.J.: Prentice-Hall, 1974, and subsequent editions), and James Axtell, *The Invasion Within: The Contest of Cultures in Colonial North America* (New York: Oxford University Press, 1985).

50.   Eric Wolf, *Europe and the People Without History* (Berkeley: University of California Press, 1982), 5–9, 13–19, 21–23, 385.

51.   Berkhofer, "Political context," 357–82; James Merrell, "Some thoughts on

colonial historians and American Indians," *William and Mary Quarterly,* 3d ser., 46 (1989), 94–99, 117–19; James Axtell, "Colonial America without the Indians: Counterfactual reflections," *Journal of American History,* 73 (1987), 981–96.

52.   Nash, *Red, White, and Black;* Axtell, *Invasion Within;* Daniel Usner, *Indians, Settlers, and Slaves in a Frontier Exchange Economy: The Lower Mississippi Valley Before 1783* (Chapel Hill: University of North Carolina Press, Published for the Institute of Early American History and Culture, 1989); Colin Calloway, *The American Revolution in Indian Country: Crisis and Diversity in Native American Communities* (New York: Cambridge University Press, 1995); James H. Merrell, *The Indians' New World: The Catawbas and Their Neighbors from European Contact Through the Era of Removal* (Chapel Hill: University of North Carolina Press, Published for the Institute of Early American History and Culture, 1992); Donald Fixico, *Termination and Relocation: Federal Indian Policy, 1945–60* (Lincoln: University of Nebraska Press, 1986); Jack Forbes, *Warriors of the Colorado: The Yumas of the Quechan Nation and Their Neighbors* (Norman: University of Oklahoma Press, 1965); Jack Forbes, *Apache, Navaho, and Spaniard* (Norman: University of Oklahoma Press, 1960); Michael D. Green, *The Politics of Indian Removal: Creek Government and Society in Crisis* (Lincoln: University of Nebraska Press, 1982); Matthew Dennis, *Cultivating a Landscape of Peace: Iroquois-European Encounters in Seventeenth Century America* (Ithaca: Cornell University Press, 1993); Daniel K. Richter, *Ordeal of the Longhouse: The Peoples of the Iroquois League in the Era of European Colonization* (Chapel Hill: University of North Carolina Press, Published for the Institute of Early American History and Culture, 1992); Theda Perdue, *Slavery and the Evolution of Cherokee Society, 1540–1866* (Knoxville: University of Tennessee Press, 1979); Peter C. Mancall, *Deadly Medicine: Indians and Alcohol in Early America* (Ithaca: Cornell University Press, 1995); Richard White, *The Roots of Dependency: Subsistence, Environment, and Social Change Among the Choctaws, Pawnees, and Navajos* (Lincoln: University of Nebraska Press, 1983); Richard White, *The Middle Ground: Indians, Empires, and Republics in the Great Lakes Region, 1650–1815* (New York: Cambridge University Press, 1991).

53.   Peter Iverson, *When Indians Became Cowboys* (Norman: University of Oklahoma Press, 1994); Stephen Cornell, *The Return of the Native: American Indian Political Resurgence* (New York: Oxford University Press, 1988).

54.   Melissa L. Meyer, "Signatures and thumbprints: Ethnicity among the White Earth Anishinaabeg," *Social Science History,* 14 (1990), 305–45; Melissa L. Meyer, *The White Earth Tragedy: Ethnicity and Dispossession at a Minnesota Anishinaabe Reservation, 1889–1920* (Lincoln: University of Nebraska Press, 1994); Alexandra Harmon, "Lines in sand: Shifting boundaries between Indians and non-Indians in the Puget Sound Region," *Western Historical Quarterly,* 26 (1995), 429–54.

55.   For instance, Edward Spicer, *Cycles of Conquest: The Impact of Spain, Mexico, and the United States on the Indians of the Southwest, 1533–1960* (Tucson: University of Arizona Press, 1962); White, *Middle Ground;* Usner, *Indians, Settlers, and Slaves.*

56.   See, for example, Usner, *Indians, Settlers, and Slaves;* Merrell, *Indians' New World;* White, *Middle Ground.* For creation of entirely new peoples in between Indians and whites, see Jacqueline Peterson and Jennifer S. H. Brown, *The New Peoples: Being and Becoming Métis in North America* (Lincoln: University of Nebraska Press, 1985).

57.   Edward Countryman, *Americans: A Collision of Histories* (New York: Hill and

Wang, 1996); Colin Calloway, *New Worlds for All: Indians, Europeans, and the Remaking of North America* (Baltimore: Johns Hopkins University Press, 1996).

58. Richter, "Whose Indian history?" 379–93.

59. Fixico, *Termination and Relocation;* Clara Sue Kidwell, *Choctaws and Missionaries in Mississippi, 1818–1918* (Norman: University of Oklahoma Press, 1995); K. Tsianina Lomawaima, *They Called It Prairie Light: The Story of Chilocco Indian School* (Lincoln: University of Nebraska Press, 1994).

60. Native Americans did have effects on both: snack foods come from corn and potatoes; capitalists used gold and silver. Jack Weatherford, *Indian Givers: How the Indians of America Transformed the World* (New York: Crown, 1988), 38, 110–11; see also Jack Weatherford, *Native Roots: How the Indians Enriched America* (New York: Crown, 1991).

61. Bruce E. Johansen, *Forgotten Founders: Benjamin Franklin, the Iroquois, and the Rationale for the American Revolution* (Ipswich, Mass.: Gambit, 1982); Bruce E. Johansen, "Native American societies and the evolution of democracy in America, 1600–1800," *Ethnohistory,* 37 (1990), 279–90; Donald Grinde, "The Iroquois and the development of American government," *Historical Reflections/Reflexions Historiques,* 21 (1995), 301–18.

62. For example, see Elisabeth Tooker, "The United States Constitution and the Iroquois League," *Ethnohistory,* 35 (1988), 305–36; Elisabeth Tooker, "Rejoinder to Johansen," *Ethnohistory,* 37 (1990), 291–97.

63. Rebecca L. Robbins, "Self-determination and subordination: The past, present and future of American Indian governance," in *The State of Native America: Genocide, Colonization, and Resistance,* M. Annette Jaimes, ed. (Boston: South End Press, 1992), 87.

64. M. A. Jaimes Guerrero, "Afterword: Shifting paradigms for an anti-colonialist discourse," *Historical Reflections*/Reflexions Historiques, 21 (1995), 387.

65. White, *Middle Ground,* 52–53.

66. Christopher Miller and George R. Hamell, "A new perspective on Indian–white contact: Cultural symbols and colonial trade," *Journal of American History,* 73 (1986), 311–28.

67. Mancall, *Deadly Medicine,* 8, 84, 100.

68. Shepard Krech III, "Retelling the death of Barbue, a Gwich'in leader," in Brown and Vibert, *Reading Beyond Words,* 214.

69. Chakrabarty, "Postcoloniality and the artifice of history," 1.

70. See, for example, Buff, "Tecumseh and Tenskwatawa," 277–300.

71. For Jaimes, *State of Native America,* see note 63 above. Joel Martin and M. A. Jaimes Guerrero's jointly edited issue of *Historical Reflections/Reflexions Historiques,* vol. 21 (1995) can serve as an introduction to this scholarship.

72. Guerrero, "Afterword," 385.

73. Ibid., 387.

74. Lenore A. Stiffarm and Phil Lane, Jr., "The demography of native North America: A question of American Indian survival," in Jaimes, *State of Native America,* 33–36; David Stannard, *American Holocaust: Columbus and the Conquest of the New World* (New York: Oxford University Press, 1992).

75.   M. Annette Jaimes, "Sand Creek: The morning after," in Jaimes, *State of Native America,* 3, 6.

76.   David Rich Lewis, *Neither Wolf nor Dog: American Indians, Environment and Agrarian Change* (New York: Oxford University Press, 1994); see, for example, Lewis's conclusions, 168–74.

77.   The leading figures in the debate were Francis Paul Prucha and Reginald Horsman. Prucha, whose position largely triumphed, wrote a summary narrative of American policy in *The Great Father: The United States Government and the American Indians,* 2 vols. (Lincoln: University of Nebraska Press, 1984); for Horsman's position see Reginald Horsman, *Expansion and American Indian Policy, 1785–1812* (East Lansing: Michigan State University Press, 1967), ii, 173. Horsman's *Race and Manifest Destiny: The Origins of American Racial Anglo-Saxonism* (Cambridge: Harvard University Press, 1981) eventually made a forceful case for racialism in American society in general.

78.   Bernard W. Sheehan, *Seeds of Extinction: Jeffersonian Philanthropy and the American Indian* (Chapel Hill: University of North Carolina Press, Published for the Institute of Early American History and Culture, 1973); Clyde Milner II, *With Good Intentions: Quaker Work Among the Pawnees, Otos, and Omahas in the 1870s* (Lincoln: University of Nebraska Press, 1982).

79.   Frederick Hoxie, *A Final Promise: The Campaign to Assimilate the Indians, 1880–1920* (Lincoln: University of Nebraska Press, 1984), 113. For a judicious evaluation of Collier's policy and intention, see Graham D. Taylor, *The New Deal and American Indian Tribalism: The Administration of the Indian Reorganization Act, 1934–45* (Lincoln: University of Nebraska Press, 1980).

80.   The collection is by "noted American Indian authors and activists." Jaimes, *State of Native America,* back cover.

81.   Ibid., 76, 101, 104, 106, 148, 167, 328, 363, 386.

82.   See, for example, Robbins, "Self-determination and subordination," 95–98, 100–107; M. Annette Jaimes, "Federal Indian identification policy: A usurpation of indigenous sovereignty in North America," in Jaimes, *State of Native America,* 128.

PART 4

FIVE TOPICS FOR
NATIVE AMERICAN STUDIES

10 *Rennard Strickland*

The Eagle's Empire
Sovereignty, Survival, and Self-Governance in
Native American Law and Constitutionalism

To many the eagle symbolizes sovereignty. This majestic bird with arrows in extended talons is an image of majesty and power. We often describe the eagle as "sovereign of the sky." Understanding the concept of sovereignty is easy for students of Native American studies if they imagine the eagle as the sovereign and each arrow held in the claws as the embodiment of the attributes of sovereignty. Our task then is not only to describe the eagle itself but to learn how it uses the arrows as it soars. If the free-flying eagle is sovereign, what is the status of the Native American tribes that Chief Justice John Marshall described as "domestic dependent nations" that "possess aspects of sovereignty"?[1] What arrows does it still hold? As this chapter unfolds, we see the tribal eagle with fewer of the arrows of sovereignty in place, but nonetheless still a sovereign, free-flying and powerful.

This chapter explores the survival of sovereignty and self-governance in historical and contemporary Native American life, law, and constitutionalism. The first section outlines the basic legal concepts of Native American sovereignty, self-governance, and constitutionalism. The second introduces an alternative contextual approach to refine and promote our understanding of all three. Unfortunately, because of the technical legal basis of much of sovereignty, Native American studies has too often dismissed these issues. An understanding of sovereignty is crucial for all students of Native American studies as Indian nations move into the twenty-first century and a new national policy of self-governance. Without this knowledge, survival of Native Americans and their tribes is at far greater risk. Native American law is too important to be left exclusively to lawyers or legal scholars. Therefore, mastery is a cornerstone for Native American studies and a central ingredient in the formulation and modification of Indian policy.

The Basic Legal Concepts

From the beginning of the Republic, the courts have acknowledged that Native American government is rooted in an established legal and historical relationship between the United States and Native American tribes or nations. This is at the heart of Native American constitutionalism and grows from precontact tribal sovereignty. It is this "government to government" relationship that distinguishes Native American questions from those of other ethnic or minority groups. The rights and obligations of Native Americans, unique to Indian law, derive from a legal status as members or descendants of a sovereign Indian tribe, not from race.[2]

Over the last two centuries, the courts have found the questions of tribal power, sovereignty, and self-governance to be extraordinarily complex, rich, controversial, and diverse. Native American cases, both old and new, weave a fabric with threads drawn from international law, American constitutionalism, federal jurisdiction, conflicts of law, corporations, torts, domestic relations, procedure, trust law, intergovernmental immunity, and taxation. All these fields, and many others, meld to produce the principles and doctrines of Native American jurisprudence: the result is unique and has been so recognized since the earliest Supreme Court pronouncements. Because of this complexity and the uniqueness of coexisting sovereignty, no area of constitutional litigation has more severely tested the United States' commitment to the rule of law. No other area of law is more frequently misunderstood or misapplied.

For the Native American, law and the courts have been seen alternatively as shields of protection and swords of extermination, examples of balanced justice and instruments of a conquering empire. Felix Cohen, author of the classic *Handbook of Federal Indian Law* (1942), thought of the treatment of Native Americans as a barometer that "reflects the rise and fall in our democratic faith," with the Indian "like the miner's canary [marking] the shift from fresh air to poison gas in our political atmosphere."[3] The nineteenth-century French observer Alexis de Tocqueville, by contrast, noted that while the "conduct of the Americans of the United States towards the aborigines is characterized . . . by a singular attachment to the formalities of law," the United States through law accomplished an extermination of much of her Indian race "with singular felicity, tranquility legally, philanthropically . . . without violating a single great principle of morality in the eyes of the world." Tocqueville concluded: "It is impossible to destroy men with more respect for the laws of humanity."[4]

Constitutional and historical scholarship in recent years has tended to affirm Tocqueville's contemporary observation of the manipulation of Indian law to achieve the expansionist objectives of the United States. American Indian policy has been characterized as "genocide-at-law." [5] Many scholars agree that in the nineteenth century law was the principal tool for both land acquisition and cultural extermination.[6] Others have seen law and the courts as ineffective but not malevolently motivated. Some historians, such as Father Francis Paul Prucha, prefer to describe the legal and political treatment of the American Indian as failed "paternalism" and completely reject the term "genocide." [7] Among legal scholars, however, the prevailing view is that of Angie Debo, one of America's most perceptive historians of the implementation of American Indian policy: "Because of the magnitude of the plunder and the rapidity of the spoliation . . . such treatment of an independent people by a great imperial power [should] have aroused international condemnation . . . but the Indians . . . were despoiled individually under the form of existing law." [8]

In recent years, Robert Williams, in *The American Indian in Western Legal Thought* (1990), has placed much of the rationalization and legal justification for the genocidal thrust within the Supreme Court itself.[9] He argues, for example, that Chief Justice John Marshall provides a court-sanctioned blueprint for the destruction of the Indian land base in his seminal opinion of *Johnson v. McIntosh* (1823). Vine Deloria and Clifford Lytle in *American Indians, American Justice* (1983) more bluntly note that Marshall in *Johnson v. McIntosh* "created a landlord–tenant relationship" between the government and the Indian tribes, under which the federal government, "as the ultimate landlord, not only possessed the power to terminate the 'tenancy' of its Indian occupants but also could materially affect lives of Indians through its control and regulation of land use." [10]

There is little argument over the magnitude of the Native American holocaust. The genocide is well documented. Russell Thornton describes the demographic collapse of the Native American population as so severe that in the three centuries up to 1800 "the total United States Native American population had been reduced to 600,000 from 5+ million." Between 1800 and 1900, the Native American population, according to Thornton, decreased "from about 600,000 in 1800 to a mere 250,000 between 1890 and 1900." [11] The latest census reports document a small increase throughout the twentieth century with a total self-declared Native American population of approximately two million, but Native Americans remain less than one percent of the entire population. Tecumseh, the great Shawnee leader, asked the important question: "Where today are the Pequat? Where are the Narrogansett, the Mohican, the Pokanoket, and many other once powerful tribes of our people?" He answers, "They have vanished before the avarice and the oppression of the white man, as snow before a summer sun." [12]

Tecumseh did not live to see the restorative power of the attributes of sovereignty. The Pequats whom he eulogized as a vanished people are now one of the most powerful and richest tribes in the eastern United States. The tribes, exercising their sovereignty as operators of gaming enterprises, now provide basic services, health care, and educational, employment, and entrepreneurial opportunities to their members, other Indians, and often non-Indians as well. As one looks at the revitalization of tribes and tribal enterprise, the power of retained sovereignty becomes increasingly clear. While the Cherokees took the mythological Phoenix bird as their tribal symbol, dozens of other native groups once thought to be at the end of the trail have themselves arisen. Many tribes written off as remnants or even extinct have petitioned for federal and state recognition. At the end of the twentieth century, tribes once described as slumbering have now awakened as vital and functioning governmental entities.

To understand tribal sovereignty and the relationship of law and the Native American requires an appreciation of precontact Indian civilizations. Tribal sovereignty on this continent long predates the U.S. Constitution or even the arrival of the European in the Americas. Early white explorers, soldiers, and settlers looking among Indian tribes for leather-bound statute books and balanced scales of justice found none and thus concluded that the hemisphere's native peoples were lawless savages. They failed to see the operational governments all around them. Sovereignty, legal authority, and governmental structure as conceived by native peoples were simply different, designed to serve other purposes than those of the feudal Europeans. In fact, long before the Magna Carta, sovereign tribal governments were highly developed in the Americas. In recent decades both scholars and legislators have begun to acknowledge the debt of the struggling young colonies to the legal and political ideas of the continent's original inhabitants.[13]

On the two hundredth anniversary of the U.S. Constitution, Congress passed a joint resolution affirming the significance of the League of the Iroquois as a federal constitutional model and acknowledged the guiding principles behind the Constitution borrowed from the Indian founding fathers and governing mothers. Yet even today lawyers and scholars tend to forget the sophistication of traditional tribal law and define Native American law as imposed (i.e., non-Indian) Federal Indian Law, which is limited to statutes and regulations promulgated by the United States to govern land claims and jurisdictional conflicts with Native American tribes. The traditional governance of Native American people is still, too often, dismissed as primitive custom or religious superstition, as when the Supreme Court in *Duro v. Reina* (1990) barely acknowledges longstanding tribal court systems with jurisdiction over nonmember Native Americans.[14]

The constitutional and legal history of America's sovereign Indian tribes demonstrates that law is more—much more—than powdered wigs, black robes, leather-bound statutes, silver stars, and blindfolded ladies with balanced

scales. It is also a Cherokee priest listening to the spirit world while holding the sacred wampum, and a Cheyenne soldier-society warrior draped in
the skin of a wolf. In fact, a command from the spirit world can have greater
force as law than the most elaborate decision devised by the highest and most
honored of court judges.[15]

As recently as 1990, Oren Lyons, the Faithkeeper of the Turtle Clan of the
Onondaga Nation, was asked, "What law are you living under?" He replied:
"United States government law? That's Man's law. You break Man's law and
you pay a fine or go to jail—maybe. That's the way it is with Man's law. You
can break it and still get around it. Maybe you won't get punished at all. . . .
But they forget there's another law, the Creator's law. We call it Natural law. . . .
Natural law prevails everywhere. It supersedes Man's law. If you violate it,
you get hit. There's no judge and jury, there's no lawyers or courts, you can't
buy or dodge or beg your way out of it. If you violate this Natural law you're
going to get hit and get hit hard." [16]

The roots of Native Americans' sovereignty and the laws of her sovereign
nations stretch back long before the black robes or the blue coats came and
built their courthouses and guardhouses. Law, in the context of Native American society, cannot be separated from the life and life ways of Indian people.
To Native Americans, as in all balanced civilizations, law is organic. Law
speaks a language that reflects the ways of a people. The Native American experience demonstrates that law cannot be separated from the environment in
which it matured. Thus law is to Native Americans a part of a larger world
view, an embodiment of a relationship of Earth and her people, a command
from the spirit world. It continues to be so to this day.

As the United States prepares to enter the twenty-first century, ancient concepts of Native America guide native peoples. From the forests of the League
of the Iroquois in the far Northeast to the Everglades of the Seminoles on
the Florida coast, across the continent to the salmon-rich rivers of the Pacific
Northwest, to the tribal villages and inlets of Alaska on to the desert of the
far Southwest, and throughout the great woodlands and plains between, the
original inhabitants of this continent still retain a remarkably rich traditional
heritage of sovereign self-governance under law. It is a system of laws that
guides daily lives in both formal and informal ways, setting values that run
deeper than the secular laws of the Republic and the decisions of the U.S.
Supreme Court.

And yet, despite the survival of precontact sovereignty, federal Indian laws
and policies adopted by Congress and interpreted by the courts dominate
the lives of Native Americans. Much contemporary confusion results from
the duality of traditional tribal law and federally enforced regulations. Today
Native Americans are controlled by laws in ways barely comprehensible to
other U.S. citizens. Legal questions pervade tribal relations with the federal

government. The courts have powers of life-and-death proportion over tribal existence. The nature of U.S. constitutional law and public policy is such that legal issues loom large in even the smallest details of Native American cultural, economic, and political life. More than four thousand statutes and treaties controlling relations with Native Americans have been enacted and approved by Congress. Federal regulations and guidelines implementing these are even more numerous. The tribe's own laws, and some state statutes dealing with Indians, further complicate this legal maze. Many thousands of reported court decisions interpret the treaties, statutes, regulations, and policies; solicitors' opinions, administrative rulings, and Bureau of Indian Affairs directives seem to be endless. To understand "the intricacies and peculiarities of Indian law" requires, as Associate Justice Felix Frankfurter noted, "an appreciation of history and understanding of the economic, social, political and moral problems in which the more immediate problems of that law are entwined." [17]

The historical principles of tribal sovereignty and self-government predate white contact and form the basis for the exercise of modern constitutional powers. The Supreme Court has consistently recognized that the present rights of Native Americans and of American Indian tribes flow from a preexisting sovereignty, limited, but not abolished, by their inclusion within the territorial bounds of the United States. Tribal powers of self-government today are recognized by the Constitution, legislation, treaties, judicial decisions, and administrative practice. Under the best circumstances they are observed and protected by the federal courts in accordance with a relationship designed to ensure continued viability of Indian self-government. The courts' recognition of tribal self-government, embodied in legislation and treaties, serves to preempt competing assertions of state authority. The exercise of tribal governing power may itself preempt state law in areas where, absent tribal legislation, state law might otherwise apply. Neither the passage of time nor the apparent assimilation of the Indians can be interpreted as diminishing or abandoning a tribe's status as a sovereign self-governing entity.

Perhaps the most basic principle in Native America law, supported by a host of Supreme Court decisions, is that powers that are lawfully vested in an Indian tribe are not, in general, delegated powers granted by express acts, but rather "inherent powers of a limited sovereignty" that have never been extinguished. The Supreme Court has held that Indian tribes are "domestic dependent nations" that still possess those aspects of sovereignty not voluntarily surrendered or withdrawn by treaty or statute. This principle guides determination of the scope of tribal authority. The tribes began their relationships with the federal government possessing all of the sovereign powers of independent nations. They were, in fact, independent sovereign states under international legal principles. The United States from the beginning permitted, then protected, the tribes' exercise of their internal government. In so doing, the United States applied a general principle of international law to the particular situation of the Native Americans. The Supreme Court has upheld the established tradition of tribal independence within a tribe's territory despite the admission of new states, recognition of Indian citizenship, and dramatic changes in native life ways. Today, the Supreme Court continues to affirm that the tradition of tribal sovereignty furnishes the backdrop against which all Native American life and law must be seen.

From the date of the adoption of the Constitution, the primary initiative on Indian questions has rested with the federal Congress. Native American law is primarily federal in nature. The Supreme Court has played a decisive role in the formulation of Indian law and the interpretation of native policy. It has been characterized as playing an activist role in creating a federal American Indian common law both defining and delimiting native rights. The formative role of the courts in Native American law arose, in part, because of silence and ambiguity. Indians are expressly mentioned only three times in the Constitution. "Indians not taxed" are excluded by both Article I and the Fourteenth Amendment from the count for apportioning taxes and representatives to Congress among the states. The only grant of power that specifically enumerates Native Americans is the commerce clause, which includes the Indian commerce clause. Congress is authorized to "regulate commerce with foreign nations and among the several states, and with the Indian Tribes."[18]

Other constitutional powers have been applied in the federal management of Native American affairs. The treaty clause, granting exclusive authority to the national government to enter into treaties, has been a principal foundation for federal powers over Indian affairs. Before the Civil War, the treaty power received extensive use in the negotiations with Indian tribes. The early dominance of the treaty clause, at least during the first century of federal authority, illustrates that Indian affairs were more an aspect of military and foreign policy than the subject of domestic or municipal laws.

Although Native American treaties remain in force, the practice of treaty making was discontinued by Congress in 1871. As a result, recent decisions of the Supreme Court have often referred to the Indian commerce clause as the primary constitutional provision supporting modern exercises of federal power over Indians. The power of Congress under the property clause to dispose of and regulate "the Territory or other Property belonging to the United States" has been considered an additional source of authority over Indian affairs. These grants of power are implemented by two other constitutional provisions. The necessary and proper clause gives Congress broad authority to execute the enumerated powers. In addition, when federal constitutional power over Indian affairs is validly exercised, it is the "Supreme Law of the Land" and supersedes conflicting state laws or state constitutional provisions pursuant to the supremacy clause.

Supreme Court opinions most often refer to the Indian commerce clause, the treaty clause, and the supremacy clause in discussing the source of federal power over Indian affairs. While those provisions are most directly relevant, it is misleading to consider each of them separately. For the purpose of constitutional analysis, in most cases it is correct to conclude that there is an amalgam of the several specific constitutional provisions that taken together constitute a single power over Indian affairs. This approach of recognizing a broad federal power over Native American affairs, coupled with the supremacy clause when state powers are involved, has emerged as the dominant theme in the protection of Native American tribal government and as the modern constitutional basis of Native American law.

Throughout U.S. history the courts' interpretations of Native American law, like Congress's enactment of Native American policy, specifically follow currents in the mainstream of American thought. Therefore, Native American legal policy is in constant flow from era to era. Native American law and policy are marked by idealistic periods such as the early years of the Republic, when Congress pledged that "the utmost good faith shall be observed toward the Indian," and the 1930s, when a commitment was made to revive tribal governments. Other eras were more damaging: the Jacksonian period of removal, when hundreds of tribes were evicted forcibly from their ancestral homelands; the allotment era during the late nineteenth century, which resulted in the loss of more than ninety million acres of tribal lands; and the 1950s termination period, when more than one hundred tribes were stripped of their special relationship with the federal government and, in the majority of cases, of their land. The U.S. treatment of Native Americans, both in the courts and in Congress, can be broken down into five eras or periods.[19] These are generally classified by Indian law scholars as follows:

1. The Formative or Treaty Era (1789–1871)
2. The Period of Assimilation and Allotment (1871–1928)
3. The Time of Reorganization and Reestablishment (1928–42)
4. The Termination Movement (1943–61)
5. The Era of Self-Determination and Tribal Revitalization (1961–present)

Historical perspective has been crucial in the courts' treatment of Native Americans. Native American law is perhaps the most historically dependent of all areas of constitutional interpretation. In so many ways the collection of decisions and doctrines called Indian law is a mirror reflecting what is called Indian policy. And that policy, in turn, reflects the collective value judgments of society at any given moment. Native American law grows from, and is merged into, the historical experience. The content of Native American law depends upon society's definition at any given point in time of the so-called

Indian problem. The conception of the problem, moreover, defines its legal dimensions.

Historical evidence demonstrates that law follows policy, which follows shifts in public perception. This relationship is clear in the early Jeffersonian civilization policy, corresponding to the age of trading posts and federal factors, when the instruments of civilization such as plows and spinning wheels were distributed to Indian tribes by men who were officially called "agents of civilization." In yet another time, after the American Civil War, operation of Indian policy was turned over to the churches. Christian denominations were paid directly to conduct U.S. Indian policy. The nineteenth-century age of military conquest saw a shift: when the "Indian problem" is seen as a military problem, American Indian administration is entrusted to the War Department. There were times when the proposed solution was "Americanization," education, urban resettlement, or any of the dozens of others. The important fact is that when the United States saw Native American issues as a matter of saving souls, the policy-makers turned to men of God; when the United States saw the problem as securing military victory, the nation turned to soldiers; when the United States saw it as training and education, the country turned to farming agents or teachers.

Just as in the past the nation turned to traders, missionaries, soldiers, and teachers, in recent years Indians themselves have turned to lawyers and to the courts. A significant factor in this redefinition of the Indian question as a legal one has been the emergence of Native American people trained as lawyers. These new Native American lawyers, many attracted by the Special Scholarship Program in Indian Law of the American Indian Law Center at the University of New Mexico, now number more than a thousand. As Tocqueville concluded, in America, eventually, every political problem becomes a judicial one. From the mid-1960s through the 1980s, the Supreme Court was the forum of choice for Native American tribes and their members. As the nation moved into the 1990s, the Supreme Court has, again, been replaced by Congress as the public forum in which native peoples seem most comfortable submitting their claims and resolving their conflicts. Recent congressional shifts may be leaving tribes without a forum.

As Native American peoples prepare to move into the twenty-first century, the issues facing tribes are not substantially different from those faced over the last five centuries. The challenge for Native American studies, particularly in the area of sovereignty and constitutionalism, is to identify the core value issues that the legal system struggles to preserve. The miracle of the past five hundred years is that Native American people and their values have survived in the face of the most unbelievable onslaughts. There is little question that the law and the courts have been, and will continue to be, a major battlefield in the struggle for sovereign survival.

In this struggle there is an ever present danger of converting this basic legal concept of sovereignty into a modern day "Ghost Dance shirt" that Native American leaders and lawyers believe will make them invincible. Sovereignty is a weapon, not an end in itself. Many scholars of American Indian law believe that sometimes an exercise of tribal sovereignty muscle may not, in fact, be the wisest policy. A decision to compact or cooperate with other levels of government (state, county, municipal) may be the highest and best exercise of sovereignty. A sovereign tribe acting as a governmental unit may, in the best use of its sovereign judgment, conclude that cross-deputization of law enforcement officers or joint water-quality standards or common health centers promotes the interest of tribal peoples better than going it alone. Such a thoughtful governmental decision arrived at through the exercise of tribal sovereignty may, in fact, enhance—not diminish—historical constitutional rights and powers.

In reviewing the court cases and the legal and political struggles that developed the principles of Indian law, it is impossible to understand the treatment of Native Americans without reference to the varying times in which particular doctrines or statutory provisions evolved. Without this historical perspective, Indian law and the treatment of native peoples seems a mystifying collection of inconsistencies and anachronisms. At every session of the Supreme Court, cases arise in which the validity of present claims of Native Americans depend upon what the law was at a particular point in some earlier period. In assessing the rights of Native Americans, the court continually struggles with statutes long repealed that have created legal rights, duties, and obligations that endure and that can be understood only by reference to repealed legislation. And, in turn, the repealed legislation must also be read and understood in the context of the changes created by subsequent legislation.

The classic example of sovereignty, the treaty-making experience, demonstrates how this history is crucial in understanding the Supreme Court's doctrinal development of Native American law. Treaty making involved matters of immense scope: the transactions totaled more than two billion acres, and some individual treaties dealt with land cessions of tens of millions of acres. At the same time, treaties included such simple daily considerations as scissors, hoes, and sugar. Yet, out of the felt needs of the parties to treaty negotiations, comprehensive principles evolved: the sanctity of Native American title, the exclusion of state jurisdiction, the sovereign status of Native American tribes, and the special trust relationship between Native American tribes and the United States. These principles endured beyond the four corners of the negotiated treaties and long after Congress ended treaty making in 1871. The same principles are embodied in the "treaty substitutes" that followed—in agreements, executive orders, and statutes. The original treaties, of course, continued in force and provided the basis for the late twentieth-century protection of not only Indian lands, but such reserved rights as hunting, fishing, and gathering.

Charles Wilkinson and other strong proponents of the view of the Supreme Court as protector of Native American rights cite cases upholding the preservation of Indian treaty-reserved hunting and fishing rights.[20] Their point is well illustrated with the series of cases in the State of Washington in which the rich fish harvest is reserved for use "in common" by Indians as well as non-Indian fishers. Rights to fish, hunt, and gather, reserved in treaties, have similarly been recognized for the Chippewa and Menominee in Wisconsin. Other areas that court advocates praise include use of reserved water rights, tribal rights of self-government, recognition of land claims, child-welfare protection, freedom of Native American religion, and powers of tribal taxation. A series of tribal victories in the so-called modern era, beginning with *Williams v. Lee* (1959), is currently under attack as the Supreme Court again shifts to follow changing economic and political viewpoints. These shifts are particularly notable in areas such as religious freedom and environmental protection. Tribal spiritual practices came under state restrictive controls in *Oregon v. Smith* (1990), which limits sacramental use of peyote by members of the Native American Church; tribal rights to zone are limited in *Brendale v. Yakima Nation* (1989); the right to protect the environment also suffered a setback when tribal religious practices clashed with the ease of timber harvesting in *Lyng v. Northwest Cemetary Protective Association* (1988). The Supreme Court's Florida Seminole case is the most recent pronouncement seeming to narrow or shift tribal authority.[21]

Native American law, as interpreted by the Supreme Court of the United States, developed from legal concepts and precedents established by the European colonists in their relations with Native Americans. Most basic principles of native sovereignty and of federal Indian law cited by the courts even today are rooted in those early international sources. For example, the early colonial principle that land can be acquired from Indians only with their consent and through treaties involved three assumptions that still form the basis of contemporary Supreme Court decisions: (1) that both parties to treaties were sovereign powers; (2) that Native American tribes had some form of transferrable title to land; and (3) that acquisition of Native American lands was solely a governmental matter, not to be left to individuals. In theory, if not in practice, these tenets rooted in medieval concepts of sovereignty were adhered to in the earliest dealings between European settlers and Indians and provided Justice John Marshall with many of the tenets of Native American law invoked in his famous "trilogy" of cases: *Johnson v. McIntosh* (1823), *Cherokee Nation v. Georgia* (1831), and *Worcester v. Georgia* (1832).[22]

Chief Justice John Marshall is, without question, the leading figure in the development of Native American jurisprudence. His decision in *Worcester v. Georgia* remains one of the five most frequently cited Supreme Court cases of the pre–Civil War era. The Supreme Court has repeatedly affirmed the *Worcester* decision. Matters affecting Indians in Indian Country are thus, as a rule, exempted from the usual application of state law. The *Worcester* decision was based on two principles: first, that the Constitution delegated to the federal government broad legislative authority over Indian matters; and, second, that the Cherokee treaties reserved tribal self-government within Cherokee territory free of interference from the State. The Supreme Court has further grafted onto the body of Native American law a concept that has become known as "the trust doctrine." It requires the federal government to observe the highest standard of trusteeship in federal relationships with Native Americans.

The Cherokee removal controversy illustrates the inability of the Supreme Court as an institution effectively to protect the rights of Native Americans—rights that the Court's own decisions pronounced. In *Worcester,* the court declared a series of Indian acts of Georgia to be void as repugnant to the Constitution, laws, and treaties of the United States. These acts included seizing tribal lands, executing Native American citizens who were precluded from testifying in court, and requiring the minister Samuel Worcester to have a Georgia permit to live in Cherokee Country. The failure to enforce the Supreme Court mandate in *Worcester* left the Cherokees with a decision in their favor but no place to turn. Whether or not Andrew Jackson actually said, "Marshall has made his law, now let him enforce it," the result was the same. It was as if President Eisenhower had chosen to align with Governor Faubus of Arkansas after *Brown v. Board of Education* (1954) and sent troops into Little Rock to prevent the integration of Central High School. Georgians remained on Cherokee soil, enforcing Georgia law, while Samuel Worcester languished in a Milledgeville prison. In the following years, legal rhetoric gave way to military reality as Justices Marshall and Story were replaced by Generals Woal and Scott. Despite a Supreme Court decision upholding their rights, Cherokee land was lotteried away, and troops drove the Indians into prison stockades to await the forced marches from Georgia.

In the winter of 1838–1839, even with that Supreme Court decision declaring them to be "domestic dependent nations who possessed aspects of sovereignty," sixteen thousand Cherokees were drive at gunpoint from their ancestral homeland over what has become known as the Trail of Tears. More than four thousand of their number died on the way; the ultimate population of the tribe was reduced by ten thousand because of the removal. There is surely a lesson of law and constitutionalism in the fate of the Cherokees, who took their struggle, rooted in the stated laws and values of the society, to the United States' highest court. "In truth," the Cherokees wrote in their 1835 Memorial to Congress, "our cause is your own." The shared fate of all Americans under law has rarely been more poignantly evoked. "It is the cause of liberty and justice," they naively asserted. "It is based upon your own principles, which we have learned from yourself; for we have gloried to count your Washington and your Jefferson our great teachers." [23]

There is little doubt that the experience of the Native American over the last two hundred years suggests the institional impotence of the Supreme Court. Other constitutional historians allege that the Court was an active partner in the Native American holocaust. The bitter irony of the Cherokee Nation's Supreme Court victories in both the nineteenth and the twentieth centuries illustrates the truth of Tocqueville's observation that in the United States respect for law did not prevent, indeed may have justified, the destruction of Native peoples. Today, more than a century and a half have passed since the Supreme Court decided in favor of the Cherokees in *Worcester v. Georgia.* The Cherokees have returned to the Supreme Court upon a number of occasions since this ill-fated victory. The most recent of those cases, *Choctaw Nation v. Oklahoma* (1970) and *United States v. Cherokee Nation of Oklahoma* (1987), involved the Arkansas Riverbed. Again, the initial decision was in their favor, but the legal victory was no more effective than the Marshall Court decision in the era of American Indian removal.[24]

The Supreme Court held in the Riverbed case that the Cherokees, along with the Choctaws and Chickasaws, were the rightful legal owners of part of the bed of the Arkansas River and were entitled to the income from its sand, gravel, and oil leases. Subsequently it was determined that the riverbed had been taken for the federally funded Arkansas Navigation Project of the Kerr-McClelland waterways; that taking had a total value of $177 million. Just as the *Worcester* Court had no soldiers, the Riverbed Court had no treasury. Despite an initial decision in their favor by the highest court in the land, the Cherokee Nation has waited more than two decades since the original Riverbed decision in 1970. Every imaginable legal and extralegal roadblock has been put up against the tribe. The tribe has returned, repeatedly, to Congress and to the courts seeking funds for Riverbed property that the court originally found to have been theirs under the terms of the 1835 Treaty of New Echota—ironically, the treaty forced on the tribe after the failure to execute the mandate of the Supreme Court in *Worcester v. Georgia.*

Again, the tribe, the court, and the American people have come full circle. An editorial by the Indian journalist Elias Boudinot, written in 1830 for the tribal newspaper *Cherokee Phoenix,* has contemporary relevance. "We will merely say," Boudinot concluded, "that if the highest judicial tribunal in the land will not sustain our rights and treaties we will give up and quit our murmuring." After all, it was in a dissent, not the majority opinion, that Hugo Black concluded: "Great nations, like great men, should keep their word."[25]

Despite court affirmations of sovereignty and tribal power, the Native American has suffered, for most of the more than two hundred years of American constitutionalism, from a prevailing national view that the Native American as "savage" stood on the wrong end of the scale of progress. The Native American was to the non-Indian a part of a hostile environment that had to be overcome if the white man was to fulfill his destiny to conquer and civilize this new world. The Native American symbolized the past in a nation of the future. There was pity for the plight of the Native American, an understanding of his "problem." In many Supreme Court pronouncements, the pity was, no doubt, sincere, but to the Court, like other citizens, the Native American and Indian culture were the inevitable victim of civilized progress. Arguably, for most of its history the Supreme Court has created a "jurisprudence of justification" that rationalized legal grounds for the conquest and the conquerors' will. Nonetheless, the Court has, within the limits of European-Judeo-Christian international legal concepts, attempted to create a constitutionally recognized system of law protecting Native American rights as long as those rights are defined within the western progressive tradition.

In the late eighteenth century, Sagowah, the Cherokee warrior, was asked by a missionary about changes being wrought by the non-Indian. He answered, "I do not understand, for I was born in another world. Your people and my people speak a different language." When Sagowah drew the contrast between Indian and non-Indian, he was speaking metaphorically. He understood, as scholars have only recently come to acknowledge, that peoples have different goals and values and senses of law and of law's function. "We have our land," he continued, "and your people want it." Law, Sagowah understood, is indeed a language. In the end, it is clear that in the task of conquering the continent, despite its constitutional humanitarianism and commitment to tribal sovereignty and the "rule of law," the Supreme Court spoke the language of the European and not the language of the Native American.[26]

Refining Our Understanding

Scholarship and understanding of Native American sovereignty, law, and constitutionalism depend upon the precise and detailed evaluation of cases and statutes in the context of broader historical, economic, cultural, and political movements. Furthermore, a meaningful understanding requires that the cases and statutes be viewed over a long period. Too often, single cases, policies, statutes, and regulations are analyzed in isolation so that the details are understood but the cumulative impact is lost. As an illustration of cumulative contextuality, let us examine a series of cases and the climaxing federal legislation in one area of tribal sovereignty. The cases and statutes herein considered are *Ex parte Crow Dog* (1883), the Major Crimes Act (1885), *United States v. Kagama* (1886), *Talton v. Mayes* (1896), the Indian Civil Rights Act (1968), and *Santa Clara Pueblo v. Martinez* (1978).

The analysis of tribal law, constitutionalism, and sovereignty that follows is an example of the flow among and between a series of historical events and legal enactments. The nexus of these is the point in sovereignty where the tribe and the state have differing regulations. Were tribes pure sovereign nations with no overlapping regulation, rather than "domestic dependent" nations retaining "aspects of sovereignty," there would be no problem. The test of Indian law and Indian sovereignty comes at those points where applying tribal law, state law, and federal law produces different outcomes.

Our analysis begins with *Ex parte Crow Dog*. The case was argued on November 20, 1883, and decided on December 17, 1883, by a unanimous Court.[27] The warrior Crow Dog, a leader of the Brule Sioux, was tried and convicted for the murder of another Sioux, Sin-Ta-Ge-Le-Scka (known as Spotted Tail). In late 1883, as the Supreme Court heard his case, Crow Dog waited under the sentence of death in the Dakota territorial jail, adjudged guilty by the First Judicial District Court of the Dakota Territory, a conviction affirmed, on a Writ of Error, by the Supreme Court of the Dakota Territory. Crow Dog sought release on a Writ of Habeas Corpus, arguing that tribal law and not federal law should apply because the courts for the territory lacked jurisdiction over crimes committed by one Indian against another Indian in Indian Country.

Sioux tribal law required that Crow Dog as punishment for murder must support Spotted Tail's dependent relatives but did not subject him to execution. This enraged residents of the Dakota Territory and induced the prosecution. Crow Dog's attorney, J. A. Plowman, petitioned the Supreme Court, claiming that Crow Dog was not amenable to the criminal laws of either the Dakota Territory or the United States. The United States maintained that federal criminal jurisdiction over Indian Country was acquired under the Sioux Treaty of 1868, interpreted in connection with general federal Indian statutes.

The Court granted the Writ ordering Crow Dog's release, finding that the Dakota Court was without jurisdiction. Crow Dog was governed in his relationship with other reservation Indians solely by the tribal laws of the Brule Sioux and was responsible only to the tribal law enforcement authorities. In *Crow Dog* the Court recognized exclusive criminal jurisdiction over tribal members as a surviving attribute of tribal sovereignty, despite treaty language appearing to submit the Sioux to the laws of the United States.

The *Crow Dog* decision did not deny the power of Congress to legislate over Native American affairs and to curtail, if it saw fit, the scope of Indian self-government. The Court relied upon the fact that Congress had not done so in any clear fashion, and thus no intent to limit Native American self-government could be implied. The Court in *Crow Dog* acknowledged that the tribes retained their right of "self-government [and] the maintenance of order and peace among their own members." Unless this power is removed by explicit legislation or is given up by the tribe, either expressly or as a part of its coming under the protection of the United States, exclusive tribal judicial jurisdiction over reservation Indian affairs is retained. Thus, today, most tribes operate their own tribal court systems, and, except to the extent demanded by the Indian Civil Rights Act (1968), the structure and procedure of such courts may be determined by the tribes themselves.

The decision in *Crow Dog* prompted action by nineteenth-century reformers who wanted the Native Americans to be absorbed into the mainstream of American life. One goal of the assimilationists (known as "friends of the Indian") was to have the same Anglo-based laws applied to Native Americans as applied to all other citizens and to outlaw the Indians' own "heathenish" laws and customs. The fact that Crow Dog could not be executed for murder shocked them and their congressional supporters. Agitated by the *Crow Dog* decision, Congress appended to the Appropriations Act of March 3, 1885, an Indian section known as the "Major Crimes Act," specifying seven crimes over which the federal courts were authorized to exercise jurisdiction. Thus, within two years, in reaction against *Crow Dog,* Congress enacted new legislation making it a federal crime for one Native American to murder another within Indian Country. Today, under the amended Indian Major Crimes Act, there are fourteen enumerated offenses.

Despite legislation aimed at reversing its specific outcome, *Crow Dog* remains a key case. It affirms that treaties and statutes are interpreted in favor of retained tribal sovereignty, self-government, and property rights against competing claims under state law. Doubts and ambiguities in treaties and statutes are resolved in Native Americans' favor, and federal Indian laws are interpreted liberally toward carrying out their protective purposes. *Crow Dog* establishes that federal protection of tribal self-government has never depended on any particular tribe's social structure or political format.

Crow Dog remains a crucial statement of tribal sovereignty and the fundamental constitutional principle that federal laws do not preempt tribal authority unless the congressional purpose to do so is certain. Congressional intent to limit or invade tribal self-government must be clearly demonstrated. Furthermore, congressional intent to include tribes within the scope of laws applying generally to persons, groups, corporations, or associations must be firmly established because of the tribe's unique status. The broadest concepts of tribal self-government articulated in *Crow Dog* continue as a basic constitutional guide in contemporary Native American law.

Our next case is *United States v. Kagama.* It was argued on March 2, 1896, and decided on May 10, 1896, with Justice Miller writing for a unanimous Court.[28] The case reached the Court by certificate of division. The question arises on a demurrer to a federal indictment that Kagama, known as Pactah Billy, an Indian, murdered Iyouse, alias Ike, another Indian, in Humboldt County, in the State of California, within the limits of the Hoopa Valley Reservation.

Three years earlier, in *Crow Dog,* the Court had decided that tribal law and not federal law applied in crimes committed by one Indian against another

Indian in Indian Country. Congress, as noted above, responded with the "Major Crimes Act." The certified questions concerned whether or not the Major Crimes Act is "a constitutional and valid law of the United States."

In *Kagama* the Court sustained the validity of a prosecution of Native Americans in federal court for murder under the newly enacted Major Crimes Act. The Supreme Court found that the protection of the Native American constituted a national obligation, which in turn implied the power to sustain the Indian Major Crimes Act. *Kagama* was the earliest Supreme Court decision applying the *Worcester v. Georgia* (1832) principles to a reservation established by unilateral federal action and within a state. The offense occurred on a reservation established in California after statehood by statute and executive order. Defendants argued that state jurisdiction was exclusive, but the Court indicated that even in the absence of federal jurisdiction under the Major Crimes Act, state courts would lack jurisdiction. Native American affairs has long been an area of broad federal preemption, and that factor alone is sufficient to conclude that the states cannot punish Indian defendants in Indian Country.

In *Kagama* the Court found the statute to be outside the authority of the Indian commerce clause but sustained its validity nonetheless. The Court relied on *Worcester*'s wardship analogy to sustain federal court jurisdiction over crimes by reservation Indians. Despite the Court's language, the federal–Indian relationship is unique and differs in important ways from the common law of guardianship. Federal trust relationships and guardianship principles arise out of the constitutional plan to delegate authority over Native American affairs to the federal government and the duties of protection undertaken by treaty and federal statute. *Kagama* concludes that one of the primary reasons for broader federal jurisdiction is that the states have historically been considered the Indians' "deadliest enemies."

Today *Kagama* is most frequently cited in connection with the legislative power of the federal government in dealing with Native American tribes. Although the Supreme Court in *Kagama* suggested that congressional power over Native Americans may be implied from necessity, that concept has been supplanted by the analysis that Indian statutes are subject to constitutional restrictions and must be tied rationally to the trust obligations of Congress. The teaching of modern cases is that acts of Congress affecting Native Americans are subject to judicial review, and that although congressional power is broad, ordinary constitutional protection may be invoked by Indians in their relationships with the federal government. Thus, while courts refer on occasion to the "plenary power" of Congress over Indians, the term is not synonymous with "absolute" or "total." Rather, the phrase appears to be used as a summary of constitutionally limited congressional powers over Native Americans. Although there have been many changes in governing laws, statutes, and interpretation of treaties over the last century, the courts continue to recognize the *Worcester* principles of Indian self-government within tribal territory as articulated in *Kagama*.

Finally, we come to *Talton v. Mayes*. This case was argued on April 16 and 17, 1896, and decided on May 18, 1896. The decision was written by Justice White, with Justice Harlan in dissent.[29] *Talton v. Mayes* was an appeal from the Circuit Court of the United States for the Western District of Arkansas of a petition for habeas corpus from a murder conviction in the Supreme Court of the Cherokee Nation, Cooweeskoowee District. Talton, the petitioner, awaited execution in the Cherokee National Jail at Tahlequah, Indian Territory, in the custody of Washington Mayes, high sheriff of the Cherokee Nation. Talton, a Cherokee citizen, was convicted of the murder of another Cherokee citizen within the geographic boundaries of the Cherokee Nation by a Cherokee court applying the Cherokee homicide statute. The petitioner alleged that he was deprived of his liberty without due process of law and was in confinement in violation of the Constitution and laws of the United States because the indictment was returned by a grand jury of only five members, which was insufficient under the Constitution and laws of the United States but adequate under the laws adopted by the legislature of the Cherokee Nation.

After reviewing the history of the Cherokee Nation, the Cherokee Treaties of 1835 and 1868, as well as U.S. statutory and constitutional provisions, the Court determined that the murder was an offense against the local laws of the Cherokee Nation and that the Fifth Amendment did not apply to local legislation of the Cherokee Nation. In reaching this decision in *Talton v. Mayes,* the Court considered the independent origin of and limitations on tribal power. The question was whether the Cherokee Nation's own criminal courts were U.S. courts subject to the Fifth Amendment requirements relating to indictment by a grand jury. The Court held that they were not. The Cherokee government was recognized by the federal government, but not created by it. Tribes have retained the sovereign power to make and interpret their own laws and ordinances, and their interpretations will be followed by the federal courts unless they violate some provision of federal law specifically made applicable to tribal governments.

Talton v. Mayes has been interpreted to mean that constitutional restraints on the federal and state government do not by their own force limit Native American tribes. The Court held that the Fifth Amendment's requirement of grand jury indictment did not limit the authority of the Cherokee Nation to prosecute a person under its jurisdiction. It has held that tribes exercising governmental powers are not limited by many provisions of the Constitution that limit federal or state governments in their infringements on basic liberties of citizens. Indian tribes are not states of the union within the meaning of the Constitution, and the constitutional limits on states do not apply to tribes. In the years since *Talton v. Mayes,* provision of the Indian Civil Rights Act (1968) have modified *Talton* and placed limits on sovereign governmental rights by imposing on tribes certain enumerated standards taken from the U.S. Constitution and designed to address the individual liberties of Indian people.

The "Indian Civil Rights Act" (ICRA) was adopted as a rider to the Civil Rights Act of 1968.[30] Designed to correct perceived problems between Indian tribes and the federal constitutional system, Title II, on the "Rights of Indians," is popularly referred to as the "Indian Bill of Rights." The most important and controversial provisions of this act limit the power of tribal governments by applying portions of the Bill of Rights to Indian tribes, including the equal protection and due process clauses. Not all Bill of Rights provisions have been extended to the tribes. This is an example of a federal limitation on governmental options available to tribes in exercising their sovereignty.

Courts had held, beginning in 1896 with *Talton v. Mayes,* that Native American tribal governments were generally not subject to restraints placed upon the federal and state governments by the Bill of Rights and the Constitution. This act put in place a number of federal restraints. Congress originally contemplated a bill that would have imposed the same limitations on tribes that the Constitution imposes on the federal government but eventually enacted a more limited bill imposing only certain specified restraints. Thus, tribes still retain some options to exercise their sovereign governmental decision making. While the right of habeas corpus was extended to actions by Native American tribes, ten enumerated restrictions on tribes were imposed by the bill:

No Indian tribe in exercising powers of self-government shall—

make or enforce any law prohibiting the free exercise of religion, or abridging the freedom of speech, of the press, or the right of the people peaceably to assemble and to petition for a redress of grievances;

violate the right of the people to be secure in their persons, houses, papers, and effects against unreasonable search and seizures, nor issue warrants, but upon probable cause, supported by oath or affirmation, and particularly describing the place to be searched and the person or thing to be seized;

subject any person for the same offense to be twice put in jeopardy;

compel any person in any criminal case to be a witness against himself;

take any private property for a public use without just compensation;

deny to any person in a criminal proceeding the right to a speedy and public trial, to be informed of the nature and cause of the accusation, to be confronted with the witnesses against him, to have compulsory process for obtaining witnesses in his favor, and at his own expense to have the assistance of counsel for his defense;

require excessive bail, impose excessive fines, inflict cruel and unusual punishments, and in no event impose for conviction of any one offense any penalty or punishment greater than imprisonment for a term of six months or a fine of $500, or both;

deny to any person within its jurisdiction the equal protection of its laws or deprive any person of liberty or property without due process of law;

pass any bill of attainder or ex post facto law; or

deny to any person accused of an offense punishable by imprisonment the right, upon request, to a trial by jury of not less than six persons.

Many constitutional limitations imposed on federal and state governments are not included in the Indian Civil Rights Act. Notable omissions are the guarantee of a republican form of government, the prohibitions against an established religion, the requirement of free counsel for an indigent accused, the right to a jury trial in civil cases, the provisions broadening the right to vote, and the prohibitions against denial of the privileges and immunities of citizens. The legislative history of the act indicates that these omissions reflect a deliberate choice by Congress to limit its intrusion into traditional tribal sovereignty and independence. Therefore, tribes retain in these areas their pre-contact rights as operational governments exercising the sovereign's options in internal policy making.

In *Santa Clara Pueblo v. Martinez* (1978), the Supreme Court sustained Congress's authority to impose ICRA limitations but held that federal court enforcement of the standards is limited to habeas corpus jurisdiction on behalf of persons in tribal custody.[31] The court held that the ICRA had not limited the tribe's immunity from suit, so the act cannot be enforced directly against tribes. Thus, the Court in *Santa Clara Pueblo* indicated that the ICRA is primarily enforceable in tribal forums. The act, as interpreted by the Supreme Court, is thus a limited intrusion on tribal sovereignty.

Understanding these and other Supreme Court cases provides a foundation for students of Native American studies to appreciate the exercise of tribal sovereignty. A review of these cases and statutes illustrates how tribal sovereignty, constitutionalism, and law are modified over the decades. Without an understanding of the many separate legal authorities, one cannot appreciate the contextual concepts of contemporary Indian law and policy. Too often, isolated doctrinal analysis focuses upon the single event to the exclusion of the full evolving series of events. The greatest need in Native American scholarship addressing law and sovereignty is broader contextual, doctrinal analysis focusing upon specific rights and responsibilities.

Individual contextual case analysis is not a new technique, and yet it has rarely been applied in depth in the field of Native American law and constitutionalism. A recently published study by C. Blue Clark, *Lone Wolf v. Hitchcock: Treaty Rights and Indian Law at the End of the Nineteenth Century,* serves as a model for such scholarship, joining legal analysis with an understanding of the culture and history of the Kiowa tribe. David Brugge's *The Navajo–Hopi Land Dispute: An American Tragedy* gives us a more personal perspective from the viewpoint of a consultant to the Navajo Nation. Law professor Edward Lazarus captures the sweep of law and native nationalism in his popular study *Black Hills / White Justice: The Sioux Nation Versus the United States, 1775 to the Present.* Additional case-focused scholarship is needed to fully appreciate Indian law, sovereignty, and constitutionalism.[32] This is crucial as we move into an era of expanded tribal self-government and compacting in which the Bureau of Indian Affairs is assigning budgetary and regulatory authority to tribal entities.

In recent years, the study of tribal law, sovereignty, self-government, and constitutionalism has drawn the attention of a group of outstanding legal scholars who are trained in history, anthropology, sociology, economics, and international affairs, as well as law. The richness of their work has begun to illuminate our understanding.[33] Unfortunately, much of their work has focused upon the broadest terrain, and there is still need for detailed study of the actual operation of tribal governmental sovereigns. We need scholars who are prepared to step beyond the theory of sovereignty and explore it in practice.[34] The more than five hundred federally recognized tribes, bands, and villages are working laboratories of self-governance in the later days of the twentieth century. It is a truly rich field that provides an opportunity for scholarship in the grand tradition. The agenda for Native American studies research over the next decades must include tribally focused exploration of the operational application of sovereignty. We need to know how the theoretical becomes the actual if the constitutional basis of sovereignty is to survive in a meaningful way.

Conclusion: Spreading the Eagle's Wings

We began this analysis with the image of the eagle as sovereign. If one thinks of the fate of the eagle as symbol for the precontact peoples of the Americas, we know that the great bird has often come close to extinction. Just as the bald eagle has been on the endangered species list, there have been moments when the symbolic bird of sovereignty has seemed to disappear from the sky. At the end of the nineteenth century, observers predicted the end of the tribal state, and yet Native American people and their tribes survived removal, allotment, and termination. The Native Americans' eagle still flies high, spreading those majestic wings of power and sovereignty over the empires of the original Americans. The tribal eagle still holds in its talons all those arrows of sovereignty that have not been surrendered by treaty or removed by specific congressional action. The arrows remain strong and secure as guardian protectors. As scholars, we must know more about survival and how law, self-governance, and sovereignty helped keep the eagle in flight. That is an agenda worthy of the majestic eagle and the Native American peoples it has come to symbolize.

Notes

1.   For the major scholarly interpretation of Marshall's continuing influence on the jurisprudence of Indian law, see Philip P. Frickey, "Marshalling past and present: Colonialism, constitutionalism, and interpretation in federal Indian law," *Harvard Law Review,* 107 (1993), 81–440. The cases that constitute the so-called Marshall Trilogy are *Johnson v. McIntosh,* 21 U.S. 543 (1823); *Cherokee Nation v. Georgia,* 30 U.S. 1 (1831); *Worcester v. Georgia,* 31 U.S. 515 (1932).

2.   The standard treatise on Indian law is Rennard Strickland, ed., *Felix Cohen's Handbook of Federal Indian Law,* 3d ed. (Charlottesville: Michie, 1982). A first-rate introduction to the field is William C. Canby, Jr., *American Indian Law in a Nutshell,* 2d ed. (St. Paul: West, 1988). The major casebooks on Indian law are David Getches, Charles Wilkinson, and Robert Williams, *Federal Indian Law,* 3d ed. (St. Paul: West, 1994), and Robert Clinton, Nell Jessup Newton, and Monroe Price, *American Indian Law* (Charlottesville: Michie, 1991).

3.   Felix S. Cohen, "The erosion of Indian rights, 1950–53: A case study in bureaucracy," *Yale Law Journal,* 62 (1953), 349, 390; cited in Strickland, *Cohen's Handbook,* v.

4.   Alexis de Tocqueville, *Democracy in America,* H. Reeve trans. (New York: Knopf, 1945), 336–55.

5.   Rennard Strickland, "Genocide at law: An historic and contemporary view of the Native American experience," *University of Kansas Law Review,* 34 (1968), 714–55.

6.   See, for general background, Robert A. Williams, Jr., *The American Indian in Western Legal Thought: The Discourse of Conquest* (New York: Oxford University Press, 1990).

7.   Francis Paul Prucha, *The Indians in American Society: From the Revolutionary War to the Present* (Berkeley: University of California Press, 1985), 2–5.

8.   Angie Debo, *And Still the Waters Run: The Betrayal of the Five Civilized Tribes* (Princeton: Princeton University Press, 1940), ix–x.

9.   Williams, *Discourse,* 308–17.

10.   Vine Deloria, Jr., and Clifford M. Lytle, *American Indians, American Justice* (Austin: University of Texas Press, 1983), 26–27.

11.   See generally Russell Thornton, *American Indian Holocaust and Survival: A Population History Since 1492* (Norman: University of Oklahoma Press, 1987), 90.

12.   John W. Shleppey Notebooks, Document Book No. 2, Item No. 14, McFarlin Library, University of Tulsa.

13.   A good reflection of these discussions and debates can be found in the *American Indian Law Review* published by the College of Law of the University of Oklahoma. Donald A. Grinde, Jr., has been among the most articulate proponents of the propositions of influence. See his initial arguments in *The Iroquois and the Founding of the American Nation* (San Francisco: American Indian Historian Press, 1977).

14.   *Duro v. Reina,* 495 U.S. 676 (1990). See the analysis in Alex Tallchief Skibine,

"Duro v. Reina and the legislation that overturned it: A power play of constitutional dimensions," *California Law Review,* 66 (1993), 767–806.

15. This argument is developed in Rennard Strickland, *Fire and the Spirits: Cherokee Law from Clan to Court* (Norman: University of Oklahoma Press, 1975).

16. Oren Lyons, "Listen to the Wisdom." For the full text of the Oren Lyons discussion, see Harvey Arden and Steve Wall, *Wisdom Keepers: Meeting with Native American Spiritual Elders* (Hillsboro, Oregon: Beyond World, 1990), 64–71.

17. Cited in Foreword to *Felix S. Cohen's Handbook of Federal Indian Law* (Albuquerque: University of New Mexico Press, 1971 [1942]), v.

18. Robert N. Clinton, "The dormant Indian commerce clause," *Connecticut Law Review,* 27 (1995), 1055–249.

19. These divisions reflect the original organizational structure of the 1942 edition of the Cohen *Handbook.*

20. Charles F. Wilkinson, *American Indians, Time, and the Law: Native Societies in a Modern Constitutional Democracy* (New Haven: Yale University Press, 1987). See also Ronald N. Satz, *Chippewa Treaty Rights: The Reserved Rights of Wisconsin's Chippewa Indians in Historical Perspective,* Wisconsin Academy of Sciences, Arts and Letters, Transactions, vol. 79, no. 1 (Madison, 1992). Rick Whaley with Walter Bresette, *Walleye Warriors: An Effective Alliance Against Racism and for the Earth* (Philadelphia: New Society Publishers, 1994).

21. I use these cases as the basis for my concluding analysis in the Fiftieth Cleveland-Marshall Lecture, published as Rennard Strickland, "Indian law and the miner's canary: The signs of poison gas," *Cleveland State Law Review,* 39 (1991), 483–504.

22. See sources in note 1.

23. The original Jefferson speech to the Cherokees is reprinted as appendix 4 in Strickland, *Fire and the Spirits,* 237–38. Thomas Jefferson, *The Writings of Thomas Jefferson,* vol. 16: 455–58.

24. Rennard Strickland, "A tale of two Marshalls: Reflections on Indian law and policy, the Cherokee cases, and the cruel irony of Supreme Court victories," *Oklahoma Law Review,* 47 (1994), 111–26.

25. *Cherokee Phoenix,* July 3, 1830; *Federal Power Commission v. Tuscarora Indian Nation,* 362 U.S. 99 (1960) (Hugo Black dissent).

26. Cherokee Files, Sagowah, Rare Books and Special Collections, McFarlin Library, University of Tulsa.

27. *Ex parte Crow Dog,* 109 U.S. 557 (1883).

28. *United States v. Kagama,* 118 U.S. 375 (1886).

29. *Talton v. Mayes,* 163 U.S. 376 (1896).

30. 25 USC §§ 1301–1341 (1968).

31. *Santa Clara Pueblo v. Martinez,* 436 U.S. 49 (1978).

32. Carter Blue Clark *Lone Wolf v. Hitchcock: Treaty Rights and Indian Law at the End of the Nineteenth Century* (Lincoln: University of Nebraska Press, 1994); David M. Brugge, *The Navajo–Hopi Land Dispute: An American Tragedy* (Albuquerque: University of New Mexico Press, 1994); Edward Lazarus, *Black Hills / White Justice: The Sioux Nation Versus the United States, 1775 to the Present* (New York: Harper Collins, 1991).

33. Some of the best examples of recent scholarship addressing the broadest issues of tribal law, sovereignty, and constitutionalism are the following: S. James Anaya, *In-*

digenous Peoples in International Law (New York: Oxford University Press, 1996); Nell Jessup Newton, "Let a thousand policy-flowers bloom: Making Indian policy in the twenty-first century," *Arkansas Law Review,* 46 (1993), 25–75; S. James Anaya, "A contemporary definition of the international norm of self-determination," *Transnational Law and Contemporary Problems,* 3 (1993), 132–64; Judith V. Royster, "Equivocal obligations: The federal-tribal trust relationship and conflicts of interest in the development of mineral resources," *North Dakota Law Review,* 71 (1995), 328–64; Robert N. Clinton, "Redressing the legacy of conquest: A vision quest for a decolonized federal Indian law," *Arkansas Law Review,* 46 (1993), 77–159; Joseph William Singer, "Well settled? The increasing weight of history in American Indian land claims," *Georgia Law Review,* 28 (1994), 481–532; Alex Tallchief Skibine, "Reconciling federal and state power inside Indian reservations with the right of tribal self-government and the process of self-determination," *Utah Law Review,* 1995 (1995), 1105–56; Joseph William Singer, "Publicity rights and the conflict of laws: Tribal court jurisdiction in the Crazy Horse case," *South Dakota Law Review,* 41 (1996), 1–44; Charlene L. Smith and Howard J. Vogel, "The wild rice mystique: Resource management and American Indians' rights as a problem of law and culture," *William Mitchell Law Review,* 10 (1984), 743–801; Alex Tallchief Skibine, "Applicability of federal laws of general application to Indian tribes and reservation Indians," *U.C. Davis Law Review,* 25 (1991), 85–140; Chadwick Smith and Faye Teague, "The response of the Cherokee Nation to the Cherokee Outlet centennial celebration: A legal and historical analysis," *University of Tulsa Law Journal,* 29 (1993), 263–302; Nell Jessup Newton, "Indian claims in the courts of the conqueror," *American University Law Review,* 41 (1992), 753–854; Frank Pommersheim, "A path near the clearing: An essay on constitutional adjudication in tribal courts," *Gonzaga Law Review,* 27 (1991/92), 393–421; Frank Pommersheim, "Tribal-state relations: Hope for the future?" *South Dakota Law Review,* 36 (1991), 239–76; Dean B. Suagee, "Self-determination for indigenous peoples at the dawn of the solar age," *University of Michigan Journal of Law Reform,* 25 (1992), 671–749; Dennis W. Arrow, "Federal question doctrines and American Indian law," *Oklahoma City University Law Review,* 14 (1989), 263–389; Robert N. Clinton, "Tribal courts and the federal union," *Williamette Law Review,* 26 (1990), 841–936.

34.   A model of what can be done in the specific context of tribal government and politics is Loretta Fowler, *Arapaho Politics, 1851–1978: Symbols in Crises of Authority* (Lincoln: University of Nebraska Press, 1982).

11 *John H. Moore*

Truth and Tolerance in Native American Epistemology

Epistemology is the study of the canons and protocols by which human beings acquire, organize, and verify their knowledge about the world.[1] It is perhaps the most abstract of philosophical enterprises — thinking about thought. The vocabulary of epistemology is largely a product of scholarship within the western European tradition. It allows philosophers to compare the philosophical and religious schools of thought within the European tradition, and to compare the western tradition with other major philosophical and religious systems, such as Confucianism, Buddhism, Marxist materialism, and so on. The vocabulary of formal epistemology includes such terms as "nominalism," "idealism," "empiricism," and "realism," which are used to compare selected portions and propositions of formal philosophical systems.

Robin Horton and other anthropologists have argued, however, that these formal concepts are not sufficient for considering philosophies that are outside the "great traditions" of the world. They have encouraged the use of "modes of thought" to emphasize the radically different nature of the logical and conceptual frameworks used by many nonliterate, small-scale societies outside the European tradition.[2] In this examination of Native American philosophies, I adopt and endorse Horton's concept and approach to emphasize the radically different nature of Native American thought, although I will also use here some conventional concepts of philosophical epistemology. My general remarks are confined to the smaller-scale and more egalitarian societies living north of Mexico before the coming of Europeans.

271

In seeking to understand the epistemology of Native Americans, whether one uses a traditional approach or not, the fundamental questions remain the same. How is knowledge structured? How is it acquired? How is it evaluated? That is, within any culture, how do we know something is true? To these essentially philosophical questions, anthropologists have added other, sociological questions. Who controls knowledge? Where in society is special knowledge located? How is new knowledge integrated into an existing system of ideology? Anthropologists are also interested in how philosophical knowledge is acted out in ceremonies and in the activities of priests, shamans, and other intellectuals. We are especially interested in certain kinds of historically known, ideological events that seem to have a regular structure and recur globally—for example, nativistic and millenarian movements, and the rise and fall of prophets and charismatic leaders.

Usually, the central framework for knowledge among tribal societies is not a systematic logical philosophy, as with western traditions (e.g., "cogito, ergo sum"; the principle of the excluded middle; materialism). Instead, it is a spatially constructed native cosmology. These cosmologies typically comprise an overview of the natural world, its sectors and their boundaries, geographic features, and flora and fauna. It is the content of this cosmology that most often provides the substance of human knowledge, to which rules of epistemology are applied.

It is extremely important to note, in keeping with the notion of "modes of thought," that the cosmologies and epistemologies maintained by Native North American philosophers are not only different from those of western philosophy, but radically different among themselves. This is to be expected from a group of human societies with deep and various historical roots, who speak scores of distinct languages making up eight or more language families. Questions as fundamental as the definition of God, the significance of human life, and the purpose of religion receive different, often contradictory answers among intellectuals representing different Native American traditions.

Among Native American people, also, philosophical questions are necessarily religious questions, since there is no formal tradition of secular philosophy anywhere in the Americas. Although there are secular, skeptical, and even irreligious people in Native American societies, and probably always have been, nevertheless the formal traditions concern religious quests for knowledge, not secular quests through logic and empirical science. While Native American societies have made significant scientific advances in such fields as astronomy, agronomy, art, and architecture, these advances were consistently couched in religious language, and surrounded by ritual and supernatural beliefs. Corn farming and the observation of planets, for example, were accompanied by prayer and ritual, and each new discovery had to be placed within the existing structure of cosmology and ceremony.[3] This is not to say that the individual "inventor" has been unimportant in the development of Native American cultures. The tradition of the "prophet" and the "culture hero" are firmly ensconced in Native American history. However, these were religious personages, not scientists, no matter how useful their innovations may have been for practical purposes. Sweet Medicine and Corn Woman, Stone Breaker and Hiawatha are all shrouded with supernatural blessings and prophetic certainties.

Several fundamental questions already emerge from these preliminary remarks. The first and probably most important is: How different are the various Native American philosophies and cosmologies among themselves, and is there any hope for extracting from them an overarching "Native American philosophy," representing the whole body of knowledge maintained by Native American intellectuals? Second, and more to the point here: Is there a consistent "Native American epistemology" shared widely in the Americas, by which Native American people have come to know the content of their cosmologies and by which they organize their lives and their thinking? The third question, which is the most important for the future success of Native American studies, concerns the issue of epistemology both as subject and as pedagogy. That is, suppose that we can in fact extract and define "Native American epistemology" as a consistent, continental, pan-cultural way of learning, is this the way that Native American cultures should be taught in the classroom? To put it another way, is Native American epistemology merely a subject to be taught, or is it a way to organize the curriculum?

Cheyenne Cosmology, Ceremonies, and Epistemology and Mvskoke Philosophy

To examine these questions, in the following sections I discuss the cosmologies and epistemologies of two cultures well known to me, the Cheyenne people, or Tsistsistas, and the people known to ethnologists as Creeks and Seminoles, who call themselves Mvskokullke, or Muskogee People. These cultures are extremely different from one another, but I have had the opportunity to discuss religious matters with intellectual and ceremonial leaders of both groups, the Cheyennes between 1969 and 1982, and the Mvskokes between 1981 and 1993. During most of these years I lived in Oklahoma, and I attended the ceremonies of both groups during the times listed.

Cheyenne Cosmology, Ceremonies, and Epistemology

I have elsewhere described Cheyenne formal cosmology and religious practice at some length; here, I merely present a brief synopsis.[4] Fundamentally, the Cheyennes see the universe as layered, with concentric hemispheres from the surface of the earth to the location of the high god, Maheo, at the zenith. From top to bottom, the layers comprise the Blue Sky-Space, the Nearer Sky-Space, and the Atmosphere. Downward from the earth's surface there are two layers, the Fertile Earth and the Deep Earth. Each of these five layers is populated by specific spiritual entities—birds, animals, plants, and named anthropomorphic spirits—with the more sacred entities in the ascendant layers.

Symbolically, the layers of the earth represent the transition from the male principle, or "all-father," at the zenith and the female principle at the nadir. The male principle is entirely spiritual, not material; the female principle is entirely material, not spiritual. All living things between, from stars in the sky, to the birds, animals, and plants, to rocks and boulders on and under the earth's surface, represent some mixture of male spirituality and female materiality.

As far as I know, no stories in Cheyenne tradition explain how the earth came to be structured in layers. There are stories about the origins of bird and animal behavior, language, other tribes, hunting techniques, the family, political structures, et cetera. The stories said to be the oldest describe how the first man and woman discovered their sexuality, and how they invented the first clothing and made simple tools and weapons. But all these origin stories are set in a world that was already created.[5] First principles, for Cheyennes, constitute the explanations for why people and animals behave the way they do.

Against this background of a created world, Cheyenne literature is most concerned with the quest for spiritual power—the search for ritual techniques by which men and women can acquire spiritual energy that can be used to accomplish their life's tasks. Typically, the hero in Cheyenne literature is a male who sets out alone and cultivates relationships with mysterious people and creatures in order to receive power from them, usually implemented and symbolized by the gift of a sacred object, song, or ceremony.

The current vision quests of Cheyennes to Bear Butte, South Dakota, and other sacred places reflect this ideal way of receiving sacred knowledge from powerful spiritual sources. It is significant that Cheyenne narratives of religious experience do not differentiate between what white people would call "reality" and the dreams and other visions stimulated by prayer, smoking, fasting, loss of sleep, and drugs such as peyote. While a white person might want to know whether a buffalo or wolf "really" visited a supplicant on Bear Butte, a Cheyenne religionist is indifferent to this question, which he considers irrelevant to the religious quest, and perhaps a rude attempt to discredit native religion. Cheyennes frequently relate to other Cheyennes their dream experiences, in which they not only encountered powerful spiritual entities, but perhaps talked to dead relatives, visited faraway places, or learned of death or disease in other families. Confirmation of the "reality" of these experiences comes from people who narrate that they were visited. During World War II, for example, a prominent Cheyenne spiritualist, Ralph White Tail, claimed to have visited Cheyenne soldiers in Europe to comfort and reassure them. When they returned, the soldiers confirmed that they had been visited.

Many kinds of knowledge are received and confirmed in this manner. Often the cosmological structure is elaborated during a religious experience, as when a bear encountered in a vision reveals himself as the "Red Star," known to white people as the planet Mars. New associations are made between birds and animals, plants and animals, stones and stars, all of which are original associations, but consistent with the existing principles of taxonomy and cosmology. Thus, one fundamental principle of Cheyenne epistemology is that new knowledge must be consistent, at some level, with old knowledge. The Cheyennes value and encourage the accumulation of new and novel perspectives on the universe, if they fit within the general framework.

For example, a supplicant of my acquaintance had an experience in which a blue egg was transformed into a blue snake, thence into a sacred bird, which people call a roadrunner. He brought back from his vision quest a blue, egg-shaped stone that represented these transformations, and his new religious power. Although his instructor and other religionists had never heard of these particular symbolic associations, his interpretation of events was quickly endorsed and legitimated because it followed the principles outlined in sacred stories, and in the experiences of other men. Just as a man could find a similitude between the black crescent on a flicker's neck and the crescent moon, so could a man find that blue eggs, blue snakes, and a roadrunner were spiritually and cognatically connected. Although the association was new, it followed well-established cognatic principles.

Cheyennes also respect old knowledge, but they expect that part of it will become obsolete while a core of knowledge will be maintained.[6] The general and ongoing framework of old knowledge is presented in annual ceremonies. This framework is reaffirmed year after year. It is not expected to be reorganized or replaced. This core of old knowledge, acted out in the Arrow Ceremony and Sun Dance, concerns the fundamental structure of the universe, the locations of spirits, sacred places, flora and fauna, and the biography of their culture hero, Sweet Medicine. Other old knowledge, which they expect to be replaced, is represented by the contents of personal medicine bundles in the possession of older men and some women. These are used during the lifetimes of the religionists. Each one is usually buried with the person who initiated it, although some people pass along their bundle and the means of using it to younger people. So, while the annual ceremonies represent the stable core of religious beliefs, it is personal medicine bundles, pipes, and other objects that represent the evolution of religious beliefs through the changing religious experiences of Cheyenne supplicants. A strict boundary is maintained between *tribal,* collective, religious objects, which are in the keeping of elected keepers, and personal objects that are under the control of individuals or families.

Formerly it was possible for personal medicines—objects, songs, and rituals—to "graduate" at the death of a medicine man into the body of shared ceremonial tradition. Some objects now in use during ceremonies are said to have been the personal property of famous priests. Within my memory, only two objects have been offered in this manner, a peyote button and a famous historical pipe. Both were finally rejected, failing to get a unanimous endorsement from the community of priests.

In Cheyenne tradition, religious inquiries or supplications, both ceremonial and personal, are directed by persons who are characterized in English as instructors. Whether one wishes to fast and smoke on a local hilltop, pray at Bear Butte, enter a sweat lodge, or participate in the major ceremonies, a man must have an instructor. A woman must also have an instructor, and sometimes a surrogate man to participate in her stead. Instructors mediate between the general framework of shared cosmology, represented in the annual ceremonies, and the new knowledge gained by their apprentices. Instructors for personal vision quests are usually people who also serve as priests in the ceremonies. In both roles, they may meet together to discuss difficult issues of religious philosophy. For example, when a dream impels a person to make an ambitious request of other religionists, or when pipes are crossed or mistakes made in a ritual or ceremony, knowledgeable religionists may have to meet to decide what to do. Epistemological principles for the incorporation of new knowledge, even contradictory principles, are invoked and discussed at great length on these occasions.

In a recent case, the issue was how to dispose of a sacred animal skin that had been part of one of the tribal medicine bundles, but was removed because it was falling apart. Unfortunately, no one could remember how the previous skin had been disposed of. One priest advised that the skin should be stuffed into a badger hole, because that was how a skin from a different medicine bundle had been disposed of. Another priest said that his family had always disposed of such items by tying rocks to them and sinking them in a stream. A third said that the skin should be buried with the next priest who died.

The discussion that followed, for nearly a full day, illustrates not only the epistemological principles that are important to Cheyennes, but also the one that was ultimately upheld above the others. Some argued for a particular means of disposal because it had greater antiquity. Others argued for a different means because it was used by deceased priests of high status. But the technique that was finally used was selected because of the continued good health and high reputation of the people who used it, and their descendants. It was argued that since the people who used the badger hole burial had not suffered particularly from disease, accident, or early death, they must have performed the ritual properly. Ultimately, then, an *empirical* test prevailed— not empirical in the experimental, scientific sense, but empirical in its logic: if the results were good, then the ritual must have been correct.

In approaching knowledge from the white man's world, some Cheyennes use traditional kinds of logic and methods, some do not. To make their automobiles run and their computers operate without error, some Cheyennes rely on eagle feathers and sacred red paint, and also their technical knowledge. Others put religious methods behind them and adopt the "white man's road" exclusively, with the idea that white man's knowledge can only be gained by white man's methods. Most Cheyenne college students, for example, adopt a new epistemology—a systematic philosophy, formal logic, and empirical standards of proof—in the university. Yet they do not reject traditional standards of truth. In a traditional context, they might employ traditional epistemology; in the white man's world, they use the same standards of validity as white people. It would not occur to a Cheyenne engineering student, for example, to pray and sing to master his homework; this is in the province of the white man's world. Students do not believe that healthy professors are any more knowledgeable than sick or disabled professors, although they would be loath to accept a sick or injured priest as an instructor for a major religious role.

My experience is that the Cheyenne students who are most successful in the university do not worry too much about the differences or contradictions between their own culture and the culture of the dominant society. They become truly bicultural, sliding smoothly between being a traditional Cheyenne and being an educated Indian. Teachers in public schools, universities, and Native American studies programs may do a great disservice to American Indian students by encouraging them to concern themselves too much about the differences—to emphasize the theme of "the person caught between two cultures." Some American Indian students do not know that they are caught between two cultures until a teacher tells them.[7] Just as it is possible for a Native American person to be truly bilingual without engaging in the study of comparative grammar, so is it possible for him or her to be truly bicultural without understanding, at a philosophical level, differences in the source and evaluation of knowledge and in the different structures of the universe implied in native and western cosmologies and epistemologies.

Cheyenne intellectuals, therefore, expect that their philosophical knowledge will come from two sources: tradition and personal religious experiences. Traditional knowledge, from oral literature and ceremonies, is not evaluated; it is accepted. The core of old knowledge, represented in the annual ceremonies, is learned by the apprentices of priests, but without seeking new knowledge or attempting to change the songs, stories, or ritual procedures.

The new knowledge offered by dreamers and vision seekers as the result of dreams or fasting, however, is carefully scrutinized, especially by an instructor. At least four different principles are used to decide its value: (1) did the knowledge have a traditional source, here a bird, animal, or spiritual being? (2) did the supplicant perform his fasting or other rituals properly? (3) are the new symbolic associations parallel or analogous to existing associations? (4) did the new knowledge have good effects on the supplicant and his family?

If all four conditions are satisfied, the new knowledge is legitimated by the community of religionists, becomes part of the shared tradition, and might be built upon or extrapolated by subsequent religious seekers.

Mvskoke Philosophy

Even at first glance, the philosophical framework for Mvskoke cosmology and ceremonies is clearly entirely different from that of the Cheyennes. While the Cheyenne perspective emphasizes spatial dimensions, the contrast between male and female "principles," individual religious quests, and the relationships between instructor and apprentice, the Mvskoke perspective is concerned with the duality of world and underworld, of good and evil, and the avoidance of pollution created by animals, the underworld, and the menstruation of women.[8] While the Cheyennes emphasize the dichotomies between zenith and nadir and among the cardinal directions, Mvskokes are focused on the animals and other phenomena that characterize their clans, and on the herbs and ceremonies that protect them from disease. Mvskokes, like the Cheyennes, celebrate the four directions; yet entirely different entities are associated with these directions, united for the Mvskokes by the symbolism of the ceremonial fire. Among Cheyennes, fire is entirely missing among the sacred symbols.

For Cheyennes, misfortune and disease are caused by ritual mistakes, the failure to participate in ceremonies, and the undisciplined and unchanneled release of cosmic energy. For Mvskokes, misfortune and disease are caused by evil people, evil creatures, and the practice of witchcraft. While the Cheyennes, who lack clans and are bilateral in their kinship structure, participate as individuals and as extended families in their ceremonies, the Mvskokes, who have matrilineal clans and a "Crow" kinship system, participate as matrilineal groups—lineages, clans, phratries, and tribal towns. The central theme in the practice of Cheyenne religion is acquiring energy, but the central theme in Mvskoke religion is avoiding pollution.

Unlike Cheyenne tradition, Mvskoke oral literature is highly concerned with cosmological origins. Mvskoke cosmogony comprises three stages of creation, which occurred in a particular order. Each stage is narrated in different versions, some of which are shared with those peoples who were neighbors of the Mvskokes in the southeastern United States during or before the nineteenth century.

The first stage of Mvskoke creation is narrated against a background in which there were only air and water, and mysterious creatures of the air and creatures of the water. In earliest times, it is said, these creatures had a long discussion among themselves, and decided that they wanted the universe to have some dry land. To accomplish this, they enlisted the aid of a water creature, in most versions a crayfish, to bring mud from the bottom of the water to form land. The shape of this traditional continent is seen by Mvskokes as square, although Cherokees and other neighboring peoples say that it is round.

Three levels of the universe resulted from these early efforts, according to Mvskoke religionists. They are a sky vault, which is blue, solid, and stone-like; the earth-continent with surrounding water; and a mysterious underworld populated by people, plants, and creatures who are similar to those on the surface, but who embody powers beyond and different from those attained on the surface. Glimpses of this underworld can be gained by looking into deep water, caves, and crevices, into swamp fires, or into the bottoms of sink holes. Caves and crevices lead to the underworld, and fogs, mists, and strange odors emanate from there. Mvskoke people see the earth's surface not as solid and secure, as the Cheyennes conceive it, but as crumbly, muddy, and treacherous, perhaps reflecting in cosmology the geographic conditions of their homeland in Georgia, Alabama, and northern Florida.

The high god and subordinate gods, in the Mvskoke world, live in the sky vault and are mostly benevolent to the earth and its creatures, and largely meteorological in their behavior, sending rain and sunshine to benefit the creatures below. These gods are the subjects of stories told to children. But in contrast to the Cheyenne tradition, these ascendant Mvskoke gods are not said to be the origins of help or power for human beings, and are not prayed to or entreated. Instead, the people, creatures, and other phenomena of the underworld are the primary focus of religious attention, and the source of potential personal power, for good or evil. Unlike Cheyenne stories, which show how apparently mysterious creatures are in fact the source of benevolent power, Mvskoke stories are terrifying and describe the underworld and its creatures as evil and unknowable. While the Cheyennes have creation stories, they are of a different sort, explaining the origins of sexuality and clothing, of institutions like soldier societies or the chief's council, and of the colors and markings of animals.

The second stage of Mvskoke creation stories concerns the origins of clans and phratries. According to these stories, when the earth's surface was originally created, new creatures came into being who would populate the surface. At this time a thick, pervasive, and continual fog prevented these creatures from seeing each other. They knew of the presence of other creatures only because they would occasionally bump into them in the fog. Creatures who lived near one another became familiar with and helped one another, though they could not see each other.

After a while, the high god took pity on these creatures of the surface living in perpetual darkness. Taking the form of Master of Breath, he blew away the fog so that the creatures could see one another. As the fog blew away, the creatures began to form themselves into neighborhood groups or phratries of creatures who lived near one another, and then, as the fog cleared further, clans were formed from similar creatures within each phratry. When the fog first began to clear, certain groups of humans discovered that they had been living among beavers, otters, alligators, and fish, so they joined with them in a water phratry. Some of these humans discovered that they had been associating specifically with beavers, and so they joined with them in a beaver clan. The specifics of which animals became associated with which other animals, and why, are very different among the independent Mvskoke communities, called Etvlwa or tribal towns, because each of them comprises different clans, which have roles in the town that are different from the roles of the same clans in other towns.

After the clans were formed, according to origin stories, and the fog had disappeared entirely, human beings came together to form their own communities, but they maintained their clan identities and their special relationships with the animals and other phenomena who had been their allies during the time of the fog.

The third stage of Mvskoke cosmogonic tradition explains where they came from geographically. These are migration stories. According to these, the component groups of the Mvskokes, originally separate tribes such as the Coosa and Arbeka, migrated east from the Red River area of Texas and Louisiana to occupy a new homeland in the area centering on the major rivers of Georgia and Alabama. Like the ancient Hebrews, their journey was accompanied by regular supernatural signs that they were traveling in the right direction, and when they arrived in Georgia they were told to settle in that place.

Mvskoke religious practices, and traditional Mvskoke political structures, center on the interactions among clans within the tribal town. For social and ceremonial purposes, each tribal town has traditionally maintained its own ceremonial ground, also called busk ground or stomp ground, which is physically organized according to the cardinal directions and the identity and status of the clans that are present in the town. A fire is maintained in the center of the grounds during the ceremonial season, with four logs pointing to the cardinal directions that are continually pushed into the fire to maintain it. Around the fire and dance circle are four arbors with benches likewise oriented to the cardinal directions, where the leaders and elders sit according to clan and phratry. Outside the dance ring are camp houses where the people of the town live during several weeks of annual ceremonies.

Among the Cheyennes, political leaders or "chiefs" have no role in the annual ceremonies unless they have achieved some religious rank by apprenticing to a priestly instructor. But among the Mvskokes, political leaders lead the ceremonies. They are assisted by priests whose roles are very restricted. The priests make the black drink and apply scratches to legs and arms as part of the ceremony, but otherwise are supposed to stay in the background. Compared with Cheyenne religious practice, Mvskoke practice is very secular; the ceremonies are more social than supernatural. While the leaders of Cheyenne ceremonies frequently retreat to private tipis for esoteric rituals, at the busk ground nearly everything is in the open, although parts of the ceremony are conducted at night and certain sacred objects are exhibited only to a restricted audience.

At a sociological level, the difference between Cheyenne and Mvskoke religious practice is a matter of how social standing is acquired—the difference between what social scientists call achieved and ascribed status. While any Cheyenne man can apprentice himself for any religious role within the tribe, a Mvskoke man cannot. Born a member of his mother's clan, a Mvskoke man can only perform the ritual duties of that clan as defined within a particular tribal town. To be a priest at the busk grounds, his father must have been a priest. That is, while ceremonial roles mostly are organized by clan, priests or medicine men usually inherit their role from the father's side, although they might perform it in a different town.

Within traditional Mvskoke religion as currently practiced, there is not much room for innovation. Most often, the celebrants at the fifteen or so existing ceremonial grounds are hard pressed to muster enough knowledgeable people to perform their annual summer ceremonies at all. Each decade more songs and dances are lost, so that Mvskoke religionists see themselves as part of a shrinking tradition. At the ceremonial grounds, there is no new knowledge against which a native epistemology can be applied. But this is not so with the medicine men, sorcerers, and seers in Creek and Seminole society. While the ceremonies annually diminish in significance, the numbers and reputations of Mvskoke shamans and healers may be increasing. For simplicity's sake I will refer to this whole community of shamanistic religionists, whatever their specialty, as medicine people.

If there is an epistemology of Mvskoke ceremonies, it is simply the test of antiquity. Songs, stories, and dances are valid if they are old. There is no innovation except the occasional insertion of Jesus among the gods of the sky vault addressed in prayer. For educated Mvskoke people, their cosmology has been largely criticized and displaced by the white man's cosmology, or, more specifically, his astronomy. Compared with Cheyenne cosmology, the Mvskoke cosmology has been vulnerable to displacement. While the Cheyenne cosmology speaks of spaces and allows for a Blue Sky-Space of infinite size, the idea of a solid blue sky vault in Mvskoke tradition is difficult to support in the face of evidence supplied by space vehicles and travelers to the moon. Consequently, even the most sincere Mvskoke religionists talk about their traditional cosmology not as something they personally believe, but as something that Mvskoke people "used to" believe.

Mvskoke migration legends are also under attack. Some archaeologists dispute the assertion that Mvskokes came from the west, and insofar as a class in history, anthropology, or Native American studies comprises archaeology, it is an attack on Mvskoke tradition. The origins and structure of the Mvskoke earth-continent have also become something that Mvskoke people "used to" believe. Like the sky vault itself, the concept has succumbed to white man's empirical science, his maps, globe of the world, astronomy, and space travel.

Despite these setbacks, Mvskoke tradition continues to thrive in the form of the knowledge and experiences of medicine people involved in private practice with patients and clients. It thrives because it is differently formulated, has different epistemological standards, and is irrefutable by white man's logic and evidence. It is also protected by its esoteric nature and the secrecy practiced, for good reasons, by Mvskoke medicine people. To understand the practice of Mvskoke medicine people, one must first understand the Mvskoke theory of disease and their notions of good and evil in the moral universe, because the practice of Mvskoke medicine is intended to cure disease and expunge the effects of immoral acts by oneself or other people.

In Mvskoke philosophy, disease is caused by animals—by physical contact with them and especially by the abuse of animals who serve as clan symbols. Most of the names of diseases recognized by Mvskokes can be literally translated in such forms as "squirrel did it," "beaver did it," "deer did it." The symptoms, or at least the array of symptoms of the different diseases, are unique. It is the medicine person's first task to diagnose which animal or symbolic entity has caused the disease.

Cures for diseases were originally provided by Master of Breath in the form of medicinal herbs. Most specific diseases have a specific plant that cures them, so that animals and plants therefore occur in cognatic pairs. Medicine people know which plant cures the disease caused by which animal. Mostly these plants are brewed and drunk; some are applied externally as a poultice. Here, as with Cheyenne epistemology, the test of efficacy is empirical. The test of whether a medicine person is good, and whether the herb selected was correct, is whether the patient gets better. Most often, a small payment is made to a medicine person for treatment, and a larger payment at recovery.

Other kinds of human illnesses are caused not by pollution from animals, but by a person's own bad behavior, or the often involuntary bad thoughts of other people. The purpose of the black drink taken at ceremonies is to cause the effects of bad behavior and bad thought, in the form of a black, red, brown, or yellow glob, to be expelled from the stomach by the emetic drink. Expelling the glob is often preceded or followed by formal apologies, sometimes with weeping, by the person for his or her bad behavior, or by another person for his or her bad thoughts or gossip. Some congregations of Mvskoke Baptists, nominally Christians, hold an annual ceremony during which people meet each other in the woods surrounding the rural churches, two by two, and apologize for their bad conduct in the past year. Offender and offended weep, embrace, and pray together.

Sometimes a person harms another person on purpose. To do so, he or she obtains the services of a medicine person who is in league with a "familiar" from the underworld, one that has the power to do harm. The symbol of the harm is placed near the target person, or his or her home, office, or automobile, in the form of an amulet containing such symbols as owl feathers and dog feces.

People who believe themselves to be the objects of attack by witchcraft can obtain the services of a medicine person who either knows the defense against certain attacks or has a familiar who can struggle with the familiar of the attacker's medicine person. Sometimes there is a great and extended battle between two medicine people and their familiars.

Medicine people get control over familiars by personal quests into dangerous places, especially caves, swamps, and other areas where there are mists or fogs. These are the marginal places between world and underworld. By secret means, the medicine person gains control over the familiar, who then enters the body of the medicine person. When medicine people die, the familiars are said to leave their bodies in the form of snakes, lizards, worms, and other strange and frightening creatures from the underworld.

The knowledge of Mvskoke medicine people is secret for several reasons. First, it is secret because it is their way of making a living, and one can gain the knowledge only by being a patient or client or by becoming an apprentice. Second, it is secret because the "witching" aspect of medical practice is regarded as immoral. Medicine people do not want to advertise that they can perform witchcraft, because of public disapproval, although some do not mind letting people know that they can probably help with witchcraft. Third, Mvskoke medicine people are secretive because in the past they have been prosecuted under the law for practicing medicine without a license. Even now, certain physicians will report medicine people to the police or sheriff when they have the opportunity.

While Cheyenne religionists constitute a community of priests who are almost universally admired in their society, Mvskoke medicine people are as much feared as respected. They are respected because of their role in the busk ceremonies, but feared because of their potential to be involved in witchcraft. Some medicine men assure their patients and clients that they are only familiar with good and benevolent spirits and creatures from the underworld, and thus attain a status similar to that of Cheyenne priests. But others intentionally cultivate the reputation of "black priest."

As with Cheyenne ritual practice, the proof of a Mvskoke medicine person's power is in the results. If the patient recovers, if a target person sickens and dies, or if a target is protected, then the medicine person is validated. But here, the identity of the operative supernatural forces is secret. Among the Cheyennes, religionists proudly admit to friends and family the identity of their spiritual contacts. Among Mvskokes, the public learns only whether medicine people were successful, and not how they did it.

An important contrast between Cheyenne and Mvskoke epistemology centers on the issue of collective validation of religious knowledge. While Cheyenne religionists constitute a community that can meet to discuss a ceremonial mistake or the validity of a vision quest, Mvskoke medicine people do not constitute a community, except for each small group of apprentices and their mentor. Instead, they are individual practitioners who are often on opposite sides of supernatural struggles. Several years ago, a naive but highly educated Cherokee man received grant to convene a conference of medicine men to discuss matters of common interest. Not surprisingly, no legitimate medicine people showed up: some feared the witchcraft manipulations of other medicine people who might be present, and nobody wanted to share knowledge with anyone else. Conversely, Cheyenne priests regularly meet together because they share a cosmology and ceremonial practice and have no secrets from one another, although they do have areas of specialized knowledge that are mutually respected.

Discussion

Despite some striking differences in cosmology, cosmogony, and religious practice, Cheyenne and Mvskoke philosophy share some fundamental premises and attitudes. First, the two traditions are agreed that human beings are not the centers of the universe, but are instead weak and helpless creatures, surrounded by spiritual and natural forces that are much more potent than they are. Neither religious tradition exalts the power of human spirituality or mentality. Birds, animals, and spirits are all alleged to be the real sources even of the limited power that humans have, and the philosophy of humanism, even religious humanism, is entirely missing.[9] Human faculties of logic and reason likewise are neither celebrated nor mentioned. Consistent themes in both tribal traditions emphasize the ignorance, helplessness, and lack of power of humans as compared with the other spiritual and moral forces of the universe.

But Cheyenne and Mvskoke traditions go about soliciting these nonhuman forces in entirely different manners. For the Cheyennes, all power is good, and can be legitimately harnessed by any person who is properly instructed and uses correct rituals. For Mvskoke people, only a few designated people have the power to marshal supernatural powers, and these people, in the role of shaman or healer, must be solicited as intermediaries. For the Cheyennes, new religious knowledge is interpreted by the community of priests; for the Mvskokes, each medicine person is his or her own ultimate judge of legitimacy. In both traditions, empirical criteria are used by apprentices, clients, and patients to evaluate the power accumulated by a religionist.

Both Cheyenne and Mvskoke tradition respect the role of elder as repository of cultural knowledge. The antiquity or traditional status of a bit of knowledge—a symbolic association, a ritual, a dance, or a story—must be confirmed by a knowledgeable elder. The issues considered by the two traditions are different, however. The Cheyennes, participants in an expanding religious tradition, must decide whether new symbols are consistent with old ones. The Mvskokes, participants in a shrinking ceremonial system, must often split the differences among the cultural traditions of tribal towns with different dances and traditions, thrown together at the same busk grounds because of a reduced ceremonial community. Among the Mvskokes there is no one to judge the status of a medicine person's knowledge, because that knowledge is personal, secret, and potentially harmful to others.

Several other aspects of knowledge and epistemology shared between Cheyenne and Mvskoke tradition are obvious, but still need to be mentioned by way of marking some contrasts with the secular or scientific tradition of Euro-Americans. First, in both Native American traditions, the attainment and exhibition of knowledge require ritual and ceremony. Prayers precede and follow every event in which important cultural knowledge is exhibited; there is no secular philosophy, and this fact is emphasized at every opportunity. In both traditions I have seen elders interrupt meetings and gatherings of various kinds if the conversation turns to serious religious matters and no prayer has been said. This behavior emphasizes both the religious nature of knowledge and the role of elders in transmitting knowledge.

Second, both societies discussed here recognize the boundaries between personal religious knowledge and collective cultural knowledge. For Cheyennes, a vision quest, a sweat lodge, or a visit with a healer or herbalist are personal matters, and no one is socially outraged at the results. The tribal ceremonies are different, however, and the proper conduct of these annual events is considered everyone's business. The sociologist Emile Durkheim would not be surprised to see the collective, moral order of Cheyenne society so carefully segregated from personal life.[10] The same is true for the Mvskokes. The proper conduct of the Green Corn and other ceremonies is a public, collective concern, but the activities of medicine people, seers, and herbalists are outside the collective realm, except for the medicines administered at the busk ground. In sociological terms, this distinction between the two religious spheres for both traditions is preserved by differentiating the priestly roles associated with ceremonies from the shamanistic roles of medicine people.[11]

The shared or collective aspect of Cheyenne and Mvskoke cultures is not only ceremonial but cosmological. It can be argued that both groups act out or dance out their cosmologies at their tribal ceremonies. In song and action, the tribal ceremonies celebrate the structure of the universe, and the universe is represented in the structure of the ceremonial grounds and its activities. Healers and medicine people, however, do not try to appeal to the collective tradition. Instead, their emphasis is on their personal powers, their individual relationships with the spirits, and the knowledge necessary to heal a person, manipulate human events, or injure an enemy.

In 1977, in connection with research for the American Indian Religious Freedom Act, I attempted to build bridges between Cheyenne and Mvskoke religionists by taking them with me to each other's ceremonies.[12] In both cases, the behavior of the hosts and of the guests was very similar. When I took two Mvskoke medicine men to the Cheyenne Sun Dance that summer, the Cheyenne priests were honored and pleased. Special places were found for their Mvskoke visitors in the lodges and tipis they visited, and they were honored to share the special ceremonial food, blessed for the occasion. They ate and otherwise participated politely in the activities, but seemed very uncomfortable. After a whispered discussion early in the evening, they wanted to leave.

A few weeks later, I took two Cheyenne priests to a Mvskoke Green Corn Dance. Although welcomed and embraced by the Mvskoke religious leaders (one Cheyenne was in fact married to a Mvskoke woman), they never felt quite at home. They did not know where to sit and constantly feared that they were doing something wrong. They were especially worried that they might step inside the dance ring or have contact with a menstruating woman, after a Mvskoke leader told them about the importance of such matters. In this case, they began to feel more secure and more anonymous as darkness fell, so they stayed the night in a Mvskoke camp house.

The most interesting result of the exchange visits, surprising to me, was that each of the four men, in the weeks following their visits and despite their obvious discomfort at the time, told me that attending the foreign ceremony was one of the most important and significant events of his life. But they did not follow up the social contacts, as I had hoped, and as far as I know never again attended a ceremony at the ceremonial site that they had visited. What to make of this combination of fascination, respect, and perhaps fear in the presence of each other's ceremonies? I will return to this question later.

Generalizing about Native American Religion

Since I first began learning firsthand about Cheyenne religion, comparing what I learned with what I had read about other Native American groups, I have been skeptical that anyone could make generalizations about Native American religion broad enough to include all traditions. What I had read about Pueblo and Northwest Coast traditions, for example, seemed so different as to resist any philosophical synthesis with the Cheyennes. My skepticism was reinforced a decade later when I began to learn firsthand about Mvskoke religion, a tradition based on principles that seemed different both from Cheyenne religion and from other Native North American religions I had read about. I admit, however, that written accounts of religious traditions can be quite different from the traditions as known to the participants, either because of the secrecy of the practitioners, as with *The Book of the Hopi,* or because of the misrepresentation of the author, as with *Seven Arrows.*[13] For that reason, I confine my attention here to the two Native American traditions with which I am personally familiar. The question in comparing these religions with each other and with other Native American traditions is whether there are any fundamental generalizations that can describe "Native American religion."

If we could isolate and define "Native American religion," and identify a unified epistemology shared by all varieties, the task facing scholars and teachers of Native American culture would be considerably simplified. It would not be necessary to teach about Cheyenne religion, Mvskoke religion, Hopi religion, or Nootka religion—only to teach a course about Native American religion with collateral discussions about how this religion is represented locally among the various tribes and nations of North America.

Attempts to describe and explain "Native American religion" have been written by people of diverse background and interest. Those written by non-Indians tend to be both foolish and transparently self-interested, emphasizing either the supposedly savage and mysterious nature of the "Indian mind" or the fact that Native Americans unconsciously represent the values that are important for Boy Scouts, YMCA Indian Guides, Catholics, Methodists, Mennonites, or even some cult or political party.[14]

There are several classic works, however, which were written by Native American scholars both familiar with their subject and motivated by a desire to expose, as well as they could, the underlying unity of Native American religion and its embedded epistemology. Here I examine the attempts of Charles Eastman and Vine Deloria, Jr., to see what propositions from their personal, knowledgeable standpoint they isolate as pan-tribal in their significance. We can then see if the propositions apply legitimately to Cheyenne and Mvskoke philosophical systems, as I have described them above, and perhaps to other traditions as well.

Charles Eastman was perhaps the most famous Native American of his generation. Raised as a traditional Dakota until he was fifteen, he became a physician and the author of the autobiographical *An Indian Boyhood* (1902).[15] He gained wide experience with other tribal traditions in his work as a physician and in his work for the Bureau of Indian Affairs, translating Indian names and entering them into official records. His attempt to describe Native American philosophy overall was published in 1911 as *The Soul of the Indian.*[16] He explains in the foreword that he has "attempted to paint the religious life of the typical American Indian as it was before he knew the white man" [17] and acknowledges that "my little book . . . is as true as I can make it to my childhood teaching and ancestral ideals." [18] The book is short, consisting of six chapters: "The Great Mystery," "The Family Altar," "Ceremonial and Symbolic Worship," "Barbarism and the Moral Code," "The Unwritten Scriptures," and "On the Borderland of Spirits."

The "great mystery" of chapter one he explains as a "consciousness of the divine," [19] emphasizing that worship of the divine does not depend on priests or temples. As the chapter proceeds, Eastman is clearly using the Plains Indian vision quest as the core of Native American religion. He explains the superiority of the vision experience over other forms of religious practice:

The red man divided mind into two parts—the spiritual mind and the physical mind. The first is pure spirit, concerned only with the essence of things, and it was this he sought to strengthen by spiritual prayer, during which the body is subdued by fasting and hardship. In this type of prayer there was no beseeching of favor or help. All matters of personal or selfish concern, as success in hunting or warfare, relief from sickness, or the sparing of a beloved life, were definitely relegated to the plane of the lower or material mind, and all ceremonies, charms or incantations designed to secure a benefit or to avert a danger, were recognized as emanating from the physical self.[20]

Eastman has listed here, as aspects of the lower mind, precisely the most frequently stated, explicit motivations for performing the Cheyenne Sun Dance: maintaining good health, recovering from illness, and gaining worldly success. And he has elevated to the upper plane the personal vision quest, which he claims can be conducted without the assistance of any priest or instructor. Later in the chapter, he attacks organized, presumably Christian religion for its concern with wealth and power, especially the "moneyed church" and its "paid exhorter." [21] But the philosophy of Christianity he endorses toward the end of the chapter, saying that "the spirit of Christianity and of our ancient religion is essentially the same." [22]

In the same chapter, Eastman outlines a proposition that is a good candidate for universality among Native North American religions—the idea that everything in nature is alive: "that the spirit pervades all creation and that every creature possesses a soul in some degree. . . . The tree, the waterfall, the grizzly bear, each is an embodied Force, and as such an object of reverence." [23] In concordance with this belief, Cheyennes say that mountains and rocks are alive, and that stones move about animately. Mvskoke people regard topographic features as animate, an attitude expressed, for example, when they say that caves can eat a person, and that rivers bark and growl as they roll along.

In chapter two, Eastman describes moral and religious instruction as the job of the mother and father, and says that marriage was a decision between two people, who go off into the woods to "taste their apotheosis alone with nature." [24] Overall, Eastman's ethnographic comments about family life are not consistent with other Dakota narratives of the period, and probably represent his own experience, moving from reservation to town at age fifteen and raised by his Christian father.[25] But in this chapter, rife with ethnographic errors, we find again a philosophical proposition with a good claim for universality among Indian people. Eastman says of the "typical Indian": "Every act of his life is, in a very real sense, a religious act." [26]

In chapter three Eastman considers ceremonies, which he has already characterized as institutions of a lower order than the personal religious quest. He asserts that the few Plains Indian ceremonies represent a transition toward Christianity.[27] At the time he was writing, Eastman himself had become a Christian, and regarded the early reservation ceremonies reported by ethnographers as inspired by Christian influences, especially the " 'Black Robe' priests, the military, and . . . the Protestant missionaries." [28] He describes the Sun Dance as "a horrible exhibition of barbarism," [29] although he blames the barbarism not on Indian tradition, but on Christianity; the Ghost Dance he characterizes as a "craze . . . of distinctively alien origin." [30] He also speaks disparagingly of the medicine lodge and medicine people, an attitude perhaps to be expected from a serious, practicing physician in the Anglo-American tradition.

The next chapter is devoted to the moral order. Briefly, Eastman says that the cornerstones of personal morality are to know God, to perceive goodness, to love what is beautiful, and to keep silence. Here also he presents a full panoply of generalizations about social morality, many of which are candidates for universal significance among Indian people—generosity, chastity, modesty, honesty, bravery in warfare. His illustrations and discussions constitute an endorsement of the values that scholars associate with the concept of *gemeinschaft* or community.[31] Both here and in previous chapters, Eastman castigates the values and behavior he associates with civilization, such as greed, selfishness, glibness, and what Karl Marx characterized as the "commodification" of everything from sexual favors to the earth itself.[32]

In the fifth chapter, Eastman deals explicitly with philosophical and epistemological issues. He narrates the creation story of the Dakota people, and declares the sun to be male and the earth female. The first person created was a man called "First-Born" who grew to maturity and then, out of loneliness, created a younger brother, Little Boy Man, to whom he taught everything he knew. Prominent, even pervasive in this chapter is the theme that elder brother knows best. Constantly in danger from the earth's creatures, Little Boy Man always receives good advice from First-Born. And so he learns to trust him completely.

The last chapter of the book is anticlimactic. It is not a summary or synthesis of Native American beliefs, but describes Dakota funerals and the activities of prophets and seers. Eastman believes in the accuracy of Native American prophecies, and urges the reader also to believe in them.

Another classic synthetic Native American philosophy is contained in Vine Deloria's *God Is Red*.[33] As everyone on the Indian scene knows, Deloria is the author of *Custer Died for Your Sins* and a host of other books and articles.[34] Born a Dakota, like Eastman, Deloria is a professor at the University of Colorado. Also like Eastman, Deloria was raised in a Christian family, the son of an Episcopal missionary. Consequently he, like Eastman, is in a position to compare Native American philosophy with western traditions at a very sophisticated level.[35]

Deloria is a creature of the Native American movement, and in fact one might argue that he helped invent "Native Americans" as a national, pan-tribal political and cultural movement. Before him, there were only "Indians" and tribes. If he did not invent "Native American" culture, he was at least a catalyst for it, as both a writer and an active participant in most of the important Native American organizations of the last thirty years.

God Is Red is largely written in the same entertaining, witty, intellectual style as *Custer Died for Your Sins.* Here, I am less concerned with his wit than with the more serious moments of the book where he addresses philosophical issues, especially in the practice of religion. Like Eastman, Deloria recognizes that Native American philosophy is necessarily a religious philosophy.

Ethnographically, it is easy to fault Deloria for a lack of knowledge of the Native American traditions he discusses, but one should remember that the non-Dakota traditions are as unfamiliar to him as to any non-Indian. Like Anglo-Americans, he has had to read about these traditions in books and articles, many of which he cites in his bibliography.

Early in his book, Deloria presents an eloquent characterization of Native American religion overall, consistent with Eastman's notion of the "Great Mystery," as well as other of Eastman's observations discussed above.[36]

> The relationships that serve to form the unity of nature are of vastly more importance to most tribal religions. . . . The task of the tribal religion, if such a religion can be said to have a task, is to determine the proper relationship that the people of the tribe must have with other living things and to develop the self-discipline within the tribal community so that man acts harmoniously with other creatures. . . . Recognition that human beings hold an important place in such a creation is tempered by the thought that they are dependent on everything in creation for their existence . . . the awareness of the meaning of life comes from observing how the various living things appear to mesh to provide a whole tapestry.[37]

Deloria also asserts that "tribal religions find a great affinity among species of living creatures. . . . Other living things are not regarded as insensitive species. Rather they are 'people' in the same manner as the various tribes of human being are people." [38] And he notes that "for some tribes the idea extends to plants, rocks, and natural features that Westerners consider inanimate." [39]

Certainly these generalizations crafted by Deloria apply both to the Cheyennes and to the Mvskokes. Most of the intellectual energy of these traditions is concerned with defining the attributes of the creatures and places of the natural world, and explaining their relationships to people. In contrast, for both Eastman and Deloria, Christianity is mostly about the relationship between humans and a monotheistic high god. Eastman's and Deloria's ideas about the substance of Native American religion and philosophy, then, and its salient differences from Christianity, are very similar: the substance of religious and philosophical thought should be the natural world and the relationships among the creatures and spirits who live there.

Deloria's assertions about the universality of sacred places in tribal religions, however, are more difficult to support from North American ethnography. The Cheyennes clearly have a sacred place, Bear Butte in the Black Hills, but the Mvskokes do not. The Mvskokes' sacred place is the ceremonial ground where their fire is located, and the fire can be moved geographically to any location. When the Mvskokes moved from Alabama to Indian Territory in the nineteenth century, for example, they took their fires with them; thus, the western ceremonial grounds became sacred. Mvskokes do not have the same reverential attitude toward their previous locations in Alabama and Georgia as the Cheyennes have toward Bear Butte. They might travel to Alabama or Georgia to visit old sites, but not to worship. Some other Native American nations in North America have sacred places, some do not.

Deloria is on very shaky ground in trying to contrast Native American and Christian religions in terms of a dichotomy between spatial and temporal emphases. He alleges at length that Native American religions are unconcerned with creation and the beginning of time on the one hand, and prophecy and the end of time on the other. He is clearly wrong about the Cheyennes, who have origin stories about the first people and many other things, and for whom the prophet Sweet Medicine spoke about the coming of the white man and an ultimate apocalypse. Mvskokes likewise have elaborate creation stories at the center of their religion, as related above, and even today maintain prophets and seers who predict future events, including the end of the world.

Also troubling to both serious ethnographers and Native American elders who preserve tribal traditions is Deloria's assertion that no Native American religions have an anthropomorphic God. As we have seen, the high god of the Cheyennes is Maheo, the All-Father, and the high god of the Mvskokes is Master of Breath, the creator of the universe, both manlike or anthropomorphic gods. One can only conclude that Deloria, despite being a Native American, is not a very well read ethnographer. In fairness, the book was not written as ethnography. Its purpose, which it serves well, is to engage non-

Indian Christians in a dialogue about respecting Native American religions and protecting sacred places. Along the way, he presents the eloquent passages about Native American religion quoted above, butchers his ethnographic resources, and ends with some stimulating suggestions about future relationships between Native Americans and non-Indians (which are discussed below).

While Eastman seems to have disapproved of tribal ceremonies, Deloria seems generally respectful but does not say much about them, except for making fun of alleged ancient ceremonies made up for naive New Age religionists by enterprising Native American entrepreneurs. Also missing from Deloria's book is a discussion of personal or social morality, other than a plea for white people to take moral responsibility for the protection of sacred places. Altogether, Deloria's tone and style are political and journalistic; Eastman's book is a more consistently serious and personal religious statement.

Thus, Eastman and Deloria agree about which are the most important, most fundamental, and most widely shared aspects of Native American philosophy. They agree that the real substance of native thought is religion, especially the relationships between humans and aspects of the natural world. They are also in agreement about epistemology—the means by which people legitimately learn religion. There are two routes: personal religious experience and the instruction of elders. Neither Eastman nor Deloria leaves much room for innovation.

Although Deloria and Eastman both wrote from a Dakota point of view, we can see that their attempts at generalization are broad enough to include the Cheyenne and Mvskoke perspectives described above. Probably this is because the personal experiences of both authors were pan-tribal, as a result of Eastman's translating work and other projects for the Bureau of Indian Affairs, and Deloria's work as an advocate for groups all over the United States. Perhaps there are Native North American groups whose viewpoint falls outside the generalizations above, but none come easily to mind. And we should note that neither the Cheyennes nor Mvskokes represent even the same language family as the Dakotas: the Cheyennes are Algonquians and the Mvskokes part of the Muskogean family.

Pedagogical Issues and Epistemological Distractions

At one point in *God Is Red,* Deloria emphasizes that Native American philosophy and its attitudes toward the world make sense only from the perspective of an American Indian community. The substance of Native American religion and the shared epistemological principles for understanding the natural world require a proper social and cultural environment for presentation. This brings us head on against one of the thorniest problems of Native American studies in colleges and universities.

Pedagogical Issues

The fundamental problem is that undergraduate programs are organized and structured, spatially and temporally, according to principles about the world very different from the Native American principles that Native American studies programs would like to communicate.[40] Contrast for example, the Anglo-American pedagogical experience in a state university with serious religious instruction as accomplished among Cheyennes and Mvskokes, which I have personally observed.

First, a university student who pays tuition and enrolls in a class can expect to be anonymous and to be treated as a client or even a customer. Normally, students do not expect to create a personal relationship with their professor, and they feel free to complain if they do not get their money's worth. The relationship between student and teacher is largely a pecuniary and impersonal one. It is also a time-bound relationship. Both student and professor begin the relationship at a certain time and end it on the minute (for example, MWF at 8:30–9:20). The content of the course is defined in advance in the title and the syllabus; neither the professor nor the student expects that the student will embrace the content spiritually or emotionally, but only that the student will learn the facts. No one examines students' motivations for taking the class, or the professor's for teaching it. In fact, to do so would be regarded as unethical, an invasion of privacy. There is competition for grades. Professors are freely and publicly criticized for being dumb, unfair, or rude. The student is the center of attention.

Now consider how a young Cheyenne man or woman would undertake to learn something important—for example, the information necessary to undertake an important ceremonial role. First, young people would be encouraged to adopt a serious attitude about the learning, and to decide introspectively whether they truly wanted to undertake a course of study. Then the question "Who would be the instructor?" is discussed in the family. The person selected is approached indirectly about serving as instructor. If they are agreeable, a gift is presented and perhaps a pipe is smoked.

Specifically, suppose that some young Cheyenne men wanted to fast and paint themselves for the Sun Dance. Today, there are sometimes so many of these young men that they are formed into classes and instructed as a group. The time is set (something like "Wednesday afternoon"), and when everyone arrives, the class starts. Everyone shakes hands. They then file into a tipi or into someone's living room. The instructor begins by first saying a long prayer and then, on the first day, commenting in turn on the family of each student and his friendship with them over the years. Sometimes there are other elders present besides the instructor. The instructor soon begins to talk of serious matters; the students drop their eyes and put their hands in their laps in a respectful listening posture. The instructor speaks in a quiet tone about the importance of the ceremonies and the underlying ideas. He tells creation stories. He describes the structure of the universe and the proper relationships among people, plants, and animals. He passes around drawings of the structure of the Sun Dance arbor. No one takes notes. No one asks questions. Everyone listens intently. He talks for an hour or two, perhaps more, and when the instructor stops, the class is over and all the students say, "Huagh" or "Ah-ho" in a loud, appreciative tone. The instructor's family feeds the students, and after the meal there is another prayer, and everyone shakes hands again. The students leave.

The Mvskokes have a more hands-on approach to pedagogy. Like the Cheyennes, they sometimes instruct young people in groups. They begin by shaking hands and eating a meal prepared and brought by the families of the students. However, the instructors are also in groups; in fact, in preparation for the Green Corn Ceremony there might be as many instructors as students. The students' families are also present. Instruction begins with the teachers telling creation stories and explaining the importance of the ceremonies and the songs and dances within the ceremonies. But then, unlike the Cheyennes, they require each student to dance or sing by himself, accompanied by an instructor, and surrounded and witnessed by everyone. When a student does well, his family and friends say, "Hmmm," loud enough to be heard. If the student falters, they sing along and prompt him. Missing a step, the student finds the instructor's hands on his and his feet very near, physically guiding him through the movements, as in an Arthur Murray dance studio.

Neither the Cheyennes nor the Mvskokes award grades to students. For the students, their reward is that they are allowed to participate in the ceremonies, telling stories, manipulating sacred objects, singing, and dancing. They are allowed to practice until they get it right. When they finish, they give their instructor a gift, sometimes an expensive or valuable one.

Teaching at the University of Oklahoma, I sometimes had classes in which half or more of the students were Native American. In these classes I tried to create a sense of community, the sort of environment that Deloria says is essential for learning in the Indian manner. We began each class by shaking hands. In the first week, students were encouraged to talk about their backgrounds, their families, and their motivations for taking the class. Playing "who's your— " for a while, I usually discovered a personal connection with each Native American student, someone in their family or tribe that I knew personally. Following the example of the Native American students, non-Indians also warmed up and talked about family and home, adding to the community atmosphere. My friend and colleague Robert Fields, a Pawnee, goes even farther in his classes by distributing gifts to students—keychains and other beadwork. He feeds them in class. It gives him a chance to discuss sharing, generosity, and hospitality as Native American values, and creates a personal relationship.

Problems sometimes develop in trying to create a Native American atmosphere, however. With Native American elders as guests, I usually asked them to lead a prayer, to make them feel more comfortable. Once a professor from another department, visiting the class, cornered me afterward and objected to this violation of the separation of church and state. On another occasion, some Native American students gave me a gift on the last day of class, before the grades were awarded, perceived as a "bribe" by some non-Indian students.

Whenever an atmosphere of community and "Indianness" was created, Native American epistemological principles emerged to crowd out those of the dominant society. There was respect for those primary criteria by which knowledge is legitimated in the Native American world—personal experience and the opinions of elders. People in class spoke frankly about vision and religious experiences and were not contradicted by others with different experiences. Students listened with respect to the presentations of elders of various tribes. The only questions were requests for elaboration, not the juxtaposition of contrary opinions and traditions, except for the occasional Christian Indian student who wanted to argue. But there were not many of these.

For good or ill, the dialectical, argumentative, debating modes by which western scholarship is supposed to refine itself and progress to a higher level were entirely missing from these classes. While the different tribal traditions were described and discussed, they were not argued, reflecting the general Native American attitude that what I believe is okay, and what you believe is okay also. Those students who took the class to argue about religion and philosophy were disappointed.

How can one teach about the singular and sacred nature of the individual religious experience if the class intends to argue about the metaphysics and epistemology—the "truth"—revealed by a unique experience? How can one learn to respect the different varieties of tribal cosmologies and ceremonies if they are going to be compared and criticized? In this regard, let me quote a remark from an Indian student in a graduate seminar, who spoke in response to a non-Indian student's paper comparing the structure of various Plains Indian songs. After listening patiently, the Indian student said, breaking the usual tolerant etiquette of the class: "You make me feel like a butterfly pinned to a cardboard. You want to know if I am redder than other butterflies and whether I have spots. You want to know what key I sing in and how long my song might last. My song is my song, and I love it because I love my family and my tribe. But I like the songs of other tribes. I like other butterflies. It is nobody's business to compare songs, or compare butterflies either. They are dead, after all."

These words, spoken in anger rather than as part of academic discourse, nonetheless suggest, I think, the existence of two other principles that are essential for understanding Native American epistemology, and for conducting successful classes in American Indian studies. The words that characterize these principles are "respect" and "tolerance." Both are the deadly enemies of western philosophy and religion, and mark a profound difference between Anglo-American and Native American modes of thought. Perhaps the western perspective derives historically from the fact that European universities were originally run by the church. These universities were not organized to teach tolerance for Islam and other competing religions, but rather to show the truth and superiority of Christianity. These attitudes about the quest for truth, I believe, were carried over into a whole range of academic disciplines when universities were secularized, mostly in the nineteenth century. Except that in the secular university, it was not the truth of Christianity that was being sought, but the truth of particular views about physics, chemistry, or philosophy. And whether the ivy-covered halls were religious or secular, the university was still defined as the place where one sought, by academic debate and discourse, the truth about the world, and about human behavior.

In astronomy, as taught in the university even now, one does not learn to respect astrology, or the archaeoastronomical systems of Babylon or Yucatan. Instead, the student is taught, based on the most recent communications from the Hubble telescope, a true and correct view of the structure of the universe. In biology classes, we still devote a block of time to criticizing the Lamarckians, who foolishly believed that acquired characteristics could be inherited, and we make fun of the creationists, who believe that species were called into existence quite recently by a supernatural creator. In my many years at universities, I have never heard professors use the words "respect" or "tolerance" in discussing these contrary views. Instead, we hear only an endorsement of the true and correct theories that have won out in the "marketplace of ideas."

Contrast these attitudes with the behavior exhibited by the Cheyenne and Mvskoke religionists I escorted to each other's ceremonies in 1977. None of them felt obliged to rise to their feet and condemn what was going on around them, even though the cosmology and social values being acted out ceremonially were completely contradictory to their own. Instead, they later referred to their experiences as among the most positive and most interesting of their lives.

Let me provide another illustration, if I may intrude a little on the privacy of my friend and former student, the aforementioned Robert Fields, a traditional Pawnee Indian. When he was called upon to defend his doctoral dissertation in 1991, he was asked to comment on Franz Boas, whom he had quoted and cited in his dissertation. In his response, Fields spoke warmly and positively about Boas's contributions. Then he was asked about the criticisms of "historical particularism" aimed at Boas by Marvin Harris, and about the criticisms of functionalists such as A. R. Radcliffe-Brown. But the doctoral candidate had nothing but praise for these other theorists.

After about an hour of trying to provoke Mr. Fields into saying something critical about anyone at all, the committee, of which I was chair, dismissed the candidate to the hallway to discuss among themselves what the dickens was going on. It was mentioned that Mr. Fields had also been reluctant to include criticisms in the written part of his dissertation, saying that these men were "great theorists," and who was he, a novice, to criticize such people. That is, he considered them the "elders" of the anthropology tribe, worthy of respect and immune to criticism. So what should we do as an academic committee? Should we insist that he be mean, critical, and nasty to satisfy the demands of the western intellectual tradition?

The question we came around to was whether there was something wrong with Mr. Fields, or something wrong with the western system of epistemology, or, more specifically, something wrong with an Anglo-American system of pedagogy that insists on maintaining the conflict and competition of ideas. Unable to resolve this issue in the half-hour remaining, we passed him. Had we been running on Indian time, maybe we could have talked longer.

Some Pedagogical Recommendations

The programs in Native American studies with which I am familiar vacillate between conducting classes in an entirely Anglo manner and trying to create something approaching the American Indian mode I try to describe above. Sometimes a class is a confusing pastiche of American Indian and Anglo modes of thought and learning. One problem concerns young instructors. Older American Indian students in particular have trouble learning from a young instructor, especially a non-Indian one. Never mind that the teacher has a Ph.D. from some respected university; he or she perhaps has not lived very long, has not had children and grandchildren, has not resided in American Indian communities, does not know anybody, and consequently is not worth listening to. It is a mistake, I believe, to put such instructors in classes where the topic is of a traditional nature. By American Indian standards, they are not believable.

On the other hand, I believe that young instructors, even non-Indians, can be successful if they appear to the class not as an "authority," but as an age-mate or seeker after knowledge, respecting the traditional epistemological means by which important knowledge is verified—personal experience and the opinions of elders. They must deemphasize the extent to which they have gained their knowledge from a book.

All instructors, young and old, must be careful about distinguishing between values and attitudes which are common to all Native North American people (as described eloquently by Eastman and Deloria, whose accounts I have tried to supplement in my discussions of "respect" and "tolerance") and those traditions which are tribally specific. When it comes to cosmologies, ceremonies, and the interpretation of specific animals and spirits, the traditions are different. But all Native Americans, I believe, agree about what kind of knowledge is important: knowledge about relationships among all the entities of nature, including people. And they are agreed about how this knowledge is properly gained—by personally engaging nature as a religious seeker, and by consulting elders. Non-Indians, and books written by non-Indians, are not regarded as legitimate sources of knowledge, no matter how sincere or sensitive, or how logical and comprehensive, the writer may be. American Indian narratives in printed form, however, are different. In my experience, most American Indian people give these texts the same status as a talk from an elder. But these texts should not be presented casually. They should be presented with the same respect and reverence with which one would introduce a real, live tribal elder.

Programs in Native American studies also contain courses and subjects that are not part of American Indian tradition: tribal management, Indian law, and social work. I believe it is a mistake to try to teach such subjects in an American Indian manner. Teachers of the subjects probably learned them in a non-Indian manner, and they will have difficulty translating the substance of the course into an American Indian pedagogical mode. However, courses about Native American history, religion, and other aspects of traditional culture *should* be approached in a traditional manner, in terms of both the substance of the course and in the way it is taught. In fact, I would argue that these are *inseparable.*

Epistemological Distractions

It would be wonderful, of course, if all students came to a program of Native American studies with curious and open minds. It would be wonderful if the instructor could write on these blank slates exactly what the students needed to know about American Indian philosophy, religion, and culture, the kinds of propositions presented above. But as it is many students come to class with much ideological baggage: competing philosophical agendas that tend to confound and disrupt the process of teaching about Native American culture. Consequently, instructors in Native American studies must often spend much time "unteaching" what students think they already know.

In my classes, I typically spend the first two weeks on stereotypes and caricatures of Native Americans. To illustrate the stereotypes, I show excerpts from such movies as *The Searchers, Two Tickets to Broadway,* and *Peter Pan.* For a more authentic view of American Indian life, they watch *Pow-Wow Highway* and read excerpts from modern Native American essayists and writers of fiction. Some students begin to understand that much of what they think they know is based on silly stereotypes, but some students seem "invincibly ignorant," to use a phrase from Catholic theology—that is, they are so rooted in Anglo stereotypes that they cannot find their way out of the maze of ethnocentric expectations. Even Native American students are not immune to stereotypes about themselves or other tribes. Overall, these stereotypes constitute competing philosophies, pedagogies, and epistemologies about Native American life and beliefs that must constantly be beaten back to accomplish real education. The four most common I have labeled "Native Americans as 'nature folk,'" "Native Americans as 'personal fantasies,'" "found Native Americans," and "New Age Aquarians."

Indians as Nature Folk. Of all the institutions in American society, the Boy Scouts of America have probably done the most damage in miseducating the public about Native American cultures. Although their "Indian Lore" merit badge has recently experienced a dramatic improvement through the advice of anthropologist David Hurst Thomas, the honorary society called Order of the Arrow annually initiates thousands of boys into the martial, romantic version of Indian culture through ceremonies drawn from the writings of Longfellow and James Fenimore Cooper. More than 175,000 American boys have been through these ceremonies and subsequent activities, and many of them are drawn to classes in Native American studies when they attend college.

Several authors have written elegantly about the assumptions and expectations of this class of students as they approach the subject of native cultures.[41] Essentially they see American Indians as primitive versions of themselves, except a little farther down the evolutionary tree. They expect to see the alleged ancient characteristics of their own cultures represented among American Indians. They see Indians as Robin Hood or Sir Lancelot or Davy Crockett. They embrace and exaggerate the significance of any apparent similarity between Native American culture and their own, especially those descriptions which present Native Americans as warlike individualists, moral do-gooders obsessed with martial honor and personal vengeance, like Cooper's Chingachgook.

Such students, with such expectations, do not like to hear that many Native American cultures were and are highly collective rather than individualistic in their values, that they were familial, communalistic in their attitudes toward land and personal property, and "heathen" in their religious views. Rather than listening to these propositions, these students want to know how to make a weapon, or make a drum, or make a "costume" that will allow them to dance about and endorse what they perceive to be Native American values—which are actually the values of their own culture, dressed up in beads and feathers. To continue this celebration of the American Indian stereotype into later life, Boy Scouts become hobbyists, forming clubs patterned after the Boy Scout organization.[42]

In an odd and ironic twist, hobbyists often say that they dress up like American Indian people to "honor" them. I once witnessed an angry confrontation at an Oklahoma powwow between several American Indian dancers and a cos-

tumed non-Indian who wanted to participate. Challenged about his right to
dance, the non-Indian protested that he did so to honor American Indians. One
Indian dancer, a Vietnam veteran, angrily responded, "Why is it, then, that
when I look at you, I don't feel honored?"

Missing from the Boy Scout/hobbyist stereotype of Native Americans is the
Native American as intellectual, as inventor, as rational politician, or even as
woman. Instead, the hobbyists focus on the American Indian as warrior, as
dancer, or as the epitome of the stereotype, the war dancer. I wish I could report success in persuading former Boy Scouts in my classes to take a broader
view of Native American culture, but I cannot.

The epistemology presented by this perspective on Native Americans is
bluntly Spencerian, social evolutionist, social Darwinist. Native American
people are alleged to represent the same values, attitudes, and commitments as
Euro-Americans in an earlier, primitive, rustic stage of development. "Indian
lore" of this genre is intellectually easy, and contains no surprises. Never mind
tackling the difficult intellectual issues presented by the Cheyenne concept of
energy or the structure of the Mvskoke cosmos; those interested in Native
Americans as nature folk move immediately into the ethnography of warfare
and dancing. Everything else about Native American culture, the part that is
to me and to serious students the most interesting and most challenging, is
dismissed as "primitive."

Consequent to the adoption of this Spencerian or social evolutionist perspective, we have books like *Sweet Medicine,* by Father Peter Powell, in which
Cheyennes are portrayed as primitive religious practitioners who are trying
very hard to be Christians but somehow cannot get it exactly right, and the
book *Hanta Yo* by Ruth Beebe Hill, in which a Lakota warrior, although surrounded by buffaloes and by other "savages" like himself, nonetheless, and
amazingly, anticipates the beginnings of capitalist democracy and adopts the
mind-set of a Silicon Valley entrepreneur. This book has been cleverly characterized by my friend Ray DeMallie as "Hiawatha meets Ayn Rand," and in
truth, in the real world, Ruth Beebe Hill was once Rand's roommate. Attempts
of Anglo writers to rank Native American cultures into an evolutionary hierarchy ending with The White Man inevitably demean the genius of Native
American cultures, and stultify the intellectual development of our students
by characterizing Native American philosophy and religion as dull, illogical,
or primitive.

Indians as Personal Fantasies. Fantasists constitute another class of students
whom I have found largely ineducable. Their fantasies, though highly variable,
are tenacious and resist criticism from peers and teachers. In my experience,
the fantasy-bearers tend to be behaviorally unorthodox by the standards of
their own Euro-American culture. For example, in the 1970s many white students in Native American studies classes were convinced that Indians were

hippies, and they liked to point out that Native Americans grew their hair long, used drugs (Native American Church), and were unemployed. So, therefore, they must be fellow hippies, and many embarrassing and uncomfortable scenes were enacted on Indian reservations in those days when hip students arrived from the campus or the city in their vans, expecting to be greeted with open arms by Indian residents. They were very disappointed to learn that many Native American people were highly structured and conservative in their values and behavior, and thus they concluded that Indians were not as "hippy" as they used to be.

Similarly, in my experience gay and Lesbian students often expect American Indian people to be more tolerant of their sexual preferences than are mainstream Americans. Having read about berdaches and women warriors among American Indian peoples, such students want to believe that they will be accepted and accommodated by American Indian people if they make their sexuality known—for example, in a class that includes American Indian students. These students likewise are frequently disappointed.

The most common fantasy among non-Indians, often a component of other fantasies, is the adoption fantasy. Such people believe that, although abused and despised in their own society, for being a hippy or being gay or whatever reason, they in fact embody virtues that, unrecognized by family and classmates, will be immediately appreciated by Indian people. Once these virtues have been discovered, Native American people will respond by having a ceremony in the person's honor, bestowing an Indian name, giving gifts, and perhaps imparting some American Indian secrets. This scenario, of course, occurs frequently in the romantic genre of American Indian literature. In many versions, the outsider must pass some tests or endure a physical ordeal to get a name. In the words of the poet and artist Edgar Heap of Birds, "They don't want Indians; they just want our names."

Found Indians. Many students begin a class in Native American studies without exhibiting any trace of American Indian culture or behavior. By the time the class is over, they have by various means actually become American Indians. Strange as it may sound to someone who has never taught a class in Native American culture, it is commonplace for students to come to the teacher in mid-course and allege that, through a dream or some other kind of revelation, they have discovered that they have American Indian ancestors, or that they are the spiritual reincarnation of some particular Indian person. In my classes over the last twenty years I have had reincarnations of Sacajawea, Crazy Horse, "Chief Red Dog," Pocahontas (twice), and an Indian named "Pretty Bird" who was killed at the Sand Creek Massacre.

Sometimes students can document that they have some American Indian ancestry and thereby become experts on matters Indian. A student with a new-found genealogical connection is a dangerous character in class, an instant expert on such topics as "Indian religion," "Indian character," and even such practical matters as putting up a tipi. They take the fact that traditional Native Americans often find them interesting as evidence of the authenticity of their new persona. Almost inevitably, found American Indians are hostile to students and teachers who have learned about Native American culture "out of books" or only from personal experience. They sometimes hold that one cannot truly understand Native American culture, or learn a Native American language, without having Native American ancestry. Somehow, it is supposed to be in your genes.

Found Indians sometimes find their way into programs of Native American studies as teachers, staff, or consultants. Their epistemological beliefs tend to be very damaging to the educational process. If learning is merely a matter of biology and genetics, then why bother having classes? Allegations that one cannot learn the Kiowa language without being a Kiowa are very discouraging to non-Kiowas.

If anthropology has made any contribution at all to academe, it is the discovery that language and culture are learned, not inherent. My favorite example of this truth among American Indian people is a young Lakota man I met in the 1970s who had, literally, been found along the road as a baby by an Indian family. By the time I met him, he was a tall, slim, ordinary-looking white man, dressed in "Indian cowboy" attire with auburn hair. What was interesting about him was that his first language was Lakota, and he had only a rudimentary understanding of English, despite his appearance. He spoke English with a Lakota accent, and his behavior and body movements, also, were just like any other Lakota's. For me, it was odd to see someone of Anglo-American appearance behaving so emphatically like an American Indian person.

All of us, I am sure, know people who represent the opposite in behavior and appearance—"full-blood" Indian people raised entirely in Anglo-American society, frequently as adoptees of white families. Many of them end up in college courses about Native American culture, trying to recapture their roots. For them and those who know them, their Native American ancestry is not in doubt; it is written on their faces. Consistently, I have found that these are among the most hardworking students, trying to make up for lost years. And I cannot explain why, but I have noticed that such students seldom assume that they have an advantage in learning over other students because of their ancestry. That belief seems to be the domain of students who are less visibly Native American.

New Age Aquarians. The most recent addition to the list of religious supplicants gathered around American Indian culture are the New Age devotees, who come in many varieties. What they share, and what differentiates them from older generations of supernaturalists, is the belief that all supernatural experiences are valid, and that these experiences are global in their distribution. Consequently New Agers take courses in Native American studies to find examples or illustrations of their preexisting beliefs in universal principles of astrology, crystalology, mantras, numerology, auras, or whatever.

Seeing a slide of the Pawnee star chart, for example, they look for constellations that resemble their own and are indifferent to the Pawnee cultural context that made the constellations different and made the chart meaningful for Pawnees. Hearing about medicine bundles, they want to know whether crystals were included, and will not accept any explanation of the crystals other than the one they want—that crystals were used to focus cosmic energy and foretell the future. Like the believers in American Indians as nature folk, the New Agers pick and choose from Indian cultures the items they want and need, for their own reasons. Intent on building a global supernatural belief system that transcends individual cultures and beliefs, they are indifferent to the internal structures of belief—cosmologies and attendant epistemologies— that characterize the rich variety of North American Indian cultures.

Summary. While found Indians and students with individual fantasies are merely distractions in teaching about Native American culture, both Spencerian evolutionism and New Age beliefs provide full-scale philosophical systems that are genuine competitors to Native American belief systems. Not only that, but these competitive systems are parasitic to Native American philosophical systems, sucking off bits and pieces to construct alternative systems that are antithetical and hostile to Native American philosophies, and emphatically Euro-American.

Over the last two hundred years, several sectors of Euro-American society have conspired to satisfy the real curiosity that non-Indians have about Native American culture, and that Native American students have about tribes other than their own. The Boy Scouts and the New Agers provide silly, ethnocentric, and simpleminded answers to truly profound questions about the values and commitments of Native American culture, and the behavior of Native American people. It is a tragic solution. It is as if students who truly wanted to learn Latin were being taught Pig-Latin instead and told that it was Latin, or students who wanted to learn Japanese were being taught Bamboo English and told that it was Japanese.

Conclusion

Programs in Native American studies were created in part to provide more authentic, but consequently much more difficult, answers to basic questions about Native American cultures. After a few decades of effort, Native American studies programs have still not found a formula for consistently communicating the facts about Native American culture and history in a popular and attractive manner. In this chapter I have described a few of the problems, at the philosophical level, that must be overcome. Prominent among these is the need to deemphasize western notions about the competition of ideas in academia, and the need to replace this quest not only with *tolerance* for the whole spectrum of possible human ideas about important intellectual issues, but also with *respect* for the holders of these ideas, no matter how strange and different these ideas might seem at first.

Notes

1. Cornelius Ryan Fay and Henry F. Tiblier, *Epistemology* (Milwaukee: Bruce, 1967).

2. Robin Horton and Ruth Finnegan, eds., *Modes of Thought: Essays on Thinking in Western and Non-Western Societies* (London: Faber and Faber, 1973).

3. Ray A. Williamson and Claire R. Farrer, eds., *Earth and Sky: Visions of the Cosmos in Native American Folklore* (Albuquerque: University of New Mexico Press, 1992).

4. John H. Moore, *The Cheyenne* (Oxford: Blackwell, 1996).

5. George Bird Grinnell, *By Cheyenne Campfires* (New Haven: Yale University Press, 1962).

6. George A. Dorsey, *The Cheyenne,* 2 vols. (Chicago: Field Columbian Museum, 1905).

7. In Native American literature, the traditional theme of the Indian person caught between two cultures has been dramatically revised by the image of the "mixed blood" as a person enjoying participation in both cultures, as in N. Scott Momaday, *The Names: A Memoir* (New York: Harper and Row, 1976).

8. John R. Swanton, "Religious beliefs and medical practices of the Creek Indians," in *Forty-second Annual Report of the Bureau of American Ethnology* (Washington, D.C.: Smithsonian Institution, 1928), 473–672.

9. Corliss Lamont, *Humanism as a Philosophy* (New York: Philosophical Library, 1949).

10. Emile Durkheim, *The Elementary Forms of the Religious Life* (New York: Free Press, 1965 [1915]).

11. S. A. Thorpe, *Shamans, Medicine Men and Traditional Healers: A Comparative Study of Shamanism in Siberian Asia, Southern Africa and North America* (Pretoria: University of South Africa, 1993).

12. This was in connection with generating interest in public hearings held preliminary to the passage of the American Indian Religious Freedom Act in 1978.

13. Frank Waters, *Book of the Hopi* (New York: Viking, 1963); Hyemeyohsts Storm, *Seven Arrows* (New York: Harper and Row, 1972).

14. The continuing sources of romantic misinformation about Native American culture, especially religion, are Henry Wadsworth Longfellow and James Fenimore Cooper. See Henry Wadsworth Longfellow, *The Song of Hiawatha* (Boston: Ticknor and Fields, 1859); James Fenimore Cooper, *The Last of the Mohicans* (Chicago: Donohue, Henneberry, 1890).

15. Charles A. Eastman, *An Indian Boyhood* (New York: McClure, Philips, 1902).

16. Charles A. Eastman, *The Soul of the Indian* (Boston: Houghton Mifflin, 1911).

17. Ibid., ix–x.

18. Ibid., xii.

19. Ibid., 6.

20. Ibid., 12–13.

21. Ibid., 20.

22. Ibid., 24.

23. Ibid., 14–15.

24. Ibid., 38.

25. Compare Ella C. Deloria, *Dakota Texts* (New York: Stechert, 1932).

26. Eastman, *Soul of the Indian,* 47.

27. Ibid., 53.

28. Ibid., 54.

29. Ibid., 53. See also Peter J. Powell, *Sweet Medicine,* 2 vols. (Norman: University of Oklahoma Press, 1969).

30. Eastman, *Soul of the Indian,* 64. See also James Mooney, *The Ghost-Dance Religion and Wounded Knee* (New York: Dover, 1973 [1896]); Russell Thornton, *We Shall Live Again: The 1870 and 1890 Ghost Dance Movements as Demographic Revitalization* (New York: Cambridge University Press, 1986); Alice Beck Kehoe, *The Ghost Dance: Ethnohistory and Revitalization* (Chicago: Holt, Rinehart and Winston, 1989).

31. Ferdinand Tönnies, *Community and Society* (New Brunswick: Transaction, 1988).

32. In the second part of his second discourse, Rousseau alleges that most of the evils of civilization derive from the private ownership of land. In a similar vein, Engels describes in *The Origin of the Family* how the evolution of capitalism ultimately requires the "commodification" of everything. See Jean-Jacques Rousseau, *The First and Second Discourses,* Roger D. Masters, ed. (New York: St. Martin's Press, 1964); Frederick Engels, *The Origin of the Family, Private Property and the State,* Eleanor B. Leacock, ed. (New York: International Publishers, 1972).

33. Vine Deloria, Jr., *God Is Red: A Native View of Religion,* 2d ed. (Golden, Colo.: Fulcrum, 1994 [1972]).

34. Vine Deloria, Jr., *Custer Died for Your Sins: An Indian Manifesto* (New York: Macmillan, 1969).

35. Arlene Hirschfelder and Martha Kreipe de Montano, *The Native American Almanac* (New York: Prentice-Hall, 1993), 115, 204.

36. Deloria, *God Is Red,* 88–90.

37. Ibid., 88.

38. Ibid., 89.

39. Ibid., 90.

40. Thomas Thompson, ed., *The Schooling of Native America* (Washington, D.C.: American Association of Colleges for Teacher Education, 1978); Hap Gilliland, *Teaching the Native American* (Dubuque: Kendall/Hunt, 1988).

41. Raymond W. Stedman, *Shadows of the Indian* (Norman: University of Oklahoma Press, 1982); Michael Hilger, *From Savage to Nobleman* (London: Scarecrow Press, 1995); Stephen E. Feraca, *Why Don't They Give Them Guns?* (New York: University Press of America, 1990).

42. See the manual for the "Indian Lore" merit badge, *Indian Lore* (Irving, Tex.: Boy Scouts of America, 1996).

Kinship
The Foundation for
Native American Society

No topic relating to Native Americans is of more importance than kinship, yet none has been more completely ignored by Native American studies. The family, culturally defined and embedded in a social system of greater or lesser structural complexity, is basic to understanding Native American peoples. Kinship is the necessary starting point for such understanding. Kin terminologies, descent and inheritance systems, marriage and residence patterns all combine in the family to shape the texture and dynamics of daily life, and serve as the foundation for Native American societies. But there is more to kinship than social relationships among family or tribal members, for in virtually every American Indian society kinship is culturally defined to include the relationship of human beings to all other forms of existence in a vast web of cosmic interrelationship in which humans stand at the bottom or on the periphery. As a social phenomenon, kinship weaves related individuals into solidary groups; as a cultural phenomenon it defines relationships (sets of statuses), prescribes normative patterns for behavior among relatives (roles), and extends those patterns outward to the universe.

This chapter provides a historical overview of the study of Native American kinship systems, characterizes the diversity of kinship systems in Native North America, presents brief descriptions of particular kinship systems, samples some of the richness of meaning of kinship systems, and suggests some of the practical uses for the scholarly study of kinship in the context of Native American studies.

Kinship Studies in Historical Perspective

Given its significance to all aspects of Native American studies, it is remarkable that kinship studies have remained the preserve of anthropology. Perhaps that is accounted for by the close relationship between kinship studies and the profession of anthropology. In the United States, anthropology began in the mid-nineteenth century with Lewis Henry Morgan's study of Iroquois kinship, and virtually every major theoretical development in social-cultural anthropology since then has come from the study of kinship systems. Nonetheless, scholars today, including many anthropologists, frequently dismiss kinship studies as arcane and irrelevant to such larger concerns as politics, economics, or religion. But the latter are institutions of Euro-American society, and if they are taken to define the terms of study, scholars are bound to miss the holism that is fundamental to American Indian life. Kinship, society, politics, economics, religion are not for Native American peoples differentiated into independent institutions as they are in mainstream America. As members of face-to-face communities, Native Americans interact with one another first and foremost as relatives—engaged in specific relationship roles as structured by the kinship system—at the same time that they interact in other social, political, economic, or religious roles. The individual's place in the web of kinship is always fundamental.

The following sketch does not attempt to provide a complete history of the development of Native American kinship studies but outlines some of the important figures and ideas that have become fundamental to this specialization within the field of anthropology.

Evolutionary Approaches

Lewis Henry Morgan, a lawyer, studied the kinship system of the Iroquois among the Seneca of New York in the 1840s. Two features especially impressed him. The first was the matrilineal character of the kinship system, by which property and rights descended through women—that is, a man inherited from his mother's brothers, not his father. This rule of descent was reflected in the organization of Iroquois society into matrilineal clans (unilineal descent groups, with every Iroquois individual belonging to the clan of his or her mother). From Morgan's legalistic perspective, the distinctive characteristic of this matrilineal descent system was "the perpetual disinheritance of the son."[1] (See fig. 12.1. *B* inherits from *A*, *C* inherits from *B*. Note that kinship diagrams show the structure of systems, not actual genealogies. Thus *A*, *B*, and *C* label categories of relatives, not individuals.) The second feature was the classification of father's brothers with father, the classification of mother's sisters with mother, and the subsequent classification of the children of all fathers and mothers as brothers and sisters. Again, in Morgan's terms,

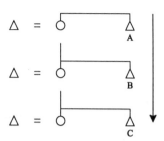

Figure 12.1. Iroquois line of inheritance through mother's brothers

"No distinction was made between the lineal and collateral lines." [2] (Collateral lines are those descended from one's siblings and cousins and the siblings and cousins of one's parents, parents' parents, and so on as far back as remembered.) This prevented the family from subdividing into collateral branches. In modern terminology, the system classified a man and his brothers and male parallel cousins together in a single social status, and classified a woman and her sisters and female parallel cousins together. Thus from the point of view of an individual (ego), the relatives in his or her generation were of two types: siblings and parallel cousins of the same and opposite sex as ego (brothers and sisters), and cross cousins of the same and opposite sex (male cousins and female cousins). The children of same-sex siblings and cross cousins were classified as son and daughter, while the children of opposite-sex siblings and cross cousins were classified as nephews and nieces. Moreover, by classifying as grandchildren the children of sons and daughters and of nephews and nieces, the system ultimately merged all the lineal and collateral lines. (See fig. 12.2.) Morgan assumed that the Iroquois kinship system was specifically adapted to the matrilineal clan system, and that the peculiarities of their kinship system were unique inventions of the Iroquois as a people. In 1857 he presented a paper on the subject to the annual meeting of the American Association for the Advancement of Science.[3]

In the summer of 1858, at Marquette, Michigan, where he had traveled on business, Morgan had the opportunity to interview some Ojibwe Indians and record their kin terms. "To my surprise somewhat, and not a little to my delight," he wrote, "I found this system was substantially the same as that of the Iroquois." [4] Shortly thereafter, Morgan discovered virtually the same system in use by the Dakota. Thus the existence of a system structurally identical among tribes of three greatly divergent linguistic families—Iroquoian, Algonquian, and Siouan, respectively—suggested to Morgan that this "primary institution" could be used to prove a genetic relationship among American Indians, a relationship so ancient that linguistic differences masked the common ancestry.

Morgan began a vigorous research project to record as many sets of kin

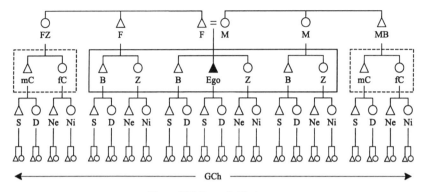

Figure 12.2. Iroquois kin terms

Note: Siblings and parallel cousins are enclosed in a solid line; cross cousins are enclosed in the dotted lines.

terms as possible, not only from American Indians, but from other peoples around the world. He depended on correspondents for much of his data, but, disappointed at the results of circular letter he mailed in 1859,[5] he decided to record American Indian data himself. From 1859 to 1862, Morgan took a steamboat up the Missouri River each summer, recording whenever possible kin terms from the various tribes living along the banks.[6] This produced a wealth of data, which substantiated his general thesis that in the merger of collateral and lineal lines, American Indian kinship systems were all alike. Since he considered such a classification unnatural (because it did not correctly represent biological relatedness), Morgan concluded that it must be the product of conscious thought. Therefore, the similarity of their kinship systems proved the genetic unity of American Indians. Moreover, although he found the system to be "special and complex," nonetheless "it rested upon definite ideas, which stood to each other in such intelligent and fixed relations as to create a system." [7] Morgan prepared a questionnaire with blanks to record more than two hundred terms for each language, reckoned four generations above and below ego (great-great-grandparents to great-great-grandchildren).

Morgan's discovery that American Indian kinship systems rest on logical principles different from those on which Euro-American systems are based forms the foundation for all subsequent studies of kinship. The importance of understanding kin terminologies as logical *systems* by which consanguines (relatives by blood) and affines (relatives by marriage) are classified cannot be overemphasized. Besides laying the basis for the study of kinship, it also pointed the way to understanding American Indian thought systems, not as illogical, but as based on different principles of classification, different ways of perceiving the world. Morgan used his discovery, however, as evidence for the origin of American Indians in Asia, once he learned that the Tamil and Telugu kinship systems in India were based on the same principles.[8] Expanding his study with data provided by correspondents from around the world, Morgan ultimately compiled his material for publication by the Smithsonian Institution. It included data on 80 Native American systems (77 American Indian groups and 3 Eskimo groups), compiled into a table that fills ninety large, closely printed pages. *Systems of Consanguinity and Affinity of the Human Family*[9] differentiated the world's kinship systems into two types. The classificatory—characteristic of American Indians and of the peoples of Asia—merged the lineal and collateral lines; the descriptive—characteristic of European and Semitic peoples—kept the lineal and collateral lines separate. In other words, the former *classified* the two types of lines together, while the latter (from Morgan's perspective) correctly *described* them as separate.

The simple historical conclusion of Morgan's study—that American Indians originated in Asia—was not deemed of sufficient importance to justify publishing such a massive work at public expense, so the secretary of the Smithsonian requested Morgan to elaborate on the significance of his work. In a brief final section entitled "General Results," he outlined a conjectural history of the progress of humanity based on the type of family as hypothesized from the structure of the kin terminology.[10] Starting at an imagined stage of promiscuous intercourse (prior to any institution of marriage), Morgan conjectured a logical sequence of "reformatory movements" that resulted in increasingly complex forms of the family and ultimately the "overthrow" of the classificatory system and its replacement by the descriptive. Such a reform, Morgan conjectured, was necessary with the growth of property so that inheritance passed from a man to his children and their children in turn, and was not dispersed along collateral lines. In other words, by distinguishing between a man's sons and the sons of his brother (sons versus nephews), the descriptive system laid the foundation for modern capitalism. The generality of these conclusions and the relevance of the kinship data to the evolution of humankind as a whole won publication of the work by the Smithsonian in an oversized book of six hundred pages.

Morgan drew on the material in *Systems* to write a popular book, *Ancient Society*,[11] which expanded his conjectural history of humankind. On the basis of the development of both "inventions and discoveries" (technological progress) and "primary institutions" (government, family, and property), Morgan reconstructed a series of seven stages ("ethnical periods") through which he believed humanity had passed from savagery to barbarism to civilization.[12] In Morgan's estimation all humans had the same potential (through every stage of social evolution the "operations of the mental principle have been uniform," though the brain itself expanded in proportion to the progress of ideas and institutions), and the inevitable development of civilization was, in Morgan's view, the result of divine providence.[13] Yet the transition from one stage to the next was hard-won, reflecting the growth of institutions from "a few primary germs of thought"; progress occurred in a geometric ratio, so that each stage was shorter than the preceding one, and saw proportionally greater progress.[14]

In Morgan's scheme most North American Indians, by the time of European contact, had reached the lower stage of barbarism (which he arbitrarily chose to mark by the invention of pottery), while a few had reached the middle stage of barbarism (marked by irrigated corn horticulture and the building of houses with adobe brick or stone).[15] In the book Morgan presents ethnographic material on American Indians, much of it drawn from his own field studies, to place the various tribes within his larger framework of evolutionary development. *Ancient Society* became, in effect, the first textbook of anthropology.

In 1879, when John Wesley Powell founded the Bureau of Ethnology (after 1895 called the Bureau of American Ethnology) at the Smithsonian Institution, Morgan's *Ancient Society* provided the intellectual framework for defining problems to study. By establishing this first institutional base for the development of anthropology as a profession, Powell was able to gather together a diverse group of individuals from a wide variety of backgrounds—military men, missionaries, scientists—and provide them means for studying American Indian peoples full-time. Powell's greatest insight was to insist that whenever ethnologists worked directly with particular groups of Indian peoples over sustained periods, their investigation "must have a firm foundation in language." [16] In this way, all cultural phenomena would be situated within the cognitive framework characteristic of each tribal group.

One of the founding members of the bureau was James Owen Dorsey, who had formerly been a missionary to the Ponca and was able to speak their language. In 1878, even before the official establishment of the bureau, Powell sent Dorsey to study the Omaha, close relatives of the Ponca who spoke the same language. Dorsey was assigned to work on completing his grammar and dictionary of the language, and to record a body of linguistic texts. At the same time he collected further data on kinship and social organization. In the spring of 1880, after returning from his first bureau-sponsored fieldwork, Dorsey read a paper to the Philosophical Society of Washington that outlined his findings on the social system of the Omaha.[17] (Following Powell's terminology, the Bureau used "gens" to designate patrilineal descent groups, "clan" to designate matrilineal ones; in modern terminology, both are referred to as clans.) Dorsey's paper presented a complex system based on moieties (a symbolic dual division of society), with five clans in each moiety. In the printed discussion following the paper, Powell emphasized the theoretical importance of Dorsey's findings, which supported Morgan's contention that kinship is "the

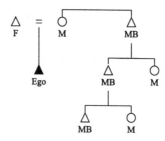

Figure 12.3. Omaha kin terms, mother's brother's patrilineage

foundation of social organization, and therefore of government," and that "in the North American Indians the tribal organization has its origin in government by kinship." [18]

Dorsey's study of Omaha kinship terms was also of particular significance because Morgan had reported an anomaly among certain of the earthlodge village tribes of the Missouri Valley. Among the patrilineal Omaha, for example, Morgan's kinship charts showed that an individual called his mother's brother, his mother's brother's son, and his mother's brother's son's son all by the same term; thus mother's brothers seemed to replicate themselves down through the generations *ad infinitum*. Similarly, the sisters of mother's brothers were all called mother. This is now designated the Omaha system (fig. 12.3). (A parallel feature was reported among the matrilineal Hidatsa whereby father's sister, father's sister's daughter, and father's sister's daughter's daughter *ad infinitum* were likewise called by a single term; their brothers were all called father. This is now designated the Crow system.) Morgan drew attention to these anomalies as the only instances among his American Indian kinship data in which a collateral line was not over time merged with the lineal.[19] In *Omaha Sociology* Dorsey confirmed this characteristic of Omaha kinship and put it into the context of a full exposition of the system from an Omaha point of view. However, since the purpose of his report was to present ethnographic description, he did not attempt to hypothesize the reason for the anomalous use of the terms for mother's brother and mother. Instead, he drew the reader's attention to the fact that the Omahas used kin terms "with considerable latitude, and not as we employ them." In short, Dorsey recognized kin terms as cultural categories, labels for statuses in society, each associated with particular rights and duties.[20]

Culture-Historical Approaches

The work of the Bureau of American Ethnology laid the foundation for the professionalization of anthropology in the United States. As universities established departments for the training of graduate students—Harvard University (1887), Columbia University (1899), University of California, Berkeley (1901)—anthropology gradually became differentiated from other academic disciplines and formed the four fields that characterize it today: archaeology, physical anthropology, anthropological linguistics, and ethnology (social and cultural anthropology).[21] Franz Boas, who began teaching at Columbia University in 1896, rapidly took the lead in training graduate students and defining the parameters and direction of academic anthropology.[22] His student, Alfred L. Kroeber, founded the department at Berkeley. Although Boas himself did significant work in all fields of anthropology, his students tended to specialize in one or two, and over time the four fields became increasingly autonomous.

Within the field of social and cultural anthropology, the description of kinship systems became a standard and expected component of ethnographies. The rationale for their significance, however, changed over time. Boas promulgated a historical approach that required as full a description of a native people's culture and society as possible, based to the extent possible on documentary materials (dictated or written texts) in the native language. Comparing one group with another, starting with contiguous peoples, then moving farther out into larger areas, Boas's method could reconstruct the history of interactions among native groups in a particular geographic or cultural area. Thus the groups themselves, increasingly over time referred to as "cultures," assumed primary importance as bounded social units.

Boas's approach was in opposition to that of Morgan and Powell, which conceptualized all of humanity as a single evolutionary stream in which particular groups provided no more than exemplars of stages in the progress of the development of ideas and institutions. For the evolutionists, kinship systems were significant because they could be used to reconstruct stages in the development of the family, from the various types of polygamous marriages of savages and barbarians to the monogamous marriages that were the foundation for the civilized family. Boas saw the matter entirely differently. As early as 1889 he wrote that the variety of marriage customs and kinship usages could not be explained "so long as science sought to solve the question of the development of the family from the standpoint of our culture." Instead, it was crucial to realize that even something as basic as the emotional relationship between a father and child is not to be understood as natural; rather, like "our ability and knowledge," so too "the manner and ways of our feeling and thinking" are products of our culture.[23]

Boas's perspective clearly gained the ascendency.[24] By 1910 the majority of American anthropologists had abandoned the approach of reconstructing evolutionary sequences of marriage patterns from kinship data; the various essays on kinship, family, marriage, and associated topics in the Bureau of American Ethnology's 1907–1910 *Handbook of American Indians* make no mention of it.[25]

Much work on kinship during the late nineteenth and early twentieth centuries was done by British anthropologists working in Australia, Oceania, and Africa. In 1900 W. H. R. Rivers published an article in which he described his use of extensive genealogies to record kin terms during an expedition to the Torres Islands.[26] The method was essentially the same as that used by Dorsey in his study of the Omaha. Rivers used the kinship data for a wide variety of purposes, including tracing the inheritance of color blindness, documenting the frequency of polygyny, and reconstructing marriage patterns among clans. In a subsequent publication Rivers suggested that Morgan's evolutionary scheme had been at least in part correct in suggesting that the origin of the classificatory system of kinship must have been in group-marriage— that is, a group of brothers and male cousins married communally to a group of sisters and female cousins. But he argued that the kin terms were to be thought of as status markers, rather than as specifically designating blood relationship. Assuming that the social system was exogamous at the time of the origin of the classificatory system of kinship (a moiety system being the most basic type, in which marriages took place across the moiety boundary), and assuming matrilineality, an individual would call the active men of his moiety mother's brothers, while the active men of the other moiety would be fathers; the women, respectively, would be mothers and father's sisters. On the basis of the patterning of kin-term usage, Rivers felt justified in conjecturing a past form of group marriage as the origin of the classificatory system.[27]

Joining the debate, Kroeber represented the antievolutionary trend of Boas's students.[28] He looked at kinship terminologies as linguistic classifications representing cultural categories and argued that they could not be used to reconstruct social or marital patterns. Kroeber showed that kin terminologies were based on eight categories:

1. Generation
2. Lineal versus collateral
3. Age difference within generation
4. Sex of relative
5. Sex of speaker
6. Sex of person through whom the relationship exists
7. Blood relatives versus relatives by marriage
8. Condition of life of person through whom the relationship exists (e.g., related by blood or marriage; alive or dead; married or marriage terminated)

Each of these categories might be more or less systematically expressed in any particular terminology; Kroeber noted that the English system is based on only four categories (generation, blood versus marriage, lineal versus collateral, and sex of relative), each category used relatively completely, while American Indian systems were based on more categories, each used less completely. Thus Kroeber's approach reduced kin terminologies to linguistic taxonomies.

Boas's students continued to debate the relationship between forms of marriage practice and the patterning of kin terminology. Boas himself contributed incidentally to the discussion by suggesting that the recognition of kinship groups and therefore of exogamy is a universal phenomenon. In those cases in which the incest group expanded in size over time, the extension of brother-sister kin terms would have served to distinguish individuals belonging to the incest group from others. From this might logically develop an association of names and other associations with the incest group, which would develop into descent groups. Such a process could in specific cases explain the classificatory system of kinship, as well as the development of totemism (the differentiation of clans and lineages on the basis of cultural activities or association with natural phenomena such as plants and animals).[29]

Throughout the first decades of the twentieth century, anthropological monographs on American Indians continued to include kinship terms, sometimes reduced to little more than lists unrelated to other aspects of culture.[30] In 1917 Robert Lowie asked, rhetorically, why descriptive monographs included lists of kin terms, adding, "The reason is far from obvious."[31] In a long essay entitled "Terms of Relationship," Lowie developed the idea that kin terms are not merely lexical items but are "correlated with specific social usages," and thereby can serve as an "index of tribal relationship."[32] Each kinship system was a unique historical development that could be understood only through study of the culture and through comparison with the kinship systems of neighboring peoples. In 1920 Lowie published *Primitive Society,* the first major summary of kinship studies since Morgan.[33] In this work Lowie brought together data on North American Indians to investigate kinship in relation to marriage, the family, and clan organization. He acknowledged his indebtedness to Rivers and brought together the threads of debate relating kinship to social forms.

During the 1920s a number of Boas's students undertook major projects on kinship. Leslie Spier, for example, summarized what was known about American Indian systems by differentiating them into eight types based on the classification of cross cousins.[34] Accompanying maps of the distribution of kinship types in North America reveal no simple patterns; most types are represented throughout North America, and most culture areas are represented by more than one type. This study provided a graphic demonstration that the question of the distribution of kinship types in North America was not a simple one that could be easily resolved into patterns of diffusion.

Taking an ethnographic approach, Gladys Reichard set out to remedy a deficiency in the literature on the Navajo by investigating social life, focusing on the clan. Using the genealogical method and sampling from various parts of the reservation, she recorded information on some 3,500 individuals, and published the data in full.[35] The study showed that the approximately fifty Navajo clans were to a strong degree localized, reflecting in part the tendency for two clans to intermarry with one another over time.[36]

Theresa Durlach undertook a comparative study of the kinship systems of the Tlingit, Haida, and Tsimshian peoples of the Northwest Coast.[37] The question she set out to investigate was whether social or linguistic forces were stronger in shaping kin terminologies. To answer it, she chose three groups speaking different languages but with similar social organization based on matrilineal clans. Following Boas's suggestion, she turned to native language texts, including genealogies, as the primary sources of data. Since most kinship systems were recorded in the field on the basis of the anthropologists' questions, Boas reasoned that mistakes were inevitable. Listening to people talk to one another to ascertain kin terms in actual use was the preferable method, but most anthropologists did not have the linguistic ability to understand conversation. Texts were the next best source, since, Boas commented, like conversation, they "give us nearly the same unhampered expression of the people themselves." [38] The conclusions of the study were no surprise. Social factors were clearly more determinative of kin terminology than was language. Comparison among the systems allowed for significant historical reconstructions reflecting diffusion; for example, Durlach concluded that both the Tlingit and the Haida had borrowed from the Tsimshian the system of reciprocal terms for affinal relatives—a clear case of borrowing a pattern of kin-term use across linguistic boundaries.[39]

Another of Boas's students, Alexander Lesser, was assigned the task of proofreading Durlach's book, and it so interested him that he asked Boas if he might undertake a similar study for his dissertation. Boas suggested a comparison of the various Siouan peoples.[40] The special interest here lay in the diversity of kinship types within the same linguistic family. Lesser's dissertation dealt with seventeen distinct kinship systems.[41] For the western Dakota he based his analysis on an extensive genealogy provided by Ella Deloria, a Lakota, who was working with Boas on the Lakota language. For several groups, Lesser was able to record lists of kin terms from native speakers of the languages while doing fieldwork in Oklahoma. And for all the groups he combed the literature, starting with Morgan's *Systems*. In the case of the Omaha-Ponca, he was able to use Dorsey's extensive texts to provide examples of kin terms in use.

Lesser reported that the Siouan kinship systems were of three types. The first, exemplified by the Dakota, was organized in bilateral bands, lacking unilineal descent; kin terms were structured generationally, the basic distinction being between offspring of the same sex and generation (siblings) and those of the opposite sex and same generation (cross cousins). The second, exemplified by the Omaha, was patrilineal, with kin terms structured so that relatives in the father's clan were classified as fathers and father's sisters. The third, exemplified by the Crow, was matrilineal, with kin terms structured so that relatives in the mother's clan were classified as mothers and mother's brothers. Although Lesser found instances of borrowing that demonstrated linguistic processes affecting the terminology, on the whole, like Durlach, he concluded that there was a close correlation between kin terminologies and social factors.

The issue of cousin terminologies took on renewed interest with the documentation of cross-cousin marriage systems, disproving Kroeber's earlier assertion that such marriage forms were not found among North American Indians. In 1929 William Duncan Strong reported the practice of cross-cousin marriage among the northern Naskapi of Labrador.[42] In 1930 A. Irving Hallowell discussed the historical sources for Ojibwe kinship that suggested cross-cousin marriage, and in 1937 he described the system as it was then practiced by the Berens River Ojibwe.[43] Cross-cousin marriage allowed these societies, organized in bilateral bands, to forge multiple bonds within a relatively small group and perpetuate these bonds through generations, thus forming tightly knit social groups.[44]

By 1930 Boas and his students (and some of their students, in turn) had taken the study of American Indian kinship systems out of the realm of evolutionary speculation on the history of humanity at large and integrated it into the culture-historical method, based on a combination of detailed ethnographies and comparative studies designed to test the relative significance of linguistic and social factors for the development of kin terminologies. In the process, kin terminologies became one more significant trait complex—comparable to religious practices, men's societies, mythological motives, or items of material culture—whose detailed study could help unravel the patterns of borrowing that reflected the historical processes leading to the distribution of cultural traits as recorded by anthropologists during the preceding half-century.

Social Anthropological Approaches

In the fall of 1931 a new approach to American Indian kinship systems was introduced when the British social anthropologist A. R. Radcliffe-Brown took up what was to be a five-year position at the University of Chicago. Radcliffe-Brown had been Rivers's first student in anthropology and had done fieldwork with the Andaman Islanders in order to write a culture history. However, he subsequently became strongly influenced by the writings of the French sociologist Emile Durkheim, from whom he borrowed the concept of function: if society is analogized to an organism, the function of each constituent institution is to maintain the structure of the whole.[45] The study of social structures, the patterned relationships among individuals and groups within a society, was for Radcliffe-Brown the most fundamental aspect of social anthropology.[46] The method of his social anthropology was synchronic: rather than historical developments, he was interested in understanding how the institutions of a society functioned at one point in time, and he hoped ultimately on the basis of comparison to develop laws of society on the model of natural science. Just before coming to Chicago, he had demonstrated his method with a comparative study of social organization among the tribes of Australia, a brilliant synthesis based on his own field studies that classified each group according to social structure and made sense of the intricate variations on the clan system characteristic of Australia.[47]

At Chicago, Radcliffe-Brown set out to repeat for American Indian groups what he had accomplished in Australia. Fred Eggan, a graduate student in anthropology, was given the position of research assistant to Radcliffe-Brown, and his first assignment was to summarize and organize the published data on the subject.[48] Although Radcliffe-Brown's own work on American Indians was limited to the study of Morgan's *Systems,* he stimulated a number of the students at Chicago to undertake fieldwork on American Indian kinship systems.

In 1937, when Radcliffe-Brown left Chicago for a professorship at Oxford University, his students honored him with a Festschrift entitled *Social Anthropology of North American Tribes.* It included detailed analyses of five American Indian kinship systems classified as follows: two bilateral (Kiowa Apache and Chiricahua Apache); one matrilineal, lacking clans (Cheyenne-Arapaho); one matrilineal, with clans and Crow-type terminology (Cherokee); and one patrilineal, with clans and Omaha-type terminology (Fox).[49] While far from a systematic survey of North America, it was nonetheless a solid beginning.

In that volume Eggan briefly summarized Radcliffe-Brown's approach to the study of society, contrasting it with historical approaches. He wrote, "An alternative method of achieving insight into the nature of social organization is by means of a comparative study of the correlated phenomena in a series of tribes." (By "correlated phenomena" Eggan meant types of social institutions—for example, social units, such as bands and clans; kin terminologies; and kinship usages, such as joking, respect, and avoidance behaviors.) This required comparisons "within a class or type," so the classification of social organizations was the necessary first step. Such a classification should ideally be made on the basis of social structure, whose function, according to Radcliffe-Brown, is "to achieve social integration." Radcliffe-Brown therefore suggested various indices to correlate social structure with the range and complexity of the social group. These indices include size and population density of the group, territorial arrangement, divisions by sex and age, the kinship system, and other formal group organizations. Eggan wrote: "Of these indices, the kinship system has proved the most useful index of social integration; in some cases the kinship system represents practically the total social structure of the group." The kinship system, in turn, "consists of all the social usages—or patterns of behavior—between relatives in a given community." Such usages include the kin terminology, but the social usages themselves are more important than the terminology.[50]

Of Radcliffe-Brown's students, Eggan most consistently devoted himself to the study of American Indian kinship systems.[51] He brought together the social anthropology of Radcliffe-Brown with American culture-historical approaches in a creative synthesis that developed a fuller picture of American Indian cultures. The limitation of Radcliffe-Brown's method was that, by focusing so narrowly on the interactional patterns and institutions of social structure, he eliminated from study the cultural detail that was the mainstay of American anthropology. Eggan sought to do both.

In 1932–1933 Eggan carried out his first fieldwork, spending six months with the Hopi, where he was able to record the material on kinship, clan, ceremonial organization, and political organization needed for his doctoral dissertation.[52] This was the advantage of Radcliffe-Brown's method: the narrow focus allowed for relatively efficient fieldwork. By searching the published literature Eggan wrote comparative sketches of the other Western Pueblos— Hano, Zuni, Acoma, and Laguna—and defined a common Western Pueblo pattern. Then, following the American tradition, he suggested explanations for divergences from the common pattern in terms of such factors as ecology and historical circumstances.

In 1933 Eggan spent two months carrying out fieldwork with the Cheyenne and Arapaho in Oklahoma, which resulted in a study of the structures of kinship and society, including descriptions of patterns of behavior among relatives and of the major life cycle events.[53] Again drawing on the published literature, he presented a comparative classification of Plains Indian kinship systems, differentiating two main types, generation and lineage, and proposing subtypes. He drew attention to the tendency on the Plains toward generational systems and concluded that "tribes coming into the Plains with *different* backgrounds and social systems ended up with *similar* kinship systems." [54] Rather than the result of diffusion, Eggan believed these similarities could be better explained as adaptations to life on the Plains.

In 1933 Eggan also made a brief field trip to the Mississippi Choctaw. In summarizing the data on the Southeast for Radcliffe-Brown, Eggan had found in Morgan's *Systems* an intriguing series of variations on the Crow system. In the Choctaw data he found that the expected transgenerational line of father's sisters in ego's father's matrilineage was instead a line of fathers in ego's father's sister's son's patrilineage (fig. 12.4). He hypothesized that there must have been a shift caused by historical circumstances, and he hoped to find some evidence of the older system still in use. Such was not the case, but on returning to Chicago he discovered that an early nineteenth-century report on

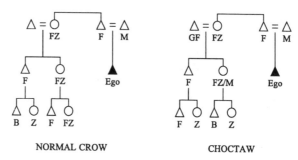

Figure 12.4. Normal Crow kin terms and Choctaw variant

the Choctaw, predating Morgan's data, confirmed that the older system was of the normal Crow type.[55] This was an important discovery, documented evidence of historical change in the Choctaw system. Summarizing his findings, he wrote: "In the Southeast, patterns of kinship terminology have turned out to be remarkably sensitive indicators of social and cultural change." [56]

Throughout his long career Eggan continued to nurture American Indian kinship studies, and he twice wrote valuable syntheses of the literature. In an expanded edition of the Radcliffe-Brown Festschrift, Eggan systematically reviewed the progress of studies from 1937 to 1955.[57] Again in 1964, in the first annual Lewis Henry Morgan lectures delivered at the University of Rochester, Eggan summarized the field.[58] These surveys have inspired successive generations of students. In 1994, after his death, a group of his students honored Eggan's memory with a collection of essays that present new analyses of a wide variety of Native American kinship systems.[59]

Further Approaches to Kinship

Anthropological study of kinship systems has continued to develop new approaches, virtually all of which have been tested with data from American Indian societies. Only a few of the most salient need to be mentioned here.

George Peter Murdock, combining American and British approaches, undertook an ambitious comparative study of kinship and social organization based on material from 150 societies worldwide. This resulted in a volume that provided a thorough classification of the types of social institutions and provided information based on statistical correlations. For example, Murdock found the most diagnostic factor in determining kinship terminology to be the pattern of residence after marriage: "The rule of residence is normally the first aspect of a social system to undergo modification in the process of change from one relatively stable equilibrium to another." [60] Perhaps more importantly, Murdock's study revealed how difficult and imprecise it was on the basis of the ethnographic record to classify societies in terms of descent, residence, family structure, and kin terminology. For example, two societies might be classified together as characterized by bilateral descent, but one had an actual descent system based on both patrilineal and matrilineal descent, while the other may have had no actual rule of descent at all and been classified as "bilateral" for lack of any other category. Murdock's was the first attempt to work out social laws through statistical study, but his book demonstrated how difficult it is to make human social phenomena fit a systematic scientific classification.

Drawing inspiration from structural linguistics, as well as from Durkheim and Marcel Mauss, Claude Lévi-Strauss developed a method of structural analysis in anthropology intended to reveal the unconscious workings of culture.[61] His approach to kinship began with what he called the atom of kinship, consisting of the nuclear family together with the wife's brother. The essential problem for continuity in society was therefore the exchange of women between men, which, given the universality of the incest taboo, forced families (or larger social groups) to cooperate with one another. Marriage was seen from the perspective of alliance, the bringing together of two groups in relationships of exchange—this in opposition to the British social anthropologists' emphasis on descent. Within what came to be called alliance theory, anthropologists were particularly concerned with patterns of preferential or prescribed marriage.[62]

Formal semantic analysis (also called componential analysis) attempted to provide the field of kinship studies with a scientific method for discovering the structure of kin terminologies. Harking back to Kroeber's early study, formal analysis seeks to deduce the components from which kinship terminologies are constructed. Floyd Lounsbury introduced the method in 1956, using the data on Pawnee kinship from Morgan's *Systems*.[63] While Lounsbury was able to demonstrate the principles of classification on which the Pawnee system is based, he was forced to state up front that his analysis did not take into account "metaphorical extensions" of terms such as the use of the term "mother" for corn, or of "father" for sun. The underlying assumption of formal analysis is that kinship is about biological relationships that can be expressed genealogically, which necessarily reduces complex cultural systems to reflections of Euro-American definitions of kinship.

The irregularities of kin-term use, and in particular the use of "incorrect" or alternative terms for relatives standing in the same genealogical position in relation to ego, became a focus of investigation for David M. Schneider in his study of Zuni kinship. He suggested that the classifying and role-designating functions of kin terms could be seen as varying independently; genealogical position, therefore, was not the only determinant of kin-term use among relatives.[64] Over the course of his career Schneider became convinced that kinship, as it had been defined in anthropology, was a distinctive product of Europoean culture. If one assumes that the genealogical grid does not have the same value or meaning in every culture, then, Schneider suggested, kinship becomes an empirical question, not a universal fact. Cultures, by definition, are sets of symbols and meanings, patterned in unique ways; the anthropologist's job is to describe each culture in its own terms rather than impose analytical concepts from the outside.[65]

The Lessons of Kinship Studies

During the century and a half that American Indian kinship has been a topic of formal study, a great deal has been learned through the application of various theoretical approaches to data recorded from a large number of different societies throughout North America. From these studies generalizations have emerged that are significant for understanding kinship not only among Native Americans but throughout the world.

The first lesson of kinship studies is that kin terms in every society form a logical system. Although there is considerable variation among them, they represent a small number of types (first classified by Spier). Because these types seem to represent a limited number of possibilities for structuring relationships in the family, the existence of the same type in different areas does not imply historical connection between them. Each kinship terminology is a linguistic classification based on a relatively small number of variables (discussed by Kroeber and by the formal semantic analysts). At the same time, kinship terminologies are cultural classifications based on principles sometimes strongly contrasting with those of mainstream American culture. Although they involve genealogical connections, kin terminologies usually classify persons and phenomena beyond actual webs of biological relatedness, and genealogy may not be the defining criterion of kinship in any Native American culture.

Kin terms are important for classifying relatives, but, even more importantly, each pair of relationships is specified in terms of culturally defined patterns of rights and obligations, proper behaviors, and attitudes or emotions. These "social usages," as Eggan called them, are the fundamentally important features of a kinship system.

The relation of kinship to other aspects of social organization is important for seeing beyond the individual to the group. Using Durkheim's analogy, the function of social structure is to integrate society. Each social institution, in Eggan's words, offers a different index to social integration. Kinship is the most sensitive index because it permeates all aspects of social life. In conjunction with marriage and descent patterns, kin terms divide society into constituent groups, the most simple of which are dual divisions (moieties). Often moieties are in turn divided into clans, which are further divided into lineages, as with the Omaha. Kin terms can be shown to pattern social units, so that, for example, from an individual's point of view, one lineage may represent mothers and mothers' brothers, while another may represent fathers and fathers' sisters. Patterns of preferential marriage over time can perpetuate and localize relations between particular clans or lineages. Much less work has been done on bilateral societies in North America, yet kinship provides social integration even in the absence of unilineal descent groups. Kin units such as clans and moieties may be invested with symbolic value, such that all taken together provide a model of the cosmos, and also invested with political and religious functions, so that they may be the dominant institutions for all aspects of social life.

Types of Native American Kinship Systems

Kin Terminologies

Recognition of the webs of relationship created by marriage and descent is a human universal, but the patterning and meaning of those relationships are cultural characteristics unique to each society. Thus the categories of relationship expressed in English and the pattern of bilateral descent from the mother's and father's sides of the family, which seem natural to members of American society, are in fact culturally specific and shaped by historical forces. The kinship system of modern America is different from the patterns characteristic of Native American systems in very basic ways.

It is necessary to understand that although the biological relationship between parents and children is universally recognized in Native American systems, terms equivalent to "father," "mother," "son," and "daughter" are not used in most of the systems to designate only those specific biological relatives. As Morgan discovered, for example, the terms "mother" and "father" frequently included mother's and father's same-sex siblings and parallel cousins. Thus in most American Indian societies an individual has many mothers and fathers. This does not mean, for example, that mother's sisters are *like* mothers; they *are* mothers. In other words, the status of mother is defined in terms of patterns of relationship surrounding, but not limited to, the act of giving birth. The biological mother is no more or less a mother to her children than are all those women she calls sister. Learning to think about biological categories and kin categories independently of one another is the first step in understanding American Indian kinship.

Native Americans frequently speak of kinship in terms of patterns of cooperation and respect, concepts that are expressed in the native words equivalent to the English concept of kinship. Often blood is a symbol of relatedness. The Eskimo concept of kinship is labeled by the word *ila,* according to Joseph Maxwell, which in its most general sense means 'part'; it is used to designate

any partner or companion, and in a kinship sense contrasts with a word meaning 'stranger'. Maxwell found that although genealogical relationship was a
necessary component of kinship, when questioned about relationship Eskimos
emphasized mutual help, love, concern, and lack of fear as prominent characteristics of kinship.[66] The Cheyenne term *navóohestoto,* according to Anne
Straus, designates biological relatives; Cheyennes relate this term to the word
for 'heart'; all tribal members share the same blood.[67] The Navajo concept of
kinship, expressed in the verbal prefix *k'e,* according to Gary Witherspoon,
connotes love, kindness, peacefulness, friendliness, and cooperation.[68]

Kinship terms delineate specific patterns of cooperation and relatedness for
particular societies. More than labels, kin terms are inextricably linked with
patterns of behavior, attitudes, and emotions. In this way they provide a normative structure within which individuals act as they go about their daily lives.
Historically, since most Native American societies were of such a scale that
everyone within a community knew (and was related to) everyone else, the
patterns of kinship offered standards of proper conduct. In larger-scale societies, kinship terms and their associated behavioral patterns provide blueprints
for interaction, even between individuals who are strangers to one another.

To a large extent, these kinship patterns still hold in many Native American
societies. Among the Navajo, for instance, kin terms are patterned according to
clan membership. Each individual is related to many clans through descent and
marriage; knowing the clan affiliation of another individual provides at least
one way of designating that individual by a kin term, with clans being considered as corporate units such that all the members of that clan stand in parallel
kin relationship to ego. Among the Lakota, kin relationship with strangers
was determined by genealogical connection or, failing that, by the conscious
choice of an appropriate kin term. Such relationships are "fictive" from a
Euro-American viewpoint, but are considered genuine (and permanent) kin
relationships by the Lakota. The norms of kin behavior are, of course, ideals,
and must not be understood as limiting the expression of individual personalities; instead, they provided models for relationships of respect, avoidance,
joking, and cooperation.

Family and Social Divisions

Throughout Native North America the nuclear family is a fundamental unit
of social life. Consisting of husband, wife, and children, nuclear families have
greater or lesser importance from one social system to the next but may be
said to be the only unit of social structure common to all the peoples of Native
North America. Nuclear families are residential units that have direct responsibility for the care of children. Additionally, in most areas, extended families
are important social units. Also residential units, extended families include

members from more than two generations—for example, a widowed parent or parent-in-law, or a married child with his or her spouse and children. Many peoples practiced polygyny, in which a man married more than one woman, usually sisters to one another; polygynous families are another type of extended family, though not infrequently the wives occupied separate dwellings. In some areas joint families were important social units, consisting of two or more brothers, or two or more sisters, with their spouses and children.

Multigenerational families formed another larger and more complex form of residential unit in some areas, consisting of multigenerational lines of women (grandmothers, mothers, daughters, granddaughters), together with their spouses and unmarried male children; or multigenerational lines of men with their spouses and unmarried female children. These types of family units were not always linked with descent patterns, nor were they necessarily year-round arrangements. Pawnee earthlodges, for example, housed multigenerational lines of women, but the Pawnee lacked a formal descent system.[69] The Omaha had a patrilineal descent system, but during the spring and fall, while they were living in their permanent village, each earthlodge was inhabited by a matrilineage. During the summer and winter hunts, the Omaha lived in buffalo-hide tipis, each inhabited by a nuclear family.[70] Seasonal variations in economic activities were reflected in variations of residential pattern in many areas of North America.

The descent groups of Native American peoples are referred to as clans. Every individual was born into the clan of his or her father (in patrilineal systems) or mother (in matrilineal systems). These were permanent identities that did not change throughout life. Some societies comprised a small number of clans: historically, the Cherokee, for example, had seven, while the Omaha had ten.[71] Other societies have many more. The Navajo, for example, recognize more than sixty clans, but they are organized into nine main sets of affiliated clans (phratries).[72] Despite the similarity in structure, there are real differences in the nature of clan systems throughout North America. The Omaha, for example, refer to each clan by a word meaning "village," with the implication that the tribal unit represented a coming together of previously independent clan groups.[73] This is the direct opposite of the Navajo, whose traditions refer to four original clans that have grown into the sixty of today. As a further dimension of contrast, the Omaha clans were historically all resident in a single village while the Navajo clans are localized and spread across Navajo country.

In addition to clans and phratries, some societies were organized in moieties (dual divisions). Omaha moieties, for example, symbolically divided the tribe into five clans representing earth and five representing sky. In some other societies dual divisions exist in the absence of clans. The Tewa of San Juan, for example, are divided into Summer and Winter moieties, which function entirely in ceremonial affairs and are not related to kinship or political organization. Recruitment to the moieties is in general patrilineal, but there is no definite rule.[74]

Kinship and Political Units

Kinship is fundamental to the political organization of Native American peoples. Minimal band organization represents the least complex type. For example, historically, among the Shoshoneans of the Great Basin and the Eskimo of the Arctic, local kin groups—perhaps only a few nuclear families—formed politically independent units. Political status and kin status were one; leadership was the responsibility of the oldest functioning male. Links to other groups were through bonds of kinship. The Shoshoneans practiced a wide variety of marriage types to ensure the continuation of alliances among bands, including the levirate (when a man died, one of his brothers married his widow), the sororate (when a woman died, one of her sisters married the widower), brother–sister exchange (providing two marriage links between bands in a single generation), and cross-cousin marriage (the continuation of the brother–sister exchange over generations) (fig. 12.5).

Tribal societies based on bands were characterized by a clearer distinction between kinship and political organization. The band organization of Plains tribes like the Cheyenne, Lakota, and Comanche was based on extended families, but political organization was invested in formally recognized leaders who were supposed to concern themselves with the interests of the group as a whole, putting the common interest above individual kinship obligations. According to normative accounts of Cheyenne society, the tribe had a council of forty chiefs, formally elected for ten-year terms; the council included four representatives from each of the ten bands, headed by four chiefs who had served in the previous council. Historically, the Cheyenne divided in the early nineteenth century into northern and southern groups, each apparently attempting to replicate the structure of the whole.[75] In contrast, Lakota and Comanche leaders were selected in a less formal manner for their personal qualities, including success in war and generosity. They functioned as leaders as long as they were effective; members of their bands were free to leave and follow other leaders as they wished. Given the great disparity in size—the Cheyenne numbered perhaps only 2,000 in the mid-nineteenth century, while the Comanche and Lakota were both several times more populous—the divisions of the Comanche and Lakota may be better conceptualized as independent tribes.[76]

Among clan-organized peoples, kinship and tribal political organization sometimes coincided. The Iroquois provide a good example, where each clan had a separate council and its own chiefs, hereditary in specific matrilineages. Fifty of these chiefs made up the General Council of the League. William Fenton characterized the relationship between kin, clan, and political organi-

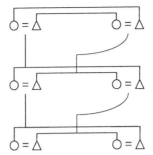

Figure 12.5. Brother-sister exchange through generations

zation in this way: "Iroquois political structure extends the basic patterns of social structure and local organization to a wider context. As one moves from the lineage to the clan, to the moiety, to the tribe or nation, to the League, the projected use of kinship terms becomes more fictional and the expected behavior more symbolic." [77] Similarly, Kalervo Oberg writes that among the Tlingit, "the clan is pre-eminently the political unit." [78] A historical example is provided by the ethnohistorical studies of the Chippewa by Harold Hickerson. On the basis of early documents, he concluded that before European contact, the Chippewa lived in politically autonomous, localized clan villages, which were tied to one another through cross-cousin marriage. Only after the start of the fur trade was there a need to mobilize larger groups, resulting in the formation of multiclan villages.[79]

More commonly, however, clans themselves did not have explicit political functions. Among the Cherokee, for example, the village council house was a seven-sided structure, members of each clan having their own side. Although the unity of a village was expressed in terms of the cooperation of members of all seven clans, the clans had no direct governing functions except relating to the obligations of clan members toward one another. Village chiefs were supposed to act as though they had no clan affiliation, placing the welfare of the whole village first. The clan system bonded the far-flung Cherokee villages together with a common identity, providing a social mechanism that reinforced the common bonds of language, culture, and religion. Among the Cherokee, one of the most significant functions of the clan was to regulate marriage: one could not marry into one's own clan or that of one's father; an individual was free to joke with members of his own clan (except mothers), but with members of one's father's clan an individual maintained relationships of respect.[80]

Identifying the actual political units in Native North America presents many difficulties. Some areas were characterized by networks of small bands loosely related by marriage, common language, and common culture. The Great Basin Shoshoneans are a good example. In other areas bands or villages were loosely affiliated, but lacked political unity. The Cherokee in the Southeast, Hopi in the Southwest, and Comanche on the Southern Plains, normally thought of as discrete tribes, in fact lacked political unity. The Lakota had an ideology of unity, and a flexible political structure that allowed any number of Lakota groups to come together and function, at least in the short term, as a political unit. The Cheyenne also had the ideology of unity, though there is no historical evidence of the Cheyennes functioning as a single unified tribe in the nineteenth century. The five Iroquois tribes, joined in historical times by the Tuscarora, constituted a political alliance that, while brittle, functioned to maintain peace among the League. Current efforts by a large number of groups to be federally recognized as tribes has complicated historical definitions of tribe. The Bureau of Indian Affairs has been forced to provide legal parameters for proving claims to tribal identity, one of which, demonstrating unbroken political identity over time, presents a formidable obstacle. Inability to provide adequate documentation for political continuity, for example, has so far stymied efforts by the Miami of Indiana to regain the tribal status capriciously taken away from them in the last century.[81]

The nature of leadership in Native American societies also requires a word of explication. Chiefs or leaders, whether hereditary, elected, or chosen informally, generally lacked coercive power. Their authority came from their status, underscored by their role as successful elder males, and consisted largely of moral suasion. Strategic marriages of siblings and children were important in most groups to build political networks that would provide support for individuals in their role as leaders. But no matter how democratically selected, or how representative of the people, in most Native American societies chiefs lacked the right to speak for the people except to the extent that they were so authorized by band or tribal councils representing the will of the people at large.

Kinship in Social and Cultural Perspective

Differentiating social and cultural perspectives on Native American kinship systems provides a useful way of understanding the multiple dimensions of kinship. This approach builds directly on Eggan's work.

The social perspective focuses on the patterned use of kin terms and the normative definitions of appropriate behavior between kin that use of the terms implies. The definition of each pair of kin relationships comprising the system as a whole offers a skeletal view of social life. Relationships can be described along two intersecting continua, one ranging from avoidance to intimacy, the other from respect to obligatory joking. Some generalizations hold: throughout North America the relationships between a man and his mother-in-law and a woman and her father-in-law are characterized by avoidance, while those between grandparents and grandchildren are characterized by intimacy. Relationships between an individual and his or her parents are characterized by respect, while relationships with a sibling-in-law of the opposite sex are frequently characterized by obligatory joking. It is the differences between systems that are diagnostic: for instance, the nature of the relationship between a man and his mother's brother, a woman and her father's sister, and the relationships between siblings, parallel cousins, and cross cousins.

The system provides norms for behavior, but in social interaction those norms are not always met—perhaps not even frequently met. When behavior and norms become noticeably out of sync, changes in the terminology may follow, offering clues to earlier patterns of behavior. The system offers a structure for social life in which people are comfortable, one that seems natural and is, in a sense, contextual; the proper behavioral patterns among kin are unconscious features of daily life that require explication only to small children (and visiting anthropologists).

At the same time, kinship is never just a system of mechanical behavioral patterns. It is a central part of the culture and provides a rich field of meanings and metaphors, symbols that create cognitive worlds. Many American Indian peoples conceptualize kinship in terms of sharing, generosity, and nurturance. These symbols structure relationships between humans and superhumans—what the ethnographer of the Ojibwe, A. I. Hallowell, called "other-than-human 'persons,' " the spirits beyond human understanding that animate the world.[82] The symbols of kinship are also used to characterize the relationships among spirits.

In his study of Navajo kinship, Gary Witherspoon makes effective use of the dual perspectives of social and cultural analysis to explicate what is unique about the Navajo system. The Navajo word *dine* designates "people," differentiated into the holy people (spirits) and earth surface people (humans). The proper relationship among all *dine* is called *k'e,* connoting love, kindness, peace—all the characteristics of kinship and friendship. The ideal symbol of this concept is the relationship between an individual and his or her mother, with whom the strongest bond of *k'e* exists; the strength of relationship diminishes as one goes from mother to family, to clan, and to the Navajo people as a whole. The bond shared by Navajos related by descent is called *ke'i,* a special case of *k'e,* relatives whom one treats as carefully as possible according to the norms of the kinship system. Relatives by descent include the members of one's own clan as well as the clan of one's father; an individual is born *of* his mother's clan, and born *for* his father's clan. Membership is only in the mother's clan, but the relationship to the father's clan is also important, though it is not inherited by an individual's children.[83]

At the same time, Witherspoon explicates a rich web of symbols, expressed in myths and ceremonies as well as in everyday life, that reveal the central importance of kinship in Navajo culture. If the central symbol of kinship is the life-giving bond between mother and child, then all kin are in a sense "mothers." The term for "mother" is used not just for human mothers; the sheep herd, corn, the sacred mountain soil bundle—all are called mother. Changing Woman, personification of earth, is likewise mother. Witherspoon suggests, "Maybe it is the earth who is really mother, and human mothers merely resemble the earth in some ways and are not really mothers." [84] Moreover, he concludes, "The symbols of motherhood and the k'e solidarity which they symbolize pervade Navajo culture and provide the patterns and sentiments which order Navajo social life." [85]

Witherspoon's account of Navajo kinship makes it clear that a mere description of the terms used among relatives by descent and marriage, and a description of the normative behavioral patterns, would only begin to suggest the pervasive importance of kinship in Navajo life.

How Kinship Systems Work

It is difficult to appreciate the centrality of kinship systems to historical Native American life without extended ethnographic presentation of specific examples. In this section I look at kinship in historical context for two Plains groups that offer a strong contrast in kinship type. The Lakota were a good example of a bilateral kinship system, while the Omaha had a classic patrilineal system. Lakota society was based on a system of fluid bands, while the Omaha lived in a single village. They represent two strategies for living in the Plains area.

The Lakota

The Lakota were nomadic buffalo hunters whose annual cycle of camp movements mirrored the congregation and dispersal of the buffalo herds. Kinship was the adaptive mechanism that provided the flexible structure to maintain social relations among individuals who spent most of the year apart. Kin terms served to structure all social discourse. Among humans, individuals must necessarily have kin designations for one another in order to carry out any kind of meaningful interaction; strangers were potentially dangerous, and to establish relationships with them they must literally become related as kin. Thus adoptions, formal and informal, were regular means by which the Lakota extended kinship to all with whom they interacted.[86]

The unity so essential to Lakota thought was symbolized visually by a circle: it described the living space within a tipi, was the shape of the ceremonial camp, and represented the wholeness of the universe. It also called to mind the bonds of kinship that united humans with the spirit world. In prayer, the use of kin terms—"father," "grandfather," "mother," "grandmother"— placed the petitioner in the role of the pitiful child, begging for help from nurturing older relatives. The quality of pitifulness was equally applicable to interactions among humans.

The locus of kinship was the nuclear family, the residential unit that inhabited a single tipi. But no nuclear family was self-sufficient, and people lived in extended families, typically comprising a set of brothers and male cousins with their wives and children. This is the social unit the Lakota call the *tiyoshpaye* (literally, 'lodge group'), usually translated as "band." The bands were organized by the mid-nineteenth century into seven "tribes" (*oyate*): the Oglala, Brule, Minneconjou, Sans Arc, Two Kettle, Blackfoot, and Hunkpapa. Together they made up the *Titunwan,* said to mean "Prairie dwellers." Today the Lakota use the word "nation" for this highest-level unit, though in the nineteenth century it, too, was designated *oyate.*

The size of Lakota camps varied with the season. During the winter, camps were small as the bands dispersed to maximize hunting potential, each locating in a protected area. Winter camps focused around particular *tiyoshpaye,* but because people frequently moved about visiting relatives, camps ordinarily included families from other bands as well. During the summer, as the buffalo herds congregated, so did the Lakota, coming together in tribal camps for the Sun Dance and for communal buffalo hunts and war expeditions. Thus throughout the year individuals came into contact with large numbers of people beyond their immediate kin networks, and through their interactions extended bonds of kinship widely.

The bands were named, usually with nicknames. Membership in bands was by choice; by residing in a particular band, individuals could decide to count themselves as members of it. Children were considered to belong to the band of the father or mother, but residence, rather than descent, seems to have been the operative category. Each band was governed by a council of adult males who had achieved prominence in warfare; leaders were appointed to represent the consensus of the council, and police (*akichita*) were appointed to maintain order when necessary—for example, when moving camp or preparing for a major ceremony or communal hunt. When various bands congregated during the summer, their councils combined into one and recognized a variety of tribal leaders who in a sense acted as the symbolic fathers of the camp, putting aside individual and band interests for those of the tribe at large.

Order was maintained in daily life through the kinship system. Within the camp, no matter how large, every individual was potentially related to everyone else. Interactions were structured by the normative patterns of kin behavior. There were two distinct types of relatives: those who centered on the family of birth (*titakuye,* 'lodge/band relatives') and those who centered on the family of marriage (*takuye,* 'relatives'). These categories do not designate

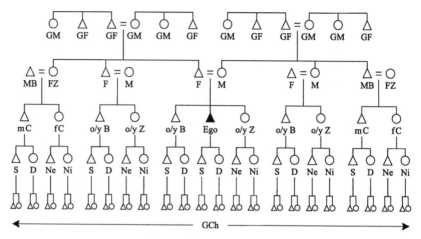

Figure 12.6. Lakota kin terms

a clear-cut distinction between consanguineal and affinal relatives, however, as will become obvious below. An assumption basic to understanding the structure of the Lakota kinship system is that a man is equated with his brothers and male parallel cousins, while a woman is equated with her sisters and female parallel cousins.

Referring to figure 12.6, we may start with ego's generation. Terms for older and younger brothers are used to designate male siblings and parallel cousins (the male children of fathers). Similarly, terms for older and younger sister are used to designate female siblings and parallel cousins (the female children of mothers). Terms for male and female cousins are used to designate cross cousins (the children of mothers' brothers and fathers' sisters). (Different terms are used by males and females for relatives in this generation). Relationships between brothers were culturally defined as very close; brothers could not refuse one another's requests without giving offense. Relationships between sisters were also close, but not so restrictive. Historically, relationships between brothers and sisters were characterized by conspicuous respect; after the age of puberty they did not look directly at one another or speak to one another. Cousins, although terminologically differentiated from siblings, were in fact treated as siblings.

In the parental generation, fathers and fathers' brothers are called father, while mothers and mother's sisters are called mother; figure 12.6 does not show the parents' parallel cousins, who are also called father and mother. Terms for mothers' brothers and fathers' sisters are extended to the spouses of those individuals; thus some mothers' brothers and fathers' sisters are consanguineal relatives, others affinal, but no distinction was made between them. The relationship between fathers and sons was one of respect and formality;

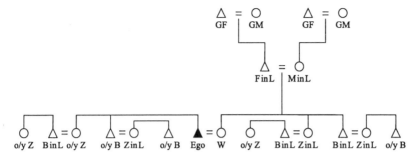

Figure 12.7. Lakota affinal kin terms

mothers and daughters were less formal. Mothers' brothers were also respect relatives, but they had responsibility for the practical training of their nephews; fathers' sisters had parallel responsibilities toward nieces. Relationships between mothers' brothers and their nieces, and between fathers' sisters and their nephews, were warm and supportive.

Anyone who is the parent of a father, mother, mother's brother, or father's sister is grandfather or grandmother, as are all grandparents' siblings, cousins, and spouses; in fact, the grandparental terms are extended to any elder. Relationships between grandparents and grandchildren were intimate and indulgent.

In one's children's generation, the children of ego and his or her same-sex siblings, parallel cousins, and cross cousins are son and daughter, while the children of opposite sex siblings, parallel cousins, and cross cousins are nephew and niece. (Males and females use gender-specific terms for nephew and niece.)

The children of sons, daughters, nephews, and nieces are all called grandchild.

Affinal relatives are shown in figure 12.7, drawn from the perspective of male ego, though there are no differences for female ego. No kin terms of address or reference were used between spouses, though a variety of other referential terms for husband and wife were sometimes used. Wife's brothers and sisters' husbands were classed as brothers-in-law, while wife's sisters and brothers' wives were classed as sisters-in-law. Relationships between siblings-in-law involved obligatory rough joking, and were particularly strained between brothers-in-law. Special "friend" terms, however, might be used between same-sex siblings-in-law, if they got along, to smooth social relations. Similarly, opposite-sex siblings of brothers-in-law and sisters-in-law could be classed as sisters and brothers, thereby removing them from the category of marked affinal relatives; alternately, they could be called brother-in-law and sister-in-law. (Males and females had distinct terms for siblings-in-law.)

One additional kin term, not shown on the chart, was used in ego's generation to designate co-parents-in-law—that is, the parents of anyone married to ego's sons and daughters. It was a respect relationship.

Parents of one's spouse were classified as father-in-law and mother-in-law, using terms derivative of the grandparental terms. These were relations of extreme respect; mother-in-law and son-in-law practiced total avoidance, while the other relationships were characterized by partial avoidance.

Parents of parents-in-law were classed as grandparents, removing them from the category of marked affinals.

Not shown on the chart, the spouses of children, nephews, nieces, and grandchildren were called by a child-in-law term derived from the grandchild term. Individuals had little direct relationship with these relatives.

In all interactions with others, Lakotas based their relationships not simply on personalities and common interests, but on the basis of structured pairs of kin relationships. Some relationships were structured to be close—for example, a man and his brothers and male cousins; others, such as the relationship between a man and his brothers-in-law, were structured to be distant, and in this case marked by obligatory joking. If brothers-in-law became friends (for instance, when a married couple was living in the wife's camp), they might decide to use a special friend term applied specifically to brothers-in-law who got along. A parallel term existed for sisters-in-law. In this way, a marked affinal relationship could be transformed into a family relationship. The structure of the kinship system explains why the typical winter camp was patrilocal. A group of brothers and male cousins formed the core of the camp, since they were the relatives culturally defined as cooperating most smoothly with one another; if the camp had been matrilocal, the group of cooperating men would have been brothers-in-law to one another, culturally defined as a difficult relationship.

Whichever residence pattern was in use, one spouse or the other lived among marked affinal relatives. Most frequently it was the woman, who must be constantly vigilant to the respect relationships involved. But there were always family relatives in the camp as well (the affines of her affines), fathers and mothers, sisters and brothers, in whose presence she could be less guarded and act more freely.[87]

The effect of the Lakota kinship system was to extend kin relationships widely, to the entire social network. Terms were structured generationally, although the actual age of individuals varied enormously; adults were likely to have fathers and mothers younger than themselves, and sons and daughters who were older than they. Most importantly, the system provided structure to all social relationships. No two people were ever left to figure out all the dimensions of their relationship on their own, as happens in Euro-American society; the kinship system offered guidelines to shape relationships, providing mutually understood expectations for proper behavior.

The Omaha

The Omaha had a dual economy based on horticulture and hunting. In the spring they returned to their earthlodge village, where they planted corn, beans, and squash. During the summer they traveled as a tribe, holding religious ceremonies and engaging in communal buffalo hunts. They returned to the earthlodge villages in the fall to harvest their crops, then dispersed in small groups to hunt during the winter.[88]

In contrast to Lakota holism, dualism permeated all aspects of Omaha culture. The Omaha believed that human beings originated from the union of Sky people and Earth people, and these became the names of the Omaha moieties. The tribe comprised ten patrilineal clans, five in each moiety. In earlier times the moieties were believed to have been exogamous, but by the late nineteenth century, although marriages between moieties were considered ideal, the clans themselves were the actual exogamous units. Each clan had its own origin story, and the five clans in each moiety were believed to have been associated with one another before the moieties came together to form the Omaha tribe.

Kinship played much the same role among the Omaha as among the Lakota: personal names were not used for address, and all individuals called one another by relationship terms. Considering the small size of the population (estimated at about 1,300 in the mid-1840s), it is likely that kinship links could be found between any two individuals. Kin terms also were the vehicle for prayer, and all spirit beings (*Wakanda*) were addressed by kin terms.

For every individual, the clan was the most significant social unit. Everyone belonged to the clan of his or her father unless the mother was Omaha and the father non-Indian; in such cases the children were considered to be members of the mother's clan. Clan names were apparently ancient; they are not easily translated, and their significance is not always clear. Each clan had distinctive ritual objects, ceremonies, taboos, a haircut for young boys, and a stock of personal names that were reused generation after generation. Symbolically, the Earth people were associated with the material welfare of the people—including war and hunting—while the Sky people were associated with their spiritual welfare. An elaborate web of symbols, however, united the moieties into a single entity. During the summer the Omaha lived in tipis in one large camp circle, the opening oriented to the direction in which the tribe was traveling, though always oriented to the east during ceremonies. As one faced the opening of the circle, the Sky people camped to the right, the Earth people to the left, and within each half of the circle every clan had its assigned camping place. The summer camp circle therefore resembled a cosmic tipi, uniting earth and sky.

Each clan was composed of patrilineages. The numbers varied, since some clans were small and others large; one Earth people clan, the *Thatada*, was divided into four subclans, each equivalent in size to other clans. The patrilineages were social units equivalent to Lakota bands.

When the Omaha were in their earthlodge village, each lodge was inhabited by a multigenerational line of women with their husbands and unmarried male children and grandchildren. During the summer hunts they lived in the tribal camp circle, organized by clan. During the late fall and winter, the people dispersed; it seems likely that groups based on patrilineages stayed together at this time of year.

The clans were not political units. According to a sacred legend, the governmental council of seven chiefs was inaugurated in order to hold the people together. In the beginning, each of seven clans was given a sacred pipe to symbolize the position of chief. Later, however, the chieftainship became competitive among the clans, each of which developed a chiefly lineage. The seven council chiefs were men of the highest prestige in Omaha society, and more than one man from a single clan might serve on the council at the same time. Membership was for life. Two of the chiefs held the highest positions in the council, and by the mid-nineteenth century only two of the pipes remained. These two principal chiefs came from opposite moieties, thereby representing the wholeness of the tribe. The council of chiefs had the authority to speak for the tribe. At their council meetings the formal use of kinship terms symbolized the chiefs' responsibilities to the people. The council was devoted to the maintenance of peace and order and was responsible for appointing the camp police, who organized camp moves, ceremonies, and communal hunts. The council also punished offenders; anyone who murdered another tribal member, for example, was exiled from the tribe for a period of three or four years.

Omaha kin terms were divided into two categories that parallel the Lakota, one centering on, but not limited to, relatives by birth, and the other referring to marked affinal relatives. Behavioral patterns were also very much as described for the Lakota. Figure 12.8 presents the kin terms in the first category. The terms in the central portion of the chart, together with those for the grandparental generation, are identical to the Lakota system. That is, father is classed with father's brother, mother is classed with mother's sister; all the children of fathers and mothers (ego's siblings and parallel cousins) are classed as brothers and sisters (differentiated into older and younger, with distinct terms used by males and females), and the children of same-sex siblings are called son and daughter, while the children of opposite-sex siblings are called nephew and niece. The parents (and their siblings) of all fathers and mothers are grandfather and grandmother. In the parental generation, there are special terms for fathers' sisters and mothers' brothers.

Here the resemblances to the Lakota system end. On the father's side, the husband of father's sister is called brother-in-law (rather than mother's brother, as in Lakota); their children, ego's patrilateral cross cousins, are called nephew

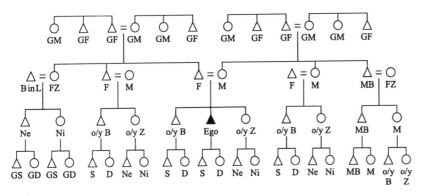

Figure 12.8. Omaha kin terms

and niece (seemingly lowering them a generation), and their children are called grandchild. On the mother's side, the wife of mother's brother is called father's sister (as in Lakota), but their children, ego's matrilateral cross cousins, are called mother's brother and mother (seemingly raising them a generation). In the subsequent generation, the children of mother's brother are again mother's brother and mother (this continues *ad infinitum*) and, expectedly, the children of mother are son and daughter. These, of course, are the diagnostic features of an Omaha-type system.

Affinal kin terms were structured the same as the Lakota, except that the Omaha had distinct son-in-law and daughter-in-law terms (instead of classing them together as in Lakota). It is unclear whether the opposite-sex siblings of siblings-in-law might be classed as siblings (in the manner of the Lakota), or whether they remained siblings-in-law.

The Omaha terms appear confusing when presented on a generational chart because they are, unquestionably, not structured entirely generationally. They become much clearer if we draw charts that refer to particular patrilineages. Figure 12.9 shows ego's patrilineage. All relatives within the patrilineage are differentiated by generation. Older in-marrying women are mothers and grandmothers, in-marrying women of ego's generation are sisters-in-law, and in-marrying women of generations younger than ego are daughters-in-law. All men who marry women of ego's patrilineage are called brother-in-law, without regard for generation, and all children of women of ego's patrilineage are called nephew and niece, again without regard for generation. These are strong arguments for the conceptual significance of the patrilineage (and therefore the clan) in Omaha kinship.

Further evidence can be gained by looking at other patrilineages. That of ego's mother, for example (fig. 12.10), clearly shows the conceptual unity of the patrilineage (the forms in square brackets are conjectural). All the women

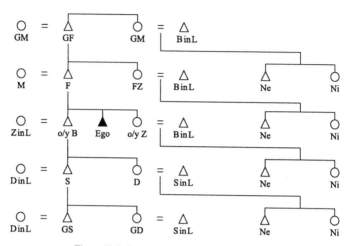

Figure 12.9. Omaha kin terms, ego's patrilineage

of the patrilineage are mothers; the men in generations older than ego's mother are grandfathers, while all the others are mothers' brothers. Women married to grandfathers are grandmothers, and women married to mothers' brothers are fathers' sisters, regardless of generation. All the men who marry women of ego's patrilineage are fathers, and all the children of mothers and fathers are brothers and sisters, again without regard to generation.

Kin terms could therefore be determined by actual genealogical reckoning between two individuals, but when uncertainty existed, simply knowing an individual's clan would be sufficient to determine a proper relationship.

Marriages were conceptualized as long-term alliances between patrilineages or clans. Anyone a man called sister-in-law was a potential wife. The rule of the sororate required men to marry their brothers' widows, and such potential marriage links were systematically recognized in the kinship system. For example, a man calls his father's sisters-in-law mother. Reciprocally, anyone a woman called brother-in-law was a potential husband according to the rule of the levirate. Her children recognized this by calling her brothers-in-law father. In this way the marriage alliance between clans was perpetuated through time.

The overall effect of the Omaha system was to extend kin relationships along patrilineages; generation was deemphasized outside one's own clan. For example, from the perspective of a male ego, the men of his mother's clan have special obligations to him, no matter what their generation, and so they are classed together as mother's brothers. In this way an individual's perspective on society from the point of view of his own kinship network corresponded with the lineal structure of Omaha clans.

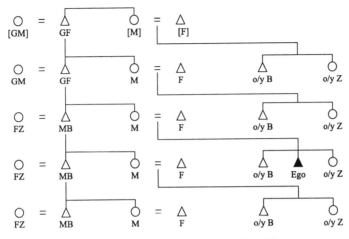

Figure 12.10. Omaha kin terms, ego's mother's patrilineage

The Uses of Kinship

The study of kinship systems requires patience for sorting through large bodies of data and making generalizations about the structure and content of kinship behavior. Analyzing the terms as linguistic systems is a first step, but studying kinship in practice makes those systems meaningful. It also allows for explanations of seeming irregularities, "mistakes," and individual variation in kinship. Like all other cultural phenomena, kinship is always in a state of change, and it is particularly sensitive to changing social practices. Yet studying kinship systems through time often reveals great stability. An understanding of kinship is essential for understanding Native American peoples both in the past and in the present, because kinship provides the foundation for social life.

For Understanding Social Systems

Knowing the social units of any Native American people and understanding how those units are built on kinship is the essential starting place for describing distinctive Native American ways of life. The realm of kinship provides the social framework that is the context for daily life; relating to kin, both near and distant, is the work of daily life. The social world built on informal bilateral bands is significantly different from one built on unilineal clans. Customs and behavioral patterns that seem to make no particular sense when looked at in isolation may frequently be understood as central to kinship obligations when the principles of the system are clarified.

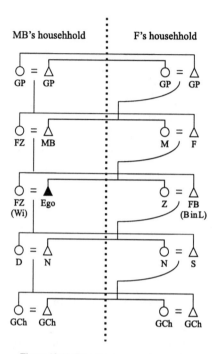

Figure 12.11. Tlingit cross-cousin marriage

One custom that has attracted a good deal of attention in the anthropological literature, presumably because it seemed exotic, is the practice of the avunculate. Found among a wide variety of Native American peoples, this custom dictates that a boy, sometime before the age of puberty, move from the household of his parents to that of a mother's brother. There, his mother's brother will take responsibility for his upbringing, and usually the nephew will inherit his mother's mother's property after the latter's death. This custom was practiced historically by the Tlingit. Characterized by matrilineal clans organized in a moiety system, Tlingit society also emphasized social rank: the clans were ranked in relation to one another, the matrilineages within the clan were ranked, and the individuals within the matrilineage were ranked, so that—with the exception of commoners and slaves—no two individuals shared exactly the same rank. Within each matrilineage (a household group), the ranking man faced the problem of identifying a successor and finding men of the proper social rank to marry his daughters. This is where the avunculate fit in with the system.[89]

Figure 12.11 depicts how the system works diagrammatically, showing two intermarrying households.[90] A boy moves from his father's household to his mother's brother's household. When he becomes an adult, he ideally marries a father's sister (one of his mother's brother's daughters, a cross cousin). He sends his son in turn back to his own father's household, where, when he grows, he will marry a cross cousin. There is no question about parity of rank, since husband and wife share the same grandparents. The diagram is only a model, of course, and if actual genealogies were studied, multiple households would be involved, but the structure would be the same. The kin terminology begins to resemble a Crow-type system (with a multigenerational line of father's sisters), but it breaks down after two generations and is not a true Crow system. Rather, it is a system uniquely adapted to cross-cousin marriage (through the avunculate) as a means of perpetuating the alliance between two clans over time.

The avunculate, however, was practiced elsewhere in North America for very different purposes and is not in any way specifically linked with matrilineal clan organization or cross-cousin marriage. The custom was practiced historically by the Pawnee of Nebraska, who lacked unilineal descent. Extended families dwelling in the village earthlodges centered on multigenerational lines of women and their husbands; however, brothers of those women were always welcome and could return at any time to the household in which they had grown up. Partly in response to this debt owed by a man to his sister, a woman might send her son at about the age of ten to live with his mother's brother in the household into which he had married. The mother's brother took responsibility for the boy's upbringing, and as he matured, the mother's brother's wife or wives introduced the boy to sex. The nephew called the children of his mother's brother (his matrilateral cross cousins) son and daughter. Lesser argued that from the point of view of the kinship system, a nephew was identified with his mother's brother as though they were brothers. The resulting pattern of kin terms resembles a Crow-type system, but in the absence of matrilineal descent. If his mother's brother were to die, the nephew might marry his widow(s) under the rule of the levirate.[91]

The important lesson of the avunculate example is that the same social form in different groups may have very different origins and functions and cannot be assumed in advance to have the same significance wherever it is found.

For Understanding Cultural Systems

Because kinship is so much a part of the context of Native American life, the extent to which it permeates all aspects of culture is easily overlooked. One area in which it is difficult to miss is religion. Myth, cosmology, and ritual consistently revolve around the structures and meanings of kinship.

The Lakota may again serve as an example.[92] The foundational myth of Lakota society and culture is also the story of the origin of kinship, a gift from the spirits to humankind. Long ago, before the Lakota were a people, two young men were sent out to scout for buffalo during a time of famine. As they lay upon a hill, they discovered something approaching in the distance. When it got near, they saw that it was a beautiful young woman, carrying a bundle. One of the young men proposed that they have sex with the woman, but his friend refused, warning that this was a sacred being. But the first young man approached the woman anyway, and when he went to embrace her, a mist descended. When it lifted, the other young man saw that his friend was nothing but a skeleton lying on the prairie. The woman spoke, telling the survivor that if he did as she said, he would be able to get any woman he wished as his wife. She instructed him to return home and report that she would arrive the next morning bearing a gift for the people. A special tipi was prepared for her and she arrived bearing her bundle, which contained the sacred Buffalo Calf Pipe, the first pipe, that would be the means of prayer by which the people would ask for help from the spirits. The people and the buffalo would be like brothers and sisters to one another, and as long as humans offered their prayers through the tobacco smoke of the pipe, there would be no famine. The woman stayed in the camp many days and taught the people the fundamentals of Lakota life. She named the kin relationships, explained the obligations among kin, and taught ceremonies that would help the Lakota in the future. When she left, she transformed herself into a buffalo as she disappeared on the prairie. She is known today as the White Buffalo Woman.

The story presents a charter for the Lakota way of life. Besides originating kinship, the story institutes marriage; because he recognized the woman as a sacred being and rejected promiscuous sexual behavior, the young man of the story is promised the woman of his choice, thus confining sexual activity to its proper place, between husband and wife. The story also explains the origin of prayer and of religious ceremonies. In fact, kinship and prayer are two ways of conceptualizing the relatedness that characterizes the Lakota universe. *Wachekiya,* in the human realm, means to call someone by kinship term; in the religious realm, it means to pray. In both senses the term implies activating a relationship.

In Lakota thought, all things in the universe were related. That wholeness was called *Wakan Tanka,* "great holy," the totality of all sacred things, and was symbolized by the circle. Humans formed only a small part of that wholeness, which they shared in in two ways. In the first place, at birth, each infant acquired four different types of spirits that animated the body. Later, through dreams and visions, individuals could acquire power (*wakan*) that put them more directly in touch with the sacredness of the universe. The relationships between the spirits and humankind provided the prototypes of human kin relationships.

Today, some of the specific beliefs and practices of Lakota religion have changed, adapting to changed circumstances. But the central symbols of kinship remain constant. The spirits are addressed as "Grandfather," and in seeking visions, participating in the Sun Dance, and performing many other ritual activities, individuals humble themselves, make themselves pitiful, and beg for help from the grandfathers. Embodying that universal kinship is the benediction used by participants in virtually all rituals: *Mitakuye oyas'in,* "All my relatives."

For Reconstructing Historical Changes in Social Systems

Kinship studies can reconstruct change over time in two ways. First, comparing kinship systems within particular language families allows for the linguistic reconstruction of proto-systems that can be at least tentatively identified as the common basis from which the contemporary systems developed. Such reconstruction has been carried out for the Algonquian, Athabascan, and Siouan families.[93] Second, we can look for inconsistencies within systems and attempt to explain them as the result of historical change. Neither method offers uncontested results, but the process of undertaking such study helps immeasurably in explicating kinship systems.

The comparative study of Siouan kin terms will serve to exemplify the method of linguistic comparison. This family is particularly significant for historical study, since it includes the Dakota, Crow, and Omaha—three type cases whose names have been used to designate, respectively, bilateral, matrilineal, and patrilineal systems. Lesser compared the terms for all the Siouan kinship systems and concluded that the proto-Siouan system was bilateral and generational, like the Dakota system but lacking terms for cross cousins. He interpreted changes in terminology in the various systems as the result of the systematic practice of the sororate and levirate. These led the Dakota system to create terms for cross cousins to differentiate them from siblings, while maintaining the old Siouan bilateral system. The Crow and Omaha systems, he argued, resulted from historical influences from tribes in the Southeast (through the Pawnee and Arikara, in the Missouri Valley) and the Midwest (the Central Algonquians), who respectively introduced matrilineality and patrilineality. The distinctive Crow and Omaha features of the systems resulted from the extension of the sororate and levirate marriages through generations.[94]

In a more rigorous linguistic study, resulting in the reconstruction of the terms of the pre-Siouan system, G. Hubert Matthews arrived at a different conclusion. He reconstructed multigenerational terms that he considered strong evidence that the parent system had Omaha-like kin terms structured around patrilineages. The evidence is not conclusive, but suggests the value of continued study.[95]

The Dakota cross-cousin terms mentioned above offer an example of the

Using plants in curing ceremonies is an important demonstration of knowledge systems. Early ethnographers often dismissed the healing practices of American Indian curers as blatant trickery, asserting, for example, that the objects a curer sucked from a patient's body were only palmed and then revealed. On the other hand, more recent studies have sometimes tended toward the too credulous, claiming that Indians had cures for everything from simple toothache to cancer.[46] Scientists have always, however, acknowledged plants' effects on the human body, and historically a number of plants used by Native Americans have been listed in the U.S. pharmacopoeia.[47]

An intriguing possibility is that Native Americans may have learned some things about plants by observing animal behavior. Although we certainly cannot generalize from this single example, chimpanzees in the wild in Africa have been observed to chew and swallow one particular species of *Aspilia* that has a bioactive component and simply to browse the leaves of other species of the plant. Observation of animals' ability to discriminate among plants and of their subsequent behavior might confirm that certain plants have noticeable and curative effects. It is possible, and possibly a subject of future research, to determine how humans could learn about bioactive plants from systematic observation of animal behavior.[48]

Older studies of ethnobotany and medical practices were often purely descriptive lists of plants that might or might not include Native American, common, and botanical names. Scholars recognize that Native Americans have utilized a variety of plants. In the upper Great Lakes region, for example, American Indians used some 220 species of plants for food and medicine.[49] Little attention was paid, however, to the ways in which American Indians might classify plants.[50] Frances Densmore studied the numerous ways Chippewas in Minnesota used plants and provided extensive lists of plants by common and botanical names and their bioactive components. She noted only in passing, however, that medicinal plants were generally used in combinations (a form of grouping plants together), and that a woman said she would have recognized a plant as having medicinal value because of the size and shape of its root, even though she had not seen it before.[51] More recent ethnobotanies are much richer in details concerning environment and cultural beliefs of communities. Janis Alcorn's work, for example, includes a lengthy discussion of Teenek (Maya) cultural beliefs and ways of relating to their environments; Richard Felger's description of the Seri gives a complete picture of the people and their cultural relationship with their homeland on the edge of the Sonoran desert.[52]

way in which anomalies can be used to infer change.[96] Among the Siouan peoples, only the Sioux (Dakota and Lakota) and Assiniboine (Nakota) have terms specifically designating cross cousins. The terms used for cross cousins consist of the sibling-in-law terms to which is added the suffix -shi, which is a marker of respect. Beginning with the early work of Rivers, and continuing with Eggan, these cross-cousin terms have been interpreted as evidence of the former practice of cross-cousin marriage, with the assumption that at some past time that custom was abandoned, and the new status of cross cousins (formerly siblings-in-law) was indicated by suffixing the respect marker. Since cross-cousin marriage was practiced by some neighboring tribes, notably the Ojibwe, it is reasonable to conjecture that it was also practiced by the Dakota and Assiniboine.[97] Eggan's argument for the abandonment of cross-cousin marriage, based on the work of Royal Hassrick, was an ecological one: as the Dakota moved onto the plains and became engaged in buffalo hunting, cooperation between larger groups of men became essential. Since relations between brothers-in-law were strained, cross cousins were removed from the category of brother-in-law, and the close relationship between brothers was extended to cross cousins.[98]

Taking an opposite approach to the problem, Lesser suggested that the introduction of cross-cousin terms reflected the systematic practice of the sororate and levirate. As these marriage practices became obligatory, but restricted to the range of siblings (including parallel cousins), terms were needed to differentiate cross cousins (presumably previously classed with siblings), who were outside the range of relatives involved in the sororate and levirate.[99] Again, the evidence is not conclusive, but Lesser has the advantage of proposing a single argument, the practice of the sororate and levirate, to explain both the Omaha-Crow and Dakota systems. Only further comparative study of Siouan kinship systems is likely to provide greater clarification.

The question of change in the Dakota kinship system is not merely of theoretical interest. It gets at the very nature of the social system. If cross-cousin marriage was practiced historically, it functioned to perpetuate bonds between social groups over generations—that is, as a mechanism for intensifying social ties between groups. Then, if the Dakota decided to outlaw cross-cousin marriage, the effect would be to unite more distant social groups, perhaps less intimately, but forging a wider network of alliances between bands. Clearly, this is consistent with the exigencies of Plains Indian life. On the other hand, written records clearly show that the Dakota were dependent on communal buffalo hunting at least since the mid-seventeenth century, and as far east as western Wisconsin. Thus the pattern of interband cooperative networks must be older than earlier scholars realized, and this argues for the sororate and levirate as effective means of perpetuating alliances between bands over time.

Answers to questions like these will ultimately help to extend our knowledge of the development of American Indian societies back beyond written sources.

For the Writing of History

The writing of Native American history has become a major focus of scholarly work in recent decades but it is fair to say that few histories have seriously and systematically attempted to reconstruct social and kinship systems and use them as the basis for interpreting the dynamics of past action. Robert K. Thomas, the Cherokee anthropologist, was fond of saying, "All Indian history is family history." [100] Without knowledge of kinship and of how bands, villages, lineages, and clans actually function in daily life, and how they affect political and economic decisions, it is not possible to write meaningful accounts of the past with any understanding of native perspectives. Lacking a grounding in social realities, history is limited to Euro-American perspectives.

The field of ethnohistory brings together anthropological and historical methods and interests in the attempt to forge new and deeper, culturally based interpretations of the Native American past. [101] Exemplifying this approach, a number of works have appeared in recent years that attempt to use kinship and social groups as a means for understanding the Dakota and Lakota past. John Wozniak has studied the dynamics of intermarriages between non-Indian fur traders and Dakota women, and the alliances among the mixed-blood families that resulted. Earlier studies assumed that the increasing dependency of the Dakota on trade goods ultimately undermined their society. [102] Wozniak, however, offers a more sophisticated model of social relations between Dakotas and whites in Minnesota that shows how the bonds of kinship effectively provided the political structure for Indian–white relations during the eighteenth century, and outlines stages in the decline of that relationship. Gary Clayton Anderson picked up the same theme and used it to develop a full-scale ethnohistory of the Dakota from 1650 to 1862. [103] Both works argue that the dissolution of kinship as the metaphor for Indian–white relations and the unwillingness of whites in the nineteenth century to continue to operate within the terms of Dakota cultural expectations of relationship ultimately erupted in violence during the Dakota Conflict of 1862. The relationships based on actual bonds of kinship and marriage, and on kinship metaphors, are the foundation for that accommodation between American Indians and Euro-Americans that Richard White later designated the "middle ground." [104]

For the Lakota, Catherine Price has written a history of the Oglala that uses anthropological sources to develop a model of social and political life based on the band system. The work is important for what it attempts, though ultimately most of the social analysis remains outside the narrative history. The challenge of integrating the two, given the paucity of historical documentation of specific band and kinship relations, is great.[105] In a brief article, I used the proceedings of Plains Indian treaty councils to demonstrate the tactical uses of kinship in establishing political relationships. U.S. commissioners, for example, were quick to refer to Indian peoples as the president's "red children." Lakota leaders took two strategies to counter this, which they must have seen as an attempt to establish kin relationships. One was to call the commissioners brothers, implying equality (and in Lakota kinship the relationship between brothers was such that one could not refuse a brother's request without giving offense); the other was to call them fathers, stress that the Lakota people were "pitiful," and beg the commissioners to act like good fathers and provide them what they requested. These relationships, highlighted by treaty negotiations, were characterized by misunderstanding on both sides, but from an analytical perspective, and a knowledge of Lakota kinship, it is easy to see the political strategies at work.[106]

Historical studies based on the investigation of kinship systems and social groups hold great potential. Only by rooting history in the lived realities of daily life will it be possible to produce studies that truly explicate the past from Native American perspectives. For example, a history of any of the Central Algonquian tribes that reconstructs the role of clans and clan interrelationships in shaping historical events would be a major contribution to the ethnohistorical literature.

For Understanding Native American Societies Today

The study of kinship systems can also reveal more recent changes related to the interaction of Native Americans with non-Indian people. Building on Eggan's study of changes in Choctaw kinship, during the late 1930s Alexander Spoehr documented the kinship systems of a number of southeastern tribes to discover whether the type of change Eggan had discovered, shifting from a Crow-type system to a generational one, was characteristic of the entire area. Spoehr made a particularly detailed study of the Seminole, comparing groups in Florida, who had not left their homeland, with those in Oklahoma, who had been forcibly removed from Florida a century earlier. He also studied the Creek, Cherokee, and Choctaw. Using historical documents and recording contemporary kinship data using the genealogical method, Spoehr discovered a series of systems that he argued represented the stages by which the Crow-type systems had progressively changed to bilateral ones. Like Eggan, he argued that the cause of the change was acculturation to Euro-American society and culture.[107]

Valuable as Spoehr's data are for documenting change, a great deal more can be said about the causes of change. By presenting his kinship data in the form of genealogies, Spoehr failed to record information essential to their interpretation. Intermarriages with members of other tribes and with non-Indians doubtless explain some anomalies, but the more significant questions, perhaps, have to do with education and with language use. The Bureau of Indian Affairs imposed a system of inheritance and surnames, giving an emphasis on patrilineal descent formerly unknown to these matrilineal peoples. The introduction of English also brought with it an entirely different classification of kin. The context in which a particular relationship was invoked, and the language spoken between relatives, were significant factors. Rather than representing stages in kinship change, Spoehr's genealogies may represent the aggregate of individuals' decisions about whether to use the traditional Crow-type system or the bilateral American one.

A parallel study was undertaken by Edward Bruner during the early 1950s on the Fort Berthold Reservation in North Dakota among the Hidatsa and Mandan, whose historical kinship systems were also of the Crow type. Rather than intermediate types, he found that his consultants used either the Crow-type system or the bilateral one; there was no mixing of systems. Since Hidatsa was the language of daily interaction, the Crow system was more frequently used. When speaking English (since most people were bilingual), individuals used English terms in the patterns of the Crow system, which Bruner argued represented not an alternate system, but merely a translation of the structure of one system into the words of another. The second kinship pattern in the community consisted of English terms used in the American generational pattern. This pattern was used in acculturated families, and when addressing non-Indians outside the village. Anomalies in kinship usage were largely explicable in terms of intermarriages with Indians from other tribes and with non-Indians.[108]

In 1970 I recorded kin terms on the Cheyenne River Sioux reservation in South Dakota and found the same pattern as described by Bruner.[109] Virtually everyone with whom I discussed kinship was clearly aware of the differences between the historical Lakota system and that of English. Children talked about being laughed at in school when they referred to their "mothers" or "fathers," and soon learned to use the acceptable expression, "Indian mother," or "father, Indian way." Personal names—usually nicknames acquired during an individual's school years—had largely replaced kin terms for daily interaction, but in times of crisis or need, kin terms, either in Lakota or in English, were invariably invoked. Virtually all serious requests were prefaced with a kin term. Hoping to discover evidence for change in the system, I was delighted one day when an elderly woman gave me the mother's brother term when I asked for father's brother, and the father's sister term when I asked for mother's sister. When I returned to check this with her, she commented, "Of course, that's not what I would say." Then it hit me: I had framed the question as, "What do I call my *X*," and making allowances for the English kin term system, my consultant had dutifully given me what she thought I wanted.

The only changes I could discover in the structure of the Lakota system represented borrowings. Since the Lakota system lacked terms for brother or sister
in general (without specifying age), when speaking Lakota people would incorporate the English words "brother" and "sister" into Lakota grammar—a
rare case of borrowing in a language normally very resistant to it.

As a final example, Anne S. Straus studied kinship among the Northern
Cheyenne of Montana during the 1980s and compared modern usage with
that recorded by Eggan for the Southern Cheyenne in 1933. She found that
the Northern and Southern Cheyenne systems were identical, and that only
a few minor changes had occurred in a half-century. Some Cheyennes, she
reported, used the mother's brother term for father's brother. Some speakers
also used an alternative word for mother's sister, meaning "second mother,"
to designate father's sister as well. The influence of the English kinship system
was apparent, although, on the basis of a consultant's comments, Straus concluded that gender was also a relevant factor; males continued to differentiate
mothers' brothers from fathers' brothers, and females continued to differentiate mother's sisters from fathers' sisters. The use of personal names in place
of kin terms paralleled the Lakota practice.[110]

Kinship in Native American Studies

Kinship has attracted virtually no attention in the field of Native American
studies. The reasons for this are not clear, but one of them is probably that kinship has always been the concern of anthropology, and that the maze of charts
and kin terminologies makes it an esoteric and seemingly irrelevant scholarly
preoccupation. A well-meaning colleague once invited me to write an article
on American Indian kinship systems, but quickly added, "Spare us the charts!"
I declined. Kinship is, in fact, an elaborated focus of anthropological study
that has a long history. Thinking and behaving in terms of kinship is second
nature to Native American people; objectifying the principles that underlie
kinship behavior makes kinship systems seem formidably complex. Yet, like
languages, they are simple enough for children to learn in every society.

Nothing is more convincing of the significance of kinship than to see what
happens when kinship fails as a social mechanism. Anastasia M. Shkilnyk's
study of the Grassy Narrows Ojibwe in Ontario presents such a case study.
Until 1963 the people lived on their traditional lands, isolated from Canadian
society, camping during the summer on their reserve, and going in the winter to
trap. Hunting, fishing, and gathering provided much of their livelihood, supplemented with occasional wage labor. They lived in extended families of twenty
to twenty-five people, organized around two or more brothers, or a man and
his sons. Ojibwe society is based on patrilineal clans; at Grassy Narrows the
extended families (patrilineages) were economically self-sufficient and were

the most important social units. The band itself gathered for only a few social events, including naming ceremonies for children and feasts for the dead.[111]

In 1963 the government moved the Grassy Narrows people to a new reserve only five miles to the south, to establish a school, provide electricity, and give the people access to a nearby town. At the same time alcohol was introduced to the reserve. In the move the extended families were uprooted and dissolved; the seasonal pattern of trapping and making a living from the land came to an end. Even fishing ended. In 1970 the provincial government discovered that the rivers and lakes in the area were so polluted with mercury (originating in pulp and paper plants upstream) that the fish were unsafe for human consumption.[112] Within a decade, Shkilnyk writes, the traditional patterns of behavior between kin had disintegrated; promiscuity and sexual assaults had become general, with an escalating number of births out of wedlock and very young girls becoming mothers; families began to engage in binge drinking; crime and violence, formerly unknown in the community, escalated; health declined; children were neglected and abused; the death rate for infants and children soared. Shkilnyk reports the chilling words spoken by one community member summing up the social situation in the early 1980s: "The only thing I know about alcohol is that alcohol is a stronger power than the love of children. It's a poison, and we are a broken people." [113]

When talking about the past, Shkilnyk reports, the people of Grassy Narrows "invariably begin by describing their close ties to the family—the grandparents, parents, aunts, uncles, and cousins who formed the community of residence on the winter trapline and in the summer encampment." Can that past be recaptured? Again, a community member summed it up poignantly: "I don't think so." Too much has been lost; the people are weak, and would be unable to survive on the trapline. But there is even more loss: "When we lived as families on the old reserve, we had our spiritual elders. . . . Now, this religion is missing from the new reserve. There is no knowledge to give to the next generation. . . . Now we have nothing." [114] The disintegration of kinship, then, not only affects the relations among community members, but has cut the people off from the kin relationships with other-than-human beings that gave meaning to life and allowed humans to share in the power of the spirits.

Grassy Narrows is an extreme case, but it is not atypical. The problems of alcohol and drugs, gangs and violence, plague Native American communities today. One resource that can be effective in countering contemporary problems is the potential that lies in traditional kinship and social systems. On the Pine Ridge Reservation, for example, leaders have been talking for many years about utilizing the traditional band or extended family (*tiyoshpaye*) system to rejuvenate community life. Recently, with grant support from the Northwest Area Foundation, organizations have been created to develop the human potential of the reservation. At Oglala Lakota College, the Lakota Elders Traditional

Government Omniciye (LETGO) was founded in 1991 and held a series of forums on topics intended to reorganize tribal government from the bottom up, basing a renewed tribal government on the fundamental unit of society, the *tiyoshpaye*. Placing authority in the hands of the *tiyoshpaye* would involve the people in government in a manner not possible now, when councilmen are elected from eight reservation districts established under the Indian Reorganization Act constitution in 1934. According to a 1992 report, the first forum addressed the roles of men and women, giving primacy to the kinship system on which the *tiyoshpaye* depend.[115]

Lakol Ikce Oyate Peta Ilekiyap ("Rekindling the Camp Fires of a Nation"), a community development project, resulted from the forums of 1992–93. According to its 1995 report, the project is designed to provide leadership in revitalizing traditional culture and social structure. The report estimates that the number of *tiyoshpaye* on Pine Ridge is between sixty and one hundred. The project seeks to empower the people and encourage the *tiyoshpaye* to work together.[116]

Such organizations reveal commitment to revitalization, not to preservation. The clear objective is to transform traditional social organization into a mechanism for government in the modern world. Membership in *tiyoshpaye* would be determined first by a census of lineal descendants of the original *tiyoshpaye;* then the community could accept others as members who were not descendants. The plan is idealistic, and founded on years of experience with Bureau of Indian Affairs record keeping, but nonetheless outlines an active strategy for rejuvenating communities and dealing with the social problems of today on the basis of the traditional strengths of the kinship system.

Kinship is fundamental to every aspect of Native American studies, from literature to history to the social sciences. It is time that scholars in the field begin to explore the richness of the Native American social heritage, and find creative ways to build on it for the future.

Notes

1. Lewis H. Morgan, *League of the Ho-de-no-sau-nee, or Iroquois* (Rochester: Sage and Brother, 1851), 84.

2. Ibid., 85.

3. Lewis H. Morgan, "Laws of descent of the Iroquois," *Proceedings of the American Association for the Advancement of Science,* 11 (1857), 132–48.

4. Lewis H. Morgan, [Journal of progress on the study of American Indian systems of consanguinity], October 19, 1859, 6, Lewis Henry Morgan Collection, Special Collections, Rush Rhees Library, University of Rochester. See Fred Eggan, *The American Indian: Perspectives for the Study of Social Change* (Chicago: Aldine, 1966), 1–8.

5. Lewis H. Morgan, [Circular letter], October 1, 1859. Morgan Collection, University of Rochester.

6. Leslie White, ed., *Lewis Henry Morgan: The Indian Journals* (Ann Arbor: University of Michigan Press, 1959).

7. Morgan, [Circular letter], October 1, 1859, 1.

8. Ibid., 5.

9. Lewis H. Morgan, *Systems of Consanguinity and Affinity of the Human Family,* Smithsonian Contributions to Knowledge, vol. 17 (Washington, D.C.: Smithsonian Institution, 1871). See also reprint ed. with an introduction by Elisabeth Tooker (Lincoln: University of Nebraska Press, 1997).

10. Morgan, *Systems of Consanguinity and Affinity* (1871), 479–94.

11. Lewis H. Morgan, *Ancient Society, or: Researches in the Lines of Human Progress from Savagery Through Barbarism to Civilization* (Chicago: Charles H. Kerr, 1908 [1877]).

12. Ibid., 3–6, 36.

13. Ibid., 8, 563.

14. Ibid., 18, 37–38. Morgan's evolutionary scheme provided the inspiration for Engel's 1884 work, *Origin of the Family, Private Property, and the State,* Ernest Untermann, trans. (Moscow: Foreign Languages Publishing House, 1954).

15. Morgan, *Ancient Society,* 10–11, 39–40.

16. J. W. Powell, *First Annual Report of the Bureau of Ethnology* (Washington, D.C., 1881), xv.

17. J. Owen Dorsey, "On the gentile system of the Omahas," *Bulletin of the Philosophical Society of Washington,* 3 (1878–80), 128–37.

18. J. W. Powell, remarks on Dorsey, "On the gentile system of the Omahas," ibid., 137–38.

19. Morgan, *Systems of Consanguinity and Affinity,* 147.

20. J. Owen Dorsey, "Omaha sociology," in *Third Annual Report of the Bureau of Ethnology* (Washington, D.C., 1884), 254.

21. Regna Diebold Darnell, "The development of American anthropology 1879–1920: From the Bureau of American Ethnology to Franz Boas" (Ph.D. diss., University of Pennsylvania, 1969), 467.

22. Melville J. Herskovits, *Franz Boas: The Science of Man in the Making* (New York: Charles Scribner's Sons, 1953).

23. Franz Boas, "The aims of ethnology," in *The Shaping of American Anthropology, 1883–1911: A Franz Boas Reader,* George W. Stocking, Jr., ed. (New York: Basic Books, 1974), 69.

24. George W. Stocking, Jr., "The basic assumptions of Boasian anthropology," in *The Shaping of American Ethnology,* 1–20.

25. Most of these essays were written by J. N. B. Hewitt, a long-time bureau member, and by two students of Boas, John R. Swanton (also on the bureau staff) and Robert H. Lowie. *Handbook of American Indians North of Mexico,* Bureau of American Ethnology Bulletin 30, Frederick Webb Hodge, ed., 2 vols. (Washington, D.C.: Government Printing Office, 1907–10).

26. W. H. R. Rivers, "A genealogical method of collecting social and vital statistics," *Journal of the Royal Anthropological Institute,* 30 (1900), 74–82.

27. W. H. R. Rivers, "On the origin of the classificatory system of relationships,"

in *Anthropological Essays Presented to Edward Burnett Tylor in Honour of His 70th Birthday Oct. 2 1907* (Oxford: Clarendon Press, 1907), 309–33. Subsequently, Rivers abandoned his belief in evolutionary explanations and embraced diffusionism to account for similarities of culture. See David M. Schneider, "Rivers and Kroeber on the study of kinship," in W. H. R. Rivers, *Kinship and Social Organization,* London School of Economics Monographs on Social Anthropology, No. 34 (New York: Humanities Press, 1968 [1914]), 7–16.

28.   A. L. Kroeber, "Classificatory systems of relationship," *Journal of the Royal Anthropological Institute of Great Britain and Ireland,* 39 (1909), 77–84.

29.   Franz Boas, "The origin of totemism," *American Anthropologist,* 18 (1916), 319–26; reprinted in Franz Boas, *Race, Language and Culture* (Chicago: University of Chicago Press, 1982 [1940]), 316–23.

30.   For example, in a classic paper on Lakota kinship published in 1914 in the *American Anthropologist,* the printer setting up parallel columns jumbled the relationship between the Lakota terms and their English equivalents—a fact that seems to have gone unremarked in the literature until 1982. James R. Walker, "Oglala kinship terms," *American Anthropologist,* 16 (1914), 96–109; James R. Walker, *Lakota Society,* Raymond J. DeMallie, ed. (Lincoln: University of Nebraska Press, 1982), 4, 46–49.

31.   Robert H. Lowie, *Culture and Ethnology* (New York: Douglas McMurtrie, 1917), 98.

32.   Ibid., 99, 175.

33.   Robert H. Lowie, *Primitive Society* (New York: Harper and Brothers, 1961 [1920]).

34.   Leslie Spier, "The distribution of kinship systems in North America," *University of Washington Publications in Anthropology,* 1, no. 2 (1925).

35.   Gladys A. Reichard, *Social Life of the Navajo Indians, with Some Attention to Minor Ceremonies,* Columbia University Contributions to Anthropology, vol. 7 (New York: Columbia University Press, 1928).

36.   Ibid., 20.

37.   Theresa Mayer Durlach, *The Relationship Systems of the Tlingit, Haida and Tsimshian,* Publications of the American Ethnological Society, vol. 11 (New York: G. E. Stechert, 1928).

38.   Ibid., 14–15.

39.   Ibid., 164–65.

40.   Alexander Lesser, personal communication.

41.   Although it was written in 1929, administrative oversight and lack of funds to publish it kept Lesser's dissertation from being formally submitted until thirty years later. Alexander Lesser, "Siouan kinship" (Ph.D. diss., Columbia University, 1958). The conclusions of the dissertation were published in Alexander Lesser, "Some aspects of Siouan kinship," *Proceedings of the Twenty-Third International Congress of Americanists* (1930), 563–71.

42.   W. D. Strong, "Cross-cousin marriage and the culture of the northeast Algonkian," *American Anthropologist,* 31 (1929): 777–88.

43.   A. I. Hallowell, "Was cross-cousin marriage formerly practiced by the North-Central Algonkian?" *Proceedings of the Twenty-Third International Congress of Americanists* (1930), 519–44.

44. See discussion in Fred Eggan, "Social anthropology: Methods and results," in *Social Anthropology of North American Tribes,* enlarged ed., Fred Eggan, ed. (Chicago: University of Chicago Press, 1955), 532–38; Eggan, *The American Indian,* 78–111.

45. A. R. Radcliffe-Brown, "On the concept of function in social science," *American Anthropologist,* 37 (1935), 394–402.

46. A. R. Radcliffe-Brown, "On social structure," *Journal of the Royal Anthropological Institute,* 70 (1940), 1–12.

47. A. R. Radcliffe-Brown, *The Social Organization of Australian Tribes,* Oceania Monographs, no. 1 (Melbourne, 1931).

48. Fred Eggan, "Among the anthropologists," *Annual Review of Anthropology,* 3 (1974), 8.

49. Fred Eggan, ed., *Social Anthropology of North American Tribes* (Chicago: University of Chicago Press, 1937).

50. Fred Eggan, "The Cheyenne and Arapaho kinship system," ibid., 39–41. Eggan later developed his ideas about comparative study into a formal method. See Fred Eggan, "Social anthropology and the method of controlled comparison," *American Anthropologist,* 56 (1954), 743–63.

51. See Raymond J. DeMallie, "Fred Eggan and American Indian anthropology," in *North American Indian Anthropology: Essays on Society and Culture,* Raymond J. DeMallie and Alfonso Ortiz, eds. (Norman: University of Oklahoma Press, 1994), 3–12.

52. Written in 1933, the dissertation, in revised form, was published in 1950. Fred Eggan, *Social Anthropology of the Western Pueblos* (Chicago: University of Chicago Press, 1950).

53. Eggan, "The Cheyenne and Arapaho kinship system," 35–95.

54. Ibid., 93.

55. Fred Eggan, "Historical changes in the Choctaw kinship system," *American Anthropologist,* 39 (1937), 34–52.

56. Eggan, *The American Indian,* 38.

57. Eggan, "Social anthropology: Methods and results," 485–551.

58. Eggan, *The American Indian.*

59. DeMallie and Ortiz, *North American Indian Anthropology.*

60. George Peter Murdock, *Social Structure* (New York: Macmillan, 1949), 183.

61. Claude Lévi-Strauss, *Structural Anthropology* (New York: Basic Books, 1963).

62. The best discussion is in David M. Schneider, "Some muddles in the models: or, How the system really works," in *The Relevance of Models for Social Anthropology,* Association of Social Anthropologists of the Commonwealth Monographs, no. 1, Michael Banton, ed. (London: Tavistock, 1965).

63. Floyd G. Lounsbury, "A semantic analysis of the Pawnee kinship usage," *Language,* 32 (1956), 158–94.

64. David M. Schneider and John M. Roberts, *Zuni Kin Terms,* Laboratory of Anthropology, University of Nebraska, Notebook no. 3, Monograph 2 (Lincoln: Laboratory of Anthropology, 1956), 17–18.

65. David M. Schneider, *A Critique of the Study of Kinship* (Ann Arbor: University of Michigan Press, 1984), 193–201.

66. Joseph Maxwell, "Biology and social relationship in the kin terminology of an Inuit community," in DeMallie and Ortiz, *North American Indian Anthropology,* 36.

67. Anne S. Straus, "Northern Cheyenne kinship reconsidered," ibid., 153.

68. Gary Witherspoon, *Navajo Kinship and Marriage* (Chicago: University of Chicago Press, 1975), 120.

69. Gene Weltfish, *The Lost Universe: With a Closing Chapter on "The Universe Regained"* (New York: Basic Books, 1965), 14–19.

70. Dorsey, "Omaha sociology," 219.

71. William H. Gilbert, Jr., "Eastern Cherokee social organization," in Eggan, *Social Anthropology of North American Tribes,* 287; Dorsey, "Omaha sociology," 219–20.

72. Witherspoon, *Navajo Kinship and Marriage,* 40.

73. Alice C. Fletcher and Francis La Flesche, *The Omaha Tribe, Twenty-Seventh Annual Report of the Bureau of American Ethnology for the Years 1905–1906* (Washington, D.C., 1911), 135.

74. Alfonso Ortiz, *The Tewa World: Space, Time, Being, and Becoming in a Pueblo Society* (Chicago: University of Chicago Press, 1969), 43–44. For a valuable discussion of clans and moieties, see Elisabeth Tooker, "Clans and moieties in North America," *Current Anthropology,* 12 (1971), 357–76.

75. For discussion of Cheyenne bands, see John H. Moore, *The Cheyenne Nation: A Social and Demographic History* (Lincoln: University of Nebraska Press, 1987), 27–51.

76. Royal B. Hassrick, *The Sioux: Life and Customs of a Warrior Society* (Norman: University of Oklahoma Press, 1964), 3–31; Thomas W. Kavanagh, *Comanche Political History: An Ethnohistorical Perspective, 1706–1875* (Lincoln: University of Nebraska Press, 1996), 1–27.

77. William N. Fenton, "Northern Iroquoian culture patterns," in *Handbook of North American Indians,* vol. 15, *Northeast,* Bruce Trigger, ed., William C. Sturtevant, gen. ed. (Washington, D.C.: Smithsonian Institution, 1978), 314.

78. Kalervo Oberg, *The Social Economy of the Tlingit Indians,* American Ethnological Society Monograph, no. 55 (Seattle: University of Washington Press, 1973), 23.

79. Harold Hickerson, *The Chippewa and Their Neighbors: A Study in Ethnohistory* (New York: Holt, Rinehart and Winston, 1970), 49–50.

80. Gilbert, "Eastern Cherokee social organization," 296.

81. Stewart Rafert, *The Miami Indians of Indiana: A Persistent People, 1654–1994* (Indianapolis: Indiana Historical Society, 1996), 283–96.

82. A. Irving Hallowell, "Ojibwa ontology, behavior, and world view," in *Culture in History: Essays in Honor of Paul Radin,* Stanley Diamond, ed. (New York: Columbia University Press, 1960), 21–23.

83. Witherspoon, *Navajo Kinship and Marriage,* 42, 120.

84. Ibid., 21.

85. Ibid., 126.

86. This section draws on Raymond J. DeMallie, "Kinship and biology in Sioux culture," in DeMallie and Ortiz, *North American Indian Anthropology,* 125–46; see Ella Deloria, *Speaking of Indians* (New York: Friendship Press, 1944), 24–49.

87. For an especially effective presentation of this contrast in kinship behavior in novelistic form, see Ella Cara Deloria, *Waterlily* (Lincoln: University of Nebraska Press, 1988), 162–87.

88. This section is based on Dorsey, "Omaha sociology"; Fletcher and La Flesche, *Omaha Tribe;* and R. H. Barnes, *Two Crows Denies It: A History of Controversy in Omaha Sociology* (Lincoln: University of Nebraska Press, 1984).

89. This section is based on Oberg, *Social Economy of the Tlingit Indians,* 23–38.

90. Adapted from Oberg, ibid., 36.

91. Alexander Lesser, "Caddoan kinship systems," *Nebraska History,* 60 (1979), 267–68; Weltfish, *Lost Universe,* 21.

92. This section draws on DeMallie, "Kinship and biology in Sioux culture."

93. Charles F. Hockett, "The Proto Central Algonquian kinship system," in *Explorations in Cultural Anthropology: Essays in Honor of George P. Murdock,* Ward H. Goodenough, ed. (New York: McGraw-Hill, 1964), 239–57; Isidore Dyen and David F. Aberle, *Lexical Reconstruction: The Case of the Proto-Athapaskan Kinship System* (London: Cambridge University Press, 1974); Lesser, "Some aspects of Siouan kinship"; Lesser, "Siouan kinship"; G. Hubert Matthews, "Proto-Siouan kinship terminology," *American Anthropologist,* 61 (1958), 252–78.

94. Lesser, "Some aspects of Siouan kinship," 567–68; Lesser, "Siouan kinship," 319–20.

95. Matthews, "Proto-Siouan kinship terminology," 275.

96. The Dakota cross-cousin terms are also discussed in DeMallie, "Kinship and biology in Sioux culture," 240–41.

97. Rivers, *Kinship and Social Organization,* 69–70; Eggan, *Social Anthropology of North American Tribes* (1955), 544–45; Eggan, *The American Indian,* 98–104.

98. Eggan, *The American Indian,* 53–56, 99–100; Royal B. Hassrick, "The Teton Dakota kinship system," *American Anthropologist,* 46 (1944), 338–47; Symmes C. Oliver, *Ecology and Cultural Continuity as Contributing Factors in the Social Organization of the Plains Indians,* University of California Publications in American Archaeology and Ethnology, vol. 48 (Berkeley: University of California Press, 1962).

99. Lesser, "Siouan kinship," 217–18, 221–22.

100. Personal communication, 1970s, at the Newberry Library, Chicago, and at Indiana University.

101. For discussion of the potential of the ethnohistorical method, see Raymond J. DeMallie, " 'These have no ears': Narrative and the ethnohistorical method," *Ethnohistory,* 40 (1993), 515–38.

102. John S. Wozniak, *Contact, Negotation and Conflict: An Ethnohistory of the Eastern Dakota, 1819–1839* (Washington, D.C.: University Press of America, 1978).

103. Gary Clayton Anderson, *Kinsmen of Another Kind: Dakota–White Relations in the Upper Mississippi Valley, 1650–1862* (Lincoln: University of Nebraska Press, 1984).

104. Richard White, *The Middle Ground: Indians, Empires, and Republics in the Great Lakes Region, 1650–1815* (Cambridge: Cambridge University Press, 1991).

105. Catherine Price, *The Oglala People, 1841–1879: A Political History* (Lincoln: University of Nebraska Press, 1996).

106. Raymond J. DeMallie, "Touching the pen: Plains Indian treaty councils in ethnohistorical perspective," in *Ethnicity on the Great Plains,* Frederick C. Luebke, ed. (Lincoln: University of Nebraska Press, 1980), 38–53.

107. Eggan, "Historical changes in the Choctaw kinship system"; Alexander

Spoehr, "Kinship system of the Seminole," *Field Museum of Natural History Anthropological Studies,* vol. 33 (2); Alexander Spoehr, "Changing kinship systems," *Field Museum of Natural History Anthropological Studies,* vol. 33 (4).

108. Edward M. Bruner, "Two processes of change in Mandan-Hidatsa kinship terminology," *American Anthropologist,* 57 (1955), 840–50.

109. This discussion draws on Raymond J. DeMallie, "Change in American Indian kinship systems: The Dakota," in *Currents in Anthropology: Essays in Honor of Sol Tax,* Robert Hinshaw, ed. (The Hague: Mouton, 1979), 221–41.

110. Straus, "Northern Cheyenne kinship reconsidered," 158–64.

111. Anastasia M. Shkilnyk, *A Poison Stronger Than Love: The Destruction of an Ojibwa Community* (New Haven: Yale University Press, 1985), 2, 80.

112. Ibid., 187–89.

113. Ibid., 45–48.

114. Ibid., 79–85.

115. Gerald One Feather and Elgin Bad Wound, *A Report on the Lakota Elders Traditional Government Omniciye* (Pine Ridge, S.D.: Oglala Lakota College, 1992).

116. *Lakol Ikce Oyate Peta Ilekiyap: A Community Development Project on the Pine Ridge Reservation,* annual report (Martin, S.D., 1995).

13 *Clara Sue Kidwell and Peter Nabokov*

Directions in Native American Science and Technology

There are profound cultural differences in the ways contemporary Americans understand their relationship to the natural world and the ways Native Americans understood it before European contact and up to the mid-twentieth century. Both understandings, however, constitute the essence of science, defined in the broadest sense as modes of explaining the phenomena of the natural world. George Sarton, founder of the discipline of the history of science, for example, offered as a definition "systematized positive knowledge." [1]

The positivism of western science represents a particular intellectual stance toward the nature of knowledge. The practice of that science, however, depends upon systematic observation of natural phenomena, the assumption that natural phenomena act in regular patterns susceptible to human understanding, and the belief that, through manipulation of events, people can discern causal relationships among natural phenomena. Native Americans also practiced systematic observation of phenomena, recorded their observations in various permanent forms (e.g., markers, building alignments, hieroglyphic writing in Mesoamerica), and recognized patterns in the behavior of natural phenomena.

In both western and Native American science, knowledge of patterns allows for the prediction of events, and with the ability to predict comes an element of control over the environment. The divergence of western and Native American scientific activities came with the emphasis on experimentation, which was a hallmark of the western European scientific revolution of the seventeenth century. Galileo supposedly tested the rate of acceleration of falling bodies by dropping cannon balls from the Leaning Tower of Pisa, verifying empirically his mathematical law that speed was uniform despite differences in weight. Although that event may not have occurred, the account demonstrates a shift in emphasis toward a physically real world rather than a mathematically abstract and ideal one.[2] Thus, the development of experimental science rested on the positivist assumption of the knowability of the physical world.

Native people in North and South America saw "natural" phenomena as manifestations of spiritual forces that exhibited will and volition, or "personhood." [3] Beyond the seasonal growing cycles of plants and animals and the movements of celestial bodies, natural phenomena acted in ways that often defied patterns. Native Americans sought to influence the actions of environmental forces by establishing personal relationships with them through ceremonial activity.

In western science, experiments allow people to predict with some certainty the degree to which events will recur given similar circumstances; manipulation of variables allows for testing of hypotheses about the outcome of events. In Native American cultures, however, human beings affect the ultimate outcome of natural processes. Appropriate symbols of reciprocal exchange and proper adherence to ritual protocols assure that the spirits will respond appropriately. Thus, sun-watchers in the traditional Hopi villages in Arizona still preserve the ancient practice of watching the horizon at sunrise every day for approximately a month before the date of the winter solstice. They mark the passage of the sun's daily rising by certain physical features of the landscape and note when it reaches its northern house, the farthest northernmost point of rising. The solstice is essential to the timing of the Soyal ceremony, held to give the sun the energy it needs to leave its northern house and begin its journey back across the sky toward its summer house. The Hopi would not think of experimenting by foregoing the Soyal ceremony to see if the Sun would remain in the north. To do so would be to risk the prospect that the seasons would not change and their harvest would fail. Such a result would destroy the Hopi as a people.[4]

The study of Native Americans has been the province of anthropology, a positivist yet culturally based enterprise. Early ethnographers studied Native Americans from the perspective that they represented "primitive" ways of thinking from which advanced cultures evolved.[5] Anthropologists also studied material culture—that is, human-made objects—as they constituted the basis for definition of "culture areas." [6] This primarily materialist approach to culture saw environmental management as an economic system. Some studies examined the evidence for independent invention of environmental management techniques in the Americas as opposed to older diffusionist models of cultural spread; for example, did the Iroquois use fish as a fertilizer before European contact?[7] Others tested the empirically verifiable results of native practices.[8] The study of Native American "science" has also occurred in a variety of other disciplines; however, these studies—of "ethno-" geography, biology, zoology, and botany—have been generally descriptive rather than analytical.[9]

Behind these varying approaches and disciplinary methods, we need to find a unifying framework. By defining native science, we can bring these disparate bodies of knowledge together. Taken together, the studies can provide insight into Native American intellectual processes from systematic understanding of human relationships to the physical environment, and a greater appreciation for activities that can be defined as scientific.

The major areas to be explored in this chapter are the intellectual realms of observation and recording of long-term cycles in the heavens (archaeoastronomy, calendar systems, and mathematics), native knowledge about plants and their uses (ethnobotany), methods of controlling the environment (resource management and agriculture), and technology in the use of natural materials (metallurgy, weaving, and architecture).

Archaeoastronomy and Ethnoastronomy

Native peoples throughout the Americas were keen observers of celestial phenomena and kept accurate records of the movements of the sun, moon, stars, and certain planets. In the temperate latitudes, the emphasis was upon observation of events along the horizon, particularly solstices and the rising and setting of certain stars. In the tropics, the orientation was directly above, as the movement of the stars was overhead.[10]

We find the greatest correlation between native practices and contemporary science in astronomical observation. Astronomy is an observational, not an experimental, science. It depends upon systematic observation and the accumulation of data over extended periods, periods usually greater than the lifetime of a single observer. It also requires some form of record keeping. There are many intriguing research questions to be addressed in the study of archaeoastronomy. Is there a connection between the development of the state and the rise of complex astronomical systems? Why should astronomy, of all human endeavors, serve as a focus for organizing social activity? What institutions are supported by astronomical knowledge, and how do they promote the development of astronomy?[11]

The major sites for archaeoastronomical research are in more sedentary, agricultural, and incipient state societies where writing systems existed. Mayan scholars produced hieroglyphic records of their observations, although very few escaped destruction after the Spanish conquest of Mesoamerica. Named after the European library in which it was eventually discovered, the Dresden codex contains mathematical notations describing the movements of the

planet Venus and a table of lunar eclipse predictions. Although the numerical values in the Dresden codex table are consistent in recording the 584-day
cycle of Venus, they contain corrections to bring the dates of actual sightings of the appearance and disappearance of the planet into alignment with
the mathematical pattern of notation. The table is not a record of actual observations but likely a marker for ceremonial or political events. It was made to
correspond, however, to observational data, much as the Gregorian calendar
adds a corrective leap year.[12] The Paris codex offers some evidence that the
Mayans might have had an ecliptic and a zodiac.[13]

Other records of astronomical observations are found in buildings such as
the Caracol Tower at Chichen Itza, the ruins of a Mayan site in the Yucatan Peninsula dating to about A.D. 800. The Caracol, a circular tower rising
two stories above a flat-topped base, may be an astronomical observatory. Its
four outer doors are oriented toward the cardinal directions. Inside is a circular corridor, from which four doors open into yet another circular corridor
that surrounds a central core within which a spiral staircase leads to the top
of the tower. Near the top of the tower three shafts pierce the thick walls,
and their orientations align with the vernal and autumnal equinoxes. One can
observe the disappearance of the Pleiades from the sky on the date of the vernal equinox. The alignments also correspond to the further northernmost and
southernmost helical rising of the planet Venus, the most important celestial
body after the sun and moon for the Maya.[14] In North America there is a physical marker of astronomical observation at Fajada Butte near the Pueblo ruins
in Chaco Canyon, New Mexico. A spiral carved into a rock face is bisected by
a dagger of light on the day of the summer solstice.[15]

The Pleiades were an important point of reference for astronomical observation in many cultures. In the northern hemisphere they appear in the night
sky in the fall and remain visible until the spring, when they disappear below
the horizon. The dates of their first and last appearance depend upon the latitude of the observer, but they appear at about the time of the first killing frost
and they remain in the sky until about the time of the last frost. They are thus
a distinctive marker of the seasons for agricultural people.

At approximately 42° north latitude, the Seneca communities in present-day
New York State observe the first rising of the Pleiades generally between October 10 and 15, which often corresponds to the first frost, and their disappearance generally between May 15 and 19, when the last frost generally occurs.
Seneca corn requires approximately 120 days of frost-free weather to appear
and mature, and the zenith passage of the Pleiades marks the midpoint of the
frost season. It was also the signal for the beginning of the traditional Midwinter ceremony. The disappearance and reappearance of the Pleiades encompass
a period of 153 to 163 days, a comfortable margin for the growth of corn.[16]

Although solstice observation is generally associated with agriculturalists, there is evidence that it was also practiced by hunter peoples in North America. Medicine wheels in Saskatchewan indicate that the Blackfeet may have oriented their tipis on a north–south axis that allowed observation of eastern sunrise solstice sites, and oral traditions tell of calendar men who observed the sun to predict certain ceremonies.[17] The medicine wheel in the Big Horn Mountains of Wyoming, a circle of stones with spokes and cairns that form sighting alignments for the summer solstice and possibly for the helical rising of certain bright stars, was created about A.D. 1500 by people who were hunters.[18]

The study of native knowledge of the sky has provided new insights into contemporary cultural world views.[19] An anthropologist studying Mescalero Apache culture was puzzled that an Apache singer could time his singing to end precisely at sunrise, thus "pulling the sun over the horizon" during the girls' puberty ceremony. She finally observed him watching the stars of the Big Dipper move overhead through the opening at the top of the tipi in which the ceremony was held. He was able to time his songs according to their passage.[20]

The Mayan calendar system is renowned for its ability to record cycles of long duration. It builds on the observations of earlier cultures, particularly the Olmec culture (1500–600 B.C.) that preceded it.[21] The Mayans counted time by two systems. One was a sacred calendar of 260 days (the *tzolkin*), which worked like the months in the Gregorian calendar—that is, the numbers 1 to 13 were counted with twenty named days (as we name the days of the week) until the cycle returned to its original point.

The 260-day year is unique among calendar systems, and its origin is obscure. One theory is that it was first devised near the city of Copan, approximately 20° north latitude, where the sun passes directly overhead twice a year. The two zenith passings divide the solar year into periods of 260 and approximately 105 days, and the latter period is the typical planting season.[22] The *tzolkin* may relate to the cycle of the planet Venus, to the 260-day gestation period of the human female, or to the base 20 numerical system of the Maya. Its purpose in the lives of the Maya was, and remains, the prediction of events in a person's life—its astrological significance.[23]

The other part of the calendar system was the 365-day solar year. The Maya calendar did not insert a leap year, and over time the calendar months drifted through the seasons: in terms of a modern calendar system, the month of May would at some point occur in midwinter. Modern scholars have named this solar year the Vague Year. It was marked by eighteen named months, each consisting of twenty numbered days. Five days with special religious significance were added at the end of the cycle. They marked a period of uncertainty before the next cycle of months and days began. Although modern scholars are uncertain about the Vague Year's significance, it was probably used to mark certain ceremonial or political events, since it did not correlate strictly with the seasons, and thus it indicated concerns beyond those of pure subsistence. The relatively recent advance of scholarship in deciphering Mayan glyphic writing has contributed significantly to the interpretation of the Mayan calendar system.[24]

The Sacred Year and the Vague Year created another conjunction, a fifty-two-year cycle. Like two interlocking gears, the 260-day *tzolkin* and the 365-day year began at one point and revolved against each other until that same point was reached. It took 18,980 days (or fifty-two years) to complete this cycle, which was known as the calendar round. The combination of day names in the *tzolkin* and the Vague Year round gave a unique identity to each day in the cycle, which made it possible to record unique historical events.[25]

Finally, the Maya had their important day count, by which they reckoned the absolute number of days in their history. A significant amount of scholarship has been expended on attempts to correlate the Mayan and Julian calendars to determine some historical reality for the Mayan system. Using best estimates from interpolations of the Maya calendar, their day count went back to approximately the third millennium B.C. One specific date is August 12, 3113 B.C.[26]

The Mayan calendar system was important for noting the completion of the fifty-two-year cycle of conjunction between the solar and the ceremonial calendars. This time was marked with special ceremonial observances in both Mayan and Aztec culture. The Aztec, relatively late comers to the Valley of Mexico (in the thirteenth century), inherited the Mayan calendar system and celebrated a ceremony called the "Binding of the Years," which marked the end of the fifty-two-year cycle. It involved the sacrifice of a captive to feed the sun with blood to sustain its strength for the next cycle.[27] Although claims have been made for the impressive accuracy of the Mayans in determining the length of the solar year, it is obvious that whatever the basis for their observations, their overriding concern was the prediction of the continuation of their world, which was based on the elaborate cosmology within which they worked.

In North America we find evidence of a sophisticated knowledge of the correlation between the solar and lunar calendars. A calendar stick made by a Ho-Chunk (Winnebago) religious leader in the nineteenth century recorded not only two precise, nonarithmetic records of observable lunar years of twelve months, but also notations that incorporated a thirteenth intercalary month every three years to bring the lunar calendar into phase with the solar tropical year. This stick represents "the most complex astronomical-calendric, problem-solving device known from the Americas," outside those in Mexico and South America. Its "underlying observational conceptual base" does not originate from those "high" cultures; rather, it is part of an ancient inheritance of hunter-gatherer knowledge carried over from Asia.[28]

Mathematical sophistication in recording large numbers was a characteristic of the Mayan calendrical system, although the numerical system was not used for computational purposes. Mayan mathematics used a base-20 system.

Numbers proceeded as units up to 20, and by powers of twenty afterward, except that, because the numbers explain the calendar system, the third number stood for eighteen units rather than twenty—that is, the number of months in the calendar year, rather than the number of days in the month. Numerals consisted of dots for numbers one to four, a bar for five, and combinations of dots and bars for six through nineteen. Powers were indicated by the vertical placement of sets of dots and bars, higher powers being written above lower powers. An eye-shaped symbol indicated that one sequence of twenty was complete and that another was beginning.

Although the Mayans have gained a reputation for developing the concept of zero long before Europeans adopted the Arabic numerical system with its zero, scholars disagree about the importance of the sequence marker in Mayan mathematics. A zero is important in the manipulation of numbers in division and multiplication, but there is no evidence of these operations in the numerical records that the Mayans left behind. Although one can count the numbers, the concepts behind the system are still to be explored. Codices and stelae can provide clues about the Mayan mathematical system. The system of dots, bars, and ovals used to record numbers can be correlated with such patterns as the frequencies of eclipses of the moon. As Floyd Lounsbury has noted, however, scholars must work through the interpretation of data from solution to problem. We may know the answers, but we do not necessarily know what questions were being asked.[29]

The Aztecs, who succeeded to the intellectual legacy of the Mayans, had entered the Valley of Mexico, subdued tribes around Lake Tezcoco, and established their capital city of Tenochtitlan on an island in the lake by 1325.[30] As military conquerors they compelled subject tribes to pay tribute, and they may have put their inherited numerical system to use in recording amounts of tribute and areas of land.[31]

In North America, a standardized unit of measure appears in physical form in the alignment of mounds in certain sites. Computer analysis of twenty-eight mound sites in the lower Mississippi River Valley revealed a regular pattern of orientation in the rectangular mounds. The native engineers who constructed these mounds around ceremonial plazas had all adopted a common distance measure of 47.5 meters, or increments thereof. Dubbed "the Toltec Module," after an Arkansas site with clear solstitial orientation, this standardized unit of measure might vary slightly—not unlike the inexact use of the "league" in eighteenth-century Europe and America—but American Indian builders throughout the region appeared to use it to space mounds starting from one key mound in a given complex. In the great Mississippian city of Cahokia, for instance, this basic module was "extended in magnitude out to 22 times and even 44 times." Similar spatial distances between earthworks were found at the great Spiro site in eastern Oklahoma. It was also apparent that fully 75 percent of the Mississippian mound sites analyzed featured one or more solar alignments. The alignment of mounds helped to alert a widespread population to the time for harvesting and planting their floodplain gardens. Sites with several mounds generally had one that functioned as the prime observation platform, with sightings generally privileging the winter solstice alignments. But it was clear that the summer solstice as well as equinoctial and even some stellar sightings (most commonly Vega and Sirius) were also important.[32]

The still-young field of archaeoastronomy holds rich promise for future research. For example, Native American peoples have recently begun to produce their own accounts of their knowledge of stars to stand beside the older accounts collected by ethnographers.[33] A comparison of the two should yield both similarities and differences. This and other related topics are clearly within the purview of Native American studies.

Ethnobotany and Medicine

Classification systems are an essential part of the intellectual work of organizing a culture's view of the world. The Linnean system of biological classification is one of the great achievements of western science. It organizes the natural world into culturally specific categories based on form, sexual characteristics, and modes of reproduction of plants. Although Durkheim and Mauss denied to "Naturvolker" the capacity to classify objects because they had no capacity to differentiate themselves from things in their environments, later scholars have given serious attention to native ability to observe and categorize the phenomena in nature.[34] The importance of classification systems to native people is demonstrated by the special status of beings whose form or behavior crosses boundaries within the system. Southeastern Indians, for instance, gave special symbolic significance to bears, turtles, flying squirrels, and Venus flytraps, beings that fell into two of their categories (humans, plants, animals, and birds: Venus flytraps, for example, hunted for their food like humans).[35] The dog has ambiguous status among Northwest Coast people because it can be classified either as an animal or, because of its domesticated status, as human. As humans, dogs may be able to usurp human prerogatives and thus they are feared; for example, there is a fear that they might usurp human speech.[36]

In the 1960s anthropologists began to study native systems of classification of plants and animals in an attempt to understand native cognitive processes and belief systems. Such research, based primarily on analysis of language and linguistic categories, was termed "ethnoscience." Native American systems' proximity to or distance from the categories and explanatory paradigms of western science provided some insight into the cognitive structures of a world view.[37]

Most studies of native classification systems have taken either the ethnoscience approach, based in a theoretical preoccupation with the importance of language as a system of classification, or the "folk science" approach, which takes into account the actual relationship of human beings to their environments.[38] Brent Berlin, Dennis Breedlove, and Peter Raven describe their study of Tzeltal plant classification as botanical ethnography, or "that area of study that attempts to illuminate in a culturally revealing fashion prescientific man's interaction with and relationship to the plant world."[39] Although one might argue with the assertion that native "interaction with and relationship to the plant world" are prescientific, Berlin and his colleagues have made a significant contribution to an understanding of native science.

Native botanical systems are generally based on relationships among plants and between plants, animals, and human beings. The Navajo organize much of their world by gender. Everything from plants to houses to rain is either male or female, based on size, strength, or, for plants, the relative hardness or softness of their stems and foliage. The system is based on analogy to personality traits distinguishing men and women, rather than plants' physical sexual characteristics.[40] The Aztecs used three major categories of plants: form—trees (*quauhtli*), bushes (*quaquauhzin*), and herbs (*xihuitl*); use—food (*quilitl*), ornamental (*yochitl*), medicinal (*patli*); and economics, depending on whether plants were used for building, clothing, or material objects, for which a number of suffixes were used.[41]

Association is another important principle of classification not necessarily based on physical properties. The Navajo, for example, classify bats and insects together because of an origin tradition in which they lived together in a previous world. Badgers belong with predatory animals such as the wolf, mountain lion, bobcat, and lynx, since Navajo stories describe the badger as their "friend."[42]

The Thompson Indians of British Columbia named some plants according to medicinal use, such as *ilie'litu'nEl*, "cough medicine," or *cuxcuxuza*, "grizzly bear berry," berries eaten by grizzly bears. They also based categories on the fact that certain plants generally grew together, so that they could predict the presence of the one by the other. Thus they named the wood betony *(Pedicularis bracteosa) skikens a sha'ket*, meaning "companion of willow weed," because they found it with the willow.[43]

Among the Tzeltal of Chiapas, Mexico, one finds relatively few of the modern botanical categories of plants. Within what western science calls a species, the Tzeltal can distinguish a number of different kinds of beans that are important to them. On the other hand, they may lump numbers of species together under single names when those species are not important to their subsistence.[44] Further, Native American people along the Columbia River distinguish easily among various species of the genus *Lomatium,* making fine discriminations that botanists find difficult to perceive.[45]

Environmental Management and Agriculture

There were no major domesticated animals for food sources or burden bearing in North America, and few in South America. Their absence in North America may have been a result of the belief that animals were under the control of spirits who exercised will and volition. To control their behavior would be an act of arrogance. The Andean peoples of South America domesticated camelids (llama and alpaca) as beasts of burden and sources of wool, and the guinea pig as a minor source of food.[53] Native people were keenly aware of the impact of their activities on the environment. Their intervention in the lives of plants and animals was not immediately apparent because it generally required at least one growing season, sometime more, to take effect. But continuing observation of changes in the environment led to continuing intervention. Knowledge of natural seasonal cycles allowed for prediction of outcomes, and the result was native ability to alter the environment and manage resources. The modern science of ecology has done much to make contemporary Americans more aware of the effect of their actions on the environment, and with that awareness has come a greater appreciation of native practices of environmental control and management.

The major tool for environmental control used by native people was fire. In contemporary society, the U.S. Forest Service has recently recognized the value of frequent, controllable fires in clearing forest areas of accumulations of undergrowth. California Indians systematically burned off areas of chaparral, the low-growing pinon/juniper/scrub oak shrubbery characteristic of the Sierra foothills, to promote new growth as browse for animals. Deer feeding on fired areas produce more and healthier offspring than those in other areas.[54] On the plains, fire drives were used for buffalo hunting, and they also caused the growth of new grass in the burned-over areas. This periodic burning not only replenished the browse for the buffalo; it also held back the perimeters of forests and maintained the extent of grasslands.[55] On the east coast, early European travelers and explorers described the parklike aspect of the forests, where stands of trees shaded grassy areas that were maintained by periodic burning. The brushy understory characteristic of the New England forests today was burned off frequently enough that it never accumulated to provide material for very hot fires. Consequently, burns took place without damaging the large trees, and new grasses grew back to provide browse for deer. The parklike environment made it easy for hunters to move through the forests and use their bows without hindrance.[56] Mayan communities used fire in swidden agriculture, where areas were burned over to clear fields for planting. Ash enriched the soil, and fire warmed it in preparation for planting.[57]

Even in areas where agriculture was not practiced, native people could manage the growth of wild plants for their own needs. Basketmakers in California, for example, deliberately cultivated the soil around stands of wild plants to encourage the growth of long, straight roots, and they pruned back shrubs to promote their production of long, straight, flexible new withes.[58]

Water is another essential element of environmental control. Several native peoples practiced irrigation. Hohokam farmers in southern Arizona developed extensive irrigation systems that allowed the rise of a sizable community around A.D. 800. Field cultivation and water control made the development of agriculture possible on the high and arid reaches of the Colorado Plateau.[59]

Too much water can be as much of a problem for farmers as too little, however. In Mesoamerica, where lowland tropical areas were often flooded, Aztec people created *chinimpas* in Lake Tezcoco—artificial islands made from the rich bottom mud from swamps and lakes. Although scholars have theorized that the demise of the Classic Mayan civilization that flourished from about 200 B.C. to about A.D. 950 resulted from exhaustion of food sources under population pressure, Mayan farming techniques were varied and productive enough to support a large population. They produced crops in highlands by terracing and in swampy lowlands by raised-bed farming.[60]

The development of agriculture in the Americas, as in the Middle East, represents a form of science because it involves systematic observation of and interaction with plants. Recent scholarship on Native American agriculture is revising opinions about the sequence of domestication of plants in North America. New research techniques such as seed flotation and electron microscopic analysis of the form and thickness of seed coats now allow scholars to study with much greater specificity the process of human domestication of wild plants.[61]

The theory of agriculture is that plants that flourish naturally in flood-disturbed riverbed environments move into human-modified environments around villages. There, people, primarily women, foster a mutual dependency between themselves and plants as they gather seeds and fruits. Wild plants produce large numbers of small seeds that drop easily from the plant, but gatherers favor larger and tighter seed and fruit clusters that do not disperse. Because of selection, plants lose much of the ability to spread their own seeds. Humans must take on that responsibility by deliberately harvesting and planting seeds. Morphologically, larger seeds and thin-coated seeds mark domesticated plants. Agriculture is thus a form of environmental control based on a mutual dependency of plants and humans.[62]

Maize has long been considered the progenitor of Native American agriculture, a gift from the advanced civilizations of Mesoamerica to the peoples of North America. However, recent research indicates that the eastern woodlands of North America were an independent agricultural hearth in which a number of plants were domesticated around 1000 to 500 B.C., long before the arrival of corn about A.D. 200. The earliest domesticated plant in the Northeast was probably a variety of sunflower (*Helianthus tuberosus*), whose tuberous root, the Jerusalem artichoke, was a major food source.[63] Other domesticated plants included sumpweed (*Iva annua* var. *macrocarpa*), goosefoot (*Chenopodium bushianum* Allen), maygrass (*Phalaris caroliniana* Walt.), and giant ragweed (*Ambrosia trifida* L.). The ability of all to withstand a wide range of environmental conditions made them good candidates for domestication.[64]

Mesoamerica was the hearth for squashes and gourds, which appeared with corn as domesticates in the American Southwest by approximately 3500 to 3800 B.P. Bottle gourds (*Lagenaria siceraria*), and devil's claw (*Proboscidea parviflora*) were also part of the agricultural complex in the Southwest, the former used for containers and the latter for its fibers, which were woven into baskets.[65] The eastern United States was, however, a site of independent domestication of squashes and gourds (*Cucurbita pepo*), previously thought to have been introduced from Central America. Similarly, the wild native gourd *Cucurbita texana* is the likely progenitor of domesticated squashes in the Southeast.[66]

Maize is still generally considered the triumph of Native American agriculture, nevertheless. It was domesticated in Northern Mexico from teosinte around 4000 B.C.; its earliest forms were popcorns, kernels held in hard coats that had to be exploded with heat.[67] The dispersion of pollen from male stamen to female tassels was essential to the reproduction of the plant, and although wind and insects accomplished this task to some degree, deliberate human spreading of pollen must have played a part. Pueblo and Navajo peoples have always prayed in their traditional ways with words and the casting of a handful of corn pollen into the air at dawn. Native Americans were not practicing breeding in a modern scientific sense in selecting certain plants to gather. They were, however, conscious of the differences in the plants they cultivated, and they contributed to the genetic diversity in modern corn through their belief in the power of corn pollen as a sacred substance.[68]

In at least one case, we have evidence of genetic specialization in the development of a corn plant. The Hopi produced a corn plant whose seed is adapted to the arid growing conditions of their mesas. The seed can be planted about eighteen inches deep because the seedling will grow that long before breaking the soil and putting out its first leaves. The tap root grows about a foot to reach down to the underlying subsurface moisture.[69] Hopi continue to preserve seed of pure colored cobs—red, white, blue, and yellow—for use in ceremonials where the offerings of colored corn meal are important.

In the Andes, Native Americans domesticated a rather amazing variety of potatoes: some 3,000 different species of potatoes can be identified from Andean sources. Indeed, because of this diversity, the Andes contributed the domesticated potato as a food source that was to be extraordinarily important in subsequent human history, and the potato readily takes its place beside corn as a major contribution to European food supplies.[70]

Contemporary commercial agriculture is based on large-scale growing of selected hybrid crops. Such monocultural practices are highly susceptible to outbreaks of disease or insect pests. Farmers have begun to realize the value of genetic diversity in crops.[71] On a small scale, the Native Seed/SEARCH organization in Tucson, Arizona, collects and disseminates seeds of native plants such as tepary beans and devil's claw. Native agriculture, a symbiotic relationship between plants and humans, can offer some essential lessons to modern agriculturalists.

Native American Technology

Technology is the practical application of scientific principles in human life, and the basic principle of science at work in technology is the application of energy. Leslie White equated the evolution of culture with increasingly efficient ways of utilizing energy, from solar-powered subsistence to fossil fuels, to electrical energy, to atomic power.[72] In contemporary American society, technology is often equated with mass production of very complex products utilizing massive amounts of energy. Native Americans utilized various forms of energy, human and mechanical, to control their environments and to manipulate material into new forms to serve human ends.[73] They also displayed a high degree of sophistication in both activities.

The purpose of mechanical devices is to enhance exponentially the force exerted upon them. Native Americans used the same kinds of basic machines as did Europeans, although they did not theorize about why they worked. Of the five simple machines of classical Greek mechanics, they used the wedge, the inclined plane, the lever, and the pulley. (There is no evidence of use of the screw.)

On the Northwest Coast, where the environment provided abundant food sources to sustain relatively large populations and large-scale materials in the form of massive fir and cedar trees, cultural conventions were manifested and elaborated in large-scale dwellings and massive totem poles denoting rank and privilege. Native artisans used mechanical devices to deal with the sheer scale of their materials. Gigantic cedar trees were sometime felled by chipping cavities into their sides with an adz (an application of the wedge) and setting a slow fire therein so that the tree burned through until it finally toppled. Cedar is straight-grained and splits easily. To split cedar logs into planks, men would open a small split in the side of a log and then widen it with a series of wooden wedges until a plank could be peeled off.[74]

In a more immediately applicable example, a simple pulley was used in a plains medical technique. To reset a dislocated joint, a man would tie a rawhide rope around the affected limb, throw the rope over a tree branch, and pull on it. This was a simple but generally effective method of exerting sufficient force to pop the joint back into place.[75]

Simple techniques joined in complex activities can have remarkable results. Weaving is such a marriage of natural materials and human skill. It is probably the oldest human technology throughout the Americas. Archaeological evidence of sandals and slings woven from plant fibers predates pottery. Women separated the fibers and wove them into strands by the simple act of rubbing them together against their thighs.

People along the western coast of South America were using spindles, looms, wool fibers, and dyes by about 500 B.C.; however, the Inca brought the skill to the state of an art during the period before the Spanish conquest. They domesticated llamas and alpacas, both as beasts of burden and as sources of wool; they hunted the vicuna for its coat.[76] Cloth was to the Inca what metal was to European society. It was the prime medium of exchange: Inca rulers demanded it as tribute from subject peoples. It was weaponry: warriors wore cotton armor and threw projectiles with cotton slings. It, rather than ceramic vessels, was the means of storing and transporting goods. Cloth also provided the basic medium for storing information: quipus, colored strings tied in sequence and knotted in distinctive patterns, encoded information for record keeping and possibly mnemonic purposes.[77]

As the Hohokam people in what is now southern Arizona domesticated cotton (perhaps as early as 300 B.C.) and traded it with other tribes, weaving techniques appeared and evolved. The development of the loom in Mesoamerica and its spread into the ancient cultures of the Southwest (Mogollon, Anasazi, and Hohokam) led to production of larger fabrics for clothing. Weavers mastered various techniques of plain weave, twill, tapestry, and brocading to produce intricate patterns and textures in cloth.[78] When Spanish colonists arrived in 1598, they were accompanied by sheep. Pueblo women soon learned to use wool for weaving; Navajo women, relative latecomers to the Southwest, adapted their basketmaking skills to the Pueblo loom. Today, some Navajo women (and a very few men) have become renowned for their skill.[79] Navajo weaving demonstrates very importantly the persistence of native technologies as a medium for the transformation of native aesthetics through time.

The manipulation of metals is essential in the history of western civilization—the Iron Age, the Bronze Age, and the Steel Age characterize the periodization of western history. (Hittite invaders armed with iron weapons, it will be recalled, overcame bronze-armed Mesopotamians to determine the course of western history.) The working of gold and silver in Mesoamerica is one of the most visible examples of this technological achievement among native people in the Americas.

The Inca of Peru elaborated on traditions of metalworking learned from the

Mochica culture along the southern Peruvian coast. The Mochica hammered gold into a thin foil with which they plated objects. Andean peoples developed a technique of smelting *tumbaga,* an alloy of gold, silver, and copper. The resulting ingot was then beaten and annealed many times. Each annealing produced a copper oxide that was removed with a saline rinse. By progressively removing the copper, the process brought the gold to the surface of the increasingly thin metal sheet. The silver was then removed with a paste of iron sulfate and salt. The gold remained in a granular state at the surface of the metal sheet, and it was heated and burnished to produce the shiny golden surface that is characteristic of Andean metal work.

This process not only produced works of lasting beauty, but also invested external forms with an inner essence, *camay,* which embodied religious and social power.[80] The process destroyed most of the copper and silver substrate in order to bring to the surface the gold that embodied the spiritual essence. Gold was a metaphor for spiritual and political power in South American societies. Metallurgy to the craftsmen of the Andes was not simply technology, the ability to use energy to melt and reform metals. It was the power to transform the very essence of material and imbue it with religious significance, an inner form that was more important than the outer form.[81]

Metallurgy did not develop in North America because of the rarity of metal ores, which appeared only in copper deposits in the Great Lakes region. Native copper was highly valued because of its rarity and was traded widely throughout North America. Copper weapons and tools have been found in graves, an indication of the status of the dead because of the value of metal. Copper repousse works of art are also found in prehistoric Woodland culture sites, and copper ornaments appear throughout the loose network of townships making up the temple mound cultures of Mississippian times (circa 1100 to 1500 A.D.).[82]

Technology means manipulating natural materials into new forms. The forms may be utilitarian (woven cloth) or ceremonial (golden figurines or vessels, copper weapons). It is apparent, however, that to most native peoples the processes of production were and are as important as the end product. Contemporary Navajo weavers create a break in the pattern of their textiles that is often called the spirit trail. It is a way of releasing the danger that comes from something being totally enclosed or surrounded.[83] This concern for process characterizes native approaches to technology.

Architecture

In their manipulations of the built environment, one can readily survey many principles of Native American science and technology. Architecture is the largest form of material culture crafted by Native Americans and provided within a great range of climates what amounted to secondary protective skins.

Practical wisdom would suggest that the limitations of technology and available materials would be primary determinants for the appearance and efficiency of native architecture. But separating out the "hard" data of climate variables and material options from the other social, economic, religious, and historical factors that had equal or even greater influence upon the layouts of native towns and villages, or upon the roof profile, construction methods, and underlying meanings of individual Native American building types, has done a disservice to the multiplicity of cultural needs that were served by Indian buildings and village arrangements.

Nonetheless, focusing upon technology alone does often underscore native ingenuity, and can remind us that when those other determinants of form demanded some new feat of architectural ingenuity, Native American engineering was up to the task. When the clan organization of the Iroquois (in the eastern woodlands) and the status principles of the Coastal Salish (in the Pacific Northwest) required bark or plank-covered buildings more than three or four hundred feet long, Native American builders performed successfully. Likewise, they were successful when the social or ceremonial requirements of the Chaco Canyon Anasazi called for stone buildings six stories high and for oversize circular meeting chambers (the so-called Great Kivas of the eleventh and twelfth centuries).

While we were aware of the diversity of traditional Native American building styles, many of which are no longer available for analysis, we are still learning new facts about how precontact structures were constructed and used. Even in the case of a well-studied region such as the Southwest, new information is appearing about the diversity of building methods during the years before the Spanish ever arrived.[84] We know, for instance, that adobe bricks were hand-fashioned in various sizes, ranging from the elongated "Vienna-roll" bricks, which involved hand-formed wet adobe molded around bundles of dropseed or Indian rice grass, to smaller, chunkier adobe bricks that were also made by hand, dried in the sun, and then mortared together into thick walls finished with plaster, applied either directly by hand or by wooden paddle. Construction methods from pre-Hispanic sites as varied as Casa Grande, Picuris Pueblo, the Chama Valley, and Chaco Canyon have been described, including the piling of crescent-shaped "turtleback," loaflike pads of wet adobe, and especially the widespread use of "coursing" adobe, or raising walls, layer by layer, with hand-shaped moist mud.

The Spanish have always been credited with introducing uniformly molded bricks into southwestern Indian technology. Their standardized blocks were set wet into wood or slab-stone forms and then spread out for sun-drying. However, at least two archaeological sites that predate the sixteenth century by two hundred years—Fourmile Ruin near Taylor, Arizona, and the proto-Hopi site of Homol'ovi—contain evidence of just such manufacture. Regarding the Fourmile location, Douglas A. Johnson has hypothesized that the Salado people who built this 500-room pueblo in the fourteenth century may have seized upon the relative dryness of late summer in order to form their bricks with wooden or sandstone slab forms, stockpiling them for future use as the need arose. In the case of the Homol'ovi III pueblo, about fifty miles south of today's Hopi mesas, Charles S. Adams found rooms from the site's final years that likewise appear to be raised with mold-made bricks.

In the pre-Hispanic southwest, the thick walls built from adobe brick or sandstone block were technologically effective in providing acceptable degrees of comfort for early Indians. In order to conserve energy and keep inhabitants warm throughout the cold winters, they functioned as passive heating units. At Pueblo Bonito in Chaco Canyon, for instance, while external temperatures might fluctuate during a January day by 35 degrees Fahrenheit, the internal temperature could be controlled so that it wavered by only a few degrees. This was accomplished through the same manipulations of siting, construction, and usage that would remain part of Pueblo Indian housing strategy down to the present day.

First, because Pueblo Bonito's curved wall opened to the south, maximum exposure to the low-lying (or "weakened," as the Pueblos conceptualize it) winter sun warmed the walls during the darker months. Second, the stepped tiers of the house block design provided enough sleeping rooms for the entire pueblo population to enjoy this southerly exposure. Third, the dense, thick, earth-and-stone walls functioned as a heat-sink, absorbing the daytime heat, then gradually radiating it indoors after sunset. Although temperatures might vary outdoors, the pueblo's sheer massiveness slowed the transmission of this variability within the rooms, maintaining a livable temperature that was abetted by small cooking fires (burning relatively smokeless wood) to replace the solar heat that was lost overnight. Finally, the north wall of Chaco Canyon, which loomed just behind the semicircular pueblo, helped to reflect the day's heat into the community well past sundown.[85]

Engineering a different insulation strategy kept Native Americans alive and even comfortable all across the 4,000-mile circumpolar rim. Rather than raising rooms aboveground, as was the southwestern approach, around A.D. 1000 members of the widespread so-called Thule culture began excavating the floors of their winter houses into tundra or snow banks. They then added lengthy entryway tunnels with cold traps, insulated the interiors with organic material, and even toggled additional skin liners to maximize retention of the heat that emanated from soapstone lamps burning seal oil, as well as from the resident human bodies during the long Arctic nights.

In the central Arctic, where the unique snow-block house form was elaborated, additional techniques contributed to this basic temperature-control approach. Starting with a ring of fresh snow blocks, preferably cut from the prospective floor area, the builder used a snow knife to shave their edges into a tight fit and then to recut them into an encircling ramp. Subsequent blocks then spiraled up around this semi-subterranean floor until only a central roof gap was left open, into which was fitted a "key" block to cap the catenary arch roof. Directly over the snow-block entry tunnel, which could easily be reshaped this way or that in order to avoid prevailing winds, an ice block cut from a freshwater source was sunk to allow illumination into the hemispherical interior. Depending on how cold it got outside, this structure could be further insulated by padding the entire shell with loose snow using driftwood snow shovels, while the inside could be lined with tentskins; both the floor and a semicircular communal sleeping deck could be covered with furry skins.[86]

In the subtropical region of south Florida, offshoots of the southern Creek federation emerged under the names of Seminoles and Miccosukees in the late eighteenth century. In their refugee hamlets deep in the Everglades, yet a third climate-control strategy was adapted. Built within clearings hacked from the natural islandlike "hammocks" that dot the Everglades, their homesteads featured various forms of the house type known as "chickee" for cooking and for sleeping and working, with oversize structures for hosting guests. Preferably framed with heart-of-cypress posts (which resist insect infestation), using cypress saplings for beams and purloins, and roofed with a palmetto-leaf thatch, these buildings perfectly suited the topography and the climate, and this housing style persisted into the twentieth century.

For the cooking chickee, with its "star" fire of long dry poles that were pushed inward as the flames burned away their tips, the eaves were left entirely open to vent the smoke. For the sleeping and working structures, however, the eaves drooped over pole framing that extended well beyond the living space to invite any breeze and allow for maximum shade. Inside these buildings tablelike platforms lifted sleepers above ground insects and reptiles, as well as periodically flooding waters. Come morning the bedding was rolled up to create a raised working environment for women to sew the tribe's trademark cloth-applique garments on old Singer sewing machines.[87]

Whether Native Americans constructed and lived in hide-covered conical tipis, beehive-shaped grass houses, voluminous lodges framed with cotton-wood and covered with earth or sod, or lofty gable-roofed summer houses sheathed with elm bark—or whether they spent as much time as possible under the shade of bough-shrouded summer arbors—most tribespeople walked around with more than one structural "blueprint" in their minds. Each new season called either for technical adjustment of a principal dwelling or for construction of a different building altogether. In addition, some form of cultural building code generally dictated the positioning and arrangement of these dwellings, based upon principles related to social status and wealth or to some key aspect of the tribe's cosmology.

We do not want to diminish the significance of reaching acceptable degrees of comfort in the evolution of these traditional house-forms. Generally, this was not terribly hard to achieve, as Wendy Hawthorne found out when she undertook a comparative simulation study of the "sustainability" of the Alaskan winter house, the Navajo corbeled-log hogan, the Ojibwa wigwam, and the Pawnee earthlodge. In the far north, while temperatures might plummet to minus 60 degrees F outside, the well-insulated, massive, and airtight winter houses built of driftwood, whalebone, and turf by Alaskan natives had little problem maintaining an indoor climate of 80 or 90 degrees above zero. While the Pawnees of eastern Nebraska did not excavate their earthlodge floors as deeply as did the Alaskans, the same general strategy kept their larger interiors around 65 to 75 degrees in January, when outside temperatures ranged around zero. Within the smaller, bark-and-mat dome-shaped winter wigwams of the Lake Superior Ojibwe, Hawthorne found that similar interior temperatures prevailed, although the lakeshore winds might howl at minus 15 degrees out-of-doors. As for the hogan, Hawthorne's analysis showed that when the Arizona desert temperature was down to around 10 degrees, inside the hemispherical dwelling a centrally placed fireplace maintained a livable temperature of 65 to 75. Finally, Hawthorne calculated the relative energy efficiency of these native dwellings, compared with both a frontier-period log cabin and her own 1960s-style suburban ranch house. She estimated that the traditional Alaskan native house, for instance, "would have used only 5% of the energy for heat that the early wood-heated Euro-American consumed, and only 3% of the energy required to bring the modern house to liveable temperature levels." Hawthorne concluded that "while tools and materials have allowed people today to build slightly more efficient dwellings on a per square foot basis, we have countered any savings with personal consumption, or more appropriately, over-consumption." [88]

Today some Native American engineers who have been schooled in both traditional and academic settings have tried to update the forms and functions of classic native dwellings. A Navajo archaeologist, Charlie Cambridge, teamed up with a faculty member at the University of Colorado's College of Environmental Design to experiment with "solarizing" the basic form of his tribe's "female" hogan style. Properly consecrated with a Blessingway ceremony by a Navajo "singer" or medicine man, their three buildings were erected outside Boulder, Colorado. All had the defining features of a traditional hogan: east-facing door, attention to four directions, organization around a central, circular room. While the first of the buildings was "traditional," the designers called the second "transitional," since it exhibited fiberglass glazing on three south-facing walls, which became the building's primary heat source. The third, more modern structure mixed passive with active solar technologies by having insulated glass windows on the southern walls as well as photovoltaic cells that heated water in the building's 120-gallon tank.[89]

Conclusion

Studies of indigenous knowledge systems provide new ways of exploring the relationships of human beings to their environments in various cultures.[90] Native Americans established control over the physical resources of their environments through a combination of systematic observation and recording of cyclical patterns in the natural world. In this respect their activities can be called scientific.

Native Americans understood their resources both as recurring patterns of events that they observed and as the variability in nature that they understood to be the will of a host of spiritual forces, a view in many ways remarkably similar to the European view in 1492 of a natural world full of animating forces, Aristotelian concepts of natural place, the alchemical transmutation of elements under the influence of philosophers' stones, and mysterious forces of magnetism. Native Americans recorded the patterns of natural phenomena in such physical markers as buildings aligned with celestial phenomena and medicine wheels. Their oral traditions explained how their physical world intersected with the spiritual world, as in the Chippewa account of the Thunderbird, which explained the regular passage of birds and storms and the highly variable violence of storms.[91]

Tribal people influenced natural cycles both through their subsistence practices and through ceremonies that they performed to ensure that the spirits would be pleased with their relationships with human beings and would continue to bring the rain and crops and animals upon which Indian people depended. Native and European world views diverged when European scientists began to insist that all natural phenomena operated according to fixed laws. Patterns and cycles became governing principles rather than the regular behavior of spiritual beings. Where western scientists experimented to test their assumptions about the uniformity of natural processes, Native Americans continued to see themselves as part of the process of nature, and they maintained its regularity through ceremonies. Although Native Americans in North and South America were capable of keen observation, sophisticated recording systems, and manipulation of certain aspects of their environments, at heart they were actors in the physical and spiritual environment rather than controllers of it.

Studies in archaeoastronomy, ethnobotany, agriculture, and architecture have done much to reveal the sophistication of native observation and understanding of the processes of the environment. The results of these studies have generally been discipline-specific and have reached relatively limited academic audiences. Research on the efficacy of native herbal medicines has sparked contemporary interest in the medicinal values of plants and a search for new plant-based pharmaceuticals. The advent of flotation techniques and electron microscopy in the field of archaeology has allowed for increasingly sophisticated studies of plant domestication and has provided strong evidence that the eastern woodlands of North America were an independent agricultural hearth.

Such disciplinary studies, however, present a fragmentary picture of the intellectual achievements of native people in the Americas. By providing a definition of native science and showing how it differs from European science of the seventeenth century and after, we have sought to provide a conceptual framework within which the results of native scientific activities can be presented and within which future research can be framed.

Studies of Native American science and technology raise important new research questions for scholars. What role does astronomical observation play in the rise of human social order? What are the mechanisms and sites of domestication of plants in North America? How did Native Americans evaluate the medicinal value of plants? Is there evidence of experimentation in native processes of dealing with their environments? (Certainly plant domestication might be interpreted as a form of experimentation.)

The field of research about Native American science should yield rich results as contemporary scientists examine the evidence from past Native American cultures. In some cases the persistence of cultural practices can give insight into physical evidence from the past. In other cases, such as architectural design, agricultural techniques, and uses of herbal medicines, native scientific knowledge may continue to have practical application in contemporary society.

Notes

1. George Sarton, *A History of Science* (Cambridge: Harvard University Press, 1952).

2. Stillman Drake, *Galileo* (Oxford: Oxford University Press, 1980).

3. A. Irving Hallowell, "The self and its behavioral environment," in *Culture and Experience* (Philadelphia: University of Pennsylvania Press, 1955), 98.

4. Stephen C. McCluskey, "Historical archaeoastronomy: The Hopi example," in *Archaeoastronomy in the New World,* A. F. Aveni, ed. (Cambridge: Cambridge University Press, 1982), 39–42.

5. Robert Redfield, "The primitive world view," in *Proceedings of the American Philosophical Society,* 96 (1952), 30–36; Paul Radin, *The World of Primitive Man* (New York: Henry Shuman, 1953).

6. Clark Wissler, *Man and Culture* (New York: Thomas Y. Crowell, 1923), 49; Clark Wissler, *The American Indian: An Introduction to the Anthropology of the New World,* 2d ed. (New York: Oxford University Press, 1922), 220.

7. Lynn Cesi, "Fish fertilizer: A native North American practice?" *Science,* 189 (1975), 26–30; see letters to the editor and Cesi's response in *Science,* 189 (1975), 945–48.

8. Bernard Ortiz de Montellano, "Empirical Aztec medicine," *Science,* 188 (1975), 215–20. Ortiz de Montellano analyzed the chemical components of a number of herbal

medicines reported in Aztec sources and concluded that sixteen of twenty-five plants studied would indeed have the effects mentioned in Aztec sources.

9. John Peabody Harrington, *The Ethnogeography of the Tewa Indians,* 29th Annual Report of the Bureau of American Ethnography to the Secretary of the Smithsonian Institution, 1907-8 (Washington, D.C.: Government Printing Office, 1909); Leland C. Wyman and Flora L. Bailey, *Navaho Indian Ethnoentomology,* University of New Mexico Publications in Anthropology, vol. 12 (Albuquerque: University of New Mexico Press, 1964); Edward F. Castetter and Ruth Underhill, *The Ethnobiology of the Papago Indians,* University of New Mexico Bulletin, Biological Series, no. 4 (Albuquerque: University of New Mexico Press, 1935); Junius Henderson and John Peabody Harrington, *Ethnozoology of the Tewa Indians,* Bureau of American Ethnology Bulletin, no. 56 (Washington, D.C.: Government Printing Office, 1914); Huron H. Smith, *Ethnobotany of the Ojibwa Indians* (Milwaukee: Public Museum of the City of Milwaukee, 1932).

10. Anthony F. Aveni and Gary Urton, "Introductory Remarks" in *Ethnoastronomy and Archaeoastronomy in the American Tropics,* Anthony F. Aveni and Gary Urton, eds., Annals of the New York Academy of Sciences, vol. 385 (New York: New York Academy of Sciences, 1982), vii-ix; Owen Gingerich, "Summary: Archaeoastronomy in the tropics," ibid., 333-36.

11. Brian S. Bauer and David S. P. Dearborn, *Astronomy and Empire in the Ancient Andes* (Austin: University of Texas Press, 1995), 1.

12. Anthony Aveni, *Skywatchers of Ancient Mexico* (Austin: University of Texas Press, 1980), 189-90.

13. John Eric S. Thompson, *A Commentary on the Dresden Codex: A Maya Hieroglyphic Book,* Memoirs of the American Philosophical Society, vol. 93 (Philadelphia: APS, 1972); Gregory M. Severin, *The Paris Codex: Decoding an Astronomical Ephemeris,* Transactions of the American Philosophical Society, vol. 71 (Philadelphia: APS, 1981).

14. Anthony Aveni, Sharon L. Gibbs, and Horst Hartung, "The Caracol Tower at Chichen Itza: An ancient astronomical observatory?" *Science,* 187 (1975), 977-85; Aveni, *Skywatchers,* 261-62, 64-66.

15. Anna Sofaer, Volker Zinser, and Rolf M. Sinclair, "A unique solar marking construct," *Science,* 206 (1979), 283-91.

16. Lynn Cesi, "Watchers of the Pleiades: Ethnoastronomy among native cultivators in northeastern North America," *Ethnohistory,* 25 (1978), 306-8.

17. Thomas F. Kehoe and Alice B. Kehoe, "Stones, solstices, and Sun Dance structures," *Plains Anthropologist,* 22 (1977), 85-96.

18. John A. Eddy, "Astronomical alignment of the Big Horn Medicine Wheel," *Science,* 184 (1974), 1035-43.

19. See the stories in Ray A. Williamson and Claire R. Farrer, eds., *Earth and Sky: Visions of the Cosmos in Native American Folklore* (Albuquerque: University of New Mexico Press, 1992).

20. Claire R. Farrer, *Living Life's Circle: Mescalero Apache Cosmovision* (Albuquerque: University of New Mexico Press, 1991), 38-59.

21. Floyd G. Lounsbury, "Maya numeration, computation and calendrical astronomy," in *Dictionary of Scientific Biography,* vol. 15, Charles C. Gillispie, ed. (New York: Scribners, 1970-80), 813.

22.   Vincent H. Malmstrom, "A reconstruction of the chronology of Mesoamerican calendrical systems," *Journal of the History of Astronomy,* 10 (1978), 105–16.

23.   Aveni, *Skywatchers,* 148; Barbara Tedlock, *Time and the Highland Maya* (Albuquerque: University of New Mexico Press, 1982).

24.   Linda Schele, *The Mirror, the Rabbit, and the Bundle: "Accession" Expressions from the Classic Maya Inscriptions,* Studies in Pre-Columbian Art and Archaeology, no. 25 (Washington, D.C.: Dumbarton Oaks, Trustees for Harvard University, 1983); Linda Schele, *Maya Glyphs: The Verbs* (Austin: University of Texas Press, 1982); Linda Schele and David Freidel, *A Forest of Kings: The Untold Story of the Ancient Maya* (New York: Morrow, 1990).

25.   Lounsbury, "Maya numeration," 765.

26.   J. E. Teeple, *Maya Astronomy* (Washington, D.C.: Carnegie Institution of Washington, 1931), 35; J. Eric Thompson, *A Correlation of the Mayan and European Calendars,* Field Museum of Natural History, publication 241, Anthropological Series, vol. 17, no. 1 (Chicago: Field Museum of Natural History, 1927); Lounsbury, "Maya numeration," 766; J. Eric Thompson, *Maya Chronology: The Correlation Question* (Washington, D.C.: Carnegie Institution of Washington, 1935).

27.   E. C. Krupp, "The 'binding of the years,' the Pleiades and the nadir sun," *Archaeoastronomy: The Bulletin of the Center for Archaeoastronomy,* 5 (1982), 9–13.

28.   Alexander Marshack, "A lunar-solar calendar stick from North America," *American Antiquity,* 50 (1985), 27–51. Marshack is a Harvard University researcher whose career has been devoted to studying time-marking devices throughout the Americas.

29.   Lounsbury, "Maya numeration," 759–818.

30.   Stanley E. Payne and Michael P. Closs, "A survey of Aztec numbers and their uses," in *Native American Mathematics,* Michael P. Closs, ed. (Austin: University of Texas Press, 1986), 213.

31.   Ibid., 225–26; Herbert R. Harvey and Barbara J. Williams, "Decipherment and some implications of Aztec numerical glyphs," in Closs, *Native American Mathematics,* 238–59.

32.   P. Clay Sherrod and Martha Ann Rolingson, *Surveyors of the Ancient Mississippi Valley,* Arkansas Archeological Survey Research Series, no. 28 (1987), 130, 134–37.

33.   See Berard Haile, *Starlore Among the Navaho* (Santa Fe, N.M.: Museum of Navajo Ceremonial Art, 1947); Ronald Goodman, *Lakota Star Knowledge: Studies in Lakota Stellar Theology* (Rosebud, S.D.: Sinte Gleska University, 1992).

34.   Emile Durkheim and Marcel Mauss, *Primitive Classification,* Rodney Needham, trans. and ed. (Chicago: University of Chicago Press, 1963), 6–7.

35.   Charles Hudson, *The Southeastern Indians* (Knoxville: University of Tennessee Press, 1976), 139–40.

36.   Pamela Amoss, "A little more than kin, and less than kind: The ambiguous Northwest Coast dog," in *The Tsimshian and Their Neighbors of the North Pacific Coast,* Jay Miller and Carol M. Eastman, eds. (Seattle: University of Washington Press, 1984), 292–305.

37.   William C. Sturtevant, "Studies in ethnoscience," in *Culture and Cognition: Rules, Maps, and Plans,* J. P. Spradley, ed. (San Francisco: Chandler, 1972), 130. Stur-

tevant defined ethnoscience as "the system of knowledge and cognition typical of a given culture."

38. Eugene S. Hunn, *Tzeltal Folk Zoology: The Classification of Discontinuities in Nature* (New York: Academic Press, 1977).

39. Brent Berlin, Dennis E. Breedlove, and Peter H. Raven, "Folk taxonomies and biological classification," *Science,* 154 (1966), 61–65.

40. Leland Clifton Wyman and Stuart K. Harris, *Navajo Indian Medical Ethnobotany,* University of New Mexico Bulletin, Anthropological Series, vol. 3, no. 5 (Albuquerque: University of New Mexico, 1941).

41. *The de la Cruz-Badiano Aztec Herbal of 1552,* William Gates, trans. (Baltimore: Maya Society, 1939), xvii; Emily Walcott Emmart, *The Badianus Manuscript* (Baltimore: Johns Hopkins Press, 1941); Francisco Guerra, "Aztec science and technology," *History of Science,* 8 (1969), 41.

42. Gladys A. Reichard, "Navajo classification of natural objects," *Plateau,* 21 (1948), 7–8.

43. James A. Teit, "Ethnobotany of the Thompson Indians of British Columbia . . . , based on field notes by James A. Teit," Elsie Viault Steedman, ed., *Forty-fifth Annual Report of the Bureau of American Ethnology to the Secretary of the Smithsonian Institution, 1927–1928* (Washington, D.C.: Government Printing Office, 1930), 450–51, 468, 500.

44. Hunn, *Tzeltal Folk Zoology,* 3–5.

45. Eugene S. Hunn, *Nch'i-Wana "The Big River": Mid-Columbia Indians and Their Land* (Seattle: University of Washington Press, 1990), 99.

46. Daniel R. Moerman, *American Medical Ethnobotany: A Reference Dictionary* (New York: Garland, 1977); Margaret B. Kreig, *Green Medicine: The Search for Plants That Heal* (Chicago: Rand McNally, 1964), 297.

47. Virgil J. Vogel, *American Indian Medicine* (Norman: University of Oklahoma Press, 1970).

48. E. Rodriguez, M. Argullin, T. Nishida, S. Uehara, R. Wrangham, Z. Abramowski, A. Finlayson, and G. H. Towers, "Thiaubrine A, a bioactive constituent of aspilia (Asteraceae) consumed by wild chimpanzees," *Experientia,* 41 (1985), 419–20.

49. Richard A. Yarnell, *Aboriginal Relationships Between Culture and Plant Life in the Upper Great Lakes Region,* University of Michigan Anthropological Papers, vol. 23 (Ann Arbor: University of Michigan Press, 1964).

50. Smith, *Ethnobotany of the Ojibwa Indians;* Huron H. Smith, "Ethnobotany of the Menomini Indians," *Bulletin of the Public Museum of Milwaukee,* 4 (1923), 1–174.

51. Frances Densmore, "Uses of plants by the Chippewa Indians," in *Forty-fourth Annual Report of the Bureau of American Ethnology to the Secretary of the Smithsonian Institution 1926–1927* (Washington, D.C.: Government Printing Office, 1928), 325, 329.

52. Janis B. Alcorn, *Huastec Mayan Ethnobotany* (Austin: University of Texas Press, 1984), 69–485; Richard Stephen Felger and Mary Beck Moser, *People of the Desert and Sea: Ethnobotany of the Seri Indians* (Tucson: University of Arizona Press, 1991). See also Gary Paul Nabhan, *The Desert Smells Like Rain: A Naturalist in Papago Indian Country* (San Francisco: North Point Press, 1982).

53. Michael Moseley, "The evolution of Andean civilization," in *Ancient Native*

Americans, Jesse D. Jennings, ed. (San Francisco: W. H. Freeman, 1978), 498. Animals suitable for domestication show herding behavior and a lack of aggressive territoriality that makes it possible for humans to subsume the position of a dominant male in the group; see Bruce Smith, *The Emergence of Agriculture* (New York: Scientific American Library, 1995), 26–28.

54. Henry T. Lewis, *Patterns of Indian Burning in California: Ecology and Ethnohistory,* Ballena Press Anthropological Papers, no. 1 (Socorro, N.M.: Ballena Press, 1973).

55. Carl Sauer, "Grassland climax, fire and man," in *Land and Life: A Selection of the Writings of Carl Ortwin Sauer,* John Leighly, ed. (Berkeley: University of California Press, 1963).

56. Calvin Martin, "Fire and forest structure in the aboriginal eastern forest," *Indian Historian,* 6 (1973), 38–42; Gordon Day, "The Indian as an ecological factor in the northeastern forest," *Ecology,* 34 (1953), 329–46.

57. Calvin Martin, "Fire and forest structure," 38–42.

58. Kat Anderson, "Native Californians as ancient and contemporary cultivators," in *Before the Wilderness: Environmental Management by Native Californians,* Thomas C. Blackburn and Kat Anderson, compilers and eds. (Menlo Park, Calif.: Ballena Press, 1993), 151–74; David W. Peri and Scott M. Patterson, "The basket is in the roots, that's where it begins," ibid., 175–94.

59. Emil W. Haury, *The Hohokam: Desert Farmers and Craftsmen* (Tucson: University of Arizona Press, 1976); Michael Glassow, *Prehistoric Agricultural Development in the Northern Southwest: A Study in Changing Patterns of Land Use* (Socorro, N.M.: Ballena Press, 1980).

60. William M. Denevan, "Aboriginal drained-field cultivation in the Americas," *Science,* 169 (1970), 647–54; Pedro Armillas, "Gardens on swamps," *Science,* 174 (1971), 653–61; B. L. Turner II, "Prehistoric intensive agriculture in the Mayan lowlands," *Science,* 185 (1974), 118–24; Ray T. Matheny, "Maya lowland hydraulic systems," *Science,* 193 (1976), 639–45; Ray T. Matheny and Deanne L. Gurr, "Ancient hydraulic techniques in the Chiapas highlands," *American Scientist,* 67 (1979), 441–49.

61. Stuart Struever, "Flotation techniques for the recovery of small-scale archaeological remains," *American Antiquity,* 33 (1968), 353–62; Deena S. Decker-Walters, "New methods for studying the origins of New World domesticates: The squash example," in *Foraging and Farming in the Eastern Woodlands,* C. Margaret Scarry, ed. (Gainesville: University Press of Florida, 1993), 91–97.

62. Bruce D. Smith, *Rivers of Change: Essays on Early Agriculture in Eastern North America* (Washington, D.C.: Smithsonian Institution Press, 1992), 11–15.

63. Charles B. Heiser, Jr., "Some botanical considerations of the early domesticated plants north of Mexico," in *Prehistoric Food Production in North America,* Richard I. Ford, ed., Museum of Anthropology, University of Michigan, Anthropological Papers, no. 75 (Ann Arbor: University of Michigan, 1985), 61–62; Hugh C. Cutler, "Food sources in the New World," *Agriculture History,* 28 (1954), 44.

64. C. Wesley Cowan, "Understanding the evolution of plant husbandry in eastern North America: Lessons from botany, ethnography and archaeology," in Ford, *Prehistoric Food Production,* 207–17.

65. Heiser, "Some botanical considerations," 63–67.

66.   Sandra L. Dunavan, "Reanalysis of seed crops from emge: New implications for late woodland subsistence-settlement systems," in Scarry, *Foraging and Farming.*

67.   Walton C. Galinat, "Domestication and diffusion of maize," in Ford, *Prehistoric Food Production,* 245–48; Smith, *Emergence of Agriculture,* 154–55.

68.   Paul Weatherwax, *Indian Corn in Old America* (New York: Macmillan, 1954); Paul C. Manglesdorf, *Corn: Its Origin, Evolution and Improvement* (Cambridge, Mass.: Belknap Press of Harvard University Press, 1974), 35, 64.

69.   G. N. Collins, "A drought-resisting adaptation in seedlings of Hopi maize," *Journal of Agricultural Research,* 1 (1914), 293–306.

70.   Stephen B. Brush, Heath J. Carney, and Zosimo Huaman, "Dynamics of Andean potato agriculture," *Economic Botany,* 35 (1981), 70–88; William H. McNeill, "American food crops in the Old World," in *Seeds of Change,* Herman J. Viola and Carolyn Margolis, eds. (Washington, D.C.: Smithsonian Institution Press, 1991), 43–59.

71.   Gary Paul Nabhan, *Enduring Seeds: Native American Agriculture and Wild Plant Conservation* (San Francisco: North Point Press, 1989), 88–90.

72.   Leslie A. White, *The Evolution of Culture* (New York: McGraw-Hill, 1959); Leslie A. White, *The Science of Culture: A Study of Man and Civilization* (New York: Farrar, Straus, 1949).

73.   Robert F. G. Spier, *From the Hand of Man: Primitive and Preindustrial Technologies,* (Boston: Houghton Mifflin, 1930), 2.

74.   Philip Drucker, *Cultures of the North Pacific Coast* (New York: Chandler, 1965), 28.

75.   David Zeisberger, "History of the North American Indians," Archer B. Hulbert and William N. Schwarze, eds., *Ohio Archaeological and Historical Quarterly,* 19 (1910), 149.

76.   A. H. Gayton, "The cultural significance of Peruvian textiles: Production, function, aesthetics," *Kroeber Anthropological Society Papers,* no. 25 (1961), 114–19; Marcia Ascher and Robert Ascher, *Code of the Quipu Databook* (Ann Arbor: University of Michigan Press, 1978).

77.   Marcia Ascher and Robert Ascher, *Code of the Quipu: A Study in Media, Mathematics, and Culture* (Ann Arbor: University of Michigan Press, 1981); Marcia Ascher, "Mathematical ideas of the Incas," in Closs, *Native American Mathematics,* 261–90.

78.   Kate Peck Kent, *Prehistoric Textiles of the Southwest* (Albuquerque: University of New Mexico Press, 1983), 11–13, 29, 198–99.

79.   Joe Ben Wheat, *Patterns and Sources of Navajo Weaving* (n.p.: Harmsen Western Americana Collection, 1977), 11–14.

80.   Heather Lechtman, "Andean value systems and the development of prehistoric metallurgy," *Technology and Culture,* 25 (1984), 30–33.

81.   Ibid.

82.   Harold Driver, *The Indians of North America,* 2d ed., rev. (Chicago: University of Chicago Press, 1969), 166–67. Chippewa Indians around Lake Superior considered large nuggets of copper as deities; see William W. Warren, *History of the Ojibway Nation* (Minneapolis: Ross and Haines, 1970), 472; *Ancient Art of the American Woodland Indians* (New York: Harry N. Abrams, 1985), 25, 89, 148–49.

83.   Noel Bennett, *The Weaver's Pathway: A Clarification of the "Spirit Trail" in Navajo Weaving* (Flagstaff: Northland Press, 1974), 30–31.

84. Michael Moquin, "Early Pueblo and Hispanic adobe," *Traditions: The Adobe Journal,* 8 (1992), 10–27.

85. Ray A. Williamson, *Living the Sky* (Norman: University of Oklahoma Press, 1984), 145–47.

86. Peter Nabokov and Robert Easton, *Native American Architecture* (New York: Oxford University Press, 1989), 195–99.

87. Ibid., 115–20.

88. Wendy Hawthorne, "Elements of sustainable design in traditional Native American architecture," manuscript, Boulder, Colorado, n.d., 8.

89. Hassel G. Bradley, "Solar hogans: Houses of the future," *Native Peoples,* 4 (1990), 44–50.

90. Robin Horton, "Levy-Bruhl, Durkheim, and the scientific revolution," in *Modes of Thought: Essays on Thinking in Western and Non-Western Societies,* Robin Horton and Ruth Finnegan, eds. (London: Faber and Faber, 1973).

91. A. Irving Hallowell, "Some empirical aspects of northern Saulteaux religion," *American Anthropologist,* n.s., 36 (1934), 394–95.

Who Owns Our Past?
The Repatriation of Native American Human Remains and Cultural Objects

On the morning of Friday, October 9, 1993, a small group of Northern Cheyenne arrived at the Smithsonian Institution's National Museum of Natural History. They had come for their dead. Almost 115 years earlier, on January 9, 1879, at least 83 members of a band of 149 Northern Cheyenne led by Dull Knife (a.k.a. Morning Star) had been massacred by U.S. government soldiers near Fort Robinson, Nebraska, after a final, desperate attempt at freedom. The Northern Cheyenne had fled toward their homelands in Montana, after having been moved to a reservation in Oklahoma to live with the Southern Cheyenne in 1877. They were captured and held in the stockade at Fort Robinson with little food, water, or even heat. They attempted to escape after two weeks. At least 57 Northern Cheyenne were killed during the attempt. Thirty-two others found a brief freedom, until they were trapped on January 22 at the edge of Antelope Creek, where 26 of them were killed during the resulting massacre. Most Cheyenne killed in the escape attempt were buried near the fort; those killed at Antelope Creek were buried nearby in a mass grave. The bones of 17 of the Northern Cheyenne were collected after their brutal deaths for scientific study by the U.S. Army Medical Examiner. Nine of these were obtained from the mass grave at Antelope Creek, which was exhumed in 1880. The bones—mostly crania—were later transferred to the Smithsonian's National Museum of Natural History. The bones were from Cheyenne ranging in age from forty-nine to a three-year-old child massacred at Antelope Creek. All were now being returned to their people in a joint repatriation with the Peabody Museum of Archaeology and Ethnology at Harvard, which also had some skeletal remains from the Antelope Creek massacre, collected about a month before those of the Army Medical Museum by a Peabody museum curator.

At the repatriation ceremony the human bones were officially turned over to the Northern Cheyenne delegation. The delegation was impressive. The Northern Cheyenne were represented by the tribal chair, the Crazy Dogs society of warriors, the Elk Horn society, Sun Dance priests, four women who were fourth-generation descendants of Dull Knife, and, most important, James Black Wolf, Keeper of the Sacred Buffalo Hat. The remains were carefully arranged on small Pendleton blankets; a pipe ceremony was performed, words and prayers were said, and a drum was played and songs were sung. Each person's bones were then wrapped in a blanket and interred in cedar boxes for the journey home to Montana and final rest. During the ceremony, it was discovered that a shattered lower part of a skull from the Harvard museum matched an upper part of a woman's skull from the Smithsonian. Either at death 115 years earlier or sometime afterward, the woman's head had been broken into two pieces, with each piece ending up at a different location. She was collected as two different people, one part of her going to the Army Medical Museum and eventually the Smithsonian, the other part going to the Peabody. On that day, October 9, 1993, not only was the young Northern Cheyenne woman reunited with her people; her skull itself was reunited.

During the ceremony, a young Native American man from the Smithsonian came up to me and told me about the three-year-old's skull. "The child was a little girl. I saw her. She was dressed in white and had yellow ribbons in her hair. I told the Cheyenne I had seen her, and that she was now happy. They were very pleased. They thanked me for telling them."

After the ceremony in Washington, the remains were taken to Montana for burial. A stop was made on October 12 at Fort Robinson, Nebraska, for ceremonies. The journey then continued to Busby, Montana, where a wake, giveaway, and offerings to the dead took place. A small teddy bear was given to the little girl and placed on the cedar box with her remains. Her remains and those of the other massacred Cheyenne were buried shortly after noon on October 16, 1993, on a hill near Two Moon Monument.

I attended the ceremony in Washington, D.C., as the chair of the Smithsonian Institution's Native American Repatriation Review Committee, which was created by the Congress of the United States to oversee the return of Native American human remains and grave objects held at the Smithsonian Institution. It was an even more meaningful ceremony for me than it would ordinarily have been. My mother had died a few days before; I had stopped in Washington to attend the ceremony while on my way to Vian, Oklahoma, for her funeral the following day. At the ceremony in Washington, I kept thinking that my mother would be laid to rest only a few days after her death, but that these Northern Cheyenne had waited in museums for over a century before they could be buried. My mother had a long, full life and died peacefully. The Northern Cheyenne men, women, and children had short lives, ended by violent, cruel deaths.

Repatriation of Human Remains and Cultural Objects

The repatriation of the Native American human remains and also of funerary and other cultural objects is occurring today because of determined efforts by Native Americans to achieve legal changes in American society. It reflects perhaps a new significance for Native Americans in American society, and an important development in the relationship between Native Americans and that society. This legally mandated repatriation is also recognition of tribal sovereignty: remains and objects are repatriated to tribal entities (individuals may make claims if they can prove direct descent), though the transfer is not from U.S. government to tribal government, but from museum to tribal government. Repatriation certainly should be an important contemporary topic within Native American studies.[1] It has additional significance for the ways native peoples and the scholarly community relate to each other, including how their respective ethics, values, conceptions, and even bodies of knowledge come together.

Native American Remains as Objects of Study

It has been estimated that skeletal remains of "tens and tens of thousands," possibly "hundreds of thousands," of Native American individuals are held in various universities, museums, historical societies and even private collections in the United States: one number frequently given is 600,000.[2] (Skeletal remains of Native Americans are also held in other countries.) Whatever the actual figure, these estimates show a sizable problem. How many objects belonging to Native American groups these collections hold is pure speculation. In addition to funerary objects (included in burials, made specifically for burials, or designed to contain human remains), there are "objects of patrimony" owned by the entire people, such as wampum belts and sacred objects, such as medicine bundles. It is also estimated that the skeletons, or more typically pieces of them, of several hundred Native Americans and the countless objects buried with them are uncovered every year in highway, housing, and other types of construction.[3]

Native American remains and grave goods have been objects of study and fascination to non–Native Americans for centuries. In 1620 Pilgrims searching for caches of Indian corn to rob uncovered a grave containing "the bones and head of a little child . . . strings and bracelets of fine white beads . . . and some other odd knacks. . . . We brought sundry of the prettiest things away with us," they wrote, "and covered the corpse up again." [4] Reports of systematic excavation of Native American burial sites and mounds date from the eighteenth century. Thomas Jefferson excavated burial mounds on his property in Virginia, and in so doing became the "father of American archaeology." He wrote of his excavation of a mound, "I first dug superficially in several parts of it, and came to collections of human bones, at different depths, from six inches to three feet below the surface. These were lying in the utmost confusion, some vertical, some oblique, some horizontal, and directed to every point of the compass, entangled, and held together in clusters by the earth. . . . I conjectured that in this barrow might have been a thousand skeletons." [5]

Native American crania became objects of particular scientific interest in the early nineteenth century, and remain so today. Scholars evaluated theories of migration to North America from Asia by comparing Native Americans with Asians. They sought physical evidence to explain physical and cultural differences among native peoples and between them and other peoples; often cultural differences were seen as a result of racial ones. Various scholars actively collected Native American remains, including Albert Gallatin and Samuel G. Morton.[6] In 1839, Morton published *Crania Americana,* reporting that Caucasians had larger brain capacities and therefore higher intelligence than Native Americans.[7] The "science" of phrenology soon developed, and collecting crania became more widespread as scholars attempted to relate intelligence, personality, and character to skull and brain size.

The Smithsonian Institution opened in 1846 and provided further impetus for the development of American archaeology, physical anthropology, and ethnology. Native American remains and cultural objects were, of course, important. The U.S. Army also became very much involved as its mandate to handle the "Indian problem" expanded after the U.S. Civil War.

On May 21, 1862, Surgeon General of the United States William Hammond suggested that an Army Medical Museum be established in Washington, D.C.,[8] to "facilitate the study of methods to diminish mortality and suffering among soldiers." [9] This was during the Civil War, and for the first several years most specimens acquired related to "the injuries and diseases that produce death or disability during war." [10]

After the Civil War, as the former Union Army turned its attention westward to confront Native Americans on the plains, the Army Medical Museum sought to update its collections to reflect this new conflict. On April 4, 1867, Surgeon General J. K. Barnes requested that medical officers also collect:

1. Rare pathological specimens from animals, including monstrosities.
2. Typical crania of Indian tribes; specimens of their arms, dress, implements, rare items of their diet, medicines, etc.
3. Specimens of poisonous insects and reptiles, and their effects on animals.[11]

Nine months later, on January 13, 1868, Surgeon General Madison Mills wrote to army medical directors at the Department of Missouri at Fort Leavenworth (Kansas), the Department of the Platte at Omaha (Nebraska), the Department of New Mexico at Santa Fe, and the Department of Dakota at Fort Snelling (Minnesota), urging them to have their medical officers collect "specimens of Indian crania and of Indian weapons and Utensils." [12] "The Surgeon General," he wrote, "is anxious that our collection of Indian Crania, already quite large, should be made as complete as possible." [13]

By September 1868, the museum had a collection of 143 crania, 47 of which were Native American, representing various tribes. A memorandum issued then said that the museum "chiefly desired to procure sufficiently large series of adult crania of the principal Indian tribes to furnish accurate average measurements." [14] In 1870 Dr. G. A. Otis, then the curator of the museum, reported his conclusions to the National Academy of Sciences during a meeting held there: "Judging from the capacity of the cranium, the American Indians must be assigned a lower position in the human scale than has been believed heretofore." [15]

More than four thousand Native American skulls were eventually collected —from burial scaffolds, graves, and ossuaries, and from battlefields and sites of massacres—and then sent to the Army Medical Museum. Many other museums participated in the collecting of Native American skeletal remains, including the Peabody Museum at Harvard University, the American Museum of Natural History in New York, and the Field Museum of Chicago, which obtained some Native American remains originally sent to Chicago for the 1893 World's Columbian Exposition.

Human ancestors began to bury their dead in some fashion more than 200,000 years ago. Native Americans developed a variety of methods of caring for their dead. These ranged from merely leaving them on the ground, sometimes covering them with stone, to placing them in wooden coffins on the surface of the ground or in caves, to placing them on scaffolds or in a tree, to burial underground, even under the floor of their homes, to cremation.[16] Some tribes kept the remains of their dead in special houses or ossuaries. For example, The Inca, Garcilaso de la Vega describes a burial temple in the province of Cofachiqui: "Along all four walls the Indians had set wooden chests. . . . Within the chests . . . , the infidels had entombed the bodies of their dead without any more preservatives against decomposition than if they were giving them burial in the earth." [17]

Most Native American peoples attach an important spiritual quality to the remains of their ancestors. Chief Seattle, for example, explained: "To us the ashes of our ancestors are sacred and their final resting place is hallowed ground, while you wander far from the graves of your ancestors and, seemingly, without regret." [18] During battles, rival tribes would sometimes attempt to destroy the ossuaries, knowing how much pain this would inflict on their enemies. Many native people think that treating their ancestral remains as objects of curiosity or scientific study is also disrespectful to them and their ancestors. To the Zuni, the removal of human remains from their ancestral lands so desecrated their ancestors that they cannot be returned to Zuni Pueblo for reburial![19] Many cultural objects are of spiritual significance, sometimes sacred to Native Americans. That skeletons of ancestors and sacred tribal objects are held by museums, scholarly and other institutions, and even private individuals is painful to most contemporary native peoples.

Collecting Human Remains and Objects

Many human remains and objects subject to legal repatriation were obtained appropriately, with the permission if not actual support of Native Americans at the time. However, many were not; that human remains and objects were obtained by "grave robbing," theft, and fraud adds to Native American discomfort and further legitimizes claims for repatriation, as the four cases briefly described below illustrate.

A major smallpox epidemic among Indian tribes of the central and northwest regions of the United States in the early 1800s killed the great Omaha chief Washinga Sakba ("the Blackbird"). The artist George Catlin, who traveled among Native Americans from the Dakotas to Indian Territory in the 1830s and 1840s, painting the natives he encountered, describes Washinga Sakba's funeral in his journal. Catlin writes that Washinga Sakba was buried on a bluff above the Missouri River, mounted on his favorite white horse, "with his bow in his hand, and his shield and quiver slung—with his pipe and his *medicine-bag*—with his supply of dried meat, and his tobacco-pouch replenished to last him through his journey to the 'beautiful hunting grounds of the shades of his fathers'." When he visited the grave site, Catlin adds, he dug up Washinga Sakba's skull to add it to "others which I have collected on my route." [20]

On December 29, 1890, several hundred Sioux men, women, and children were massacred by troops of the First Squadron of the Seventh Cavalry at Wounded Knee Creek.[21] The Sioux had fled their reservation to practice their new religion—the Ghost Dance. The massacre occurred after the troops had captured them and were attempting to disarm them. The cavalry left with their dead and wounded after the massacre, and sent out a burial detail a few days later. Meanwhile, other Sioux learned of the massacre and collected some of their own dead. When the burial detail arrived on January 1, 1891, a heavy blizzard had covered the remaining bodies with snow. Eighty-four men and boys, 44 women and girls, and 18 children were collected and buried in a mass grave. Some Sioux had been wearing sacred Ghost Dance shirts; they were stripped of these shirts before being dumped into the grave.

Six shirts ended up at the National Museum of Natural History; one was displayed in a museum exhibit with the caption stating that it was taken from the Wounded Knee "Battlefield." In the fall of 1986, I was a fellow at the museum. I remember vividly a trip one afternoon with a curator into the building's attic to examine some of the North American Indian collections. He volunteered to show me these shirts. He pulled out a drawer from a large cabinet, and there they were. Almost a hundred years after it occurred, I was a witness to the legacy of the massacre at Wounded Knee. The shirts have bullet holes and are stained with blood; some still have medicine bags attached.

The Smithsonian officially had twenty-nine "objects" taken from those massacred at Wounded Knee. Besides the six Ghost Dance shirts, they include a blanket from "a dead body," a pair of boys' moccasins, and baby jackets and caps. Their return to the descendants of those slain at Wounded Knee occurred in September of 1998. The Cheyenne River Sioux Tribe represented the descendants in negotiating the request.[22]

Ales Hrdlicka, recognized as a father, if not the father, of physical anthropology, visited Kodiak Island off the coast of Alaska in the 1930s. Representing the Smithsonian Institution, he removed the remains of about a thousand people and 144 associated burial items from an archaeological site called Uyak. The people later said that they resented the intrusion and the removal of the remains, but Hrdlicka was a representative of the government, and they did not know what to do. They never gave him permission. But "he had no regard for the people here. And we had no laws. None that we knew about. We just stood by." [23]

A final, well-known example occurred at the American Museum of Natural History. In 1897, Robert Peary brought to New York City from Greenland six Inuit (Eskimo) and the famous Cape York meteorite, a sacred object to the Inuit. Four of the six soon died of tuberculosis; one, Uisaakassak, eventually returned to Greenland.[24] The sole remaining Eskimo was the well-known Minik, who lived until 1918, after returning to Greenland in 1909, and then coming back to the United States in 1916 to live in New Hampshire. The first of the four to die was Qisuk, father of the then-eight-year-old Minik. After his death, in January 1899, his "bones were preserved, boiled and varnished and mounted as a perfect skeleton." [25] The other three Inuit who died were likewise dissected, and their skeletons added to the museum's collections. Hrdlicka published a paper on Qisuk's brain in 1901, complete with pictures (he called him Kishu or Kissuk).[26] A fake burial had been performed for Qisuk. It was noted by a young anthropologist, Alfred Kroeber, who had studied the six Eskimos in New York and wrote a paper on the Eskimo of Smith Sound without leaving the city. Kroeber indicated that Minik was instructed to "visit the (supposed) grave of his father." [27] Later, Minik discovered that his father's bones were actually on display in the museum. "I can never be happy till I can bury my father in a grave," he lamented. "It makes me cry every time I think of his poor bones up there in the museum in a glass case, where everybody can look at them. Just because I am a poor Esquimau boy why can't I bury my father in a grave the way he would want to be buried?" [28]

The answer, in his case as in the other three described here, was that the bones were being kept in the interest of science.

Important Research

Nearly all of the 4,000 crania at the Army Medical Museum were eventually transferred to the Smithsonian's National Museum of Natural History and added to the remains of approximately 14,500 other Native Americans there (along with non–Native American remains). This supposedly represents the largest single collection of Native American remains in the United States, followed by some 13,500 held by the Tennessee Valley Authority. The University of California also has a very large collection. The Hearst (formerly Lowie) Museum at its Berkeley campus has "the third largest number of catalogued skeletal entries in the United States (more than 11,000)." [29] Most of these remains, "representing more than 8,000 individuals," are from California's northern coast and Sacramento Valley. As for artifacts, there are "roughly 1 million or more pieces" at Berkeley. UCLA and other campuses of the University of California system have smaller numbers of Native American human remains and artifacts.

Research on native skeletal remains has generated much important knowledge about such diverse topics as population size and composition, cultural patterns of tooth mutilation, diseases present among Native American populations and treatments for those diseases, life expectancies, growth patterns, population affinities, origins and migrations, and diets, including dates at which corn was introduced among various peoples of North America.[30] We now know from studying these remains that tuberculosis was present in this hemisphere before European contact in 1492, as were some infectious diseases, including treponemal infections, that certain native groups had serious iron deficiencies from a diet heavily dependent on corn,[31] and that among some groups males with more social prestige—as reflected by burial objects—were physically larger than males with less social prestige (perhaps because they had better diets, perhaps because bigger men were simply given more prestige).

Native American skeletal remains have become even more important as objects of study, scholars assert, given recent advances and probable future advances in scientific technology, including the detection of immunoglobulin and DNA sequencing from bone. The study of immunoglobulin could enable scholars to establish explicit disease histories for the skeletons; deciphering their DNA code could enable scholars to establish genetic relationships among historical populations. Moreover, science progresses, and unforeseen and foreseen advances will enable scholars to generate increasingly greater knowledge from the skeletal remains.[32] This is no small issue, and much of the knowledge to be gained could benefit both Native American and other peoples of the world.

Some Views

Native American views that repatriation must occur are typically held despite any scholarly or public good, past or future, derived from the study or display of the remains and objects. Scholars and others assert that the scientific and public value of the remains and cultural objects outweigh any claims Native Americans may have. As scholars attempt to reconstruct histories of Native Americans, they argue that the scientific benefits are important not only to the public at large, but also to native peoples themselves. Some have even sued to be allowed to retain or study remains or objects, as is the case with a recent discovery: Native American remains 9000 years old (or older) and showing some "caucasoid features," an individual dubbed the "Richland" or "Kennewick Man." [33] Other lawsuits have involved the ability to study the remains before actual repatriation.[34]

A related view is that the remains and objects now housed in museums and educational institutions belong not to Native Americans but to all Americans, even to all peoples of the world. They are part of the heritage of all people, not only Native American people. Another view is that the scholars are keeping and studying the remains because Native Americans do not know what they are doing when requesting repatriation. "Someday," they say, "Native Americans will want this knowledge. It is up to us to preserve it for them." (This assertion that scientists are "saving the Indians from themselves" is both patronizing and insulting.)

Native Americans, conversely, assert that other factors outweight science and education, noting that our society places all sorts of restrictions on research. Obviously, research that physically harms humans (and, to a lesser extent, animals) is prohibited. Under conventional ethical standards, one must get "informed consent" from subjects who are aware of the nature and implications of the research, the research must not harm subjects psychologically, and subjects may not be identified without their permission. Yet studying the human remains of their ancestors, for example, causes great psychological pain, Native Americans argue.

Native Americans also point out that skeletons obtained from battlefields and massacres, as many of those in the Army Medical Museum were, are remains of Native Americans who died defending their homelands: all of the United States of America was once Native American land. American society has given much attention to returning to the United States the remains of Americans killed in World War II, the Korean Conflict, the war in Vietnam, and other wars. Do we owe less to those who defended America against the Europeans and the Euro-Americans who took their land? Are Native American warriors killed in battle less deserving of an honorable burial than American military personnel who died for the United States? (And what about "civilians" killed in battles and massacres?) Most Americans strongly support efforts to repatriate the remains of all fellow Americans who died in Vietnam and elsewhere. What would be the reaction if the Republic of Vietnam refused to return the skeletal remains of American service men and women killed there? What if they said: "We want to keep them and study them. They have much scientific value"?

The Repatriation Movement

Native Americans have attempted legally to prevent the collection of their human remains and cultural objects for more than a century.[35] During the last few decades, they have increasingly demanded that ancestral remains and sacred objects be returned to them for proper disposal or care. This effort is a social movement: "a concerted and continued effort by a social group aimed at reaching a goal (or goals) common to its members. More specifically, the effort is directed at modifying, maintaining, replacing, or destroying an existing social institution." [36] Thus, social movements are determined and organized group efforts to bring about some objectives, particularly types of social change. Repatriation is an organized effort to return Native American human remains and cultural objects to the communities from which they came.

Social movements are shaped by societies and cultures; goals and objectives are achieved by means available and acceptable at particular times in particular societies and cultures. Social movements in American society today often involve such political processes as obtaining public support and sympathy, lobbying legislators, and getting specific laws passed. This is exactly what occurred in the repatriation movement.

Repatriation is also a pan-Indian movement in two ways: it involves many different Native American peoples, with or without strong tribal affiliations (though, as noted, repatriation is only carried out with tribes or direct descendants); and Native American tribes have joined in it to pursue common, though tribally specific, interests. For many Native Americans, with strong tribal ties or otherwise, the repatriation movement ranks in importance with the social movements of other groups in American society—the civil rights movement, the women's movement. The repatriation movement has given Native Americans a new sense of respect—from American society and also for themselves.

Repatriation might also be considered a revitalization movement, a "deliberate, organized, conscious effort by members of a society to construct a more satisfying culture." [37] My own view is that a revitalization movement is a special type of social movement designed "to create a better social and/or cultural system while reviving or reaffirming selected features." [38] Repatriation is truly revitalizing and breathing new life into Native American communities by seeking to recover what has been taken from them.

During past decades, the pan-Indian repatriation movement became successful through the passage of federal and state laws not only calling for the repatriation of human remains and objects to descendants, if known, or, otherwise, appropriate tribes, but also preventing the further disenfranchisement of remains and objects. (Native peoples in Canada have raised similar issues, but similar changes in Canadian law have not yet occurred.) Not only has the success of the repatriation movement revitalized Native America and provided new self-esteem; the task of actually winning repatriations of human remains and cultural objects has also revitalized communities by bringing members together for this struggle as well as reaffirming important knowledge about many cultural and sacred objects.

It is not always an easy undertaking, although the result may be worth it. "As difficult as implementation of the repatriation policy and laws may be in the non-Native world," Suzan Shown Harjo comments, "the truly complex issues are being examined by Native Peoples, who must arrive at a consensus in matters for which most lack specific historical and ceremonial context. Each detail of repatriation, including whether or not to request repatriation, must be worked out within each family, clan, society or nation." [39]

This process can be very important when it comes to sacred objects, sources of much power or "medicine." How does one handle them? Can one handle them? Much of this knowledge was lost by Native Americans, and they may find it difficult to know exactly what to do. One may compare Native American sacred objects with the Ark of the Covenant containing the ten commandments, a source of great power in some religions. What would people do if the Ark was suddenly discovered? Would they open it? Would they touch the stones on which the ten commandments are carved? The ten commandments are on stone given by a god or creator, and Native American sacred objects also may be of stone, given by a creator.

I attended the 1995 Southeast Alaska Indian Repatriation Conference, sponsored by the Tlingit and Haida Indian Tribes of Alaska in Juneau. During the conference, a TeleVideo hookup with the National Museum of Natural History allowed tribal members to view objects held there. It was gratifying to see a packed room at the University of Alaska Southeast Campus where tribal members ranging from elders to young children had gathered to view important objects. The moderator of the conference, David Katzeek, caretaker (*Hit–s'aati*) of the Shangukeidee clan (Thunderbird of Klukwan, Eagle moiety), and his mother, Anna Katzeek, followed ceremonial protocol and wore regalia as a sign of respect for all involved. Responses by members of other clans also followed the protocol. During the TeleVideo session, elders talked and debated about the masks, hats, and bear knife shown on the video screen, sharing their knowledge with tribal members. It appeared to be a time of real intellectual revitalization for the Tlingit and Haida. One respected participant responded after the conference: "Everything has power, has spirit. The power was strong there this morning, and emotions were strong. . . . One day all the things that have been lost will be returned." [40]

It is important to note, however, that the costs of repatriations, legal or otherwise, may be considerable, straining limited tribal resources.

Much of the early focus of the movement was upon the Smithsonian Institution, since it is the national museum of our country. I was a visiting scholar at the Smithsonian's National Museum of Natural History in 1985–1986. At that time one curator of physical anthropology was Douglas Ubelaker, whose forensic work was popularized in his book *Bones*.[41] Ubelaker has also done extensive scholarly work on the population history of North American Indians, one of my own topics of interest.

At that time, the Smithsonian Institution was being subjected to extreme political pressure from national pan-Indian organizations to return its Native American skeletal collections to Native American tribes. The decision was made by Smithsonian administrators to inform tribes of the skeletal collections and suggest to them that some ancestral tribal members might be among the skeletons of the Smithsonian.

Ubelaker sought my advice. We talked about the draft of a letter informing the tribes of the Smithsonian's holdings along with a computer printout detailing the geographical origin of the Native American skeletons. I made a suggestion or two, and the revised letter was sent by Adrienne L. Kaeppler, then chair of the Department of Anthropology, to 225 federally recognized tribes.[42] I thought from the beginning that the tribes would show little interest. They were generally focused on local issues; repatriation was not yet an issue of concern to them—at least I had not heard much about it from tribal people. Rather, I told Ubelaker that the demands for repatriation were mainly articulated by "urban" Native Americans. Tribes might very well be supportive of those demands and might eventually become involved, but they had not yet done so to a significant extent. The likely response, I thought, would be no response. My prediction proved correct. Only a handful of responses came in.

National Native American leaders, such as Walter Echo-Hawk of the Native American Rights Fund and Suzan Shown Harjo of the National Congress of American Indians, continued to seek the repatriation of human skeletal remains from the Smithsonian and elsewhere. Native American organizations, such as the American Indians Against Desecration (AIAD), a project of the

International Indian Treaty Council, issued a statement calling for repatriation.[43] Native American protests took place at specific museums, such as the Illinois State Museum at Dickson Mounds. Professional associations such as the Council for Museum Anthropology, Society for American Archaeology, American Anthropological Association, and American Association of Museums became involved and issued position papers. A Panel for a National Dialogue on Museum/Native American Relations was established.[44] Various universities also debated the issues, forming committees and panels to develop policies. The University of California system formed a "Joint Academic Senate–Administration Committee on Human Skeletal Remains" in 1990 to develop a policy for the system, and individual campuses formed local committees to implement the policy.[45]

Senator Daniel K. Inouye (Democrat of Hawaii) took up the cause as chair of the Select Committee on Indian Affairs and, as discussed below, linked it to the acquisition of the collection of the Museum of the American Indian in New York City to form the National Museum of the American Indian. One idea considered but discarded was to establish a national mausoleum where Native American remains " 'which are not useful for scientific inquiry' would be buried, 'giving due regard to the religious and ceremonial beliefs and practices of those Indians, Aleuts and Eskimos whose ancestors may be included in the Smithsonian collection.' " [46]

The private sector also became involved in the repatriation movement, just as it did in the civil rights movement. Elizabeth Sackler purchased three Hopi and Navajo ceremonial masks for $39,050 at a Sotheby auction in New York City in May 1991. Her intent was to return them to the tribes. She then established the American Indian Ritual Object Repatriation Foundation to help native groups win the return of important cultural objects in the hands of private individuals and organizations.[47] The foundation continues to be active in repatriation.

State and Federal Laws

Repatriation legislation was enacted on both the state and federal levels.

"All states have laws that address in some manner the disposition of prehistoric aboriginal remains and grave goods," concludes Marcus Price. Although some states "merely apply their criminal laws against grave robbing, trespass, and vandalism, or their general public health and cemetery laws," ever more, he notes, they are establishing "legislation specific to the problem," yet, "there is little consistency in approach." [48] An important example of state legislation was Iowa's reburial statue of the mid-1970s, which protects "prehistoric burial mounds and unmarked cemeteries and presumes ultimate reburial of ancient remains." [49] The landmark state legislation, however, probably was Nebraska's

1989 Unmarked Human Burial Sites and Skeletal Remains Protection Act. In passing the act, Nebraska became the first state with a general repatriation statue. It provides for the protection of unmarked burial sites throughout the state and the repatriation (within one year of a request) to relatives or American Indian tribes of human remains and associated burial goods held in state-sponsored or state-recognized public bodies.[50] In 1991 California, after much effort by Assemblyman Richard Katz, established a new law providing for the repatriation of Native American human remains and funerary objects.[51] The original bill was vetoed by the governor in 1990, but after further amendments was passed again and approved by the governor on September 6, 1991.[52] In large part, Katz's efforts were inspired by the large number of Native American remains held by the University of California system. The University of California had lobbied against the law, preferring instead to develop its own repatriation policy.[53]

The federal government has repeatedly enacted legislation aimed at protecting the rights of Native American groups vis-à-vis ancestral remains and sacred objects. Twentieth-century legislation may be dated from the Antiquities Act of 1906, which granted the federal government jurisdiction over all aboriginal remains and artifacts on federal property. Other important legislation includes the Historical Sites Act of 1935 (supplemented by the Reservoir Salvage Act of 1960), the National Historic Preservation Act of 1966, the Department of Transportation Act of 1966, and the National Environmental Policy Act of 1969.

Recent federal legislation has been sparked by the outspokenness and political sophistication of Native Americans themselves. Native groups have successfully lobbied lawmakers and obtained public support for their repatriation efforts. On August 11, 1978, Senate Joint Resolution 102, the American Indian Religious Freedom Act (AIRFA), made it "the policy of the United States to protect and preserve for American Indians their inherent right of freedom to believe, express, and exercise the traditional religions of the American Indian, Eskimo, Aleut, and Native Hawaiian." Included in this freedom was "use and possession of sacred objects." [54] The Archaeological Resources Protection Act (ARPA) of 1979 soon followed, specifically mandating that the AIRFA be considered in the disposition of archaeological resources, and that "archaeological resources recovered from Indian land are the property of the tribe." [55]

The next important federal legislation on repatriation was Public Law 101-185, the National Museum of the American Indian Act of November 1989, which established the National Museum of the American Indian (NMAI) as part of the Smithsonian Institution. A component of this law mandates that "if any Indian human remains are identified by a preponderance of the evidence as those of a particular individual or as those of an individual culturally affiliated with a particular Indian tribe, the Secretary [of the Smithsonian], upon the request of the descendants of such individual or of the Indian tribe shall expeditiously return such remains (together with any associated funerary objects) to the descendants or tribe, as the case may be." [56]

In October 1990, Public Law 101-601, the Native American Graves Protection and Repatriation Act (NAGPRA), was established. It specifically considers the disposition of Native American human remains and artifacts in federal agencies (other than the Smithsonian), mandating that "any institution or State or local government agency, including any institution of higher learning, that receives Federal funds and has possession of, or control over, Native American human remains or cultural items must comply with NAGPRA." [57] NAGPRA will, therefore, affect most of the approximately eight thousand museums in the United States.

The law increases the protection of Native American graves on federal and tribal land, makes illegal the commercial traffic in Native American remains, requires the inventorying and repatriation to culturally affiliated tribes or descendants of all collections of Native American remains and associated funerary objects held by federal agencies and federally funded museums (and universities), and also requires the repatriation of Native American sacred objects and cultural patrimony. Human remains, funerary objects (either associated or unassociated with currently held remains), sacred objects, and objects of cultural patrimony shall all "be expeditiously returned." [58] ("Cultural affiliation" as defined in NAGPRA means "that there is a relationship of shared group identity which can be reasonably traced historically or prehistorically between a present day Indian tribe or Native Hawaiian organization and an identifiable earlier group.") Under the provisions of NAGPRA, a seven-person review committee monitors and reviews repatriation activities. Three of the members are appointed from a pool nominated by Native American groups and religious leaders; at least two of them must be "traditional Indian religious leaders." Three members are appointed from nominees of museum and scientific organizations, and one member is appointed from a list suggested by the other six members.

The Smithsonian Institution decided to follow Public Law 101-601 as well as Public Law 101-185, thereby extending the mandate of repatriation to include not only human remains and funerary objects but also sacred objects and objects of cultural patrimony. In the fall of 1996, an amendment to the NMAI Act was introduced into the U.S. Senate by Senator McCain (Republican of Arizona), and passed a few months later. It amends the act along the lines of the NAGPRA legislation, setting a strict time schedule and legally requiring the repatriation of objects of cultural patrimony and sacred objects. [59] The Smithsonian is committed to completing its inventory of Native American human remains and funerary objects by June 1, 1998; a summary of ethnographic objects was sent to all tribes shortly after the December 31, 1996 deadline.

The NMAI Act of 1989 contains a provision whereby a Repatriation Review Committee is appointed "to monitor and review the inventory, identification, and return of Indian human remains and Indian funerary objects." This committee is composed of five individuals, at least three of whom are to be selected from individuals nominated by Native American groups. The committee was empaneled in March 1990 and four of the five members were selected from those nominated by Native American groups; two of these are American Indians.[60] The 1996 amendment to the act added two members to the committee, both of whom are to be traditional religious leaders.[61]

The collections of the Smithsonian's newly created National Museum of the American Indian, however, are not under the purview of this committee; rather, the museum's repatriation activities are the responsibility of its own board of trustees, as stated in the act. Consequently, NMAI has its own policies and procedures for repatriation, established in 1991.[62] Recently, the NMAI has been criticized by both Native Americans and museologists for its handling of repatriation.[63] In fact, the Smithsonian Institution as a whole has not been immune to criticism in this regard.[64] Some changes are underway.

International Developments

U.S. federal and state laws for repatriation pertain only to claims made by Native American groups in the United States, and only for remains and objects in the United States. For example, human remains of Native Americans from Mexico or Central or South America are not within the purview of the laws, nor are wampum belts from Iroquois in Canada.[65] Similarly, U.S. law does not apply to remains or objects in any other country. Nevertheless, ever more native groups in the United States are attempting to recover their ancestors and histories from elsewhere in the world. For example, the Zuni are recovering war gods from other countries, and the Wounded Knee Survivors' Association is attempted to recover from the Kelvingrove Museum in Glasgow, Scotland, a Ghost Dance shirt "reputedly taken from a body at Wounded Knee." The response of the museum in the latter instance was that "it is a very difficult issue for us. It could be seen as a precedent that could open up our collection to other claims for repatriation." [66]

There are important recent developments concerning international repatriation, however. The Inuit Circumpolar Conference (ICC) is held every four years. This international organization represents around 115,000 Inuit in the Arctic regions of the United States (Alaska), Russia (Chukotka), Canada, and Greenland. Its purposes are to further Inuit unity, rights, and interests, foster policies that safeguard the Arctic environment, and be a full partner in the development of the circumpolar regions. At its 1995 conference, held in Nome, Alaska, the Keepers of the Treasures* Alaska sponsored a symposium on international repatriation. (The Keepers of the Treasures, a national organization, is dedicated to preserving, affirming, and celebrating Native American cultures.) Speaking at the symposium, I commented that "all repatriation in the United States is international repatriation, given what should be an independent status of native tribes. Unfortunately, it didn't turn out this way. Native groups are forced to negotiate with museums and institutions rather than with the federal government as equal entities."

Only a month before the ICC, a diplomatic conference was held in Rome to discuss the adoption of the draft UNIDROIT Convention on the International Return of Stolen or Illegally Exported Cultural Objects. Delegates from some seventy countries, with observers from eight, voted to approve the text of the convention, derived after "eleventh hour negotiations following weeks of debate between the art-rich 'source countries' and the so-called 'market countries' where most of the trade in cultural objects takes place." [67] It calls for the return of stolen and illegally exported cultural objects under certain specified conditions.[68] The United States eventually approved the act, a small but important step in international repatriation.

In the international repatriation movement, Native Americans join with other exploited peoples of the world to claim the objects of their history, plundered by thieves as well as colonial or war-occupied governments. The objects at stake include art looted during World War II and the Elgin marbles, Greek works currently in London.[69]

Some Repatriations

According to its own established procedures, some 2,500 of the approximately 18,500 skeletal remains in the collections of the National Museum of Natural History have been repatriated by the Smithsonian to Native American groups, including some to Hawaiian Islanders. To date, the largest number of repatriated remains were returned to Larsen Bay, Alaska, in October 1991. These were the remains of about a thousand people from the site on Kodiak Island excavated by the Smithsonian physical anthropologist Ales Hrdlicka between 1932 and 1936.[70] In January 1992 the associated funerary objects were returned.

The Smithsonian has also returned human remains to the Cheyenne River Sioux (including the brain of Leon Pretty Voice Eagle), Yankton Sioux, Devil's Lake Sioux, Sisseton-Wahpeton Sioux, Oglala Sioux (the remains of Chief Smoke were returned to a descendant), Two Kettles Sioux (the remains of Chief Puffing Eyes were returned to his family), Southern Arapaho, Shoshone-Bannock, Makah, Pawnee, Southern Cheyenne, Yerington Paiute, Ninilchik, Spokane, the Warm Springs Confederated Tribes, and various Alaskan villages. (Some remains were returned before the federal legislation; in 1984 remains including the skull of the well-known Captain Jack were returned to the Modoc; others were restored to the Blackfeet in 1988.) Funerary objects have been returned to Alaskan groups, and to the Pawnee and the Cheyenne River Sioux. Included in the Warm Springs repatriation were 86,085 objects, mostly beads.

Among the remains repatriated to the Southern Cheyenne were those of Native Americans killed at the infamous massacre at Sand Creek, Colorado Territory, on November 29, 1864. The Colorado militia led by Colonel John Chivington had dismembered and decapitated victims on the spot, sending some to the Army Medical Museum. The remains repatriated to the Pawnee included the crania of six Pawnee, believed by some to have been beheaded after being killed by the U.S. Army only one month after their honorable discharge from the U.S. Army as scouts.[71] A repatriation ceremony for these and other Pawnee remains from the Smithsonian, complete with a military escort, was held at Fort McNair in Washington, D.C., on June 6, 1995. The small wooden boxes containing the remains of the six scouts had folded U.S. flags on top, acknowledging their status as veterans. Senator McCain, the chair of the Select Committee on Indian Affairs, spoke and apologized to the Pawnee on behalf of the U.S. government for what had happened and for the fact that it had taken the government so long to return their dead. The following day, the remains were taken under a military escort to former Pawnee lands at Genoa, Nebraska, for burial. At Genoa, the location from which the Pawnee had earlier been removed to Oklahoma, the remains were buried with other Pawnee remains at the cemetery and covered with a slab of concrete to prevent further disturbance. (Pawnee cemeteries in and around Genoa had been looted for a century by scientists and others seeking bones and artifacts.)[72] A week later, as is the custom of the Pawnee, a final feast for the dead was held by the Pawnee tribe in Pawnee, Oklahoma, where they are now centered.

Other museums, institutions, agencies, and collectors have also returned Native American skeletal remains, both before NAGPRA and as a response to it. California Indian remains have been repatriated to appropriate groups by the Catholic church; the state of Nebraska has returned Pawnee and Omaha skeletons; the University of Minnesota returned 150 sets of remains to the Devils Lake Sioux; Stanford University returned remains of some 550 individuals to the Ohlone; and the University of Tennessee returned 190 sets of remains to the Cherokee.

Cultural and sacred objects have also been returned, by the Smithsonian and other museums, institutions, and private individuals. The Smithsonian repatriated a few cultural objects to the Zia Pueblo (in 1982) and Zuni Pueblo (in 1987) before the legislation, and some others to Native Hawaiians since the legislation. Wampum belts, masks of the False Face Society, a *kano:wa* or ceremonial turtle rattle, and two antler hair combs have been returned to the Iroquois;[73] various ceremonial shields and weapons and altar figurines have been repatriated to the Jemez Pueblo by the NMAI; and medicine bundles and prayer boards have been returned to the Navajo and Hopi. Hopi kachinas have also been repatriated;[74] and several dozen twin War Gods or *Ahayu:da* have been repatriated to the Zuni—nearly all that were missing.[75] Finally, the Omaha's sacred pole was returned to them by the Peabody Museum, as were the skeletal remains and burial offerings of almost one hundred Omaha held by the University of Nebraska.

The NAGPRA legislation of November 16, 1990, gave institutions five years (with a possible extension) to complete inventories of human remains and funerary objects, and three years to provide summaries of unassociated funerary objects, sacred objects, and objects of cultural patrimony. After the inventory, six months are allowed for notifying tribes of affiliated remains and funerary objects. Therefore, only now, at the end of the decade, are full repatriation efforts under NAGPRA commencing, and the Smithsonian is ahead of most other museums and institutions, if not all, in actual repatriations. Nevertheless, many issues remain to be settled in implementing NAGPRA. Two important ones are whether nonfederally recognized tribes are entitled to repatriated remains and objects (as they are by the Smithsonian), and what are institutions to do about remains or objects where cultural affiliation cannot be established? In 1997 an interim rule established penalties for noncompliance with NAGPRA.[76]

New Views, New Ideas, New Knowledge

The repatriation process has great potential for bridging the gap between native worlds and the larger society. As it developed, the issue of the repatriation of human remains became polarized between advocates of reburial and advocates of study and preservation in repositories. Little compromise occurred; yet some compromise is not only necessary but desirable. Native Americans and scholars, particularly physical anthropologists, must learn to relate to one another in new ways. Science and scholarship have much to offer to Native Americans, as Native Americans attempt to recapture their lost histories. Native Americans are no longer powerless in American society, but are important actors, and Native American values, wishes, and perspectives must be respected by scholars. Although some disciplines such as anthropology have histories of applied work with Native Americans, the repatriation process is providing new challenges for the application of scholarly disciplines to Native Americans' real-life concerns. Native American studies seems to be ideally situated to assist in these applied matters.

Who "Owns" What?

Important in the repatriation process are different conceptions of property and ownership between Native American groups and the larger American society. "Cultural patrimony" as defined above is an important concept in repatriation;

it means simply "group ownership," and is in itself an important recognition of the rights of Native American ownership as defined by Native Americans. However, it may have different interpretations.

Many native tribes are organized as clans. Native groups argue that the idea of cultural patrimony must be extended to the clan, not only the entire group. For example, the Tlingit became organized with the Haida Indians in 1912, under the Alaskan Native Brotherhood, and then the tribe was federally recognized under the Central Council of Tlingit and Haida Indian Tribes of Alaska. They later became a part of the Sealaska Corporation under the Alaska Native Claims Settlement Act of 1971. However, in Tlingit culture the "basic property-holding unit" was the matrilineal clan, with the "Hit" representing "both the physical structure and matrilineage associated with a house" and the house being the clan subunit. So, "a Tlingit individual acquires ownership to clan property through his/her membership in a clan. Ownership rights are not inherited or assigned independently of clan membership." Moreover, clan property may not be transferred in any manner unless agreed upon by all clan members. Similarly, individuals owned few possessions, including personal clothing. Clans owned not only physical items but also crests, songs, and stories, with crests typically being the most important symbols of the clan. Clan members may use clan property, including symbols, but this ends at death. There is no transfer of the privilege. Use rights might be extended to nonclan members—for example, by grandparents to grandchildren who are not clan members—but never ownership. The "title" to clan property is vested in the *Shaadeihani* (head man) or *Hits'aati* (trustee), but that individual only holds the property for the clan and "does not have the authority to sell or dispose of clan property." Thus, the Tlingit argue that such objects as clan hats depicting crests fall within the category of cultural patrimony, although they are not extended to the entire group. Moreover, all clan hats outside clan possession were obtained, by definition, illegally from the Tlingit.[77]

The Kiowa have their own view of the ownership of symbols. One important cultural expression is the Tipi with Battle Pictures. "Ornamented with fine pictures of fighting men and arms on one side and wide, horizontal bands of black and yellow on the other," [78] the tipi has been reproduced in various forms since 1845, but only "according to distinctive principles relating to the individual ownership of intangible property." [79] Although the Kiowa have experienced broad changes in their society and culture over the past century, "many concepts regarding rights and restrictions over intangible property remain based on a traditional legal system." One important concept is that individuals own their various "accomplishments and the right to control their representation," be they exploits in battle, songs, designs, or names.[80]

In 1994 I gave a lecture on repatriation at Cameron University in Lawton, Oklahoma. Afterward, a young Kiowa man came to me and asked about a

Kiowa Tai-me in the National Museum of Natural History. Tai-me is the central figure of *kado,* the Kiowa Sun Dance ceremony, "a central group ritual, reaffirming the spiritual and physical unity of the group."[81] When the Kiowa acquired Tai-me, he was, in the words of the Kiowa author N. Scott Momaday, "from that moment the object and symbol of their worship, and so shared in the divinity of the sun."[82] James Mooney describes Tai-me as "a small image, less than 2 feet in length, representing a human figure dressed in a robe of white feathers, with a headdress consisting of a single upright feather and pendants of ermine skin, with numerous strands of blue beads around its neck, and painted upon the face, breast, and back, with designs symbolic of the sun and moon. The image itself is of dark-green stone, in form rudely resembling a human head and bust."[83] It is kept in a rawhide box. "The Tai-me bundle is not very big, but it is full of power."[84] From time to time, the Tai-me has been stolen, and then the Kiowa Sun Dance was not held; for example, the Osage stole it in 1833 and did not return it until 1835, "at the persuasion of the Americans."[85]

The Kiowa have their Tai-me, as the young Kiowa man told me. But an image, a reproduction of Tai-me is at the Smithsonian. "It is ours," he said. "Can it be repatriated?" The image of Tai-me is Kiowa property, as is the image of the Tipi with Battle Pictures. Who had the right to reproduce it? Who had the right to make a graven image of it? Who owns the reproduction? Is it a reproduction?

Who Are Ancestors?

A difficult question often arising in repatriation is: who is ancestral to whom? Our knowledge of Native American histories is very incomplete, based in part on the very human remains and cultural objects that are being repatriated. Contemporary Native American groups did not typically have just one ancestral group, but several, and one ancestral group did not typically have just one descendant but several. Conceptually, the problem may be viewed as one of "cladistic" affiliation (from Greek *clados,* 'branch') versus "rhizotic" affiliation (from Greek *rhiza,* 'root'). As John Moore explains, "Cladistic theories emphasize the significance of a historical process by which daughter populations, languages, or cultures are derived from a parent group. Rhizotic theories emphasize the extent to which each human language, culture, or population is considered to be derived from or rooted in several different antecedent groups."[86] Specific native peoples today may have several ancestor groups, and, most importantly for repatriation, different native peoples today may have the same ancestral group. The complexity of these and other repatriation issues may be seen in a case recently considered by the Smithsonian Institutions Native American Repatriation Review Committee.

Some Native American people lived from about A.D. 1000 to about A.D. 1250

just north of present-day Kansas City. In archaeological terms, they represent what is called the "Steed-Kisker" Phase of cultural traditions. In the late
1930s, a Smithsonian archaeologist named Waldo Wedel excavated some sites
in the area and took some human remains and funerary objects to the National
Museum of Natural History. As part of a broader repatriation request by the
Pawnee Tribe of Oklahoma, it was determined by the museum's Repatriation
Office that the Steed-Kisker Phase might be affiliated with what is called the
larger Central Plains Tradition, to which the Pawnee of today are definitely
affiliated. The Pawnee requested the repatriation of the (minimum of) 53 individuals and 178 funerary objects, based on the belief that the preponderance of
available evidence indicated a cultural affiliation with them. The Smithsonian
Repatriation Office declined, stating that further research was necessary. They
argued that the Steed-Kisker Phase might be more closely affiliated with
Middle Mississippian people, and that the Steed-Kisker area might be only
an outlier or colony of the Middle Mississippian area of Cahokia, located at
that time just across the Mississippi River from present-day St. Louis. Or, the
phase might be connected with other traditions such as the Middle Missouri or
Oneota Tradition in Missouri and elsewhere. The Pawnee Tribe of Oklahoma,
represented by their attorney, Walter Echo-Hawk, asked the Repatriation Review Committee to consider the case. We did so.

In considering the issue of cultural affiliation with the Pawnee, or, more
precisely, the Central Plains Tradition, we examined several types of evidence
available from Steed-Kisker Phase excavations: ceramics, house type, mortuary practices, physical anthropological evidence, settlement patterns, subsistence patterns, and tools; we also considered the geographic location of the
sites and Pawnee oral traditions. The Repatriation Review Committee concluded that the house type of earthlodges and rectangular structures, the geographic location adjacent to known Central Plains Tradition areas, the settlement pattern of dispersed houses without mounds (which are a characteristic
of Middle Mississippian Tradition), and Pawnee oral traditions telling of origins in the area indicated a cultural affiliation with the Central Plains Tradition
and the Pawnee of today. We also concluded that the type of ceramics indicated
a possible Middle Mississippian affiliation, while the evidence from physical
characteristics, mortuary practices, subsistence, and tools was inconclusive for
any affiliation. Thus the preponderance of the *available* evidence at the time
indicated that the remains and objects should be repatriated to the Pawnee.

We also thought, as did the Pawnee, that other contemporary groups representing other traditions at that time might also be affiliated with the Steed-
Kisker Phase; therefore, the people and culture in that area at that time might
be ancestral to several different groups today. Because of this possibility, the
Repatriation Review Committee recommended also that other contemporary
tribes potentially affiliated with the Steed-Kisker Phase be notified of the intention to repatriate to the Pawnee and be given the opportunity to present their

case for the remains and objects.[87] This was done, and some other tribes—the Iowa Tribe of Oklahoma, the Kaw Nation of Oklahoma, the Osage Nation of Oklahoma, the Otoe-Missouria Tribe of Oklahoma, and the Ponca Tribe of Oklahoma—also expressed interest in the Steed-Kisker remains and objects. Procedures for a formal consideration of the various requests and corresponding evidence were set by the Review Committee. However, the tribes themselves sought to undertake a joint repatriation. The Osage eventually withdrew their claim, stating that "where there is some dispute as to the origins of the remains, the Osage Nation will not seek to repatriate such remains." [88] The remaining tribes formed a Steed-Kisker Joint-Repatriation Committee (SKJRC), chaired by Charles Lone Chief of the Pawnee. They eventually agreed to a Memorandum of Understanding whereby the tribes would engage in a joint repatriation of the remains and objects.[89] They are now reburied.

A Note on Oral History and Archaeology

Repatriations under the law, NAGPRA or otherwise, have thrust Native Americans into new interactions and partnerships with archaeologists, and vice versa. Native Americans have been made "administrators over archaeology," [90] as Roger Echo-Hawk has termed the relationship, in that they act as watchdogs and are often given the final say; however, Native Americans need to be much more than administrators. What is needed, Echo-Hawk writes, is a blending of archaeology and Native American oral tradition, thereby "creating exciting new avenues of research on ancient Indian history." [91] As he further notes, "The successful integration of oral evidence from archaeology and physical anthropology holds great potential for reshaping the essential character of academic constructions of ancient human history." [92] Oral traditions offered by the Pawnee in the Steed-Kisker dispute were both very important in their own right and very helpful in interpreting the archaeological record. They indicate the formation of the four bands of Pawnee—Pitahawirata, Chaui, Kitkahahki, and Kawarakis—out of diverse groups. The oral traditions also indicate two major Caddoan groups of the Steed-Kisker Phase: one group, on the west side of the Missouri River, eventually becoming Arikara, the other group, on the east side, eventually becoming Pawnee. Testimony in this regard by Roger Echo-Hawk was based on both oral traditions and the archaeological record, and one helped clarify the other.[93] This is an important relationship that will likely increase in importance in the future.

Implications for Native American Studies

The repatriation of Native American human remains and cultural objects represents only one area—but an important, applied area—in which Native American studies has the potential to assist Native American communities.

Help can take the form of consultation and workshops with local communities so that they may make actual repatriation requests to museums and institutions. It can take the form of assisting communities with the actual return of the remains and objects and deciding what to do with them when they are physically returned. Decisions regarding human remains are generally simple. Most groups want to and do rebury the remains, although some have allowed universities and museums to keep them for the group (for example, a repository for Chumash remains is cared for by the physical anthropologist Philip Walker at the University of California, Santa Barbara). Decisions regarding objects are more complex. Native groups may want to develop museums for them, somewhat along the lines of the Makah of Neah Bay, who built a new tribal museum to house objects recovered from the archaeological excavation of a former village. They may even allow museums to keep and display them. For example, the Cheyenne and Arapaho Tribes of Oklahoma and the Smithsonian Institution have recently signed an agreement whereby 36 Cheyenne funerary objects subject to repatriation may remain at the National Museum of Natural History.[94]

Native American studies can also assist groups with the actual documentation needed to establish both cultural affiliation with the remains and objects in question and the sacred or cultural status of the objects themselves. Native American studies, with its interdisciplinary nature, could be at the forefront in generating new knowledge about the histories of native peoples derived from and reconciling diverse sources of information. Native American studies could help to generate new knowledge about the objects as communities explain their purposes, uses, and creation. As in so many other instances, the dichotomy between applied and scholarly issues involved in repatriation may be a false one.

Notes

This chapter is a much revised and greatly extended version of my "Repatriation of human remains and artifacts," in *Native America in the Twentieth Century: An Encyclopedia,* Mary B. Davis, ed. (New York: Garland, 1994), 542–44. An earlier, shorter version was presented at Festival II: A Celebration of Diversity, Cameron University, Lawton, Oklahoma, in 1994.

1. Other important applied areas include Native American tribal economic development, on reservations and elsewhere, gambling and casinos, museology, health and related issues, language development, legal and political tribal development, social welfare issues, and education on all levels.

2. See Douglas J. Preston, "Skeletons in our museums' closets," *Harper's* (February 1989), 67.

3. These estimates were obtained from H. Marcus Price III, *Disputing the Dead: U.S. Law on Aboriginal Remains and Grave Goods* (Columbia: University of Missouri Press, 1991), 1.

4. *Mourt's Relation: A Relation or Journal of the English Plantation Settled at Plym-*

outh in New England, by Certain English Adventurers Both Merchants and Others, Dwight B. Heath, ed. (New York: Corinth, 1963 [1622]), 28.

5.   Thomas Jefferson, *Notes on the State of Virginia,* William Peden, ed. (Chapel Hill, N.C.: University of North Carolina Press, published for the Institute of Early American History and Culture, 1954 [1787]), 98–99. (This edition retains the integrity of the original version published in English by the bookseller John Stockdale of London in 1787 with Jefferson's permission. A French version was published in Paris in 1786.)

6.   See Robert E. Bieder, *Science Encounters the Indian, 1820–1880: The Early Years of American Ethnology* (Norman: University of Oklahoma Press, 1986), 16–103.

7.   Samuel G. Morton, *Crania Americana; or: A Comparative View of the Skulls of Various Aboriginal Nations of North and South America, to which is Prefixed an Essay on the Varieties of the Human Species* (Philadelphia: n.p., 1839).

8.   William A. Hammond, Surgeon General's Office, Washington, D.C., Circular no. 2, May 21, 1862, in *A History of the United States Army Medical Museum, 1862 to 1917,* Dr. D. S. Lamb, compiler (Washington, D.C.: n.p., n.d.), 2.

9.   Lamb, *History of the Medical Museum,* p. 4.

10.   Ibid., 43.

11.   Ibid.

12.   Madison Mills, Surgeon General's Office, Letter to Generals, January 13, 1968; see also Lamb, *History of the Medical Museum,* 47. Mills explained that he was writing a letter rather than issuing a printed circular as "making this task obligatory might make it distasteful."

13.   Mills, Letter to Generals. He also indicated that "we should preserve likewise illustrations of the weapons of the fast disappearing tribes."

14.   The collection included the following numbers of Native American crania: "Tsuktshi, 1; Flathead, Chenook, Selipsh, Nisqually, 13; Californian, 2; Piegan, Spokane, Mandan, 3; Arickaree, Gros Ventre, 2; Sioux, Kaw, Minatree, Menominee, 6; Cheyenne, Kiowa, Arrapahoe, Wichita, 10; Navajo and Apache, 5; doubtful or mixed breeds, 5." Lamb, *History of the Medical Museum,* 51.

15.   Ibid., 56A.

16.   Harold E. Driver, *Indians of North America,* 2d ed., rev. (Chicago: University of Chicago Press, 1969), 375–76. See also Roger C. Echo-Hawk, "Pawnee mortuary traditions," *American Indian Culture and Research Journal,* 16 (1992), 77–99; David I. Bushnell, *Burials of the Algonquian, Siouan and Caddoan Tribes West of the Mississippi,* Bureau of American Ethnology, Bulletin no. 83 (Washington, D.C.: U.S. Government Printing Office, 1927).

17.   The Inca, Garcilaso de la Vega, *The Florida of the Inca,* John Grier Varner and Jeannette Johnson Varner, trans. and eds. (Austin: University of Texas Press, 1951 [1605]), 312–13; see also 319.

18.   Quoted by Ernest Turner, "The souls of my dead brothers," in *Conflict in the Archaeology of Living Traditions,* Robert Layton, ed. (London: Unwin Hyman, 1989), 191.

19.   See Zuni Tribal Council Resolution no. M70-90-1017, November 16, 1989, Zuni, N.M. Since the remains cannot be returned to Zuni, the tribal council requested "museums and other institutions to continue to respectfully care for and curate any desecrated Zuni ancestral human remains."

20. George Catlin, *Letters and Notes on the Manners, Customs and Conditions of the North American Indians,* vol. 2 (New York: Dover, 1973 [1844]), 6.

21. The Seventh Cavalry was the regiment commanded by General George A. Custer, who was defeated by the Sioux, Northern Cheyenne, and other tribes on June 25, 1876, in the Battle of Greasy Grass, better known as the Battle of Little Big Horn.

22. Following the Wounded Knee Massacre, there was some trade in "fictitious" items supposedly obtained from the massacre site. One issue in this repatriation is establishing whether the items are "real."

23. Tamara L. Bray and Thomas W. Killion, eds., *Reckoning with the Dead: The Larsen Bay Repatriation and the Smithsonian Institution* (Washington, D.C.: Smithsonian Institution Press, 1994), 18.

24. See Kenn Harper, *Give Me My Father's Body: The Life of Minik, the New York Eskimo* (Iqaluit, Northwest Territory: Blacklead Books, 1986).

25. "Give me my father's body," *World* (magazine supplement, January 6, 1907), 3.

26. Ales Hrdlicka, "An Eskimo brain," *American Anthropologist,* 3 (1901), 454–500.

27. Alfred L. Kroeber, "The Eskimo of Smith Sound," *Bulletin of the American Museum of Natural History,* 12 (1899), 316.

28. "My father's body," 3.

29. "Summary description of UC collections of human skeletal remains and artifacts," unpublished statement, University of California, n.d.

30. Jane E. Buikstra, "Diet and disease in late prehistory," in *Disease and Demography in the Americas,* John W. Verano and Douglas H. Ubelaker, eds. (Washington, D.C.: Smithsonian Institution Press, 1992), 87–101.

31. These and other topics are discussed in Verano and Ubelaker, *Disease and Demography.*

32. See, for example, Douglas H. Ubelaker and Lauryn Guttenplan Grant, "Human skeletal remains: Preservation or reburial?" *Yearbook of Physical Anthropology,* 32 (1989), 249–87.

33. According to the U.S. Army Corps of Engineers, which has control over them, the remains should be repatriated to the Umatilla Indians under the provisions of NAGPRA. The corps has been sued to prevent the repatriation; two of the eight plaintiffs are anthropologists at the Smithsonian Institution. See *Bonnichsen et al. v. U.S. Army Corps of Engineers,* Complaint CV '96-1481 JE in the U.S. District Court for the District of Oregon, October 16, 1996.

34. For example, a lawsuit was brought by the Hawaiian organization Hui Malama I Na Kupuna O Hawai'i Nei, seeking to prevent the U.S. Navy from conducting an inventory and study of the remains of 1,582 people excavated on Oahu in 1939–40 and held at the Bishop Museum. See *Na Iwi v. Dalton, et al.,* Civil No. 94-00445 DAE, in the U.S. District Court for the District of Hawaii. The suit was filed on June 14, 1994; a summary judgment rendered on July 25, 1995, stated that the inventory that was conducted did not violate NAGPRA.

35. See, for example, Douglas Cole, *Captured Heritage: The Scramble for Northwest Coast Artifacts* (Seattle: University of Washington Press, 1985), 120–21.

36. Preston Valien, "Social movements," in *A Dictionary of the Social Sciences,* Julius Gould and William L. Kolb, eds. (New York: Free Press, 1964), 658. For vari-

ous definitions of social movements, see Paul Wilkinson, *Social Movement* (New York: Praeger, 1971); see also Rudolph Heberle, *Social Movements* (New York: Appleton-Century-Crofts, 1951); Neil Smelser, *Theory of Collective Behavior* (New York: Free Press, 1963); David F. Aberle, *The Peyote Religion Among the Navaho,* 2d ed. (Norman: University of Oklahoma Press, 1991 [1966]), 315–333; Orrin E. Klapp, *Collective Search for Identity* (New York: Holt, Rinehart and Winston, 1969); Anthony Oberschall, *Social Conflict and Social Movements* (Englewood Cliffs, N.J.: Prentice-Hall, 1973); Jo Freeman, ed., *Social Movements of the Sixties and Seventies* (New York: Longman, 1983); Daniel A. Foss and Ralph Larkin, *Beyond Revolution: A New Theory of Social Movements* (South Hadley, Mass.: Bergin and Garvey, 1986); Aldon D. Morris and Carol McClurg Mueller, eds., *Frontiers in Social Movement Theory* (New Haven: Yale University Press, 1992); Enrique Larana, Hank Johnson, and Joseph R. Gusfield, eds., *New Social Movements: From Ideology to Identity* (Philadelphia: Temple University Press, 1994); Sidney Tarrow, *Power in Movement: Social Movements, Collective Action and Politics* (Cambridge: Cambridge University Press, 1994).

37. Anthony F. C. Wallace, "Revitalization movements," *American Anthropologist,* 58 (1956), 265.

38. Russell Thornton, "Boundary dissolution and revitalization movements: The case of the nineteenth-century Cherokees," *Ethnohistory,* 40 (1993), 359–83; see also Aberle, *Peyote Religion,* 315–33; Ralph Linton, "Nativistic movements," *American Anthropologist,* 45 (1943), 230–41; Wallace, "Revitalization movements," 264–81. For considerations of specific Native American revitalization movements, see James Mooney, *The Ghost-Dance Religion* (Lincoln: University of Nebraska Press, 1991 [1896]); Cora Du Bois, *The 1870 Ghost Dance,* Anthropological Records, no. 3 (Berkeley: University of California Press, 1946); Aberle, *Peyote Religion;* Hazel W. Hertzberg, *The Search for an American Indian Identity: Modern Pan-Indian Movements* (Syracuse: Syracuse University Press, 1971); Anthony F. C. Wallace, *The Death and Rebirth of the Seneca* (New York: Vintage, 1972); Joseph G. Jorgensen, *The Sun Dance Religion: Power for the Powerless* (Chicago: University of Chicago Press, 1972); R. David Edmunds, *The Shawnee Prophet* (Lincoln: University of Nebraska Press, 1983); Fred W. Voget, *The Shoshoni-Crow Sun Dance* (Norman: University of Oklahoma Press, 1984); Russell Thornton, *We Shall Live Again: The 1870 and 1890 Ghost Dance Movements as Demographic Revitalization* (New York: Cambridge University Press, 1986); William G. McLoughlin, *Cherokee Renascence in the New Republic* (Princeton: Princeton University Press, 1986); Omer C. Stewart, *Peyote Religion: A History* (Norman: University of Oklahoma Press, 1987); Joel W. Martin, *Sacred Revolt: The Muskogees' Struggle for a New World* (Boston: Beacon Press, 1991).

39. Susan Shown Harjo, "Introduction," in *Mending the Circle: A Native American Repatriation Guide* (New York: American Indian Ritual Object Repatriation Foundation, 1996), 7.

40. Chuck Smythe, "Observations of experimental video conference consultation with NMNH," manuscript, National Museum of Natural History, March 29, 1995.

41. Douglas H. Ubelaker with Henry Scammell, *Bones: A Forensic Detective's Casebook* (New York: HarperCollins, 1992).

42. Adrienne L. Kaeppler, Chairman, Department of Anthropology, National Museum of Natural History, letter to tribal representatives, November 22, 1985.

43. See, for example, Jan Hammil and Robert Cruz, "Statement of American

Indians against desecration before the World Archaeological Congress," in Layton, *Archaeology of Living Traditions,* 195–200.

44.   See "Report of the Panel for a National Dialogue on Museum/Native American Relations," presented to the Senate Select Committee on Indian Affairs, Washington, D.C., 1990.

45.   "Report of the University of California Joint Academic Senate–Administration Committee on Human Skeletal Remains," Office of the President, University of California, Oakland, Calif., August 1990.

46.   "Indians seek burial of Smithsonian skeletons," *New York Times* (December 8, 1987).

47.   The foundation has published *Mending the Circle* (1996) and is distributing it free of charge to assist native groups with their repatriation efforts.

48.   Price, *Disputing the Dead,* 43.

49.   Ibid., 65.

50.   See Robert M. Peregoy, "The legal basis, legislative history, and implementation of Nebraska's landmark reburial legislation," *Arizona State Law Journal,* 24 (1992), 329–89; see also Price, *Disputing the Dead,* 43–115, for a survey of state laws.

51.   See Assembly Bill No. 2577, introduced January 8, 1990 in the California Legislature, 1989–90 Regular Session, amended in Assembly, February 16, 1990, amended in Assembly, March 26, 1990.

52.   See California Legislature at Sacramento, 1989–90 Regular Session, 1989–90 First Extraordinary Session, Assembly Final History, Synopsis of Assembly Bills, Constitutional Amendments, Concurrent, Joint, and House Resolutions, vol. 2:1695; California Legislature at Sacramento, 1991–92 Regular Session, 1991–92 First Extraordinary Session, 1991–92 Second Extraordinary Session, Assembly Final History: Synopsis of Assembly Bills, Constitutional Amendments, Concurrent, Joint, and House Resolutions, vol. 1: 83.

53.   See "Report of the University of California."

54.   Francis Paul Prucha, *The Great Father: The United States Government and the American Indians,* abridged ed. (Lincoln: University of Nebraska Press, 1986 [1984]), 369.

55.   Price, *Disputing the Dead,* 30–31; see pp. 19–42 for a discussion of the ARPA and other federal laws.

56.   Public Law 101-185, 1989, sec. 11, pt. c.

57.   Francis P. McManamon, "Memorandum to Universities, Colleges, Departments of Anthropology, Schools of Medicine," National Park Service, U.S. Department of the Interior, August 15, 1994, Washington, D.C.

58.   Public Law 101-601, sec. 7, pt. a. For a history of this law, see Jack F. Trope and Walter R. Echo-Hawk, "The Native American Graves Protection and Repatriation Act: Background and Legislative History," *Arizona State Law Journal,* 24 (1992), 35–77.

59.   See Public Law 104-276, 104th Congress, October 9, 1996; see also Memorandum, Office of Government Relations, Smithsonian Institution, "S. 1970, Amendments to the National Museum of the American Indian Act of 1989 (repatriation)," September 9, 1996.

60.   Specifically, the committee's duties, as stated in Public Law 101-185, are: "(1) with respect to the inventory and identification, ensure fair and objective consider-

ation and assessment of all relevant evidence; (2) upon the request of any affected party or otherwise, review any finding relating to the origin or the return of such remains or objects; (3) facilitate the resolution of any dispute that may arise between Indian tribes with respect to the return of such remains or objects."

61.　See Public Law 104-278; see also Office of Government Relations Memorandum, "S.1970."

62.　See "National Museum of the American Indian Policy Statement on Native American Human Remains and Cultural Material," unpublished statement, National Museum of the American Indian, Washington, D.C., n.d.

63.　See Carol Kalafatic, "A fox in the henhouse? Repatriation at the National Museum of the American Indian," *News from Indian Country: The Nations Native Journal* (Late July 1996), 7A; Judith Brandin, "A museum turned upside down," *Washington Times* (October 11, 1996).

64.　See Thomas G. Watts, "Delays in repatriation blamed on law," *Dallas Morning News* (November 17, 1996).

65.　In a case involving an Iroquois wampum belt from Canada at the National Museum of Natural History, the Canadians let the United States Iroquois handle the repatriation, which has been approved.

66.　"Sioux seek return of sacred red shirt," *British Weekly* (April 16, 1995).

67.　Helen J. Wechsler, Program Manager, International Program, "Report on the UNIDROIT Convention," American Association of Museums, October 1995.

68.　See "Final Act of the Diplomatic Conference for the Adoption of the Draft Unidroit Convention of the International Return of Stolen or Illegally Exported Cultural Objects," Rome, June 24, 1995.

69.　See John Henry Merryman, "Who owns the Elgin marbles?" *ARTnews, 85* (1986), 100–109.

70.　Bray and Killion, *Reckoning with the Dead,* xiv.

71.　James Riding In, "Six Pawnee crania: Historical and contemporary issues associated with the massacre and decapitation of Pawnee Indians in 1869," *American Indian Cultural and Research Journal, 16* (1992), 111; see also William T. Billeck, Erica B. Jones, Stephanie A. Makseyn-Kelly, and John W. Verano, "Inventory and assessment of human remains and associated funerary objects potentially affiliated with the Pawnee in the National Museum of Natural History," Repatriation Office Case Report no. 88-007, National Museum of Natural History, January 19, 1995.

72.　See Orlan J. Svingen, "The Pawnee of Nebraska: Twice removed," *American Indian Culture and Research Journal, 16* (1992), 121-37.

73.　See William N. Fenton, "Return of eleven wampum belts to the Six Nations Iroquois Confederacy on Grande River, Canada," *Ethnohistory, 36* (1989), 392-410; "Sacred masks go back to tribes," *New York Newsday* (November 24, 1993), 65, 101; and "Keepers' board members involved in repatriation cases," *Keepers of the Treasures* (June 1996), 1-3.

74.　See Jake Page, "Return of the kachinas," *Science 83, 4* (1983), 58-63.

75.　See William L. Merrill, Edmund J. Ladd, and T. J. Ferguson, "The return of the *Ahayu:da,*" *Current Anthropology, 34* (1993), 523-67.

76.　"Native American Graves Protection and Repatriation Act; Interim Rule," *Federal Register, 62* (January 13, 1997), Rules and Regulations, 1820-23.

77.	Rosita Worl, "The Tlingit Indian tribe," manuscript, Juneau, Alaska, n.d.

78.	N. Scott Momaday, *The Way to Rainy Mountain* (Albuquerque: University of New Mexico Press, 1969), 45.

79.	Candace S. Greene and Thomas D. Drescher, "The Tipi with Battle Pictures: The Kiowa tradition of intangible property rights," *Trademark Reporter,* 84 (1994), 420.

80.	Ibid., 420, 423.

81.	*A Chronicle of the Kiowa Indians (1832–1892)* (Berkeley: R. H. Lowie Museum of Anthropology, University of California, n.d.), 2.

82.	Momaday, *Rainy Mountain,* 6.

83.	James Mooney, *Calendar History of the Kiowa Indians* (Washington, D.C.: Smithsonian Institution Press, 1979 [1898]), 240. Mooney writes "the present *taime* is one of three, two of which came originally from the Crows, through an Arapaho who married into the Kiowa tribe, while the third came by capture from the Blackfeet."

84.	Momaday, *Rainy Mountain,* 80.

85.	*Chronicle of the Kiowa,* 5.

86.	John H. Moore, "Putting anthropology back together again: The ethnogenetic critique of cladistic theory," *American Anthropologist,* 96 (1994), 925.

87.	Russell Thornton, Andrea A. Hunter, Roger Anyon, Lynne Goldstein, and Christy G. Turner II, "Recommendations regarding the dispute between the Pawnee Tribe of Oklahoma and the National Museum of Natural History Repatriation Office over the Steed-Kisker Phase human remains and funerary objects," unpublished report submitted to Secretary I. Michael Heyman, October 10, 1995, Washington, D.C.

88.	Leonard M. Maker, letter to Pawnee Tribal Repatriation Committee, February 6, 1997.

89.	See Memorandum of Understanding between the Iowa Tribe of Oklahoma, the Kaw Nation of Oklahoma, the Otoe-Missouria Tribe of Oklahoma, the Pawnee Tribe of Oklahoma, and the Ponca Tribe of Oklahoma, April 14, 1997. A memorandum of understanding (MOU) or a memorandum of agreement (MOA) may become an important mechanism in repatriation. With a MOA, Native American groups will enter an agreement whereby another party will simply represent both groups in a repatriation case. With a MOU, there will be an understanding that several Native American groups will engage in a joint claim and repatriation. Through such understandings and agreements, Native American peoples are able to resolve potential repatriation disputes and prevent institutions from playing one group against the other (sometimes in order to conduct further research or study on the human remains) when cultural affiliation is unclear or cannot be established.

90.	Roger Echo-Hawk, "Forging a new ancient history for native America," paper presented at the Annual Meeting of the Society for American Archaeology, 1996 New Orleans.

91.	Ibid., 2; see also Roger Echo-Hawk, "*Kara Katit Pakutu:* Exploring the origins of Native America in anthropology and oral traditions" (M.A. thesis, University of Colorado, 1994).

92.	Echo-Hawk, "Forging a new ancient history," 4. For another successful attempt see J. Douglas McDonald, Larry Zimmerman, A. L. McDonald, William Tall Bull, and Ted Rising Sun, "The Northern Cheyenne outbreak of 1879: Using oral history and archaeology as tools of resistance," in *The Archaeology of Inequality,* Randall H. McGuire and Robert Paynter, eds. (Cambridge: Blackwell, 1991), 64–78. For writings considering the relationship between ethnohistory and archaeology, see J. Daniel Rogers and Samuel M. Wilson, eds., *Ethnohistory and Archaeology: Approaches to Postcontact Change in the Americas* (New York: Plenum Press, 1993).

93. See, for example, Thornton et al., "Recommendations"; Echo-Hawk, *Kara Katit Pakutu.*

94. Agreement between the National Museum of Natural History, Smithsonian Institution, and the Cheyenne and Arapaho Tribes of Oklahoma regarding Cheyenne funerary objects in the collection of the National Museum of Natural History, December 5, 1996.

Russell Thornton and C. Matthew Snipp

A Final Note

This volume is, we hope, a step in the proper direction for the development of Native American studies. Contributors have attempted to present problems and prospects for Native American studies, for many problems are to be overcome, but many prospects also are to be realized. History is history, but history is remembered. Native American studies emerged in certain ways for certain reasons. Good or bad, the legacy of the past is with us. To the detriment of Native American studies today, that legacy means that it is more a political phenomenon than an intellectual one. Perhaps this volume will convince some otherwise, or at least suggest its intellectual potential and its importance.

Native American Studies in the Twentieth-First Century

As we near the end of this century, it is worthwhile to contemplate the future of Native American studies in connection with the future of the people to whom this scholarship is devoted. If Native Americans had vanished, as most observers in the late nineteenth century expected, it seems altogether likely that this volume would not exist. At most, Native American studies would be an arcane academic topic not too unlike other fields devoted to long-extinct cultures.

Long before Native American studies appeared in the course catalogues of colleges and universities, historians, anthropologists, and other scholars devoted considerable energy to studying Native Americans. In view of this tradition, one may wonder why Native American studies has appeared in the academy only in recent decades. In part, the answer to this question lies with Native Americans themselves. Defying expectations, Native Americans did not disappear in this century and are actually far more numerous today than a century ago. Indeed, the vibrancy of Native American studies as a subject of intellectual discourse stems directly from the vibrancy of modern Native American communities, be they reservation, rural, or urban.

As we have seen, it is no coincidence that Native American studies appeared in academe at a time when Native American communities themselves were asserting their place in American society. The civil rights movement was successful in opening institutions of higher education to racial and ethnic communities that had historically been all but excluded. As numbers of minority students, including a small number of Native American students, pursued their studies of history, culture, and science, they found their own people profoundly absent, their contributions to society ignored, discounted, or appropriated. Native American students in particular found that their people were ignored or at best minimized (in history) or treated as relics and specimens (in anthropology), despite five hundred years of contact and struggle for the western hemisphere. Knowledge about contemporary Native American communities was entirely missing from disciplines such as sociology and political science.

The students' response was to demand the representation of their people in the curricula of postsecondary education. When these demands were ignored or rejected, the students' frustration escalated. One of the first outbursts occurred at San Francisco State University in 1968, where a strike initiated by African-American students was soon joined by students of many racial and ethnic backgrounds, including a small group of Native Americans. Administrators at San Francisco State reluctantly acceded to the students' request for an ethnic studies program. In the process, they created the first Native American studies program in the nation, followed shortly by others at the University of California's Berkeley, Davis, and Los Angeles campuses, the University of Arizona, the University of New Mexico, and the University of Minnesota. These programs were grudgingly incorporated into university life, but were also perceived by most as marginal, staffed by marginal faculty, teaching marginal students. The program at the University of California at Davis was literally located at the farthest edge of campus in temporary buildings.

Underfunded, understaffed, and generally unsupported at most institutions, Native American studies struggled to survive and has done so now for three decades. In that time, journals have been established, books and monographs published, curricula and academic majors developed, and Native American studies, as an academic field, has moved toward the intellectual mainstream, though it is not there yet. As we approach the next century, it is a good time to contemplate the academic challenges that will confront Native American studies in the decades ahead.

What Should Be Done?

Argued, discussed, and documented here, the study of Native Americans and Native American studies have much to offer to traditional disciplines, though the disciplines may constrain both. English and comparative literature have embraced Native American literature, with mostly positive results for all, though one might question the impact of some Native American literature upon Native Americans ourselves. Native American languages are important for Native American studies and, of course, for Native Americans as well. Linguistics is, however, only part of the academic solution. Anthropology has long embraced the study of Native Americans; yet its effects have been mixed for Native Americans and Native American studies, and both have had to distance themselves from the discipline. American history has yet fully to consider Native Americans as relevant, let alone important, actors in American society at virtually any point in time. Until our society and its history fully legitimate Native Americans as agents in history, then all will continue to suffer, and Native American studies will remain an illegitimate academic offspring.

Native American studies ought to be much more than the typical study of Native Americans within existing disciplines. Individual disciplines are important in the study of Native Americans, and together they are very important. Nevertheless, the disciplines remain limited in their ability to encompass Native American experiences, either traditional, historical, or contemporary ones. The chapters in this volume offer guidelines for the future of Native American studies—particularly those in Part 1, which articulate questions faced uniquely by Native American scholars, students, and peoples. Population and identity issues, the trauma of history, literature and writing literature, history and writing history, language, sovereignty, epistemology and religion, kinship and family, science and technology, and repatriation of human remains and cultural objects are among the more important topics; but this is not an exhaustive list.

Native American studies' ambitious objective is to understand Native Americans, America, and the world from Native American perspectives and thus broaden the knowledge and education of both Native Americans and non-Native Americans. Its accomplishment will require Native American studies to develop its considerable intellectual potential in the next century, and colleges and universities to recognize the educational and intellectual legitimacy of Native American studies, neither of which has been done to date. Native American studies is still hindered by romantic, fantasy-based, and stereotyped notions about, lack of appreciation and respect for, and even an unwillingness to accept Native Americans. It is also still hindered by the fact that colleges and universities have typically failed to consider Native American studies as a serious intellectual endeavor. At the same time, some people who teach in Native American studies departments fail to appreciate or even understand the system of higher education; sometimes they even fail to appreciate or understand Native American peoples, especially traditional or tribal ones. Some Native American studies faculties are even today dominated by non–Native Americans or Native Americans too distant from Native America. To appreciate and understand both academe and Native American peoples and their diversity are critical for Native American studies. It makes no sense to be involved in higher education if one is unwilling to embrace the values and objectives of higher education; it makes no sense to be involved in Native American studies without a realistic understanding of Native Americans. Native American studies needs to develop the intellectual richness of Native Americans and their societies and cultures, and incorporate it into colleges and universities in ways understood by both academe and Native Americans. This, of course, is no easy task.

Some Suggestions

The First Convocation of American Indian Scholars held at Princeton University in 1970 was a landmark event.[1] It established a national agenda for the study of Native Americans; the report of the convocation lists seventeen resolutions passed, covering such areas as Native American participation in the study of Native America, communication between Native American groups, support for educational endeavors at various levels, an examination of the newly emerging field of Native American studies, and support for Native American arts and artists.[2] Another national convocation, in 1970, was focused on Native American water rights, though education, Native American studies, and other issues were considered as well.[3] Two and one-half decades have passed since the Second Convocation; it seems time for another to consider issues in the study of Native Americans and Native American studies, as did the First Convocation. The initial resolution passed at the First Convocation was "to continue the Convocation as an annual event";[4] Alfonso Ortiz said, "As Native American scholars we have an enormous responsibility which we must come together and carry out."[5] We have not done this; because we have not, others have too frequently determined the course of Native American studies.

Major national universities must make commitments to developing Native American studies as a major academic endeavor equal to other endeavors on their campuses. Resolution 12 of the First Convocation "called for a conference or workshop to be organized to undertake an examination of the current and proposed Native American Studies programs in the universities of Canada and the United States, composed of both Indian and non-Indian representatives of the institutions of higher education involved in such programs." [6] To our knowledge this was never done, although conferences on Native American studies have been held. In a 1980 conference, participants acknowledged the difficulties of incorporating Native American studies into major institutions, particularly the Ivy League universities.[7] They also acknowledged that it is in the interest of academe and larger society for Native American studies to "accept its conception of society and scholarship, so as not to present it with any challenges" — even though "it is precisely this challenging role which ethnic studies can and must take." Therefore, "this is reason enough to promote Native American Studies programs of all types, at all kinds of institutions of higher learning." [8] A national conference bringing together important Native American scholars and intellectuals with deans and other administrators from major universities to consider intellectual issues in Native American studies and its incorporation into universities would be extremely helpful to the development of the field.

A broad national scholarly and professional association for Native American scholars has been discussed for some time, and various attempts to found one have been made. At one conference of directors of Native American studies held in 1980, "the strongest area of agreement was the necessity of forming more numerous and more effective linkages between Native American scholars in universities." [9] Some half-dozen conferences of Native American professors have been held over the years; yet little resulted from them, and many prominent professors have not attended.

Native American studies cannot "heal itself," it seems; major assistance is undoubtedly needed. It would be helpful if major foundations promised to develop the rich intellectual potential of Native American studies, including consideration of the experiences and problems of Native Americans in contemporary America. Resolution 17 of the First Convocation stated that foundations should "not support with funds any program or activities for or about American Indians and Native Peoples, which are not directed and controlled by Indian groups, organizations or tribes." [10] Over a quarter of a century later, reaffirming this is still necessary. A national program to fund research on Native Americans and Native American studies, with funding decisions made by leading Native American and other scholars familiar with Native American studies and Native American tribal people, would be desirable. A related national effort might be made to attract highly qualified young Native American students into graduate programs in areas important to Native American studies; concomitantly, an effort might be made to encourage bright young scholars of Native Americans in various disciplines to become involved in Native American studies, at least intellectually if not organizationally as well.

Ultimately, the future will and should be determined by those involved in

Native American studies, particularly the Native Americans involved. This group must include substantial numbers and proportions of Native American scholars doing the finest scholarship. As we look back over three decades of Native American studies, it sometimes seems that the Crow chief Plenty Coup was right when he said, "He loves His white children most." Plenty Coup advocated the importance of education for American Indians to overcome their disadvantage in American society. He noted that the Great Spirit gave Indians "patience and love of home and children," but not knowledge of "how to do the many wonderful things His white children are doing." [11] Those involved in Native American studies have yet to do all the wonderful things their colleagues are doing in the traditional academic disciplines and other scholarly areas. Eventually they must do so. And they should do so in ways that make sense to Native American peoples themselves.

Notes

1. For the proceedings of this convocation, see *Indian Voices: The First Convocation of American Indian Scholars* (San Francisco: Indian Historian Press, 1970).

2. Ibid., 378–82.

3. For the proceedings of this convocation, see *Indian Voices: The Native American Today: A Report on The Second Convocation of American Indian Scholars* (San Francisco: Indian Historian Press, 1974).

4. *First Convocation,* 378.

5. Roxanne Dunbar Ortiz, ed., *Final Report from the Round Table of Native American Studies Directors in Forming the Native American Studies Association* (Albuquerque, N.M.: Native American Studies Association with the Institute for Native American Development, University of New Mexico, 1980), 33.

6. *First Convocation,* 381.

7. Ortiz, *Final Report,* 13, 20–21.

8. Ibid., 20–21.

9. Ibid., 22.

10. *First Convocation,* 382.

11. Annette Rosenstiel, *Red and White: Indian Views of the White Man, 1492–1982* (New York: Universe Books, 1983), 158.

Index

Index

Acoma Pueblo: kinship system of, 319; mentioned, 114. *See also* Pueblo Indians
Adams, Charles, 374
Africa, 366
African American: students, 87, 417; intellectuals, 97; literature, 119, 120; slavery of, 194; mentioned, 4, 25, 43, 83, 191, 202. *See also Brown v. Board of Education;* Civil Rights Act of 1868
Ahenakew, Freda, 172
Alaska Native Claims Settlement Act of 1971, 404
Alaskan Native Brotherhood, 404
Albuquerque, New Mexico, 30
Albuquerque Indian School: founding of, 86
Alcatraz Island: Native American occupation of, 112
Alcoholism, 61, 68, 233, 349
Alcorn, Janice, 366
Aleutian Islanders: arrival of ancestors in Western Hemisphere, 21; population size of, 27; mentioned, 8, 397, 398
Aleuts. *See* Aleutian Islanders
Algeria: indigenous population history of, 17
Algonquian Indians: languages of, 52, 157, 173, 174, 175, 180*n44,* 292, 308, 343; kinship system of, 343, 346
Allen, Paula Gunn, 111, 137–38, 145–46
American Academy of Child Psychiatry, 69
American Anthropological Association, 397
American Association for the Advancement of Science, 308
American Association of Museums, 397
American Indian Chicago Conference, 94
American Indian Ethnohistoric Conference. *See* American Society for Ethnohistory
American Indian Movement, 41, 116, 235, 236. *See also* Clyde Bellecourt; Lehman Brightman; Dennis Banks; Russell Means
American Indian Religious Freedom Act of 1978, 64, 286, 398
American Indian Ritual Object Repatriation Foundation, 397
American Museum of Natural History, 389, 391
American Society for Ethnohistory: founding of, 93, 185; mentioned, 182
Anadarko, Oklahoma, 84
Anasazi: weaving by, 371; Great Kivas of, 373; mentioned,199. *See also* Southwest Indians

Anchorage, Alaska, 30
Andaman Islanders, 317
Andean Indians: domestication of potatoes
by, 369–70; metallurgy of, 372; mentioned,
367. *See also* Inca; Mochica
Anderson, Gary Clayton, 345
Anishinaabe Indians. *See* Ojibwe Indians
Antelope Creek, 385
Antiquities Act of 1906, 398
Apache Indians: 1990 population of, 24; cere-
monies of, 68. *See also* Chiricahua Apache
Indians; Fort Apache Reservation; Jicarilla
Apache Reservation; Kiowa Apache Indi-
ans; Mescalero Apache Indians; San Carlos
Reservation; Southwest Indians
Apess, William, 125, 146
Appalachian Mountains, 50
Appiah, K. Anthony, 136
Arapaho Indians: kinship system of, 318, 319;
Southern Arapaho, 401; Cheyenne and
Arapaho Tribes of Oklahoma, 408. *See also*
Plains Indians
Arbeka Indians, 280. *See also* Mvskoke
Indians
Archaeological Resources Protection Act of
1979, 398
Arikara Indians, 405. *See also* Fort Berthold
Reservation; Plains Indians
Arkansas Navigation Project of the Kerr-
McClelland waterways, 259
Arkansas River, 259
Ark of the Covenant, 395
Aryan Nation: writing history of, 226–27
Aspen Institute for Humanistic Studies, 94
Assiniboine Indians, 344. *See also* Nakota
Indians; Plains Indians; Sioux Indians
Athabascan languages. *See* Athapaskan lan-
guages
Athapaskan languages, 161, 343
Atmosphere, 274
Australian Aborigines: population history of,
17; kinship system of, 318
Axtel, James, 230
Aztec: Binding of the Years, 362; Tenochtit-
lan, 363; categories of plants, 365; creation
of *chinimpas* in Lake Tezcoco, 368

Bacone, Almon: founding of Bacone College
by, 84
Bacone College: founding of, 84

Bailyn, Bernard, 203
Baja, California, 80
Baker, Mark, 159
Bakhtin, Mikhail, 132, 146
Baldwin, James, 120
Ballard, Louis, 114
Banks, Dennis, 112. *See also* American Indian
Movement
Baraga, Frederick: Ojibwe grammar by, 175
Barnes, J. K., 388
Barthes, Roland, 140
Basso, Keith, 189
Bates, Russell, 145
Bear Butte, South Dakota, 274, 276, 291
Beaver, Fred, 114
Beck, Peggy V., 145
Bellecourt, Clyde, 112. *See also* American
Indian Movement
Bemidji State University, 89
Bennett, Robert, 115
Bennett, William, 140
Bergman, Martin, 65
Beringa, 20, 21
Berkhofer, Robert, 185
Berlin, Brent, 365
Berlin, Irving, 69
Bevis, William, 138
Bierwert, Crisca, 176
Big Dipper, 361
Big Horn Mountains, 361
Bird, Gloria, 145
Birmingham corpora: used for the *Collins
Cobuild English Grammar,* 163
Black, Hugo, 259
Black Death, 22. *See also* Bubonic plague
Black Elk, 70
Blackfeet Indians: Medicine Wheel of, 361;
mentioned, 114, 402. *See also* Plains Indians
Black Wolf, James, 386
Blaeser, Kimberly, 141, 145
Blatchford, Herb, 115
Bloomfield, Leonard: plan for researching and
documenting Native American languages,
166; mentioned, 153, 157, 162, 173
Blue Sky-Space, 274, 281
Boas, Franz: study of kinship by, 315, 316,
317; mentioned, 156, 161, 296, 313. *See also*
Boasians
Boasians, 183, 184. *See also* Franz Boas
Boston, Massachusetts, 101

Boudinot, Elias, 259
Boulder, Colorado, 376
Boyd, Robert, 22
Boy Scouts of America: Order of the Arrow, 299; mentioned, 287, 299, 300, 303
Brain, Jeffery, 25
Brant, Beth, 138, 144
Brave Heart, Maria Yellow Horse, 9, 66, 73, 74*n*8
Breedlove, Dennis, 365
Breinig, Jeane, 145
Brendale v. Yakima Nation, 257. *See also* Yakima Indians
Brightman, Lehman, 112. *See also* American Indian Movement
British and Foreign Bible Society, 93
British Columbia Indian languages, 167
Bronze Age, 371
Brown, Dee, 234
Brown, Jennifer, 193
Brown v. Board of Education, 258. *See also* African Americans
Brugge, David, 267
Bruner, Edward: study of kinship by, 347
Bubonic plague, 20, 22. *See also* Black Death
Buffalo Calf Pipe, 342
Bureau of American Ethnology: emphasis on linguistics, 155; founding of, 155, 311; mentioned 312, 313
Bureau of Ethnology. *See* Bureau of American Ethnology
Busby, Montana, 386
Bushotter, George, 118
Byrd, William, 81, 82

Cabeza de Vaca, Álvar Núñez, 91
Cahokia, 363, 406
Cahuilla Indians, 115, 118. *See also* California Indians
California Indians: languages of, 167; use of fire by, 367; as basketmakers, 368; human remains of, 392; repatriation of human remains to, 402; mentioned, 23, 64, 234. *See also* Cahuilla Indians; Covelo Indian Community of Confederated Tribes of the Round Valley Reservation; Chumash Indians; Hoopa Valley Reservation; Mission Indians; Modoc Indians; Ohlone Indians; Pomo Indians; Tolowa Indians; Yuki Indians; Yurok Indians

Calloway, Colin, 230, 231
Cambridge, Charlie, 376
Cameron University, 404
Campbell, Janet, 114
Canadian Rocky Mountains, 20
Cape York meteorite, 391
Captain Jack, 401
Carlisle, Pennsylvania, 85
Carlisle Indian School: founding of, 85–86; mentioned, 153, 154
Carrier language, 167
Carr-Saunders, A. M., 17
Casa Grande, 373
Catawba Indians, 25. *See also* Southeast Indians
Catlin, George, 390
Central Council of Tlingit and Haida Indians, 404. *See also* Haida Indians; Northwest Coast Indians; Tlingit Indians
Central Plains Tradition, 406. *See also* Plains Indians
Certificate of Degree of Indian Blood, 27
Chaco Canyon: Pueblo Bonita, 374; mentioned, 373. *See also* Anasazi; Pueblo Indians; Southwest Indians
Chafe, Wallace, 160
Chakrabarty, Dipesh, 233
Chama Valley, 373
Chamberlain School: founding of, 86
Changing Woman, 330
Charles City, Virginia, 80
Cherokee Academy: founding of, 84
Cherokee Female Seminary: founding of, 84; mentioned, 89
Cherokee Indians: history of, 11; Trail of Tears, 23, 55, 194, 258; 1990 population of, 24; tribal membership requirements of Eastern Band of Cherokee Indians, 28; enumerated in 1980 U. S. census, 29; enumerated in 1990 U.S. census, 29; tribal membership of, 29; recognition of groups by Georgia, 55; education of, 83, 86; intellectuals, 122; future study of, 200; Phoenix as symbol of, 250; 1835 Memorial to Congress, 258; *Cherokee Phoenix,* 259; 1835 Treaty of New Echota, 259, 264; National Jail, 264; Treaty of 1868, 264; kinship system of, 318, 327, 346; political organization of, 328; repatriation of human remains to, 402; mentioned 93, 114, 251, 259, 279,

Cherokee Indians (*continued*)
    345. *See also Cherokee Nation v. Georgia;*
    Worchester v. Georgia; Southeast Indians;
    Talton v. Mayes
Cherokee Male Seminary: founding of, 83–84
Cheyenne Indians: Northern Cheyenne his-
    tory, 225, 226; epistemology of, 273–78;
    Arrow ceremony of, 275; Sun Dance of,
    275, 286, 288, 293–94, 386; comparison
    with Mvskoke Indians, 278–84 *passim,*
    284–86, 291, 292, 293, 294, 296; Blue Sky-
    Space, 281; kinship system of, 318, 319,
    324, 325, 326; political organization of,
    328; comparison of Northern Cheyenne
    and Southern Cheyenne kinship systems,
    348; massacre of Northern Cheyenne at
    Fort Robinson and Antelope Creek, 385–86;
    Northern Cheyenne repatriation, 385–87;
    Crazy Dogs society, 386; Elk Horn society,
    386; Keeper of the Sacred Buffalo Hat, 386;
    repatriation of human remains to South-
    ern Cheyenne, 401, 402; Cheyenne and
    Arapaho Tribes of Oklahoma, 408; men-
    tioned, 11, 85, 251, 286, 287, 300. *See also*
    Fort Robinson Massacre; Plains Indians;
    Sand Creek Massacre
Cheyenne River Sioux Tribe: reservation of,
    347; repatriation of Wounded Knee objects
    to, 391; repatriation of human remains to,
    401; repatriation of objects to, 402. *See also*
    Lakota Indians; Sioux Indians
Chiapas, Mexico, 365
Chicago, Illinois, 93, 182, 389
Chickasaw Indians: education of, 84, 86;
    mentioned, 200, 259. *See also* Southeast
    Indians
Chief Puffing Eyes, 401
"Chief Red Dog," 301
Chief Seattle, 389
Chief Smoke, 401
Chilocco Industrial School: founding of, 86;
    study of students at, 201
Chingachgook, 299
Chinook language, 162
Chippewa Indians. *See* Ojibwe Indians
Chiricahua Apache Indians: kinship system of,
    318. *See also* Apache Indians
Chivington, Colonel John, 402. *See also* Sand
    Creek Massacre
Choctaw Academy: founding of, 83
Choctaw Indians: 1990 population of, 24;

schools for, 83, 84; education of 84, 86;
    kinship system of Mississippi Choctaw,
    319–20; kinship system of, 346; men-
    tioned, 200, 259. *See also Choctaw Nation v.*
    Oklahoma; Southeast Indians
Choctaw Nation v. Oklahoma, 259
Cholera, 20, 23
Chomsky, Noam, 157, 158, 159, 160, 162
Chumash Indians, 408. *See also* California
    Indians
Churchill, Ward, 145
Civil Rights Act of 1968, 265
Cladistic affiliation, 405
Clark, C. Blue, 267
Clark, William, 155
Cleveland, Ohio, 112
Clifford, James, 186, 222
Cloquet, Minnesota, 85
Coastal Salish: architecture of, 373. *See also*
    Northwest Coast Indians
Coast Tsimshian language, 167. *See also*
    Tsimshian language
Cofachiqui, 389. *See also* Southeast Indians
Cohen, Felix, 28, 248
Colgate University, 90
College of Ganado, 85
College of William and Mary: founding of, 81
College of the Menominee Nation: founding
    of, 85. *See also* Native American tribal
    colleges
Collier, John, 27, 47, 235
Colorado River, 52
Columbia University: Department of Anthro-
    pology, 313
Columbus, Christopher, 43
Comanche Indians: kinship system of, 326;
    political organization of, 328; mentioned,
    85. *See also* Plains Indians
Comas, Juan, 45
Comrie, Bernard: linguistic questionnaire with
    Smith, 163
Cook, Captain, 186–87
Cook-Lynn, Elizabeth: definition of Native
    American studies of, 4, 116; mentioned, 97,
    133, 138, 143, 145
Cooper, James Fenimore, 299
Coosa Indians, 280. *See also* Mvskoke Indians
Copan, 361
Cornell, Stephen, 230
Cornell University: American Indian Program,
    89, 99, 148*n12;* mentioned,119

Corn Woman, 273

Coronado, Francisco, 91

Corte-Real, Gaspar, 91

Costo, Rubert, 115, 116, 118, 128*n25*

Council for Museum Anthropology, 397

Countryman, Edward, 231

Covelo Indian Community of Confederated Tribes of the Round Valley Indian Reservation, 25. *See also* California Indians; Yuki Indians

Crazy Horse, 301

Creek Indians: 1990 population of, 23; education of, 83, 84, 86; kinship system of, 346; mentioned, 11, 14, 281. *See also* Mvskoke Indians; Southeast Indians

Cree language, 10, 157, 172

Crockett, Davy, 299

Cronon, William, 225, 226

Crow Dog, 260, 261, 262

Crow Indians: as allies of United States, 194; kinship system of, 278, 312, 317, 318, 319–20, 341, 343, 346, 347; mentioned, 421. *See also* Plains Indians

Cruikshank, Julie, 176

Cultural affiliation: definition of, 95–96, 399

Dakota Conflict of 1862, 345. *See also* Dakota Indians

Dakota Indians: kinship system of, 316, 343, 344, 345; history of, 345; mentioned, 114, 131. *See also* Dakota Conflict of 1862; Sioux Indians

Dakota language, 90

Dakota Wesleyan University, 89

D'Arcy McNickle Center for the History of the American Indian: American Indian Family History Project, 202; American Indian Historical Demography Project, 202; mentioned, 182, 202. *See also* Newberry Library; D'Arcy McNickle

Darnell, Regna, 155–56

Dartmouth College, 6, 11; founding of, 82; Native American studies, 89, 99; Hovey Murals, 100; fantasies about Native Americans, 101; Native American faculty, 102, 122; faculty teaching Native American literature, 119. *See also* Moor's Indian Charity School; Samson Occom; Eleazar Wheelock; Nathaniel Whitaker

Davis, California, 85

Debo, Angie, 249

Deep Earth, 274

Deganiwidah-Quetzalcoatl University (D-Q U): founding of, 85. *See also* Native American tribal colleges

de la Vega, Garcilaso, The Inca, 389

Delaware Indians: Lenape, 52; mentioned, 83

Deloria, Ella, 118, 122, 146, 316

Deloria, Vine, Jr.: definition of Native American studies of, 4; call for end of anthropology, 188; comparison with Eastman, 290–92 *passim;* Native American religion of, 290–92; mentioned, 9, 44, 96, 112, 113, 115, 116, 140, 145, 249, 287, 297

DeMallie, Raymond, 11, 12, 138, 225, 226, 227, 300

Demmert, William, 115

Demographic regime: definition of, 22

Denevan, William: aboriginal population estimates of, 18

Dennis, Matthew, 230

Densmore, Frances, 147, 366

Department of Dakota (at Fort Snelling, Minnesota), 389

Department of Missouri (at Fort Leavenworth, Kansas), 389

Department of New Mexico (at Santa Fe), 289

Department of the Platte at Omaha (Nebraska), 389

Department of Transportation Act of 1966, 398

Derrida, Jacques, 138

Des Moines, Iowa, 101

De Soto, Hernando, 91

de Ullola, Antonio, 91

Diphtheria, 20

Dobyns, Henry: aboriginal population estimates of Western Hemisphere, 18; aboriginal population estimates of North American (north of Mesoamerica), 19, 23; criticisms of his population estimates, 34*n12,* 199

Dogrib language, 171

Dorris, Michael, 122, 145

Dorsey, James Owen, 311, 312

Douglas, Frederick, 120

Dozier, Edward, 115, 118

Duchene, Marlys, 5

Dull Knife (a.k.a. Morning Star), 385, 386

Duponceau, Peter: creation of the term "polysynthetic," 155

Duran, Bonnie, 9, 32, 149–50*n25*

Duran, Eduardo, 9, 32, 149–50*n25*

Duran, Fray Diego, 60
Durkheim, Emile, 91, 92, 285, 317, 321, 322, 364
Durlach, Theresa: study of kinship by, 316, 317
Duro v. Reina, 250
Dysentery, 20

Earth People, 335–36
Eastern Hemisphere: population of in 1492, 18
Eastern Washington University, 97
East Indian School, 80
Eastman, Charles: on Native American religion, 287–90; mentioned, 82, 146
Ebola, 199
Echo-Hawk, Roger, 407
Echo-Hawk, Walter, 396, 406
Edmunds, David, 230
Eggan, Fred: study of kinship by, 318–20, 322, 328, 344, 346
Egypt: indigenous population history of, 17
Eisenhower, Dwight D., 258
Elgin marbles, 401
Ellison, Ralph, 120
Emmanuel College, 81. *See also* University of Saskatchewan
Engles, Frederick, 91, 183
Epistemology: definition of, 271; in contrast to Horton's "modes of thought," 271–72
Erdrich, Louise, 121, 122, 138, 176
Erickson, Erik, 42, 43, 65
Eskimos. *See* Inuit
Ethnohistory, 10, 182–204 *passim, 206n11;* discussion of at The Newberry Library Conference on Indian Studies, 93; importance to Native American studies, 95; of Lakota Indians, 225; of Northern Cheyenne Indians, 225–26
Ethnopoetics, 132
Evers, Larry, 137, 141, 142, 189, 190, 196
Ex parte Crow Dog, 260, 261–62. *See also* Sioux Indians

Faubus, Governor of Arkansas, 258
Faulkner, William, 124
Felger, Richard, 366
Fenton, William: study of kinship by, 326–27
Field Museum, 389
Fields, Robert, 294, 296–97
First Born, 289
First Convocation of American Indian Schol-

ars: presenters at, 115–16, 127n18; impact of, 116, 419; Resolution 12, 419–20; Resolution 17, 420; mentioned, 13, 94, 114–15, 116
Fixico, Donald, 230, 231
Fogelman, Eva, 65–66
Fogelson, Raymond, 8–9, 41
Fond du Lac Tribal and Community College: founding of, 85. *See also* Native American tribal colleges
Forbes, Jack, 113, 118, 128n27, 145, 230
Formosa: indigenous population history of, 17
Fort Apache Reservation: 1990 population of, 28. *See also* Apache Indians
Fort Belknap College: founding of, 85. *See also* Native American tribal colleges
Fort Coffee, I. T. (Oklahoma), 84
Fort McNair, District of Columbia, 402
Fort Marion, Florida, 85
Fort Robinson, Nebraska, 385, 386
Fort Sill, I. T. (Oklahoma), 85
Foucault, Michel, 132
Fought, John, 156
Fourmile Ruin, 373–74
Fox Indians: language of, 156, 168; kinship system of, 318. *See also* Great Lakes Indians
Frachtenberg, Leo, 156
Frankfurter, Felix, 252
Franklin, Benjamin, 81, 155
Freud, Sigmund, 91, 138
Fried, Morton, 51

Galileo, 358
Gallatin, Albert, 388
Ganado, Arizona, 85
Geertz, Clifford, 144, 187
Genoa, Nebraska, 402
Georgetown, Kentucky, 83
Ghost Dance: shirts, 256, 390, 391, 400; mentioned, 192, 196, 289. *See also* Tatanka Iyotake (Sitting Bull) and Wokiksuye (Bigfoot) Memorial Ride; Wounded Knee Massacre
Gila River Reservation: 1990 population of, 28. *See also* Southwest Indians
Gilbert, William Harlen, Jr., 25
Gill, Sam, 223
Glasgow, Scotland, 400
Gorman, R. C., 114
Gould, Janet, 145
Grand River Reservation, 93. *See also* Mohawk Indians

Great Lakes Indians: metallurgy of, 371; mentioned, 366. *See also* Fox Indians; Menominee Indians; Ojibwe Indians; Stockbridge Indians; Winnebago Indians
Green, Graham, 122
Green, Michael, 89, 230
Gregorian calender, 360, 361
Grimm, Jakob, 155
Grimm, Wilhelm, 155
Grinde, Donald, 232
Guerrero, M. Annette Jaimes. *See* Jaimes, M. Annette

Haida Indians: kinship system of, 316; mentioned, 395, 396, 402. *See also* Central Council of Tlingit and Haida Indian Tribes; Northwest Coast Indians
Haisla language, 167
Hale, Janet Campbell. *See* Campbell, Janet
Hale, Kenneth, 160
Hallowell, A. Irving: study of kinship by, 317
Hammond, William, 388
Hampton Normal and Agricultural Institute. *See* Hampton University
Hampton University: history of, 85
Handsome Lake, 196
Hano Pueblo: kinship system of, 319. *See also* Pueblo Indians
Hanover, New Hamphire, 82, 101
Haraway, Donna, 223
Harjo, Joy, 114, 121, 126
Harjo, Suzan Shown, 395, 396
Harlan, Justice of the Supreme Court, 264
Harlem, Montana, 85
Harmon, Alexandra, 230
Harris, Marvin, 296
Harvard University: Native Americans at, 6, 89, 99; founding of, 81; Department of Anthropology, 313; Peabody Museum of Archaeology and Ethnology, 386, 389, 403; mentioned, 119, 133
Haskell Indian Junior College. *See* Haskell Indian Nations University
Haskell Indian Nations University: history of, 84–85
Haskell Institute. *See* Haskell Indian Nations University
Hassrick, Royal: study of kinship by, 344
Haudenosaunee. *See* Iroquois Confederacy
Havana, Cuba, 80
Havighurst, Robert J., 86

Hawaiian Islanders. *See* Native Hawaiians
Hawthorne, Wendy, 376
Heap of Birds, Edgar, 301
Heart of the Earth Survival School, 87
Hegel, Georg W. F., 91, 182. *See also* Hegelian
Hegelian, 229. *See also* Hegel, Georg W. F.
Hegeman, Susan, 220–21
Hemish Indians. *See* Jemez Pueblo
Henrico College, 80
Henrico, Virginia, 80
Henry, Jeannette, 115, 128*n*25
Hernandez-Avila, Ines, 145
Herring, D. Ann, 22
Hewitt, J. N. B., 118
Hiawatha, 273, 300
Hickerson, Harold: study of kinship by, 327
Hidatsa Indians: kinship system of, 312, 347. *See also* Fort Berthold Reservation; Plains Indians
Hill, Roberta, 176
Hill, Ruth Beebe, 300
Historical Sites Act of 1935, 398
Hitler, Adolph, 234
Hoa-sjela (Stone or Boulder Lake), 227. *See also* Jicarilla Apache Reservation
Hobsbawam, Eric, 223
Ho-Chunk Indians. *See* Winnebago Indians
Hockett, Charles: on Bloomfield, 166
Hohokam: farming by, 368; domestication of cotton by, 371; weaving by, 371; mentioned, 199. *See also* Southwest Indians
Hoijer, Harry, 157
Homol'ovi, 373–74. *See also* Southwest Indians
Hoopa Valley Reservation, 262. *See also* California Indians
Hopi-Navajo land dispute, 196
Hopi Pueblo: 1990 population of, 28; Soyal ceremony, 358; maize agriculture of, 369; repatriation of objects to, 402–3; mentioned, 287, 397. *See also* Hopi-Navajo land dispute; Pueblo Indians
Horsman, Reginald, 235
Horton, Robin, 271
Howe, Oscar, 114
Hoxie, Fred, 202
Hrdlicka, Ales, 47, 391, 401
Humboldt State University, 88
Hupa Language, 156
Huron Indians, 81
Hurston, Zora Neale, 120

Huxley, Aldous, 5
Hymes, Dell, 132, 162, 175, 176, 189

Illinois State Museum at Dickson Mounds, 397
Inca: weaving by, 371; metalworking by, 371–72. *See also* Andean peoples
India: indigenous population history of, 17; mentioned, 310
Indiana University, 89, 93
Indian Bill of Rights. *See* Indian Civil Rights Act
Indian Child Welfare Act of 1978, 69
Indian Civil Rights Act of 1968, 262, 264–65, 266
Indian Claims Commission. *See* United States Indian Claims Commission
Indian Education Act of 1972, 87
Indian Reorganization Act. *See* Wheeler-Howard Act
Indian Self-Determination and Educational Assistance Act of 1975, 87
"Indians not taxed," 253
Indian Territory, 23
Influenza, 20, 22, 24
Inouye, Daniel K., 397
Institute of American Indian Arts, 114
International Indian Treaty Council: American Indians Against Desecration, 396–97
Inuit: arrival of ancestors in Western Hemisphere, 21; population size of, 24, 27; kinship system of, 323–24, 326; architecture of (igloo), 374–75, 376; mentioned, 8, 391, 397, 398. *See also* Inuit Circumpolar Conference
Inuit Circumpolar Conference, 400, 401. *See also* Inuit
Iowa State University, 90
Iowa Tribe of Oklahoma, 407
Iron Age, 371
Iroquoian language, 308. *See also* Iroquois Confederacy
Iroquois Confederacy: influence on U.S. Constitution, 11, 204, 228, 232, 250, 268*n13;* 1990 Iroquois population, 24; education of, 81; kinship system of, 307–9, 326–27; General Council of the League, 326; use of fertilizer by, 358–59; repatriation of objects to, 402; mentioned, 25, 48, 52, 251, 328, 400. *See also* Grand River Reservation; Mo-

hawk Indians; Onondaga Indians; Seneca Indians; Tuscarora Indians
Iverson, Peter, 230
Iyouse (a.k.a. Ike), 262

Jackson, Helen Hunt, 122
Jacobs, Melville, 156
Jacobs, Wilbur, 185
Jahner, Elaine, 124
Jaimes, M. Annette: definition of Native American studies of, 6, 154; mentioned, 7, 57*n22,* 97, 143, 234
Java. *See* Netherlands Indies
Jefferson, Thomas: linguistic questionnaire of, 155; excavation of mounds by, 388; mentioned, 48, 83
Jemez Pueblo: repatriation of objects to, 402; mentioned, 227. *See also* Hoa-sjela; Pueblo Indians
Jesuit College of Quebec, 81
Jicarilla Apache Reservation, 227. *See also* Apache Indians
Johansen, Bruce, 232
Johnson, Douglas A., 374
Johnson, E. Pauline, 125
Johnson v. McIntosh, 249, 257
Jones, William, 168
Jorgensen, Joseph, 196
Jucovy, Milton, 65
Julian calender, 362
Juneau, Alaska, 395

Kaeppler, Adrienne L., 396
Kagama, 262
Kaniatobe, Robert, 115
Kansas City, Missouri, 406
Kaskaskia Indians, 83. *See also* Plains Indians
Katz, Richard, 398
Katzeek, Ana, 396
Katzeek, David, 395
Kaw Nation of Oklahoma, 407
Keepers of the Treasures, 401
Keepers of the Treasures* Alaska, 400
Kegg, Maude, 172
Kehoe, Alice Beck, 66
Kelly, Jane Holden, 142
Kelvingore Museum, 400
"Kennewick Man" ("Richland Man"), 393, 410*n33*

Keshena, Wisconsin, 85
Kidwell, Clara Sue, 12, 89, 230, 231
King, Martin Luther, Jr.: assassination of, 87
King, Thomas, 138
King George III, 173
King James I, 80
King Philip, 52
Kiowa Apache Indians: kinship system of, 318.
    See also Apache Indians
Kiowa Indians: education of, 84, 85; Dohasan
    Kiowa Winter Count, 85; Tipi with Battle
    Pictures, 404, 405; Sun Dance, 405; men-
    tioned, 111, 187, 267, 302. *See also* Plains
    Indians
Klein, Kerwin, 10, 12, 221
Knox, Henry, 83
Kodiak Island, 391, 401
Korean Conflict, 394
Krashen, South Dakota, 164–65
Krauss, Michael, 153, 166
Krech, Shepard, 233
Krestenberg, Judith, 65
Krestenberg, Milton, 65
Kroeber, Alfred L., 184; aboriginal population
    estimates of, 17–18; founding of Depart-
    ment of Anthropology at Berkeley by, 313;
    study of kinship by, 314, 315, 317, 321, 322;
    mentioned, 52, 156, 184, 391
Kroeber, Karl, 135–36
Krupat, Arnold, 135, 137, 141

Lac Seul, Ontario, 172
LaFlesche, Francis, 118
La Florida, 80
LaFrance, Ron, 130
Laguna Pueblo: kinship system of, 319;
    mentioned, 111. *See also* Pueblo Indians
Lakehead University: researching and teaching
    languages at, 173, 174
Lake Superior, 168
Lake Tezcoco, 363
Lakota Indians: language of, 171; history of,
    225, 345–46; kinship system of, 316, 324,
    325, 330–34, 341–43, 345, 346, 347, 348,
    353n30; bands of, 331; Sun Dance, 331, 342;
    comparison of kinship system with Omaha,
    335–38 *passim;* mentioned, 131, 139. *See
    also* Dakota Indians; Nakota Indians; Pine
    Ridge Reservation; Cheyenne River Sioux
    Reservation; Sioux Indians

La Ronge, Saskatchewan, 172
Larsen, Clark Spencer, 22, 23
Larsen Bay, Alaska, 401
Lawrence, Kansas, 84
Lawton, Oklahoma, 404
Lazarus, Edward, 267
League of the Iroquois. *See* Iroquois Confed-
    eracy
Leaning Tower of Pisa, 358
Leap, William, 176
Lebanon, Connecticut, 82
Lesser, Alexander: study of kinship by, 316–
    17, 341, 344
Levenworth, Kansas, 84
Lévi-Strauss, Claude: study of kinship by, 321;
    mentioned, 184, 187, 219, 221
Lewis, David, 234, 235
Lewis, Meriwether, 155
Leyva, Don Alfonso Florez, 189
Limpieza de sangre ("clean blood"), 45
Linguistic Society of America, 157
Linnekin, Jocelyn, 187
Linton, Ralph, 191
Lips, Julius, 49
Little Boy Man, 289
Little Rock, Arkansas, 258
Lomawaima, K. Tsianina, 201, 231
Lomayesva, Frederick, 46
London, England, 401
Lone Chief, Charles, 407
Lone Wolf Mission: founding of, 84
Lono, 186, 187
Los Angeles, California, 30
Louis, Adrian, 131
Louisiana Purchase: explored by Lewis and
    Clark, 155
Lounsbury, Floyd: study of kinship by, 321;
    mentioned, 363
Lowie, Robert: study of kinship by, 315;
    mentioned, 156
Lumbee Indians: 1990 population of, 24;
    mentioned, 25, 200. *See also* Southeast
    Indians
Lumberton, North Carolina, 84
Lushootseed language, 176
*Lyng v. Northwest Cemetary Protective Asso-
    ciation,* 257
Lyons, Oren, 251
Lyotard, Jean-François, 219, 221, 222
Lytle, Clifford, 249

McCain, John, 399, 402
McFee, Malcolm, 192
McGrath, Janet, 22
Macgregor, Gordon, 65
McKenzie, Fayette Avery, 92
McNeil, William, 22
McNickle, D'Arcy, 115, 118, 138, 146. *See also* D'Arcy McNickle Center for the History of the American Indian
Madura. *See* Netherlands Indies
Magna Carta, 250
Maheo, 273, 291
Maize agriculture, 368, 369
Major Crimes Act of 1885, 260, 262, 263
Makah Indians: museum of, 408; mentioned, 401. *See also* Northwest Coast Indians
Malaria, 20
Malinowski, Bronislaw, 184
Malthus, Thomas, 91
Mancall, Peter, 230, 233
Mandan Indians: kinship system of, 347. *See also* Fort Berthold Reservation; Plains Indians
Mansfield, Connecticut, 82
Manson, Spero, 67
Maori: population history of, 17; mentioned, 54, 186
Marquette, Michigan, 308
Marshall, John, 247, 249, 257, 258, 268*n1*
Martin, Calvin, 187, 188, 193, 219, 220, 221, 223
Marx, Karl, 91, 92, 183, 289
Mashantucket Pequot Indians, 50, 249, 250. *See also* New England Indians
Mashpee Indians: attempt at legal recognition by, 188, 222; mentioned, 200. *See also* New England Indians
Master of Breath, 279–80, 282, 291
Mathews, John Joseph, 118, 122, 138, 145, 146
Matthews, G. Hubert, 343
Mauss, Marcel, 321, 364
Maxwell, Joseph: study of kinship by, 323–24
Maya: calender of, 359–63 *passim;* Dresden codex, 359–60; Caracol Tower at Chichen Itza, 360; Paris codex, 360; *tzolkin* (Sacred Year), 361, 362; Vague Year, 361–62; use of fire by, 367; farming techniques of, 368; mentioned, 187, 366
Mays, Washington, 264
Means, Russell, 112, 122. *See also* American Indian Movement

Measles, 20, 21, 22
Medicine, Bea, 114, 115
Medicine Wheels, 361
Medler, Andrew, 153, 154
Meister, Cary, 23
Menand, Louis, 147
Menominee Indians, 154, 257. *See also* Great Lakes Indians
Menomini language: Bloomfield's Menomini grammar 166; mentioned, 157
Meredith, Howard, 84
Meriam Report of 1928, 86, 92, 94
Merrell, James, 193, 230
Mescalero Apache Indians, 361. *See also* Apache Indians
Mesoamerica: agriculture in, 368, 369; development of the loom in, 371; metals of, 371; mentioned, 199, 357, 359
Mestizo, 46. *See also Métis*
Methodist Episcopal Society school, 84
Methodist New Hope Academy, 84
Métis: population size of, 24; ethnogenesis of, 193, 200; mentioned 25. *See also mestizo*
Meyer, Melissa, 10, 12, 230
Miami Indians (of Indiana), 328
Miccossukee Indians: architecture of, 375. *See also* Mvskoke Indians; Seminole Indians; Southeast Indians
Middle Missippian Tradition, 199, 372, 406
Middle Missouri Tradition, 199, 406
Mille Lacs, Minnesota, 172
Mills, Madison, 389
Milner, Clyde, 235
Milton, John R., 113, 114, 127*n10*
Minneapolis-St. Paul, Minnesota, 30, 112
Minik, 391–92
Mission Indians, 80. *See also* California Indians
Mississippi River, 406
Missouri River, 390, 407
Mithun, Marianne, 160
Miwok Indians, 144, 189. *See also* California Indians
Mochica: metallurgy of, 372
Modern Language Association: Native American literature in, 119
Modoc Indians, 402. *See also* California Indians
Mogollon: weaving of, 371; mentioned, 199. *See also* Southwest Indians
Mohave Desert. *See* Mojave Desert

Mohawk Indians, 93, 144. *See also* Iroquois Confederacy

Mohican Indians, 249. *See also* New England Indians

Mojave Desert, 52

Molina, Felipe S., 141, 142, 189, 190, 196

Momaday, N. Scott: winning of Pulitzer Prize, 87, 111, 114, 125; presentation at Convocation of American Indian Scholars, 115; printing of *House Made of Dawn,* 127*n11;* support of Martin's thesis, 188; mentioned, 9, 115, 116, 121, 126, 138, 176, 405

Montana State University, 89

Mooney, James: aboriginal population estimates of North American (north of Mexico), 18, 19, 23; survey of triracial groups, 25; mentioned, 405

Moore, John, 11

Moor's Indian Charity School: founding of, 82

More's Indian Charity School. *See* Moor's Indian Charity School

Morgan, Lewis Henry: study of kinship by, 307–10, 310–12 *passim,* 314, 315, 316, 318, 319, 321, 323; mentioned, 61, 92, 183, 313, 320

Morgan, Thomas Jefferson, 47, 49–50, 55, 59*n36*

Morrison, Toni, 120

Morton, Samuel G., 388

Mother Earth, 223

Mourning Dove, 146

Mowatt, Albert, 170

Murdock, George Peter: study of kinship by, 320–21

Murray State College, 85

Museum of the American Indian, 397. *See also* National Museum of the American Indian; Smithsonian Institution

Muskogean language, 292

Muskogee Indians. *See* Mvskoke Indians

Muskogee, Oklahoma, 84

Mustee. *See mestizo*

Mvskoke Indians: kinship system of, 278; cosmology of, 278, 279, 280, 281, 282–83, 284, 300; ceremonies of, 278, 280, 281; creation tradition of, 278–80; comparison with Cheyenne Indians, 278–84 *passim,* 284–86, 291, 292, 293, 294, 296; Green Corn Ceremony of, 285, 286, 294; mentioned, 273. *See also* Arbeka Indians; Coosa Indians;

Creek Indians; Seminole Indians; Southeast Indians

Myth of blood, 45, 46–47, 49

Myth of nomadism, 49

Myth of the tribe, 51

Nabhan, Gary Paul, 142

Nabokov, Peter, 12

Na-Dine: arrival in Western Hemisphere, 21

Nahua, 187

Nakota Indians, 131. *See also* Assiniboine Indians; Sioux Indians

Nandy, Ashis, 223

Narrogansett Indians, 249. *See also* New England Indians

Nash, Gary, 230

Naskapi Indians: kinship system of, 317; mentioned, 49

National Academy of Sciences, 389

National Endowment for the Arts, 172

National Endowment for the Humanities Summer Seminars, 137

National Environmental Policy Act of 1969, 398

National Historic Preservation Act of 1966, 398

National Museum of Natural History: Repatriation Office, 406; mentioned, 385–86, 391, 392, 395, 396, 401, 405, 406, 408. *See also* Smithsonian Institution

National Museum of the American Indian, 115, 397, 398, 400, 402. *See also* Museum of the American Indian; Smithsonian Institution

National Museum of the American Indian Act (Public Law 101–185): described, 398–99; amendment to, 399; mentioned 95, 400

National Science Foundation, 202

Native American Church, 192, 196, 257, 301

Native American Graves Protection and Repatriation Act (NAGPRA) (Public Law 101–601): described, 399; review committee, 399; mentioned, 41, 48, 95–96, 399, 402, 403, 407

Native American language stocks of North America, 156

Native American population: aboriginal size of U.S. and Canada, 14*n16,* 18–19, 21, 24; history of U.S. and Canada, 14*n16,* 21–22, 2426; aboriginal size of Western Hemisphere, 17–18; history of Western Hemi-

Native American population (*continued*)
sphere, 17–18, 21; U.S. Census definitions
of, 26; of U.S. states, 30; of U.S. cities, 30;
Canadian definitions of, 39*n80;* of Canadian
provinces, 39*n81;* of Canadian cities, 39*n84*
Native American studies: definition of, 4, 5, 6,
7, 418; name vs. American Indian studies,
7–8, 151*n49*
Native American tribal colleges, 83–84,
85, 86–87, 104*n33. See also* College of
the Menominee Nation; Deganiwidah-
Quetzalcoatl University; Fond du Lac Tribal
and Community College; Fort Belknap College; Navajo Community College; Ogalala
Lakota College; Salish Kootenai College;
Saskatchewan Indian Federated College;
Sisseton-Wahpeton Community College
Native American tribal membership: requirements of U.S. tribes, 27, 28, 57*n21, 57n22,*
328; Confederated Salish and Kootenai
Tribes tribal membership requirements, 28;
Eastern Band of Cherokee Indians tribal
membership requirements, 28; Navajo
Nation tribal membership requirements,
28; Walker River Paiute tribal membership
requirements, 28; Cherokee tribal member-
ship, 29; Navajo Nation membership, 29;
size of in U.S., 29; size of Canadian bands,
39*n80. See also* Certificate of Degree of
Indian Blood
Native Hawaiians: population decline of, 17,
23; encounter with Captain Cook, 186–87;
mentioned, 8, 54, 398, 399, 401, 410*n34*
Native Seed/SEARCH organization, 370
Navajo Community College: founding of, 85.
See also Native American tribal colleges
Navajo Indians: 1990 population of, 24, 29;
tribal membership requirements of, 28;
language of, 156; kinship system of, 315–
16, 324, 325, 329; categories of plants,
365; use of pollen in prayer, 369; weaving
techniques of, 371; architecture of (hogan),
376; repatriation of objects to, 403; mentioned, 267, 397. *See also* Hopi-Navajo land
dispute; Navajo Reservation
Navajo Reservation: 1990 population of, 28;
schools on, 86. *See also* Navajo Indians
Nazi holocaust: survivors of, 60, 62, 65, 66,
73; and Native American genocide, 9, 234;
mentioned, 73
Neah Bay, 408

Nearer Sky-Space, 274
Nebraska 1989 Unmarked Human Burial
Sites and Skeletal Remains Protection Act,
397–98
Neel, James, 22
Neihardt, John, 122
Netherlands Indies: indigenous population
history of Java and Madura, 17
New Agers, 302–3
Newberry Library: Conference on Indian
Studies, 93, 106*n61;* mentioned, 137, 182.
See also D'Arcy McNickle Center for the
History of the American Indian
New England Indians: "praying Indians," 80;
education of, 81; use of fire by, 367. *See also*
Mashantucket Pequot Indians; Mashapee
Indians; Mohican Indians; Narrogansett
Indians; Pokanoket Indians; Stockbridge
Indians
New York City, New York, 30, 101, 389, 391,
397
Nichols, John, 172, 173
Ningewance, Patricia, 172
Ninilchik Indians, 401
Nisga'a language, 167
Noble Savage, 237
Nome, Alaska, 85
Nootka Indians: language of, 156; mentioned,
287. *See also* Northwest Coast Indians
Nora, Pierre, 221
Northeastern State University, 89
Northern Arizona University, 90
Northwest Coast Indians: architecture of,
373; mentioned, 52–53, 230, 234, 251, 257,
316, 364, 365, 370. *See also* Coastal Salish;
Haida Indians; Makah Indians; Nootka
Indians; Tlingit Indians; Tsimishian Indians
Northwest Community College, 85
Nyholm, Earl, 172

Oberg, Kalvero: study of kinship by, 327
Obeyesekere, Gananath, 187
Occom, Samson, 82, 122, 146
Occum, Samson. *See* Samson Occom
Oglala Lakota College: Lakota Elders Tra-
ditional Government Omniciye, 349–50;
mentioned, 131. *See also* Native American
tribal colleges
Ohlone Indians, 402. *See also* California
Indians
Ojibwe Indians: language of, 10, 90, 153–54,

157, 158, 159, 168, 171, 172, 173, 174, 175, 308; 1990 population of, 24; writings of, 113; Algonquin dialect of language, 170–71; Temagami Ojibwe, 173; Red Lake Ojibwe, 200; White Earth Ojibwe, 230; Berens River Ojibwe kinship system, 317; kinship system of, 329, 344; study of Grassy Narrows Ojibwe, 348–49; Lake Superior Ojibwe architecture (wigwam), 376; account of Thunderbird, 377; mentioned, 153, 169, 172, 173, 257. *See also* Great Lakes Indians

Oklahoma City, Oklahoma, 30

Oklahoma State University, 89

Old Agency Village, South Dakota, 85

Olmec, 361

Omaha Indians: kinship system of, 311, 312, 314, 315, 316, 318, 323, 325, 330, 335–39, 343; earthlodges of, 325; tipis of, 325; *Thatada* clan of, 335–36; comparison of kinship system with Lakota, 335–38 *passim;* repatriation of remains to, 402, 403; repatriation of sacred pole and objects to, 403; mentioned, 390. *See also* Plains Indians

Oneida language, 171

Oneota Tradition, 406

Onondaga Indians, 251. *See also* Iroquois Confederacy

Opechancanough, 80

Oregon v. Smith, 257

Ortiz, Alfonso, 59, 115, 116, 118, 134, 419

Ortiz, Simon, Jr., 132, 138, 144

Orwell, George, 94–95

Osage Indians: education of, 84; Osage Nation of Oklahoma, 407

Otis, G. A., 389

Oto Indians: Otoe-Missouria Tribe of Oklahoma, 407; mentioned, 145. *See also* Plains Indians

Ottawa language, 173

Owens, Louis, 134, 138, 146

Oxford, Mississippi, 124

Oxford University, 318

Pablo, Montana, 85

Pactah Billy. *See* Kagama

Paiute Indians: Southern Paiute language, 156; mentioned, 131

Paleo-Indians: arrival in Western Hemisphere of, 21

Palomar College, 89

Panel for a National Dialogue on Museum/ Native American Relations, 397

Papago Reservation: 1990 population of, 28. *See also* Tohono O'odam Indians

Parkman, Francis, 183, 184

Pawnee Indians: as allies of United States, 194; kinship system of, 321, 325, 341, 343; earthlodges of, 325, 376, 406; repatriation of human remains to, 401, 402; Pawnee Tribe of Oklahoma, 406; oral traditions of, 406, 407; repatriation of human remains and objects to, 406–7; bands of, 407; mentioned, 145, 294, 407. *See also* Plains Indians

Pawnee, Oklahoma, 402

Pellagra, 20, 392

Pembroke State University: history of, 84; Native American Studies at, 89

Pentland, David, 173

Pequat Indians. *See* Mashantucket Pequot Indians

Perdue, Theda, 230

Perry, Robert, 391

Perseus Project of classical Greek, 171

Peterson, Jacqueline, 193

Pettitt, George, 79

Philippines: indigenous population history of, 17

Philosophical Society of Washington, 311

Phoenix, Arizona, 30

Phoenix School: founding of, 86

Picuris Pueblo, 373. *See also* Pueblo Indians

Pikogan, Quebec, 170

Pilgrims: grave robbing by, 387–86

Pine Ridge Reservation: 1990 population of, 28; leaders on, 349; Lakol Ikce Oyate Peta Ilekiyap, 350. *See also* Lakota Indians; Sioux Indians

Pipestone School: founding of, 86

Plains Indians: wars with the United States, 194; kinship systems of, 319, 330, 346; organization of, 344; medical techniques of, 370–71; mentioned, 48, 52, 85, 142, 288, 289. *See also* Arapaho Indians; Arikara Indians; Assiniboine Indians; Blackfeet Indians; Cheyenne Indians; Comanche Indians; Crow Indians; Dakota Indians; Hidatsa Indians; Iowa Indians; Kaskaskia Indians; Kiowa Indians; Lakota Indians; Mandan Indians; Nakota Indians; Omaha Indians; Oto Indians; Pawnee Indians; Ponca Indians; Sioux Indians; Wichita Indians

Plateau Indians, 53
Pleiades, 360
Plenty Coup, 421
Plowman, J. A., 261
Pocahontas, 46, 80, 301
Pokanoket Indians, 249. *See also* New England
    Indians
Pomo Indians, 144, 189. *See also* California
    Indians
Ponca Indians: kinship system of, 316; Ponca
    Tribe of Oklahoma, 407; mentioned, 311.
    See also Plains Indians
Popular, Montana, 131
Population bottleneck, 19
Powell, John Wesley, 155, 156, 313
Powell, Peter, 225, 226, 227, 228, 300
Powhatan, 52
Pratt, Richard H.: founding of Carlisle Indian
    School by, 85
Presbyterian Union, 84
Prescott, Arizona, 85
Pretty Bird, 301
Pretty Voice Eagle, Leon, 401
Price, Catherine: history of Lakota by, 345–46
Price, Marcus, 397
Princeton University, 94, 115
Prucha, Francis Paul, 249
Pueblo Indians: 1990 population of, 24;
    Pueblo girl, 66; Western Pueblo kinship
    system, 319; Fajada Butte (near Chaco
    Canyon), 360; use of pollen in prayer by,
    369; weaving of, 371; architecture of, 373–
    74; mentioned, 52, 196. *See also* Acoma
    Pueblo; Hano Pueblo; Hopi Pueblo; Hopi-
    Navajo land dispute; Laguana Pueblo;
    Picuris Pueblo; San Juan Pueblo; Southwest
    Indians; Taos Pueblo; Tewa Indians; Zia
    Pueblo; Zuni Pueblo

Qisuk (Kishu, Kissuk), 391–92

Radcliffe-Brown, A. R.: study of kinship by,
    317–19; mentioned, 296
Radin, Paul, 156, 227
Rand, Ayn, 300
Ranger, Terence, 223
Raven, Peter, 365
Red Schoolhouse Survival School, 87
Red Star (Mars), 275

Reichard, Gladys: study of Navajo clans by,
    315–16; mentioned, 156
Republic of Vietnam, 394. *See also* Vietnam
    War
Reservoir Salvage Act of 1960, 398
Rhizotic affiliation, 405
Rice, Keren: grammar of Slave Indians by, 161
Richter, Daniel, 230, 231
Rivers, W. H. R.: study of kinship by, 314;
    mentioned 317
Riverside School: founding of, 86
Robbins, Rebecca, 232
Robin Hood, 299
Roemer, Kenneth, 137
Rogers, Will, 145
Rolfe, John, 46
Rome, Italy, 401
Rosaldo, Renato, 130, 146, 151*n51*
Rosebud Reservation: 1990 population of 28.
    See also Lakota Indians; Sioux Indians
Rothenberg, Jerome, 132
Round Table of Native American Studies
    Directors (1980), 13, 420
Ruoff, A. LaVonne Brown, 119, 126–27*n9*,
    128*nn28, 137*

Sa, Zitka, 146
Sacajawea, 301
Sackler, Elizabeth, 397
Sadock, Jerrold, 160
Sagowah, 260
Sahlins, Marshall, 186, 187
Said, Edward: call for end of anthropology by,
    188
St. Lawrence River, 80
St. Louis, Missouri, 406
Salish Kootenai College: founding of, 85. *See
    also* Native American tribal colleges
San Carlos Reservation: 1990 population of,
    28. *See also* Apache Indians
Sand Creek Massacre, 234, 301, 402. *See also*
    Arapaho Indians; Cheyenne Indians; John
    Chivington
Sandefur, Gary, 19
San Diego State University, 89
San Diego, California, 80
Sando, Joe, 227
San Francisco, California, 101
San Francisco State University, 89, 417
San Juan Pueblo, 325. *See also* Pueblo Indians

Santa Clara Pueblo v. Martinez, 260, 266. *See also* Pueblo Indians

Santa Fe, New Mexico, 114

Santa Fe School: founding of, 86

Sapir, Edward, 156, 157

Sarris, Greg, 144, 189, 190

Sarsi language, 156

Sarton, George, 357

Saskatchewan Indian Federated College, 89–90. *See also* Native American tribal colleges

Savala, Refugio, 142

Scarlet fever, 21

Schneider, David M.: study of kinship by, 321–22

Scholder, Fritz, 115

Scott, General of the United States Army, 258

Sealaska Corporation, 404

Second Convocation of American Indian Scholars: focus of, 419; mentioned, 94, 116

Select Committee on Indian Affairs, 397, 402

Seminole Female Academy: founding of, 84. *See also* Seminole Indians

Seminole Indians: education of, 84, 86; architecture of, 375; mentioned, 251, 257, 281. *See also* Miccossukee Indians; Mvskoke Indians; Southeast Indians

Seneca Indians: agriculture of, 360; mentioned, 196, 197. *See also* Iroquois Confederacy

Senungetuk, Joseph, 115

Seri Indians, 366

Setzler, Frank, 47

Shaffer, Lynda, 199

Shakespeare, William, 123

Shanley, Kathryn, 10, 150*n28*

Shawnee Indians: education of, 84; mentioned, 249

Sheehan, Bernard, 235

Sherzer, Joel, 162–63

Shkilnyk, Anastasia M.: study of Ojibwe by, 348–49

Shoemaker, Nancy, 200

Shoshonean Indians: kinship system of, 326; political organization of, 327; Shoshone-Bannock, 401

Silko, Leslie Marmon, 121, 125, 138

Simms, William Gilmore, 46

Simpson, O. J., 45

Sin-Ta-Ge-Le-Scka. *See* Sinte Gleska

Sinte Gleska, 261

Siouan kinship system, 316, 343

Siouan language, 308

Sioux Indians: 1990 population of, 24; ego identity of, 42; Brule Sioux, 261; Treaty of 1868, 261; creation story of (Dakota), 289; kinship system of, 344; Oglala Sioux, 401; Sisseton-Wahpeton Sioux, 401; Two Kettles Sioux, 401; Yankton Sioux, 401; Devil's Lake Sioux, 401, 402; mentioned, 43, 65, 72, 116, 194, 267, 287, 302, 308. *See also* Assiniboine (Nakota) Indians; Cheyenne River Sioux Tribe; Dakota Indians; Ghost Dance; Lakota Indians; Pine Ridge Reservation; Plains Indians; Rosebud Reservation; Wounded Knee Massacre

Sirius, 364

Sir Lancelot, 299

Sisseton Wahpeton Community College: founding of, 85. *See also* Native American tribal colleges

Six Nations. *See* Iroquois Confederacy

Sky People, 335

Smallpox, 20, 21, 22

Smith, Bruce, 12, 199

Smith, Martin Cruz, 145

Smith, Norval: linguistic questionnaire with Comrie, 163

Smithsonian Institution: founding of, 155, 388; Secretary of, 398–99; mentioned, 310, 311, 391, 398, 399, 400, 401, 402, 403, 405. *See also* National Museum of Natural History; National Museum of the American Indian; Bureau of American Ethnology; Smithsonian Institution Native American Repatriation Review Committee

Smithsonian Institution Native American Repatriation Review Committee: duties of, 412–13*n60;* mentioned, 12, 386, 400, 405, 406–7

Snipp, C. Matthew, 13, 19, 57*n22.*

Social Science Research Council, 184, 191

Society for American Archaeology, 397

Sotheby's, 397

South American Indians, 221

Southeast Alaska Indian Repatriation Conference, 395–96. *See also* Haida Indians; Tlingit Indians

Southeast Indians: architecture of, 375; mentioned, 52, 364. *See also* Arbeka Indi-

Southeast Indians (*continued*)
ans; Catawba Indians; Cherokee Indians;
Chickasaw Indians; Cofachiqui; Coosa
Indians; Creek Indians; Lumbee Indians;
Miccosukee Indians; Mvskoke Indians;
Seminole Indians
Southwest Indians: architecture, 373; mentioned, 52, 251. *See also* Anazasi; Apache
Indians; Hohokam, Mogollon; Navajo Indians; Pueblo Indians; Sarsi Indians; Tohono
O'odam; Yaqui Indians
Spicer, Edward, 142
Spier, Leslie: study of kinship by, 315, 322
Spiro mounds, 363–64
Spoehr, Alexander: study of kinship by, 246,
347
Spokane Indians, 114
Spotted Tail. *See* Sinte Gleska
Spruhan, Paul, 46
Standing Bear, Luther: life of, 13*n4;* mentioned, 3, 4, 102
Stanford University: Native Americans at, 7,
99; mentioned, 111, 115, 119, 402
Stannard, David, 23
Steed-Kisker Joint-Repatriation Committee,
407, 414*n89. See also* Steed-Kisker Phase
Steed-Kisker Phase: repatriation of human
remains and objects associated with, 406,
407, 414*n89. See also* Steed-Kisker Joint-
Repatriation Committee
Steel Age, 371
Stockbridge Indians, 83. *See also* New England
Indians; Great Lakes Indians
Stone Breaker, 273
Story, Justice of the Supreme Court, 258
Stoughton, John, 81
Straus, Anne S.: study of kinship by, 324, 348
Strickland, Rennard, 11
Strong, William Duncan: study of kinship by,
317
Studi, Wes, 122
Sun Dance; of Cheyenne Indians, 275; of
Lakota Indians, 331; of Kiowa Indians, 405;
mentioned, 42, 196
Sutchin language, 156
Sweet Medicine, 273, 275, 291

Tahlequah, Oklahoma, 84, 89, 264
Tai-me: description of, 405
Takelma language, 156

Talton (citizen of the Cherokee Nation), 264
Talton v. Mays, 260, 264–65. *See also* Cherokee Indians
Tamil: kinship system of, 310
Taos Pueblo, 27. *See also* Pueblo Indians
Tasmania: indigenous population history of, 17
Tatanka Iyotake (Sitting Bull) and Wokik-
suye (Bigfoot) Memorial Ride, 72. *See also*
Lakota Indians; Sioux Indians; Wounded
Knee Massacre
Taylor, Charles, 143–44
Taylor, Arizona, 373
Tecumseh, 249
Tedlock, Dennis, 132, 162
Telugu: kinship system of, 310
Tennessee Valley Authority, 392
Tenskwatawa, the Shawnee Prophet, 196, 227
Tewa Indians, 325–26. *See also* Pueblo Indians; San Juan Pueblo
Teyoninhokarawen, John Norton, 93
Thomas, David Hurst, 299
Thomas, Dylan, 42
Thomas, Robert, 67, 118, 345
Thompson Indians: names of plants of, 365
Thornton, Russell: definition of Native American studies of, 4, 5, 6; Native American
population history by, 8, 249; aboriginal
population estimate of Western Hemisphere
by, 18; aboriginal population estimate for
North America (north of Mexico) by, 19,
249; speech at UCLA's Fourth Annual Conference on Contemporary American Indian
Issues by, 96–97
Thornton, William, 140–41
Thorp, George, 80
Thorpe, Jim, 85
Thule culture: architecture of, 374–75
Thunder Bay, Ontario, 173
Tierra del Fuego Indians, 91
Tishomingo, Oklahoma, 85
Tlingit Indians: kinship system of, 316, 327,
340; clans of, 404; mentioned, 395, 396. *See
also* Central Council of Tlingit and Haida
Indian Tribes; Northwest Coast Indians
Tocqueville, Alexis de, 248, 249, 255, 259
Tohono O'odam Indians, 143. *See also* Papago
Reservation; Southwest Indians
Tolowa Indians, 23, 25. *See also* California
Indians
Tonkawa language, 162

Tonnies, Ferdinand, 192
Torres Islands, 314
Trade and Intercourse Act of 1834, 46
Treponemal infections, 20, 392. *See also*
  Venereal disease
Trosper, Ronald, 224
Trout, Lawanna, 137
Tsaile, Arizona, 85
Tsimshian Indians: kinship system of, 316. *See
  also* Northwest Coast Indians
Tsimshian language, 171. *See also* Coast
  Tsimshian language
Tsistsistas. *See* Cheyenne Indians
Tuberculosis, 20, 392
Tucson, Arizona, 370
Tufts University, 171
Tulsa, Oklahoma, 30
Tuscarora Indians, 25, 83, 328. *See also*
  Iroquois Confederacy; Southeast Indians
Twain, Mark, 140
Twin Cities, Minnesota. *See* Minneapolis-St.
  Paul, Minnesota
Two Moon Monument, 386
Tyler, Stephen, 141
Tylor, Edward, 183
Typhoid fever, 20
Typhus, 22
Tzeltal (plant), 365
Tzeltal Indians: kinds of beans used by, 365

Ubelaker, Douglas H.: aboriginal population estimate of North America (north of
  Mexico) by, 19; mentioned, 396
Uisaakassak, 391
UNIDROIT Convention, 401
United States Army Medical Museum: Medi-
  cal Examiner, 385; collection of Native
  American remains, 386, 388–89, 392, 393,
  402; founding of, 388
United States Bureau of Indian Affairs: Branch
  of Acknowledgment and Recognition, 54,
  328; Eastman's work for, 287, 292; men-
  tioned, 26, 27, 30, 52, 94, 194, 196, 252,
  267, 287, 347, 350
United States Civil War, 51, 85, 253, 255, 388
United States Commissioners of Indian
  Affairs, 346
United States Constitution: influence of Iroquois Confederacy on, 11, 204, 228, 232,
  250, 268*n13*; mentioned, 194

United States Forest Service, 367
United States Indian Claims Commission:
  formation of, 92–93, 185; mentioned 48,
  190
United States Indian Health Service, 68, 76*n42*
United States Office of Education: National
  Study of Indian Education, 86–87
United States Office of Indian Affairs. *See*
  United States Bureau of Indian Affairs
United States v. Cherokee Nation of Oklahoma,
  259
United States v. Kagama, 260, 262–64. *See
  also* Hoopa Valley Reservation
United States War Department, 255
University of Alaska, Fairbanks, 89
University of Alaska, Southeast, 395
University of Alberta, 90
University of Arizona: Native American fac-
  ulty at, 102; mentioned, 6, 90, 137, 142, 417
University of Calgary, 89, 90
University of California (system of higher
  education): Native American students, 112;
  Native American remains, 392; Joint Aca-
  demic Senate-Administration Committee on
  Human Skeletal Remains, 397; repatriation
  policy of, 398
University of California, Berkeley: Depart-
  ment of Anthropology, 313; Native Ameri-
  can remains at Hearst (formerly Lowie)
  Museum, 392; mentioned 88, 90, 98, 112,
  119, 190, 417
University of California, Davis, 89, 90, 119,
  417
University of California, Irvine, 88
University of California, Los Angeles: Fourth
  Annual Conference on Contemporary
  American Indian Issues, 96–97; Native
  American faculty, 102; Native American
  remains, 392; mentioned, 88, 90, 97, 119,
  417
University of California, Riverside, 88
University of California, Santa Barbara, 408
University of Chicago, 94, 317, 318, 319
University of Colorado, 89, 97, 376
University of Hawaii, 89
University of Illinois, Chicago Circle, 117
University of Lethbridge, 89
University of Manitoba: researching and teach-
  ing languages at, 172, 173, 175; mentioned,
  89

University of Michigan, 119
University of Minnesota, Twin Cities, 88, 90, 99, 100, 190, 402, 417
University of Montana, 89
University of Nebraska, 403
University of New Mexico, 89, 255, 417
University of North Carolina, 89
University of North Dakota, 89
University of Northern British Columbia: preservation of Indian languages at, 167; mentioned 89, 90
University of Oklahoma, 89, 117, 294
University of Regina, 89
University of Rochester, 320
University of Saskatchewan, 81
University of South Dakota, 89
University of Tennessee, 402
University of Texas at Arlington, 137
University of Tulsa, 89, 90
University of Washington, 89, 90
University of Wisconsin–Green Bay, 119
University of Wisconsin–Madison: Native American faculty, 88; mentioned, 119
University of Wisconsin–Milwaukee, 89
Upper Skagit Indians, 176
Usner, Daniel, 230

Valentine, J. Randolph, 10
Valley of Mexico, 362, 363
Van Kirk, Sylvia, 193
Veblen, Thorstein, 96, 102,
Vega, 364
Veile, Alan, 117, 118
Venereal disease, 20. *See also* Treponemal infections
Venus, 360, 361
Vespucci, Amerigo, 43
Vian, Oklahoma, 386
Vietnam War: veterans of, 300; remains of soldiers killed during, 394; mentioned,79, 131. *See also* Republic of Vietnam
Virgin soil epidemics, 21, 233
Vizenor, Gerald, 99, 113, 139, 176
Voegelin, Charles, 173

Waco Baptist Academy: founding of, 84
Wakan Tanka, 342
Walker, Alice, 120
Walker, Philip, 408
Wallace, Anthony F. C., 41, 93, 196, 197, 200

Walpole Island, Ontario, 153
Walters, Anna Lee, 144–45
"Wannabees," 41, 55
Warm Springs Confederated Tribes: repatriation of remains to, 401; repatriation of objects to, 402
Warrior, Robert Allen, 4, 9, 145
Washinga Sakba (the Blackbird): death and burial of, 390
Washington, Booker T., 120
Washington, District of Columbia: 386, 388
Wayne, Anthony, 83
Weatherford, Jack, 232
Weber, Max, 92
Wedel, Waldo, 406
Welch, James, 122, 130, 138
West, Richard, Jr., 115
West, Richard, Sr., 114
Westerman, Floyd, 44
Western History Association, 182
Wheatley, Phyllis, 120
Wheeler-Howard Act of 1934, 27, 195, 350
Wheelock, Eleazar: founding of Moor's Indian Charity School by, 82; song about, 100
Whitaker, Nathaniel, 82
White, Hayden, 187
White, Justice of the Supreme Court, 264
White, Leslie, 184, 370
White, Richard, 10–11
White Buffalo Woman, 342
Whitecalf, Sarah, 172
White Tail, Ralph, 274
Whooping cough, 20
Wichita Indians: education of, 84. *See also* Plains Indians
Wilkinson, Charles, 257
Willard, William, 145
Williams, Angeline, 173
Williams, John, 84
Williams, Robert, 249
Williams v. Lee, 257
Wilson, Michael, 145
Winnebago Indians: calender stick of, 362; mentioned, 84, 227–28. *See also* Great Lakes Indians
Wishram language, 156
Witherspoon, Gary, 324, 329, 330
Woal, General of the United States Army, 258
Wolfart, H. Christoph, 172
Wolfe, Eric, 229, 330

Womack, Craig, 145
Woodbury, Anthony, 162–63
Woody, Elizabeth, 138
Worchester, Samuel, 258
Worchester v. Georgia, 257–60, 263, 264. *See also* Cherokee Indians
Wordsworth, William, 42
World's Columbian Exposition, 55, 389
World War II, 274, 394, 401
Wounded Knee Creek, 390
Wounded Knee Massacre: objects taken from, 391–92; repatriation of objects taken from, 392, 400; mentioned, 70, 72, 390. *See also* Ghost Dance; Pine Ridge Reservation; Tatanka Iyotake (Sitting Bull) and Wokiksuye (Bigfoot) Memorial Ride; Wounded Knee Survivor's Association
Wounded Knee Survivor's Association, 400. *See also* Wounded Knee Massacre
Wozniak, John: study of Dakota by, 345
Wright, Richard, 120

Yakima Indians, 200, 257
Yana language, 156
Yanomamo Indians, 22–23

Yaqui Indians, 141, 142, 189, 190, 196. *See also* Southwest Indians
Yavapai College, 85
Yeats, W. B., 187
Yellow fever, 20
Yerrington Paiute, 401
YMCA Indian Guides, 287
Young Bear, Ray, 138
Yuki Indians, 25. *See also* California Indians; Covelo Indian Community of Confederated Tribes of the Round Valley Indian Reservation
Yukon Indians, 176
Yupik language, 171
Yurok Indians, 42, 43. *See also* California Indians

Zepeda, Ofelia, 142
Zia Pueblo, 402. *See also* Pueblo Indians
Zuni Pueblo: 1990 population of, 28; kinship system of, 319, 321–22; removal of human remains from, 390, 409*n19;* war gods, 400, 403; mentioned, 402. *See also* Pueblo Indians